S0-AYA-829

ERRATUM

❧ ACKNOWLEDGMENTS

It is quite impossible to study domestic architecture without the assistance of benevolent owners. As anyone who has tried to investigate the private property of strangers will know, this type of research poses special challenges: suspicious caretakers, houses shut off behind high walls, perimeters patrolled by dogs with fangs, not to mention burglar alarms and electronic eyes. The sense of gratitude is therefore doubled when a welcoming or knowledgable inhabitant appears. This book would not even have been started without Giuliana Salvadori at Santuccio and Sir Harold Acton at La Pietra. Both were not only wonderfully generous and hospitable, but they actively encouraged the research project, enabling repeated visits with questions, tape measures and photographic equipment. Since then, many others have kindly opened their doors or provided information on individual villas, including Francesca Baldry, Maurizio Burlamacchi, Mark Roberts, Helen Spande and Kim Wilkie.

I am indebted to the following institutions who supported the research, writing and publication of this book: the Courtauld Institute of Art, the University of London, the Fondazione di Studi di Storia dell'Arte 'Roberto Longhi', the Italian Government, the University of York Research and Innovations Fund, the Harvard University Center for Italian Renaissance Studies at Villa I Tatti and the Lila Acheson Wallace / Reader's Digest grant towards illustrations. My colleagues in the History of Art Department at the University of York have covered teaching and administration during my sabbatical leave with unfailing good humour. The librarians and archivists whose help I have most regularly and deeply appreciated are those of the Warburg Institute and the Conway Library in London, and of the Archivio di Stato, the Kunsthistorisches Institut and Villa I Tatti in Florence. In the publication process my first thanks go to Richard Schofield and Paul Davies, the most encouraging of general editors for the series on Architecture in Early Modern Italy, while at Cambridge University Press I have benefitted from the patience and editorial skills of Rose-Shawe Taylor, Beatrice Rehl and Michie Shaw of TechBooks.

Inspiration, advice, practical help, and bibliographic or archival nuggets were supplied by friends and colleagues, among whom I particularly thank Caroline Anderson, Crispin de Courcey Bayley, Jane and Bob Black, Eve Borsook, Jill Burke, Howard Burns, Suzy and Humfrey Butters, Georgia Clarke, Sam Cohn, Gino Corti, Simon Ditchfield, Caroline Elam, Sabine Eiche, Lynda Fairbairn, Chris Fischer, Giorgio Galletti, Richard Goldthwaite, Ernst Gombrich, Rab Hatfield, Bridget Ikin, Roger Jones, Bill Kent, Christiane Klapisch-Zuber, Hermione Lee, Paola Peruzzi, Brenda Preyer, Charles Robertson, Elaine Rosenthal, Pat Rubin, Nicolai Rubinstein, and Anna Teicher. Among these friends two deserve an extra mention: Kate Lowe for consistently helping to cheer flagging spirits, and managing to stiffen my resolve during weak moments. And Daniela Lamberini, as co-explorer of the Florentine contado, whose keen eye taught me more than any art historical tome.

FLORENTINE VILLAS IN THE FIFTEENTH CENTURY

AN ARCHITECTURAL AND SOCIAL HISTORY

AMANDA LILLIE

CAMBRIDGE
UNIVERSITY PRESS

CAMBRIDGE UNIVERSITY PRESS
Cambridge, New York, Melbourne, Madrid, Cape Town, Singapore, São Paulo

Cambridge University Press
40 West 20th Street, New York, NY 10011-4211, USA

www.cambridge.org
Information on this title: www.cambridge.org/9780521770477

© Amanda Lillie 2005

This book is in copyright. Subject to statutory exception
and to the provisions of relevant collective licensing agreements,
no reproduction of any part may take place without
the written permission of Cambridge University Press.

First published 2005

Printed in the United States of America

A catalog record for this publication is available from the British Library

Library of Congress Cataloging in Publication Data
Lillie, Amanda.
  Florentine villas in the fifteenth century : an architectural and social history / Amanda Lillie.
    p.   cm. – (Architecture in early modern Italy)
  Includes bibliographical references and index.
  ISBN 0-521-77047-5
    1. Architecture, Domestic–Italy–Florence.   2. Architecture–Italy–Florence–15th century.
3. Florence (Italy)–Buildings, structures, etc.   4. Florence (Italy)–History.   I. Title.   II. Series.
NA7594.L55   2004
728′.0945′5109031 – dc22   2004045674

ISBN-13   978-0-521-77047-7 hardback
ISBN-10   0-521-77047-5 hardback

Cambridge University Press has no responsibility for
the persistence or accuracy of URLs for external or
third-party Internet Web sites referred to in this book
and does not guarantee that any content on such
Web sites is, or will remain, accurate or appropriate.

Contents

ILLUSTRATIONS

Abbreviations

For short titles of published material, consult the bibliography. All manuscript references are to collections in the Archivio di Stato, Florence, unless otherwise indicated.

Dates between January 1 and the Florentine New Year on Ascension Day, March 25, are given in modern style (eg, 24 February 1454 in Florentine style is 1455 in modern style).

ASF	Archivio di Stato, Florence
BNF	Biblioteca Nazionale Centrale, Florence
Burl. Mag.	*Burlington Magazine*
Capponi	Archivio Capponi (ASF and BNF)
Cat.	Catasto (ASF)
Decima Repub.	Decima Repubblicana (ASF)
IGM	Istituto Geografico Militare
JWCI	*Journal of the Warburg and Courtauld Institutes*
Litta	P. Litta, *Famiglie celebri italiane*
MAP	Archivio Mediceo avanti il Principato (ASF)
Mitt.KhIF	*Mitteilungen des Kunsthistorischen Institutes in Florenz*
Not. Antecos	Notarile Antecosimiano (ASF)
Pupilli	Pupilli avanti il Principato (ASF)
Repetti	E. Repetti, *Dizionario geografico, fisico e storico della Toscana*
Strozziane	Carte Strozziane (ASF)

Currency and Measures

L. – *lira*   s. – *soldi*   d. – *denari*
1 *lira* = 20 *soldi*
1 *soldo* = 12 *denari*

F. = *fiorini*   s. – *soldi*   d. – *denari*
1 *fiorino* = 20 *soldi*
1 *soldo* = 12 *denari*

1 *braccio* = 58.3 cm.
1 *staio* = 24.4 litres or c. 2/3 bushel
1 *moggio* = 24 *staia* or 585 litres or c. 17 bushels
1 *staioro* = 525 square meters (1 hectare = 5.6 *staiora* or 1 acre = 7.6 *staiora*)
1 *barile* (barrel) of wine = 45.58 litres
1 *soma* = 2 *barili* of wine, 91.16 litres
1 *cogno* = 10 *barili* of wine
1 *orcio* or *barile* (barrel) of oil = 33.42 litres
1 *dodicina* of linen = 12 *libbre* or 4.074 Kg.

❧ INTRODUCTION

It is largely due to the traditional view of the Renaissance as an urban phenomenon that art historians have tended to focus on the city and to regard fifteenth-century art and architecture as the products of a purely civic culture created for an urban environment. Scholars have continually fallen prey to an ancient literary construct – but one which is still very much alive – according to which the countryside is perceived as the antithesis of the town.[1] This adversarial model was an ideological commonplace in the fifteenth century, to the extent that authors as diverse as Franco Sacchetti and Lorenzo de' Medici made it the subject of jests and ironic treatment.[2] By presenting the topos in an exaggerated or burlesque form, audiences were invited to step back and laugh at the urban-rustic antithesis, to see it in a critical light. It was clear at that time and ought to be clear to us now that this dichotomised approach was only one short version of a long and complicated story about the countryside.

This book takes as its starting point a very different view, one established by Nicola Ottokar, Johan Plesner, Armando Sapori, Enrico Fiumi and Philip Jones, that urban landowners of late medieval Florence maintained one foot in town and the other in the country, and that these were the two interdependent halves of a single social and economic world.[3] Although this view has been widely accepted by historians since the late 1950s, there have been few attempts by art historians to examine the material evidence or the artefacts produced by that integrated society. The

main task of this study, therefore, is to start to redress the balance by investigating the rural activity and villa architecture of Florentines in the fifteenth century.[4] The fundamental questions that motivate this investigation are: what sort of buildings did Florentines of the so-called early Renaissance inhabit when they were out of town, and what sort of lives did they live there?

What emerges is, in art-historical terms, an anti-canonical view of the Florentine villa in this period. For this is not a book about the Renaissance in any obviously recognisable way. The impact of humanism on the villa, a subject with which many have long been concerned, is willfully disregarded, because the purpose here is to escape from the idealised and fictional construction of the 'Renaissance Villa', and to reach towards the everyday experience of people in their country houses. The evidence for this investigation is drawn from unpublished tax returns, account books, diaries, notarial records and letters. Indeed, the approach is largely driven by the archival data, so that villas are explored by way of a variety of documents, while taking particular pains to seek out and exploit the detail retrievable in the richest sources, such as the building accounts and letters relating to the Strozzi villa of Santuccio or the notarised document of Division for the Sassetti villa at La Pietra. Since all sources are to some degree tendentious, it is important to be aware in this case that an abundance of financial documentation tends to lead to a perception of an economically oriented society. This is offered here not as the only interpretation, but as a counterbalance to the view based on pastoral poetry, *novelle*, and humanist panegyric.

Nor is this a book about the Medici. Until now the entire canon of early Renaissance Florentine villas could be said to consist of just five houses: Trebbio, Cafaggiolo, Careggi, Fiesole and Poggio a Caiano, all belonging to the Medici. How is it possible to understand the whole development of villa architecture during the period from this tiny and unrepresentative group of buildings? How is it possible to explore material culture in the countryside, or attitudes to rural life, via one ruling family? As an alternative to the Medici, this book examines the properties of two other clans of the landowning class: the Strozzi and the Sassetti. In doing so, it not only attempts to broaden the canon by looking at imposing but neglected houses, but it also attempts to look beyond the canonical criterion entirely, to find out what more ordinary country houses might have been like and to gain a sense of a whole range of buildings in the fifteenth-century countryside, including labourers' as well as landowners' houses.

It follows that the approach is not based on value judgement, in that the buildings included in this book were not originally selected according to artistic or aesthetic criteria. Most studies of villas have taken architectural merit as the prerequisite for selection or have catalogued the most remarkable buildings within one region, but this is an investigation of two families and all their country houses, whatever their physical appearance may be. Some of these buildings have disappeared or are unrecognisable, others survive in a transformed state with few or no discernible fifteenth-century features, while, in a few cases, the fifteenth-century villa structures have been preserved. The two most complete surviving fifteenth-century landowners' houses belonging to the Strozzi and Sassetti families form the basis for architectural analysis in Parts I and II of this study.

In one further important respect, this work differs from most architectural histories of the villa, for the land and agriculture are treated with the buildings as integral themes. Here the justification is twofold. Firstly, farming was quite simply the economic raison

d'être behind almost every country house; secondly, this approach derives from and is consistent with the fifteenth-century concept of the villa. In and around Florence in this period, the word *villa* was used in three interrelated ways, firstly to mean the countryside in general;[5] secondly, it was applied to a hamlet, unfortified village, or small town in open countryside;[6] and thirdly, it referred to a country estate embracing the landowner's house (*casa da signore*), any related farmhouses (*case da lavoratore*) and outbuildings, together with gardens and farmland.[7] In this book the word villa is largely employed in this third sense to refer to country estates in which the conglomerate of land and buildings are treated as a unity. Apart from the *casa da signore*, the complex of *case da lavoratore*, outbuildings (granaries, stables, dovecotes) and other buildings related to the estate economy (mills, kilns, and country inns) are integrated into a holistic treatment of the estate or villa.

The book is in two parts, each dedicated to a family and its country properties. The two case studies were selected to complement each other, for the Strozzi in Part I are an example of a big, once-powerful clan with vast inherited estates suffering opposition from the ruling Medici faction, whereas the Sassetti in Part II typify a small family of Medici partisans attempting to boost their status through art and architectural patronage and the aquisition of new estates. The many branches of the Strozzi clan managed to survive the demographic crises of the second half of the fourteenth century, emerging with more than forty households in 1427.[8] They were one of the most powerful families in Florentine politics from the election of their first member of the *signoria* in 1284[9] until the exile of four Strozzi in 1434.[10] Even after the return of the Medici, the size of the Strozzi clan, their entrenchment in Florentine patrician circles, the Medicean sympathies of several members, and their caution, resilience and shrewdness ensured their survival under Medicean domination.[11] The Sassetti, on the other hand, had never been a huge family and lost many of their number in the plague of 1383, leaving only five households by 1427.[12] As an old Ghibelline family, they were in political disfavour during the fourteenth century,[13] and it was only as Medici employees and supporters that the brothers Bartolommeo and Francesco Sassetti were elected to public office after 1452.[14]

A close examination of one individual and his main country residence forms the nucleus of each section. Whereas the wide range of rural buildings drawn into this study by including all the residential villas owned by Strozzi and Sassetti kinsmen has made it possible to explore diverse building types of the *contado*, the detailed analysis of two villa owners and their houses – Filippo Strozzi at Santuccio and Francesco Sassetti at La Pietra – sheds light on the stylistic development of villa architecture in this period. In these two case studies Santuccio can be described as a typical fifteenth-century *casa da signore*, while the house at La Pietra emerges as an exceptionally grand and innovatory design that was applauded by humanists and

was far from utilitarian in appearance or function. Yet it is important not to isolate the case of La Pietra and put it on an art-historical pedestal, because it is above all in relation to the buildings around it that we can begin to imagine how a great country house like this might have looked to fifteenth-century Florentines, and it is in the context of the lives of the Sassetti family that we can best understand what this villa might have meant to them and their contemporaries. Apart from investigating the formal characteristics of villa architecture, a key aim of this study is to integrate the buildings with the family history, to use the villas as evidence for understanding the people, particularly the motives and purposes that gave impetus to their lives in the country and, vice versa, to use family history to shed light on the functions and forms of the houses.

 PART ONE: THE STROZZI

THE HISTORY OF THE FLORENTINE VILLA IN THE EARLY RENAISSANCE has been almost entirely built around five houses belonging to the Medici.[1] It is no coincidence that this now obsolete historiographical model should have focussed exclusively on the buildings of the hegemony, but in this case the idea of *Herrschaftsarchitektur* has been carried to extremes, reduced to the buildings of one branch of a single ruling family.[2] It is lamentable that this tiny sample should still be considered representative of fifteenth-century Florence, a republican oligarchy in which not only the vast majority of elite families, but also a substantial section of what might be called the artisan class, and even a surprising number of unskilled urban workers, sharecroppers and tenant farmers, owned some land and a place to stay in the country. Ultimately, the Medici examples may emerge far closer to those of their well-off co-citizens than has been realised, but until the sample is widened to include a larger group of buildings, we shall never be able to evaluate the Medici country houses in context, let alone investigate the broader category of Florentine villas in the early Renaissance.

As members of the ruling class, the Strozzi may seem a dubious choice in the attempt to widen the canvas. Yet, they are also an obvious alternative to the Medici: they were their pre-eminent rivals, an older, larger clan, who were richer and more powerful than the Medici at the beginning of the fifteenth century. Like the Medici, there were important patrons of art and architecture in the family, especially Palla di Nofri Strozzi who acquired key palace and villa sites and commissioned works by Gentile da Fabriano, Fra Angelico, Ghiberti and Michelozzo; and Filippo di Matteo Strozzi, whose most famous commissions were his great palace occupying a whole block in the centre of Florence and his frescoed burial chapel in the church of S. Maria Novella. The Strozzi also provide the opportunity to explore whether opposing factions suffered from cultural, as well as political and financial, exclusion under the Medici regime. Moreover, the surviving archival records of the Carte Strozziane are unsurpassed, even considering the extraordinary wealth of family documentation in the Archivio di Stato in Florence.

The Strozzi family's prominent role in Florentine political life lasted for 150 years from the election of Ubertino di Geri Strozzi as prior in 1284 until 1434 when the Medici regime banished Palla di Nofri Strozzi, together with his kinsmen Smeraldo di Smeraldo Strozzi and Matteo di Simone Strozzi.[3] Between 1282 and 1399 the Strozzi held more posts in the city government than any other family.[4] Their political power was sustained by financial prosperity acquired mainly through international banking and the wool industry. When the new property tax was instituted in 1427 the Strozzi were still the wealthiest clan in Florence, owning "2.6 percent of the total net taxable capital of the city",[5] including Palla di Nofri Strozzi, who was by far the richest individual Florentine, declaring a taxable wealth of 162,925 florins.[6] The Medici regime's suppression of their opponents from 1434 meant that the Strozzi lost their political power, and simultaneously entered a period of financial decline.[7]

Yet the sheer size of the clan, living in about forty-five households in 1427,[8] ensured their survival; while the retention of their social status is demonstrated by their continuing intermarriage with the Florentine oligarchy.[9] Another indicator of wealth, their investment in and use of the state dowry fund (*Monte delle doti*), shows that throughout the fifteenth century more Strozzi women (113) were endowed by the dowry fund, and more Strozzi men (78) married women assisted by the same fund, than in any other clan.[10] Moreover, several branches of the family were Medici partisans who managed to prosper and attain government posts until, in the last two decades of the century, the status of the whole clan was boosted by the extraordinarily successful financial career of Filippo di Matteo Strozzi whose fortune was worth more than 112,000 florins by 1483.[11]

It is clear, therefore, that extremes of wealth and poverty were achieved at different times within the fifteenth century, as indeed they coexisted within the family network.[12] Despite the tendency of historians to concentrate on rich and powerful individuals such as Palla di Nofri and Filippo di Matteo Strozzi, the poor members of the clan outnumbered their wealthier kin. Similarly, political destinies swung during the fifteenth century and, whereas Palla, Smeraldo and Matteo died in exile, and the majority either shunned or were excluded from the political limelight altogether, four key Strozzi – Francesco and Antonio di Benedetto, Messer Marcello di Strozza and Palla Novello – all prospered as Medici supporters. It is partly this range of fortune that makes the Strozzi clan a suitable case study in the quest for a more representative view of rural life and rural buildings. Although they should not be considered as a paradigmatic model, taken as a whole, the Strozzi may characterise broad trends in property holding and development. Above all, the Strozzi are a prime example of urban merchant-bankers who were major landowners in the surrounding countryside while retaining their city base.[13] The origins of their landholdings remain obscure, but widespread purchases are documented from the late thirteenth century until the Black Death in 1348, picking up again in the last quarter of the fourteenth and early fifteenth centuries.

I · THE ACQUISITION AND ALIENATION OF COUNTRY PROPERTY

Families sought to establish their identity in many ways: most obviously through the adoption of a family name and in the display of pictorial and representational signs such as heraldic devices, personal emblems or portraits, or alternatively through written records such as *ricordanze*, geneaologies and even the preservation of family archives. Another tactic operated firstly by way of territorial association, through the occupation and ownership of land or space,[1] and secondly, with the creation of a material identity consisting of inhabited buildings, their contents and all possessions. This material identity, once established, could be passed from generation to generation and became the patrimony. The preservation of a patrimony was considered universally desirable in late medieval and Renaissance society.[2] Nevertheless, it would be wrong to think of its form as fixed, for it was constantly being modified, either augmented and embellished or eroded and transformed. Since the management of property is a continuing process of negotiation, this chapter considers the manoeuvres and strategies that the Strozzi family adopted in their attempt to preserve their rural patrimony during the fifteenth century.

INHERITANCE[3]

Belonging to a well-established, landed family, the fifteenth-century Strozzi mostly inherited their country estates, and wherever possible they retained those ancestral lands. Of the twenty-two Strozzi villa owners listed in the first *catasto* of 1427,[4] fourteen were able to pass their principal country estate to their sons and grandsons, who declared the same villa in the last *catasto* of 1480[5] (Fig. 1 and Appendix B). The remaining eight examples demonstrate that the sale of country estates usually took place under duress. Two of these owners died childless, two were exiled, another family emigrated to Ferrara and another sold land to pay debts. The tenacious attitude to ancestral estates is illustrated by Alessandra Macinghi Strozzi, whose husband, Matteo di Simone, had died in exile and who reluctantly sold her land piece by piece to support her banished sons. She managed to keep the inn at Quaracchi for nearly thirty years after her husband's death, only selling in 1462; and when her son Filippo finally returned, she still owned the farm at Pozzolatico, which had belonged to her father-in-law at the turn of the century.[6]

Thus, the great majority of Strozzi landowners tried to retain their real estate even in the face of misfortune, and a moderate degree of debt was not usually enough to bring about sale. On the contrary, poverty was often cited as a reason for keeping a country house. For example, Bernardo di Giovanni at Signano, Ubertino di Tommaso at Montughi, Carlo di Marco at Il Palagio and Marco di Goro at Fornello all claimed to live in the country because they were too poor to reside in town.[7] Only two members of the clan seem to have sold their main country residence because of debts: Rinieri d'Antonio sold his villa at Brozzi to a richer Strozzi cousin, Francesco di Benedetto in 1441 and Lionardo di Stagio sold his villa at Casi to Francesco Sassetti in 1477.[8]

Nor did the Strozzi sell country lands in order to buy houses in town or to construct new palaces there. Later we shall see that, although Francesco Sassetti bought the site for a new town house, he did not sell country property so as to raise the capital to build in Florence. The wealthiest members of the Strozzi clan, Palla di Nofri and Filippo di Matteo, had sufficient funds to build a palace in the city while maintaining their country estates. Only Palla di Palla and his sons sold rural property in order to build their new town palace, the Strozzino, although significantly they chose to sell land and scattered farm houses while managing to keep their main country residence at Soffiano. In tax returns there are many complaints from Strozzi who could not afford a town house, yet only one of the family, Rinieri d'Antonio, took up the option to sell his villa in order to retain urban property.

It has been suggested that country property was a less highly esteemed component of the Florentine patrimony than urban real estate,[9] but the Strozzi evidence, demonstrating that there was a firm and widely held policy of preserving inherited villas,[10] shows that it is unwise to contrast attitudes to town and country property in black and white terms. The most pragmatic reason for holding on to ancestral lands is that inheritance is the only form of acquisition that requires no capital outlay. But above all, the retention of old property as well as the choice of new sites in Strozzi-dominated districts, demonstrates that the association of family identity with ancestral country estates remained powerful throughout the century. There was no rush to sell out and build new villas in new places.[11] Filippo di Matteo was unusual because he returned to Florence in 1470 with a great fortune in capital but no real estate and had the opportunity to begin on fresh ground as well as the means to build on a grand scale. Nevertheless, he is a paradigmatic example of the traditional clansman, investing modestly and conservatively in the old family areas, buying back the

villa at Santuccio, which had previously belonged to his uncle and where his family had owned the patronage rights to an oratory since the 1370s, acquiring a house at Capalle that his kinsman had owned and was close to other cousins, and finally purchasing land at Le Miccine where several Strozzi grazed their livestock.

The notion of ancestral lands has been challenged by P. J. Jones, who suggested that such estates were not as ancient as genealogists had implied and that they were acquired in the thirteenth or fourteenth centuries rather than in the eleventh or twelfth.[12] However, the desire of fifteenth-century landowners and diarists to represent properties aquired by their fathers and grandfathers as ancestral, is itself significant, and reveals their wish to appropriate the signs of dynastic stability and old wealth in an accelerated timescale. Strozzi dominance in the districts of Campi and Capalle was indeed relatively recent. Campi Bisenzio had been a feudal estate of the Mazzinghi family from the tenth century,[13] until the Strozzi began to buy into the area around 1295, increasing their holdings as the Mazzinghi fortunes sank during the fourteenth century.[14] The Strozzi fortress at Campi was not built until the 1370s by Carlo di Strozza, who enlisted funds for construction from other members of his clan.[15] Similarly, Capalle had long been a rural haunt of the archbishop of Florence, who owned a palace next to the ancient *pieve* there.[16] In this case too, the Strozzi probably only gained their foothold in the *castello* in the early fourteenth century,[17] but they were certainly a dominant presence by the end of the fourteenth century and retained three large estates at Capalle throughout the fifteenth century.[18]

Although most Strozzi inherited their estates directly from their father or grandfather, a few members of the clan benefited from non-patrilineal or collateral inheritance. For example, Piero di Carlo's estate was entirely made up of bequests from various members of his family. He inherited his first town house from his sister Maddalena who died in 1430,[19] but nevertheless preferred to reside at the Villa of Querceto near Ponte a Mensola, which he initially rented from his naturalised Ferrarese cousins Niccolò, Lorenzo, Uberto

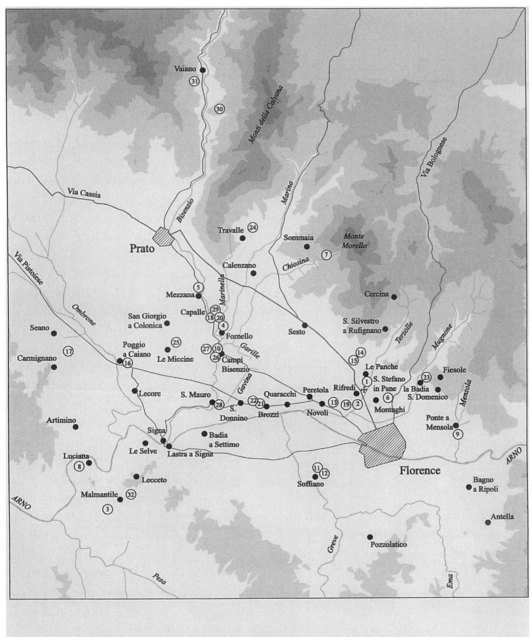

1. Map of the Floren-
tine *contado* showing
the location of Strozzi
villas in the fifteenth
century. The numbers
correspond to the list
of Strozzi villas in
Appendix B (drawn
by Steven J. Allen,
adapted from IGM,
1:100,000, Folio 106,
'Firenze', 1956).

N

0   10 km

1. Alle Gore/Le Panche	9. Querceto	17. Trefiano	25. Le Miccine
2. Poate in Mezzo	10. Rocca di Campi	18. Capalle	26. Il Palagio
3. Le Corti	11. Soffiano	19. La Loggia/Macia	27. Signano
4. Fornello	12. Soffiano	20. Capalle	28. Santuccio
5. L'Agio del Santo/Mezzana	13. Novoli	21. In Cantone	29. Il Palagione
6. Montughi	14. Petraia	22. Brozzi	30. Maglio
7. Loiano/Rocca di Morella	15. Il Palagetto	23. Palaiuola	31. Il Mulinaccio/Casi
8. Castelio di Luciano	16. Ambra	24. Galluzzo	32. Malmantile

and Tito di Nanne Strozzi. It was later confiscated and came into his own possession in 1436 (Fig. 2).[20] In 1438, his brother Salamone died and a codicil in their father's will came into effect ensuring that his farms at Campi went to Piero rather than to Salamone's own children.[21] Finally, in 1449, a first cousin, Strozza di Smeraldo, bequeathed his town house and his estate at Loiano on Monte Morello to Piero. By then, he owned two of the grandest and best-situated of all Strozzi villas, Loiano and Querceto, and was so well provided for that he could afford to sell the scattered and less valuable lands at Campi.[22]

Given the great variety in fortune and career patterns observable across the many branches of the Strozzi clan, the consistency and tenacity with which they held on to old rural estates is remarkable. It is also clear from the rich documentation that the main landowner's house or *casa da signore* was the most persistently guarded single item in the portfolio of inherited and bequeathed country properties. Scattered lands and smaller houses were more frequently and easily sold because they were a less important part of the patrimony, whereas the *casa da signore*, perceived as a crucial part of the family's sense of identity, was retained even in adverse circumstances.

SHARED OWNERSHIP AND DIVISION

The desire to maintain intact major dynastic estates came inevitably into conflict with the need to divide property among heirs.[23] Since the rule of primogeniture was not observed in central Italy,[24] a landowner could either leave his estate to be shared among his sons or heirs *per non diviso*, or he could separate his properties and distribute them among the individual heirs. Many country estates were maintained jointly by a widow and her sons until the widow's death or the sons' maturity,[25] and most of the Strozzi estates were shared between brothers at some time.[26] This shared arrangement seldom survived into the heirs' middle age, however, and even more rarely into the next generation. The selfish desire for sole possession, the urge towards economic independence, and the sheer inconvenience of housing several families under the same

roof led to the eventual division of households. So although a shared household was an experience suffered by the majority, it rarely lasted a lifetime, and the overcrowding that occurred when brothers married and produced children often precipitated division. At this point, the property might either be sold outside the family, or an exchange might be negotiated within the family. This sort of exchange took place between Francesco and Zanobi di Benedetto Strozzi, who originally shared their villa at Brozzi. When Francesco was forty with a wife and seven children his brother Zanobi gave up his half of the *casa da signore* in return for land in the district. Zanobi Strozzi, the manuscript illuminator and painter, was then twenty-two and had already bought another villa for himself at Palaiuola below the Badia Fiesolana.[27]

Moreover, it was usually the principal family residences – in town or country – which were coveted by the whole family and which represented a large capital unit that could not be divided and apportioned as easily as pieces of land, shops or small houses. Thus, in 1430 and 1433, Francesco and Zanobi still shared the Brozzi villa, while all their other country lands and farmhouses had already been divided between them.[28] Similarly, in 1427, Messer Marcello and Rosso, the sons of Strozza Strozzi, submitted separate tax returns for all their property except for the Rocca di Campi and its lands, for which they wrote a third, joint tax return,[29] delaying the problem of division until the next generation.[30]

The differences and quarrels arising from shared property are documented in tax returns and *ricordanze*. The ambiguity of these arrangements left much room for manipulation and exploitation within the family and almost inevitably gave rise to complex notarised exchanges, if not full-scale litigation.[31] In one family, Giovanni, Tommaso and Begni, the sons of Jacopo d'Ubertino, all disagreed about the division of their patrimony and particularly their villa at Ponte di Mezzo, which was swapped from one brother to the other. It belonged to Giovanni in 1430 and was declared jointly by all three in 1442; but after a legal settlement in 1446, it was allotted to Tommaso, although Giovanni was still complaining in 1451 that he owned no country property and that

2. Querceto in the parish of S. Martino a Mensola, Nanne di Carlo Strozzi's house, that was confiscated and sold to Piero di Carlo Strozzi c. 1438.

the settlement was unfair, whereupon he was compensated for the loss of the main villa with a farm above Sesto.[32]

Another division between the three sons of Benedetto di Marcuccio Strozzi is a typical example of a distribution that strove to provide each male heir with his fair share from a legacy that was not quite big enough to furnish each son with the ideal combination of a town and a country house. Marco lived with his wife and two children in his half of a town house in San Pancrazio while also owning a farm in Le Miccine.[33] His brother Bernardo, who had no wife or offspring, let the other half of the town house to one distant Strozzi cousin while he boarded in the house of another cousin Francesco di Zanobi, at the same time maintaining a farm in the Mugello inherited from his mother.[34] The third brother Giovanmaria inherited the principal family villa in Le Miccine and had to manage without a house in town.[35] For the purposes

of this division, therefore, the main country estate with its *casa da signore* was considered to be the equivalent of half a town house plus a farm.

Divisions might also be drawn up on paper for tax evasion or to document a legal agreement rather than as a true reflection of the living situation. This was the case for Marco di Goro, who owned two large rural estates with *case da signore* in the first half of the fifteenth century. The tax returns submitted by Marco and his sons in 1427, 1430 and 1433 state that they were living at the villa of Fornello while Mezzana remained uninhabited.[36] By 1442, Marco's son had died and separate returns were submitted by his daughter-in-law, who claimed to be living alone at Fornello, while eighty-eight-year-old Marco and his six grandsons all resided at Mezzana.[37] This was highly implausible, but the apparent division reflected separate patrimonies, that of the grandfather with his grandsons and heirs, and that of the daughter-in-law who had reclaimed her

supervised the Gianfigliazzi farms and rebuilding in the Val di Pesa.[72] It is possible that her purchase of Il Corno from her brother Battista for 640 florins was a form of loan, since the household and farm accounts suggest that Battista continued to live at the villa,[73] and, as a rich widow, Selvaggia was certainly in a position to offer charity to her family.

PURCHASE

The most frequent type of purchase made by the Strozzi during the fifteenth century was small scale and involved odd pieces of land either near established family farms or intended to complement the type of land that the family already owned. The level of prosperity was not sufficient for most members of the clan to afford new farms let alone a whole new estate.

Francesco di Benedetto Strozzi was unusual in that he was a Medici partisan and, although he never rejected his Strozzi kin, he continued to prosper in the 1430s and 1440s.[74] Thus Francesco bought his second villa just along the street from his first in the village of Brozzi, and his sons extended the Brozzi lands with eight extra fields that they bought in the late 1450s and 1460s.[75] His son Vanni di Francesco created a large estate at Galluzzo near Travalle, northwest of Calenzano.[76] The formation of this estate gives a clear idea of how such a villa was created in the fifteenth century. The *casa da signore* and its farm formed the nucleus of the holding, and a family bequest helped provide the impetus for expansion (Fig. 3). The *casa da signore* at Galluzzo was acquired in two halves, the first bought for a mere thirty florins in June 1458 and the second given the following year by a female relative, Antonia di Lorenzo d'Uberto Strozzi. This donation may have been foreseen because a series of land purchases and exchanges began in July 1458. Meadows and woods in adjacent parishes were bought, and more distant lands were given in exchange for pieces adjoining Galluzzo. By 1469, the lands at Galluzzo were listed in seventeen pieces, farmed by one family of sharecroppers.[77] Consolidation and extension continued throughout the 1470s when another tenant farmer's house and an oil press were bought together with woods, meadows and arable fields.[78]

At both the beginning and the end of the century, Palla di Nofri (before his exile) and Filippo di Matteo (after his years in exile) acquired large rural estates, which are the only outstanding examples among the Strozzi of large-scale rural investors. However the similarity between their policies ends there, for, despite Filippo's great wealth, his country properties were not exceptionally extensive: three villas for his own habitation and other farms mostly clustered around those villas. Palla, on the other hand, declared far more country land than any other Florentine in his tax returns of 1427, 1430 and 1433, and his properties extended as far afield as Pisa, Carmignano and Prato. He owned at least eight *case da signore*, although only two or three seem to have been furnished for his own habitation.[79] In his accumulation of country property, Palla di Nofri Strozzi was continuing a project initiated by his father,[80] just as construction and decoration of the Sacristy of Santa Trinita in Florence was initiated by Nofri.[81] When Nofri died in 1417, he already owned large expanses of land, and Palla went on to extend them, creating the vast holdings he declared in 1427, which were not equalled by any other Florentine until Lorenzo de' Medici's extravagant purchases of the 1480s and early 1490s.[82] The year 1427, however, marked the high point of Palla's wealth, for property tax and the series of forced loans made by the commune in the late 1420s and early 1430s hit him hard, and he had already sold a number of properties by the time of his exile in 1434.[83]

Although his wealth was comparable, Filippo di Matteo's attitude was in direct contrast to Palla di Nofri's. He made no attempt to accumulate huge estates distributed over a wide area. The first villa bought after his return was a clannish choice, an old Strozzi property at Capalle that had belonged to Ubertino di Tommaso and was sold to Filippo by Marcuccio di Carlo Strozzi and his brothers Niccolò, Girolamo and Paolo for 1,000 florins on 18 May 1475.[84] Filippo continued to enlarge this estate, buying the surrounding fields at Ciriegio and storage buildings within the *castello* walls at Capalle.[85]

Two years later, Filippo bought his main residential villa at Santuccio between the villages of San Donnino and San Mauro for 1,250 florins.[86] Although he bought the *casa da signore* and its farm from the heirs

3. Galluzzo in the parish of S. Maria a Travalle, Val di Marina, Vanni di Francesco Strozzi's house, rebuilt c. 1460–80.

of Giovanni degli Alberti, this property had belonged to Filippo's great uncle Pinaccio di Filippo Strozzi in the 1420s and early 1430s[87] until it was confiscated and consigned to the Alberti in payment of a debt in 1436.[88] Moreover, the next-door oratory of San Giovanni Battista with its farm had come to the Strozzi from the Manfredi in the fourteenth century when Lena di Filippo Manfredi married Filippo's great-great-grandfather Messer Lionardo di Loso Strozzi.[89] Pinaccio together with other Strozzi had administered the oratory farm in the 1430s, and this land together with the patronage rights to the oratory were inherited by Filippo and his brother Lorenzo.[90] The purchase of Santuccio should therefore be regarded as the reacquisition of an ancestral property further motivated by their continuing patronage of the adjacent oratory.

In early 1484, Filippo bought his third villa, in the Bisenzio valley at Maglio. The initial cost was less, but the development of the farms required more labour, and he continued to enlarge and improve his lands there until his death. As late as August 1490, Filippo bought another farm at Maglio including a large farmhouse complex with extensive lands.[91]

In addition to the three residential villas, Filippo bought a big farm at San Donato in Fronzano in June 1483[92] and four farms at Le Miccine between 1482 and 1490.[93] This policy of expansion was continued by Filippo's widow Selvaggia and her sons. Filippo had bought two kilns at San Cresci a Campi with land for quarrying, which were meant to serve the needs of the palace building project in town.[94] After his death, Filippo's heirs bought more land at San Cresci a Campi and vineyards next to their other kiln at San Piero a Ponti, as well as more fields at Santuccio and Maglio.[95]

RENTING

It was not common practice to rent *case da signore* in the fifteenth century. The reasons for this are that, although it may appear that they were only inhabited by the landowner in the summer and for brief periods during the rest of the year, in fact there was usually a servant or factor in residence, and visits from the children and women of the family were more frequent and lengthy.[96] Availability to the extended family, and in time of heat or plague, or when whim dictated, was a key factor in villa-owning. Besides, a surprising number of the Strozzi were living year-round at their villas in this period, so their *case da signore* were not for rent.

An exception to this practice was made by Filippo di Matteo who let his newly purchased villa at Santuccio to Lucrezia Tornabuoni, widow of Piero de' Medici for five years from 1477 to 1482 at nine florins per annum. Lucrezia did not inhabit the villa herself, but handed it on to her attorney (*mallevadore*) Bernardo Baroncelli.[97] As a young artist, the miniaturist Zanobi di Benedetto Strozzi had lived in his villa near the Badia Fiesolana, but in 1446 he moved into town and let his country house to four widows, one of whom was a vowess (*pinzochera*). In this case, the rented villa may have functioned as a religious retreat for a small group of pious women or as an inexpensive abode for poor widows.[98] This property was particularly suitable for this purpose because it was relatively close to town, there were gardens but no farmland to administer, and the rent was only five florins a year. On the other hand, Piero di Carlo Strozzi paid a far higher rent of fifty florins a year for the lease of the villa of Querceto, which included the crops from the large estate.[99] This was a long-term arrangement between Piero and his first cousins Niccolò, Lorenzo, Uberto and Tito, whose father Messer Nanne Strozzi had long since settled in Ferrara. Their failure to pay taxes eventually led to the villa's confiscation and sale at a cheap price to the tenant Piero di Carlo.[100]

The wish to keep property within the clan is reflected in urban rent arrangements, a large proportion of which were between relatives. Bernardo di Benedetto, for example, let his half of a town house to one relative for fifteen florins per annum, while he himself was paying twenty-four florins for board and lodging ('*la tornata e spese*') to another relative.[101] Bernardo's brother Marco mostly lived at his villa at Le Miccine, but on his visits to town he moved from one relative to the next: 'I live most of the time in the country, and when I come into Florence I sometimes stay with one and sometimes with another of my relatives, and still I need to rent a house'.[102] A relative could also be trusted to care for and repair

clan property. Niccolò di Lionardo and his brother Jacopo lived abroad all their working lives and let their Florentine house to Niccolò di Jacopo d'Ubertino Strozzi. Niccolò di Lionardo, known for his extraordinary portrait sculpted in marble by Mino da Fiesole (see Fig. 116 in Chapter 7), was busy managing his bank in Rome and complained that he needed a tenant to prevent the old family residence from falling down, although much of the rent was consumed by the cost of repairs.[103]

The dense network of family ties is nowhere better illustrated than in these mutual arrangements for renting town property.[104] Intense activity in the rental market also reflects the scarcity of large sums of capital in the family in this period. Residential mobility among the Strozzi did not reflect the large choice afforded by prosperity, but rather the shortage of housing in Florence and financial insecurity. Although he was no longer poor by the 1440s, Piero di Carlo's movements are characteristic of the local situation. Apart from his villa at Querceto where he frequently stayed, Piero was renting a palace in town from Rinieri d'Antonio Strozzi for twenty-two florins a year, at the same time as he was letting his own town house for thirteen florins.[105] To pay his debts, however, in 1441 Rinieri d'Antonio sold his villa at Brozzi where he had been living and took his town palace back in 1442.[106] Piero di Carlo was then obliged to reside at the Querceto villa for a few years, with the intention of moving back into his town house on the Corso degli Strozzi, which he had been letting.[107] The general picture gained from such documents is of frequent shifts between town and country bases and equally frequent moves within town itself. Although Piero is the only member of the Strozzi family who rented his main country residence at one stage, the greater desirability, the shortage and the expense of town houses meant that many of the family were obliged to rent palaces or apartments in Florence.[108]

When cash was short, rural proprietors could loan their property to creditors as a convenient method of payment. Benedetto di Pieraccione let his villa Il Cortile at Capalle to Conte Spinelli for five years as a way of repaying his debt to him. During this time Spinelli was to receive the produce from the farm and, according to their agreement of 24 July 1441, if he had not been entirely repaid in kind, after five years he was entitled to sell the land.[109] Similarly, Francesco di Benedetto's sons owed 200 florins to their relative Giovanni di Caroccio Strozzi, but instead of cash they leased him their farm at Ruballe and later gave him their house at Fiesole free of rent with the produce from the farm.[110]

The most common leases in the country were, of course, those contracted between a landowner and his tenant farmer, which are discussed in the following chapter on agriculture. Yet not all country property was for the use of the *signore* or the *lavoratore*. Village houses were often let to local shopkeepers, such as Francesco di Benedetto and Carlo di Marco Strozzi, who both owned butcher's shops in the villages beside their villas;[111] whereas Simone di Filippo had an inn that he let to country innkeepers, and four other houses at Quaracchi and Campi that were let to local residents.

SALE

Just as the purchase of property is an obvious indication of prosperity, so the sale and stagnation of real estate are clear signs of hard times. Therefore, if one accepts that the exile of Palla, Matteo and Smeraldo had a disastrous political and economic effect on the clan as a whole, it is perhaps surprising that a greater number of the main Strozzi villas were not sold after 1434. In many cases the sale of scattered pieces of land and farms deferred the sale of a *casa da signore*. Benedetto di Pieraccione Strozzi, the humanist scholar and scribe, managed to retain the house at the heart of his Capalle estate, although he had to sell large blocks of land to pay debts. Of his eight or nine original farms, only two were left for his heirs in 1469.[112] Carlo di Marcuccio Strozzi is another example of someone who chose to retain his principal residence in the country, while selling his last foothold in town. Although he complained of poverty, debts and the need to provide dowries, he kept all his country property intact and lived off the land in his villa, called Il Palagio, at Campi.[113]

On the other hand, for at least one member of the clan, life in town took precedence. Rinieri d'A Antonio and his nephew Giovanni di Caroccio chose to keep their palace on the Via Larga de' Legnaiuoli (the present Via Tornabuoni) and sell the villa at Brozzi. The death of his brother Lionardo meant that Rinieri had to repay the widow's dowry, for which he sold four shops in town, land and farmhouses at Brozzi, a farm and a mill at Lecore and another farm at Campi. To cover other debts, Rinieri sold the family villa of Il Cantone at Brozzi with its garden, a series of vineyards and grain lands round about and part of a mill on the Arno.[114] Yet it is significant that Il Cantone did not pass out of the family, for it was bought by another Strozzi, Francesco di Benedetto, who owned the house next door on the village street in Brozzi.

Apart from the exiles, only three other families seem to have sold a large villa between 1427 and 1480. Stagio d'Antonio's villa, known as Il Mulinaccio, in the Val di Bisenzio was convenient to his urban residence in Prato, and a strong attachment to the estate is suggested by the choice of his son's name, probably called Lionardo after the ancient *pieve* of S. Lionardo a Casi, whose patronage rights accompanied ownership of the villa. In 1477, however, Lionardo di Stagio was reduced to selling Il Mulinaccio along with the church patronage rights, to Francesco Sassetti.[115]

Marco di Goro had been complaining of debts and the burden of a numerous family since 1395[116] and managed to hold out for fifty years before finally selling one of his two villas, L'Agio del Santo at Mezzana, in October 1445. It was bought for 2,100 florins *di sugello*, by the Hospital of S. Maria Nuova, who then sold it to Messer Dietisalvi Neroni.[117] Although this must have been an imposing villa in the early fifteenth century with its fortified *casa da signore*, dove-tower, courtyard and meadows, surrounded by five farms with their *case da lavoratore*, its usefulness as a residence was diminished by the proximity of Marco di Goro's other villa at Fornello, where he lived most of the time. Mezzana was declared uninhabited in 1427 and 1430,[118] as its site and functions reproduced those already afforded by Fornello.

The steadily increasing sales of country property by Messer Palla Novello and his sons Agnolo and

4. Soffiano, the houses that originally belonged to Messer Palla Novello Strozzi and to Palla and Carlo di Francesco Strozzi.

Carlo Strozzi shed light on their construction of the Strozzino palace in Florence. The sale of a group of lands for a total of 480 florins to Palla di Nofri Strozzi in 1429 probably had more to do with Palla Novello's business crisis in 1426 and predates plans for a new palace,[119] but the sale of other properties all through the 1430s and 1440s marks the initiation of the urban building scheme, for the first town house on the site of the new palace was bought in 1435, two more houses were purchased in 1440 and 1441, a further two in 1448, another two in 1451 and the final house in 1457. The total cost of the new site seems to have been the remarkably low sum of 600 florins, whereas the sale of country lands between 1430 and 1457 brought 735 florins and the sale of three town houses over 1,500 florins more.[120] A detailed study is required to discover exactly how the site and construction of the Strozzino was funded, but it seems likely that the sale of country land, together with the three town houses, went a considerable way towards paying for the new

palace. A renewed need for cash is reflected in the sale of more country properties in the 1460s. A farm at Mosciano was sold for 139 florins in early 1461, another farm and a meadow at San Giorgio a Colonica were sold for 200 florins and, in 1465, a farm and *casa da signore* at Signano fetched the large sum of 2,200 florins.[121] These were probably intended to cover the cost of a second phase of construction at the palace, during which the main façade was completed (1462–5).[122] It is remarkable that while these other properties were sold, Palla Novello and his sons took care to retain their country house at Soffiano, which is the only villa consistently described as a *casa da signore* in all their tax returns (Fig. 4).

The estate of Carlo and Palla di Francesco derived from the same patrimony as Carlo and Agnolo di Palla Novello – through their common grandfather.[123] Many of their lands were in the same locations, distributed in the area between Soffiano and Settimo on the south bank on the Arno. The pattern of depletion

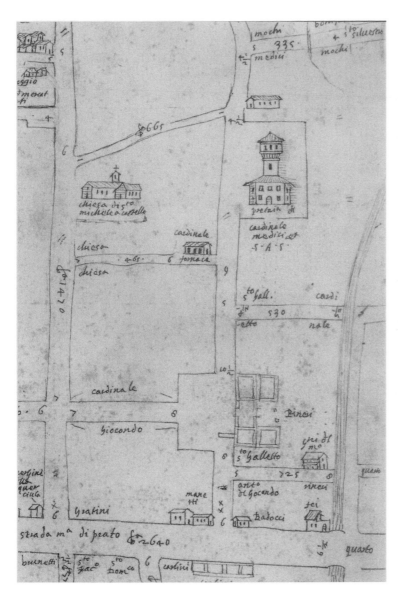

5. Parish of S. Michele a Castello, Messer Palla di Nofri Strozzi's villas of Petraia (shown in elevation, labelled 'Pretaia del cardinale Medici...') and Il Palagetto (shown in plan below with its own piazza, labelled 'Rineri'). Detail of *Piante di popoli e strade – Capitani di parte guelfa – 1580–1595*, II, c. 375.

found in so many Strozzi estates during the fifteenth century is also exemplified in the case of Palla and Carlo di Francesco. The brothers had to sell one farm to pay their sister's dowry and, by 1446, Palla, the elder and poorer of the two, had sold his remaining farms and was reduced to living in a crumbling town house while letting another small house for a pittance. In the same year, Carlo let his country houses in order to help provide his daughters' dowries. He had inherited a small family villa at Soffiano, but he sold it before 1469 and kept two farms there and a house and land in the *castello* of Quarantola in the Val di Pesa.[124]

In summary, only three Strozzi sold their main country residence: Lionardo di Stagio, Carlo di Francesco and Rinieri d'Antonio. Marco di Goro did sell a large ancestral villa, but it was not his only estate and had not been his home for some time. By far the largest number of sales, however, were made by the families of the exiles Palla di Nofri and Matteo di Simone. Smeraldo di Smeraldo ('Smeraldino'), the third Strozzi who was exiled in 1434, left his estate in the hands of his brother Strozza, who grew poorer and sold his one and a half farms at Campi but managed to retain the old family castle of Loiano until his death, when he bequeathed it to his first cousin Piero di Carlo.[125]

The sale of Palla and Matteo's properties did not take place immediately after their departure. F. W. Kent has traced some of the complex methods employed by Palla di Nofri in his effort to retain his Florentine patrimony.[126] In order to avoid taxation and sequestration or outright confiscation, Palla sold his properties at cheap rates to trusted relatives and friends on condition that, should he return to Florence, he could buy back the property for the same amount. Thus, one of the two houses that formed Palla's town residence was sold to his wife's nephew, Messer Marcello Strozzi, who agreed to relinquish the house if Palla required it, while the other house was leased to the Abbot of San Pancrazio in order to be available in case Palla or his sons returned.[127] Other real estate was seized by the commune in payment for Palla's taxes and resold below its true value to selected parties. After the exile of Palla's son Lorenzo in 1438, it was more difficult to guard and administer what was left of his vast estates, and he turned to his son-in-law Giovanni Rucellai as the person he could most trust to assist him. Giovanni bought back a series of Palla's properties that had passed into other hands, including Poggio a Caiano and the ancestral villa of Trefiano.[128]

Another solution adopted by Palla di Nofri was to transfer his property to the women of the family since the commune could not seize the possessions of wives, who were not subject to tax and who were legally entitled to claim property equivalent to their dowry.[129] Thus, Palla's three other most valued estates were initially kept by his wife Marietta and his daughter-in-law Alessandra Bardi-Strozzi. Marietta owned the villa of Petraia from before 1442 until 1446, when it was handed over to the Abbot of San Pancrazio,[130] who let the villa to Alessandra in 1456 and then finally sold it to her in 1458.[131] After the exile of her husband in 1438, Alessandra also owned the property called Il Palagetto on the Piazza below Petraia[132] (Fig. 5), as well as Palla's main residential villa at Novoli.[133] However all three villas were sold soon afterwards. Il Palagetto was sold in 1460 to Bernardo Rinieri and Novoli in the same year to Girolamo Giachinotti, whereas Alessandra sold

Petraia to Agnolo di Nerone di Nigi Dietisalvi in 1463, the year after Palla's death.[134]

Matteo di Simone's real estate was also destined to be sold, although the circumstances were quite different. Matteo died within two years of his departure from Florence,[135] and his widow, Alessandra Macinghi Strozzi, claimed his entire estate in restitution for her dowry which had been large (1,600 florins[136]), but was probably not worth Matteo's palace on the Corso degli Strozzi, another town house, an inn at Quaracchi, four other country houses, four farms and scattered lands.[137] Alessandra's legal ownership and her presence in Florence, which enabled her to supervise the estate and placate tax officials, kept Matteo's patrimony safe from confiscation. Nevertheless, these were hard years for Alessandra, who, in 1442, claimed to owe 600 florins to the commune.[138] She managed to hold off the sale of real estate until 1446, when she sold a town house in Via San Gallo and two pieces of land at Petriolo. It was another ten years before she sold two farms at San Piero a Calicarza, which were among the least valuable of Matteo's properties,[139] and this was not the immediate result of her husband's exile, but an attempt to inject capital into her sons' growing business.[140] When her sons were exiled in 1458, it was her decision to join them that finally caused Alessandra to sell the properties in the heart of Strozzi country at Quarracchi and Campi.[141] Every year from 1459 to 1465, she sold at least one piece of real estate, raising more than 2,000 florins.[142] By an ironical twist of fate, in 1466, when she had sold all except the farm at Pozzolatico, the ban was lifted and Filippo and Lorenzo were free to return home.[143]

In all their property transactions it is evident that, despite political misfortune and widespread financial restraints, the Strozzi clung to their inherited rural properties and particularly to their main residential estates. Since the clan had more real estate than capital in this period, property, and especially agricultural produce or income generated from its sale, was frequently used as a substitute for cash in dowry and debt settlements. A great range of practices involving the purchase, lease, sale and exchange of rural property is documented in the Strozzi archives, but certain strategies predominate: an engagement in frequent and complex legal negotiations demonstrating versatile systems of property management, a tendency to redistribute property within the clan whenever possible, and an ambition to own residences in both town and country, coupled with a willingness to let the town palace (or part of it) in times of financial hardship.

In opposition to Richard Goldthwaite's view that 'the country house was not an ancestral seat where the noble had an independent basis of power and status',[144] the overwhelming evidence from the Florentine archives shows that a large proportion of the main residential estates owned by the fifteenth-century Florentine elite were indeed ancestral estates. In particular, proprietors' unwillingness to dispose of their principal residential villa demonstrates that its maintenance was an important symbol of dynastic longevity and family identity. Land-owning was always a source of status, in Tuscany as elsewhere. As a power base, the villa did not function in the same way as a town palace, yet it would be wrong to assume that the networks established in the countryside were not strongly supportive and highly valued. After all, land-owning itself is a form of power holding, and the dominion a proprietor could hold over a country district was both quantitatively (in the sense of covering a larger geographical area) and qualitatively (in the sense of a more complete dependence of the local population on their landlord) greater than that he could achieve in the city.[145]

On the other hand, Goldthwaite's statement that 'there was not . . . a return to the countryside' does hold true for the Strozzi and for other fifteenth-century Florentine landowners.[146] Apart from Nofri di Palla and his son's vast investment in country property in the first twenty-seven years of the century, there was no remarkable new shift towards rural investment among the Strozzi. Filippo di Matteo preferred to save cash or invest in his own banking enterprise, and although his land purchases were steady from the time of his return to Florence in 1471 and increased considerably from the mid-1480s, he reserved his major capital outlay for the great town palace.[147] Other Strozzi who had the means to buy in the country, expanded on a respectable scale, as Francesco di Benedetto did at Brozzi and his son Vanni at Galluzzo; but as a clan the Strozzi could not be cited as evidence for either refeudalisation or a return to the land in this period. It could be further argued that there was no need to return to the land because they had never (at least not since the thirteenth century) left it.

2 · THE AGRICULTURAL ESTATE

Just as a Florentine Renaissance palace is inconceivable without its urban context of streets and piazzas, so the fifteenth-century Florentine villa is unimaginable without the surrounding agricultural landscape. Architectural history has, however, tended to isolate the country house from its land and to study it as a self-contained work of art, or as an aesthetic concept exported by the city-dwelling patron and architect. Yet this academic construction does not fit what we know of fifteenth-century Tuscany, where the landowner's house and its surrounding land were bound together in a symbiotic relationship. The house was ultimately a product of its rural setting, and that setting was predominantly agricultural – whether it was the market gardens of suburban Florence, the wheatfields and vineyards of the Arno valley, or the high pasture and woodland of the upper Mugello and the Montagne Pistoiesi.

The single most important motive behind villa or land ownership was agricultural productivity or, at its most fundamental level, the need to eat, survive and, if possible, to make a profit. The priorities were epigrammatically laid out in Leon Battista Alberti's seven-page vernacular treatise entitled *Villa*. There the word *villa* clearly refers to the country estate, that is, to the buildings and the land conceived of as a unity, but with the land given absolute precedence to the point where the house could be dispensed with altogether if necessary: 'If an estate lacks a house, it will be less missed than if a house lacks land'.[1]

Of the thirty-two Strozzi estates studied here, only one country house was not attached to farm land, and that was the exceptional case of Zanobi Strozzi's small house near the Badia a Fiesole. In every other case, the country residences were supported by at least one, and usually several, farms with many additional scattered pieces of land. For a full understanding of the villa in fifteenth-century Tuscany, it is therefore essential to investigate the farming practices of these Florentine landowners and to ask how the villa functioned as an agricultural unit. The four fundamental questions investigated in this chapter are: How did landowners manage their rural estates? How was the land worked? What did the farms produce? And what was the overall shape of the landed estate?

THE MANAGEMENT OF COUNTRY ESTATES

There is a huge body of evidence for the close involvement of landowners with the practical aspects of farming.[2] The large proportion of agricultural matters in *ricordanze* and household account books shows that farm administration was not only carried out by remote control with the help of financial systems and bailiffs, but was a more direct and down-to-earth participation. Family correspondence and letters between landowners and estate managers also document the proprietor's daily concern with his estates.[3] The 'hands-on' approach of many Florentine landowners is conveyed by the famous Medicean examples of Cosimo Pater Patriae, who was reported to have grafted fruit trees and pruned his own vines at Careggi,[4] and Lorenzo il Magnifico, who went to great lengths to import new breeds of cow for his dairy farm at Poggio a Caiano.[5]

The archival and anecdotal evidence is supported by the theorists who asserted that there was no substitute for the personal supervision of property. Piero de' Crescenzi considered the productivity of the farm to be dependent on the presence of the *signore*, which in turn was facilitated by proximity to town:

> The landowner's presence is needed for the fields, and whoever abandons his vineyard will be abandoned by it. Among peasants of importunate greed only the presence of the owner and his attentiveness are feared.[6]

Alberti also emphasised surveillance of the untrustworthy *villano*, which could only be achieved through the landowner's own diligence.[7] Among the Strozzi this view is echoed by Palla di Nofri's less prosperous brother Marco, who owned four farms and five pieces of land near Prato. He had no country residence and so was obliged to ride out on horseback from his rented house in town to oversee his lands, a chore he considered essential if he were to receive any profit at all.[8]

A key person in the management of country estates was the *fattore*, the estate manager or factor.[9] The employment of an estate manager should not be taken as a sign of neglect by the owner or even as a substitute for personal involvement. Whenever an estate was composed of many farms and separate pieces of land, or was scattered over several districts; or when the landowner resided in town, travelled frequently, or owned a number of villas, an estate manager was required as a central administrator to supervise tenant farmers and see to the overall upkeep of the estate. Two of his most important tasks were to collect rents and keep the farm accounts,[10] but his duties ranged from guarding the *casa da signore* and the harvest during the owner's absence to initiating new policies regarding crop planting or buying livestock at market. On a more manual level, the *fattore* often cultivated the kitchen garden, which provided fruit and vegetables for the proprietor's own table.

It is clear from Palla di Nofri Strozzi's tax returns that he intended his factors to look after his decaying or incomplete country houses. One lived below Petraia in 'a servants' dwelling', another stayed at Poggio a Caiano in the 'dwelling called Ambra, all in ruins'; while a third lived at Trefiano in 'a palace badly situated and unfit for habitation'.[11] Together with Novoli, these were Palla's favourite villas, all intended for renovation and for his own eventual habitation. While the factors were in residence, the houses were preserved from further decay, and they could also supervise repairs or construction on the site. Above all, these villas were at the centre of large agricultural estates administered by the factors. The fragmentation of Palla's lands and their distribution over a wide area made such a system of control essential, and a master account book for his farms entitled, 'Entrata de' poderi: 1423–25', is divided according to the nine administrative centres to which crops and rents were delivered.[12] Five of these were towns or large villages where Palla owned houses for secure crop storage and redistribution: Florence, Prato, Figline Val d'Arno, Empoli and Campi Bisenzio; the other four were the villas described above: Petraia, Ambra (Poggio a Caiano), Trefiano and Novoli, the last of these his main country residences.

Filippo di Matteo Strozzi, the other example of outstanding wealth in the clan, had a consistent policy of employing relatives to manage his estates, not only because greater trust could be placed in members of the family, but because this was a form of charity a rich man could bestow on his poor relations. Most of these were not professional *fattori* in the narrow sense, but clerks or administrators who fulfilled several roles simultaneously. Marco di Benedetto was employed as clerk of the works for two construction projects in the country at Santuccio (1482–6) and Maglio (1486–7), as well as for the great Strozzi Palace in town (from 1489).[13] Although he was a paymaster and accountant rather than a farm manager, when the land at Maglio was being drained, terraced and planted, it was Marco who kept the accounts and was on the spot to supervise the agricultural work at the same time as the villa was being built there.[14] In this case, the construction of a landowners's house and farm buildings was part of the whole scheme of agricultural improvement (*bonificazione*). When the Maglio estate had been established, two other relatives were hired as factors there, Francesco di Carlo Strozzi in 1488[15] and Piero di Messer Michele Strozzi in 1489.[16]

At Capalle yet another kinsman – Pagholo di Benedetto di Pieraccione Strozzi – ran the estate. Already living on the spot, the son of the humanist scholar and scribe, Pagholo is not called *fattore* in the accounts, and he held a more priviledged position than that of the ordinary factor. Grain was delivered by the tenant farmers to the Palagione from where Pagholo either sold it or had it milled and transported to Filippo's palace in town. A separate account book was kept for each tenant farmer so that they could be scrupulously supervised. Pagholo also organised the alterations to farm houses and Filippo's residence, Il Palagione, paying the builders and purveyors and checking the work.[17]

Not all Filippo's estate managers were relatives, however, for when construction at his main residential villa of Santuccio was completed in 1486, a factor called 'Piero di Sandro da Llechore fattore del nostro maggiore al Santuccio' was hired at an annual salary of forty lire.[18] Perhaps the most responsible position of all was given to Giuliano d'Antonio from Quarantola in the Val di Pesa, whom Filippo despatched to Naples to look after Bella Vista, his farm and gardens perched above the Bay of Naples that were praised for their beauty and exotic plants in Lorenzo Strozzi's biography of his father.[19]

There was another position to be filled in the hierarchy of farm administration, that of cashier, clerk or farm secretary. Surprisingly, in a period when few educated women found employment, this job was sometimes allotted to married women with arithmetical skills.[20] Mona Checcha di Dino from Poggio a Caiano was *cassiera* at Santuccio at a salary of eight florins a year from 1491 to 1492, succeeded by Mona Nana di Jachopo in 1493.[21]

The practice of employing a different factor for each villa could only be followed by the wealthiest landowners and was by no means common. Marco di Goro Strozzi and his heirs, for example, kept an estate manager at their residential villa Fornello, whereas nearby at the equally large estate of Mezzana, they merely employed a young farmhand (*garzone*) to till the *orto* and do odd jobs.[22] In the tax return of 1457, the factor at Fornello is introduced as Francesco di Bartolo. He received an annual salary of thirty lire, but the only duties listed were to deliver provisions to Florence and to cultivate the gardens. Food and lodging were also provided for his wife and son, who helped to nurse Marco di Goro's widow, a frail seventy-year-old.[23] By 1480 the same factor was kept on as an old retainer, receiving the same salary but needing to be waited on himself.[24]

The low salaries among factors may be explained by the fact that they received lodging at the villa and could grow food and crops for their own use. It also seems to have been a recognised perk to skim a little wheat, wine or fodder from the tenant farmers' payments before they reached the *signore*. They were certainly in a good position to fiddle the accounts.

A fuller picture of the flexibility of the factors' role and some sense of their priviledged status among employees can be gleaned from the case of Filippo Strozzi's father Matteo di Simone and his trusted agent in the countryside. Agnolo di Papi di Buto da Quaracchi was a long-standing tenant, whose father had also been a tenant farmer (*fittaiolo*) of Matteo's father. From before 1425 until at least 1450, Agnolo rented the house and land next to Matteo's tavern at Quaracchi, from where he could conveniently supervise the farms, village houses and pieces of land that were scattered between the districts of Quaracchi and Campi.[25] Although Agnolo's own book of farm accounts does not survive,[26] Matteo's *ricordanze* document his activities as rent collector. In 1431 Agnolo collected grain rents from ten country tenants, delivering eighty *staia* of wheat to Matteo for household consumption and selling the remainder to a local miller. In addition, he collected the wheat for Matteo's uncle Pinaccio, who was living in London. He transported wine to the palace in town, and when the tavern at

Quaracchi was rebuilt in 1425–6, he carted bricks and paid for deliveries. In 1432, he took over the management of Matteo's tavern in partnership with the local priest.[27] Agnolo was a faithful retainer who could be trusted to look after the young Matteo on his first departure from home in 1449,[28] and who, as an old man, was determined to make the long journey to Naples to see Filippo before he died.[29] It also emerges from the correspondence of Matteo Strozzi's widow, Alessandra, that her only country residence while her sons were in exile was a house they shared with Agnolo at Quaracchi.[30]

Although factors often did indeed inhabit the *casa da signore*, house-sitting in the owner's absence, they were rarely listed as members of the household in tax returns, making it difficult to establish what proportion of the Strozzi employed estate managers in the fifteenth century. Nevertheless, six families are documented as having factors while two of these, Palla di Nofri and Filippo di Matteo, employed more than one at a time. It is likely that several more used a farm manager or hired someone to carry out those tasks on a part-time basis. It is also clear, however, that when the estate was small or a villa close to town and frequently inhabited by the landowner's family, a manager could be dispensed with, particularly if incomes ran low.

Factors occupied a key role as middlemen in the villa hierarchy, straddling the divide between *signore* and *lavoratore*, between landowner and landworker. Their position in rural society was equivalent to that of a *capomaestro* in the building industry, with responsibility for supervising a workforce (the peasant farmers), ordering supplies (seed, livestock etc.), checking production (delivery of the harvest), keeping accounts, and guarding property. They had to be literate and numerate, with agricultural expertise, and, ideally, honest, loyal, with managerial skills and the shrewdness to detect fraud in others.

FARM LABOUR AND FORMS OF TENURE

The *lavoratori* or peasant farmers were an essential part of the estate community. They cultivated the land and either surrendered half of its produce to the landowner (*mezzadria*), or paid him a fixed rent in cash or kind (*affitto*), or a combination of both.[31] Their role was not limited to the land, however; together with their families, they played a full part in villa life, as members of the estate community. It would be unwise to make rigid class distinctions when considering the hierarchy of rural inhabitants, as it would be unwise to dismiss farm labourers as vassals who tilled the fields and had little contact with the landowners. The documentary evidence suggests a much more fluid and potentially intimate relationship between the classes. *Lavoratori* were sometimes chosen as godparents to the *signore*'s children, especially when those children had been born at the villa. Likewise, the farmers' wives were considered ideal wet nurses for the landowner's babies, while their husbands were often convenient witnesses for legal transactions, especially those pertaining to rural property. It was certainly to the advantage of the *signore* to foster good relations with his *lavoratori*, for loyalty and long service benefitted the land as well as the convenience of both parties.[32]

Labour conditions, however, are not easy to summarise, for the type of tenure and relations between *lavoratore* and *signore* varied greatly from one individual to another, as did the standard of living within each group. The letters of Alessandra Macinghi Strozzi reveal what may have been a typical outlook: a preoccupation with the harvest and its value combined with pride in self-sufficiency and a pragmatic, not to say ruthless, approach to the *lavoratore*:

> This year I think I won't have to buy wine, if no other disaster occurs. Still, there's very little for us all, and the wheat still has not many stalks, but the ears are strong and feel a good weight, better than we've had for some years. I don't know yet how things will go at Pozzolatico, because I haven't a healthy farm worker, and God knows to what state it has been reduced: Piero and Mona Cilia are still alive, both frail. I have let the farm for the year after next, and it would suit me to put it in order; and those two old people, if they don't die, must go out and beg. God will provide.[33]

Alessandra's long familiarity with the aging peasant farmer Piero and his wife Cilia did not increase her compassion for them. Five months later, she took on a new *lavoratore* and wished Piero a speedy death rather than to end his life as a beggar. One senses her frustration at the decaying state of the land, while her need to justify the purchase of a single ox illustrates the parsimony that lay behind the creation of her son Filippo's fortune. Here too, is the attention to detail, the well-informed and practical approach that Florentine landowners applied to rural economy just as they did to business matters in town.[34]

In contrast, Benedetto di Pieraccione Strozzi the humanist scribe, whose land at Capalle supported the families of six or seven *lavoratori*, had a charitable attitude towards his tenant farmers. On leaving Benedetto's farm, one sharecropper still owed him three *moggia* and fifteen *staia* of wheat, but Benedetto recognised his poverty and chose to overlook the debt.[35] Another *lavoratore* had died, and Benedetto allowed his widow to go on living in his house within the village walls at Capalle.[36] Similarly, when the house next to his own courtyard burnt down and he took over the site to enlarge his courtyard, he provided another house rent free for the widow who had been living there.[37]

The type of tenure was usually arranged to suit the type of property. Matteo di Simone received fixed rents for his scattered pieces of land and his inn at Quaracchi, whereas the twenty-one pieces of land he owned at Campi were all cultivated as one *podere* and worked *a mezzo*. The fixed rents for the scattered properties were combined cash and grain rents corresponding with the fact that these were houses with a small piece of arable land attached to each. Matteo charged cash for the houses and grain for the land.[38] Palla di Nofri combined both forms of tenure by charging fixed rent and *mezzadria* payments for the same piece of land. For example, he might receive a combination of cash and half of the wheat crop or a fixed grain rent and half the wine produced.[39]

By the time Filippo di Matteo Strozzi began to buy his rural properties in the 1470s, the labour shortage had come to an end and the proprietor had 'greater contractual power'.[40] Although *mezzadria* was the most common form of tenure on compact farms owned by citizens near Florence, Filippo displayed the same ruthlessness as his mother Alessandra, in preferring to let his farms for high cash and grain rents on short contracts.[41] From the landlord's point of view, the advantages of cash or fixed rents were the steady income that did not fluctuate with a poor harvest, the reduced opportunity for cheating, the high sums that could be fixed at the level of an abundant harvest, and the short terms of lease that made dismissal easy.[42] Otherwise a *fitto* contract for a large farm like Filippo's at Capalle might closely resemble a *mezzadria* contract.[43] For example, in August 1475, Filippo made a three-year contract with two brothers to farm his newly acquired lands at Capalle, although the precarious position of the tenant farmer is still clearly revealed by Filippo's cancellation of the contract at the end of three years, when he took on three new *fittaioli* on the same terms.[44]

Another advantage of a fixed rent was that the landowner need not supervise the land so closely, an arrangement that was highly suitable for absentee landlords.[45] When Pinaccio di Filippo Strozzi lived in London in the 1420s, he let his big farm at Santuccio and other lands at Quaracchi for fixed grain rents, which were collected by the factor of his nephew, Matteo di Simone.[46] Pinaccio's brother Lionardo, who also travelled frequently on business, adopted the same solution, letting his flat lands at Quaracchi for grain rents, the hill farms at S. Martino La Palma for wine and the highest country at Vinci for olive oil rents.[47]

Several Strozzi documents confirm what historians have long maintained – that the greater involvement required by *mezzadria* also led to more intensive and more balanced exploitation of the land.[48] Benedetto di Marcuccio describes how his departure for Mantua caused him to change from *mezzadria* to *fitto*, and although the account should be read with the scepticism normally accorded tax returns, his opinion that *fitto* is less profitable for himself and less beneficial for the land, is probably an honest one:

All the said farms and lands are without oxen because when I left town from necessity, I had to sell the oxen and take back the loans; and in

July 1441 I rented out the farms ... All these properties yield as stated above a rent of 200 lira and 50 *staia* of wheat, and in the first *catasto* they and the others were taxed at a much higher level because then I was continually at the villa and it was like my workshop, and today from necessity I rent them out and they are in bad shape because they are places that need a lot of care and without the owner they don't produce anything and whoever lets them would make little profit.[49]

After his return from Mantua, he complained in 1451 that his farms had half reverted to pasture because he had not been there to look after them,[50] and by 1457 he had returned to the *mezzadria* system on at least one of his farms.[51]

FARM PRODUCE

Information about crops abounds in the Strozzi tax returns and farm accounts.[52] Of all crops grown in the Florentine *contado*, wheat was produced in far the greatest quantity over the widest area for the greatest profit.[53] The largest yields of wheat came from the big valley farms on the rich alluvial soil of the Florentine plain, but smaller amounts were sown wherever feasible in hill country (in areas never used for cereals today), diminishing as the slope grew steeper and the land less fertile.

Palla di Nofri's vast estates were said to yield 600 *moggia* of wheat,[54] which was not derived from a series of huge, compact farms, but from an enormous number of small farms and separate pieces of land scattered over a very wide area. Thus, between 1427 and 1433, his largest villas only produced an average-to-large yield, as at Petraia, where 140 *staiora* of land produced from 75 to 92 *staia* (3–4 *moggia*) of wheat a year, and at Poggio a Caiano, where 224 *staiora* of land produced between 159 and 164 *staia* (6–7 *moggia*) of wheat a year.[55] Although no other Florentine owned nearly as much land, other single Strozzi estates produced an impressive quantity of grain, considerably larger than that produced on any one of Palla's consolidated

holdings. Benedetto di Pieraccione reaped the most from one estate at Capalle where, in 1427, his eight farms yielded a massive 35 *moggia* (840 *staia*) of wheat.[56] A mile down the road at the Rocca di Campi, Messer Marcello's farms produced 20 *moggia* (486 *staia*) of wheat a year before the estate was subdivided.[57] Marco di Goro's lands at Fornello, halfway between Campi and Capalle, yielded more than 14 *moggia* (340 *staia*) and his Mezzana villa, a mile to the north, slightly more – 15 *moggia* and 14 *staia* (374 *staia*), giving a large total of 29 *moggia* for the two estates.[58] Indeed, all the biggest grain producers among the Strozzi farms were within a five-mile radius of Campi Bisenzio,[59] a reminder that agricultural motives underlay the choice of the Campigiano as one of the most popular locations for the country estates of the Florentine elite.

However lucrative the farms, the sale of surplus grain in the marketplace was not sufficient to defray huge tax bills which, ironically, were partly generated by the land and its profits.[60] Nor could an agricultural income protect a landowner from business crises when the need for capital could only be assuaged by the outright sale of real estate. Of these big grain producers, Palla went into exile, Benedetto di Pieraccione's eight farms of 1427 were reduced to two by 1457, the Rocca di Campi estate was divided between heirs, Mezzana was sold,[61] Fornello's land reverted partly to meadow,[62] while at Pinaccio's farm at Santuccio the eleven *moggia* of wheat produced in 1427 had diminished to a mere five and a half *moggia* by 1498. In 1526, the same farm at Santuccio produced even less wheat (four and a half *moggia*), much more wine (sixty barrels), various minor cereals, linen, pigeons and guano, wood, fruit, vegetables and garlic. In this case, a change from grain rents (*fitto*) to sharecropping (*mezzadria*) encouraged diversification as wheat land was replanted in other cereals, linen, vines and trees, and when observed over a century, the tendency towards a greater range of crops and less intensive monoculture of wheat, is marked.[63]

The *colombaie* or dovecotes present on most estates were not so much a decorative addition to the villa complex, as they were essential for the production of bird lime, widely held to be the most effective fertilizer for wheat.[64] The fertility of doves or pigeons ensured that they hatched four, five or even six times a year, and their meat was also much in demand.[65] If the dovecotes were plentifully supplied with food, the birds could roost inside, depositing their manure, and growing fatter than if they had to fly long distances in search of food and shelter.[66] Italian millet (*panico*) and sorghum (*saggina*) were the grains preferred for feeding pigeons in the Florentine *contado*, with Filippo Strozzi's birds, for example, consuming forty *staia* of *panico* and *saggina* at Capalle during the year 1478.[67]

The most common industrial crop of the *contado* was flax. The Strozzi tax returns show that most estates produced their own linen as a cottage industry. The sowing, weeding, pulling, rippling, retting, drying and scutching of the flax was usually done by tenant farmers and their wives, who were paid twelve or thirteen lire for twelve pounds in weight of uncombed linen. The combing or hackling was entrusted to a professional *pettinatore*, who would then return it to be spun and woven by the wives of farm workers or household servants.[68] Thus, the wife of Matteo di Simone's sharecropper wove linen cloth for Matteo from the flax grown on his farm at Campi.[69] When there was insufficient home-grown flax, landowners would buy unwoven fibre for it to be spun and woven at home, as Filippo di Matteo's wife Selvaggia bought Viterbo linen from a draper to spin at home for domestic use.[70]

Vines were grown in both the valley and the hills in the late Middle Ages, and although the valley wine was considered poorer quality, grapes were nevertheless grown there in large quantities.[71] All the big Strozzi farms in the Arno valley produced wine, from Novoli and Quaracchi, to Campi and Capalle, to beyond Prato at Galciana and Montemurlo. The largest quantity of wine from a single estate was produced on the same river flats that produced the largest quantity of wheat: Benedetto di Pieraccione declared more than 200 barrels (9,100 litres) from his Capalle farms in 1427 and 224 barrels in 1442.[72] This was a huge quantity from one estate, and even the merchant of Prato, Francesco Datini, produced much less from all his properties: between 100 and 150 barrels a year in the early fifteenth century.[73] Benedetto's wine was of mediocre quality, however, valued at between sixteen and eighteen *soldi* a barrel. Only two other Strozzi villas yielded over fifty barrels a year: Piero di Carlo's four farms around his house at Querceto beside Ponte a Mensola produced 103 barrels,[74] and Giovanni di Luigi's widow and son at Le Corti in the district of Gangalandi above Signa produced an average of ninety barrels,[75] but these were better wines, valued at twenty-six to twenty-eight *soldi*.

The variety in quality and value is neatly illustrated in Matteo di Simone's 1430 tax return in which the wine from his vineyards in the Arno valley at Campi were valued at eighteen *soldi* a barrel, that from the foothills south of the city at Pozzolatico was valued at twenty-eight *soldi* a barrel, whereas wine from the higher slopes at Calicarza towards the Mugello was priced at thirty *soldi*.[76] Yet there is no sign that the Strozzi developed estates especially to provide themselves with the best-quality wine. None of them had land in Chianti, nor in the upper Val d'Arno, where the highly prized Trebbiani grew. A range of produce, or rather provision of the two most essential victuals – wheat and wine – in abundant quantities was the main criterion, rather than sheer excellence. As Alberti expressed it in 'I Libri della famiglia':

> This is what I would do, then. I would see that the estate was, first of all, suited to yield all that might be needed to feed the family, and if not all, at least the most necessary commodities, namely bread and wine.[77]

Although in the hills the quantity of wheat and other cereals decreased, not only was better wine produced there, but olive oil, wood and livestock, all rare in the valley, were important resources derived mostly from higher country. It is clear from the lists of yields and contemporary descriptions that farms were conceived in terms of their complementary agricultural products. Matteo di Simone Strozzi refers to his lands at 'Calicarza where one gathers wood and keeps livestock and wheat' and to his farm at 'Pozzolatico where we harvest oil and cereals and fruit and wine'.[78] These were, in fact, both hill farms, the former in steeper country north of the city, and the latter in gentler, more fertile terrain to the south. Most of Matteo's rural property, however, was concentrated in his estate at Quaracchi and Campi in the Arno valley where mainly wheat was grown. If the valley farms were commercially more lucrative,[79] the hill farms were valued for their smaller yields of scarcer products, which were of direct use to the household and which also fetched good market prices.

It is on these hill farms that new efforts to diversify crops can most clearly be discerned. On the whole, long-term agricultural changes are hard to trace among the Strozzi, for they are obscured by the dominant tendency to sell and divide lands during the fifteenth century. Nevertheless, Filippo di Matteo's creation of his estate at Maglio in the 1480s involved the terracing and drainage of the whole hillside; enclosure of fields; the planting of new vineyards, olive groves and fir trees; and the acquisition of cattle, sheep and goats to forage on the higher slopes.[80] Filippo's intention was certainly to acquire a farm that would complement his other properties in the valley and provide him with the products his other farms lacked. The benefits of Filippo's scheme were reaped by his sons in the 1520s, by which time the six farms at Maglio were producing thirty-seven-and-a-half barrels of olive oil, seventy-six barrels of wine, twenty-seven *moggia* of wheat and thirty *cataste* of wood every year, as well as other fruits, cereals and animal products.[81] A similar motive lay behind the creation of Vanni di Francesco's property at Galluzzo in the Val di Marina (1458– late 1470s),[82] and Bartolommeo Sassetti's hill farms at Valcenni (1463–77).[83] These schemes are representative of a significant new trend among Florentine landowners (discernible from c. 1460) away from the intensive monoculture of wheat, or biculture of wheat and wine, towards a greater use of the high country and side valleys for more olives, fruit trees, timber and animals.[84]

Although olive oil was produced in relatively small quantities, olives were grown on all the eleven Strozzi villas in hill country. The three farms north of Florence, their slopes facing south, produced the most: Petraia yielded twelve to fourteen barrels of oil a year,[85] Loiano ten barrels in its best year[86] and Querceto five and a half barrels.[87] After that, a group of farms at Pozzolatico and Gangalandi yielded

between two and three barrels a year,[88] whereas most of the remaining farms produced only half, three quarters or one barrel of oil.[89] In a period when lard was the main cooking fat, this may have been enough for household consumption.[90]

In the fertile alluvial valley where wheat cultivation was intense and the population dense, livestock was largely confined to plough oxen and farmyard poultry,[91] but in the hills where steep terrain and poor soil made cropping less productive and where there was more room to forage, sheep and goats were herded. Sheep were more common and were valued for their cheese and wool as well as their meat and hides. Whereas Crescenzi considered mutton only fit for 'the roughest of peasants'[92] and goats' milk was preferred, sheep's cheese was highly prized.[93] Alessandra Macinghi Strozzi's letters frequently refer to gifts of *marzolino*, the fresh sheep's cheese, which was coated in wax and sent by courier to her son in Naples.[94] This was clearly a Florentine speciality, for later Filippo sent *marzolini* as diplomatic gifts to the Neapolitan court.[95] The size of flocks was small, varying from only twelve head to fifty,[96] but they were widespread because nearly all Strozzi hill properties ran sheep: north of Florence from Monte Morello to the Mugello, above Calenzano and Prato and southwest of town towards Vinci and Gangalandi. There were also some sheep in the valley, for Messer Marcello kept sheep at Campi Bisenzio, and Filippo di Matteo allowed his to forage on wheat stubble at Capalle.[97]

Communal statutes prohibited the keeping of goats within fourteen miles of the city, unless it were one or two to provide milk for invalids, and even those had to be closely guarded.[98] Goats are mentioned on only five Strozzi farms, all well removed from town, in the Mugello, in the mountains above Prato and a herd of fifty at Gangalandi.[99] Pigs were fattened on many farms by the sharecropper and the meat divided with the landowner. Palla de Nofri claimed to own twelve 'porci tenporili', which he gave to his *lavoratori* for fattening.[100] Very few cows were listed, and they may have been used as plough beast and to breed and feed young oxen, rather than for milk or meat.[101] Heifers were more common and were probably kept for their flesh since veal was the most expensive and desirable meat.[102] Oxen were the most valuable farm animals, for without them cultivation was slow, backbreaking work and their plentiful manure fertilised the fields. A friend of Matteo di Simone Strozzi, Giovanni di Ser Matteo Mainardi (father of Piovano Arlotto), was even ready to sell him his Quintilian manuscript for five florins in order to buy an ox to work his lands at the *pieve* of Macioli.[103]

Firewood and timber were other essential products of hill country. Brushwood was plentiful on Monte Morello, in the mountains above Prato and Pistoia where broom still grows wild and in the hills south of the Arno at Malmantile. Most wood provided from family estates was burnt as fuel in hearths and ovens ('legne grosse e minute da ardere'). Filippo Strozzi's household consumed twelve cartloads of firewood in 1490, eight in town and four at his villa of Santuccio.[104] Timber for construction could also be felled from privately owned woods in the hills and from smaller copses often planted along river banks in the valley,[105] although for any large-scale projects like Filippo Strozzi's new palace, bulk suppliers from further afield were used.[106]

CONSOLIDATION OF THE COUNTRY ESTATE

In order to discover where the *casa da signore* lay in relation to its land, it is essential to consider the overall shape of estates, how their lands were distributed, whether they formed a continuous block and whether the landowner's house was indeed the nucleus of the agricultural estate. Sheer quantity of land is a fundamental component in the construction of rural grandeur, and as the extent of land cannot be appreciated when it is divided and scattered, so it is more impressive when it is gathered into one large sweep with an imposing house at its centre. The dual criteria of size and compactness were already emphasised in the fourteenth century by Piero de' Crescenzi, who recommended a strategy of purchase and exchange of neighbouring properties to attain an uninterrupted expanse of fields:

> We take much delight in fields that have a beautiful and well-tended site; especially

when they are not small, rustic plots, but a great unified expanse without a break, and that have straight edges or boundaries; and for this reason, any of you who want to buy, should acquire land near your own fields rather than elsewhere, and sell off your smaller plots in other places; and exchange the superfluous and poor fields with your neighbours, and straighten the boundaries between your field and that of your neighbour.[107]

This was an arduous task in Italy, where there was a long tradition of farming small separate pieces of land scattered over a wide area. However, agricultural historians have suggested that, from the late thirteenth century, there was an increasing trend towards the concentration of scattered patches into compact farms (*appoderamento*).[108] If this is the case, we should expect to find new farms being created and previously dispersed lands consolidated. Once again, the great variety of practice means that a whole range of estate formations co-existed, while most of the Strozzi were reducing their real property rather than participating in progressive forms of agriculture.

The first impression gained from the Strozzi tax returns is of large numbers of *pezzi di terra* dispersed over wide districts. Even when one *signore*'s lands fell within one parish, cultivated by the same farmer and administered from the same *casa da signore*, the different boundaries often show that his fields were not contiguous but were separated by other owner's lands as well as roads, ditches, rivers or villages. Apart from the lands that were associated with a particular villa, there were still more isolated farms and fields that were not attached to any *casa da signore*.[109]

Yet whereas topographically the estates were loosely constructed, the conception of the villa or estate as a unit seems to have been firmly defined, its parts and boundaries frequently recorded in *ricordanze* as well as in the obligatory tax returns, being the result of a long, meticulous process of purchase, exchange and jealously guarded bequest and often the subject of tenacious legal wrangling. Moreover, on closer inspection it becomes obvious that most Strozzi villas retained a clearly defined nucleus of *casa da signore* with a home-farm attached, while other farms and pieces

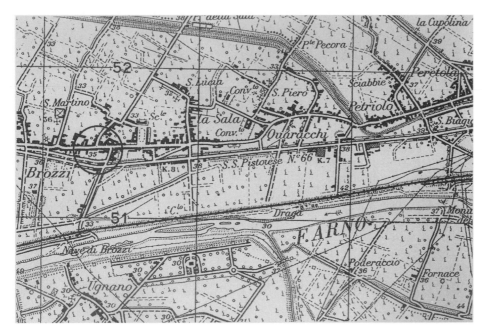

6. Map of Brozzi, Quaracchi and Petriolo along the Via Pistoiese, site of villas belonging to Francesco and Zanobi di Benedetto di Caroccio Strozzi (encircled), and the inn of Matteo di Simone Strozzi. Detail of IGM, 1:25,000, 'Campi Bisenzio'.

of land were separate but distributed within a short radius. The estate was therefore only occasionally a neat, compact unit and more often an untidy conglomerate, with a central core, some offshoots and other detached but related fragments. The *casa da signore* usually functioned as the administrative centre from which the *signore* or his *fattore* supervised the estate, as the office to which rents were paid and as the storehouse to which crops were delivered. Another organisational factor governing the shape of the land was the *lavoratore* himself, whose farm had to be of sufficient size and fertility to support him and his family. Similarly, it had to be practicable for him to farm the *pezzi di terra*, and if the pieces were gathered into a compact unit, more rational and economic cultivation would be possible.[110]

Of the thirty-two main Strozzi estates, only one *casa da signore* was not associated with any farmland. The painter and miniaturist Zanobi di Benedetto's house near Fiesole had a garden and a grove of trees (*boschetto*), but no land of commercial value and, although he bought the next-door *casa da lavoratore* with a small vineyard, he made no attempt to acquire a farm.[111] Although this is a rare example of a villa without saleable agricultural produce, it may have had another commercial function as an artist's workshop, for Zanobi's move to Palaiuola came about

because he shared a house there with his teacher Battista Sanguigni in the 1430s. Still, after Zanobi's marriage in 1438, he stayed at Palaiuola, living next door to Sanguigni, who had a complex arrangement with Zanobi's brother Francesco whereby he had a lifetime lease on the house that would then revert to Francesco Strozzi at his death.[112] Even the Palaiuola property, therefore, was not simply a 'pleasure house'[113] but was linked to Zanobi's activity as a painter, its location close to Sanguigni and also to Fra Angelico's workshop at San Domenico where both miniaturists worked.

Three other Strozzi villas consisted of houses quite separate from their lands, all being village houses with their farms outside the village. Matteo di Simone's properties at Quaracchi comprised four houses in the village with small patches of ground beside each, where grain and wine were cultivated. One of the houses was kept for his own use, another was a tavern and the other two were let to villagers. In addition, Matteo owned half a dozen pieces of land scattered around Quaracchi and Petriolo, and twenty-one pieces of land farmed as one *podere* in the neighbouring district of San Martino a Campi[114] (Fig. 6). Francesco di Benedetto's house at Brozzi was more imposing, especially after he had joined it to his cousin's house next door. The façade was on the main village street, with

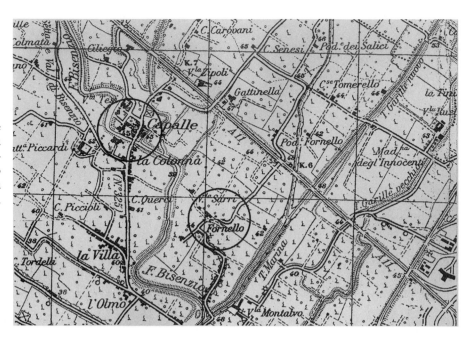

7. Map of Capalle and Fornello, site of villas belonging to Benedetto di Pieraccione Strozzi, Francesco di Giovanni Strozzi, Ubertino di Tommaso Strozzi and the heirs of Marco di Goro Strozzi. Detail of IGM, 1:25,000, 'Campi Bisenzio'.

kitchen gardens behind, while the farmlands were removed from the house but distributed around the same district. Unlike Matteo, none of Francesco's many pieces were gathered into one *podere*, and they were worked by different labourers.[115] Another reason for the fragmentation of these lands may have been the density of population in the parishes of Brozzi and Quaracchi, which were among the most crowded in the whole Florentine *contado*,[116] so that urban characteristics came into play, making it more difficult to acquire large stretches of land. This does not apply to Niccolò di Barla Strozzi, who inherited farms in the hills of Gangalandi with no *casa da signore*. To remedy this, he bought a house in the nearby *castello* of Malmantile from where he could administer his land and was a cheap alternative to life in town.[117]

These exceptions apart, the Strozzi villas all retained a clearly defined central complex of *casa da signore* with one or more home-farms attached. This applies both to the large sprawling estates and to the more compact single-farm villas. There were seven big composite estates, each with three or more farms surrounding the *casa da signore*. The Rocca at Campi had 770 *staiora* of land,[118] all within the parish of San Lorenzo at Campi, of which forty *staiora* were occupied by farmhouses, threshing yards, market gardens, cane thickets and river bank, while all the rest was

arable.[119] Yet this estate probably owed its consolidation to a long process of accumulation during the fourteenth century, culminating in Carlo di Strozza's construction of the Rocca in the 1370s.[120] Although the family did its utmost to keep the land intact in the fifteenth century, it was broken up to pay debts and divide the patrimony.[121]

In contrast, at Fornello in 1427 four *case da lavoratori* were dotted like satellites around the *casa da signore* (Fig. 7). Although the land was all contained within the area between the Garille Vecchio and the Bisenzio rivers, each farm was composed of separate pieces of land sprinkled around that area. There was no attempt to join the pieces or to rationalise the tenure system by entrusting a group of fields in close proximity to one farmer; thus, three peasants worked fields in one *luogo* at Garille, three men worked lands at Capallese and so on, so that a list of the components of the four farms suggests a policy of dispersal or, at the very least, haphazard purchase rather than consolidation. It is likely, however, that the tenure system at Fornello was an old one, surviving from the time of Goro and Niccolo di Iacopo before 1350,[122] and it was certainly considered unsatisfactory by the 1450s when the Strozzi began to rent intervening fields to facilitate access from one part of the fragmented estate to the next.[123] Although Mezzana, also a fourteenth-century

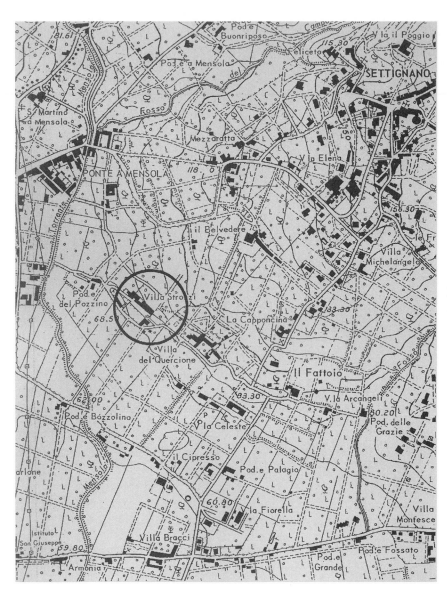

8. Map of Ponte a Mensola, site of the villa of Querceto (labelled 'Villa Strozzi') belonging to the heirs of Nanne Strozzi and, after their move to Ferrara, to Carlo di Piero Strozzi. Detail of Amministrazione Provinciale di Firenze 1:10,000, 'Firenze'.

estate, was a more tightly constructed unit consisting of five farms, there, too, intervening pieces of grain land and pasture were being rented by 1442 to accommodate the sharecroppers.[124]

In the 1420s and 1430s, Benedetto di Pieraccione's villa at Capalle, the largest single Strozzi estate, had eight or nine farms in five different locations, all within the parish of S. Quirico a Capalle[125] (see Fig. 7). As at Fornello, each *casa da lavoratore* stood on its own piece of farmland, but the sharecropper also worked other lands scattered round about. Therefore, the *podere* was not conceived as a geographical unit but as an agglomerate of lands worked by one family of *lavoratori*. At

Capalle, Benedetto di Pieraccione's own house was placed next to the *castello* walls and although none of the farms adjoined it, they were nearby. Of the original nine farms, the most profitable, Il Cortile, and one other large farm, Tra Salci, remained in the family throughout the century. By 1457, however, seven other farms had been partly sold and partly incorporated into the two big farms.[126] Here, therefore, the process of sale and reduction led to the concentration of lands in fewer farm units. The old form of *appoderamento* that had taken place prior to 1427 with many separate pieces farmed by many families of *mezzadri* was being replaced by fewer, more compact farms, at

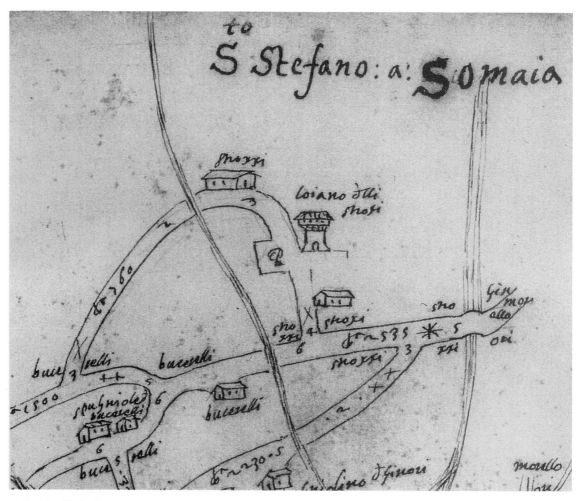

9. Parish of S. Stefano a Sommaia, Rocca di Loiano (labelled 'Loiano delli Strozi'). Detail of *Piante di popoli e strade – Capitani di parte guelfa – 1580–1595*, II, c. 438.

the same time as the unfavourable political climate, the burden of heavy taxes and the inevitable division of patrimony caused Benedetto di Pieraccione to sell the marginal and less valuable properties.

Capalle was also the location of Francesco di Giovanni and his son Chiricho's villa. One large stretch of land across four fields, eight other pieces of land, a farmhouse and five other houses that had been burnt down with their remaining threshing floors and market gardens were described as one *podere* and farmed by three brothers in 1427.[127] Here again the word *podere* is a bracket term for a multifarious group of lands and buildings considered as one unit for the purpose of cultivation and administration. In addition, Francesco owned a dozen more pieces of land and houses, some in ruins, in Capalle. The heyday was certainly over,

for not only were the ten ruined houses not repaired, but fields were consigned to the women for dowries and others were sold by 1451.[128] Nevertheless, the *casa da signore* and the largest block of land at La Chinata were still intact in 1498.[129]

Only two of the big, composite estates escaped depletion during the fifteenth century, and it is significant that these also seem to have been the most compact villas. Querceto, like the Rocca di Campi, had been created before Carlo di Strozza left Florence in 1378.[130] Its lands were in one block, divided into four *poderi*, and the boundaries and site descriptions are unequivocal in placing the *casa da signore* at the centre with all the farms adjoining each other to form a continuous sweep of land[131] (Fig. 8). Bernardo and Giovanni di Giovanni's villa at Signano was the only

10. The Rocca di Loiano nestling under Monte Morello, with olive groves on the lower slopes.

one of the old estates to increase in size. In 1427 it consisted of three farms, at least two of which adjoined the *case da signore*, and an extra house for storing crops in the *castello* of Campi.[132] Giovanni bought a fourth farm in the same parish of S. Lorenzo a Campi from Strozza di Smeraldo Strozzi in 1440.[133]

Most Strozzi villas, however, were compact single-farm estates, some with a few other detached lands nearby. For example, Ubertino di Tommaso's compact single-farm villa at Montughi had only fifty-one *staiora* of land, all in one piece that seems to have surrounded the house. This was a characteristic of residential villas, when the aesthetic component and the desire for privacy dominated. The Montughi property contrasts with Ubertino's other rural holdings, such as his farms at Capalle and Campi, composed of nine and thirteen pieces of land respectively, and of purely agricultural function.[134]

Loiano, an ancient villa belonging to Strozza and Smeraldo[135] and bequeathed to Piero di Carlo, may not have been as profitable as grain lands in the valley, but in a period when crop diversification was coming into favour, its produce was cherished (Figs. 9 and 10). There was a single farm, and other lands seem to have been contiguous. The sale of five vineyards and olive groves in 1449, 1452 and 1467[136] may have been part of a policy to replace these more intensive types of farming that were already duplicated at his main residential villa of Querceto, with pasture for sheep and firewood for the kiln since, in 1464 and 1465, Piero di Carlo bought two broom thickets and a piece of woodland, all adjacent to his other properties,[137] while his son Carlo bought four more pieces of woodland pasture in the 1470s,[138] and Carlo's son Andrea in turn bought more pasture and a mill on the Chiosina below the villa in the 1490s.[139] Singly these small purchases appear negligible, but when followed from one generation to the next, a long-term policy for the consolidation of land and diversification of crops around an ancestral villa emerges.

That the principle of compactness was well established by the fifteenth century is not only suggested by the survival of a group of late thirteenth- or fourteenth-century villas, which all display that characteristic, and by the methods employed to create new estates, such as Galluzzo and Maglio, during the fifteenth century, but can also be inferred from grander or modernised villas such as Palla di Nofri's Poggio a Caiano and Petraia and Filippo di Matteo's Santuccio, all of which were compact villas whose farms consisted of consolidated blocks of land.

Significantly, the compact estates were also most often those intended for residential purposes, the *casa da signore* functioning as a pivot around which the fields were gathered. Although there does not seem to have existed a term such as 'home farm', there was, in fact, usually one farm closely identified with the *casa da signore* (sharing the same place name and very often the same boundaries), which was an important component in this configuration, for it, together with the *casa da signore*, was the last to be sold. Therefore, an initial impression of highly fragmented, widely dispersed land holdings with houses placed at random within those scattered holdings, needs to be overlaid by an awareness of the gradual emergence of more consolidated villa nuclei.

The interdependence of the *casa da signore* and its land therefore operated on various levels simultaneously. It functioned on the ground in the placing of the owner's house near, beside or in the midst of a block of land belonging to that same owner. The two were economically dependent, in that the inhabitants of the houses were at least partly dependent on the agricultural produce of the surrounding lands, or on rents, for sustenance and income. In the social sphere, too, the various members of the estate community – owners, estate managers and farm labourers – were bound together in their attachment to a locality and in their mutual concern for the land.

3 · SITES

CHOICE OF SITES

Free from crowded conditions in town, we might imagine that villa owners had the whole countryside from which to choose.[1] Yet several factors contributed to narrow down that choice. As Chapter 1 has shown, the inheritance of family estates, the proximity of relatives and a preference for the same quarter of the *contado* as the family belonged to in town were all interrelated motives that influenced the initial selection of a country estate. On the other hand, if a property had no connection with the owner's family or their quarter, it was almost certain to be an existing villa site and preferably one whose prestige was already established. Entirely new villa sites, like *ex novo* villa buildings, were rare in the Florentine *contado* in this period.[2]

Thus, in 1445, Dietisalvi Neroni bought Marco di Goro Strozzi's villa of Mezzana, an imposing estate that was ready-made with its castellated house and five farms[3], while Messer Marcello Strozzi sold his fortified villa of Luciano, redolent of its chivalric past, to Antonio Antinori in 1448.[4] When Francesco Sassetti returned with a great fortune from abroad, he chose a Macinghi palace built by another wealthy, home-coming patriot some sixty or seventy years before.[5] More famous examples are Palla di Nofri Strozzi's villas of Petraia and Ambra, whose connection with a wealthy, wise and celebrated rival may have been as attractive to the Medici as the convenience of pre-existing buildings and established gardens.[6] It is hard to resist the conclusion that other Florentines were profiting from the Strozzi misfortunes by appropriating some of their kudos along with their sites. This further suggests that, despite the exile of four members of the clan and their heirs, their reputation was preserved to the extent that a Strozzi provenance still retained its historic aura of social prestige and power.[7]

On a more practical level, other criteria came into play. At the beginning of his *De Agri Cultura*, Cato gave precise directions on how to choose a site:

> When you are thinking of acquiring a farm, keep in mind these points: that you be not over-eager in buying nor spare your pains in examining, and that you consider it not sufficient to go over it once. . . . Notice how the neighbours keep up their places; if the district is good, they should be well kept. . . . It should have a good climate, not subject to storms; and the soil should be good, and naturally strong. If possible, it should lie at the foot of a mountain and face south; the situation should be healthful, there should be a good supply of labourers, it should be well watered, and near it there should be a flourishing town, or the sea, or a navigable stream, or a good and much travelled road. It should lie among those farms which do not often change owners; where those who have sold farms are sorry to have done so.[8]

11. Brozzi, Francesco di Benedetto Strozzi's house incorporating Lionardo d'Antonio Strozzi's house with the tower.

These recommendations were echoed with variations and additions by subsequent theorists: Varro, Piero de' Crescenzi, and Leon Battista Alberti.[9] The common sense that lay behind Cato's prescription also motivated the Strozzi in their choice of sites. Analysis of the placing and distribution of the Strozzi villas reveals that proximity to a 'flourishing town', a 'navigable stream', a 'good and much travelled road' and to suitable neighbours – in the Strozzi's case their relatives, friends and neighbours from the Quarter of S. Maria Novella in town – were all determining factors. The fertile soil of the Arno basin attracted the majority, whereas some

were drawn to sites 'at the foot of a mountain facing south'.

DISTRIBUTION OF SITES

Only seven residential Strozzi villas were situated outside the *contado* administered by S. Maria Novella, and four of these were close to town in populous and attractive areas in the foothills (Badia Fiesolana, Ponte a Mensola and Soffiano); the other three were south of the Arno above the Via Pisana (at Malmantile and

12. Brozzi from the south; tower identified as Lionardo d'Antonio Strozzi's house.

Luciano). The majority (nineteen) were grouped in two clusters in the districts of S. Stefano in Pane and Campi Bisenzio, joined by a string of houses along the Via Pistoiese (see Fig. 1 in Chapter 1). The cluster closest to town comprised seven villas, three in the parish of S. Stefano in Pane at Rifredi, Le Panche and Macia, and the other four were within two kilometres' radius at Petraia, Montughi and Novoli. From Palla di Nofri's villa at Novoli, a chain of properties ran up the Via Pistoiese through Quaracchi, where Matteo owned his house and inn, to Brozzi where Francesco di Benedetto and Lionardo d'Antonio had houses and beyond to Pinaccio's (and later Filippo's) farm of Santuccio near San Donnino.

The second large cluster gravitated around the *castello* of Campi where several families owned storage houses within the village walls and around which lay the Rocca, Signano and Il Palagio. Fornello's lands stretched towards Campi in one direction and towards its subsidiary *castello* of Capalle in the other. At Capalle there were another three villas, as well as small houses within the village. The Strozzi villas at Le Miccine and

Mezzana were also connected with this group by their lands, which stretched towards Campi and Capalle. This spreading characteristic is a special feature of all the properties along the Via Pistoiese and near Campi and Capalle, so that the picture gained from tax returns is of a patchwork of Strozzi lands stretching over the whole area from Peretola to San Donnino across the fields towards Osmannoro and up the Bisenzio as far as Mezzana, also embracing the left bank of the river westwards to Le Miccine and San Giorgio a Colonica. This wide distribution over the area and deep penetration into its settlements differs significantly from the properties outside this district, which tended either to be more discrete or were the result of a single wealthy man investing in an area as Palla di Nofri did around Carmignano or Filippo di Matteo at Maglio. The pervasiveness of Strozzi landholding in the Campigiano is likely to be a key characteristic of old clan power bases in the countryside. Their farms might have been composed of scattered pieces, their castles and farm houses in disrepair, but the drawing power of the Campi district as an ancestral locality was still strong enough to

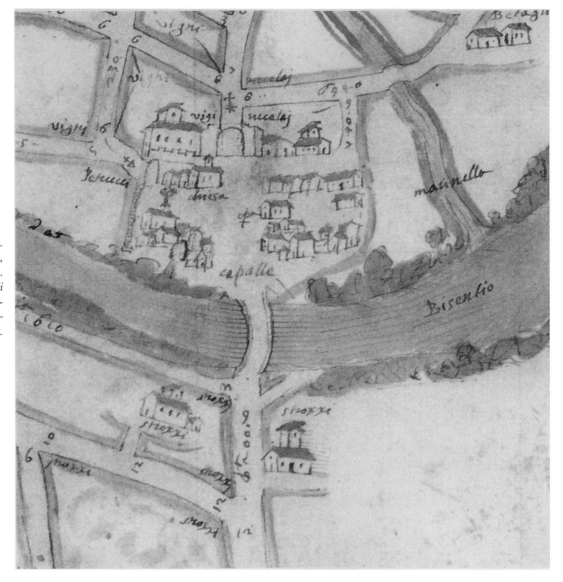

13. Parish of S. Quirico a Capalle, *castello* of Capalle. Detail of *Piante di popoli e strade – Capitani di parte guelfa – 1580–1595*, II, c. 410.

bring Filippo di Matteo back there in the 1470s and 1480s.

THE RELATION OF VILLA SITES TO LOCAL SETTLEMENT

Only five of the thirty-two residential villas were situated within the walls of a *castello* or were flanked by other houses on a village street.[10] Francesco di Benedetto and his cousin Lionardo d'Antonio's houses at Brozzi were village houses. The imposing palazzo

still standing on the village street at Brozzi is probably the amalgamated palace formed by the joining of Lionardo's house with Francesco's (Fig. 11).[11] The entrance façade is built directly on the Via Pistoicsc, which ran through the village in the fifteenth century, whereas the garden façade would have faced across the fields towards the Arno (Fig. 12). The combination of garden view on the one hand and, on the other hand, the enormous convenience of being at the centre of a busy village with tradesmen and supplies available on the doorstep, was recommended by Giovanni Rucellai down the road at Quaracchi, 'where there are carters,

14. Capalle, gate in the walls of the *castello* next to the Palagione.

mule drivers, fishermen, craftsmen and shopkeepers of every sort, which are extremely useful to the inhabitants' (see Fig. 6 in Chapter 2).[12]

Another village house was Ubertino di Tommaso's big, old tower at Capalle,[13] sold to Filippo di Matteo Strozzi in 1475. The 'torrione' of Ubertino's tax returns can be identified with the 'palagione posto sopra una delle porti di Capalle' described in Filippo's *ricordo* of purchase in 1475[14] and depicted in the Capitani di Parte map from the 1580s, where the house merges with the crenellated village wall, next to the northern gateway to the *castello* (Figs. 13, 14 and 15).

Placed directly opposite the Romanesque church of San Quirico, the Palagione had been a country residence of the Florentine bishops who administered the *castello* of Capalle throughout the twelfth and thirteenth centuries.[15] Filippo amassed more property within the walls of the *castello*, converting houses into stables and storage space for estate produce, while also extending his land into the fields that lay beyond the Palagione towards Ciliegio[16] (see Fig. 7 in Chapter 2). Such a site afforded both the security of the *castello* for residence and storage, as well as proximity to open farmland.

15. Capalle, Il Palagione from outside the *castello* walls.

16. Rocca di Campi on the banks of the Bisenzio from the south.

17. Rocca di Campi, view east from tower guarding the bridge and the *castello* of Campi.

As at Capalle, where only one of three Strozzi houses was within the walls of the *castello*, so at Campi most Strozzi preferred to have their *case da signore* within a short distance of the fortified village rather than within its precincts. The Strozzi Rocca or fortress, however, was so closely connected to the *castello* on the opposite river bank that it could hardly be described as an isolated house in open countryside (Figs. 16 and 17). Strategically placed to guard the road from Prato and a key bridge over the Bisenzio,[17] it gave protection to Campi Bisenzio itself and to one of the three main approach roads to Florence from the west – the front that was most vulnerable to attack from armies coming from the direction of Pisa or Lucca. Its tower provided a lookout along the course of the

Bisenzio River and across the plain as far as Calenzano in the north and Signa in the south.[18]

The other twenty-six residential villas were all situated in open countryside surrounded by fields. Nevertheless, most *case da signore* were within close proximity to local settlements, and a glance at Christiane Klapisch-Zuber's population map of 1427 (Fig. 18) shows that there was a marked preference for sites not only near Florence but within the most densely populated parishes surrounding the city.[19] Of thirty-two residential villas, only six were situated in parishes whose population was under 100 in 1427. The ownership of a villa within short travelling distance from Florence was motivated by the need to supervise the agricultural estate as well as the desire to maintain close contact with affairs in town. Proximity to market was another important motive and nearly all the Strozzi villas fulfilled Alberti's recommendation that the house be 'not far from the piazza' for the convenience of being able to shop easily for all provisions.[20]

ROADS AND BRIDGES

Because accessibility to local markets and Florence was an important factor, it follows that many of the *case da signore* were situated along main roads. The Via Pratese running from the Porta al Prato through Campi, Capalle and Mezzana functioned as a backbone in the villa network. Here lay Palla di Nofri's house at Novoli, as well as the concentration of Strozzi properties at Campi and Capalle, whereas the Via Pistoiese connected Matteo di Simone's inn at Quaracchi and the Brozzi houses with Pinaccio's villa at Santuccio and Palla di Nofri's at Poggio a Caiano. The Via Pistoiese had been little used and was probably incomplete in the thirteenth century, but new work began in 1319–20 to extend it across the Bisenzio at San Mauro, continuing through Signa and Lecore to Poggio a Caiano. The bridge at San Mauro was certainly built by 1358, and the massive tower of Santuccio beside the bridge may have been intended to serve a partly defensive function guarding that bridge (see Fig. 20 in this chapter, and Fig. 80 in Chapter 6). Fourteenth-century

Strozzi investment in land around Palla's future estates at Trefiano and Poggio a Caiano may well have begun as a result of the improved road to Pistoia and a new bridge built over the Ombrone at Poggio a Caiano in 1329.[21] Since viability and access were such fundamental needs, it is not surprising that many of the Strozzi villas should be near bridges. Apart from Santuccio and the Rocca at Campi both guarding strategic bridges over the Bisenzio, the three Capalle villas lay beside a third bridge over the Bisenzio. Even Casi was conveniently placed near to Vaiano, a major crossing point in the Bisenzio valley. Other locations specify the presence of a bridge: Querceto at Ponte a Mensola and Casciolle near Ponte di Mezzo.

Nor should the social function of roads be overlooked. For Giovanni Rucellai, the Via Pistoiese running past his garden at Quaracchi provided the opportunity to make a magnanimous gesture towards passersby:

> A grove of trees near the house . . . from which one receives great consolation, not so much we in the house and in the village, as visitors and passers-by in very hot weather, because on one side it borders the road to Pistoia, so that no visitor passes by without stopping for a quarter of an hour to see our garden.[22]

Referring again to the Via Pistoiese, Giovanni's son Bernardo Rucellai described in 1474 how the distribution of their property along that road had led to many friendships in the area.[23]

RIVER SITES

As many Strozzi villas were situated along the axes of the Via Pistoiese and the Via Pratese, so the Arno and especially its tributary the Bisenzio, linked many of their country houses. Palladio later favoured the placing of villas beside a river to exploit the views, the plentiful water supply, the possibility of irrigation and the convenience of river transport;[24] the practice was surely long established and not confined to the Veneto. In the Florentine countryside, certain produce including flax, fruit trees, the canes used for vineyard stakes, as well as the poplars and willows that grew fast and provided shade, windbreaks, withies and timber, grew best near water. The dependence on rivers for the whole population is made clear in the communal statutes of 1415, which protected the public right to use rivers for drinking (for animals rather than people), washing and fishing.[25] A statute prohibited the cultivation of canes, reeds or hedges ('sepem vel cannatum') in the Arno because it would prevent fish from reaching Florence.[26] On the other hand, mill dams were allowed on the Arno as long as they had a gap ten *braccia* wide to let boats pass through.[27] The right to take stones, gravel and sand from the river banks was also upheld,[28] and indeed these were basic building materials in the Florentine *contado*, and a handy supply was as useful for repairs and construction at the villa as was a nearby kiln or quarry.

Nineteen Strozzi villas had land beside a river. Nine of these were on the Bisenzio, three on the Arno and the remainder near smaller rivers of sufficient size to power a mill but not navigable: the Ombrone (Poggio a Caiano, Trefiano), the Mensola (Querceto), the Terzolle (Ponte di Mezzo, Le Panche), the Marina (Galluzzo and Fornello) and the Chiosina (Loiano). Although most landowners had access to a river, these lands were often separated from their residence, and only six *case da signore* were placed directly on the river bank and could be described as riverside properties. To what extent did the river site influence the orientation and architecture of these six houses?

The sites of the Rocca di Campi, and the castle at Luciano can be explained by their role as fortresses guarding Florentine outposts, and their architecture reflected that function. At the Rocca di Campi, the tower and machicolated parapet were designed to survey the Bisenzio River in either direction (Fig. 19 and see Figs. 16 and 17, this chapter). Whereas the tower overlooked the road and bridge, the longest section of machicolation runs parallel to the river bank. Despite their primarily military function, such features would have been appreciated in peace time for their views and commanding aspect. Like any other villa, these castles were also farm centres, surrounded by large agricultural estates that exploited the fertile

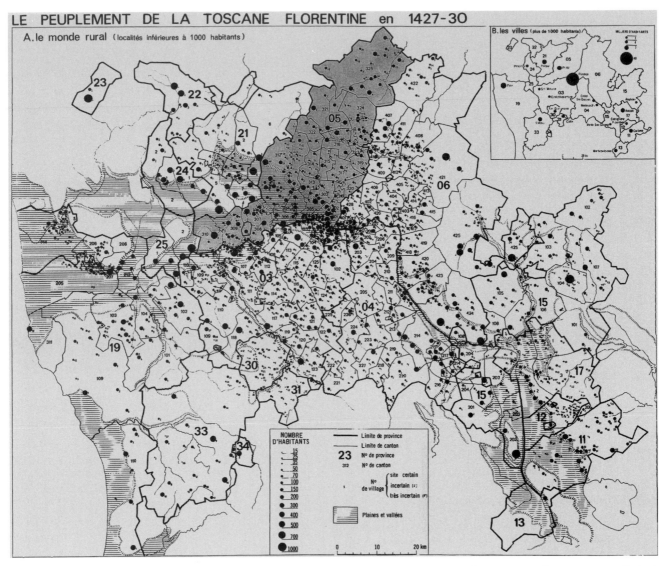

18. Map showing population distribution in Tuscany 1427–30, area under the jurisdiction of the quarter of S. Maria Novella (05) marked in grey (from Klapisch-Zuber, *Una Carta del popolamento*).

river terraces for the cultivation of wheat and other crops.

Francesco di Giovanni Strozzi's property lay further up the Bisenzio opposite the *castello* of Capalle (see Fig. 13 in this chapter). His *casa da signore* had a loggia that may have faced the water, and his garden and fields with *coltura promiscua* of wheat, millet and sorghum, interspersed with rows of vines and fruit trees, and bordered by willows, led down to the river and stretched along its banks in either direction.[29] The terse documentary references to Francesco di

Benedetto Strozzi's house at Brozzi can be supplemented with Giovanni Rucellai's more vivid description of boating and fishing at his riverside villa in the neighbouring parish of Quaracchi.[30] About 400 metres from the banks of the Arno, Francesco di Benedetto Strozzi may even have shared the view of boats enjoyed by Giovanni Rucellai from the dining table of his villa at Quaracchi:

Sitting at table in our dining hall I can see the boats passing behind me, along the Arno.[31]

19. Rocca di Campi, machicolation on east side.

If subsequent transformations have made the district of Brozzi and its connection with the Arno unrecognisable today, then the slower development of the marshy area between San Donnino and the Arno, together with the survival of Filippo di Matteo's account books, make it possible to reconstruct the fifteenth-century conditions at the villa of Santuccio more plausibly. The Capitani di Parte map from the 1580s shows the site clearly (Fig. 20). Wedged into a triangular piece of land bordered by the Bisenzio River, the Fosso Gavina and the road from San Donnino to San Mauro just before

it crosses the bridge, it was ideally placed to exploit local river transport. The Arno itself lay only a kilometre to the south, across waterlogged fields; it could be more easily reached by following the river Bisenzio down to its mouth at Signa. This area between the Arno and the Bisenzio, now reclaimed from marshland and sandbanks, then included what was known as the 'Isola d'Arno a San Donnino', which was partly farmed, partly wooded, surrounded by water mills and used by Filippo di Matteo Strozzi for the storage of timber. Wood brought upstream from Pontormo and

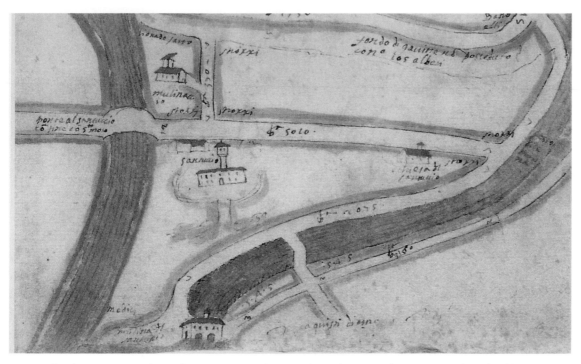

20. Parish of S. Donnino, Filippo di Matteo Strozzi's towered *casa da signore* of Santuccio with outbuildings nearby, the mill above ('mulinaccio') and the oratory ('chiesa del santuccio') to the right. Detail of *Piante di popoli e strade – Capitani di parte guelfa – 1580–1595*, II, c. 404.

Signa was delivered there[32] and later picked up and distributed, still by river transport, to one of Filippo's properties or construction sites: the palace in town, Capalle and Maglio further up the Bisenzio, Santuccio itself, the kilns at S. Piero a Ponti, the new farms in Le Miccine or other farm houses near Campi. It was their river sites that made the Isola d'Arno and Santuccio such suitable timber yards, and sawyers were regularly employed there. Filippo Strozzi's renovation of the *casa da signore* at Santuccio, however, was not designed to maximise views of the river Bisenzio on whose banks it lay. The fourteenth- or early-fifteenth-century house bought by Filippo Strozzi in 1477 consisted of a tower and a long wing running north-south, parallel to the banks of the Bisenzio. Yet Filippo's new extension was orientated on an east-west axis parallel to the road and furnished with a north loggia at ground level facing the road and an upstairs loggia facing the garden on the south side (Fig. 21, and see Fig. 76 in Chapter 6).

Therefore, despite Giovanni Rucellai's description of Lo Specchio and the proximity of Strozzi villas to river banks, there is little concrete evidence to suggest that contemporaries took advantage of river sites for aesthetic reasons. In Florence, palace owners began to build grand façades on the Lungarno from the 1450s and 1460s with the construction of the Palazzo Gianfigliazzi and the Palazzo Coverelli.[33] In the Florentine *contado*, however, it seems that, although access to the river and a distant view of it were desirable, architectural planning to make the most of river sites and to encourage a close relationship between the house and the water was not adopted either in the fifteenth century nor subsequently.

An important reason for this was the real danger of flooding and a prevailing attitude to the river, either as a potential foe or, at best, as a semi-industrial amenity harnessed for water and power. Both Alberti and Tanaglia recommend a site set well back from the river.[34] At Santuccio before Filippo Strozzi bought

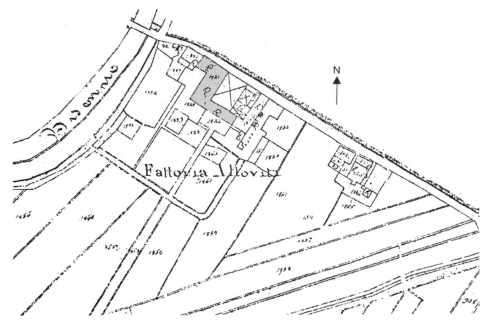

21. Santuccio, site map from Florentine *catasto* c. 1827, Filippo di Matteo Strozzi's *casa da signore* is shaded grey and marked 'R'.

the estate, its previous owners had complained of flooding:

> The said farm is badly damaged by the Bisenzio river and the Gavina river which cover it every year when they rise, and we often lose the wheat harvest.[35] The River Bisenzio causes great annoyance to me and my farm every year when it is swollen and strong; we have lost land because of the river, and we would have lost more if I didn't spend four florins and 5 *denari* every year on making riverside palisades and other repairs.[36]

More damage was caused to country property by flooding than by any other means. Already in the first *catasto* of 1427 (when taxpayers may have been less devious than subsequently), Benedetto di Pieraccione complained that twenty *staiora* of his land at Tomerello had been covered by gravel deposited by the Marina Nuova, and he declared that twenty days' work a year was needed to protect his lands from the Bisenzio and Marinella.[37] Other properties at Capalle were prone to river damage throughout the century. Ubertino di Tommaso, whose farm on the banks of the Bisenzio

was later sold to Filippo di Matteo, began to report flooding in 1442, claiming eight florins a year 'because the river causes us very great damage', and a further twenty lire a year for damage caused by the Marina to his other farm at Campi.[38] His complaints were repeated in each subsequent tax return.[39]

HILL SITES

Half the Strozzi villas were situated in the plain (sixteen out of thirty-two). Of those on elevated sites, over half were in the foothills overlooking Florence and the Arno valley: Montughi, Petraia, Palaiuola, Querceto, Soffiano, Poggio a Caiano and Trefiano, and the remaining villas were in higher country above the Golfolina at Malmantile and Luciano, or in side valleys at Travalle, Loiano, Maglio and Casi. Unlike the plain, which is now industrialised and hard to imagine as it was in the fifteenth century, the foothills are still sought after as a retreat from town and have retained more of their rural character. Among those in the Florentine foothills, the villa of Petraia below Monte Morello and that at Palaiuola on the side of the Mugnone valley below Fiesole occupy two of the most beautiful sites. One of the advantages of sites in the hills north of

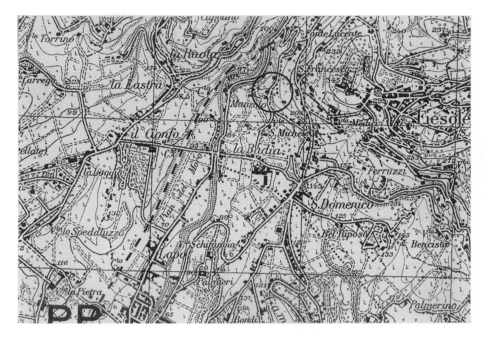

22. Map of S. Domenico and the Badia at Fiesole, with the hamlet of Palaiuola on the road leading from the Badia to Fonte Lucente. Detail of IGM, 1:25,000, 'Firenze'.

23. Palaiuola, the site below Fiesole.

24. One of three Strozzi houses at Palaiuola, here identified as Lorenzo di Francesco di Benedetto Strozzi's house.

25. Palaiuola, Lorenzo di Francesco di Benedetto Strozzi's house, doorway with inscription.

26. Palaiuola, the view from the loggia of Lorenzo di Francesco di Benedetto Strozzi's house.

Florence is that the choice southern slopes face towards the city, providing panoramic views of Florence with its cathedral dome of the type represented by artists such as Pollaiuolo and Botticini.

Palaiuola was the name given to a hamlet on what is now the Via delle Palazzine leading from the Badia Fiesolana to Fonte Lucente (Figs. 22 and 23).[40] Zanobi di Benedetto Strozzi's purchase of a house there between 1427 and 1430[41] was almost certainly motivated by his entering an apprenticeship with the miniaturist Battista Sanguigni at this time.[42] Identification of this house is complicated by the co-existence of at least two other villas at Palaiuola belonging to Battista Sanguigni and Zanobi's brother Francesco and his heirs. A clue is provided, however, by an inscription over the door in one villa at Palaiuola (Figs. 24 and 25), with the name 'Ioannis Baptistae Strozae', referring to the writer and classical scholar Giambattista Strozzi (1551–1634), which may identify the house as that belonging to his great-grandfather Lorenzo di Francesco Strozzi in the late fifteenth century, in which case this was the house inhabited by Battista Sanguingi between c. 1428 and his death in 1451.[43] In this house, the central arch of the loggia was deliberately placed to

27. Palaiuola, the view down the Mugnone valley to Florence.

frame a view of the *cupolone* (Fig. 26). Instead of the wide, expansive view of the whole Arno valley gained from higher up the hill at Fiesole, here the vista is contained between the tapering slopes of Camerata on the left and Montughi on the right, and focussed by the river Mugnone with its terraces and the Via Faentina winding their way towards Florence (Fig. 27). Restricted by the steep hillside above and the river Mugnone below, and unsuitable for growing cereals, these villas had small vineyards, groves of trees and gardens, but no cereal or wheat production. As their economic function was minimal, the aesthetic features of the site became more prominent. Close to town so that work need not be disrupted, with varied views of both hills and city, together with fresher air in summer, the advantages of a villa in the foothills surrounding Florence were as manifest then as they are now.

Villas further from the city and in higher hill country served other purposes. Screened from view of the Arno valley by the lower flanks of Monte Morello on which it stands, the Strozzi fortress of Loiano, otherwise known as the Rocca di Morello, commands a view down the narrow Chiosina valley to Calenzano and across to the other fortified houses of Sommaia and Baroncoli on their hillocks (Fig. 28). As was the case with the Rocca di Campi, the site was strategically placed for defence purposes, forming part of a network of fortified houses around Monte Morello, the mountain guarding the main approach to Florence.[44] However, unlike the Rocca di Campi, there is no record that the Rocca di Loiano was prepared for military action during this period, and whereas the Rocca di Campi is usually referred to as a 'fortezza' or 'uno palagio adatto a fortezza',[45] Loiano is simply described as a 'casa da signore' throughout the fifteenth century.[46] As a villa site it was particularly attractive, with healthy air, cool in summer but protected from the winds and worst frosts on the leeside of the mountain facing south, with plenty of pure water from mountain streams. The river Chiosina below could be easily harnessed for mill power. Set on

28. Rocca di Loiano, viewed from the slopes of Monte Morello.

what appears to be a natural platform in the hillside, its terraces still produce olives and figs as they did in the fifteenth century.

Whereas Loiano owes its location to its original function as a fortress, other Strozzi estates in hill country were created from the outset as farms with a residence for the owner. Casi and Maglio in the Bisenzio valley are two of these. The estate at Casi was formed before 1427 when the house was already described as 'a tumbledown country palace in disrepair'(Fig. 29). The distance from Florence was lamented in 1427,[47] and in 1433 the location was described as 'up in

the mountains.'[48] Unlike the other Strozzi, Stagio d'Antonio seems to have settled for a provincial life, marrying a woman from Pistoia and keeping his only urban residence in Prato.[49] Too poor or unwilling to pay for maintenance and repairs, Stagio's son Lionardo sold the villa to Francesco Sassetti, whose son Cosimo enlarged the property and rebuilt the house.[50] Maglio was on the opposite bank of the river from Casi, two kilometres away on the southern side of Poggio del Maglio. On a steeper site, Maglio had views of a wide, gently sloping, shell-shaped basin, crowned by Monte Maggiore that was forested on its upper

29. Casi, view from the presumed site of S. Lionardo over Il Mulinaccio.

30. Maglio, view from Filippo di Matteo Strozzi's 'casa da oste' towards Monte Maggiore.

slopes and well watered by streams on its lower terraces (Fig. 30). It was here that Filippo Strozzi planted hundreds of new vines and olives, kept sheep, goats and cattle, cut brushwood and planted new trees in the 1480s and 1490s.

For the wealthiest proprietors like Francesco Sassetti and Filippo Strozzi, who already owned one or more villas, an estate well removed from the city, in a rustic setting with produce that was scarce near town, was particularly attractive. As the sole residential villa in a portfolio, however, this sort of site would have been inconvenient for landowners in the middle-income bracket. The majority of Florentine citizens still made their first choice of villa site in an accessible and civilised countryside, well served by roads and bridges, near water supplies and near towns and villages where provisions and labour were easy to find. Furthermore, throughout the fifteenth century, most Strozzi were making a short and familiar journey to their rural properties, moving directly from their ancestral quarter of S. Maria Novella in town through the nearest city gate – the Porta al Prato – into that wedge of territory still administered by the quarter of S. Maria Novella.

4 · THE VILLA COMPLEX

In the fifteenth century the term *villa* not only referred to the landowner's house but to the whole country estate, which included a complex of buildings as well as the land.[1] The inhabitants of the villa complex constituted a small community that embraced the social hierarchy from the *signore* with his extended family, to the officiating priest, to the estate manager, to the tenant farmers or sharecroppers with their numerous families, not to mention the owner's household servants or slaves and casual farm labourers. Within a short radius of the estate centre another group of tenants – millers, kilnsmen and innkeepers – were often drawn into the life of the villa. Whereas in town a range of inhabitants and functions was often housed under one roof in different parts of a single *palazzo* block; in the country a fragmented complex of separate structures catered for specific occupants and functions. Apart from the landowner's house (*casa da signore*) and the farmhouses (*case da lavoratore*), hovels (*casolari*) and sheds (*capanne*) were sometimes inhabited by the poorest farm labourers and were in any case used for storing equipment, wood and crops, while the cowshed or stable (*stalla*) sheltered the beasts of burden. Since the farmhouses and outbuildings on country estates in this period were so often dispersed over a wide area, the term 'villa complex' should be understood in the broadest sense of scattered buildings serving the agricultural estate, but also including the interrelated industrial or commercial structures that formed part of the estate economy.

Because most of these buildings were primarily functional and informal structures rather than serving aesthetic or ceremonial purposes, their architectural forms were usually adapted to diverse needs and conditions. This flexibility of form and function is an important characteristic of rural architecture. It makes the strict definition of rural building types in this period a hazardous enterprise. Moreover, the transformation of rural buildings over the centuries makes an in-depth analysis of most individual structures unfeasible. This chapter, therefore, seeks to identify the main components of the villa complex and to explore their functions and their relation to the *casa da signore*.

CASE DA SIGNORE AND CASE DA LAVORATORE: TERMINOLOGICAL DISTINCTIONS

Just as the forms and functions of rural buildings were extremely versatile, so the terminological distinctions were often blurred. A whole variety of expressions was used in fifteenth-century documents to refer to the landowner's country residence, ranging from *casetta* to plain *casa* to *casamento* and *palagio*. The most common term was *casa da signore*, which was often substituted by the synonymous phrases *casa da cittadino* (town citizen's house) and *casa da oste* (landlord's house).[2] Few landowners applied one term consistently, and there was a tendency to demean the status of the house for taxation purposes. Thus, Carlo di Marcuccio Strozzi described his villa at Campi as a 'palagio' in 1427, 1430 and 1433, but in 1442 he abruptly changed his tone to describe the same house as 'a house almost in ruins' ('una chasa quasi rovina'), further reduced in 1446 to 'a covered hovel . . . which I inhabit because poverty has reduced me to living in the country' ('un chasolare choperto . . . il quale abito perchè mi sto in chontado per povertà'), adding that he needed to repair and buttress twenty-five *braccia* of crumbling wall.[3] In this case the switch from *palagio* to *casa* to *casolare* (from palace to house to hovel) reflected a deliberate policy by the owner to evoke pity in the tax officials, as well as describing the actual degradation of the building. Only three other Strozzi villas were described as *palagio* in the tax returns. The Rocca at Campi, referred to as 'uno palagio adatto a fortezza' in 1427 and 1457, as 'una fortezza' in 1446 and 1451, and as 'una possessione' in 1442, was simply a 'casa' in 1480.[4] Meanwhile, the other two country palaces were in a state of decline. Palla di Nofri's *palagio* of Trefiano was 'male abitato e situato',[5] and Stagio d'Antonio's *palagio* at Casi was 'disfacto et male in punto'.[6]

If *palagio* denotes bigger than average size and past or present grandeur, then the word *casamento* is another signal for a large and dignified dwelling. Querceto was the only villa consistently referred to as a 'chasamento da signiore' or 'chasamento in chontado chon abitazione da cittadino'[7]; although, Loiano, Lionardo d'Antonio's house at Brozzi, Messer Palla Novello's house at Soffiano and Palla di Nofri's villas at Novoli, Petraia and Castello, were all described as *casamenti* on occasion. Beyond these general implications as to size and prestige, the fifteenth-century terms are not architecturally informative. The use of vocabulary was not consistent, and there were no rules or dictionaries governing the application of words. Therefore, while it is occasionally possible to interpret the motives behind a description, as in the case of Carlo di Marcuccio at Il Palagio near Campi, the frequent oscillations between 'casa', 'casa da signore' or 'casamento' are not necessarily significant.

The distinction between the owner's house and that of his tenant or sharecropper, however, which was a distinction in class of inhabitant as well as function, was more clearly defined. All the Strozzi *case da*

signore were accompanied by *case da lavoratore*, except for those few with prominent gardens and little farm land. Palla Novello specifically states that his villa with a walled garden at Soffiano had no *casa da lavoratore* until he bought a small one towards 1480,[8] and Zanobi also lacked one at Palaiuola until he bought the little house next door in 1457,[9] whereas his nephews' neighbouring houses at Palaiuola remained without farmhouses until the end of the century.[10]

Although the distinction between *casa da lavoratore* and *casa da signore* is usually clear, even here functions tended to fluctuate. Thus, Palla di Nofri owned at least three crumbling castles or palaces that had passed their heyday and were now inhabited by farm labourers. At Casteletti near Signa, he owned 'uno abituro fu già dei signori . . . il quale casa è rovinata e abitavi uno lavoratore';[11] at San Martino a Vitiano on the Arno beyond Empoli, his ruined fortification, Il Chasteluccio, is described as, 'uno Abituro che chade . . . stavi dentro iii de' miei lavoratori cholle loro famiglie';[12] and in the parish of San Miniato alle Serre, he owned an abandoned palace called Prulli: 'Nel mezzo de' detti poderi è il palagio disfatto ed è chasolare'.[13]

There are counterexamples in which the landowner is reduced to living in a *casa da lavoratore* as Giovanni di Messer Marcello seems to have done in the Mugello,[14] or in the case of Filippo di Matteo Strozzi who used part of his fortune to resuscitate old houses and enlarge insignificant ones. The house he bought at Capalle may have once been the 'palagione' of the Florentine bishops, but in the meantime it had been left uninhabited and scarcely used by Ubertino di Tommaso, who declared it as 'uno torrione tutto guasto' and 'uno torrione che chade'.[15] The house at Santuccio was no more than a *casa da lavoratore* when Pinaccio Strozzi owned it in 1427, and it retained that label while the Alberti were in possession at least until the late 1450s.[16] At Maglio, Filippo joined the 'casa da oste' to the *casa da lavoratore*, an arrangement that is borne out by the surviving house at Maglio (Fig. 31).[17]

Such instances discourage a rigid categorisation of form and function and show that there was a relatively fluid situation, in which conversion to upgrade a modest or delapidated house was as common as the

31. Maglio, the 'casa da oste' joined to the old *casa da lavoratore* (photo: Conway Library, Courtauld Institute of Art).

neglect and decay of previous stately buildings. This view conforms with Jacques Heers's conception of the flexible structure of late medieval society[18] rather than Bentmann and Müller's interpretation of 'Die Villa als Herrschaftsarchitektur',[19] although at one end of the scale a country house certainly could present an image of dominance and prestige.

THE COMPONENTS OF THE VILLA COMPLEX AND THEIR DISPOSITION

The same question raised in Chapter 2 concerning the consolidation and unity of the farmland here applies to the disposition of buildings and whether they formed a compact unit clustered around the *casa da signore* in its function as estate centre. Unfortunately it is not possible to rely on the surviving buildings to provide evidence because, even if the *case da signore* are often preserved, the *case da lavoratore* and outbuildings have

more often been transformed over the centuries. Nevertheless, the site and orientation of some farmhouses may still reflect the original arrangement.

At Fornello, for example, the present Villa Sarri, which was almost certainly Marco di Goro's house in the fifteenth century, has a group of separate farmhouses scattered around it within a radius of half a mile (see Fig. 7 in Chapter 2).[20] This conforms with the documentary descriptions in the fifteenth century that divide the *casa da signore* and its nucleus from the four *case da lavoratore*, each of which formed a small complex on its own (Figs. 32 and 33). Here the *casa da signore* compound included a portico, a courtyard, a second smaller courtyard, a well, a small tower used as a dovecote, stables, a building for making wine, cellars and about one and three quarter acres of garden.[21] It is clear, therefore, that the owner's complex, although separate from the farm workers' buildings, did shelter some of the important agricultural activities. In addition, each of the *case da lavoratore* attached to the

32. Fornello, Marco di Goro Strozzi's *casa da signore*.

33. Fornello, one of the *case da lavoratore*.

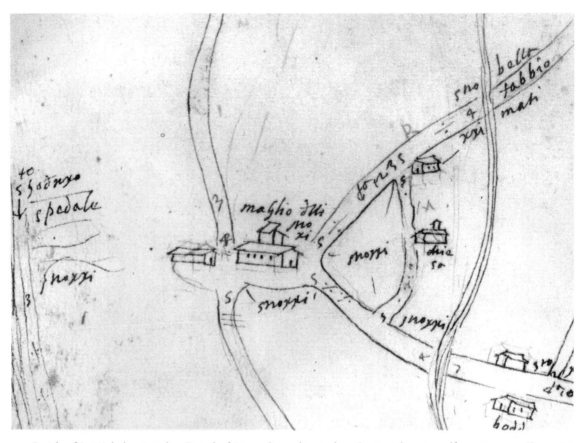

34. Parish of S. Michele a Maglio. Detail of *Piante di popoli e strade – Capitani di parte guelfa – 1580–1595*, II, c. 488.

Fornello estate is described as a distinct microcosm with its own portico, threshing yard, stall for animals, cane thicket and kitchen garden.[22]

This pattern of a *casa da signore* complex with micro complexes of *case da lavoratore* dispersed at a distance can be traced on all the big Strozzi estates and is partly due to the partition of the holding into a series of separate *poderi* worked by different farmers.[23] The descriptions of tenant-farmers' houses often convey a sense of completeness and self-sufficiency, which suggests that the *case da lavoratore* functioned as independent units, probably only using the *casa da signore* to deliver rent or consign the landlord's share of the crop or to perform assigned tasks there.

The exceptions to this configuration are to be found in distant hill villas such as Maglio and Galluzzo,[24] where the *case da lavoratore* sometimes occupied the same enclosure as the *casa da signore*, and on single-farm estates, where the landowner's house

was more likely to be closely connected with the infrastructures of the farm.[25]

Many components were duplicated in the complexes attached to both *casa da signore* and *casa da lavoratore*. Therefore, it was common for each to have a portico, a courtyard (*corte*), a well and a garden (*orto*). A bread oven (*forno*), a stable or stall for livestock (*stalla*) and a building for processing wine could also be found in either or both compounds. Certain features were more exclusive, however. The uneconomic use of land to create attractive surroundings or a dignified approach to the villa by creating formal gardens, flowery lawns or meadows (*giardini, pratelli* or *prati*) and *piazze* in front of the house, only appear in descriptions of the *case da signore*. When towers are mentioned, they tend to have been abandoned by the *signore* and only then become part of a *casa da lavoratore* complex; they are 'disfatto, a uso da lavoratore' or abandoned altogether, 'tutto ghuasto e non s'abita'.[26] The *colombaia*

35. Capalle, *casa da lavoratore* with dove tower.

is only rarely attached to a *casa da lavoratore*, which is why even in the late sixteenth century, one symbol used for *case da signore* on the Capitani di Parte Guelfa maps is a rectangular block with a dove tower attached (Fig. 34). Conversely, the *casa da lavoratore* was accompanied by areas of purely agricultural use which did not play a part in the landlord's activities: here was the threshing floor (*aia*), the market garden (*ortora* or *ortale*), the sheds for storage (*capanne*), other delapidated houses (*casolari*) and cane thickets (*canneti*).

TOWERS, DOVECOTES AND GRANARIES

Twelve of the Strozzi villas are listed with *colombaie* or dovecotes attached,[27] and some of these still survive, although they have undergone alteration since

the fifteenth century. The owner's house at Fornello (Fig. 32) was largely rebuilt in the sixteenth century, but the low tower which emerges on one side of the main block of the house, its sloping roof supported by slender brick piers, may well be the descendent of the 'torriciella dove si soleva essere cholonbaia', described in tax returns.[28] The slanting roofed dove tower incorporated into the house is the type most commonly depicted in the late-sixteenth-century maps of the Capitani di Parte Guelfa and in *cabrei* from then on. A number of such towers can still be found in the Florentine *contado*, at Gonfienti and Capalle, for example (Fig. 35), and at Brozzi (Fig. 36), where the tall tower at one end of the Strozzi house, supports its identification as Lionardo d'Antonio Strozzi's house 'in Cantone', listed in 1430 as 'una casa per loro abitazione... trae dalla cholonbaia paia 40 di pippioni l'anno e in più la spesa del bechare'.[29] The present dovecote at Filippo di Matteo's villa of Maglio is a freestanding structure with a slanting roof (Fig. 37), but two drawings of the villa made by the Capitani di Parte (Fig. 38; see also Fig. 34) show a tower protruding from the house, and although these maps are not accurate, it is possible that the present dovecote was originally the 'capanna', the 'granaio' or the 'edificio da olio diripetto a detta chasa', which are all referred to in the building accounts, or was built later,[30] whereas a *colombaia* is never mentioned and examples of freestanding dovecotes, illustrated in the frontispiece to the 1495 edition of Crescenzi (Fig. 39) or in Gentile da Fabriano's *predella* of the Strozzi altarpiece depicting the 'Flight into Egypt', seem to have been uncommon near Florence. Since all three of these Strozzi dovecotes – at Fornello, Brozzi and Maglio – are so different from each other, their slanting roofs being the only common feature, it is likely that the *colombaia*, like the villa itself, was a highly flexible type, quickly adapted to other uses, and contained within multifunctional towers, whose lower storeys were used as living rooms or granaries, or even as shops or cellars.

This applies to the tower of the Rocca di Campi (Fig. 40), whose function altered at least four times during the fifteenth century. It is listed as 'a tower which is a pigeon-loft next to the said castle' in 1427[31]; as 'an old tower for us to live in, where we need to

36. Brozzi, 'In Cantone', Francesco di Benedetto Strozzi's house incorporating Lionardo d'Antonio Strozzi's house with the tower.

put the tenant farmer because the farmhouse is in ruins' in 1446;[32] as 'a little tower' ('una torriciella') in 1451;[33] as 'a little tower which used to be a pigeon-loft next to the said castle, under which tower is a place to rent for 12 lira per annum, let to Berto di Marcho the blacksmith' in 1457;[34] in 1480 it is described by Carlo di Messer Marcello as 'A tower that used to have below it a blacksmith's workshop, which we keep for our own habitation ... and I have dismantled the said workshop and turned it into a wine cellar';[35] and finally in 1498 Carlo's brother Giovanni declares it as 'a tower where my brother Carlo used to live, and now Nanni the carter from the parish of S. Lorenzo at Campi lives there because he farms my land'.[36] From pigeon-loft to labourers' house, to smithy, to landowner's residence with wine cellar and back to farm labourer's house again, the tower beside the Rocca was adapted to the immediate needs of the family. Moreover, its original defensive purpose is never mentioned in these descriptions.

If the machicolated tower of the Rocca di Campi could be used as a pigeon-loft, presumably the same

37. Maglio, the dovecote (photo: Conway Library, Courtauld Institute of Art).

applied to the tower at Santuccio (Fig. 41 and see Fig. 79 in Chapter 6), which may be the *colombaia* referred to in a document of 1489.[37] At Capalle, Filippo di Matteo bought Ubertino di Tommaso's 'Torrione' (also known as the 'Palagione') and, apart from improving the house, Filippo's factor certainly kept many pigeons there, presumably in the upper part of the 'Torrione'.[38] Again the conflation of tower and dovecote can be inferred from the documents. The use of such large and formidable structures as the towers at Santuccio and the Rocca di Campi for the rearing of

small birds seems more plausible when we consider that only the top of the tower was used for this purpose and that pigeons were an important source of meat and fertilizer in the fifteenth century.

Granaries are not mentioned in the Strozzi tax returns which suggests that they were incorporated into other buildings, either part of the owner's or the peasant's house or other outbuildings. Account books do furnish some information about granaries, and from these it is clear that they existed in both quarters. Filippo di Matteo's factor at Capalle needed

38. Sketch of Maglio ('casa delmaglio') with its mill to the right ('Mulino'), showing plans to dam the Bisenzio River. ASF, Capitani di parte guelfa, numeri neri, filza 1005, Acque e strade, 1594.

39. Frontispiece to Piero de' Crescenzi, *De Agricultura*, Venice 1495.

40. Rocca di Campi tower, seen from the south.

a place to store the grain delivered by the tenant farmers, which was provided in the Palagione.[39] Simone di Filippo Strozzi rebuilt a *granaio* in his *palagio* at Quaracchi in 1416;[40] and Bartolommeo Sassetti's *granaio* was incorporated into the *casa da signore* at Macia.[41] Clearly, in a society that was so dependent on wheat, which was both its primary crop and yet also the one in shortest supply, in a period still subject to plague and famine, grain storage was of fundamental importance. At Santuccio, an account specifies that a granary should be built above the *casa da lavoratore's* stall for animals.[42] Granaries were probably often accommodated in lofts or small towers above the *lavoratore's* living quarters as well as over the stable, high up to protect the grain from damp, vermin and thieves.

GARDENS

Gardens were an integral part of the villa complex, situated beside the landowner's house, not only for ease of access and to embellish the setting, but also because fifteenth-century gardens were private spaces usually

41. Santuccio, detail of tower depicted in mural on the first floor of the house (photo: Conway Library, Courtauld Institute of Art).

enclosed by walls and guarded by the villa inhabitants. In this sense the distinction between farm and garden was clearly demarcated, for although it was an outdoor space, its walls and gates made the garden function like a series of rooms. In another sense, however, the fifteenth-century villa garden corresponded with the emphasis on *utilità* demonstrated by the widespread preference for villas attached to fertile and profitable farms; for the documentary evidence shows that most villa gardens were useful and productive, growing fruit, vegetables, herbs and trees. Just as Piero de' Crescenzi listed a medicinal use for almost every flower, fruit and tree,[43] so the decorative, edible or health-giving properties of plants were considered mutually enhancing and were appreciated in combination. The terminology reflects this holistic attitude for the words *giardino* and *orto* were usually interchangeable. Thus, the only use of the word *giardino* in the Strozzi tax returns was for Messer Palla Novello's 'giardino murato' at Soffiano, alternately described as 'orto murato' in

the tax return of 1442.[44] It is misleading to translate *orto* as kitchen garden and *giardino* as an ornamental or pleasure garden, for this distinction did not exist in fifteenth-century Italy,[45] where *orto* was widely used to refer to country gardens attached to both *case da signore* and *case da lavoratore*, as well as to town gardens that were undoubtedly ornamental, and even embellished with classical sculpture, such as the garden behind Palazzo Medici in Florence.[46] The word *giardino*, on the other hand, seems to have been reserved for more refined or decorative gardens with an aesthetic rather than a productive function.[47] *Orto*, therefore, like *casa*, was a blanket expression that could be applied to all types of gardens whether grand or humble, whereas *giardino*, like *palagio*, was only used for the more dignified end of the scale.

Since this is an attempt to understand fifteenth-century villa gardens and gardening practices without depending solely on agricultural theorists or the imagery of poets and painters, it might be hoped that documents would supply descriptions of their appearance. However in the case of tax returns, which make it possible to survey and compare a large group of properties, they merely mention whether a garden exists and occasionally refer to its size and yield. It is therefore only possible to say that at least nineteen of the Strozzi's residential villas were accompanied by *orti*,[48] which ranged in size between a quarter of an acre and one and three quarter acres (two to thirteen *staiora*). References to the plants grown are rare, for the produce was not considered of marketable value and only grown in sufficient quantity to meet the needs of the owner's household, if that. In 1427, however, Carlo di Marcuccio described the fruits of his *orto* beside Il Palagio at Campi, so as to assure the tax collectors that his profit was tiny and that most produce was eaten during the summer months at the villa:

> The garden, which is with the house where I live, produces 3 *staia* (c. 52 kilos) of broad beans, a quarter (c. 4 1/2 kilos) of peas, one and a quarter *moggia* of chick peas, twelve bunches of garlic, the grapes we use partly for eating and for verjuice; all the other fruit we consume in the summer without making any profit.[49]

Only a few of these descriptions in tax returns carry hints of grandeur or formality. At least six Strozzi villas were embellished with *pratelli*, which were meadow gardens or flowery lawns, usually planted with trees and sometimes including raised beds, stone seats, topiary hedges or trees and a fountain. The *pratello* was an important feature of Italian gardens, certainly from Boccaccio's day, and it was clearly perceived as a distinct entity or compartment within the whole garden area. Not only is it listed separately from the *orto* in documents, but building accounts for new Strozzi and Sassetti gardens both refer to separate walls and gates for the *pratelli*, so that we should resist the modern temptation to conceive of these as open meadows, merging with the agricultural landscape or wild grassland.[50] Nevertheless, as Ada Segre has recently suggested, the flowery meadows represented in verdure tapestries, and in paintings by Fra Angelico,

Botticelli and other fifteenth-century artists, were at least partly inspired by contemporary meadow gardens, just as gardeners were inspired by artists' representations.[51]

Bernardo di Giovanni's villa at Signano had a *prato* in front as well as a *piazza* and an *orto*.[52] Stagio d'Antonio's villa at Casi, referred to as a 'palagio disfacto' in 1427, was redeemed by its 'orto, corte et pratello'.[53] Marco di Goro's villa, L'Agio del Santo at Mezzana, had a *pratello*, and its *orto* was tended by a *garzone* before it was sold to Dietisalvi Nerone in 1445.[54] Among the Strozzi villas, it may have been those of minimal economic function with little farm land that had the most elaborate gardens. Ubertino di Tommaso's Montughi villa, attached to a small farm of about seven acres (fifty-one *staiora*), had a garden with 'chorti, pratello, citerna, perghole ... e un orto',[55] and Zanobi di Benedetto's garden at Palaiuola had three *staiora* (about half an acre) of *orto*, vines and 'un pocho di boschetto'.[56] The *boschetto*, a copse or grove of trees for summer strolls, sitting in the shade or trapping birds, was another key feature of the fifteenth-century garden. Giovanni Morelli contrasts the 'gran boschi e selve' of the high, wild country of the Mugello (the 'salvatico') with the tame 'boschetti' of the villa landscape, a cultivated Arcadia:

> Near the houses there are a great number of groves (*boschetti*) of fine oaks, and many of them have been trimmed to provide enjoyment, clear underneath, that is the ground is kept like a lawn (*prato*), so that you can go barefoot without worrying that anything will hurt your feet.[57]

Tanaglia links the *boschetto* to the presence of birds and birdsong.[58] Nor were these woods only a literary creation, for some of the finer gardens, those beside the Villa Medici at Fiesole, Giovanni Rucellai's villa at Quaracchi[59] and Francesco Nori's property at Africo near Antella,[60] all incorporated a *boschetto*.[61]

From their appearance in documents, it is possible to identify the walled garden (*orto*), the meadow garden (*pratello*) and the grove of trees (*boschetto*) as the three key components in the fifteenth-century

or from a grand country palace that retained an internal courtyard such as Sassetti's villa at La Pietra (rebuilt c. 1462–8).

Since the provision of fresh, cheap produce of the owner's choice was one of the great advantages of a country estate, many owners reserved extra land for their own personal use apart from the *orto*. Allocated 'a mia mano' or 'a nostre mani', this land was usually cultivated by the *fattore*, for whom it was a regular part of his job, or by *lavoratori*, for whom it was occasional work paid by the day in cash or kind.[68] Instead of being divided with the *lavoratori*, the harvest from this land belonged exclusively to the *signore*. It was often planted in vines to provide extra wine for the table, it might include the vineyard's essential partner the *canneto* (cane thicket) for stakes, hay meadows for horse fodder, an orchard for fruit, and other trees to provide fuel, shade and beauty.[69]

The terse items of the Strozzi tax returns are partly supplemented, in the case of Filippo di Matteo, by his surviving account books. Filippo's new garden at Santuccio was divided into two distinct areas: the *orto* and the *pratello*. They were built after the renovations to the house were completed in 1486. The *orto* had a well,[70] with stone benches (*muriciuoli*, which probably also functioned as the walls of raised beds),[71] and a boundary wall next to the Spini property, which was crenellated with battlements in 1489.[72] The *pratello* was raised and levelled with the addition of 800 cart-loads of earth.[73] It also must have been walled, for a gateway with a wooden roof was built there in 1486.[74] Unfortunately, there are few records of plants at Santuccio, although one account refers to the planting of 200 mulberry trees there in 1488.[75] Mulberries were no longer a novelty since Giovanni Rucellai had already planted several thousand at Poggio a Caiano in the early 1470s, but this nevertheless illustrates how the vogue for silk production was spreading on the country estates of the Florentine elite.[76] Equally significant is a request from Filippo's Ferrarese cousin Roberto di Nanne Strozzi in 1489 for some little fig plants with roots ('qualche piantolina con radice de' fichi brusochi').[77] This letter, like those written some thirty years before to Giovanni di Cosimo de' Medici while he was making his new garden at Fiesole, confirms that plant collecting was already established in this period and that a connoisseur's attitude to plants and gardens was beginning to develop.[78] It was through the interest and instigation of landowners and garden builders writing to relatives, friends and agents that new and exotic varieties of plants were disseminated throughout Italy.

The letter about fig plants also confirms at least one statement in Lorenzo Strozzi's biography where the description of his father's Neapolitan farm reveals that Filippo had a special interest in horticulture:

> He had, near the city of Naples, a garden called The Farm (*Masseria*) which surpassed all others in its nature and abundance; where he would often go for his own refreshment and to the delight of his friends, and he took such pleasure in its cultivation, that he did many things with his own hands, gathering there the rarest and first fruits of the season that came to Naples; from which afterwards he did not fail to adorn also his own homeland with noble plants, transporting there cultivated figs and artichokes, which had not before been brought into our region.[79]

Surprisingly, Filippo did not buy his Neapolitan farm, called Bella Vista, on the hill of Sant'Elmo below the gardens of San Martino, until July 1480,[80] some fourteen years after he first returned to Florence.[81] This makes it more likely that the purchase was motivated by a desire to garden in volcanic soil, in a frost-free climate, on a spectacular site overlooking the Bay of Naples. The association of Naples with gardening was well established by this time. Not only had Giovanni di Cosimo de' Medici's agent exported plant specimens from Naples, but both Piero de' Crecenzi and Michelangelo Tanaglia had dedicated their agricultural treatises to rulers of Naples[82]; likewise, the humanist Giovanni Pontano, who was employed by King Ferrante and his court and was a friend of Filippo Strozzi's,[83] declared in his treatise on social virtues that villa gardens were an essential element in creating a magnificent identity.[84]

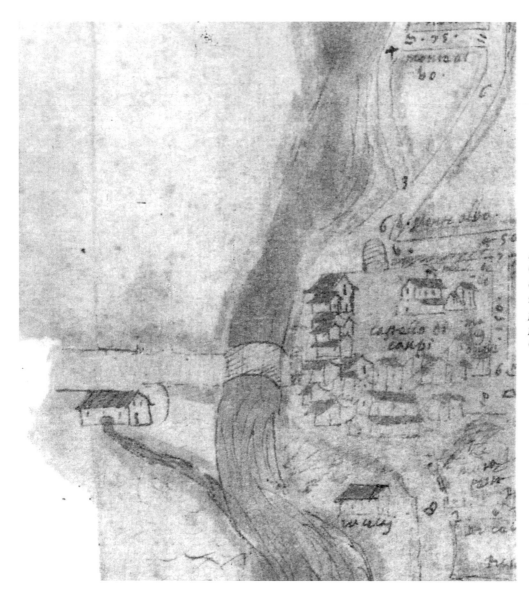

44. Parish of S. Stefano a Campi, the *castello* of Campi on the banks of the Bisenzio River. Detail of *Piante di popoli e strade – Capitani di parte guelfa – 1580–1595*, II, c. 409.

HOUSES IN THE *CASTELLO*

Although houses in fortified villages (*castelli*) were not physically part of the villa complex, they were administratively part of the whole estate and were usually closely associated with the *casa da signore* nucleus. Fear of disaster, whether attacks by brigands, war or floods, together with a deep-rooted faith in the *castello* as a safe refuge, led landowners to take the precaution of maintaining a house in the walled village or town nearest their farms. These were probably the motives behind Francesco di Giovanni, Benedetto di Pieraccione and

Filippo di Matteo's ownership of extra houses in the *castello* of Capalle (see Fig. 11 in Chapter 2) and Carlo di Marcuccio and Giovanni di Giovanni's houses in the *castello* of Campi (Fig. 44). All these landowners had farms and *case da signore* beyond the village walls except for Filippo Strozzi, whose Capalle residence was within the walls of the *castello* itself. Perhaps the vulnerability of this area to floods and attacks in wartime made it a special case.[85] It is doubtful whether the profit from letting these small houses could be the attraction for Carlo di Marcuccio, who let his house to local butchers for six florins a year,[86] whereas Giovanni di Giovanni let his little house to a shoemaker for only ten lire (c. two and a half florins) a year.[87] Occasionally, they reserved these houses for their own use, as Carlo di Marcuccio's heirs expressed it in 1469:

> The said house we keep for our own use for cereals and wheat and as a refuge for our things and our tenant farmers in times of danger or in war.[88]

On the other hand, Francesco di Giovanni's village houses at Capalle had been in ruins and were demolished and sold to make a threshing yard,[89] while Benedetto di Pieraccione used a house in the same *castello* for storing the timber used to repair his many *case da lavoratore*,[90] and Filippo di Matteo bought extra houses beside Il Palagione to use as stables and storage space.[91]

The other main reason for owning houses in a town or village, was as a substitute estate centre when there was no *casa da signore* nearby. This was the case for Marco di Nofri di Palla, who had no *casa da signore* but four farms near Prato and a small house in the town of Prato:

> A small house which we have in the walled town of Prato, in which we put all our harvest and wheat and cereals and wine.... And in the said house are various belongings, such as wicker baskets and barrels and things of little value.[92]

Similarly, Palla di Nofri's main motive for owning properties in market towns and villages was to store and redistribute the crops from his vast estates. Yet the sheer number of these houses and the fact that so many of them were let shows that this was also part of a policy of investment in provincial property. Thus, two of his three houses in the *castello* of Campi were let, his house at Capalle was let, three of his four houses in Prato were let and at Empoli he retained one house for his own use and let thirteen others, whereas a house at Figline was kept for storage, and one at Carmignano was let to a relative who was the local priest.[93] Crispin de Courcey Bayley's recent work on the rental market in Florence has revealed how renting was a crucial aspect of property management in this period.[94] The letting of small houses and shops in the towns and villages of the surrounding countryside may be an extension of this practice. Out of town, however, the income it brought in was not nearly as significant as both the need for more secure storage space than the open country could provide and the desire to extend proprietorial rights over a wider provincial territory.

COUNTRY INNS

Whereas houses in nearby villages were maintained for reasons of security, to provide storage space and only sometimes to bring in a modest rent, the economic motive was certainly dominant in citizens' ownership of country inns. In the fifteenth century, the function of a grand hotel was often performed by privately owned villas to which distinguished travellers had been referred by friends, relations or colleagues. At the other end of the scale, the poor and pilgrims stayed at hospices; most travellers, however, used wayside hostelries and inns.[95]

Country inns also illustrate how a self-sufficient economy could be run on a small scale by rural landowners. The inn created a demand for bread, meat and wine that could be supplied cheaply from the proprietor's own farm next door,[96] or, to put it another way, surplus produce from the farm could conveniently and profitably be consumed at the proprietor's own inn. Because landowners left the responsibility of running the hotel to an innkeeper but received a higher rent than for most rural property, the enterprise might seem undemanding and lucrative; however, the two Strozzi hotel owners, Palla di Nofri and Matteo di Simone, both had a succession of innkeepers and were involved in expensive improvements to the buildings. In 1427, Palla was rebuilding the house behind the inn at Poggio a Caiano as an annex for guests and received a rent of between twenty-five and thirty florins a year.[97] Palla's other, much smaller inn on the Via Pisana at Signa, was let to Domenicho detto Farfalla

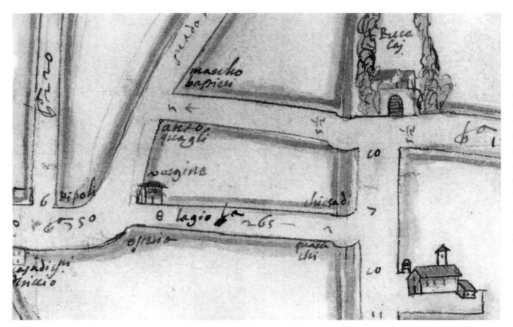

45. Parish of S. Piero a Quaracchi, detail of the place called L'Agio, with the site of Matteo di Simone Strozzi's inn marked 'osteria' near the church of S. Piero and the garden of Giovanni Rucellai's villa, Lo Specchio. Detail of *Piante di popoli e strade – Capitani di parte guelfa – 1580–1595*, II, c. 401.

for 11.6 florins in 1430 (capitalised at F.178.11.4)[98] and for a mere nine florins in 1433 (capitalised at F.144.13-).[99]

Matteo Strozzi inherited a hotel or tavern called L'Agio at Quaracchi from his father, Simone (Fig. 45).[100] The inn had a brisk turnover of seven managers (*osti*) between 1425 and 1435.[101] They were all local men from Quaracchi itself or neighbouring parishes. For over a year, from November 1432 until February 1434, Matteo's factor Agnolo di Papi di Buto and the parish priest of San Piero a Quaracchi, Ser Domenico d'Agnolo, went into partnership to run the inn. It was a convenient arrangement for Agnolo who lived in the house attached to the tavern,[102] while the priest was already concerned with its success because he had supervised renovations there in 1426–7.[103] Matteo enlarged the inn: converting the old stables into a small dining room (*saletta*), renewing a cloak-room (*guardaroba*) in the next-door chamber, rebuilding the tower chamber and building new stables.[104] He then proceeded to incorporate the house next door where the factor had lived, constructing a large dining room (*sala grande*) and making new staircases, doorways and corridors leading to more bedrooms.[105]

Whereas previous inkeepers had paid a rent of between thirty-six and thirty-eight florins a year from which six to eight florins in gabelles for meat and wine were deducted,[106] Matteo experimented with a new contract for his overseer and the priest, whom he charged only fourteen florins in rent, leaving them to cover the cost of maintenance.[107] After Matteo's exile and death, his widow Alessandra took over the inn as part repayment for her dowry.[108] She let it for only twelve florins a year in the 1450s, and in 1462 the inn was sold for 300 florins when Alessandra anticipated joining her sons in exile.

WATER MILLS

Grain mills run by water power were another profitable investment for landowners, integrated into the estate economy. Although not strictly part of the *casa da signore* complex, of the dozen rural mills owned by the Strozzi during the fifteenth century,[109] most were situated near the estate centre. Messer Marcello's mill was just across the road from the Rocca di Campi. Its site was marked by the Capitani di Parte Guelfa

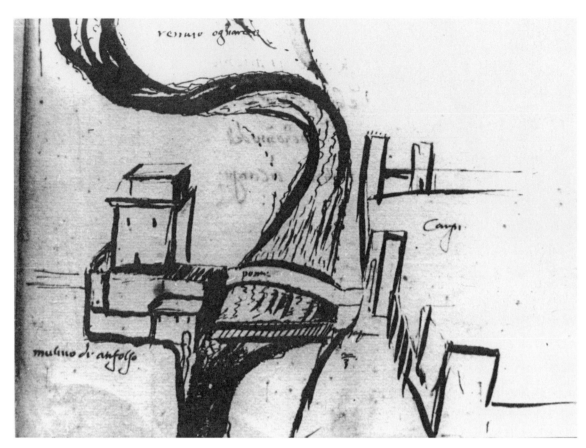

46. Sketch of the Rocca di Campi with its mill. ASF, Capitani di parte guelfa, numeri neri, filza 965, 12 September 1564.

in a sketch to accompany a report of 12 September 1564 and in their road map of c. 1585–90 in the parish of S. Stefano a Campi (Fig. 46 and see Fig. 44 this chapter).[110] The 1564 sketch only gives a very rough idea of the form of the Rocca and its mill, but it does show how close together they stood. The two low blocks of the mill were built right against the river bank, with the dam (*pescaia*) stretching flat across the water's surface and the race only slightly diverted from the main course of the Bisenzio; the tower of the Rocca behind is set slightly back from the river.

The prosperous mill owned by Filippo Strozzi's widow and sons in the early sixteenth century is the small towered *mulinaccio* placed just north of the Villa of Santuccio on the Capitani di Parte Maps (see Fig. 20, Chapter 3). This mill was called 'il Mulino del Ponte a San Moro' and was bought by Lorenzo

and Filippo the Younger in May 1518.[111] It was one of the most profitable of all Strozzi mills, rented for over 170 lire in 1517, 252 lire in 1519 and over 261 lire in 1520.[112] A summary of income from this mill in 1526 itemises the kind of rent payments: seven *moggia* of wheat (F.28), the milling of five *moggia* of flour (F.2.5.7), fifty pounds of fish and a pair of capons (F.2).[113] The use of milldams as fish ponds, a function that is spelled out in the double meaning of the word *pescaia*, was an important bonus for mill-owners.[114]

With the intensive grain production in the Arno valley, where most Strozzi villas lay, water mills were a lucrative investment for the landowner, although the tenant miller would have skimmed off some profit.[115] Repairs seem to have been costly and were eagerly declared by the tax-payers. Messer Palla Novello claimed that his mill on the Arno at Cintoia was left high and dry and needed to be moved and rebuilt at a cost of

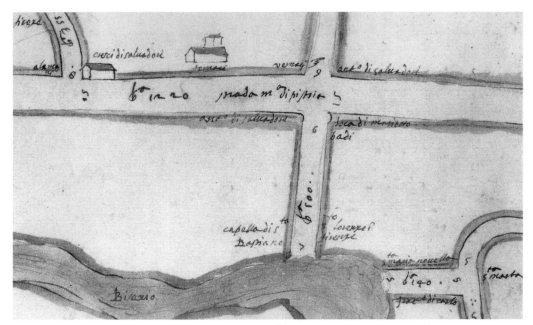

47. Parish of S. Cresci a Campi, kiln of Salvadore d'Antonio's descendents marked 'fornaci' beside the Via Pistoiese. Detail of *Piante di popoli e strade – Capitani di parte guelfa – 1580–1595*, II, c. 415.

150 florins.[116] In a similar vein, Palla di Nofri Strozzi claimed that to buy stone and repair the milldam at Poggio a Caiano would cost him over 100 florins,[117] and altogether his tax deduction for the maintenance cost of mills in 1427 was almost 500 florins.[118] Most mills only had one set of mill stones, but to make a larger profit faster, some, such as Lionardo di Jacopo's big estate on the river Elsa, had up to four sets grinding simultaneously.[119]

KILNS FOR LIME AND BRICKS

As a rural industry, lime and brick kilns were a less attractive investment for the Strozzi landowners than grain milling. Whereas eight families had mills, only four of the Strozzi claimed to own kilns.[120] This was partly because mills were of direct service to farms, and their reputation for profit making was long established.

Kilns, on the other hand, served the building industry, not agriculture, and were needed intermittently for construction projects by the few landowners who had the means to build on a large scale. For repairs and small building projects, owners had re-course to whatever kilnsmen operated closest to their estate or whose good service had been proved in previous employment. Therefore, only the two wealthiest Strozzi who engaged in large-scale property expansion and construction had more than one kiln, and, even then, their own furnaces only provided a small proportion of the baked lime and brick work needed for their projects, being a handy supplement rather than an essential source of materials.[121] Palla di Nofri had two working kilns between 1427 and 1433, both in the valley below Carmignano, at Strada Nuova in the parish of S. Marco a Seano and at Tavola in the parish of S. Maria Maddalena.[122] It seems that kilns needed frequent reroofing due to the great heat of repeated firing, for the kiln at Tavola was reroofed in 1421 and again two years later.[123] In these years, Palla also had a kiln working at Petraia since baked lime for the sacristy of S. Trinita was provided from there in 1420 and the same kiln was repaired in 1422–3.[124] However, by 1430 it was described as disused,[125] and the likely explanation for this and other mentions of abandoned kilns in the *contado*[126] is that those belonging to urban landlords were only activated to serve a particular building scheme or series of construction projects. Palla's kilns at Tavola and Seano were useful for his repairs at Poggio a Caiano and probably were also intended to serve the much larger building and restoration programme he planned, but was never able to execute, at Trefiano and Poggio a Caiano. Similarly, the kiln at Petraia was designed to provide materials for his construction of two villas there: at Petraia itself and at Il Palagetto on the piazza nearby.

When Filippo di Matteo Strozzi was financing construction of a hermitage at Lecceto in 1480, he made use of a kiln belonging to his poor relation Antonio di Niccolò di Barla Strozzi who had farms nearby. In March 1489, Filippo bought two kilns of his own in the parish of S. Cresci a Campi[127] to supply the construction of his new town palace, which had been inaugurated seven months earlier.[128] The record of purchase mentions two adjacent kilns, one for bricks and the other for lime, with living quarters, a courtyard and over half an acre of arable land with trees.[129] The right to dig clay from two pieces of land on the banks of the Bisenzio for two years was negotiated by Filippo Strozzi. He ousted the previous tenants, built a new house, and let the kiln to Salvadore d'Antonio d'Andrea *fornaciaio* for three years from 1 March 1491, on condition that they make brick-work and not lime and that the extra two pieces of land beside the Bisenzio, which was then sown in wheat, would be resown with the same amount of wheat when they left and that after quarrying, the land be left in better rather than worse condition. In return, Salvadore should pay thirty-five florins a year in three instalments.[130]

It is clear from the trouble that Filippo Strozzi went to in acquiring the extra land, that a brick kiln needed its raw material – clay – at hand,[131] as well as plenty of room to manoeuvre delivery carts with their oxen and to stack supplies and the finished products. Lack of land was the reason Palla di Nofri gave in 1433 for being unable to find a tenant for his kiln at Petraia.[132]

Although these kilns were all situated near residential villas, the danger of fire,[133] the dirty nature of the industry and the requirement for its own space to quarry and load meant that kilns would not have been placed within, or even beside, the villa com-plex. That the kiln sites were close to, but removed from, the *casa da signore* is confirmed by the Capitani di Parte maps of S. Michele a Castello and S. Cresci a Campi, which mark *fornaci* in the locations specified in the fifteenth-century accounts of Palla di Nofri and Filippo di Matteo's kilns. In the case of Petraia, the map shows a small porticoed structure labelled 'fornace' just below the villa on the road leading towards the church of S. Michele a Castello (see Fig. 3 in Chapter 1). Filippo Strozzi's kiln can be identified with the tow-ered building marked 'fornaci' on the Via Pistoiese in the Capitani di Parte map of c. 1580–95 (Fig. 47). The land around it belonged to 'Cresci di Salvadore' and 'Ant[oni]o di Salvadore', presumably descendants of Filippo Strozzi's kilnsman Salvadore d'Antonio. The villa of Santuccio was only half a mile away, down the Bisenzio River.

As was the case with farmland, the buildings of the villa complex were not gathered into one consolidated unit but were physically dispersed around the coun-tryside, usually within a radius of half a mile from the *casa da signore*. Although the landowner's house was quite separate from the tenant farmers' houses, it is clear that some agricultural functions were integrated into the owner's complex; in particular, the *casa da signore* was often used as a store house for the most valuable produce: wheat, wine, olive oil and birdlime. Thus, each structure of the villa complex served an agricultural, industrial or commercial function, and the simplified concept of a villa as the pleasure house of the elite would be hard to sustain in the face of this evidence. Further than this, a striking feature of the Strozzi landowners is the degree to which they in-vested not only in their own country residence – in the land itself and in the farmhouse complexes of the fam-ilies they needed to work the land – but also in village shops and houses, wayside inns and in the preindus-trial structures of the countryside – mills and kilns. If the Strozzi's only, or even main, interest were simply *villeggiatura*, it seems unlikely they would have spread their investment into small towns and villages and into regional commerce and industry. This tentacle-like, colonising characteristic is most easily explained by the desire to make a profit, however small, whenever possible. Structurally, however, this pervasive involvement in rural territory resembles the extraordinarily wide-reaching patronage networks spreading out from the big families of the Florentine merchant class and most famously exemplified by the Medici. The wide arena of the *contado* offered rich possibilities for extending influence and ties, and the villa complex with its community of inhabitants, dependants, employees and clientage connections in country towns and villages was integrated into this metapatronage system.

⟡ 5 · Repair, Construction and Rural Patronage

Dilapidation and Repair

For most of the Strozzi clan the fifteenth century was a period of maintenance and repair in the face of retrenchment and decline. If tax returns are relied on as a major source, it is easy to overestimate the extent of decay in buildings, since it was in the interests of taxpayers to declare and exaggerate the cost of property maintenance, which was deducted from their taxable assets. In 1427 Palla di Nofri claimed that repairs to his houses in town and country cost him more than 200 florins a year.[1] No other Strozzi landowner spent nearly as much on maintenance, and Piero di Carlo's *incarico* of five florins a year spent at Querceto, three florins a year on farmhouses at Campi and ten florins annually on the old fortified house at Loiano was larger than most claims.[2] Even allowing for some exaggeration on the tax payer's part, however, the Strozzi *catasti* convey an overall impression of stasis at best and, at worst, dilapidation. At Capalle Francesco di Giovanni's riverside estate had clearly seen better days. A group of five houses had burnt down in January 1427 and were allowed to gradually disintegrate, mentioned in each tax return until 1498, when all traces of them were apparently obliterated.[3] Francesco's houses within the village of Capalle were also neglected: two *casolari* had partly fallen down, while another four *casolari* were flattened and the site finally sold in 1451 for only four florins to make a threshing floor.[4] Although Ubertino di Tommaso seems to have looked after his residence at Montughi, his Torrione at Capalle was uninhabited

and falling down when Filippo di Matteo stepped in and bought it in 1475. Here, too, there were other *casolari* falling into ruins.[5] Tenant farmers' houses belonging to Benedetto di Piero at Capalle were no longer occupied and, once they had decayed, were used for storing wood or for processing the grape harvest.[6] Even one of the wealthier members of the clan, Messer Marcello Strozzi, is eloquent in his appraisal of the damage caused to the Rocca di Campi by lightning and of the cost of repairs to all his properties:

> To maintain the house in Florence and the properties at Campi and at Luciano we need big money. This is to inform you that, less than a year ago, lightning struck the house at Campi and did great damage, so that it will cost a lot of money to repair it; and so too we have to spend a lot on the house in Florence which is all in ruins in many places.[7]

The image of derelict country buildings or of landowners struggling to maintain old houses in need of major repair is consistent with the historians' view of the demographic crisis following the Black Death of 1348 and lasting until the mid–fifteenth century,[8] although a survey of fourteenth-century buildings is needed to establish whether many of the isolated *case da signore* and farm houses of the *contado* did pre-exist the plague of 1348.[9] Apart from the many *case da lavoratore* and *capanne* in a state of dilapidation, which are partly a testimony to the relatively low rural population compared with the late thirteenth and early fourteenth centuries, as well as the result of the concentration of land holdings into fewer *poderi*, the number of once imposing buildings fallen into decay is striking.

The building types are impressive: towers, palaces and fortified dwellings in ruins or relegated to the use of *lavoratori*. There was Ubertino di Tommaso's Torrione at Capalle, probably built by the Florentine archbishop in the early fourteenth century, and Palla and Carlo di Francesco also owned towers, one near the Badia a Settimo, which they sold before 1446, and another in the Val di Pesa, described as 'disfatta'.[10] Three Strozzi and a man from Prato all shared a tower in Le Miccine, referred to as 'Una toraccia', and as 'Una torre disfatta a uso de' lavoratore'.[11] Although towers survived when they were incorporated into larger houses as granaries, dovecotes or simply belvederes, it is likely that the isolated towers, the *case torri* of the *contado*, were slowly being phased out as they were in town.

Palla di Nofri's decaying fortifications, Il Casteluccio (Vitiano) and Castelletti (Signa), may have also been the remainders of a building type no longer in demand,[12] although his palaces stood a better chance of survival. Prulli has long since disappeared, but Trefiano, Petraia and Poggio a Caiano were rebuilt by subsequent owners.[13] Palla does not seem to have carried out renovations on the *palagi* of Trefiano and Prulli, described as 'uno palagio male abitato e situato chiamaxi Treffiano' and 'il palagio disfatto ed è chasolare, luogo detto Prulli' in 1427.[14] On the other hand Palla's *abituri*, which were also described as dilapidated in 1427, were in the process of renovation as building accounts for Petraia and Poggio between 1420 and 1423, suggest.[15] It was these *abituri*, salvaged by Palla before his exile in 1434, that were eagerly bought by other owners – the Medici, the Neroni and the Rinieri – when Palla's supporters and relations could no longer afford to retain them.

Stagio d'Antonio Strozzi's 'palagio disfacto' at Casi is another example of an old, delapidated house that found a wealthy new owner in Francesco Sassetti and was restored to grandeur by his son Cosimo Sassetti in the sixteenth century.[16] Other Strozzi managed to carry out their own restoration

and to maintain their ancestral properties, as Carlo di Marco did for Il Palagio at Campi, which had one wing crumbling away by 1446 and was listed as a 'chasolare coperto'; yet there were no claims for maintenance costs in subsequent *catasti*, and the house remained in Strozzi hands until the eighteenth century.[17]

CONSTRUCTION AND RENOVATION: A CASE STUDY OF FILIPPO DI MATTEO STROZZI'S RURAL BUILDING PROJECTS

Messer Palla di Nofri's awareness of the special status of *ex novo* construction is conveyed in the will he made in 1462 at the age of ninety. Although the country palace of Trefiano was by then small and delapidated he made provision that it should never leave the family (Figs. 48 and 49):

> And I do this because it was built from its foundations by our ancestors and forefathers, Messer Jacopo and Palla his son, father of Nofri my father, and therefore my grandfather. And I want as far as it is possible for me to ensure that the site and place and farm should remain with our family and our descendents, in memory of he who built it and raised it from its foundations, and because of the place where it is: that is Carmignano, where there have always been men the same as us and of our lineage. Although that place is now such a small thing and a sort of hovel, once it was great and beautiful and magnificent.[18]

Despite the fact that so few country houses were built from scratch during the fifteenth century, and none of these by the Strozzi, the distinction between mere alteration and additions on one hand, which were carried out regularly and thoroughly by a large number of property owners with medium to large incomes and, on the other hand, initiating a new construction ('lo edificò e fa principio') to build on a large scale 'da fondamenti', was plainly recognised. For Palla di Nofri Strozzi, it was the combination of ancestral

48. Parish of S. Piero a Seano, Palla di Nofri Strozzi's *palagio* of Trefiano marked 'trefiano de rucellai'. Detail of *Piante di popoli e strade – Capitani di parte guelfa – 1580–1595*, II, c. 553.

possession of the site and *ex novo* construction that gave his palaces in Florence and at Trefiano their special status.

The greater prestige and public exposure enjoyed by urban palaces meant that capital expenditure in a town palace was more profitable in terms of social status and reputation than a more distant, less visible country house was likely to be. When owners needed to expand their country dwellings, they tended to add to old buildings, spreading out into the available space with new wings, porticoes or outbuildings, whereas in town the lack of space to expand in was more likely

to favour the substitution of old buildings with new ones. The economic factor that governed farm life also led owners to be more pragmatic and less idealistic or ambitious in their schemes for rural building. Finally, the conservative style of country building was considered an appropriate expression of a family's ancestral presence in a district, giving the appearance of having been long settled in that country neighbourhood.[19]

Apart from Palla di Nofri, only Francesco di Benedetto's family and Filippo di Matteo seem to have been able to afford to rebuild thoroughly or to enlarge their villas. Whereas no building accounts have

49. Trefiano, Palla di Nofri Strozzi's *palagio*, later rebuilt by the Rucellai.

been found for Francesco and Zanobi di Benedetto's alterations at Brozzi or Palaiuola, nor for Vanni di Francesco's construction at Galluzzo, Filippo di Matteo's projects are thoroughly documented in his many surviving account books and *ricordanze*. As a case study in rural construction, Filippo di Matteo is also a particularly suitable candidate because he was an active patron in the country as well as in town, and projects of different scale and function were carried out in several locations simultaneously, allowing comparison between urban and rural schemes and presenting an integrated view of fifteenth-century building methods.

FILIPPO DI MATTEO STROZZI'S EARLY PROJECTS

On 22 April 1477 Filippo wrote to his brother Lorenzo that he would first attend to ecclesiastical projects before turning to his own interests:

> Since God has granted me worldly goods, I want to recompense Him for it; and starting with God's things, we can one day arrive at our own; about which I am doing all I can; but for now, no conclusion has been reached, and the more one gets involved, the

more they pull back. Manfredi is the sort who won't budge from a thousand florins, and before that is sorted out I don't want to build or I would have problems with the neighbours.[20]

In this one letter Filippo altogether refers to six projects, beginning with the design of a tomb for their dead brother Matteo, justifying his extravagance in buying the villa of Santuccio, admitting his desire to improve the *pieve* at Ripoli, and informing Lorenzo that he had just spent more than 100 florins at the church of Le Selve and expected to spend twice that at the hermitage of Lecceto. Although four of these schemes were indeed ecclesiastical and a fifth, the villa of Santuccio, was described in relation to its oratory, the sixth and most ambitious scheme was for the grand new town palace, in preparation for which Filippo was doing all he could ('fo quello posso'), only prevented from acquiring the site by an obstinate neighbour ('Manfredi è di quelli che sta duro a mille fiorini').[21] This letter provides a remarkably clear exposition of Filippo Strozzi's motives, above all illustrating how closely connected these schemes were in the patron's mind, all (apart from the palace) interwoven into the daily exercise of charitable activity. Filippo's undoubtedly genuine piety co-existed with a desire to honour his family, a keen eye for profit and the entrepreneurial spirit that led him to lay plans for his grand palace well in advance, while his other comparatively small religious projects were going ahead. This combination of motives is further articulated in the letter when he gives his reasons for buying the villa of Santuccio. High standards for the sake of family reputation, an offering of thanks to God, the practical need for accommodation and, finally, the indisputable advantage of profit, were all put forward to justify his purchase to an unenthusiastic brother:

About the expenses I have incurred at Santuccio, I know that I have overstepped the limit; but once I had laid my hands on it, it would not have done to leave that work incomplete, since it belonged to us. Since God has granted us His grace, there is no harm in recognising it in some way. My idea was

that if Giovanluigi had the benefice, he could live there, and we could go there every year for the Saint's Day [St John Baptist]. Since it didn't work out, if I had not already begun on it, I would have pulled out. But a start had been made; and I have rented it out, so that by All Saints they will have moved in. And whereas before we received 110 lire in wheat and cash, I have raised that to 160 lire with the rent, and I have worked out that we will take so much in profit that it will pay for itself and in the end it will turn out to have been a good thing for us.[22]

As the following chronological and geographical survey indicates, Filippo's statement that he was attending to religious patronage before secular patronage was not strictly true because urban and rural, religious and secular projects proceeded side by side at a steady pace from the mid-1470s until Filippo's death in 1491 (Fig. 50).[23]

On his immediate return from exile in 1466, Filippo first attended to his domestic arrangements in town, decorating the nuptial chamber to receive his bride Fiammetta Adimari and acquiring other furnishings[24] for the old family house, which had been bought by his grandfather Simone in 1416 and rebuilt in 1421.[25] Filippo's plan to replace his grandfather's house with a magnificent new residence may have taken shape soon after his return to Florence, for in September 1474 he began to buy shops and houses on the site of his future palace, continuing with nine purchases in 1475, although the last property was not acquired until 1489, the year in which building started.[26] Next door to the great palace site but separate from it, Filippo bought a house from his distant relative Strozza di Messer Marcello Strozzi, which he entirely rebuilt at a cost of 1,152 florins between 1482 and 1487.[27] This house was probably planned from the start as a temporary shelter for the family when their old house was pulled down and while the grand new palace was being built. Its elevation, as represented in Baccio d'Agnolo's view of Piazza Strozzi (Fig. 51),[28] was modest and traditional, although building accounts mention an

50. Benedetto da Maiano, terracotta bust of Filippo Strozzi, 1475. Skulpturen Sammlung und Museum für Byzantinische Kunst, Berlin, currently exhibited in the Gemäldegalerie, Berlin.

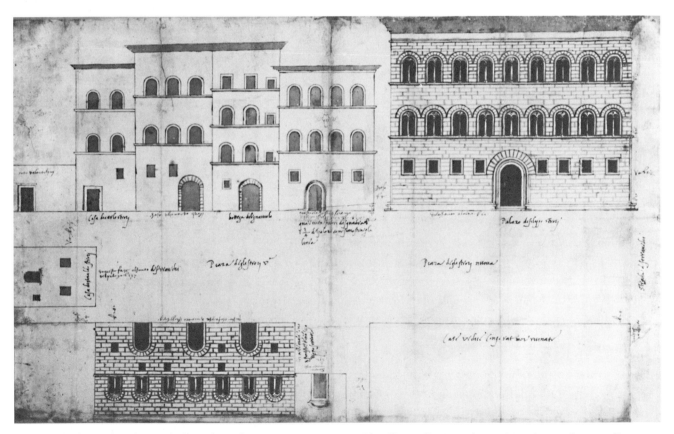

51. Baccio d'Agnolo, plan and elevations of Piazza Strozzi, 1533, with Filippo di Matteo's provisional town house adjacent to Palazzo Strozzi. Uffizi, Gabinetto Disegni e Stampe 132A (photo: Ministero per i Beni e le Attività Culturali, Soprintendenza Speciale per il Polo Museale Fiorentino, Gabinetto Fotografico).

internal courtyard overlooked by loggias ('veroni sopra la corte').[29]

Filippo's ecclesiastical patronage in town focussed on two sites: The first was S. Maria Ughi, the small parish church on Piazza Strozzi immediately opposite his town house, for which he commissioned two windows in 1472, liturgical vestments and, in 1482, a Madonna with angels and the Strozzi coat of arms frescoed by Ghirlandaio above the main door.[30] The other site was S. Maria Novella, the main church of his ancestral quarter, for which the more ambitious scheme of a burial chapel frescoed by Flippino Lippi was initiated in 1486 but not finished until twelve years after his death.[31]

Meanwhile, Filippo's rural patronage schemes had been long under way. The problem of finding a rector for the ancestral oratory at Santuccio, which had worried his mother Alessandra during the 1460s,[32] was solved when Messer Piero di Benedetto di Pieraccione Strozzi was made rector in June 1470,[33] and a book of administrative accounts for the oratory was opened at the same time to tabulate the first expenditure on new roofs for the oratory and the next-door *casa da lavoratore* in 1471.[34] At Santuccio, no other major expenses were incurred until Filippo bought the villa there in 1477.[35]

52. Capalle, Il Palagione from the piazza.

CAPALLE

The farm at Capalle was Filippo's first large rural purchase, concluded in spring 1475. He did not consider Ubertino's 'Torrione', also described in his *ricordanze* as 'a big palace over one of the gates to Capalle' ('uno palagione sopra una delle porti di Capalle'), to be fit for habitation, because he specifically mentioned the lack of a 'house to live in' in a letter to his brother in Naples and said that the estate was purely for agricultural produce or income.[36] To rectify this situation, Filippo spent over 377 florins between June 1475 and November 1476, 'in the building campaign carried out on the Palagione at Capalle'.[37] When the sitting tenant in the small house next door died in early 1479, Filippo took over that house,[38] and in late 1482 he bought two other adjacent *casette da lavoratore* from the Florentine archbishop, in return for which he had a

new *casa da lavoratore* built on the archbishop's farm.[39] Finally, Filippo bought another small house adjoining the Palagione in summer 1483.[40] From 1486 to 1487 Pagholo Strozzi, the factor, supervised the construction of new stables and a stone oven on the piazza beside the Palagione. The remaining small houses were repaired in preparation for new tenants.[41] Although it is no longer possible to see the results of Filippo's scheme of improvement for Capalle (Fig. 52) and although it was a comparatively minor project, the strategy not only to improve the residence, but also to secure possession of the surrounding houses, to expand into the neighbouring farm country, and to attend to every rudimentary hovel in the vicinity, is typical of Filippo's unremittingly tenacious and meticulous approach expressed in his statement about Santuccio: 'ma poi v'avevo messo mano, non era da

53. Villa Le Selve, Lastra a Signa, rebuilt in the sixteenth century (photo: Conway Library, Courtauld Institute of Art).

lasciare quella hopera inperfetta, esendo chosa nostra'. After all, Filippo would never have bought the house at Capalle if his poor relatives had not appealed to him not to allow the property to leave the clan ('e perchè non escha di chasa mixi sieno volto'). The sense of a clan patrimony was undoubtedly the clinching factor here, and, although the phrase 'cosa nostra' now carries different, specifically mafioso implications, the cult of loyalty revealed in Filippo Strozzi's property dealings and his fixation with the family, embracing everything that touched it, are nevertheless striking.

LE SELVE

Filippo had been introduced to the hills above Signa many years before when his sister Alessandra married Giovanni Bonsi and moved to her husband's villa overlooking the Arno at Le Selve (Fig. 53). The villa of Le Selve became the favourite country retreat not only for Alessandra Strozzi Bonsi but also for her mother and her brothers.[42] Filippo's own intimate concern with the church of S. Maria alle Selve, a short distance above the villa, may have dated from August 1473 when he buried his fourth child, Alessandro,

under the Bonsi family altar in that church.[43] Perhaps this event awakened Filippo to the need for his own altar in the church, although the death of his brother-in-law Giovanni Bonsi in 1473 and his increased sense of responsibility for his widowed sister as well as his wish to offer thanks to God ('essere ricordevole', 'faciamo...richonoscienza') in the form of religious patronage made the choice an obvious one. On 3 November 1476, the nine Carmelite friars of S. Maria delle Selve granted the patronage rights of the church to Filippo Strozzi.[44] That year he had already spent over twenty-eight florins on repairs to the villa and farm of Le Selve[45] and in 1477 he spent another 100 florins at the church.[46] Church vestments and hangings were commissioned in 1477 and 1478,[47] although Neri di Bicci did not paint his altarpiece with its tabernacle until 1482.[48] From the scattered accounts, it appears that, after the initial construction of two chapels spanning the nave of the church (1477–78),[49] Filippo's patronage took the form of occasional gifts and repairs involving fairly small expenditure. The largest task in later years seems to have been paving the cloister with bricks in early 1489–90.[50] Here visits to his sister's villa led to repairs and embellishment not only of the house but of the neighbouring convent and church.

LECCETO

Although the building of a church and hermitage at Lecceto was a purely ecclesiastical scheme, it cannot be divorced from Filippo's other rural projects that were situated nearby, overlapped in time and often employed the same builders and artists. After Le Selve, the hermitage at Lecceto became the focus of Filippo's patronage in this district of Malmantile on the hills above Signa. The area overlooked the Campigiano, where most of Filippo's country property lay, so his investment in this adjacent zone can be interpreted as territorial expansion by means of religious patronage. In another way, Filippo was involved in this district through his provision of a dowry for the daughter of a poor relation, Niccolò di Barla Strozzi, who, in exchange, provided Filippo with timber from his woods around Malmantile. Renovating villas, building and decorating country chapels and convents and supporting the families of country cousins were all part of a holistic approach to rural patronage.

The construction of an oratory at Lecceto on the hill above Le Selve was begun in 1473 by the Dominican hermit (*romito*) Fra Domenico di Piero Guerrucci who opened an account book for the project in that year and who continued to supervise all building and decoration at Lecceto until his death in 1485.[51] If the conception and initial impetus were Guerrucci's, Piero del Pugliese was the first patron of the project, donating a vineyard in 1475 and paying for building materials and a stone *occhio* for the church façade in January 1478.[52] Filippo Strozzi's involvement at Lecceto is not documented before April 1477, when he wrote to his brother that he expected to spend twice as much at Lecceto as at Le Selve, implying that he had not yet started to build there.[53] A contract with three stonemasons dated 30 July 1478[54] probably marks the first of Filippo's commissions; although the Strozzi coat of arms was already on the façade by October that year[55] and the contract stipulated construction should be completed by 1 November, he wrote to Lorenzo on 12 December 1478 that it was still not finished.[56] Indeed it was not until June 1480 when Strozzi had contracted Stefano di Jacopo Rosselli to build the choir and campanile that building work began in earnest.[57] Accounts show that the period between June and November 1480 was the busiest one, with large deliveries of bricks, lime and timber and teams of builders, stonemasons and carpenters working on the site.[58] The church was roofed at that time,[59] and the carved stonework for the campanile, the church and the sacristy including doorways, windows, steps, cornices and a coat of arms dates from the same period.[60] That construction of the church was completed during the summer and autumn of 1480[61] is corroborated by the fact that decorations were first acquired in the following year. Pugliese's altar was consecrated in May 1481,[62] while Strozzi bought a gilt and silver enamelled chalice in December[63] and a marble water stoup from Benedetto da Maiano in January 1482.[64] Another lapse, however, seems to have followed, for the choir stalls, altar and altarpiece were not completed until 1488,[65] while the frieze with its inscription was gilded by Biagio d'Antonio in 1489 together with the Frati Ingesuati's three round windows with the Strozzi arms.[66]

Lecceto was not to remain an isolated church, however, for there are references to building a 'chasa d'abitazione', a *foresteria*, an oven and stables between March 1487 and October 1489.[67] By 1484, the feast day of SS. Jacopo and Filippo was being celebrated at Lecceto at Filippo Strozzi's expense,[68] although the church remained dedicated to the Virgin until 1587.[69] Friars must have been in residence by early 1486, for on 31 January, Strozzi bought a young mule to give to the friars at Lecceto so they could go begging.[70] Barrels of wine were sent up from Le Selve and Capalle and donated to the friars of Lecceto.[71] In 1487, Strozzi even sent three matresses, sheets and bedcovers to the hermitage as winter was setting in.[72] This level of personal, practical, everyday concern is not at all what we might expect from an absentee patron and urban patrician, and it confirms Jill Burke's important new work on patronage that emphasises the mutual benefits and the 'intimate and regular' nature of the 'relationship between institution and patron' at Lecceto.[73]

The fifteenth-century conventual complex at Lecceto is still clearly recognisable today (Fig. 54). Two drawings by Fra Bartolommeo, now in the Pierpont Morgan Library in New York and identified by Chris Fischer, help to show which structures belong to the

54. Lecceto, church façade with dormitory block attached.

original building programme and which were later additions and alterations[74] (Figs. 55 and 56). The arrangement of church and hermitage resembles that of S. Marco in Florence as represented in Richa's engraving of 1758 (Fig. 57),[75] with the dormitory block attached to one side of the church and its façade flush with that of the church. As at S. Marco, the door to the cloister lies just beside the church, while a coat of arms placed under the roof at the far end of the monastery block (visible in Richa's engraving) was later removed from S. Marco but is still in place at Lecceto (Fig. 58). That the basic layout of S. Marco was a model for Lecceto is confirmed by the fact that

Lecceto was founded by a Dominican from S. Marco, Fra Domenico Guerrucci, who originally intended that Lecceto should serve as a country retreat for the friars of S. Marco;[76] indeed it was in this capacity that Fra Bartolommeo came to stay at Lecceto.[77] The elevated site in a secluded spot surrounded by woods made Lecceto an ideal summer refuge for friars wishing to escape the heat and noise of the city, fleeing to their rural hermitage as laymen did to their villas.

Comparison between Fra Bartolommeo's drawing and the present structure shows that a third storey was later added to the dormitory.[78] The church façade, on the other hand, tallies closely with the present

55. Fra Bartolommeo, 'View of the Ospizio della Madonna del Lecceto from the West', (recto) 1507. The Pierpont Morgan Library, New York, 1957.18.

structure. The *pietra serena* stonework of the main portal with its projecting cornice and lunette, the large bevelled oculus, the triangular pediment with Strozzi coat of arms and the interlocking quoins are all visible in the drawing and survive today in the recently restored church. Fra Bartolommeo's second drawing of Lecceto viewed from the north reveals that at the end of the fifteenth century, the hermitage was not constructed on three sides to form an enclosed cloister protected by the church on its fourth side, as it is today, but was a single rectangular block extending from the church to form an L. This drawing also reveals that

the house standing opposite existed in the fifteenth century. This may have been the original *foresteria* or, as today, a farmhouse.[79]

Examination of the structure of the church tallies with the building procedure outlined in the documents. The narrow arched window on the side of the church does not let light directly into the choir, for there is an oculus behind it that appears from the inside to be the direct source of light. It looks as though the choir was built as an independent structure within the already-existing curtain walls of the church. This fits the documentary evidence that Fra

56. Fra Bartolommeo, 'View of the Ospizio della Madonna del Lecceto from the Northwest', (verso) 1507, showing hermitage on left with the *foresteria* on right. The Pierpont Morgan Library, New York, 1957.18.

Domenico Guerrucci had already half built the walls of the church and completed the façade with the help of funds from Piero del Pugliese, before Strozzi came on the scene and proceeded to build the choir inside the pre-existing church walls (Fig. 59).

Eve Borsook has published the stonemasons' contract of July 1478, stipulating that the design of the choir should imitate that of S. Maria Ughi, Filippo Strozzi's parish church in Florence. Borsook also demonstrated that, although S. Maria Ughi was demolished, a very similar choir was later built for the church of S. Chiara (1493) (reconstructed in the Victoria and Albert Museum, London) (Fig. 60).[80] Apart from certain variations that are clearly specified in the contract (the substitution of oculi for tall windows, the inclusion of two round-topped doors behind the altar and the replacement of a stone moulding that probably defined a shallow *cupola* at S. Maria Ughi with the Strozzi coat of arms in the vault at Lecceto and the obvious substitution of the inscription for cherubs in the frieze), the choir at Lecceto has quite different proportions and is certainly wider and lower than that of S. Chiara. Above all, the outward sloping pilasters supporting the entrance arch, which are

57. Piazza S. Marco with the façade of the church and convent of S. Marco, Florence. Giuseppe Richa, *Notizie istoriche delle chiese fiorentine*, 1754–62, vol. 7, p. 113 (Photo: Warburg Institute).

58. Lecceto, the dormitory wing with Strozzi coat of arms at the corner.

59. Lecceto, church interior, choir.

intentionally non-vertical, are strikingly similar to those in the apse of the nearby *pieve* of S. Martino a Gangalandi, (which was commissioned by Leon Battista Alberti, but only completed after his death in 1473–4),[81] and also to the chancel of the abbey church at Settimo in the valley below (Fig. 61). The way in which this cluster of churches – Gangalandi, Settimo, Lecceto – adopted an unusual perspectival effect for the construction of their choirs is striking. In the case of Lecceto, this was a distinct departure from the urban model of S. Maria Ughi, in favour of a local, rural paradigm. The intention was presumably to make a relatively small church appear much larger, but whether this motif had originally been a perspectival experiment of Alberti's that was then respectfully imitated at Settimo and Lecceto, or was a request by the commune of Gangalandi who first supported the Lecceto project and wanted to establish a Gangalandian motif in the district or was simply a case of country builders responding to new ideas, the result was a distinctively local and short-lived architectural experiment.

60. Chapel and High Altar from the demolished conventual church of S. Chiara, Florence, 1493. Reconstructed in Victoria and Albert Museum, London (Photo: V & A Picture Library).

SANTUCCIO

On 15 July 1477 Filippo Strozzi bought what was to be his principal villa, situated between the oratory of S. John the Baptist at Santuccio and the Ponte a San Mauro over the Bisenzio (Fig. 62). At first, however, Filippo did not consider Santuccio his main country residence, for he had hoped that it could house the rector of the oratory and would be suitable for brief visits from his own family to celebrate the annual feast day of S. John the Baptist.[82] Filippo was probably also influenced by the cool reaction of his brother

Lorenzo, who was still living in Naples at the time of purchase. When Filippo wrote to tell him the news, Lorenzo replied that he did not want to contribute towards the cost of the villa because he preferred a farm that would be a delightful residence rather than being solely useful. When Lorenzo finally returned to Florence in June 1478, he came to see Santuccio and told Filippo that if he were repatriated he would endeavour to find something more attractive.[83] Given his brother's lack of enthusiasm, it is not surprising that Filippo chose not to inhabit the villa initially but let it for five years from 1 November 1478 to Lucrezia

61. Badia a Settimo, church of SS. Salvatore and Lorenzo, choir interior.

Tornabuoni, widow of Piero de' Medici. Lucrezia did not live there herself but passed it on to her guarantor (*mallevadore*), Bernardo Baroncelli, who fulfilled their promise to spend at least forty florins on improvements by installing new benches (*panche*) around the dining halls on the ground and first floors.[84] Baroncelli did not even stay the full five years, however, for by early 1483 Filippo had changed his mind and decided to renovate the villa for his own habitation. The building accounts for the villa were opened by his accountant and paymaster for the project, Marco di Benedetto Strozzi.[85]

The house was renovated in one main phase of construction lasting from February 1483 until autumn 1484.[86] The busiest year was 1483 with deliveries of timber, stone, gravel and sand continuing throughout the spring and summer. Already in August 1483 Strozzi bought inlaid woodwork ('17 pezi di tarsie de' quali ne venne 15 al Santuccio'), perhaps for redecorating the old wing of the villa, and by September construction of the new wing had probably reached first-floor level because walnut console brackets for the upper loggia were acquired ('2 pezzi di noci per ffare menssole al terrazzo sopra l'orto').[87] In the winter

62. Santuccio, the villa complex approaching from S. Donnino, with oratory and farm buildings in the foreground and towered *casa da signore* behind (photo: Conway Library, Courtauld Institute of Art).

of 1483, interior decoration was under way. Vaults were plastered, ceilings and wooden panelling were built and the first payment for painting ceilings also dates from the autumn of 1483. The carved pietra serena stonework, including columns for the portico, doors and windows, was not paid for until February 1484, although it could have been delivered some time before.[88] Decorative refinements were added in 1484 with more intarsia, *sgraffito* decoration for the façade and an iron wind vane to stand on top of the tower.[89] Although the main phase of construction and decoration was over by autumn 1484, the building accounts were not closed until January 1486 when the amount spent totalled 1,253 florins,[90] only slightly more than the cost of building the provisional town house, which was an almost exactly contemporary project (total cost in 1487: 1,151 florins) and rather less than was spent in the more drawn-out enterprise of church and convent at Lecceto (total cost in 1491: 1,561 florins).[91]

The house at Santuccio was not built *ex novo* by Filippo. It may have been one of the *case da lavoratore* mentioned in the tax returns of his uncle Pinaccio in 1427 and 1430 and owned by the Alberti from 1436 to 1477.[92] The Alberti probably converted a *casa da lavoratore* into a *casa da signore*, for whereas the tax returns until 1469 consistently refer to one or more tenant farmers' houses, the purchase contract of 1477,[93] and all subsequent documents, list a house for the owner, which must already have been a suitable habitation for Lucrezia Tornabuoni's attorney in 1478. A final account for the construction project establishes that Filippo renovated an old house by introducing new ceilings, stairs and vaults and building on a new wing with a loggia, bed chambers and a balcony. He also improved the villa complex with the addition of a kitchen, henhouse, stables or stalls for livestock and new paving and brickwork for courtyards and garden beds.[94]

63. Santuccio, portico of new wing, *pietra serena* columns with Ionic capitals provided by Girolamo d'Antonio da Fiesole, 1483–4 (photo: Conway Library, Courtauld Institute of Art).

There were two *maestri da murare*, Simone di Niccolò and Buono di Stefano da Campi, who were rebuilding Santuccio almost continuously from March 1483 until autumn 1484.[95] The carved pietra serena stonework, including columns, windows and doors, was commissioned from a stonecutter at Fiesole, Girolamo d'Antonio (Fig. 63 and see Figs. 68–70 in Chapter 6).[96] The value of the skilled craftsmen is underlined by the fact that Filippo employed many of them on other building projects. Most of the ironwork was provided by Antonio di Pagno, although special features were commissioned from other smiths

such as Niccolò di Nofri, called Caparra, who made the iron wind vane in the shape of a flag perforated with the Strozzi crescents and capped by a gilt iron ball (Fig. 64);[97] or Baldassare di Giovanni, who made iron crosses for the pediment of the oratory and its bell tower.[98] Three painters were employed. Bernardo di Stefano Rosselli (son of the building contractor) painted the new coffered ceilings (Fig. 65 and see Figs. 105 and 106 in Chapter 6) and incised the *sgraffito* decoration on the façade of the *casa da signore* (See Figs. 96 and 97 in Chapter 6);[99] at the oratory of S. Giovanni Battista, Neri di Bicci painted

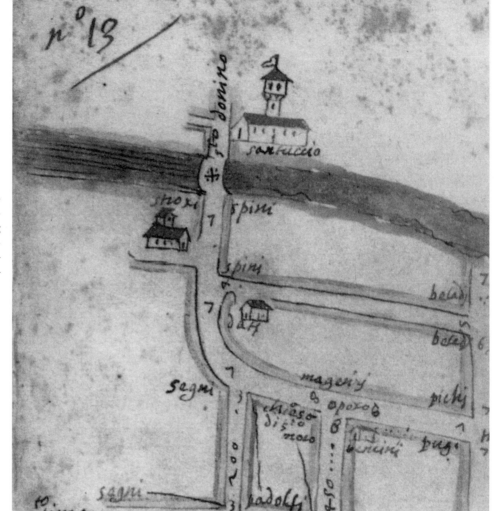

64. Parish of S. Moro, Filippo di Matteo Strozzi's villa of Santuccio with Caparra's iron flag flying from the tower roof. Detail of *Piante di popoli e strade – Capitani di parte guelfa – 1580–1595*, II, c. 421.

a crucifix for the altar in 1487;[100] and in the following year, Biagio d'Antonio painted the lunette over the door with a scene of S. John the Baptist in the wilderness.[101]

MAGLIO

As was the case with almost all of Filippo di Matteo's rural investments, his estate at Maglio grew out of an old family property that he took over and enlarged. Like Le Selve, this was not Strozzi ancestral property

but belonged to his in-laws. In 1477, Filippo's mother-in-law, Mona Antonia, daughter of Simone de' Bardi da Vernio and wife of a Bolognese Jacopo degli Orsi, repaid Filippo for a loan of 400 florins by granting him the fruits of her share of a farm at Maglio in the upper Bisenzio valley north of Prato.[102] Eventually, in 1484 and 1485, he acquired the whole of this farm, at the same time buying many more pieces of land around it.[103] With authority from the pope, he bought the land and patronage rights of the small parish church of S. Michele a Maglio, which had been destroyed in the war against Milan in the 1420s,

65. Santuccio, ground-floor *camera*, original wooden ceiling painted by Bernardo di Stefano Rosselli, 1483 (photo: Conway Library, Courtauld Institute of Art).

and rebuilt it (Fig. 66).[104] The building programme for the villa was carried out in 1486 and 1487 by Marco di Benedetto Strozzi, who had been paymaster for Santuccio and was soon to keep the accounts for the construction of the new palace in town. The final account of 8 December 1487 for 623 florins describes what was achieved in this modest scheme at Maglio:

> For the amount he assigned to be spent up until today, in having the landowner's house repaired to be able to live there on the farm at Maglio, joined to the house of his tenant farmer; and a shed and a building for the oil press behind the said house; and for

making a new farm house on Piso's field where Ghabriello di Giovenale lives with a stable and shed; and for a pipe for fresh water leading to where the head of our family plans to build a house . . . F. 623. 10. 2.[105]

Although it is clear from this that the owner's house was built onto a pre-existing farm house (Fig. 67 and see Fig. 31 in Chapter 3), it remains uncertain whether the *casa da lavoratore* was incorporated into one larger building for the owner's or factor's sole habitation or whether the tenant farmer would continue to live in the house attached. The supply of fresh water for a site where Filippo intended to build a house seems to refer to a separate location and not to the newly rennovated 'casa da oste'. This site, bought in 1486, was described in Filippo's *ricordo* as:

> A piece of land of about 3 *staiora* altogether, partly arable and olive groves, partly fallow and partly wooded, situated on the little hill where I plan to build the house to live in.[106]

This implies that Filippo had plans to build a house *ex novo* for his own habitation apart from the converted 'casa da oste'.

Unlike the book of accounts for Santuccio, which almost exclusively refers to construction, the 'quaderno in ssul quale si schriverrà debitori e creditori e spese nella muraglia chessi farrà a Maglio' includes as many accounts for farm improvement as for building work.[107] The two activities continued at the same time, along with the purchase of more land. An extended campaign for terracing and planting the farm land, together with the construction and repair of agricultural buildings, continued well into the 1490s. Filippo's opportunities to create a whole new estate with extensive landholdings were greater here than in the Arno valley close to town. Here, too, he could implement progressive agricultural methods that would yield more wine, olives and timber; would support more animals; and create a fertile, pastoral environment, attractive as a rural retreat from town. These seem to have been Filippo di Matteo's initial concerns at Maglio. While a 'casa da oste' was rebuilt

66. S. Michele a Maglio, the church.

on a modest scale for use as a temporary residence, it is likely that a site was being prepared for Filippo's own new house; in the meantime, a large workforce was employed in landscaping and cultivating the whole hillside.

SUPERVISION OF FILIPPO DI MATTEO STROZZI'S RURAL BUILDING PROJECTS

Supervision of construction was a collaborative undertaking that might involve all or any combination of the following protagonists: the patron, the accountant or clerk of the works, the architect, the foreman (*capomaestro*) or other master builders. In the country, inconvenient access meant that other people resident in the vicinity were often drawn into the project. Friends, relations or employees of the patron were obvious choices, and, as the most literate and trustworthy member of a rural community, the local priest was sometimes involved.[108] Of this group, consistent records exist only for the clerks or paymasters whose building accounts document one of their main contributions to the projects. The extent of the patron's

67. Maglio, the 'casa da oste' seen from the church of S. Michele.

and architect's involvement, especially their presence on the site and their day-to-day control, is a more elusive question. Whereas the role of master builders and *capomaestri* is seemingly more straightforward and better documented, their responsibility for direction and design details was often greater in proportion to the architect's lesser control or absence.

To coordinate a number of building projects that were proceeding simultaneously in different places, delegation to trustworthy administrators and an efficient accounting system, which made it possible to keep tight control of funds, were essential.[109] This need was still greater in the country, where Filippo himself could rarely check on progress. The first of such employees to appear in the account books is Pagholo di Benedetto di Pieraccione Strozzi, whose father was a humanist and an accomplished musician and scribe and whose brother Messer Piero was also an outstanding scribe and rector of S. Piero a Ripoli.[110] It was Pagholo's family who owned the huge but now much diminished estate at Capalle,

so when Filippo bought his own farm and houses at Capalle in 1475, Pagholo was a natural choice as manager of the new property. Filippo must have also intended to assist this distinguished branch of the clan that had fallen on hard times. He certainly wished to endow the *pieve* at Ripoli because of Messer Piero's connection with it,[111] just as he secured the rectorship of the oratory at Santuccio for Messer Piero in 1470.[112] Pagholo and Messer Piero's sister, Margherita, was a companion to Filippo's wife Fiammetta in the early 1470s and received a gift of fine linen when Filippo returned from a visit to Naples in 1473.[113] Pagholo took over the running of Filippo's estate at Capalle, gathering, selling and redistributing its produce among various Strozzi properties, enlarging and repairing the buildings, and acquiring timber that he stored or dispatched to Santuccio for construction. Between 1482 and 1484, while Filippo's accountant Marco di Benedetto Strozzi was supervising the building project at Santuccio, Pagholo kept the accounts for Filippo's new town house that was to be a temporary residence while the new palace was being built.[114]

The provisional town house was mostly built between spring 1482 and summer 1483 under the *capomaestro* Jacopo di Stefano Rosselli, who later worked on the big palace for the first six months of its construction. His father, Stefano di Jacopo Rosselli, was already a trusted employee of Filippo's having built Lecceto in 1480. Although Filippo Strozzi provided the funds, Fra Domenico Guerrucci was in charge of the scheme at Lecceto until his death in 1486 and kept his own accounts. Goldthwaite describes Stefano di Jacopo Rosselli as the *capomaestro* at Lecceto and notes that he was paid for drawings.[115] Given that the main body of the church was already built when Strozzi gained his patronage rights and that the stonemasons' contract of 30 July 1478 gave precise instructions that they follow the model of the *cappella maggiore* of S. Maria Ughi except for certain clearly specified variations, it might be inferred that there was no need for a designer and that Chimenti di Nanni the chief stonemason, who was also named as *capomaestro* on occasion, could supervise the project. However, the building accounts for Lecceto in Strozzi's 'Libro Grande', provide more precise information about Stefano Rosselli's contribution.[116]

It emerges firstly that Stefano was not a foreman or *capomaestro* in the sense that he was constantly on the site to supervise the day-to-day work, but was a building contractor who selected a team of workmen, received and distributed their pay and made occasional visits to the site. The final payment to Stefano, quoted in part by Goldthwaite, is more revealing. He was paid two florins, thirteen *soldi* and eight *denari* on 23 March 1481,

> for his labour in having gone various times to Lecceto when they were building there, to provide drawings, and for the loan of ropes and tackle and other things.[117]

The tasks of providing working drawings and visiting the site to check on progress reveal that Stefano Rosselli was what we would now describe as executant architect as well as building contractor. We should not overestimate his role, however, for it is clear that a whole group was responsible for the design of Lecceto, including Guerrucci, who first devised the hermitage scheme and was probably responsible for its similarity in layout to S. Marco; Filippo Strozzi, who stepped in as patron in 1477 and stipulated that the choir be modelled on his own urban parish church of S. Maria Ughi; the chief stonemason, Chimenti di Nanni, who probably determined the detailed form of the *pietra serena* articulation; as well as the building contractor and architect, Stefano Rosselli, who chose the labour force, provided drawings and checked the work.

The results of Marco di Benedetto di Marcuccio Strozzi's labours at Santuccio, Maglio and the big palace in town still survive in the form of his building accounts.[118] In Filippo's general account book, Marco's triple role as accountant, supervisor of the workforce and purveyor of supplies for the scheme at Maglio is clearly defined. He was paid 24 florins, five *soldi* and one *denaro*,

> for his salary for having kept account of the construction project at Maglio and for supervising the master builders and whatever was required for the said building project from the day it began until the day it finished.[119]

His task at Maglio had lasted from May 1486 until December 1487, making his salary of about sixteen florins a year a low one, although it is unlikely to have been a full-time job, and he may well have been employed by Filippo on other contemporary schemes. When he worked on the new town palace which began in the summer of 1489, a year and a half later, he was paid a salary of thirty florins a year, was sometimes described as 'proveditore della muraglia' and certainly kept all the accounts for this huge construction project.[120] Marco's first documented job for Filippo Strozzi had been at Santuccio, for which he was bookkeeper during the period of building and decoration from 1482 until 1486 and was paid 'per sua faticha di tratare la detta muraglia'.[121] It is possible that

Marco was taken on partly because he was living near Santuccio when building there was due to start. In his 1480 *catasto*, Marco declared that he had sold his town house to provide his daughters' dowries and mostly lived at his family villa in Le Miccine, about two miles west of Santuccio.[122] His poverty would have led him to seek employment with his rich relative, who then rented him a town house as well as extra pasture at Le Miccine.[123]

Despite the existence of a complete set of building accounts for the villa at Santuccio, there is no reference to an architect in the documents. More surprising is the failure to mention a *capomaestro* in the accounts. Stefano Rosselli's son Jacopo, who was the *capomaestro* for Filippo's provisional town house built in the same years, is a likely candidate, but the only reference to him in the documents is one payment for timber. It was probably deemed sufficient for the refurbishing of an old house and the addition of a new wing that two master builders with a trustworthy purveyor and accountant should run the day-to-day construction. As for the design of the new wing – with its five-bay portico, two ground-floor rooms, a barrel-vaulted *androne* and a staircase leading to an upper loggia and several more rooms – an architect or highly experienced building contractor such as Jacopo di Stefano Roselli, or his father, may have suggested the solution and provided sketches or drawings. Execution of the design, which followed a conventional formula adopted in other *case da signore* and monastic cloisters, lay well within the competence of fifteenth-century master builders.

Isolation often made supervision of rural construction a problematic undertaking. At Capalle, Santuccio and Maglio, Filippo di Matteo relied largely on his accountants who were also relatives, whereas in the case of Lecceto and the Santuccio oratory, resident priests stepped in, and at Lecceto construction and design procedure was at least partly in the hands of the building contractor and architect Stefano Rosselli. The question of quality in rural architecture is closely related to the workforce and supervision on country building projects. More investigation is needed to establish whether there was a double standard for rural

and urban buildings. Architectural irregularities and clumsy structural solutions are often attributed to unskilled labour or to less rigorous supervision of the project. This explanation has been proposed for the irregularly placed windows on the façade of Poggio a Caiano, as it has for the outward leaning pilasters at S. Martino a Gangalandi, and by extension to the same feature in the choir at Lecceto. The same excuse could be made for the disproportionately large entablature and inscription at Lecceto, where the welding together of imported prototypes of different scales produced a jarring effect. At Santuccio and Maglio, however, as well as at Lecceto, centuries of neglect, alteration and radical restoration have intervened and must be taken into account before forming any judgment about architectural detail or aesthetic quality.

Architectural patronage may be too grand a term for Filippo Strozzi's rural construction projects. This is not patronage in the sense of an impressive public display of wealth and status through the medium of great works of art and architecture. Only perhaps in the tower and loggia of Santuccio and in the inscription at Lecceto could any element approach what might be described as magnificent. Ironically, the most expensive of these schemes was the hermitage, designed as a retreat into solitude. Yet it needs to be emphasised that the scale of these enterprises was not particularly modest compared with those of his peers. Lecceto is similar to the Medici's rustic convent built for the observant Franciscans at Bosco ai Frati, Santuccio is closely comparable to *case da signore* belonging to other Florentine clans such as the Spinelli, the Nerli, the della Tosa or the Morelli, while the estates at Maglio and Capalle were very like other contemporaries' primarily agricultural investments.

If lavish display were not the main objective, what was? At the most fundamental level, Filippo Strozzi was sustaining an old patrimonial and familial network by repairing and renovating buildings that had belonged to uncles or cousins or in-laws. This campaign of renewal not only provided houses for Strozzi and his *brigata* and facilitated agricultural production through improvement of the rural infrastructure, but it is also notable how the construction process itself, by bringing a wide group of people into his employment (particularly the poor relations who administered the projects), functioned as a form of clientage. Furthermore, the construction, restoration and maintenance of buildings was widely recognised as the most effective way to assert a presence in a place or territory. After all, land could not carry coats of arms or marks of family or personal identity as buildings could.

6 · THE ARCHITECTURE OF A *CASA DA SIGNORE*: SANTUCCIO

Filippo di Matteo Strozzi's villa of Santuccio lies halfway between the parish churches of San Donnino and San Mauro on the banks of the Bisenzio River in the middle of the Florentine plain. Until 1985, the *casa da signore* survived in a dilapidated state, its *quattrocento* features recognisable but unrestored. The *pietra serena* columns of the north portico were worn, chipped and crumbly, yet the organic quality of the Ionic capitals – with the delicately carved veins and rippled surface of the laurel leaves and crisp bead necklaces running around the top of the torus ring – could still be appreciated (Figs. 68, 69 and 70). Not only did the original stonework survive, but the remains of the fifteenth-century plaster were still clinging to the façade (see Fig. 88, this chapter), incised with the Strozzi crescent moons and Filippo's devices of a falcon and a seated lamb, together with exuberant clumps of acanthus and classical urns (see Figs. 96 and 97, this chapter). Inside the house, it was still possible to reconstruct some of the fifteenth-century room functions with the help of painted coffered ceilings from the 1480s (Fig. 71 and see Fig. 65 in the previous chapter), a carved stone *lavabo* (Fig. 72), elegantly moulded doorways (Fig. 73) and an eighteenth or early nineteenth-century mural depicting the villa and its garden (Fig. 74). Much of this was destroyed in a brutal transformation campaign that created modern apartments out of one fifteenth-century *casa da signore* and its outbuildings. A full awareness of the historical significance of Santuccio might have helped

to inform the renovation project so that more of its now irrecoverable fifteenth-century features could have been conserved.[1]

Filippo Strozzi enlarged and renovated the villa at Santuccio between 1483 and 1486. A closer study of Santuccio's architecture is rewarding not only because it is so richly documented, the new wing being securely dated in the building accounts, but also because the manner in which Filippo Strozzi added an Ionic portico to a pre-existing towered structure is characteristic of the attitude to villa construction in the period. The desire to maintain the traditional and heraldic associations attached to towers and crenellation, combined with the up-to-date elegance of newly inserted *all'antica* features was not only evident earlier in the century at the Medici villas of Trebbio, Cafaggiolo and Careggi, but it also continued to be popular at the end of the fifteenth and well into the sixteenth centuries as demonstrated by the Villa Salviati at Ponte alla Badia[2] or by the Medicean restoration of Palla Strozzi's old villa of Petraia.[3]

THE TOWER AND THE 'CASA VECCHIA'

It is certain that Filippo Strozzi attached the new wing with its portico to an old house. The document of February 1486 summarising construction refers to renovations to the old house, consisting of new ceilings, stairs and vaults ('palcho e schale e volte ala chasa

68. Santuccio, portico of new wing, built 1483–84 (photo: Conway Library, Courtauld Institute of Art).

69. Santuccio, Ionic capital provided by Girolamo d'Antonio da Fiesole, 1483–4 (photo: Conway Library, Courtauld Institute of Art).

70. Santuccio, Ionic capital provided by Girolamo d'Antonio da Fiesole, 1483–4 (photo: Conway Library, Courtauld Institute of Art).

71. Santuccio, walnut console bracket with Strozzi crescent moons in ground-floor *camera* of new wing (photo: Conway Library, Courtauld Institute of Art).

72. Santuccio, *pietra serena lavabo* in first-floor *sala* of the 'casa vecchia' (photo: Lynda Fairbairn, Conway Library, Courtauld Institute of Art).

vechia').[4] It also refers to the new wing as the addition ('l'agiunta') to an existing house. Examination of the villa shows that the old house consisted of an L-shaped block with a tower at one end (Figs. 75 and 76). Although in many villas, towers were the original nucleus onto which wings were later grafted, this was not the case with the 'casa vecchia' at Santuccio. Here the tower was built on top of the two-storeyed 'casa vecchia' so that the only visible extra support is a single, short but massive wall containing a narrow service stair (Fig. 77); otherwise one is unaware of the existence of the tower inside the house. The tower was therefore not an independent structure but seems to have been built with the main block of the 'casa vecchia' as one unit.

The date of this wing is difficult to establish. It is unlikely that such a large, towered structure was described as a *casa da lavoratore* in Pinaccio Strozzi's tax returns of 1427 and 1430 and subsequently in the Alberti tax returns from 1442 until 1469.[5] On the other hand,

after the first *catasto* of 1427, later tax returns may have repeated the *casa da lavoratore* formula without reference to the real state of the building. It also remains possible that the change in terminology from *casa da lavoratore* to *casa da signore* that occurred between the last Alberti tax return of 1469 and the document of sale to Filippo Strozzi in 1477 signifies that the house was enlarged in the early 1470s. Unfortunately the architecture of the 'casa vecchia' does not present easy solutions to this question.

The tower may at first appear to be characteristic of the late fourteenth century, but comparison with the Rocca di Campi, probably built in the 1370s,[6] leads to the conclusion that Santuccio is almost certainly later, and a date well into the fifteenth century should not be ruled out. The machicolated gallery at the Rocca di Campi follows the asymmetrical structure of the castle walls, supported by long tapering brick consoles that fuse with the brick construction of the walls (Fig. 78). There is not a regular

73. Santuccio, *pietra serena* door frame in first floor *sala* of the 'casa vecchia' (photo: Lynda Fairbairn, Conway Library, Courtauld Institute of Art).

correspondence between the crenellations supporting the roof and the consoles with their bridging arches below. The tower at Santuccio, on the other hand, is more cheaply built of brick and rubble, but has *pietra serena* consoles each composed of four pieces of cut stone (Fig. 79). Narrow *pietra serena* string courses run above and below the consoles, a roll moulding below and a concave moulding above. The tower is rectangular and a symmetrical correspondence in the number and placing of the consoles and the crenellation that survived until the Second World War was maintained around all four sides (see Fig. 76 and Fig. 100). There

were twelve consoles and six battlements on the long sides with ten consoles and five battlements on the short sides of the tower. The battlements were placed directly above alternating bridging arches. There is no machicolation, suggesting that the tower was not designed for defensive purposes.[7]

The tower at Santuccio resembles those of the Medici villas of Trebbio and Cafaggiolo, probably rebuilt in the 1420s or early 1430s (Fig. 80). The brick consoles on the towers at Trebbio and Cafaggiolo, however, are considerably longer and therefore fewer were needed to support the gallery, whereas at

74. Santuccio, late eighteenth- or nineteenth-century mural on the first floor of the new wing, depicting the south façade of the house (photo: Conway Library, Courtauld Institute of Art).

Santuccio there are more, shorter stone consoles. Nor is there a regular correspondence between the consoles and crenellations at Trebbio and Cafaggiolo.[8] The symmetry of the tower at Santuccio suggests it may be closer in date to Michelozzo's Palazzo Comunale at Montepulciano begun after 1440 and completed by 1466 (Fig. 81).[9] On the parapet there we find a similar use of relatively short, triangular stone consoles with string courses running either side and battlements that are disposed symmetrically in relation to the console arches. This would reinforce the suggestion that the tower and old wing at Santuccio were built or enlarged while the Alberti owned the house between 1436 and 1477. Because of the lack of any comparable towers securely dated as late as the 1480s, it is unlikely that Filippo Strozzi rebuilt the upper part of the tower. A more extensive and detailed study of towers and castellation is urgently needed to establish the framework for such comparisons.

The architectural features of the main block of the old house are scarcely more helpful for establishing a date. The only clues offered on the east façade flanking the courtyard are two porthole windows with finely moulded *pietra serena* rims (Fig. 82), but these are probably part of Filippo Strozzi's renovations in the 1480s. One lights a narrow service stair that may be the 'scale' referred to in the concluding document of February 1486 (see Fig. 77). Inside the house, the simple beamed ceilings with carved wooden console brackets on the ground floor (Fig. 83) are less refined than those in the new wing (see Fig. 71), but they probably belong to Filippo's renovations nevertheless and mark the distinction between storage or service quarters and the new wing destined for the landowner's living rooms.

The short wing attached to the north end of the 'casa vecchia' may be an early structure. A scan of the north façade shows a row of four windows framed with large blocks of *pietra forte* and brick relieving arches

Original features
obscured by
modern building

N

☐ 'casa vecchia'

☐ **Filippo di Matteo Strozzi's new wing**

0   20 m

75. Santuccio, ground plan of the *casa da signore* (drawn by Steven J. Allen).

(Fig. 84). The ground-floor room beneath has lunette vaults, but the imposts have been covered by a layer of modern cement, offering no hint as to exactly when, within a broad span from c. 1370-1480, this wing was constructed. The same applies to the small tower at the end of this west wing (Fig. 85). Its thick walls and cross vault suggest an early date, although it is possible that this was the dove tower raised by Filippo Strozzi in 1489.[10] The creation of a courtyard in the shelter of these walls may reflect the original orientation of the house towards the river, whereas Filippo's new wing extended eastwards towards the oratory.

The resultant ⎣ shape of the villa (see Fig. 75) was probably exploited by Filippo to create two courtyards with complementary functions. The area on the west side towards the river could have served as a farmyard or kitchen garden with the *colombaia* behind,[11] whereas the eastern courtyard formed by the elegant new portico would have been intended for the use of the landowner's family and domestic purposes, since there was a well there, and the large oven adjoined the east end of the portico.[12]

There were many good reasons for retaining an old house with a tower. The prime economic motive

76. Santuccio, north courtyard with the portico of the new wing on the left and the 'casa vecchia' on the right, in a photograph taken before the Second World War (photo: copy held at Conway Library, Courtauld Institute of Art).

behind villa owning made landowners like Filippo Strozzi less willing to splash out on *ex novo* building, but it was not only a question of saving money or making use of materials and a ready-built structure that made demolition unpopular. It was a great advantage to be able to inhabit the site either immediately before and after construction or during building and decoration if that were a lengthy process. Thus, Lorenzo de' Medici stayed at Palla Strozzi's old villa, Ambra, while the dairy farm and the huge new villa were being built.[13] Francesco Sassetti listed the furnishings of his villa at Montughi in the period when it was being rebuilt, making it likely that the old villa was retained, furnished, while new construction went on around it.[14] In addition, the reluctance to dispense with an old house reflected the conservative attitude to rural architecture during this period. Old country dwellings were associated with respectability, with a

history of landowning or with the feudal origins of old Florentine families who retained a stronghold in the *contado* after they had moved to town.

Filippo's choice of Santuccio derived from his patronage of the oratory and from his uncle's and great-grandfather's ownership of the farm and farmhouse. It is scarcely surprising, then, that Filippo bought it back, and his refurbishing of the tower with Caparra's iron banner displaying the Strozzi coat of arms and capped by a gilt sphere was a display of heraldry in the traditional chivalric manner. A similar (probably nineteenth-century) wind vane with the Strozzi crescent moons still stands on top of the tower at the Rocca di Campi a mile up the Bisenzio (Fig. 86). There could scarcely be a clearer sign of dynastic pride than these flags, forged in a permanent material, flying from the Strozzi towers so as to be visible from a distance on the flat horizon of the Arno basin. Apart from the historic

77. Santuccio, 'casa vecchia', narrow stair in the thickness of a wall, lit by porthole window (photo: Conway Library, Courtauld Institute of Art).

and powerful associations of crenellated towers, they had, of course, important practical uses for housing pigeons, storing grain and drying linen flax.[15] The panoramic views from this type of tower would also have been important to fifteenth-century landowners. The villas of Filippo's relatives at Campi and Le Selve, as well as the Florentine cathedral dome, were all visible on a fine day from the tower at Santuccio.

THE PORTICO AND THE NEW WING

When it came to building the new wing Filippo Strozzi chose to add an *all'antica* portico at right angles to the main towered block of the 'casa vecchia',

thereby creating a courtyard sheltered by the two walls of the 'L' (Fig. 87; see Figs. 75 and 76). The scale of the new wing was largely determined by that of the old house. It was originally the same height; and almost exactly as long as the main block of the 'casa vecchia' (c. 32 metres); it was also one room deep, the rooms being just over seven metres wide. This unified the two parts of the building and lent balance and symmetry to what might otherwise have appeared a mismatched or piecemeal construction.

The architecture of the new wing was elegant and up-to-date. The proportions of the north-facing Ionic portico have now been spoilt by many years of accumulated silt on a site prone to flooding. The bases of the columns are still intact but can only be seen in the water-logged cellars beneath the present ground level. As a result, the columns appear stunted, and the arches and spandrels above look disproportionately large (Figs. 88 and 89). The Ionic order was not only applied to the columns and console capitals of the courtyard portico, but also to the colonettes of the upstairs loggia (*verone*) facing the garden (Fig. 90). This consistent application of a classical order was still a sign of modernity in villa architecture in the 1480s.

Although the inclusion of a loggia or portico with piers or columns was a common feature of Tuscan villas from the thirteenth century on, water-leaf capitals (like those used at the Medici and Pazzi villas of Trebbio) or octagonal columns with a flat, unadorned capital or an applied shield (like those of Bartolommeo Sassetti's villa at Macia (see Figs. 124 and 125), Giovanni Rucellai's villa Lo Specchio or the Tornabuoni villa at Chiasso Macerelli) were the most common forms until the middle of the fifteenth century. In Florence, the appearance of the Ionic order in the cloisters at the Badia Fiorentina (1436–7), S. Marco (1437–52), the Chiostro delle Donne of the Ospedale degli Innocenti (from 1437), S. Lorenzo (1457–61) (Fig. 91), and in the upper loggia of the women's cloister at the hospital of San Paolo (1465–76),[16] would have ensured that it was closely associated with monastic and hospital architecture by the second half of the fifteenth century. It was employed in a similar context in the country in the cloisters at S. Maria, Impruneta

78. Rocca di Campi, north-east tower.

(after 1439), and S. Miniato al Monte (1443–7), on the south portico of the Conventino della Maddalena at Le Caldine (c. 1460)[17] and closer to Santuccio on the side portico of S. Martino a Gangalandi (Figs. 92 and 93),[18] and in the big cloister of the Badia a Settimo (from 1461) (Figs. 94 and 95).[19] It may also have appeared regularly in villas from the middle of the century, but until more houses have been documented and dated, the emergence and development of the Ionic order in rural domestic architecture cannot be convincingly traced. Nevertheless, it was to become a widespread feature of villa architecture.[20] Jacopo d'Alamanno de'

Medici adopted it for his villa Il Sasso near Cardetole in the Mugello, built *ex novo* in the 1470s;[21] Giuliano da Sangallo introduced Ionic capitals with fluted necks at Poggio a Caiano (from 1485), and they appear on many more modest villas of the Florentine *contado* (eg, La Bartolina in the Mugello and the Villa Rucellai at Campi Bisenzio).[22]

The capitals at Santuccio bear the closest resemblance to those in the large cloister of the Badia a Settimo, begun after 1461. Some carry bead moulding at the top of the neck, and the volutes enclose blossoms. The fact that the abbey was only a mile from the

79. Santuccio, the tower (photo: Conway Library, Courtauld Institute of Art).

80. Cafaggiolo, the Medici villa.

81. Montepulciano, Palazzo Comunale.

82. Santuccio, 'casa vecchia', porthole window of stair, *pietra serena* frame (photo: Conway Library, Courtauld Institute of Art).

83. Santuccio, ceiling with wooden console brackets on ground floor of the 'casa vecchia' (photo: Conway Library, Courtauld Institute of Art).

84. Santuccio, west wing, original window surround in *pietra forte* (photo: Conway Library, Courtauld Institute of Art).

85. Santuccio, west side facing the Bisenzio River, with small tower to left and main fortified tower to right (photo: Conway Library, Courtauld Institute of Art).

86. Rocca di Campi, tower from east, iron flag with Strozzi crescent moons.

87. Santuccio, the north courtyard with raised modern roof level of the 'casa vecchia' on the right (photo: Conway Library, Courtauld Institute of Art).

villa, directly across the Arno, increases the likelihood that Strozzi would have known the new cloister and may have requested similar columns for Santuccio. Here another link can be added to the chain, for the contract for the large cloister at Settimo stipulated that it be modelled on the cloister at San Lorenzo in Florence, just completed in 1461. As in the church at Lecceto, an urban model played a crucial part in the evolution of rural architecture. The form of Ionic portico adopted at Santuccio was transmitted from the cloister at S. Lorenzo by way of the Badia a Settimo. Santuccio therefore represents a stage in the dissemination of the classical orders from town to country and from ecclesiastical to secular architecture. Strozzi's villa is also a valuable reference point because the stonework is securely documented. Girolamo d'Antonio from Fiesole was paid 350 lire (c. fifty-eight florins) on 5 February 1484 for all the decorative stonework for the villa: 'that is for doorways, windows, columns and other things'.[23]

The simplicity of the stone architrave and cornice in the entablature above was not only an inexpensive solution and in keeping with the Ionic order, but it was also a suitable framework for the figurative *sgraffito* frieze, which took the form of family emblems and coats of arms. The three crescent moons with radiating flames enclosed in roundels were incised on the spandrels between the arches (Fig. 96): In the frieze above, the remains of urns and acanthus, alternating with Filippo's emblems of a seated lamb with a scroll bearing the motto MITIS ESTO unfurled above it (Fig. 97) and the falcon plucking feathers from its wing, were all visible until the conversion campaign of the 1980s.[24] Until then, this was a rare surviving example of documented *sgraffito* work. The Santuccio building accounts record a payment of six lire, three *soldi* to Bernardo di Stefano Rosselli on 16 October 1484 'per isgraffiare fregi e archali e pilastri'.[25] It is most likely that the mention of incised 'pilastri' in the document referred to fictive pilasters etched into

88. Santuccio, portico of new wing, proportions of columns distorted by modern ground level (photo: Conway Library, Courtauld Institute of Art).

the fresh plaster between the upstairs windows.[26] If this were the case, then the upper *sgraffito* would have added a fictive superimposed arcade of pilasters to the three-dimensional arcade with columns beneath. This arrangement would have been consistent with the function of the classical members – the *sgraffito* pilasters resting on the entablature, aligned with the columns below and supporting an upper cornice at roof level – like a figurative version of the court-yard in the Ducal palace at Urbino. The existence of the *sgraffito* roundels with Strozzi moons and flames gives credence to Neilson's suggestion that Filippino

Lippi's Strozzi Madonna was painted for the villa of Santuccio.[27] The appearance of an Ionic loggia with a roundel containing crescent moons in the spandrels of the arch behind the Madonna (see Figs. 114 and 115) does seem to be a reference to the newly completed villa, and would support a date for the painting af-ter 1484 and towards 1487 when the house was being furnished.

A barrel-vaulted passage leads from the north por-tico through to the south façade (Figs. 98 and 99). This *androne* is not centralised in terms of the north portico, opening under the second bay from the left; however,

89. Santuccio, portico of new wing after restoration in mid-1980s.

90. Santuccio, upper loggia or *verone* with Ionic colonettes after restoration in mid-1980s.

91. Florence, S. Lorenzo cloister (1457–61).

92. S. Martino a Gangalandi, portico on north side of church (photo: Conway Library, Courtauld Institute of Art).

93. S. Martino a Gangalandi, north portico, Ionic capital (photo: Conway Library, Courtauld Institute of Art).

94. Badia a Settimo, large cloister, portico, after 1461.

95. Badia a Settimo, large cloister, Ionic capital (restored).

96. Santuccio, detail of *sgraffito* decoration between the arches of the north portico, Strozzi crescent moons enclosed in a roundel (photo: Conway Library, Courtauld Institute of Art).

the *androne* was not a dominant feature when seen from the north, its entry hidden under the shadow of the portico (see Fig. 68). On the other hand, when viewed from the south, it *was* centralised in relation to the full latitude of the new wing, emerging on the façade with a prominent arched stone portal (Fig. 100). The string course that runs across the southern façade, beginning from the upper loggia, marks the extent of the new wing. The barrel-vaulted passage and its large portal surmounted by a coat of arms (Fig. 101), were placed in the centre of this string course to produce a more harmonious effect, even if the reten-

tion of the old block on the left prevented the creation of a strictly symmetrical façade. Yet this old block was bound into the proportional system of the whole façade at first-floor level, for although the upper loggia (*verone*) was placed to one side, its measurements and position were precisely gauged so that the southern end of the old block and the *verone* together measured one half of the whole façade. This counterbalancing of apparent asymmetry at ground- and first-floor levels demonstrates the expertise and care employed in such conversions. The regular fenestration at first-floor level, which is probably still close to

97. Santuccio, *sgraffito* decoration in frieze above north portico, by Bernardo di Stefano Rosselli, 1484 (photo: Conway Library, Courtauld Institute of Art).

98. Santuccio, barrel-vaulted *androne* or passage looking towards the north portico (photo: Conway Library, Courtauld Institute of Art).

99. Santuccio, archway of the barrel-vaulted *androne* or passage, door on right leads to stairs (photo: Conway Library, Courtauld Institute of Art).

100. Santuccio, south façade in a photograph taken before the Second World War (photo: copy held at Conway Library, Courtauld Institute of Art).

101. Santuccio, portal on south façade with Strozzi coat of arms (photo: Conway Library, Courtauld Institute of Art).

the fifteenth-century arrangement, also helps to unify the south façade.

From the ground-floor *androne*, a single-flight staircase led up to the south loggia (*verone*) (Fig. 102). Here the unity of simple but elegant architectural forms is maintained. The *pietra serena* moulding of the wide *androne* arch is reproduced on a smaller scale in the arch leading to the stair (see Fig. 99). Like the *androne*, the staircase is also barrel-vaulted with the same roll moulding at the springing of the vault. The south *verone* is a deep space sheltered by walls on three sides, with two slender Ionic colonettes (now recut) sup-

porting the beamed roof on the fourth (Fig. 103). Looking over the garden and across the Arno to the hills above Signa, it would have been ideal for al fresco dining (were it not for the mosquitoes!).

The function of rooms at Santuccio can only be reconstructed where parts of the decoration survived. In this respect, the wooden coffered ceilings of the ground-floor rooms either side of the *androne* revealed them to have been part of a residential apartment for the owner (Figs. 104, 105 and 106). Traces of the original paintwork showed that the edge of each coffer and the friezes along the beams were painted with floral

102. Santuccio, stair to upper loggia or *verone* (photo: Conway Library, Courtauld Institute of Art).

motifs interspersed with the same Strozzi coat of arms and emblems found on the façade. The same painter Bernardo di Stefano Rosselli, who designed and executed the façade *sgrafitto*, was paid thirty-eight lire on 24 December 1483 'per dipintura di tegholi 330 a lire 5 al ciascuno e braccia 230 di liste e chornice a lire 9 soldi 6 al ciascuno'.[28] The walnut console brackets were carved with crescent moons and egg and dart cornices (see Fig. 71), another token of the superior status of these rooms in contrast to the rough ceilings on the ground floor of the 'casa vecchia'. Given the

dimensions of these two rooms (6 × 7.18 meters for the smaller and 7.08 × 9.50 meters for the larger), they may have been designated as two *camere*, although it is more likely that the larger served as the ground-floor *sala*.

The only other clue to the internal disposition of rooms is the base of a *lavabo* or washstand carved in *pietra serena* with a large rosette (see Fig. 72), imbedded in the south wall of the largest upstairs room in the *casa vecchia*.[29] This was certainly the principal *sala* or dining room of the villa (Fig. 107). Two *pietra serena* portals

103. Santuccio, south-facing upper loggia or *verone* before restoration with single remaining Ionic colonette (photo: Conway Library, Courtauld Institute of Art).

with egg and dart cornices also set this room apart from the others (see Fig. 73). A large *pietra serena* mantelpiece, finely carved with the Strozzi coat of arms set in a laurel wreath with long unfurling ribbons, originally belonged in this room but is preserved in a private collection (Fig. 108). It has been attributed to Giuliano da Maiano.

By the time Filippo Strozzi began to renovate Santuccio in 1483 he clearly intended to create something more than a lodging for the oratory rector and a shelter for his family on occasional religious feast days. Apart from Le Selve, which belonged to his sister Alessandra, this was to be Filippo's principal country retreat, and it continued to be the main villa of his son Lorenzo long after his father's death. The result was a dignified *casa da signore* with an imposing tower that could be seen from a distance and a fine classical portico to impress visitors on arrival. Heraldic devices were prominently displayed from the weather vane to the decorated plaster on the façade. The Ionic portico and upper loggia, the barrel vaults, arched portals and the stonework in the upper *sala* were all refined *all'antica* features that contributed to the elegance of the villa. At the same time this was not an

104. Santuccio, ground-floor *camera*, original wooden ceiling painted by Bernardo di Stefano Rosselli, 1483 (photo: Conway Library, Courtauld Institute of Art).

105. Santuccio, ceiling of ground-floor *camera*, Strozzi devices of falcon and crescent moons painted by Bernardo di Stefano Rosselli (photo: Conway Library, Courtauld Institute of Art).

106. Santuccio, ceiling of ground-floor *camera*, Strozzi devices of lamb with 'MITIS ESTO' and crescent moons painted by Bernardo di Stefano Rosselli (photo: Conway Library, Courtauld Institute of Art).

107. Santuccio, *sala* on first floor of 'casa vecchia' (photo: Lynda Fairbairn, Conway Library, Courtauld Institute of Art).

108. Mantelpiece from Santuccio, carved in *pietra serena* with Strozzi coat of arms, Florence, private collection.

ostentatious building. Decorum and a certain austere simplicity were the keynotes. The scale of the building, its traditional elements and its restrained decoration all ensured that it was appropriate in its rural setting. The choice of the Ionic order may also reflect a desire for a less ostentatious effect than the composite order used, for example, at Careggi; its comparative simplicity may have been considered suitable in a rural domestic setting in a period when the Doric, Tuscan and rustic orders were little known. The use of the Ionic at Santuccio, however, may derive as much from the type of two-storeyed, porticoed wing that resembled the most popular solution adopted in monastic cloisters and hospitals and was here applied to a villa. The porticoed block was therefore treated as an adaptable formula that could be grafted onto pre-existing buildings.

The design of the new wing at Santuccio was not remarkably innovative for the mid-1480s, but this is precisely what we might expect in the circumstances. After all, the purchase and development of the whole Santuccio project was expedient and reactive, rather than novel and imaginative, in the sense that Filippo was fulfilling long-established dynastic expectations, maintaining a Strozzi presence in the old localities, and renewing their material identity with dignity and a sufficient degree of elegance. Because the family connections already existed, Filippo felt morally bound to look after the place. However, it is above all in relation to the great town palace, begun just two years after Santuccio was finished, that we can sense the emergence of what might be described as an integrated building and investment policy. Filippo had been planning the palace from 1474, nearly three years before he bought the *casa da signore* at Santuccio. One of the main explanations for the relative modesty of all Filippo Strozzi's country projects was that the huge palace was constantly evolving in the background. The urban project took priority, and this prudent, successful banker took care not to overspend elsewhere. The unprecedented scale and expense of Palazzo Strozzi, occupying a whole city block on a prominent corner site, clad from top to bottom in rusticated stone, with a looming classical cornice, the most modern domestic ground plan yet conceived, and a truly magnificent courtyard, reveals what grand conceptions Filippo was capable of, but these were not what he was carrying out in the countryside.

Christiane Klapisch-Zuber has described the typical Tuscan *casa da signore* as follows:

> A rudimentary sort of house, offering little comfort... mostly furnished with only the few beds, benches, tables and chests necessary for the summer encampment of an urban family. In the countryside closest to Florence the landowner's house is more often grandly equipped and decorated, becoming a symbol of patrician life, a sign of social prestige.[1]

The 1459 inventory of Il Palagio at Campi owned by the four sons of Carlo di Marcuccio Strozzi at first appears to be a good illustration of the sparsely furnished type of *casa da signore* described by Klapisch-Zuber. Since Niccolò, Girolamo, Marco and Pagholo were all unmarried, aged respectively 25, 20, 14 and 13 in 1459, extra accomodation for offspring was not yet needed. Their father had resided at the villa for many years and had sold his third of an urban palace in 1456, so his sons divided their time between a rented house in town and the villa at Campi (Fig. 109). Although this house was described as a *palagio* in the first three tax returns, the list of rooms and their contents dispells any impression of grandeur conveyed by that title. The space allotted to service rooms and agriculture was at least as great as that devoted to family accomodation. There was a cellar, a room for making bread, a granary, a pigeon loft, stables and three kitchens,[2] whereas only one *sala* and three *camere* were maintained as living rooms for the owners. The ground floor *camera* contained a bed, five chests full of books, letters, papers, clothes, linen, several smaller boxes of papers, one box with saffron and a branding iron with the Strozzi crescent moon. In the *sala*, there was a huge dining table (ten *braccia* or nearly six metres long), a long plank of fir wood from which they later made a bench (twelve *braccia*), a trestle table, three stools, a big armchair and two medium-sized chairs, scales, brass lamps, candlesticks, fire irons, a water stoup with bucket, an earthenware jug, a sword and bow. An upstairs *camera* was barely furnished with a bed, one chest, a writing desk, a table with an old carpet on it and a stool. The *camera grande* was more comfortable with a large bed, a *lettuccio*, a tabernacle with an image of the Madonna, two chests containing jars of raisins, linen, towels and bird nets of various sorts.[3]

Although such an inventory might initially seem merely to confirm preconceptions of the comfortless late-medieval rural interior, we should beware of misjudging this type of house based on a misreading of the documentary signals and on interpreting with hindsight. The size of the great table in the *sala* suggests large-scale entertaining was planned, the presence of chairs, which were prestige items in the fifteenth century, and of a *lettuccio* with its high back and cornice add a touch of comfort,[4] while the many books and papers remind us that two of this family, Marco and Girolamo Strozzi, are known to have commissioned manuscripts and printed editions of humanist texts.[5] In any case, inventories of this type shed light on

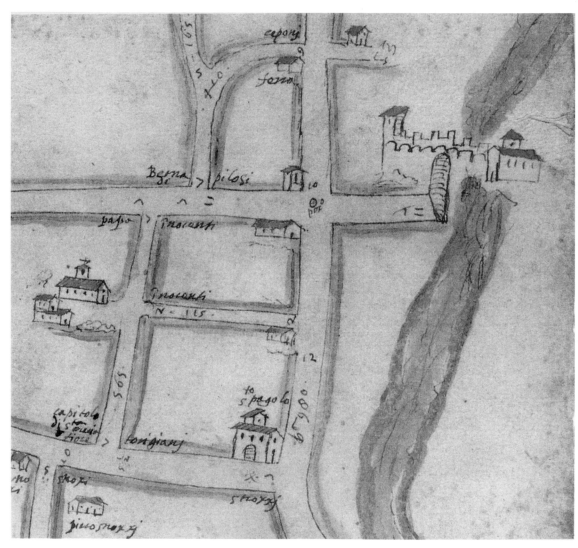

109. Parish of S. Lorenzo a Campi, with sites of Rocca di Campi (top right) and Il Palagio (marked 'piero stroxxj' and 'stroxi', bottom left). Detail of *Piante di popoli e strade – Capitani di parte guelfa – 1580–1595*, II, c. 412.

important aspects of the rural house. For example, the division of space between living and agricultural quarters was not nearly as sharp as might be imagined in a landowner's house. In Il Palagio at Campi a stair led directly from the upstairs *camera* to the pigeon loft, and the granary seems to have been incorporated into the house – most probably in a tower.[6] The presence of bird nets and cages in the *camera grande* and of garden or farm tools in the *androne* is a reminder of the daily activities at the villa as much as it conveys a rough or rustic note. Ultimately, this integration of agriculture within the *casa da signore* is consistent with what went

on outdoors, with the placing of the *casa da signore* near its home farm and with the social integration of the owner's family into country life (Fig. 110).

A comparison with the same owner's town house is also revealing, for in this case the rented house was scarsely more luxurious, consisting of a small diningroom (*saletta*) and two *camere* on the ground floor with a *sala*, a third *camera* and a kitchen on the first floor. More clothes were stored in town, but there was no sign that furnishings were more complete and not one painting is mentioned.[7] This is not, then, an example of a family who prioritised their urban lives, living

110. Il Palagio, Campi Bisenzio, rebuilt in the eighteenth century (photo: Fabio Costantini, Andrea Sordini, Francesco Tasselli and Michele Viti).

grandly in town and meagrely in the country. More-over, a closer reading of the four brothers' account book shows that Il Palagio was made more elegant and more comfortable in the late 1460s and 1470s. A renovation campaign took place from March 1469 to January 1470, focussed on a single grand apartment on the ground floor, consisting of a *sala, camera, scriptoio,* and *necessario* – dining hall, bedchamber, study and lavatory.[8] The *sala* was rebuilt, its main architectural features – a big fireplace, an *acquaio* (water stoup), doorway and window – carved in stone by Antonio di Nanni scarpellatore da Settignano.[9] The room was then whitewashed, wooden benches fitted, and door handles made. The next-door *camera* was improved at the same time, and a study and lavatory were built with new drains, veneered doors and, for the study, wooden shelves, a bench and desk.[10] The provision of these purpose-built *en suite* facilities catering specifically for the separate needs of mind and body, and forming part of an integrated apartment, brought greater convenience to country house living and raised it to a new level of modernity.[11]

The renovated apartment on the ground floor was almost certainly planned for the 1470 marriage of Niccolò, the eldest brother, and is therefore typical of a ritualistic pattern identified by Kent Lydecker, according to which the groom created a marital apartment to receive his bride, anticipating the arrival of her dowry in lavish expenditure on luxury furnishings.[12] Niccolò refers directly to this practice when he removes the cost of a very expensive suite of furniture for his new *camera* from the brothers' joint account book and debits it to his own personal account: 'It seems to me better that it should go into my account since, on taking a wife, everyone can spend his own money in his own way'.[13] In these matter-of-fact terms, he explains his extravagance as if marriage made expenditure on domestic comfort, or even luxury, morally justifiable and universally acceptable. The suite of furniture to which he refers cost ninety-five lire in March 1470 and consisted of a bed with chests around it and a *lettuccio* with its high back and cornice, all commissioned from Battista di Giovanni dello Squarta.[14]

Although a few commissions for furniture and minor structural and decorative improvements were made well before and long after the time of Niccolò's marriage, it is remarkable the extent to which most expenditure was concentrated around the wedding, particularly in the acquisition of elaborate pieces of wooden furniture: beds, settles and chests. For example, in December 1469 a bed with its plinth was veneered by Giuliano *legnaiuolo*, possibly Giuliano da Maiano who worked frequently for Filippo di Matteo Strozzi in these years.[15] In February 1470, while Mancino *legnaiuolo* was paid for a pair of *cassoni*,[16] Andrea di Lorenzo *legnaiuolo* made another grand bedroom suite in walnut with chests, a *lettuccio* and a *cassone*.[17] Just over a year later, in May 1471, Francesco di Salvadore *legniauolo* was paid for a series of carpentry jobs around the house including a further *lettuccio* for a *camera*, and for the *sala*, veneered benches with cornices and chests underneath, shelves at the water stoup, veneered surfaces for a table, a door and a *desco*.[18] In the case of this Strozzi villa at Campi, the emphasis around 1470 was not on painted decoration nor on expensive cloth but was focussed on the handiwork of *legniauoli*: elaborate pieces of carved furniture and fine wooden surfaces. It is clear from the ordering of at least three bedroom suites, that this was not simply a matter of furnishing one nuptial chamber but was an opportunity to improve the whole house.[19] Marriage therefore functioned as the trigger for a campaign of modernisation, bringing about what might individually appear to be small changes, but actually signal important developments in the organisation and decoration of domestic space. The evidence from this type of villa also suggests that, where funds allowed, programmes of renovation were underway in close parallel to developments in town:[20] architectural elements executed in *pietra serena* in an *all'antica* idiom, fine wood and intarsia introduced in furniture and panelling rather than the painted, storiated surfaces popular until the 1460s, and new semi–self-sufficient apartments created with *en suite* facilities for priviledged members of the household.

Despite an increase in elegance and comfort at Il Palagio near Campi, it is doubtful whether any of the Strozzi villas could be classified among the grand 'ville da mostra' of the *contado*, as the sumptuous furnishings listed in the inventories of the Medici villa at Careggi and the Tornabuoni villa at Chiasso Macerelli show them to have been;[21] but Filippo di Matteo Strozzi's villa at Santuccio may have fallen between the rudimentary and luxurious extremes. The account books of Filippo di Matteo Strozzi contain much useful material on his furniture, which, however, was mostly bought for his town house.[22] From this negative evidence, therefore, it can be assumed that, even in the period before Filippo built his grand new palace, he spent far more money in town. Nevertheless, some interesting aspects of Santuccio do emerge from a close consideration of the *ricordanze* of Filippo di Matteo and his heirs.

When Filippo Strozzi let his newly acquired *casa da signore* at Santuccio to Lucrezia Tornabuoni for the use of her agent Bernardo Baroncelli, Filippo removed his furniture, except for the benches (*panche*) that he had just installed around the dining halls on the ground and first floors.[23] The items removed were a new bed with two *cassapanche* (benches with chests underneath), a *lettuccio* (settle), four *cassoni* (great chests), a mattress and a bed-cover.[24] The sparseness might be explained by the fact that Filippo had just bought the villa and was only beginning to furnish it, hence also the new bed and new benches. It might also be explained by Filippo's initial intention not to spend long periods at the villa, to equip it with the barest essentials and to let it unfurnished straight away.

Very few subsequent accounts specify which items were bought for Santuccio. The first reference, from after the period when the villa was let and before construction began, records the purchase of a bed, five *braccia* long, with chests around it, bought for twenty-six lire in Empoli, strapped to a mule and brought to the villa for Filippo's own *camera*. The arrangements were made by Bernardo di Giovanni and Company, linen drapers (*linaiuoli*), who seem to have acted as furniture purveyors and upholsterers for Filippo on a regular basis. They made the under and over mattresses (*saccone* and *materasso*) for the same bed as well as a small mattress for the *lettuccio*.[25] Another bed with its bench and *lettuccio* were repaired and an under mattress filled with straw for the *camera terrena* in the *casa vecchia* at Santuccio, a room that was used by the boys' tutor.[26] The old wing was therefore at least partially furnished for habitation while construction of the new wing was under way. Rooms were whitewashed and painted a stone colour in May 1483. Fifteen pieces of intarsia made by Niccolò di Francesco and Company were also intended for the old wing.[27]

After renovation was complete, there is little information about furniture recorded in the household accounts, so it is not possible to gain an overall picture of the villa interior. Nevertheless, accounts and *ricordi* do provide details of the paintings hung at Santuccio, which shed light on Filippo Strozzi's artistic preferences. On 29 December 1487, Filippo paid Bernardo di Stefano Rosselli one gold florin for the gold leaf and labour he provided in gilding the frames of two canvasses at Santuccio, one a Madonna and the other a painting of a giraffe.[28] A later account, dated 5 July 1488, records payment of one gold florin, again to Bernardo di Stefano Rosselli, 'to make up and gild [the frames of] two Flemish paintings at Santuccio'.[29] The fact that both tasks were assigned to Bernardo Rosselli or his workshop is consistent with his role as Filippo's decorative painter, regularly employed on household jobs, repairing and painting old chests, painting ceilings and coats of arms in town and country, as well as his commissions for the *sgraffito* at Santuccio and the altar frontal at Lecceto.[30] That four paintings for Santuccio be provided with gilt frames in late 1487 and 1488 also fits into the period when other furnishings were provided for the villa. Seats, a bed, a feather quilt for the slave girl and small items for the garden were bought in the same years.[31]

More information about the villa interior is provided by a list of the contents of Santuccio divided between Filippo's heirs after his death in 1491.[32] His eldest son Alfonso, the issue of Filippo's first marriage, inherited one-third of the moveables, whereas the two younger sons Lorenzo and Giovambatista (known as Filippo from the time of his father's death), still under the guardianship of their mother Selvaggia, shared

the remaining two-thirds. Unfortunately, the Santuccio division does not list the contents according to room, so it is impossible to reconstruct the interior disposition of rooms or to discover how the contents were distributed. Unusually, the inventory only lists relatively small, portable objects – tableware, kitchen equipment, tools, linen, two hangings (a painted canvas *spalliera* and a painted linen *usciale*), nine paintings, but no furniture. This is unfortunate because accounts concerning Filippo's commissions for *lettucci* and *cassoni* from Giuliano and Benedetto da Maiano and the list of furniture inherited by Alfonso in town demonstrate that Filippo had many fine pieces of furniture there, comparable with those in the Medici and Tornabuoni palaces.[33] The list of nine paintings from Santuccio divided between the three heirs is more helpful. Alfonso received four paintings in the division:

> A Madonna on panel, and three painted cloths in frames, that is a ship, a burning house with various inventions, and a Madonna for 26 lire.[34]

Lorenzo and Filippo il Giovane inherited:

> 5 painted cloths in frames, that is an Adoration of the Magi, 2 lions, 2 great danes, a giraffe and a Madonna.[35]

The painting of the giraffe, the frame of which was gilded in December 1487, is immediately identifiable with the painting in this division. One of the two Madonnas on canvas must also be the one whose frame was gilded with the giraffe, and the two Flemish pictures, gilded in July 1488, are likely to be among the remaining seven.

The subjects of the pictures in the Santuccio division are striking. Only four of the nine were religious paintings: three Madonnas and an Adoration of the Magi. Another four paintings – the three animal pictures and the ship – might be categorised as belonging to the genres of marine views and still life, normally associated with the seventeenth century rather than

111. Piero di Cosimo, *Vulcan and Aeolus*, c. 1490. National Gallery of Canada, Ottawa.

this period. There was one historical or mythological work: a burning house with other inventions ('una chasa che arde con più fantasie').

In particular, the mention of three animal paintings at Santuccio, each an image of a single species, suggests that these may have been portraits. The document referring to gilding the frame of the giraffe is illuminating in this respect, for it shows that this must have been an image of one particular giraffe, almost certainly drawn from life by the artist. Payment to Bernardo Rosselli was made on 29 December 1487,[36] only seven weeks after Lorenzo de' Medici had received a gift of a giraffe from the Sultan of Egypt on 11 November.[37] The first live giraffe to be seen in Florence, writers and painters quickly disseminated the novel image, catering to the fashion for the exotic while satisfying their own scientific curiosity and testing their ability to reproduce such an unusual form. The example of the Santuccio giraffe illustrates exactly how fast such an image could be commissioned, painted, framed and hung in its chosen setting. Although no individual painted portrait of the giraffe has survived, Sigismondo Tizio's engraving and Piero di Cosimo's *Vulcan and Aeolus* (Fig. 111) convey how Lorenzo's giraffe was represented by fifteenth-century artists.[38]

Lions were a more familiar feature because the commune kept lions – their live heraldic beasts – behind the Palazzo de' Signori. An account dated 30 March 1475 records that Filippo Strozzi paid three florins for '2 painted cloths, one of 2 dogs and one of 2 lions and lion cubs'.[39] Since these are almost certainly the same two pictures later recorded at Santuccio, the scene with two lions and their cubs may have resembled Villani's description of how, in 1331, the commune's lion and lioness gave birth to two cubs, 'an event that attracted a great deal of attention and was regarded as a powerful omen of future prosperity.'[40] The use of the lion as the heraldic emblem of the city of Florence may partly account for its appearance at Santuccio and the Palazzo Medici where Pesellino's 'lioni nelle gratichole' hung.[41]

Great Danes figure prominently in paintings from Gentile da Fabriano's Strozzi *Adoration of the Magi* to Mantegna's Camera Dipinta.[42] Whether accompanying the Magi, the Gonzaga court or a triumphal procession painted on a *cassone*,[43] these big, powerfully built dogs were an accessory of the patrician pursuit of hunting and a sign of magnificence. It might be assumed that the painting of two Great Danes at Santuccio was a generic image of no personal significance for Filippo Strozzi, if it were not for the survival

112. Ghirlandaio workshop (attributed to Sebastiano Mainardi), central *predella* panel from Lecceto altarpiece, *The Adoration of the Shepherds*, 1487–8. Museum Boüjmans van Beuningen, Rotterdam.

of the central *predella* panel from the Lecceto altarpiece painted in Ghirlandaio's workshop between January 1487 and July 1488. First identified by Eve Borsook as the painting now in the Boüjmans van Beuningen Museum in Rotterdam,[44] it includes a representation of Filippo Strozzi in the humble role of an adoring shepherd kneeling on the right and accompanied by a large dog with a studded collar, not the usual shepherd's dog, but a Great Dane (Fig. 112). In the Strozzi *predella* the dog was partly meant to signify *fides*, as the emblem of the seated Great Dane with a muzzle did for the Gonzaga in Mantua.[45] The dog in the Lecceto *predella* sits obediently beside its master Filippo Strozzi, exercising the same virtues of faith and loyalty that Strozzi displays towards the infant Christ. The appearance of a Great Dane accompanying this portrait of Strozzi and the second appearance of two Great Danes in the painting at Santuccio is more than coincidental, and we can surmise that this was a double portrait of Filippo's favourite hunting dogs, who were probably kept at the villa.

The most intriguing of all the paintings at Santuccio, and probably the only narrative picture there, was the 'chasa che arde con più fantasie'. This may have represented the burning of Troy, or perhaps a burning house in a fantastic landscape. It is quite possible that such a work was executed by Piero di Cosimo who painted a series of fires and who certainly worked for Filippo Strozzi's son Filippo the Younger in 1510.[46] The juxtaposition at Santuccio of paintings of a giraffe and of a fire, both unusual images in this period, and the fact that Piero di Cosimo painted both these rare subjects and is known to have worked for the family, makes his presence at the villa highly plausible.

The painting of a ship ('una nave') may have been part of a vogue for marine views. Lorenzo de' Medici owned a Netherlandish canvas painted with two skiffs and a ship ('uno panno alla franzese dipintovi dua palandite [*sic*: palandrie] e una nave, di stima F. 2').[47] It is possible that the Santuccio picture was one of the 'quadri fiandreschi' referred to in the account book and is an early example of a Netherlandish marine view, although it could also have been a perspectival view with a boat in the foreground and a port in the distance.[48] Given the lack of surviving examples and documentary detail, problems of conflation tend to arise when attempting to reconstruct artistic categories for the domestic interior. It is clear that there were several genres of nautical or marine images appearing in Italian inventories from the mid–fifteenth century, including paintings of ships (perhaps specific galleys or naval vessels with which a merchant family like the Strozzi was concerned); topographical paintings, drawings or prints of cities that were ports;

113. Francesco Rosselli (attrib.), *Strozzi view of Naples*. Museo Nazionale del convento di S. Martino, Naples, on loan to Capodimonte.

intarsiaed views of ports built into panelling or furniture; and portolan maps. Filippo Strozzi may have acquired a taste for marine subjects through his acquaintance with Valencia, Barcelona and Naples and through his uncle Niccolò, his employer, from whose estate Filippo bought the bust by Mino da Fiesole, paintings, medals, hangings and two nautical or portolan maps.[49] However, although Filippo commissioned two large *lettucci* incorporating what were probably intarsiaed views of Naples in the backrest (*spalliera*) (Fig. 113),[50] and owned at least three topographical paintings of ports – one of Otranto and two of Naples – and a nautical map,[51] none of these were associated with the villa.

The three Madonnas at Santuccio have not been traced, except for the one on panel that is probably Filippino Lippi's Strozzi or Bache *Madonna and Child* now in the Metropolitan Museum in New York (Fig. 114). In fact, this is the only surviving painting that has a good claim to come from Santuccio. Although many fifteenth-century Florentine altarpieces have been discussed in the context of their original chapels, remarkably few non-Medicean domestic pictures have been analysed in relation to the houses for which they were commissioned. This may therefore be a rare example of a fifteenth-century villa picture whose original location has been identified and still exists. The date proposed for the Strozzi Madonna on stylistic grounds, c. 1485–7,[52] neatly fits the period of Santuccio's

decoration. More telling, however, is the way in which Filippino's placing of the Strozzi device of crescent moons in the spandrels of the loggia corresponded precisely to the actual *sgraffito* decoration on the entrance loggia at the villa (see Fig. 96, Chapter 6). Yet the capitals in the painting are gilded and have fluted necks or coats of arms with delicate acanthus leaves curling up towards the volutes (Fig. 115), so that they are a form of composite, quite unlike the robust and simpler Ionic capitals carved for Santuccio (see Figs. 69 and 70, Chapter 6). Likewise, the grey *pietra serena* columns at the villa have been transformed into something that resembles a warm brown *pietra forte*, but streaked with grey to look like marble. Filippino's painted background bears the same sort of relationship to the real villa landscape as his architectural details do, so that, although no element of the background scene is strictly identifiable with Santuccio in the way that the Nerli family palace in Borgo San Frediano and the Porta San Frediano are in Filippino's Nerli altarpiece, every element nevertheless relates generically and plausibly to the busy countryside around the villa. This is plainly not a portrait of the view from Santuccio, for the river Bisenzio was never visible from Santuccio's loggia since the rest of the house was in the way. Nor is there evidence that a fortified gate and village wall ever existed in S. Mauro on the other side of the Ponte al Santuccio. Yet the key juxtaposed elements of a river landscape, two bridges,

114. Filippino Lippi, *Madonna and Child* (Strozzi or Bache Madonna), c. 1485–7. The Metropolitan Museum of Art, New York, the Julius Bache Collection, 1949 (49.7.10).

115. Filippino Lippi, *Madonna and Child* (Strozzi or Bache Madonna), detail. The Metropolitan Museum of Art, New York, the Julius Bache Collection, 1949 (49.7.10).

116. Mino da Fiesole, *Bust of Niccolò di Lionardo Strozzi*, marble, 1454. Skulpturen Sammlung und Museum für Byzantinische Kunst, Berlin, currently exhibited in the Gemäldegalerie, Berlin.

a mill house, a mill dam (*pescaia*) and the fortified gate of a walled village (*castello*) are all featured in the close vicinity of Santuccio. It is possible that Filippino never saw the villa, but if he did, his intention was the same – to create a suggestive correspondence or capriccio-like evocation of this part of the *contado*, rather than an exact likeness.

Another Madonna is documented as a Santuccio commission. This was a painting of the Virgin with two little angels in a gilded frame ('un quadro di Nostra Donna con dua angioletti dallato con cornicie d'oro') bought from Perugino's assistant, Giovanni di Iacopo

Lo Spagna, for three large florins in April 1490.[53] It is worth noting that this painting, like the Madonna on canvas and the giraffe framed in 1487 and the two 'quadri fiandreschi' framed in 1488, were all specifically destined for the villa and were not castoffs from the town house.

Although the information about Santuccio's paintings may seem meagre, comparison with the works of art in other villas and town palaces sheds light on fifteenth-century interiors and helps to place Filippo's villa in a broader context. Nine paintings seems very few in a house that included two *sale*, four *camere* and at least four other residential rooms.[54] Was this villa unusually modest in its display of images and were town houses lavish by comparison? An inventory for Filippo di Matteo's provisional town house has not yet been found, but a list of the furnishings allotted to Alfonso after his father's death in 1492 gives some idea of its interior. Alfonso inherited six paintings from the town house: a large hunting picture of bulls and lions, another canvas with lions and horses, a Madonna, topographical views of Otranto and Naples and a nautical map. He also acquired four sculptures: a sculpture of the Virgin and Child; two marble roundels carved in relief, one with two heads, the other a head of Nero; and a marble portrait bust of Niccolò Strozzi.[55] The relief with two heads is probably the white marble roundel carved in relief with the heads of Charlemagne and Totila bought from Mino da Fiesole in 1473,[56] and the bust of Filippo's cousin and employer Niccolò di Lionardo Strozzi is almost certainly the portrait carved by Mino da Fiesole in Rome in 1454 (Fig. 116).[57] Compared with Alfonso's share of four paintings at Santuccio, this does indeed show there were more works of art displayed in town. If the other two brothers inherited a comparable number, there would have been about thirty paintings and sculptures in the town house, compared with nine paintings at the villa. Comparing the Strozzi example with a series of inventories of town palaces and villas demonstrates that even in the case of grand villas, there were fewer works of art in the country (see Table 1).[58] The number of paintings at Santuccio does not, therefore, suggest that this villa was more modestly decorated than, for example, the Medici villas at Fiesole, Trebbio and Cafaggiolo or the Nori villa of Lonchio, although it does confirm that there were usually fewer paintings and sculptures outside the town. One explanation is that murals and tapestries may have figured more prominently in the country. Certainly no contemporary urban equivalent has been discovered for the secular murals by Castagno at the Villa Carducci, those by Pollaiuolo at the Villa Lanfredini or those by Botticelli at the Tornabuoni villa of Chiasso Macerelli. Yet I have found no evidence to suggest that tapestries were more popular in the country. On the other hand, in their castle in

Chianti, the da Uzzano retained what may have been a traditional type of decoration appropriate to ancestral country seats when they hung their ground floor *sala* with ten shields painted with coats of arms.[59]

If visits to the country were confined to short periods or one summer stay, it is likely that owners would bring furnishings and luxury items with them from town. Portability would then be a key factor, favouring painted or woven cloths rather than heavy tabernacles and wooden panels.[60] The list of eight canvasses and one panel painting at Santuccio might support this suggestion, although these paintings seem to have been kept permanently at the villa. A glance at the other inventories shows that, although there was some preference for canvasses in the country, the tendency was not necessarily a strong one or widespread. A comparison between Lorenzo de' Medici's paintings in town and at Careggi does show that panels prevailed in town (c. sixty-two panels against c. twenty-six canvasses) and canvasses at the villa (twenty-three canvasses and six panels at Careggi), although at Fiesole and Poggio a Caiano there were as many or more panels as there were canvasses. Francesco Nori had eight canvasses at the villa and only one specified in town, but Giovanni Tornabuoni on the other hand, maintained a distinct preference for wooden panels in both town and country. Nor did Pierfrancesco de' Medici's heirs tend to keep canvasses at their villas of Trebbio, Cafaggiolo and Fiesole.

Another fundamental question concerns the subject matter of country house decoration. The proportion of secular subjects was striking at Santuccio. Did other villa owners demonstrate a similar fondness for nonreligious images? In the limited sample of inventories consulted for this study it is clear that religious images predominated in both town and country houses in the fifteenth century and most of these were devotional, nonnarrative subjects[61] (see Table 1). Even a patron like Pierfrancesco de' Medici, who owned important mythological paintings such as Botticelli's *Primavera* and *Minerva and the Centaur*, maintained a high ratio of religious subjects in his collection. Twenty-two of the thirty paintings and sculptures in the *casa vecchia* in town were religious pictures of which only one

Table 1. *Table showing the numbers of paintings and sculptures in Florentine town houses and villas.*

Owner and House	Total Number of Paintings and Sculptures	Religious Works	Secular Works	Unidentified
FILIPPO STROZZI (1492)				
Town (Alfonso's share approximately 1/3)	c. 30	1+ (c. 10%)	9+	c. 20
Santuccio	9	4 (44%)	5	–
DA UZZANO (1424)				
Town	11	10 (91%)	1	–
Cast. Uzzano	5	5 (100%)	–	–
FRANCESCO NORI (1478)				
Town	11	6 (54%)	1	–
Lonchio	5	7 (78%)	?	–
GIOVANNI TORNABUONI (1497)				
Town	35	23 (66%)	12	–
Ch. Macerelli	20	16 (80%)	4	–
Le Brache	7	7 (100%)	–	–
PIERFRANCESCO MEDICI (1498)				
Town	30	22 (73%)	8	–
Cafaggiolo	11	11 (100%)	–	–
Trebbio	8	8 (100%)	–	–
Fiesole	4	4 (100%)	–	–
LORENZO DE' MEDICI (1492)				
Town (paintings only)	86	34 (40%)	44	–
Careggi	29	17 (59%)	12	–
Fiesole	8	7 (88%)	1	–
Ambra	11	9 (82%)	2	–

of Moses and the Pharoah was a narrative. More significantly, all the images at Pierfrancesco's three villas of Cafaggiolo, Trebbio and Fiesole were devotional. Although at first sight the proportions would seem to be reversed in the case of Lorenzo Il Magnifico, this is only the case in town, where more than half the paintings were secular,[62] whereas with the exception of Careggi, there was a preference for devotional images at his villas, particularly at Fiesole and Poggio a Caiano.

The greater proportion of religious images in the country may partly derive from a conservative attitude more pervasive in the country and from the economic motive which allowed villa owners to save money in the country where expenditure was not so conspicuous and therefore less effective as a prestige symbol. A Madonna or similarly conventional devotional subject could be cheaply produced by assistants or lesser artists in the workshops and did not require the special skills and invention needed for an unusual narrative or portrait. Above all, the need for a devotional image in most, if not every, *camere* meant that Madonnas (or another nonnarrative New Testament subject) were an essential component, and their provision reflected the need to equip the room, rather than any independent display of artistic selectivity. This is clearly expressed in the list of pictures at Ambra, where the eight devotional paintings were casually described in relation to their function and support:

> Eight little pictures painted with various figures of Our Lady and other saints to use in the bedchambers, some of wood and some of those Flemish cloths.[63]

Although Filippo Strozzi certainly had few paintings and sculptures compared with Lorenzo de' Medici, it is interesting to note that these two are the only inventories in the sample to share a high proportion of secular works. Of course the relatively low ratio of religious works at Santuccio (four out of nine) may partly suggest that only four principal *camere* were decorated for habitation, but it does also show a marked taste for certain new types of secular painting, a taste Filippo shared with prominent patrons like the Medici who were at the forefront of new artistic developments.

It is tempting to relate the appearance of animal pictures to the pastoral or Arcadian associations of villa life, or to the activities of hunting and fishing centred around the villa. Yet the animal paintings listed in the Medici and Strozzi villa inventories only occasionally relate to country life:[64] Lorenzo de' Medici owned three bird paintings at his villas (a peacock; a canvas with peacocks, pheasants and other birds at Careggi; and a painting of bears, falcons, pheasants, partridges, peacocks, foxes and other birds at Fiesole), which can be associated with hunting and with the creation of aviaries, both favourite rural pursuits. Although the double portrait of Filippo Strozzi's hunting dogs, the Great Danes, are connected to country life, none of the other subjects was specifically rural. Indeed, it could be argued that the communal and patriotic associations of the lions,[65] and the Medicean resonances or modish fascination with the exotic giraffe, were primarily Florentine references. Ultimately the comparison of subject matter in palace and villa inventories demonstrates that there was no binary division; rather both locations were part of the same ideological world, unified in their references and concerns, whether it be in their spiritual or talismanic need for a bedchamber Madonna or in their desire to display dynastic motifs or patrician or *all'antica* imagery. House interiors in town and countryside were unified in their celebration of the same locality, Florence and her *contado*, as a single greater locus.

8 · VILLA FUNCTIONS AND ATTITUDES

MOTIVES FOR VILLA OWNING

There were many reasons why such a large proportion of Florentines should own country property in the fifteenth century.[1] Although profits from the land were not as spectacular as those from banking, trade and manufacturing, the risk of loss was far less.[2] Unlike moveable wealth, real property could not be lost or stolen and was less subject to market fluctuations. The income from farms might be modest but, in the welcome form of food, it was necessary to life.[3] Enrico Fiumi cites the popular description of agriculture as 'that occupation in which one never dies of hunger, but nor has one ever a penny in the pocket'.[4] Alberti went further in *I Libri della famiglia*, setting up an antithesis between urban trade, manufacturing and business on the one hand and rural landowning or agriculture on the other. Business is represented as dangerous, exposed to treachery and generating anxiety, fear, suspicion and regret, whereas the country estate is presented as secure, productive, enjoyable and, above all, honest or virtuous:

> LIONARDO: What kind of person could fail to take pleasure in his villa? The villa is of great, honorable, and reliable value. Any other occupation is fraught with a thousand risks, carries with it a mass of suspicions and of trouble, and brings numerous losses and regrets. There is trouble in purchasing, fear in transporting, anxiety in selling, apprehension in giving credit, weariness in collecting what is due to you, deceit in exchange. So in all other occupations you are beset by a multitude of worries and suffer constant anxiety. The villa alone seems reliable, generous, trustworthy and truthful. Managed with diligence and love, it never wearies of repaying you. Reward follows reward'.[5]

The idea of being independent of clients and partners was attractive. Landowners sought the sense of security that came from self-sufficiency,[6] a desire that had been reinforced by the disastrous series of plagues, famines and bankruptcies which had characterised the second half of the fourteenth century.[7] A country estate was seen as a protection against ill fortune, a source of food in hard times and an indestructible form of property that might survive when all else had gone.

Apart from functioning as a financial safety net or insurance measure, the healthy rural environment was a great advantage. The association of health with the country was one of the reasons that children spent longer periods of time there. In particular, the babies of well-to-do Florentines were often sent to country wet nurses, not only to breathe the fresh air but also to benefit from the milk of a robust and healthy country woman, ideally the wife of the *signore's* own tenant farmer.[8] Alessandra Macinghi Strozzi wrote of her delicate son Matteo's transformation after a stay at the villa, 'and he's become such a beautiful boy while he's been in the country; if you'd seen him before and saw him now, you wouldn't know he was the same boy'.[9] The countryside was regarded as psychologically, as well as physically, healthier, as is clear again from Alberti's dialogue on family life: 'As for me, to live with less vice, with less melancholy, with less expense, but more healthily, with more equanimity, yes indeed, my children, I do praise the villa'.[10]

When plague was rife in town those who could afford to leave, did so; as Alessandra Macinghi Strozzi wrote in the plague-ridden summer of 1450: 'for as long as there is plague . . . the well-off people have all left Florence'.[11] That year Alessandra stayed closer to town than her son Filippo recommended,[12] the family dispersed among various villas ('questo andare pelle ville fuggendo la moria',[13]) she herself at Antella with her brother;[14] her daughter Caterina with her husband Marco Parenti in Giovanni Portinari's villa at Camerata; her youngest son Matteo at Quaracchi.[15] The plague had begun the year before, soon spreading to the countryside surrounding the city.[16] Marco Parenti and Caterina had moved first to Camerata, but left for the Mugello in July 1449:

> I am staying at the villa like everyone else, because there is hardly anyone left in Florence and there is nothing to do there; and in a few days' time I am thinking of going to the Mugello to a place called Pulicciano. The whole of Florence has fled because it is a better environment in the countryside. In Florence between 10 and 16 people are dying every day.[17] (Marco Parenti at Camerata to Filippo Strozzi in Naples, 11 July 1449)

Matteo wrote cheerfully from Quaracchi two days before joining his sister in the Mugello:

> As long as it's a good district to be, we are here at Quaracchi in Agnolone's house, and if nothing else comes up, we will go to the Mugello to Marco and Caterina's house, or we shall go to Figline near Prato because for now there is good air in both places.[18] (Matteo

di Matteo Strozzi to Filippo di Matteo, 24 August 1449)

The plague had spread to Quaracchi by then and a move to the hills was essential. Giovanni Rucellai, who listed the plagues he lived through between 1400 and 1457, never took the risk of remaining as close as his villa at Quaracchi, but fled to Pisa (1411), Modena and Forlì (1417), Arezzo and the Pandolfini villa at Signa (1423–4), Arezzo and Ancisa (1430), Montevarchi and Pisa (1437–8), Gubbio, Perugia and, as it abated, Palla di Nofri Strozzi's villa at Petraia (1449–50), and San Gimignano (1457).[19] The Arno valley close to Florence was not considered safe during most outbreaks. In 1429, Matteo di Simone Strozzi sent wine from his vineyards at Campi up to Antella to be casked at the villa of his brother-in-law Zanobi Macinghi, 'stimando andarvi per la moria'. In the event they went further afield to Montemurlo for a whole six months from 1 May until November 1430.[20]

In 1446 Messer Palla Novello bought a country house at Monterchi in the Tiber valley specially to serve as a retreat from the plague:

> An estate that I bought from Michele di Nofri Parenti in the district of Monterchi with a house in the walled town for my own habitation. And a vineyard outside the walls now barren and disused, and arable land, in all costing 200 florins; we don't earn anything from it yet because there is no family of sharecroppers, nor oxen nor other livestock. We bought it so as to renovate it and to escape there from the plague.[21]

The frequency of outbreaks (almost every seven years) also shows that, rather than a rare occurrence for which no contingency arrangements need be made, this could have been a pressing and ever-present motive for owning a rural refuge.

The healthy and economic aspects of villa life co-existed with the pleasure motive. A *ricordo* by Filippo di Matteo reproducing the correspondence with his brother Lorenzo in Naples over the purchase of Santuccio reveals the different priorities of each brother. In July 1477, Filippo informed Lorenzo that he had bought the Alberti farm at Santuccio and gave a description and the price, adding that should Lorenzo want the farm he could have it, but if not, Filippo would keep it for himself. In his reply Lorenzo distinguishes between the profit motive ('per rendità') and the practical need for a country residence which would at the same time be a delightful place to satisfy the pleasure motive:

> He [Lorenzo di Matteo Strozzi] replied to me in his letter of the 26th that it was not to his taste because he would have liked a farm to live on as well as to provide some pleasure ('diletto') and convenience ('chomodità'). But after discussing it with Marco [Parenti] and when the two of us were both agreed that he would need it as a source of income, we decided to buy it for him or he could always give it up.[22]

Whereas for Lorenzo the questions of 'diletto' and 'chomodità' were apparently all important, Filippo had conveyed his reasons to Lorenzo in an earlier letter of April 1477 which made it clear that he had been motivated mainly by piety: wishing to offer thanks to God and provide accommodation for the oratory rector and for the family on the annual religious feast day.[23] Once involved, he ensured that he made the maximum profit from rents in cash and kind. Although their standpoints were so different, Filippo and Marco Parenti were nevertheless sensitive to Lorenzo's wishes and conferred as follows:

> I have been with Marco and I put before him the objections you made to me over the farm and what your intentions were. In the end it seems to us that we should find a place more to your taste, and this one [Santuccio] I shall take for myself, and when you are here and want somewhere, we shall sort something out between us.[24]

When Lorenzo finally came to Florence the following June, he saw Santuccio and made it clear that he would prefer something more attractive for himself:

> Then when Lorenzo was in Florence during the month of June 1478 and had seen the farm, and I asked him whether he was inclined to want it, he replied to me 'no'. And that when he moved back to Florence he would try to find something that was more to his taste.[25]

The fact that Filippo transcribed the substance of these letters into his diary or *ricordi* shows how significant this disagreement with his brother over the villa was to him, although the need to keep a record of family property disputes, especially unnotarised ones, may have been at the forefront of Filippo's mind. This is a rare example where different personal reactions to a villa are recorded. Despite the consistently pragmatic message conveyed by treatises such as Crescenzi's *De Agricoltura*, or Alberti's *Della Famiglia*, and *Villa*, and despite the vast quantity of agricultural and economic evidence from the archives, it is clear that there was not just one set of acceptable motives for the purchase of a villa. While for Filippo Strozzi dynastic identity and clan loyalties were of crucial importance, together with religious reasons and the added advantage of profit and agricultural productivity, for Lorenzo Strozzi quite another set of values was paramount: personal taste and preferences ('partito suo', 'ghusto tuo', 'se aveva l'animo a volerllo', 'piu a ghusto'), pleasure, delight ('diletto'), convenience and comfort ('chomodità').

Villas could offer an alternative to all the disagreeable features of urban life – its noise, its dirt, overcrowded conditions, the heat and bad air, the demands of work and the intrusions of public life.[26] Later, in 1537 when political pressures were nearing crisis point for Filippo di Matteo's sons, Lorenzo di Filippo wrote to his brother Filippo the Younger from his country retreat at Santuccio:

> I dearly recommend this life of mine staying at the villa and enjoying the peace and quiet, the only refuge in my indisposition, which I do

not value any less because it gives offence to no-one. . . . As for the news, here at Santuccio I have none to give you in exchange; I'm here not just for the fresh air, but to avoid hearing, so quickly and so often, thousands of things I don't want to hear, and which are anyway at times untrue . . . Santuccio, 6 June 1537.[27]

Like the passages in Alberti's *Della Famiglia*, Lorenzo Strozzi's letter echoes classical eulogies of the villa as *locus amoenus*. The attitude to villa life among the Florentine elite in the fifteenth century was certainly influenced by the writings of contemporary humanist scholars and their ancient literary models. The pastoral revival in literature encouraged country visits for the purposes of study, enlightened conversation or recreation in a rural environment. Nevertheless, there is not necessarily a direct connection between humanist interests and villa patronage. Among the Strozzi, Palla di Nofri might be cited as an example of one who combined humanism with villa building, and indeed, when he lived in exile at Padua, he specially chose to buy a villa at Arquà where Petrarch had once owned a country retreat.[28] But the classical learning of the scribe Benedetto di Pieraccione Strozzi is unlikely to have found expression in his dwindling farms at Capalle; nor is it easy to reconcile Matteo di Simone's humanist interests with his only country residence, the inn at Quaracchi. Where villas were associated with intellectual discourse, as at the Medici villa of Careggi or the Pandolfini villa at Signa, the parallels to be drawn between classical ideas and architecture are very limited, and any attempt to relate such buildings to ancient architectural models or the letters of Pliny the Younger must surely fail. Pre-existing structures and practical and economic considerations so often prevailed in the evolution of villa architecture. In the mid–fifteenth century, the Medici villa at Fiesole had the best claim to be based on classical rural prototypes, but where another grand, new, symmetrical design with *all'antica* features took shape in Francesco Sassetti's villa at Montughi, current schemes for town palaces held greater sway than archaeological or literary precedents.

VILLEGGIATURA

In the summer there was an exodus of the better-off Florentines into the country, although it would be misleading to think of villeggiatura as an exclusively seasonal phenomenon, for most sources refer to frequent short visits all year round.[29] Villani stated that prosperous families spent at least four months of the year *in contado*,[30] and there is evidence that Filippo di Matteo's family spent the six months from April to early October at the villa. At first Filippo's sister Alessandra Strozzi Bonsi's villa at Le Selve was their main country residence, but Santuccio was preferred after its renovation was complete. There are scattered accounts for food and wine consumed at Le Selve where Filippo's wife Selvaggia and the *brigata* seem to have stayed from April at least until August in 1480.[31] In the following year, supplies were again transported to Le Selve in July, although Lorenzo di Matteo's family were staying at Santuccio in September when Filippo sent a feather quilt to them.[32] In 1482, some of the family spent September and October in the valley at Capalle,[33] and in 1483, there were more payments for provisions at both Le Selve and Capalle between April and October.[34] These accounts nearly all involve the dispatch of money from Filippo in town to his wife or sister at the villa, often by way of his eldest son, Alfonso. Clearly it was the women and children who spent long stretches of time at the villa, whereas Filippo made brief sorties into the country, often returning to his business and banking in town.[35]

There is evidence that visits to Santuccio involving bird trapping and fishing had already begun while the villa was being rebuilt. Forty-eight *staia* of wheat were eaten there during the summer of 1482.[36] In May 1483 Filippo bought bird nets at Signa,[37] while in June Alfonso had a fish pond (*pescagione*) made in the river Bisenzio beside Santuccio.[38] Later fishing nets and a boat (*navicello*) were bought for Santuccio.[39] In 1491, the Ingesuati friars, who made stained-glass windows for Filippo's chapels at S. Maria Novella and Lecceto, also provided him with brass or copper wire nets for trapping birds at Santuccio.[40]

From 1487, the year after renovations were finished, Santuccio appears more regularly in the household expense accounts and the large quantity of supplies consumed at the villa demonstrate that long periods were spent there. In 1487 the *brigata* is recorded at Le Selve in May and at Santuccio from July until the feast of San Donnino on 7 October.[41] That year the amount of wheat consumed at Santuccio was less than a fifth of the amount consumed in town (35 *staia* at the villa, 188 *staia* in town); but by 1489 more than a third of the town consumption of wheat was used at Santuccio (83 compared with 238 *staia*), and the amount had more than doubled.[42] Less than twice the quantity of wine was drunk in town than at Santuccio in 1489 (64 barrels at Santuccio, and 120 barrels in town,[43]) although this was only the wine from Filippo's own estates, and other, superior wine may have been a more regular supplement in town. The amount of wood used at the villa was also large: of seventeen and a half *cataste* of logs and fifteen mule loads of brushwood, eleven and a half *cataste* and nine mule loads were burnt as fuel in Florence and six *cataste* and six mule loads at Santuccio in 1489.[44]

Births, deaths and marriages all took place at the villa. Although the ceremonies of baptism and burial were sometimes transferred to town,[45] in hot weather the villa was probably a healthier place in which to nurse an illness or bear a child,[46] and it was often the preferred setting for wedding celebrations.[47] Filippo Strozzi's second son Alessandro died at Le Selve aged eighteen months in August 1473 and was buried under the Bonsi family altar in S. Maria delle Selve.[48] His eldest daughter Lucrezia, aged twelve, also died at Le Selve on 5 September 1481.[49]

At least two Strozzi marriages took place at Le Selve in this period. Filippo introduced his kinsman and employee Girolamo di Carlo Strozzi to his niece Maddalena di Giovanni Bonsi and arranged the marriage on 4 September 1476. Girolamo visited his betrothed at Le Selve two and half weeks later, presented her with the ring on 6 October, and consumated the marriage at Le Selve two days later.[50] When Filippo himself married a second time in 1477 his bride, Selvaggia di Bartolommeo Gianfigliazzi, rode directly from Milan to her family villa of Il Corno in the Val di Pesa. The wedding mass was held on 2 September when Filippo presented the ring and the contract was drawn up on 19 September. A week later Filippo led his bride to his family villa, Le Selve, for the consumation of their marriage on 27 September. Six months later Selvaggia miscarried a boy; but at Le Selve on 9 July 1479 she successfully bore a daughter, Alessandra, who was baptised in the local *pieve* of San Martino a Gangalandi.[51]

It is clear from examing just one household of the Strozzi clan that the villa was important not only for the sake of its past and the memory of ancestors who had lived there and whose spirit lived on in that locality, and not only for the sake of its future as a form of immovable wealth that could be bequeathed to future generations and form a relatively stable part of family identity, but also because from day to day the villa performed an important function as a meeting place for the *brigata*. Here it seems, even more than in town, large family groups gathered in a place where in-laws, cousins, friends, neighbours and old retainers could all come together on an informal basis or on more ritualistic occasions.

THE VILLA AS PRINCIPAL RESIDENCE

Boccaccio told the story of Federigo Alberighi who spent all his inheritance on chivalrous entertainments to please the object of his unrequited love. His worldly goods were finally reduced to a falcon and a small farm at Campi Bisenzio from which he was obliged to live:

> and he remained poor with nothing but a little farm, on whose produce he lived very penuriously, and one falcon which was among the best in the world. More in love than ever, but thinking he would no longer be able to live as a citizen in town as he desired, he went to live at Campi where his farm was. There he spent his time hawking, asked nothing of anybody, and patiently endured his poverty.[52]

Boccaccio contrasts the courtly, refined and expensive life as a *cittadino* with the humble, rustic existence on a farm at Campi. The falcon remains as the emblem of Alberighi's patrician status. Although he can no longer afford to live as a *cittadino*, yet with his falcon to help provide, nor is he a *contadino*. By killing the falcon and serving it on a dish to his lady, Alberighi destroys the last sign of his civilised and patrician status and is on the brink of becoming a *contadino*. Yet in this gesture he reveals his truly chivalrous spirit, which is rewarded by the love of a lady whose wealth and nobility justly return him to his original class and civic life. Boccaccio's *novella* encapsulates attitudes to town and country that persisted through the fifteenth century and which were expressed as poignantly in tax returns as they were in fiction.

Living at the villa was widely recognised as a way of escaping bankruptcy and urban poverty.[53] Whereas it was not possible to survive in town on a very low income, at worst owners could live off the fruits of the land or they could supplement a meagre inheritance by letting or selling their more valuable town house. The simpler way of life in the country meant less expense on luxury goods, and although these *cittadini selvatici* undoubtedly lost face by residing in the country, they were excused from having to maintain urban standards of dress and hospitality.

Of the twenty-four Strozzi villa owners, six families lived year-round at the villa for most of the fifteenth century, all except one of whom were forced to do so because of poverty. Only Piero di Carlo chose to reside at Querceto when he probably could have afforded to live in one of his houses in Florence; nevertheless his reasons were also economic, as he stated in 1446: 'at present, because of taxes which I cannot pay, it suits me to live at the villa'.[54] The other families presented a catalogue of woe to the tax officials, who were expected to recognise that only the direst of financial difficulties could have led them to take this extreme measure signifying inevitable loss of dignity. Paradoxically, although a six-month summer stay in the country was considered respectable and desirable, to live there year-round was demeaning.[55] But more was at stake, for the fear underlying these complaints was that they be identified as *contadini* rather

than *cittadini*. Their legal, fiscal and electoral status as Florentine citizens may not have been at risk, but their social status certainly was.

Three families claimed that they were reduced to the level of *lavoratori* or *contadini*. Carlo di Marcuccio who lived at Il Palagio at Campi is a good example. Although he owned a third of a town house in 1427 it was not declared for his own habitation and was let in 1430 and 1433.[56] In 1442 he described his situation in detail:

> I have the taxable wealth and discount that you see, and we are a family of gentle folk, and in two months time we expect another child and we already have two wetnurses; so that I have trouble in making a living even when I don't pay anything to the government; and I am of the age you see [45] without a job or business, and I am in debt to various people. . . . And I am living in the country through poverty.[57]

In 1451, after listing his debts, Carlo continued to plead:

> Wanting to return to Florence, I have nothing to live off and my sons are turning into peasants. . . . As you see I have 9 children, of whom 5 are girls for whom, because of our poverty, I have not been able to invest any dowry at all with the public dowry fund. The farms have not yielded as much as I put into them, which was a lot'.[58]

In 1456 he sold his share of the town house,[59] although his sons were finally able to rent a house in town in 1469.[60]

Ubertino di Tommaso was similarly distressed to find his family living off the land. By 1446 he had left his town house and sold scattered lands in the Campi district, pasture at Gangalandi and a profitable farm outside the Porta San Gallo. He retired to his Montughi villa:

As you can see, I have had neither house nor living for more than 14 years, and during this time I have always paid my taxes out of capital because my income is barely enough for us to live off and I am destitute, and I have turned my sons into peasants'.[61]

In 1451 Ubertino had died and his son Francesco, after six months of illness, described their country residence and their labour on the farm as the worst thing that could have happened to them:

We have no house in Florence and are in debt to various people, and owe 400 florins to the commune . . . and we sold 90 florins worth of possessions to pay the expenses arising out of the illness of Ubertino our father before he died. And Francesco one of his heirs, has been sick for 6 months, so that very little is left now. And we are all living at the villa because we can't pay rent or keep a servant, and because our mother is in poor health. And we have grown-up sisters without dowries as you can see in the list of household members. And we have no-one to help us or advise us. Please believe that this is the truth, and try to distinguish between those who tell the truth and those who don't; because we have been forced to become peasants as you can understand, because there is nothing else we can do.[62]

Marco di Goro's father had been rich,[63] but in 1421 he sold the contents of his palace in town to pay debts and 'from necessity we are reduced to living in the country'.[64] They chose to sell the palace in 1441, even before they sold their second large villa of Mezzana (in 1445), and were then dependent on Marco's widow's family for accommodation in town.[65] The arrangements made for Giovanni di Marco di Goro's daughters can be taken as a measure of the family's increasing involvement in the *contado* (and correspondingly reduced contact with Florence), as Giovanni looked to Prato to find a husband for his daughter Spinetta, whose dowry was partly paid in the form of a ten-year lease on a farm at Mezzana.[66]

Another daughter, Talana, became a nun in the convent of S. Nicolaio at Prato, with part of her dowry paid in the form of crops from Mezzana to be consigned to the nunnery in perpetuity.[67] In the 1460s Marco's grandsons began to rent a town house,[68] and they still did so in the 1480s, although they claimed that of five sons one was a priest, one a soldier, one was working for Filippo Strozzi in Naples, while the two youngest, Piero and Matteo, lived at the villa with their ageing mother. Piero was managing the estate, 'looking after his mother to relieve her of the management of the house and the little land that we have; he is growing up to be a peasant and learns nothing'; while Matteo the youngest loafed about, 'living off relatives in the country; we give him lots of money for clothes and food and drink, and he is entirely useless'.[69]

Messer Niccolò di Pagnozzo was confined through poverty to Macia, and although his villa was close to town, he complained of the lack of an urban pied-à-terre:

I am living with seven people in my household as you can see, without any earnings. Through poverty I cannot live in Florence and, aged 62 1/2, when I come to Florence there is no-one with whom I can stay.[70]

In 1469 his widow Cosa was still living in the same circumstances: 'living at the villa through poverty and I have been here for the last 30 years'.[71]

Francesco di Giovanni and his son Chirico were also long-term residents in the *contado* but complained less. Francesco's commitment to rural life at Capalle was signalled by the marriage of his illegitimate daughter to a provincial from nearby Calenzano and by his choice of Chirico as a name, since the ancient *pieve* of Capalle was dedicated to Saint Quirico or Chirico. They had no town house between 1427 and 1457, and although Francesco's widow Mea rented a town house in the 1440s, her son Chirico continued to declare himself 'without any job and I have always lived at the villa'.[72] In 1478 Chirico's widow Piera left her sons a house in Florence, and although this must have provided them with an urban alternative, their tax declarations of 1480 and 1498 still refer to Capalle as their

FRANCESCO DI TOMMASO SASSETTI (1421–1490) IS BEST KNOWN FOR HIS burial chapel in the church of S. Trinita in Florence, which is one of the finest examples of fifteenth-century chapel decoration surviving in its entirety (Fig. 117). Ghirlandaio's altarpiece remains in place, his fresco cycle covers walls, vault and entrance arch, while the tombs of Francesco and his wife still rest in their sculpted niches on either side. However, it is not only because of the survival of his chapel that Francesco Sassetti is often cited as a paradigmatic patron of the arts, for he is historiographically important. In a seminal article published in 1907, Aby Warburg investigated the 'inner architecture' or psychology of Francesco Sassetti as the archetype of a Florentine Renaissance patron: wealthy banker, Medicean protégé, friend of humanists, collector of manuscripts and ancient inscriptions, whose preoccupations were revealed not only in the imagery of his chapel, but also in a remarkable document recording his last wishes (*ultima volontà*) for his sons.[1] Although this document contains detailed instructions regarding Sassetti's great country palace, and makes it absolutely clear that its construction was his proudest achievement, Warburg failed to identify the villa, as did subsequent scholars.[2] This omission has had important consequences, as in what was one of the first and most influential studies of a Renaissance patron, Warburg established the persona of Sassetti as a man focussed exclusively on urban culture.

This study of the Sassetti therefore begins where Warburg left off. Its first purpose is to consider Francesco Sassetti in his familial context. Its second and most fundamental aim is to reestablish Sassetti and his family as both town and country residents, seeking in particular to resuscitate the rural element in their lives. The survey of property acquisition and estate management in the wider Sassetti family conducted in Chapter 9 provides the essential framework for the close investigation of Francesco Sassetti's surviving villa at La Pietra, which is carried out in Chapters 10, 11 and 12.

117. Sassetti Chapel, Florence, S. Trinita (photo: Conway Library, Courtauld Institute of Art).

9 · THE SASSETTI FAMILY AND THEIR PROPERTY

During the thirteenth century the Sassetti were prosperous merchants, established in the quarter of S. Maria Novella and one of the leading Ghibelline families in Florence. From the early fourteenth century, however, with the Guelf rise to power, they faded into political insignificance and were subsequently almost killed off by the plague of 1383. The ambitions of Francesco Sassetti need to be seen against this background. He was eager to show that he was not one of the *gente nuova*, but part of the old elite, and he was determined to regain wealth and political power in order to resuscitate his lineage.

A closer investigation of Francesco Sassetti's immediate family helps to explain not only the motives behind his patronage, but how he first entered the Medici orbit and therefore had greater opportunities to make a fortune and redefine his position in society. Above all, Francesco's wider family constitutes a yardstick against which to measure and evaluate his own property and patronage schemes. Thus, the scale and grandeur of Francesco's projects are starkly revealed in comparison with the careers of his two older brothers, Federigo (c. 1405–1463) and Bartolommeo (c. 1413–c. 1490). The three sons of Tommaso di Federigo Sassetti (died 1421) are exemplary cases of the contrasting fortunes that could co-exist within a single family of the merchant class: the eldest a failure, the middle brother representing average or ordinary success, the youngest brilliantly successful until his final years.[1] To summarise: Federigo ran into debt, had his only property confiscated, fled from the tax collectors

to Rimini, only returning to Florence to collect a long-awaited but meagre bequest that made him solvent again and allowed him to retrieve the vestiges of his landed respectability. Bartolommeo reaped the benefits of his elder brother's debts by acquiring Federigo's confiscated villa. He settled into the ancestral Sassetti houses in town and country and never strayed far from Florence. This caution was reflected in his investments and patronage. On the other hand, Francesco, the youngest, sought to excel, was highly prosperous for most of his business career, travelled widely and lived for many years abroad. On his return to Florence he sold one of his inherited houses and struck out towards fresh places. He bought most of his country land outside the traditional Sassetti areas and although the site for his new town palace was in the family quarter of S. Maria Novella, he moved to another parish within it – to S. Trinita rather than S. Piero Buonconsiglio. He never managed to build the new town palace he intended, but was prompt, determined and successful in carrying out his plans for a grand palace in the country.

Yet it is clear that while the three brothers' careers were so different, their fundamental attitudes to property were remarkably similar, and certain underlying patterns emerge. First, property-owning was regarded as an essential part of their social status and identity; its loss signified failure (as in the case of Federigo), its accumulation marked success (as Bartolommeo intimated), and the form it took was an expression of their personal style. Secondly, all three brothers sought to establish a balance between town and country property – it was not considered sufficient to have one without the other. Thirdly, they all, to some extent, attempted to preserve their links with old family districts.

FEDERIGO DI TOMMASO SASSETTI'S INHERITANCE

Tommaso di Federigo Sassetti, the father of Federigo, Bartolommeo and Francesco, remains a shadowy figure.[2] What little is known of him can be pieced together from the posthumous evidence left by members of his family. He died on 10 June 1421, having bequeathed his country estate of Macia near Novoli to his eldest son Federigo and his two palaces in town to be shared between his two youngest sons Bartolommeo and Francesco. A bakery and other town houses and shops were left to his widow Betta di Bartolo Pazzi,[3] and he made a lifetime endowment of his remaining town and country property to his brother Bernardo.[4] In addition, he stipulated that his three sons should share in providing the maintenance and dowry of his youngest daughter Pippa.[5]

Federigo, Tommaso's eldest son,[6] inherited the principal family villa at Macia but no property in town. In 1427 he was letting the villa and, at the age of twenty-two, was already feeling the lack of his own independent residence.[7] By 1430 Macia had become his abode,[8] although the mere fact that he was living outside the city can be interpreted as a sign of straightened circumstances. Nevertheless, he was able to lend 500 gold florins to his younger half-brothers on 4 January 1436 to pay their sister Pippa's dowry.[9] Although Pippa was only his half-sister, Federigo was obliged to contribute towards her maintenance until her marriage, on which occasion he had to pay one-third of her dowry in accordance with his father's will.[10] It may have been this very sum of 500 florins that tipped the balance of Federigo's fortune, for, instead of a cash repayment, it was agreed a year later, on 11 February 1437, that Bartolommeo and Francesco would renounce their claim to the inheritance due to them on their uncle Bernardo's death, which should all go to Federigo in lieu of the 500 florins they owed

him.[11] It is not clear why Bartolommeo and Francesco were unable to pay their share of the dowry, nor why Federigo was content to receive a distant promise of property rather than a prompt repayment in cash. For within a month of this agreement, on 19 March 1437, he was so much in debt that he had to transfer his only property, the villa of Macia, to Bartolommeo's name.[12]

By 1440 Federigo owed 400 florins to the commune and the *gonfalone*, as well as fines of 400 lire for not having paid his taxes.[13] In December 1440 the villa of Macia was confiscated by the *Sei delle Vendite*, who forced Bartolommeo to buy it back for the sum that Federigo owed the commune.[14] In his *ricordi* Bartolommeo emphasises his initial reluctance to carry out this deal, but claims that Federigo not only encouraged him to buy back the estate from the commune, thereby freeing Federigo from debt, but also requested that Bartolommeo give him a further 200 Venetian ducats to cover the full value of the estate. Bartolommeo paid this additional sum on 23 December 1441 and subsequently considered Macia as belonging rightfully and entirely to him. While Federigo later maintained that Bartolommeo had agreed to sell the villa back to him at a future date, Bartolommeo denied that he had ever expressed such an intention after paying the final 200 Venetian ducats.[15] These complex family wrangles over Macia and the extensive self-justificatory explanations in Bartolommeo's *ricordanze* make it clear that the ancestral villa was not only a valuable piece of real estate but was an important element in the Sassetti family's identity.

Federigo fled from his debt collectors to Rimini[16] and only felt able to return to Florence when his uncle Bernardo died and he came into his inheritance in 1444.[17] He then lived either with his sister in town or in the country while letting his own town property to pay debts.[18] By 1448 he was able to buy another small farm near Macia (which he resold in 1454 to his sister Caterina Bonbeni,)[19] and in 1456 he could afford to take part in the dummy purchase for 127 florins of Francesco's palace, which he looked after in Francesco's absence and subsequently sold back to him in 1460.[20] Nevertheless this semi-itinerant lifestyle, moving between a small country estate and relatives'

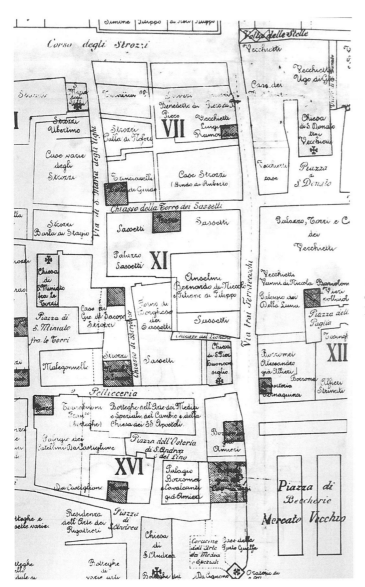

118. Map showing location of Sassetti town houses. Detail of Carocci's map of the area around the *Mercato Vecchio* in Florence, based on the 1427 *catasto*.

houses in Florence while living off the rent from his only valuable town property is characteristic of the poorer and indebted members of the land-owning classes, as the Strozzi examples have shown.

BARTOLOMMEO AND FRANCESCO'S SHARED INHERITANCE AND DIVISION

After the death of their father in 1421, Bartolommeo, aged eight, and Francesco, only three months old, were placed under the protection of the Ufficiali dei Pupilli, who appointed an administrator to manage their estate and keep their accounts.[21] Greater independence was achieved in 1428 when their mother, Mona Betta di Bartolommeo Pazzi, was elected their guardian (*attrice*), and thereafter Bartolommeo kept an account book for himself and his brother.[22]

All their property was in the parish of S. Pier Buonconsiglio, in the block bounded by the Via Ferravecchi (now the Via Strozzi) to the North, the Via del Chiasso del Forno del Borghese to the South, and the Chiasso della Torre dei Sassetti (now Via dei Sassetti) on the West side (Fig. 118).[23] It consisted of two neighbouring palaces. They lived in one on the Chiasso del Forno del Borghese, while the other, on the Canto di Borghese, was let.[24] Mona Betta was making repairs and additions to these houses and to the Forno del Borghese in the late 1420s, which Bartolommeo completed after his mother's death. Then aged about seventeen, these alterations provided Bartolommeo with his first experience of keeping building accounts.[25]

In 1430 the family rented a house in Rimini to escape an outbreak of plague in Florence, and they took up residence there on 9 July, intending to stay six months.[26] Mona Betta was taken ill with a fever, however, and died on 10 September.[27] On their mother's death, Bartolommeo and Francesco inherited the Forno del Borghese and another house on the Canto dei Ferravecchi with three workshops for smiths and metalworkers.[28] Although their estate was still nominally controlled by the Ufficiali dei Pupilli, Bartolommeo was now guardian (*attore*),[29] and it was possibly due to his prompting that, in May 1433, the Ufficiali dei Pupilli made a nominal division of the two brothers' property. The palace where they were living and the house on the Canto dei Ferravecchi with the smithies was apportioned to Francesco; while the palace on the Canto del Borghese, the bakery and one of the workshops was taken by Bartolommeo.

It is clear that, while on paper they each inhabited separate houses and therefore paid no taxes for them, they were still living together as one household under one roof. Since Francesco was only twelve at the time, it is unlikely he would set up on his own. Furthermore, Bartolommeo's *ricordo* makes it certain that this 1433 division was a tax dodge rather than an indication of the two brothers' desire to live separately:

Of this division I do not make particular mention because it was fictitious and we did it as a precautionary measure so that each of us could submit his own tax return, above all because we took the big house back from the tenants and each of us declared a house for his own habitation, which much reduced what we would have had to pay in taxes. Notwithstanding the said division we are still sharing, not only our income but all expenses as it apppears in our account books,

because we intend still to live together. But the real division was made between us in the year 1440.[30]

This document unequivocally demonstrates how tax legislation made it financially advantageous to break up the family group into separate, smaller households with each individual occupying more space, rather than sharing living quarters and letting the empty houses, which was no longer so profitable under the new regulations.

In March 1437 Francesco, aged sixteen, could officially take possession of his share of his mother's estate,[31] and it was he who instigated the actual division of their property in spring 1440 in preparation for his departure to Geneva. The decision was taken on 29 February 1440, and the division was ratified by a notary a month later,[32] with the property apportioned as it had been in the nominal division seven years earlier. In April, Bartolommeo bought Francesco's share of their slave Marta, together with the furniture and household goods. The final details were ratified on May 20, including Bartolommeo's pledge to pay Francesco's taxes during his absence.[33] Although the exact date of Francesco's departure for Geneva is not certain, it was probably in the last week of May 1440.[34]

Initially Francesco was employed as a clerk in the Medici bank in Geneva. By 1448, he was branch manager there and he continued in that employment until his return to Florence eleven years later.[35] After the 1442 levy it appears that Bartolommeo could not afford, or was unwilling to pay taxes on Francesco's behalf,[36] for in February 1446, the *Monte* officials forced the sale of half of one of Francesco's shops to his sister Ginevra to cover taxes that were mounting in his absence.[37] By early 1454 the dreaded Ufficiali delle Vendite had seized Francesco's main town house. To extract payment of the debt, they forced Bartolommeo to buy the palace by listing him as a debtor and threatening to ban him from public office until he had paid 500 florins worth of *Monte* credits to cover it. Having just held public office and no doubt unwilling to endanger his future eligibility, Bartolommeo carried this out in January 1454 and returned the house to Francesco who repaid him in July 1456. At this point, Francesco made a nominal sale of the house to his eldest brother Federigo so that Federigo would look after the property and pay taxes on it until his return.[38]

As Molho points out, the 1425 legislation that obliged a debtor's relatives to buy back his property for the amount owed to the commune, bound the family more tightly together in a network of financial obligation and dependence.[39] It was a law that both took for granted and enforced strong family bonds, although in the case of the Sassetti, this public fiscal policy induced strained relations between various members of the family.

BARTOLOMMEO DI TOMMASO SASSETTI'S LIFE AND PATRONAGE

Bartolommeo is not merely of significance as Francesco's only full brother, but is himself of special interest as the administrator of Medici building projects, as a close friend of the famous wit and cleric Piovano Arlotto, and as the writer of a series of *ricordanze* that provide rich documentation for his life over an unbroken span of thirty-six years from 1439 to 1475.[40] From these *ricordanze* Bartolommeo emerges as a continuously active rennovator and purchaser of furnishings to improve his properties in town and country. His art and architectural patronage (if that is not too grand a word for it) seems to have been mainly focussed on the domestic sphere.

Bartolommeo was probably born in 1413[41] and named after his mother's father, Bartolommeo di Beltramo Pazzi. In the 1440s and 1450s, while his younger brother Francesco was seeking his fortune as a Medici employee and partner abroad, Bartolommeo furthered his prospects working for the same family in a more modest capacity while earning political recognition and respectability at home in Florence. The earliest evidence not only for Sassetti employment by the Medici but also for the establishment of close and affectionate relations between the two families, is found in a series of letters from Bartolommeo Sassetti to Giovanni di Cosimo de' Medici written between 1437 and 1450.[42]

Bartolommeo's first letters, sent from Florence in August 1437 while Giovanni was staying at the Medici villa of Trebbio, set the tone of relaxed and affectionate intimacy combined with the respect due to one who was his employer.[43] From the letters it is clear that Bartolommeo was already working for Cosimo and Lorenzo de' Medici's household at this date,[44] since they partly serve as reports on business matters that crop up in Florence during Giovanni's absence. The early date for his employment is crucial, for if Bartolommeo were already working for the Medici by 1437, it is most likely that this contact procured his younger brother Francesco his job in the Medici bank in 1440.

By March 1441 Bartolommeo was working as paymaster or accountant for the building schemes at both S. Lorenzo and the new Medici palace since his surviving account book for both projects covers the twelve years from 1441 to 1453.[45] The letters to Giovanni di Cosimo, however, suggest that Bartolommeo was not taken on solely for the purpose of administering building projects, but was already employed as a private accountant or factotum who was on close terms with the family and in whom they invested complete trust. Not only did Bartolommeo receive money on Giovanni's behalf and deal with business correspondence in his absence,[46] he also took custody of Giovanni's prized musical instruments[47] and helped organise a hunting party for him and his friends in the hills above Altopascio in spring 1444.[48] Keeping the accounts for the building of the new church and palace was therefore just one part of Bartolommeo's job as an employee of the Medici household.[49]

The Medici connection gave Bartolommeo the corporate backing and steady income that made it easier for him to buy the villa of Macia from his brother Federigo. His payments to Federigo in 1440 and 1441 were debited to his account in the Medici bank. As a satellite in the Medici family orbit, it is not surprising therefore that Cosimo de' Medici was the mediator on Bartolommeo's behalf when he was betrothed to Antonia di Niccolo di Messer Baldo della Tosa in 1447.[50] Medicean influence must also have played a part in procuring public office for Bartolommeo who was the first Sassetti to do so when he was elected prior of the government in 1453.[51] His special pride in attaining high office is evident in his choice of Priore as the name for his first legitimate son, born in the following year.[52]

While Bartolommeo's public office marked his acceptance in Medicean political circles, his appearance in Piovano Arlotto's anecdotes gives the sense of his popularity in town. Messer Arlotto di Giovanni di Ser Matteo di Ser Mainardo (1396–1483), *pievano* of S. Cresci a Macioli, was a jovial cleric and witty raconteur whose reputation was established in his lifetime, long before the *Facezie* concerning his life were published in 1515.[53] In the *Facezie*, Bartolommeo is described as 'our virtuous compatriot, an important and trustworthy merchant, and close friend of our Piovano Arlotto',[54] a description that is corroborated in Bartolommeo's *ricordanze* where, apart from the writer himself, Arlotto is the person most frequently mentioned.

It is useful to look briefly at Bartolommeo's urban projects in order to establish the background for his rural schemes and to characterise his style of patronage. After his brother Francesco's departure for Geneva, Bartolommeo lived alone for seven years until his marriage to Antonia della Tosa in 1447. During the seven months between his betrothal on 6 February 1447 when vows were exchanged and 16 September when he presented the ring,[55] Bartolommeo made extensive alterations to his town house including the decoration of a new apartment to receive the bride. He may not have been able to afford a new palace, but within the space of a few months he transformed the interior of the old family house.

He demolished a section of the ground floor, providing in its place a new entrance portal with a projecting cornice, a hallway with a cross vault and another large *camera* with plastered brick vaults supported on stone console capitals. The comparatively inexpensive but thorough restructuring of the palace provided some of the new comforts and conveniences demanded in the mid–fifteenth century: an internal staircase, a new kitchen and lavatory, the introduction of a study (*scrittoio*), a new first floor *sala* constructed over the vaults of the ground-floor *camera* and new doorways to provide easier access from one room to the next and onto the *verone*, which functioned as an upstairs corridor. The dining and sleeping rooms were embellished with new wooden coffered ceilings and *pietra serena* stonework for doors, windows, fireplaces, *lavabi* and cupboards, all carved in the new *all'antica* idiom.[56]

While building was proceeding, Bartolommeo was buying new furnishings to make the bridal *camera* more luxurious. Its doorway was distinguished by the addition of a cornice resting on console brackets.[57] As usual, the new bed was a special feature with a gilt tin cornice around the tester provided by the decorative painter Chimenti di Lorenzo,[58] who also painted the wall around a tabernacle of the Madonna.[59] Two *cassoni* were acquired (one with walnut intarsia) and a cypress wood table.[60] Perhaps the most interesting item was a painting of the Madonna that was bought for the much higher price of forty lire from 'Domenico dipintore' on the 22 February, just over two weeks after the betrothal.[61] It is possible that this was Domenico Veneziano since the price, the date and the commission are compatible with his oeuvre.[62] That a stylish setting was provided for this marriage is also suggested by the fact that the bride's trousseau included a pair of painted marriage chests bought for thirty-two gold florins from the workshop of Apollonio di Giovanni, the most sought-after Florentine *cassone* painter.[63]

Antonia bore Bartolommeo four sons and four daughters of whom two sons and three daughters survived infancy. When Antonia died on 27 August 1470 Bartolommeo lost no time in marrying Cosa, widow of Piero Alinari and daughter of Antonio Tornaquinci.[64] It was probably the occasion of his second marriage that prompted Bartolommeo to demolish a small house between his palace and the Borghese bakery in order to build a new stairway with a stable underneath, as well as altering his own *camera* again and building a loggia or *verone* above the well.[65] Meanwhile, the growing independence of his two sons, Priore and Gentile, was marked by the creation of their own apartment within the family palace. In 1471, a storeroom in the Chiasso che va tra Ferravecchi was torn down to make way for the new ground-floor *camera* with a *scrittoio* and lavatory off it. Three *pietra serena* doorways were built to frame intarsiaed doors; in the *camera*, a coffered ceiling was constructed and intricately painted, and the walls were whitewashed, while the *scrittoio* next door was painted green.[66] The components of this new apartment with its own adjoining lavatory and study are very like those created by Niccolò di Carlo di Marcuccio Strozzi at Il Palagio just a year before.[67]

In 1476–7, elaborate preparations were made for the marriage of Bartolommeo's eldest son Priore to Alessandra di Francesco Dini. As in the case of his father, a nuptial chamber was decorated in the time between betrothal in October and the marriage in January.[68] The room had a new painted, coffered ceiling, an inlaid door with walnut veneer, a bed surrounded by chests with a canopy over it, and a *lettuccio* with a high back and prominent cornice (*capellinaio*).[69] There was a painting of the Virgin and Child with St. John the Baptist by Zanobi di Giovanni with an oil lamp lit before it,[70] and two large intarsiaed *cassoni* in the shape of sarcophagi[71] – the new type of *cassone* that was replacing the painted storiated decoration that had been fashionable when Bartolommeo first married thirty years before.

Bartolommeo's commissions to builders and artists seem to represent what was typical among Florentines of his means, and there is little to suggest that his links with the Medici or his brother Francesco formed his taste or inflated his ambitions. His schemes of building and decoration in town were closely tied to rites of passage in his family life. In particular, marriage provided the motive and the funds (in the form of the bride's dowry) to make improvements to his property.[72] Yet these were up-to-date rather than innovative, and in both town and country, he inhabited ancestral Sassetti properties and was content to carry out effective and rigorous alterations, rather than building from new foundations.

THE SASSETTI VILLA AT MACIA NEAR NOVOLI

The Sassetti villa is referred to in the fifteenth-century documents as Macìa or Novoli. It lay in the hamlet of Macia, halfway between Novoli and the Ponte a Rifredi, in the big parish of S. Stefano in Pane, three kilometres north-west of Florence (Fig. 119).[73] In the fourteenth and fifteenth centuries the area was sought after as a site for villas on flat, fertile land in a rural setting close to town,[74] but the district has now been separated from its original parish church by the construction of the main railway line, and the few early buildings are dwarfed by modern industrial and residential development. Stranded between the wholesale fruit and vegetable market and high-rise apartment blocks, Bartolommeo's villa, still known as 'Il Sassetto' or 'a Sassetti', is one of the few survivors (Fig. 120).[75]

By the late fourteenth century the estate appears in the *ricordanze* of Paolo d'Alessandro Sassetti, who describes how he went with his cousin Tommaso to measure the property in 1385.[76] Tommaso had inherited the estate jointly with his brother Bernardo, who was trading abroad in the 1380s and early 1390s[77] and accrued heavy debts as a result of failing to pay his taxes. Eventually Tommaso repaid Bernardo's debts and took possession of the estate, leaving one piece of land and a small labourer's house where Bernardo reluctantly lived.[78]

The estate that Federigo inherited in 1421 and passed on to Bartolommeo in 1441 included a land owner's house (*casa da signore*), a tenant farmer's house (*casa da lavoratore*), 106 *staiora* of farmland and an adjoining vineyard of four *staiora*. The main commercial crop was wheat, with some barley and sorghum cultivated for fodder, and wine.[79] The household benefitted from other fruits of the farm: a field of medlars (*nespoli*), fig trees planted between the vines, home-produced linen and a steady supply of pigeons from the *colombaia*.[80] The tenant farmers rented extra land from Bartolommeo on which they grew watermelons, pumpkins and turnips.

A detailed survey is needed to understand the structure and chronology of the *casa da signore* at Macia, but a brief examination of the most important architectural features may still be helpful.[81] The original nucleus of the house was the fourteenth-century tower with its enormously thick outer walls of *pietra forte* and quoins of *alberese* (Fig. 121). Although the tower has undergone many alterations, the regularity

122. Macia, U-shaped courtyard with portico now filled in.

and overall consistency of the stonework suggests that the greater part is original and only its upper storeys appear to have been transformed. Macia's other notable feature is its U-shaped courtyard enclosed on the north, west and south sides (Fig. 122). The north side survives without major transformation, its single, very wide arch resting on squat octagonal piers (Figs. 123 and 124). The loggia on the west side of the courtyard has been blocked up, but its octagonal piers are still visible (Fig. 125), revealing that an L-shaped loggia ran around the north and west sides of the courtyard. Continuity was achieved by maintaining the same height

for the wide arch on the north side as for the three narrower arches in the west loggia and by retaining the octagonal form for all the piers.[82]

The octagonal piers have simple chamfered capitals, a type that appears in Florence and its *contado* well into the fifteenth century as an alternative to the *foglie d'acqua* or shield capitals often found in combination with octagonal piers. The distinguishing characteristics of those in the west loggia of Macia are a bevelled abacus that projects strongly forwards above the neck and a narrow astragal moulding at the base of the neck to mark where the flat capital ends and the shaft of the

123. Macia, north side of courtyard, wide arch supported by two short octagonal piers.

124. Macia, short octagonal pier supporting wide arch on north side of courtyard.

pier begins. Other examples range from the staircase of the Palazzo da Uzzano (c. 1411–21),[83] to the courtyard of the Medici villa of Trebbio (c. 1422–33), to the Cortile della Dogana of the Palazzo Vecchio (begun from 1446, completed before 1469).[84] Although none of these corresponds exactly in its details to the form used at Macia,[85] the inexpensive, workmanlike solution to mark the transition between arch and pier and create a cushion to support the arch without carving a true capital is the same in each case. The traditional (undocumented) association of Michelozzo with the Medici villa of Trebbio and the Cortile della Dogana and his acquaintance with Bartolommeo Sassetti through the construction of Palazzo Medici makes the reappearance of this form tantalising, yet there is no evidence that Michelozzo contributed to renovations at Macia.

Nevertheless, examination of the documents does throw light on improvements to the villa. By 1399 the description of Tommaso Sassetti's wedding at the villa implies that the house was worthy of display,[86] and the possibility that Tommaso had renovated the villa before his death in 1421 cannot be dismissed. One of Bartolommeo's justifications for not returning the villa at Federigo's request in 1444 was that he himself had been cultivating the land and had done some building

125. Macia, west side of courtyard with filled-in portico.

there ('v'aveo murato e coltivato'.[87]) Although there is no record of large sums spent on construction in the years before 1444, Bartolommeo wrote a list nearly thirty years later, in 1471, of the major sums spent on alterations at Macia.[88] The most expensive repair was reroofing the *colombaia* at a cost of thirty-five florins. Another roof was raised to accommodate a new ceiling in an upstairs room. A vault was plastered, enclosed by walls and its doorway rebuilt. The ceiling of a north-facing room was lowered and a partition built to create a room that opened onto the *verone*, and an *anticamera* was built next to Bartolommeo's room. Although the descriptions in the document are not specific enough for them to be precisely matched with the present building, it is likely that the pigeon loft and granaries were incorporated into the main tower, and a newly constructed stair to the pigeon loft may well be the one enclosed in the projecting south wing of the courtyard (Fig. 126).

This list of alterations sheds light on a fundamental problem that arises when a villa is a farm. It is evident that the towers incorporated into many *case da signore* were used for storing crops, housing pigeons, drying flax and so on, and that the divisions between these agricultural areas and the living quarters were often scarcely demarcated. In the case of Macia, it seems that Bartolommeo's alterations were intended to make his habitation more comfortable and refined, thereby dividing his residential rooms further from the granaries, the pigeon loft and the tenant farmer's quarters. Instead of entering the *colombaia* directly from the *sala* by way of a wooden ladder as he had before, Bartolommeo had a new staircase built to provide separate access to the pigeon loft without having to go through the dining-hall. He also had a partition built to separate the granaries from an adjacent *camera*, and he removed the big oven from his own house and had one built in the tenant farmer's house instead. Improvements were made to the whole villa complex. The granaries and stables were rebuilt. A washhouse was erected beside the road, a new stable constructed for the tenant farmer, and new rooms, a fireplace and

126. Macia, projecting south wing of courtyard, enclosing staircase and well.

a front door added to the tenant farmer's house. It is clear that more menial functions such as washing clothes and baking bread were being removed from the *casa da signore* to be nearer to the *casa da lavoratore*, which was now provided with its own independent access from the road and its own stable. Thus, the list of alterations reveals that, for Bartolommeo, modernisation of his country residence meant creating a clearer division between habitation and agriculture, between the *signore* and his *lavoratori*.

We can only gain fragmented glimpses of the interior of the *casa da signore*. There is a reference to a *sala terrena* which confirms that dining and entertaining were not confined to the *piano nobile*. The account books once mention furniture destined for the *camera terrena* at the villa. In July 1462 Bartolommeo bought a bed with its frame, legs and chests to be attached around its base, and a settle (*lettuccio*) with its high back and cornice (*capellinaio*), all part of the same suite with a little intarsia decoration ('tutto con uno poco di tarsia'). They were bought for forty lire on a trial basis so that Bartolommeo could return them within two years and still receive thirty-eight lire back.[89] The phrase 'uno poco di tarsia' sums up an attitude to villa decoration, which should display a touch of elegance but not strain the pocket. It goes with the unadorned appearance of the courtyard loggia. This style was for those who embraced the cautious view that magnificence might be indecorous in a rural setting or was simply for those with limited means.

The garden (orto) at Macia was also improved by Bartolommeo. It may not have been comparable to Giovanni Rucellai's garden nearby at Quarracchi, for its pergola was only of wood, but it was enclosed by walls, its beds divided by low brick walls ('orticini murati'), with a well, a stone table for dining 'al fresco', as well as fruit trees and vegetables reserved for the use of Bartolommeo and his household.[90]

During the late 1420s and 1430s when the villa was still owned by Federigo, its fruits and accommodation were shared by all three brothers.[91] The villa provided a base for the whole family and their in-laws, as, for example, when their mother died in Rimini in 1430 and Bartolommeo and his sisters Pippa and Ginevra with her husband all stopped off on their return to Florence and spent three weeks recovering at the villa before moving into town.[92] However the convivial sharing of country life suggested by these joint accounts did not survive into the adulthood of Bartolommeo and Francesco. The villa of Macia was the bone of contention in a quarrel that divided Federigo and Bartolommeo and strained relations with Francesco too. That property, in this case a villa, should be the subject of family dispute and jealousy, can hardly be considered unusual. Yet the deep concern that Bartolommeo expresses in his *ricordanze* provides a particularly strong impression of the brothers' tenacious attitude towards this country estate:

> Below appears the way in which I bought the farm at Novoli which had belonged to my brother Federigo. After 1444 Federigo, having returned from Rimini to live in Florence, and having come to live in my house, said to me that he would like to have the said farm back and that he would return my money to me. And I replied that his request did not seem fair to me, especially because my taxes had increased so much and his had diminished, and

also because I had built there and cultivated the land. In the end he did not take it well and he began to argue saying that I had promised to give it back to him and we launched into a major quarrel, but here is not the place to describe it. . . .[93]

> It will never be found to be true or likely that I ever promised to Federigo to give it [the farm at Novoli] back to him. Even though he joined forces with Francesco to take it away from me. God will forgive them if they are worthy of it.[94]

The manifestation of sibling rivalry through property ownership is vividly conveyed by this quarrel. The situation arose because Federigo's and Bartolommeo's need of houses in both town and country had not been met in their father's will, nor was it acceptable for them to share the single country property now that they had wives and children of their own. Ultimately, the desire to own this particular house, which had belonged to their father and their ancestors and was a concrete symbol of their lineage, proved deep-seated and ineradicable. It is a recurring irony that the patrimony, which ought to cement the bonds of kinship, drove families apart; in this case, as so often, the appetite for possession proved stronger than brotherly love.

Bartolommeo Sassetti's Villa at Valcenni

If Macia satisfied Bartolommeo's need for a large country residence, reassuringly close to town, at the hub of Sassetti dynastic territory, then Valcenni was a radical alternative. Isolated from the city on a steep mountainside, on land that had to be broken in, with only rough labourers' houses to convert, this could be described as a pioneering venture. Bartolommeo Sassetti's accounts and *ricordi* covering the years 1463 to 1477 provide a detailed picture of how he set out to create a new villa that became the focus of his building activity and land purchase and cultivation during those years.[95] Valcenni lies on the south-eastern slopes of Monte Morello above the parish church

127. Monte Morello, with Valcenni visible as the last house up the mountain towards the right.

of S. Silvestro a Rufignano (Fig. 127). It is accessible from the districts of Quarto and Castello at the foot of the hill and from the Pieve of Sant'Andrea a Cercina across the Terzolle valley to the east. Today the name Valcenni still refers to two houses with their farms, which are probably the ones that Bartolommeo rebuilt.[96] Topographical references to the site (the position of roads, springs and hills) in the documents tally with those observable today. The upper house retains the tower mentioned in the building accounts, which appears on the late-sixteenth-century Capitani di Parte Guelfa Map (Fig. 128). This must have been Bartolommeo's 'casa da abitare'. Both houses retain other features that suggest an origin at least as early as the fifteenth century, for example, the thick walls and *alberese* quoins on the tower of the upper house (Figs. 129 and 130), the irregular shape of the lower house which is buttressed against the slope and follows the contour of the outcrop on which it perches (Fig. 131), and the massive jambs of the doors and windows (made of slabs of *alberese*) of the outhouse in the

yard beside the lower house (Fig. 132). Extensive alteration and restoration means that a precise reconstruction of their historic fabric would not be feasible; yet while this type of modest building is not easily placed within the history of architecture, it is a fundamental component in the range of fifteenth-century country buildings, as Bartolommeo's *ricordanze* so clearly illustrate.

The property at Valcenni consisted of many small, scattered pieces of land acquired gradually between 1463 and 1477 and consolidated into three farms. The nucleus of the estate was a tenant farmer's house with its farm and other pieces of land bought by Bartolommeo on 21 December 1463 for 300 gold florins from the three sons of a carpenter, Cerbino di Bartolommeo.[97] This was transformed into a house fit for Bartolommeo's own habitation (see Figs. 129 and 130). A second house, bought in October 1467 from the sons of Checcho Salucci,[98] was repaired for the tenant farmers' use and absorbed into the estate (see Fig. 131), and another group of fields in the vicinity

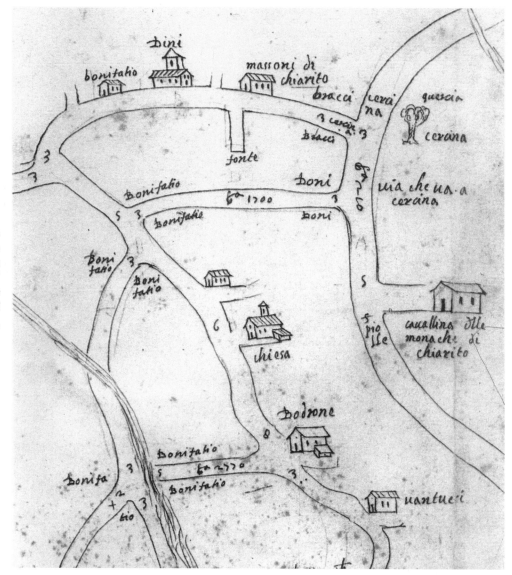

128. Parish of S. Silvestro a Rufignano, Valcenni at top with Bartolommeo Sassetti's houses marked 'bonifatio' and 'Dini'. Detail of *Piante di popoli e strade – Capitani di parte guelfa – 1580–1595*, II, c. 385.

was amalgamated to form a separate farm with a new *casa da lavoratore* known as Al Vallato.[99]

Building on the first farm began less than a month after purchase in January 1464. Loads of sand, lime, bricks, tiles, pipes and timber were hauled up to the site where the old *casa da lavoratore* was being renovated. A new roof was built, the tower was plastered, a portico was added in front of the *sala* and drains were laid. By springtime four new groundfloor windows with bars had been installed, wooden doors and more windows built.[100] In August the interior stonework, all carved in *pietra serena* (mostly by Camerata da Fiesole)

was complete, including two mantle pieces supported by consoles, an interior staircase, a frame for the *aquaio*, five windows, three doorways and a cupboard.[101]

For a more complete idea of the interior of a modest villa like this there are accounts for a secondhand bed surrounded by chests, a *panca* (bench) and a *lettuccio* (settle), all costing twenty lire, that is half of what he paid for a similar set of furniture for the grander villa at Macia.[102] Nor is there any sign of intarsia here. A year later Bartolommeo bought a new bed with two low chests,[103] a secondhand backrest with cornice and a low bench.[104] More interestingly, he also acquired

129. Valcenni di sopra, Bartolommeo Sassetti's 'casa da abitare' with a view of Florence in the distance.

130. Valcenni di sopra, the 'casa da abitare' rebuilt by Bartolommeo Sassetti in the 1460s.

131. Valcenni di sotto, one of Bartolommeo Sassetti's *case da lavoratore*.

three panel paintings of the Virgin. The first costing twelve *soldi* and including other figures, presumably saints, had *sportelli*, but we cannot be sure that its destination was Valcenni. The second, however, which only cost eight *soldi* and was 'molto vecchia' was intended for the maid's room at Valcenni; while the last and most expensive (thirty-three *soldi*) was for Sassetti's own use in the ground-floor *camera*.[105]

By far the greatest expenditure, however, was on breaking in and terracing the farmland, on the water system and on the enclosed gardens. The most time-consuming labour carried out on the new farm was the construction of drystone walls for which six Lombards and three locals were employed intermittently over four years from 1464 to 1468, building the walls when they were needed, as more livestock was acquired and more land was bought.[106] Eventually the gardens were protected by their walls, the animals separated from the crops and vineyards and the estate divided from the rough, wooded country beyond. Moreover, these were retaining walls, essential on a

steep hillside like this, where terracing was required and the material conveniently at hand. Along the tracks, in the woods and marking the terraces around Valcenni, today many crumbling drystone walls remain, the descendants of those first built by Sassetti in the 1460s.

The next lengthy task was the installation of a running water system, which served the farm as well as the garden and the house. In December 1464, a certain Donato Bocchi came to look for springs,[107] while another eleven men worked on building fountains or troughs (*fonti*) and pipelines or watercourses (*condotti*) around the estate.[108] Around the farm the abundant supply of water was channelled into a stone drainage canal with a system of tributary ditches.[109] There were at least three fountains ('la fonte disopra', 'la fonte disotto del salcio con la pila tonda', 'la fonte del botticino'), two of which were on the *pratello*, while the house itself was served with brass taps or spouts (*cannelle*) and the garden with copper spouts.[110] Like the drain pipes for the lavatory next to the tower

132. Valcenni di sotto, outbuilding next to the *casa da lavoratore*.

bedroom these features were a civilised amenity in the rustic setting.[111]

In October 1464 Bartolommeo acquired a vineyard just above his farmhouse with the intention of making a *pratello* and an *orto* there.[112] The *pratello* or meadow garden was an enclosed, landscaped garden for the use of the landowner's household that took shape during the summer of 1465 when earth was removed and the ground levelled and rolled. Stone walls were built around it with two gateways: a wooden one and a stone one towards the *orto*.[113] Later the gates were fitted with locks and keys. Two fountains were provided: a trough with a rose carved on it and the other a stone basin (*botticino*). Refinements were added in 1466 in the shape of low brick walls or benches (*muricciuoli*) to create flower beds, grass plots or paths, and seventeen cypress trees.[114] The *orto nuovo* was established after the *pratello*. It was freed of stones, tilled and enclosed in 1467. One of its gates led onto the *pratello* and the second onto the hillside. It is likely that this was the site of Sassetti's private vineyard, as the *orto vecchio* ('overo al vignuolo') certainly was.[115]

The farm was in full working order within two years of the initial investment. From spring 1464 stock was bought: a mule, a donkey and oxen, as well as a flock of twenty-seven sheep, twenty-seven lambs with the fleece still on them and a ram.[116] The sheep were shorn and sold at market or directly to a local butcher (although two lambs were retained at Easter to furnish Bartolommeo and his tenant farmer's pascal table).[117] Oxen and cattle were bought and sold in various market towns from San Piero a Sieve to Sesto.[118] The guano from the pigeon loft fertilised the farm, and the birds were eaten.[119] Arrangements were made to snare other birds, since hedges were specially planted in 1469 from which to stretch nets along one of the boundaries.[120] Brushwood (*legni di stipa*) and kindling were regularly supplied to individual buyers and to kilnsmen who provided Bartolommeo with lime, bricks and tiles in return.[121] There were crops of beans and wheat as well as the more important olive and grape harvests.

In enlarging the estate at Valcenni, Bartolommeo bought out a small holder Checcho Salucci and his sons Buono, Meo and Saluccio who had owned a farm and a number of scattered pieces of land there. After Checcho Salucci's death in October 1467, he was able to buy their *casa da lavoratore*, while their remaining land, with woods, broom thickets, olives and fig trees, was acquired in 1468 and 1469.[122] Meo Salucci

was the indispensable odd-job man at Valcenni, living in Bartolommeo's house and receiving a regular
salary 'to help build, to work as a labourer and other
things', those 'other things' ranging from fertilising
the fields to tying bundles of brushwood to digging
ditches. Although based at Valcenni, he appears in
Florence working on alterations to the town houses
and at Novoli hoeing in the garden. An idea of Meo's
movements and his position of trust within the family
is gained from a document that describes how, in June
1470, he took the Sassetti daughters from Valcenni
down to town in a cart and then spent a day working in
the *orto* at Macia before returning to the hills. In winter he chopped timber on the slopes above Valcenni
and repaired roofs in the valley at Novoli.[123]

In a comparatively isolated place like Valcenni,
supervision of employees and of a building project,
however small, is inconvenient. The main alterations
to the house were executed between January and August 1464, and during this phase the payments to suppliers and labourers on the site, and probably also
the process of construction itself, were supervised by
Messer Antonio, *pievano* of Sant'Andrea a Cercina.[124]
The *pieve* at Cercina lies at the same altitude about
four kilometres to the north of Valcenni and was directly connected to it by road. Not only did Messer
Antonio hold a position of local authority, but he was
also a close friend of Piovano Arlotto whose *pieve* was
over the next hill. Moreover, the employment of the
local priest to act as a paymaster on a country building scheme was not unusual. For example, the parish
priest of S. Piero a Quaracchi supervised the renovation of Matteo Strozzi's inn at Quaracchi in the 1420s,
and several priests oversaw payments for construction
at Poggio a Caiano in the late fifteenth and sixteenth
centuries.[125] Although Messer Antonio does not seem
to have played an active role at Valcenni after July
1464, his responsibility during the early stages of the
project implies that he may have originally encouraged
Sassetti's involvement in that district.

The network of friendships in this part of the *contado* probably contributed to Bartolommeo's choice
of site at Valcenni. Apart from the two genial priests
at Cercina and Macioli, the Baldovinetti family at

Calicarza were also part of the circle, and there were
regular interchanges between the estates at Valcenni,
Macioli and Calicarza.[126] The tavern at Uccellatoio
(just south of Pratolino) lay on the direct route between Calicarza and Macioli to the north-east and
Cercina and Valcenni to the south-west and is described as a favourite haunt of Piovano Arlotto's in his
motti e facezie.[127] Sassetti was clearly a friend and cus-
tomer too, since the innkeeper Antonio di Fruosino
was made godfather to his son Gentile, who was baptised at Calicarza in 1457. The innkeeper's elder son,
Agnolo, sold Bartolommeo wine, timber and lime,
and Piovano Arlotto arranged for the younger son
Chimenti to live with the Sassetti for nearly two
years while he learnt arithmetic.[128] Thus, the tavern
at Uccellatoio provided another link in the chain that
connected these friends and their country houses.

While Bartolommeo Sassetti was engaged in this
modest agricultural enterprise on the slopes of Monte
Morello, his younger brother Francesco was building
his country palace on a grand scale at La Pietra. The
contrast is striking. However clear the view of the
Florentine cupola is from Valcenni (see Fig. 129) and
however many mules and carts traversed this part of
the country in the quattrocento, even in its heyday it
must have remained a rustic alternative to life in town.
It is not clear from the documents how much time
Bartolommeo spent there. A brief reference mentions
food provided for the Sassetti family at Valcenni, and
there is the payment to Meo Salucci who carted the
Sassetti girls into town. As usual, evidence for people's
behaviour – and therefore, for architectural function –
is scarce. Yet it is clear from the description of the farmhouse as the 'casa da abitare' that it was intended for
Bartolommeo's own habitation.[129] Nor is it likely that
he would have spent so much and employed gangs of
workers to build and continually improve the gardens
and fountains and to introduce the carved stone features in house and garden, not to mention the odd
painting and piece of furniture he acquired for the
house, had he not intended to visit and stay on the
estate.

But the main reason for owning a secondary villa
of this sort was clearly agricultural. Bartolommeo

already owned an estate close to town, with a large house and the provisions that the valley could supply. It was to Novoli that the family repaired frequently and for longer stretches of time. Valcenni was valuable for its products, which were scarce near Florence: olive oil, firewood and livestock, especially sheep. A hill farm would also complement his principal villa in other respects by providing solitude, a simpler lifestyle, healthier air and wide views. Nor are plausible motives for choosing this particular area hard to find. The land high on Monte Morello seems to have been cheap, although that saving needs to be set against the cost of rebuilding and improvements necessary in a less intensely cultivated district. The site also had the advantage of being isolated from Florence by the steep gradient of the hillside, yet close as the crow flies and within sight of town. The plentiful supply of spring-water and building stone (*pietra forte* and *alberese*) were great assets.

Like Filippo Strozzi's scheme at Maglio in the Val di Bisenzio (begun in the 1480s), the creation of a new estate in high country at Valcenni meant the coordination of construction, agriculture and landscaping for an integrated villa project. Unlike most valley farms and villas near town, these were not ready-made estates. Steep slopes had to be terraced, water supplies channelled, open country enclosed, rough ground domesticated for gardens, and a hierarchy of buildings reconstructed to cater for the new class of owner, his tenants and their livestock. The simultaneity of these undertakings and the level of investment accorded each, underline the extent to which buildings, gardens, farms, and the wider untamed landscape were all fused in a unified vision of the rustic villa.

10 · FRANCESCO SASSETTI'S VILLA
AT LA PIETRA

Bartolommeo Sassetti's villas can be seen as a foil against which to view his younger brother's magnificent palace at La Pietra. Bartolommeo's policy was a conservative one. His biggest acquisition — that of Macia — was forced on him by the tax officials and it only took one further payment to secure the estate for his own exclusive use, thereby providing him with the rural equivalent of his ancestral house in town. His alterations to Macia were on a similar modest scale to those he carried out in town. His major construction project was the rustic villa of Valcenni, which could hardly have been in greater contrast to the scale and grandeur of La Pietra. Francesco Sassetti, on the other hand, made a deliberate move away from his ancestral rural district and away from his brothers. His brothers' quarrel over the family estate at Macia may even have led him to react against the traditional type of villa and spurred him on to a new conception of a country house that would be removed from his immediate family and in another class altogether.

HISTORY OF OWNERSHIP: THE MACINGIII, THE SASSETTI, THE CAPPONI

Francesco Sassetti returned to Florence from Geneva in 1459.[1] Conditions were ripe for him to build. He had amassed a fortune as branch manager of the Medici bank[2] while it was still profitting from Cosimo's firm management,[3] and in Geneva where the Florentine bankers held a monopoly over the exchange shops during the golden age of the international fairs there.[4] His assets were mainly in the accessible form of money held on term deposit in the Medici banks of Geneva and Milan.[5]

His landed property did not yet reflect this prosperity since he had acquired nothing in Florence during his absence, and his estate remained essentially that which he had inherited from his father: two houses, one of which he had nominally sold to his brother Federigo, and several shops in town.[6] Thus, it was probably because he had no country holdings that the first property he bought after his return was a villa near the hamlet of La Pietra in the district of Montughi.[7] Besides, if he had an urge to build, he could take advantage of the fact that it was easier and quicker to find a large site in the country. Finally, this speedy acquisition of property shows Francesco eager to reestablish himself in his hometown and to advertise himself as a man who had made his fortune and deserved a prominent place in society.

When Francesco bought the villa at Montughi from the sons of Carlo Macinghi on 7 April 1460, the notarial document of sale described the estate as:

> A farm with a house or palace for the landowner's residence, with a farmhouse, an oil press, a partly walled garden, a meadow garden, with tubs for the wine harvest, barrels, wine vats, wine press, olive press, and all the other necessary equipment to process the fruits of the said farm; and with arable land,

vineyards, olive trees, orchards, with fruit trees and other trees, situated in the parish of S Marco Vecchio, in the district of Florence, in the place called Montughi or Le Citine, bounded on the first side by the road, on the second by land belonging to Bartolomeo di Ser Santi, on the third by property belonging to the hospital of Messer Bonfiazio Lupi, on the fourth by property belonging to the Chapter of S Lorenzo in Florence. . . . With all the rocky caves, clumps of bushes,[8] ditches and the other things belonging to the said property.[9]

The name Le Citine also appears in 1344 in the earliest known reference to the villa where it is listed in the parish of S. Marco Vecchio as a 'podere cum domo, curia, furno' called 'alle Citine'.[10] Le Citine was the name given to the barren strip of land in front of the second circle of city walls (from c. 1172), created as a defensive measure to expose the enemy when approaching Florence.[11] This name is never referred to in Sassetti's time, however, when it was simply called the 'casa' or 'palagio di Montughi', and the abandonment of the old name may partly relate to the reconfiguration of that area when the new city walls were built, or, in Sassetti's case, to his orienting the main entrance of the villa towards the milestone on the Via Bolognese rather than looking south towards Florence with its defensive system. The house continued to be referred to in the sixteenth, seventeenth and eighteenth centuries as the Palazzo of the Sassetti at Montui or Montughi,[12] and it was not until Arthur Acton took up residence from 1903 that its name became Villa La Pietra.

It is significant that the house was referred to as a 'palagio' by the time the Macinghi's first tax return was filed in 1427,[13] as it still was when they sold it to Sassetti in 1460. This suggests that the house was already large and imposing. The original house was probably built by Zanobi di Neri Macinghi, who had made a fortune in Naples and returned to Florence where he was elected prior in 1393.[14] However by the late 1420s Zanobi Macinghi's son Carlo was not well-off,[15] and from the early 1440s the next generation was

deeply in debt.[16] It was to pay the dowry of one of Carlo's daughters that the Macinghi brothers, Zanobi, Neri, Ruggiero and Francesco, sold their only valuable piece of real estate, the villa at Montughi, to Francesco Sassetti on 7 April 1460 for 1625 *fiorini di sugello*.[17]

Soon afterwards, Francesco bought the two adjacent farms, thus forming one sizeable property. He bought the first from Alesso Lapaccini on 8 April 1462 for 427 florins and 8 *soldi* and the second from the hospital of Messer Bonifazio Lupi on 31 January 1463 for 531 florins. The new estate at La Pietra was now consolidated. Its boundaries remained the same not only during Sassetti's life but through the succeeding centuries until the present day, defined by the Via Bolognese, the Vicolo or Via di San Marco Vecchio and lands belonging to other owners in the south.[18]

In 1485 Francesco gave La Pietra to his son Federigo, then aged thirteen and destined for a career in the church.[19] However, Federigo died less than two years after his father, in December 1491,[20] and the estate was then left to be shared among the remaining sons Galeazzo, Cosimo and Teodoro II. This arrangement proved impractical, for in 1499 a document of division was drawn up to separate the house and land into three equal parts.[21] This solution survived until 1545, by which time both Galeazzo and Cosimo had died,[22] and while Cosimo had no children of his own,[23] one of Galeazzo's sons was in prison, leaving Filippo di Galeazzo and Teodoro II with his son Giovanbatista to make the decision to sell. This decision was ratified in April 1545,[24] and the villa with all its lands was sold on 19 August 1545 to Piero di Niccolò Capponi.[25] The terms were not favourable for the Sassetti since it was sold for the sum of 3,500 florins to Piero Capponi, who could not afford to pay the full amount but needed a loan from his uncle Giuliano di Piero; even then he paid by instalments, which were still kept up by Piero's heirs, at a fairly low interest rate of 6%, until at least 1615.[26]

Piero's son Francesco Capponi (1540–1615) was well known for his horticultural interests, and after his death, his heirs continued to cultivate and construct what must have been a beautiful and well-appointed garden.[27] Between 1616 and 1624 they enlarged the *stanza dei vasi* with a new roof and four windows with grilles; they repaired the *conserva*, levelled the *prato* before the house to be embellished by statues of lions on pedestals, stone benches and cypresses; they planted a chestnut wood, reared silkworms, pruned elaborate hedges or plants trained against a trellis (*spalliere*) and a *ragnaia* of elm; and they laid gravel for a bowling court (*pallottolaio*).[28] The first cypress avenue at La Pietra may even date from October 1612 when 102 cypress plants were bought from the friars of S. Maria Novella.[29] At the same time improvements were made to the interior of the house, and payments for six new stone doorways, bricking up around doors to the ground-floor *camere* and other new doors, may relate to a payment in 1622 to the architect Gherardo Silvani for 'a drawing for the said doors and renovations'.[30] These accounts probably refer to the conversion of the fifteenth-century loggia into a long vaulted room with baroque strap work and six doorways. Recent research by Mary Ellen Hoelscher Lawrence reveals that Scipione di Piero di Francesco Capponi employed Gherardo Silvani again between 1653 and 1665 to make further improvements to the house and gardens, whereas the raising of the roof with its new balustrade and exterior veneer were probably carried out for Francesco Pier Maria d'Alessandro Capponi by Innocenzio Giovannozzi *ingegnere* in the early 1750s.[31] Considering that the Capponi had the means and the ambition to build big palaces and villas and owned a large number of houses, it is significant that La Pietra remained in that family and retained its fifteenth-century structure. It stayed in their hands until Gino Capponi died without male heirs in 1876, when it was left to the children of his daughter Hortensia Incontri,[32] who rented it to Hortense and Arthur Acton in 1903 and sold it to them in 1907.

THE SITE

The enduring beauty of the villa at La Pietra owes much to its location. Montughi was the name given to the hillside that rises between the Mugnone and the Fosso della Lastra above the Porta San Gallo.[33] The ancient road north, the Via Bolognese,[34] runs up this hill, dividing the cluster of villas around what is now the Museo Stibbert and the Pazzi villa at Montughi (in the parish of S. Martino a Montughi) on the west side, from the area associated with the hospice of Pellegrino and the Bruni and Sassetti estates (in the parish of S. Marco Vecchio) on the eastern slope (Fig. 133). One mile from the city walls, the road curves around at the point where the Roman milestone is traditionally said to have been placed.[35] In the fifteenth century there was a hamlet there, and the spot was referred to as 'la Pietra al Migliaio', now simply abbreviated to La Pietra.

That the entrance to Sassetti's estate was here, on the Via Bolognese, is suggested by the the fifteenth-century document of division that refers to the 'loggia sulla strada alla pietra al migliaio'.[36] Such a loggia would almost certainly have served to mark the entry point to the villa, which was set a third of a mile back from the road. A glance at the map illustrates how an avenue runs from the hamlet of La Pietra straight to the centre of the palace façade. It is likely that the 'viottolo' mentioned in the 1499 division[37] is the same 'viottola' the Capponi embellished with a new gateway in the seventeenth century[38] and was in the same position as the driveway that survives today (Fig. 134).[39] While it is almost certain that the Macinghi house was on the same site and that its walled garden and *pratello* were taken over by Sassetti for the same purpose, it is clear from a comparison of the boundaries of the Macinghi property with those added when Sassetti purchased the neighbouring farms that the Macinghi did not have access to the Via Bolognese. It was only with the purchase of the third farm in early 1463, described as being 'in sulla strada grande della Pietra al Migliaio', that Sassetti's land was extended as far as the main road.[40] It was therefore Sassetti who planned to maximise the site in this way. He bought the farmland that lay between the Macinghi property and the Via Bolognese, he marked the entry to his estate at La Pietra with a loggia, and created a long straight path or driveway that allowed the visitor to make a dignified approach and appreciate the splendour of his palace from a distance. This is an early example of a strategy that takes full advantage of the large space available in the country to create a finely controlled, ceremonial approach.

133. Map of Montughi district with the Via Bolognese running northwards up the centre and Francesco Sassetti's villa marked 'V.la la Pietra'.

134. Villa La Pietra, west façade with avenue from 'la Pietra al Migliaio' to the house.

Furthermore, an understanding of the overall design and orientation of the fifteenth-century house is greatly enhanced when seen in relation to an approach from the milestone. Le Citine, the old name given to the pre-exisiting house in the fourteenth-century documents, implies that the house originally faced Florence and its fortified walls, whereas Sassetti reoriented the newly constructed villa towards the milestone on the Via Bolognese. The design of the house with two of its grand *sale*, together with its main *androne* and interior doors on axis, all opening towards 'la Pietra al Migliaio' confirm the importance of this link. Besides, a strategic entry from the milestone must have held special significance for a man whose name was stones, albeit little stones – *sassetti*. The presence of the first Roman milestone beyond the walls of Florence and the name given to that location may even have enticed Francesco to buy this villa in the first place. 'La Pietra al Migliaio' could become a ready-made family emblem, as he appropriated a very public and universally recognisable marker as his own personal sign. This could be interpreted as a larger scale pun of the type Sassetti was later to employ in

his burial chapel in S. Trinita, and it is unfortunate that nothing survives of the roadside loggia that would undoubtedly have incorporated coats of arms and devices with many stones.[41]

The palace itself was situated at the top of a rise, beyond which the land dropped sharply towards the Via Faentina in the Mugnone valley. This commanding site afforded fine views in all directions: towards Monte Morello in the west, to Fiesole in the north, over Camerata to Vallombrosa in the east and down to Florence itself with its cathedral dome visible to the south. La Pietra was so close to town that it could be used as a principal residence and it was certainly suitable for long and frequent visits and for entertaining friends at short notice. It had the double advantage of being easily accessible, yet at the same time removed from the noise, the congestion and the public life of Florence. It is easy to imagine that the site on the Via Bolognese provided travellers from the north with a refreshing stopover before descending into town. Certainly Francesco's business and his most important contacts were in the north – he was frequently on the move in that direction himself – and his

135. Villa La Pietra, walled garden on the north side of the house.

great-grandson said that Bolognese visitors were 'looked after and given lodging in his house and magnificently entertained and fed', for which he was made an honorary Bolognese citizen in 1484.[42]

THE GARDENS

Unfortunately, little information has come to light regarding the fifteenth-century gardens. There was already a partly walled garden (*orto*) and a meadow garden (*pratello*) in the Macinghi's time, but their location is not specified. The 1499 division of the Sassetti estate is slightly more helpful. There were specially designated areas of garden, each with its own character. The east side of the house facing towards the slope was paved ('il lastrico che guarda verso Camerata'). This must have been a terrace from which to admire the view across the Mugnone to Camerata and beyond. From the evidence of the document of division it is most likely that the *orto* was on the north side of the house where the walled garden is today (Fig. 135).

There were *pratelli* in front and behind the house. From the *pratello* on the west side facing towards La Pietra, an *anghuillare*, or row of vines, ran on either side ('di qua et di là') to the gate on the main road. This was probably the same as the 'anghuillare del viottolo', also mentioned, which suggests that the avenue to the house was flanked by vineyards.[43]

THE FARMS

The farmland surrounding the palace at La Pietra was an essential part of the estate. It not only served to set off the house in a wider space, to ensure privacy and to stake out a claim in the district; but its farms also provided a useful, and fairly profitable quantity of wheat, wine and olive oil. After buying the two extra farms in 1462 and 1463, Sassetti declared them as part of the one estate: 'Tutti i sopradetti poderi sono insieme', and together their value was capitalised in the 1469 tax return at over 750 gold florins, that of one large farm.[44]

The farmland was served by its outbuildings: a stable with a threshing yard, a dovecote, enclosures for hens and rabbits, an oil press and three houses for tenant farmers.[45] While there was a high turnover of tenant farmers under the Macinghi,[46] their last *lavoratore*, Mechero di Nanni detto Pecorino, must have stayed on to work for Sassetti and may have received better treatment from him, since we find his sons Nanni and Benedecto were still farming the estate in 1498,[47] and in 1499 Nanni witnessed the act of division of the farmland at La Pietra.[48] After Francesco's death his sons claimed that a factor was needed to run the estate.[49] The provision of a room for the factor in the villa suggests that a bailiff was already in residence in Francesco's day and the Capponi still employed estate managers at La Pietra in the seventeenth and eighteenth centuries.[50]

It is notable that, although two new farms were added to the original eighty *staiora* owned by the Macinghi, the yield did not even double in quantity. Sassetti received forty-eight rather than thirty *staia* of wheat, about the same amount of oil and roughly double the quantity of wine (fifty barrels).[51] Moreover, he and his sons continued to complain to the tax-officials that the land cost them more than it produced and, taken together with the upkeep of the house, it was an expensive property and a drain on their income.[52] While this should be read as a conventional plea to tax officials, by comparison with Sassetti's other estates at Gonfienti and Casi, La Pietra was certainly a poor investment, which could not be justified in purely financial terms. Indeed, here it is clear that the land was subordinate to the house. It might be said that the ideal balance between house and land, recommended by Alberti,[53] had been lost. This may partly explain why Francesco bought his big farms at Gonfienti and Casi; why, as soon as financial trouble hit, he was aware that La Pietra would have to go;[54] and why the disproportionate size of the palace site was claimed as an excuse to the tax men.

THE BUILDING HISTORY

Although no building accounts survive for La Pietra and only sparse references have been found so far, it is still possible to establish the decade within which the house was rebuilt. Having bought the original palace with its farm in April 1460, Francesco Sassetti probably began building within two years of purchase, and construction was certainly under way soon after the next farm was acquired in April 1462, for on 3 May of that year, Piero di Lapo del Tovaglia was appointed as Francesco Sassetti's procurator to supervise the construction of the villa ('pro muraglia quam facit in loco suo a Montug[h]i') while Francesco was absent from Florence. As the Gonzaga agent in Florence, Piero del Tovaglia later played an active role supervising the design and construction of SS. Annunziata in Florence. The new evidence from La Pietra reveals that Piero was already experienced in overseeing a construction project for an absent patron when he was made Lodovico Gonzaga's procurator in 1470.[55]

A valuation of his whole estate was summarised in Francesco's *Libro segreto*,[56] and although it is dated November 1462, it cannot have been completed before early 1463 because it includes the third farm bought on 31 January 1463. This list includes 2,000 florins (*di sugello*) worth of furnishings (*masserizie*) divided between the town house and the villa, which may suggest that part of La Pietra was completed at this date or that part of the old Macinghi house was retained and inhabited. *Masserizie*, however, can refer to anything from large pieces of furniture to tableware that could have been bought in anticipation or stored at the villa. Moreover, the fact that the La Pietra estate is valued at exactly the same price that Francesco paid for the three properties (ie, 2,697 *fiorini di sugello*) makes it unlikely that much building had taken place.

Four years later another summary, dated 27 November 1466, was made in the *Libro segreto*.[57] This time the furnishings in town and at the villa were worth 3,500 *fiorini di sugello*, the estate at La Pietra was valued at 5,000 *fiorini di sugello* and the building process is referred to as: 'Le possessioni di Montughi con la caxa dove s'è murato', While this use of the perfect tense should not be taken as evidence that the building was definitely complete by that date, it is certain that some construction had already taken place and at least 2,303 florins had been spent. This may not seem a large sum, especially when compared with the

12,000 florins that Francesco's great-grandson claimed had been spent on the villa.[58] We can perhaps assume that construction and decorative refinements continued during the late 1460s and that a considerably larger sum was spent.[59]

One further document from the 1460s can be plausibly connected to Francesco Sassetti's campaign of building and decoration at La Pietra. On 21 July 1464 an agreement was drawn up between Francesco Sassetti and Giovanni di Domenico *legnaiuolo*, according to which the carpenter would provide wood, labour and drawings ('designis') for Sassetti.[60] Although there is no mention of the villa in the notarial record, this is the only known building project in which Sassetti was involved at the time. Giovanni di Domencio *legnaiuolo* is almost certainly Giovanni di Domenico da Gaiole, who had close connections with the Medici and in the same year, 1464, was carving the wooden seat and backrest for the east wall of the sacristy in Florence cathedral.[61] The drawings he made for Sassetti might have been for coffered ceilings, benches or any other woodwork, rather than architectural drawings or plans. Although Gaiole claimed architectural expertise when he criticised Manetti's designs for the cupola of S. Lorenzo (for which he himself had originally submitted a model) in 1457, and he became *capomaestro* at S. Spirito from 1460 to 1461 and submitted a model for the tribune of SS. Annunziata in 1471, we have no evidence of designs for domestic architecture executed by him.[62] In any case, this new evidence fits neatly into what we already know about Giovanni da Gaiole as a provider of wood, as a virtuoso carver and designer of wooden fittings (especially benches and ceilings), and as one who obtained a series of prestigious commissions on important public buildings in the Medici orbit. For Sassetti, it provides us with the only name of an artisan who can be linked to the villa project; it tends to confirm that building and decoration were underway in the mid-1460s, and it hints at the luxury with which this interior was furnished.

By the 1470s it is most likely that the villa was complete and inhabited.[63] It is referred to in letters; it is the place where family marriage contracts were signed, and it had become a subject worthy of literary praise. Of the few letters by Francesco surviving from these years, a note written to Giuliano de' Medici on 31 August 1472 was sent from La Pietra down to Florence saying that Francesco would certainly have come to discuss a matter with Giuliano if he had thought it necessary, and he would in any case see him tomorrow if Giuliano had not already left Florence,[64] giving the sense that while Francesco was based at the villa he made frequent trips into town. As a postscript to Fonzio's letter of 11 April 1478 to Francesco Gaddi in Rome asking for medals for Cosimo Sassetti, the eldest son Teodoro Sassetti added a note on his own account to remind Gaddi of the deal they had arranged together, saying that he could fulfill his part of the exchange (of books? medals? or antiquities?) either in Florence or at La Pietra ('et promettovi ristorarvi delo schanbio o a Firenze o a Montughi quando vi sarete').[65]

Francesco Gaddi must have been just one of many distinguished visitors to the villa. Indeed, the writings of the humanist scholars Ficino, Fonzio and Verino all testify to the villa's magnificence and fame,[66] and it is possible to link some of these passages to the period when the palace was newly built and first attracted widespread admiration. The early 1470s were the years when Francesco developed his friendship with the young humanist Bartolommeo Fonzio. They may have met by the end of 1471 when Fonzio returned from the Este court in Ferrara, and their trip to Rome together probably took place in the spring of 1472.[67] In the autumn of 1473 Fonzio accompanied Donato Acciaiuoli on a diplomatic mission to France,[68] and it was on this occasion that he composed a series of epistolary poems written to his friends and mentors in Florence. In a poem addressed to Niccolò Michelozzi, he says how much he is missing Sassetti, his wife Nera and their children and how he is looking forward to return to them at La Pietra, which is worth more to him than France.[69] In another poem dedicated to Bartolommeo Scala, Fonzio introduces La Pietra and Sassetti's other estate at Gonfienti as the prime examples of grand, expensive country estates.[70] Finally, in a poem written to Sassetti himself, Fonzio cites La Pietra and Gonfienti as the most splendid examples of Sassetti's patronage, the fruits of his well-earned wealth, built to the glory of his family lineage.[71]

Ficino's undated letter describing the twin chapels in Sassetti's palace, which almost certainly refers to La Pietra, is one of a group (Liber V) that Kristeller states was mostly written between September 1477 and April 1478.[72]

On 29 August 1473 the marriage contract between Francesco's niece Fiammetta (whose father Federigo had died ten years before) and Simone Pulci was drawn up at the villa,[73] and although there is no evidence that this was where the feasting took place, it may indicate that this was Sassetti's summer residence by then. Nearly ten years later, on 27 September 1482, Francesco's eldest daughter Sibilla exchanged marriage vows with Alessandro Pulci at La Pietra.[74]

THE PLANS: VASARI THE YOUNGER AND TODAY

Among the plans of palaces and villas made by Vasari the Younger c. 1600 there is one of La Pietra, labelled 'Palazzo del S.[igno]re Franc[esc]o Capponi a Montui Luogo detto a' sassetti con un' prato dinanzi, e uno dietro' (Fig. 136).[75] As the earliest surviving plan of the house this is clearly an indispensable document. However since Vasari the Younger's plans are notoriously inaccurate and ruthlessly regularised, it should not be taken in isolation and used in an attempt to reconstruct the villa rebuilt by Sassetti some 140 years before; but when compared with the earlier documents and with the house today, Vasari's plan assumes a central position in the chain of evidence. The document of division made in 1499 by Francesco Sassetti's sons lists all the rooms and can be taken as a faithful description of the house as it was rebuilt in the 1460s. There is a close and legible correspondence between this document and Vasari's plan which suggests that major changes were not made to the structure between 1499 and 1600. Moreover, when both the division and Vasari's plan are compared with the present house it becomes clear that the essential structure of Sassetti's palace still survives today.

Two major structural alterations postdate Vasari's time and are immediately apparent in the modern house. The transformation of the ground floor loggia opening off the courtyard into a large enclosed room was carried out by the Capponi in the seventeenth or eighteenth century, perhaps at the same time as they gave the exterior its baroque face-lift. Then, in the late nineteenth century, a huge elliptical staircase was constructed, almost entirely enclosing the old courtyard (Figs. 137 and 141, room no. 23), except for its corners which were tucked out of sight behind the curving walls of the new 'rotunda' (Fig. 140). In addition, the staircase drawn by Vasari on the north side of the courtyard was removed and replaced by corridors on the ground and first floors (Figs. 137, 138, and 139, room nos. 21, 35 and 57).

If we compare the plan of c. 1600 with a modern plan of the house, the differences and similarities emerge. Vasari has drawn the outer structure and the rooms within as regular rectangles, whereas the whole villa is a trapezoid and many of the rooms have slightly irregular shapes. He shows the house to be deeper than it is wide, with the shape of the courtyard reflecting those proportions. In fact the house is slightly wider than it is deep, and the original courtyard was almost square. In Vasari the Younger's plan the walls are of uniform thickness, whereas they vary considerably in the actual structure. He has also left two interior spaces undivided, although the surviving fifteenth-century vaults show that they were each divided into two smaller rooms (see room nos. 8, 9, 13 and 14). On inspection of the house and the modern plan (see Fig. 141), the narrow service areas shown by Vasari on the south side of the house hollowed out in the space between the *androne* (7) and the *camera* (5) appear to be a solid thick wall. In many other respects, however, there is a remarkable similarity between the two ground plans. In both cases the courtyard is not placed centrally, but somewhat to the north and towards the back of the house, which also means that the entrance is placed slightly to the left of the main façade. The room disposition has remained fundamentally the same and its clarity is equally legible on both plans. Three long hallways (1, 7, 15) lead from the exterior to the open space in the centre, and the ground-floor loggia (now enclosed (11)) functions as another transitional space. These are the main arteries of the house, linking the gardens with the courtyard and the various

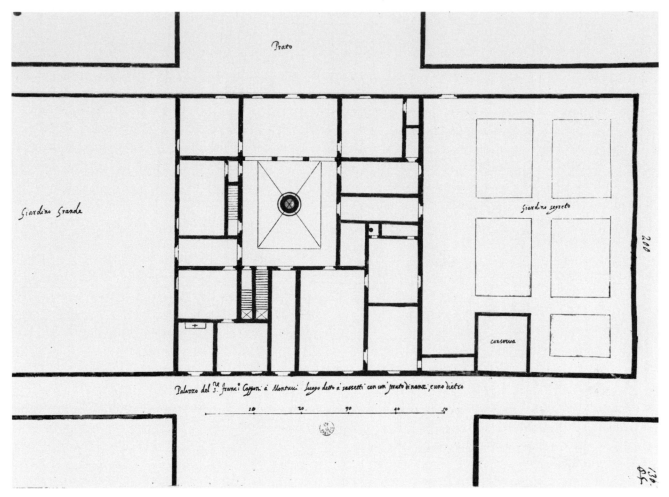

136. Vasari the Younger, ground plan of Villa La Pietra, c. 1600. Uffizi, Gabinetto Disegni e Stampe 4914 (photo: Ministero per i Beni e le Attività Culturali, Soprintendenza Speciale per il Polo Museale Fiorentino, Gabinetto Fotografico).

parts of the interior, but they also serve to divide the whole ground floor into four apartments, with one large and two or three smaller rooms in each quarter. This arrangement is at its most symmetrical in the way the loggia is balanced by the square rooms that open off it on either aside, leading to their attendant anterooms and to the *androni* beyond.

Although the villa at La Pietra is trapezoid in plan, this irregularity is not apparent in three dimensions. To the visitor on the site it appears to be a geometrically regular, compact block. Certain features reinforce this sense of symmetry. Even before entering, the eye is caught by the vista through to the end of the house and the light beyond since the doors are on

axis allowing a view through the sequence of spaces. Whereas the exterior shape of the house only seems to be square, the measurements of the original courtyard show that it was very nearly square.[76] Indeed, on examining the modern plan, certain irregularities seem to be set against and overcome by a striving for symmetry. For example, the courtyard and the rooms arranged around it on the north and east sides (10–18, 21 and 23) appear to be laid out in a regular fashion with their walls parallel and in conformity with the courtyard, whereas the south-west part of the house (1–9, 19 and 20) is not perpendicular to the rest of the house and is less rational in its internal arrangement. Attention is drawn to the conflict between the two

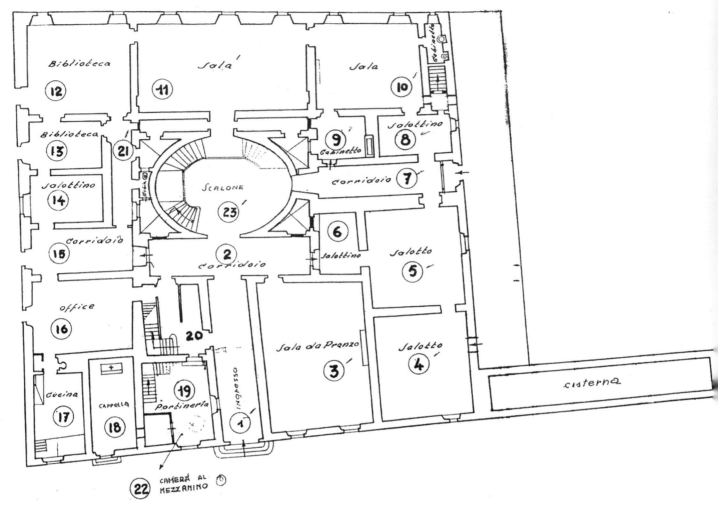

137. Ground plan of Villa La Pietra made for Arthur Acton.

axes by the way the front hallway is set at a different angle from the courtyard to which it leads. On closer inspection, it becomes evident that this hallway has been cleverly manipulated in order to resolve several problems simultaneously. The desire to create a symmetrical courtyard seems to have taken precedence, for the *androne* opens in the centre of the west wall of the courtyard, directly opposite what was the central bay of the loggia. However, the angle at which it is set demonstrates that whoever designed the villa also intended to maintain a semblance of symmetry in the façade, for if the *androne* had run perpendicular to the courtyard, the main portal would have had to be placed even further off-centre. As it is, the hall-

way is placed as centrally as possible in the façade, but not so far to the right as to deny the main axis running east-west and to destroy the vista through the house.[77]

Yet why were these compromises necessary in the first place? At this point it is possible to surmise that the less regular south-west section of the house may have incorporated a pre-existing structure which imposed certain restrictions on the architect. In that case, the positioning of the *androne* is just one illustration of how the transition was made from the older south-west part of the house to the more rationally organised and newly designed suites of rooms on the north and east sides.

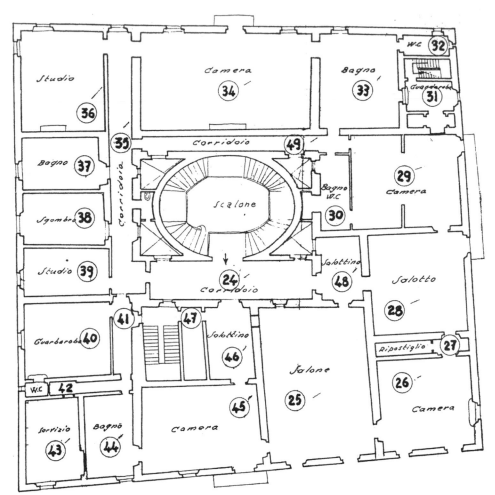

138. First-floor plan of Villa La Pietra made for Arthur Acton.

IDENTIFICATION OF ROOMS LISTED IN THE DIVISION OF 1499

On 12 May 1499, eight years after the death of Francesco Sassetti, a notary drew up an instrument of division for the estate at La Pietra. The rough draft of the division survives, as does a copy of the completed document made in 1522.[78] The palace, its gardens, the farm land and the outbuildings were to be divided between Francesco's three surviving sons, Galeazzo, Cosimo and Teodoro II. To allocate the parts, each brother drew a slip out of a hat, the first part being drawn by Galeazzo the eldest; the second by Cosimo the middle son; and the third by Teodoro the youngest. Analysis of the document and its application to the plans show that Galeazzo was to inhabit the western half of the first and second storeys, Cosimo the eastern half of the upper floors, while Teodoro's apartments covered the ground floor. The division of 1499 is of great significance for the architectural history of the villa not only because its list of rooms can be convincingly matched with the ground plans, thereby confirming the reliability of the plans and the survival of the fifteenth-century structure, but also because it provides evidence for how the interior was used in the fifteenth century.

The ground-floor rooms are the easiest to locate (Fig. 141). The 'loggia terrena' (11) and 'corte' (23) can be identified with certainty, the 'dua camere' listed with them were probably the two identical rooms flanking the loggia (10 and 12) and the unspecified number of 'anticamere' would then be the small rooms

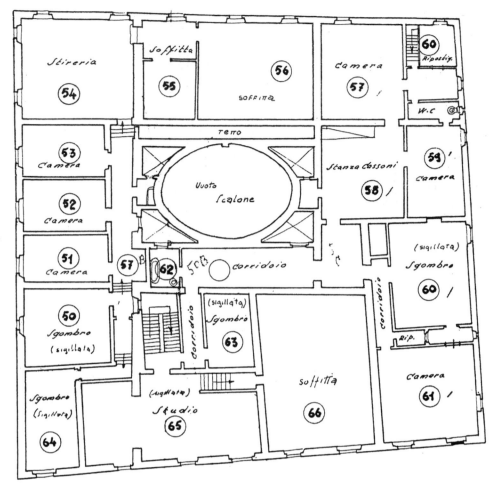

139. Second-floor plan of Villa La Pietra made for Arthur Acton.

leading off the 'camere' (8 and 9, 13 and 14). The next rooms are more difficult to find. The 'entrata dell'uscio di dreto' is probably room 7 and the 'camera del maestro' (the tutor's room or school room) is probably room 19(?). 'L'abituro dove si tiene le legne' could be a walk-in cupboard near the kitchen, or the stairs or in the corner of the courtyard. The 'sala terrena', however, can be unequivocally identified with what is still the dining room today (3), the largest room on the ground floor, its vault liberally decorated with the family coat of arms; and the 'dua camere in su essa' must therefore refer to the two rooms adjoining the 'sala' on its south side (4 and 5). The remaining areas can only be tentatively identified. The 'salotto da famiglia' could be room 6, in which case the small well in the wall shown in Vasari's plan would be the 'citernino' listed with it. The 'entrata dell'orto' was probably room 15. The 'cucina terrena' (16?), the

'camera da olio del fattore' (17?) and the 'forno' were probably near what is the kitchen nowadays in the north-west corner of the house.

These suggestions grow more tentative in the upper floors (Fig. 142). As on the ground floor where the rooms were grouped in clusters or apartments around the 'loggia terrena' and the 'sala terrena', so on the *piano nobile* the two *sale* were each accompanied by a suite of smaller rooms, followed by a third apartment and finally the kitchen and servants' quarters. The key to the division of the first floor lies in the description given to the two *sale*. The first is the 'sala di sopra che ghuarda verso la Pietra al Migliaio', which formed the nucleus of Galeazzo's portion. This must be the largest room on the west side of the first floor facing towards the Via Bolognese and situated directly above the ground-floor *sala* (25). In the list it is followed by the 'camera della stufa con le dua anticamere

140. Villa La Pietra, corner of original courtyard with exterior of nineteenth-century elliptical staircase.

e scrittoio'. Here the juxtaposition of *stufa* and *scrittoio* within a principal apartment may be a relatively early example of the 'proximity and interdependence' of bathrooms and studies noted by Dora Thornton in sixteenth-century Italy.[79] While it might seem that the 'camera della stufa' would be small like later bathrooms, the use of the word 'camera' indicates that it was much larger than, say, the bathroom in the Palazzo Ducale at Urbino;[80] and reference to the 1492 inventory made after Lorenzo de' Medici's death shows that at Careggi the 'camera della stufa' contained a bed, a settle (*lettuccio*), other furniture, as well as a painting of the Annunciation and a hanging like those in any *camera*.[81] It is most likely, therefore, that the 'camera della stufa' was a full-sized chamber or bedroom where room 45 is today with the added luxury of a bath set into an alcove or partitioned area within it. The two 'anticamere' would then be rooms 43 and 44 and the 'scrittoio' probably built into a corner of one *anticamera*.

'La camera dal canto in detta sala' must surely refer to the corner room opening off the *sala* (26), and the 'salotto in su detta sala' would then be room 28. The 'saletta da famiglia in sul verone' – the servants' small dining room opening off the upstairs loggia – is most likely to be room 46 (?), placed conveniently near the 'scala vecchia' (47) and the 'cucina vecchia a capo di scala' (40?). This area may seem cramped compared with Teodoro's spacious apartments on the ground floor, but Galeazzo also gained all the rooms on the west side of the top floor and the attics.

Meanwhile Cosimo's quarters lay on the east side of the house, as is clear from the name given to his grand reception room, the 'sala grande dipinta che ghuarda verso Camerata', which was the big room over the ground-floor loggia (34). The 'camera in su quella e l'anticamera et oratorio che si chiama la camera di Francesco' refers to the adjacent set of rooms on the south side of the *sala*: a bedchamber (33), its antechamber (31) and a room whose function is as recognisable in its form today as it was intended in the fifteenth century: a tiny cruciform chapel with a shallow dome set into its ceiling and a miniature vestibule leading into it from the *camera* (32). The phrase 'che si chiama la camera di Francesco' does not refer to the oratory alone, but rather to the *camera*, or to the three rooms that together formed Francesco Sassetti's private apartment. That the next set of rooms faced south can be inferred from the mention of a winter sitting-room, the 'camera del salotto da 'verno', which is also described as the wet nurse's room ('da balia') in the

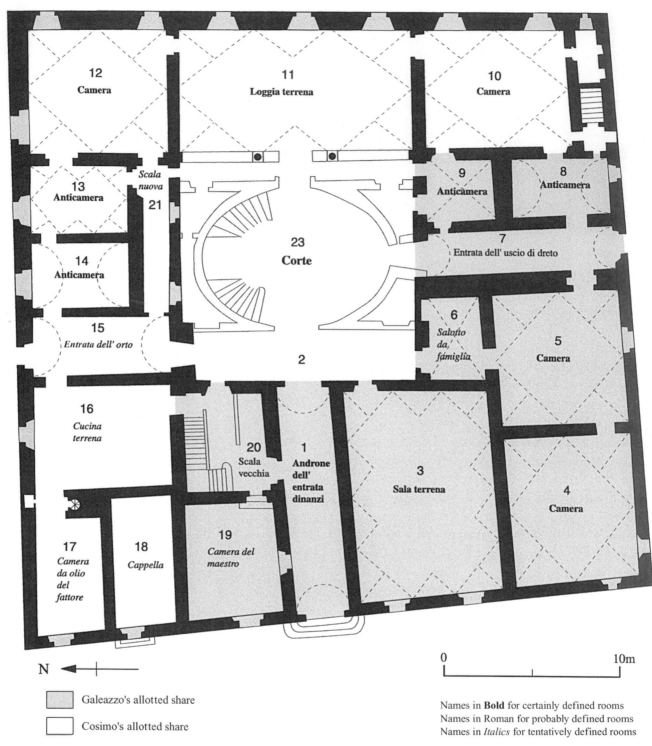

141. Villa La Pietra, plan of ground floor showing room functions listed in the 1499 document of division (drawn by Steven J. Allen).

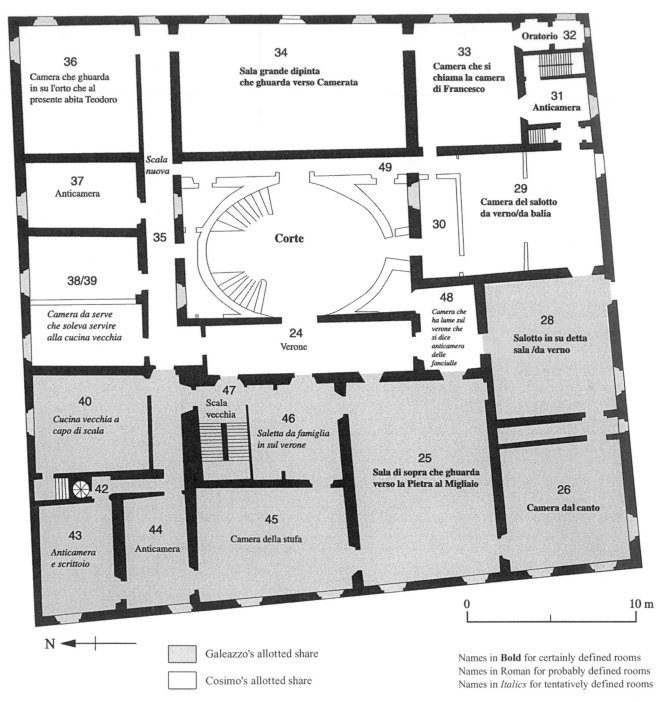

142. Villa La Pietra, plan of first floor showing room functions listed in the 1499 document of division (drawn by Steven J. Allen).

rough draft of the division (29), and the 'camera che ha lume sul verone che si dice anticamera delle fanciulle' would then be room 48 since its only light derived from the upstairs loggia and inspection of the remaining fifteenth-century *sgraffito* on the courtyard walls reveals that the *verone* was most likely to be on the west side of the courtyard where the corridor (24) is today. This would also place the girls' room conveniently near the nursery. The inventory then moved across to the north side to the 'camera e anticamera che ghuarda in su l'orto che al presente abita Teodoro' (36 and 37). This leaves the 'camera da serve', which was probably rooms 38 and 39 because it used to serve the old kitchen now in Galeazzo's portion (40?), whereas the 'cucina in sul secondo verone che si dice la cucina nuova' was on the floor above, leading onto a second-floor loggia superimposed above the first-floor loggia (Fig. 139, rooms 50 and 62).

It was remarkably convenient that the house contained three large dining halls (*sale*), so that one could be allocated to each brother. But that there were also three kitchens, each clearly distinguished by its description in the division, may have been the result of modifications made to the house in the 1490s to facilitate the creation of three apartments for the three sons. The kitchens were, in any case, likely to be tiered or placed on different floors close together in the north-west part of the house, perhaps sharing the same chimney, if not situated directly one above the other.

Galeazzo's share included the 'cucina vecchia a capo di scala et la scala vecchia'. It also stipulates that 'habbi a cchi tocca detta parte [Galeazzo's] a rimurare l'uscio che va dalla cucina vecchia alla cucina terrena perchè dette scale sono della terza parte' meaning that, since the stairs led into Teodoro's area, the door between the staircase and Teodoro's kitchen should be walled up because his apartments were confined to the ground floor, and he had no need of stairs. It is clear that a staircase ran from the old kitchen on the first floor down to the ground-floor kitchen; but this could be either the 'scala vecchia', which is shown on Vasari's plan in approximately the same position as the staircase today, or a small spiral staircase like the one built into the thickness of the present kitchen wall. On the other hand the 'scala nuova' (35) in Cosimo's part

was probably the long, single-flight staircase shown in Vasari's plan on the south side of the courtyard, leading from the *androne* [15] to a landing that must have been just outside Teodoro's *camera* [36] on the first floor. It was included in Cosimo's share because it provided essential access to the east wing, which was his allocated part of the house.

It is also possible that the 'scala vecchia' was part of the earlier Macinghi palace (perhaps originally an external staircase enclosed for Sassetti's rebuild). The irregular shape and great thickness of the wall between the main staircase (20/47) and the room next door (16/40) confirm this hypothesis. In this wall the two slightly varying axes visible in the plans meet, and the transition between them is effected within its thickness. This does suggest that the need to reconcile a pre-existing structure with the new wing caused the irregularity of its shape. In this case the wording of the division would lend credence to the theory that part of the earlier palace survived in the substructure of the new house. In addition, one of the ground-floor *androni* is described as 'nuovo' in the documents. The original draft of the division mentions the 'andito dell'orto nuovo in terreno che è tra'l pozzo e la camera del maestro in terreno'. This is almost certainly the corridor on the north side of the house (15) that forms part of the system of rooms on the north and east sides whose walls run parallel to the courtyard. The epithet 'nuovo' would then distinguish it from the two other *androni* (1 and 7) that are contained within the south-western part of the house.

The garden and outbuildings were divided at the same time as the palace; Galeazzo was given the oil press and half the poultry yard, Cosimo the field with a view towards Florence and the rabbit run, and Teodoro the *orto*, the dovecote and the other half of the poultry yard. The farms were divided three weeks later according to a contract drawn up on 5 June 1499.

Although it appears that each brother was allocated his own entrance to the house, the division was not a neat one. Access by the front (west) hallway was shared by all three brothers. Otherwise, Galeazzo was to enter from the east terrace overlooking Camerata, but Cosimo was to do likewise and also had the use of the corridor (15) leading from the north *orto*, which provided convenient access to the 'scala nuova' (21/35) in his part of the house. Teodoro had three possibilities: to enter by the west *androne*, or the corridor from the north *orto* and also presumably from the east-facing ground-floor loggia.

Not all the property was divided and, apart from the front hallway, other fundamental items were to be held in common, including the meadow gardens ('pratelli') in front and behind the house, the chapel on the ground floor, the well in the courtyard, the wine press and the loggia beside the road at La Pietra, while the drains and gutters were to be maintained by all. Although Teodoro had the advantage of the courtyard and ground-floor loggia, Cosimo and Galeazzo had the use of the upstairs *veroni* and the water catchment from the roof.

THE ORIGINAL FUNCTION AND DISPOSITION OF ROOMS

The division of 1499 provides a bare list of rooms with no inventory of their contents. Nevertheless, this list is sufficient to create an impression of a comprehensive range of rooms such as can only be provided in a palace built on a grand scale with specific requirements in mind and the means to fulfill them. The villa was built to house the growing Sassetti family. By the time Francesco started to build in 1462, Nera had given birth to three children, by 1470 they had six children and by 1479 they had ten,[82] not to mention household servants, a wet nurse, a tutor and an estate manager resident in the house for at least part of the year. The *palagio* contained large formal rooms such as the ground-floor *sala* with its heraldic emblems or the upstairs *sala* with its fresco decoration as well as modern luxuries like a hot bath, and essential facilities such as storage space for wine in the cellars, for firewood and olive oil on the ground floor, and efficient water supply from the roof and the well in the courtyard.

A careful reading of the division together with the plan reveals how the interior was arranged to provide separate accommodation for inhabitants of varying status[83] as well as a strategic distribution of private and communal rooms. The ground floor contained four separate suites, created by dividing the approximately square plan into four quarters, distributed around the courtyard, broken by the deep loggia to the east, and divided by three *androni* on the north, south and west sides. In this way the interior division is clearly recognisable in the plan. Two of the four quarters form private apartments: the *camere* either side of the loggia each with two *anticamere* (10 with 8 and 9; 12 with 13 and 14) in the north-east and south-east corners. Similarly, the *sala* (3) in the southwest is associated with the two large *camere* that open off it, although their relatively public position together with the lack of *anticamere* makes it less likely that these were sleeping rooms for members of the family. Perhaps they were guest rooms, as Shearman suggested the 'camara terrena della dua lettacho in sula salla terrena' at Cafaggiolo was, and as the rooms found in a similarly public position at Palazzo Medici and Fiesole probably were.[84] The north-west quarter was separate from the family's residential quarters. It housed the kitchen, the estate manager's room, the tutor's room and the chapel.

The plan of the first floor follows that of the ground floor very closely, so that many of the interior walls rise from their foundations up to the roof (compare Figs. 137, 138 and 139.). The functions of the rooms follow suit. The 'sala disopra' (25) lies over the 'sala terrena' (3) and the 'sala grande dipinta' (34) over the 'loggia terrena' (11) with the *camere* either side (10 and 12, 33 and 36) superimposed. There were three distinct apartments upstairs: Francesco's with its *camera, anticamera* and *oratorio* (33, 31, 32) next to the 'sala grande dipinta' (34); Teodoro's room (36) with its *anticamera* (37) overlooking the *orto*; and the room with a bath (45) and its *anticamere* and *scrittoio* (43, 44) beside the 'sala di sopra che guarda verso la Pietra al Migliaio' (5). The 'camera dal canto' (26) must have been another bed/sitting-room that communicated with the winter *salotto* (28), a south-facing room for informal dining that was convenient to the nursery (29) and girls' room (48). As downstairs, it is likely that a group of service rooms was placed close together in the north-west section: the servants' dining and sleeping rooms (46 and 39), the stairs (47) and the kitchen (40).

Since notions of public and private have not yet been fully investigated in relation to fifteenth-century domestic space, it is useful to discover whether the plan and room functions at La Pietra can throw light on these issues. Although accessibility was important for a communal *sala*, privacy may have been desirable for a study, oratory or antechamber.[85] The *sale* were the three main reception rooms of the house. Accordingly, the ground floor *sala* lay in the most accessible, public place, immediately to the right of the main entrance and opening directly off the courtyard. The *sala* (25) immediately above was within easy reach of the main stair (47) and, like its counterpart below, could be entered from outdoor space, in this case, the first-floor *verone* (24). As part of the new, symmetrical design, it is likely that the 'scala nuova' (21/35) was built to provide convenient access to the east wing with the 'sala grande dipinta' (34) in its centre. The ground-floor loggia was an analogous semi-public space intended for summer dining or simply to linger in during the hot months.

The main residential apartments all opened off these, the *camere* leading in turn to the *anticamere* or any more intimate rooms such as the study and the oratory.[86] This sequence from the very big *sala*, to the medium-large *camera*, to the smaller *anticamera*, to the tiny *scrittoio* or *oratorio*[87] can be observed in the ground-floor apartments flanking the loggia and upstairs in the bathroom apartment opening off the 'sala di sopra che ghuarda verso la Pietra al Migliaio', and in the eastern suites opening off the 'sala grande dipinta che ghuarda verso Camerata'. That the sequence in function from *sala* to *camera* to *anticamera* (and *scrittoio* or *oratorio*) matches that from large to medium-sized to small and apparently fits the gradation from public to personal to private or intimate is certainly no coincidence. Thus, the fact that at La Pietra the two most complete apartments – Francesco's *camera* with *anticamera* and oratory, and the 'Camera della Stufa' with two *anticamere*, a bath and a study – were deliberately placed in the corners of the house, taking full advantage of a position that did not permit intercommunication for the most intimate rooms, confirms that the need for privacy was a determining factor in the interior disposition of rooms.[88] Nevertheless, we should

resist the temptation to apply simplistic or modern notions of public and private to fifteenth-century domestic interiors. Probably all the *camere* and most of the *anticamere* were provided with two or more doors leading into various parts of the house.[89] This accessibility tallies with documents and contemporary fiction that reveal how bedchambers and antechambers were used as the daily living rooms of the house, as places in which to receive and talk to visitors, whether officials or friends and family, as much as for sleeping. The *camera* lay at the heart of the sociable house and should not be given a fixed place within a linear scale from public to private. Its many functions meant it could be anything at any time. This does not, however, mean that fifteenth-century Florentines had no need for what we call privacy, but the desire for secrecy, seclusion or security are likely to have been more pressing motives. At the same time a different need for a range of rooms with specific functions and, at La Pietra, the wish to construct a hierarchical sequence of spaces as part of an orderly, planned interior were also determining factors. Brenda Preyer has recently analysed the design of Florentine palaces in terms of accomodation and display for visitors, and here the grand scale, sequences of entry and provision of multiple reception spaces – the three *sale* and the loggia in the courtyard as well as the loggia beside the road – must have been conceived with the splendid entertainment of visitors in mind.[90]

It is not possible to discover exactly who lived where in the villa, since the division only mentions two rooms inhabited by individuals ('camera, l'anticamera, oratorio detto la camera di Francesco' and 'la camera che guarda in sul orto che al presente abita Teodoro'). Yet the less precise designations ('il salotto da famiglia', 'la camera del maestro', 'l'anticamera delle fanciulle' etc.) do help to establish where the servants, employees and children lived. In the case of the three kitchens, we are left to guess whether they were intended for different members of the family, for summer or winter, for grand or informal entertaining or to correspond with whichever of the three *sale* was in use.[91]

Since Vitruvius and Renaissance theorists recommend the use of separate rooms for different seasons[92] and in the nineteenth century Lady de Bunsen still

143. Villa La Pietra, west façade.

described the villa at La Pietra as having full sets of summer and winter apartments,[93] it is likely that the existence of three *sale* fulfilled that need. Vitruvius recommended that the winter dining room face the setting sun and this is true of both the ground floor *sala* and, more especially, of the dining hall directly above (25), which is elevated and therefore does actually catch the sunset. Although it, too, faces west, the breeze from the courtyard, the high vaults and thicker walls would have made the cooler ground-floor *sala* more suitable for summer entertaining. In fact, the only room specifically designated for seasonal use was the 'salotto da verno', the informal family dining room, sun-filled on the south façade, and smaller than the *sale* so easier to heat. The painted *sala* was an easterly room but protected from the draughts by the *camere* opening off it. It was probably intended for spring and autumn use, as Vitruvius suggested the easterly *triclinia* should be. Although weather was taken into consideration, the orientation of the *sale* had as much to do with the position of the main axis and the

view. Thus, two *sale* were placed on the front façade facing the main road,[94] while the third was centrally placed on the opposite side of the house overlooking the terrace and the view of distant hills.

A Description of the Fifteenth-Century Elements Surviving in the Villa

When the documents and the plan are finally compared with the house itself, the image of Sassetti's palace becomes concrete. Although the baroque verneer applied to both the interior and exterior of the villa ensures that the first impression is of eighteenth-century elegance on a magnificent scale (Figs. 143, 144 and 145); nevertheless, its fifteenth-century character is not so thoroughly disguised as to be discernable only in plan or to the documentary historian. Once it is known that the baroque elements are merely a decorative wrapping, the early Renaissance palace begins

144. Villa La Pietra, east façade.

145. Villa La Pietra, south façade.

146. Villa La Pietra, the 'Entrata dell'uscio di dreto' or south hallway (room 7 on Figures 137 and 141).

to emerge from underneath. The massive block of the house looming from its hilltop conveys a compact severity very like urban palaces of the same period. Apart from the basic structure of the whole house, the shapes of most rooms also survive from Sassetti's time, as is immediately evident when entering the house. On the ground floor particularly, the austere, if not gloomy, grandeur of the high, vaulted spaces, the deep window embrasures, the airy proportions, the cool stone and plaster framework, are again reminiscent of fifteenth-century Florentine palaces. But it is above all in the telling decorative detail that the precise date of the building is most apparent.

The three *androni* that subdivide the house and link its various parts are all barrel vaulted with simple courses of curved *pietra serena* moulding running along them (Fig. 146). This similarity of form and decoration tends to disguise the fact that they are all of different length and width and indicates instead their identical function and their role in creating a symmetrical and clearly articulated plan. Although the courtyard that we see on Vasari's plan has mostly been submerged in the structure of the elliptical staircase, its corners are still visible (see Fig. 140) and its essential square shape survives.[95] If we are to trust Vasari's plan, the court led into a loggia on the east side only – a three-bay loggia supported by two columns and two half-columns.[96] Unfortunately the loggia was walled in and the columns are presumably still embedded in the wall. Nevertheless, examination of the plaster in the corners of the original courtyard helps to solve other questions about its fifteenth-century appearance.

On both walls in the south-east and north-east corners and on one wall in the south-west corner, *sgraffito* decoration survives (Figs. 147 and 148). The *sgraffito* work is immediately recognisable as part of the fifteenth-century decoration. It is revealed in patches where the upper layers of plaster have flaked off, in these obscure corners no longer intended for public view where the surface has not been so frequently renewed. The frieze of palmettes and acanthus, the narrow courses of incised dentils, astragal and ovolo mouldings and the background of fictive ashlar compare closely with schemes dated by Christel and Gunther Thiem to the 1460s and 1470s.[97] That it was an elaborate scheme of high quality became apparent when a strip of plaster was chipped off the first-floor corridor wall (room 49). This was originally an exterior surface – a continuation of the east wall of the courtyard on which the ashlar and palmette friezes are incised higher up, but covered by the lean-to roof of an interior corridor when the elliptical staircase was built. Under this strip of plaster two winged putti dancing with swirling ribbons have been revealed (Fig. 149), part of a whole frieze that ran along the east side of the courtyard. It is fitting that this should be the most highly decorated wall, being directly above the ground-floor portico on the main west-east axis so that this was the view that greeted a visitor entering the courtyard from the front hallway. From what is visible in the present state of the building, the north and south walls may not have been enlivened by dancing putti but were mostly covered by expanses of fictive ashlar with friezes of palmettes and acanthus at attic level.[98]

It seems most likely that two *veroni* were superimposed on the west side of the courtyard.[99] This would be the simplest solution and one that conforms with the symmetrical tendencies of the plan because the upper loggias or balconies would be directly opposite

147. Villa La Pietra, south wall of courtyard, *sgraffito* decoration.

the ground-floor loggia. The presence of the 'scala nuova' on the north side of the courtyard would rule out the possibility of a balcony being there, and the thick wall running north-south across the south wing together with the lack of any interior wall parallel to the courtyard makes the existence of a loggia on the south side unlikely. The putto at first floor level on the east side would surely not originally have been incised in the shadowy recess on the back wall of a balcony. Finally, the description and sequence of rooms in the division suits the explanation that the first floor *verone* (and probably also the second floor *verone*) was on the west side of the courtyard where the wide corridor is today (24).

The ground-floor loggia has become an interior room, a wall in place of the open side with columns

148. Villa La Pietra, south wall of courtyard, detail of *sgraffito* decoration.

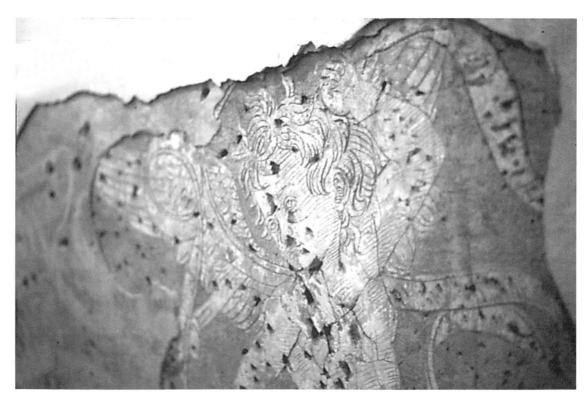

149. Villa La Pietra, east wall of original courtyard, now enclosed by a corridor, *sgraffito* putto.

150. Villa La Pietra, the 'loggia terrena' (11).

and only stucco pilasters to indicate where the columns were (Fig. 150). A layer of seventeenth- or eighteenth-century plaster strapwork covers all the walls and ceiling, but the lunette vaults are still intact with the roundel bearing the Sassetti coat of arms in the centre and tie bars spanning the depth of the old loggia. The original loggia should be envisaged as a covered extension of the courtyard, with the curtain wall at its back providing added privacy and shelter.

In the *camere* on either side of the loggia the fifteenth-century vaults survive intact. In these rooms it is likely that Arthur Acton replaced the original imposts with a reasonable approximation of what might have been there (Figs. 151 and 152) (although those in the *camera* on the north side of the loggia are of a higher quality than those on the south side) (Figs. 153 and 154). In both these rooms a *pietra serena* roundel bearing a shield with the Sassetti coat of arms is placed in the centre of the vault. The shield is of the same type as that on the della Robbia coat of arms above the entrance to the Sassetti chapel in S. Trinita. These two

camere are approximately square with an impost capital on each wall and narrow wedge-shaped imposts in each corner from which lunette groins spring.

In the *anticamera* on the north side (13) a similar flat vault with lunette groins survives (Fig. 155). But here, although the room is much smaller, its rectangular shape means that there are two console capitals on each of the long walls and one on each of the short walls to support ten diminutive lunettes. Since the curves of the vault are finely articulated and the console capitals small and delicately carved, the result is elegant and refined. Rather than the small size creating a stuffy, dark, enclosed space, the vault opens up the room making it airy and luminous. The varied forms of console capital add to the sense of vivacity (Figs. 156 and 157). The neck of each capital is carved with a different motif – with vertically or diagonally pointed leaves, with rounded scales or fluting, which in each case is contrasted with the mainly foliate forms of the volutes, the *calathos* rim and the tapering *calathos* base.

151. Villa La Pietra, *camera* (10) on south side of 'loggia terrena'.

152. Villa La Pietra, console capital in south *camera* (10).

153. Villa La Pietra, *camera* (12) on north side of 'loggia terrena'.

154. Villa La Pietra, roundel in vault of north *camera* (12) with Sassetti coat of arms.

155. Villa La Pietra, vault of *anticamera* (13).

156. Villa La Pietra, console capital in *anticamera* (13).

157. Villa La Pietra, console capital in *anticamera* (13).

158. Villa La Pietra, corner console capital in *anticamera* (9).

159. Villa La Pietra, *camera* (4), south-east corner.

Two other *anticamere* (14 and 8) have had their vaults replastered and painted with landscapes and chinoiserie probably following Giovannozzi's restoration programme of the 1750s, although it still appears from their shapes that they were originally barrel-vaulted. The fourth *anticamera* (9) is more puzzling, for the compartments of its groin vault do not fit the space of the room exactly and the wedge-shaped corner imposts are embedded in the walls (Fig. 158). Furthermore, these imposts are quite different from those in the *camere* 10 and 12 and *anticamera* 13. They are a bevelled trapezoid shape with a dentilated crest, a form commonly found in Florentine buildings of the late fourteenth and early fifteenth centuries.[100] The same form of dentilated impost is to be found in what is now the porter's room beside the main entrance (19) and in the two large *camere* on the south side of the 'sala terrena' (4 and 5) (Figs. 159, 160 and 161).

Again, the vaults here are slightly irregular (like the shape of the rooms themselves), their arcs not equally matched nor quite symmetrically arranged.[101] The effect is altogether more severe. The contrast between this earlier style of console capital and the more sophisticated classicising form (found in 10, 12 and especially 13) becomes clearer still when the two *camere* in the south-west corner are compared with the 'sala terrena' next door (Fig. 162).

This juxtaposition of the *sala* and the south-west *camere* and the linking of the three rooms in the division means that an explanation for the simpler, more old fashioned aspect of the *camere* cannot be sought in terms of their position in the house and a more modest function. It is far more likely that they survive from an earlier phase of building and were integrated into the later design. There is no doubt that the 'sala terrena' was built or rebuilt by Sassetti. The family

160. Villa La Pietra, console capital in *camera* (4).

161. Villa La Pietra, *camera* (5), east wall.

162. Villa La Pietra, the 'sala terrena' (3).

device of a sling with little stones (*sassetti*) is incorporated into six console capitals (Figs. 163 and 164), the coat of arms into the remaining four (Figs. 165 and 166), and there is a stone roundel carved with the coat of arms and *impresa* in the centre of the vault (Fig. 167). This liberal use of family symbols provides a foretaste of the iconographical method employed in the decoration of the Sassetti Chapel in S. Trinita fifteen to twenty years later.[102] There the use of family devices and puns on their names plays a part in determining the imagery: from the heroic image of David portrayed as the Sassetti arms bearer with his sling, his stone and his shield (Fig. 168) to the tomb reliefs carved with mock battles between *amorini* armed with catapults and ammunition of little stones (Fig. 169). The painted shields held by David above the entrance to the Sassetti Chapel and by the Roman soldier in the grisaille inscribed *ADLOCVTIO* above Francesco's

tomb (Fig. 170) are of the same form as those carved on the imposts and vault of the 'sala terrena' at La Pietra (see Figs. 165 and 167). The console capitals in the *sala* are of higher quality than those in any of the smaller rooms. Again, each one is different so that the *folium* is formed of palmettes in some cases and of acanthus or oak leaves in others, while the tapering *calathos* at the base is decorated with forms of tear drop, scales, bayleaves or palm fronds (see Figs. 163–166). Even the device of the sling and stones carved on the neck varies, and in one case is designed so that the tassel and loop at the ends of the sling are tucked around the curl of the volute (see Fig. 163), while in another the sling is suspended from the centre of the *abacus* blossom. The *peducci* do, however, conform to a general pattern and can be characterised by their projecting *abacus* that curves outwards from the wall on either side of the central blossom, by the simple *torus*

163. Villa La Pietra, 'sala terrena' (3), console capital with *impresa* of little stones.

165. Villa La Pietra, 'sala terrena' (3), console capital with Sassetti coat of arms.

164. Villa La Pietra, 'sala terrena' (3), console capital with *impresa* of little stones.

ring at the bottom of a prominent rounded neck and especially by the large *folia* curling downwards, almost smothering the volutes and splaying slightly onto the surface of the wall.

The small room (6) that opened onto the courtyard is now covered with mid-eighteenth-century murals and the original form of its vault disguised, but it appears to have had a cross vault of the same type as the *anticamera* (9) on the other side of the passage. This would support the suggestion that the south-west part of the house belonged to an earlier period than the courtyard and north-east wings. The irregular shape of this room (6) would mean that it marked another area of transition between the old and new parts of the house, like the unorthodox vault in room 9 and the odd shape of the wall between the main staircase (20) and the 'cucina terrena' (16).

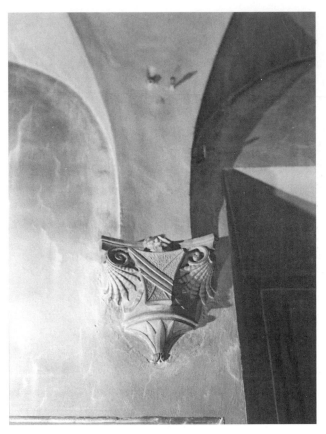

166. Villa La Pietra, 'sala terrena' (3), console capital with Sassetti coat of arms.

167. Villa La Pietra, roundel in vault of 'sala terrena' (3) with Sassetti coat of arms.

168. Sassetti Chapel, S. Trinita, Florence, Ghirlandaio's fresco to the left of the entrance arch with David as the Sassetti arms bearer.

Why, then, do the *androni* (1 and 7) and the *sala* (3), all situated in this part of the building, exhibit architectural features that so clearly belong to the 1460s? At this point it is important to underline the radical nature of Francesco Sassetti's building scheme. This was not merely a case of modifying a courtyard and tacking two new wings onto an existing palace. The old building was subsumed within the new and in the process certain parts of the earlier structure were entirely rebuilt and more modern forms introduced, while other sections (*camere* 4 and 5, *salotto* 6, *anticamera* 9 and room 19) retained their earlier character, which was not deemed inappropriate for their function in the new house. The joins where the two differing axes meet may be seen in the plan and in the

169. Sassetti Chapel, S. Trinita, Florence, reliefs below Francesco Sassetti's tomb, *amorini* playing with slings and little stones.

house itself in details such as the door leading into the courtyard from the south *androne* (7), which is placed off-centre in the corridor wall so that it could directly face the well in the centre of the courtyard. Overall, however, the planning of the house reflects the skill with which the graft was carried out: in the way the corridors in the old part of the house are coordinated with the loggia and the new third corridor in order to lead into the courtyard and create the four main apartments; in the way the old *camere* in the south-west corner form a suite with the *sala* and can be read in the same way as the two *camere* flanking the loggia with their corresponding sets of anterooms; and in the degree to which doors and rooms are arranged so that a streamlined axis is apparent on the site. The seam was so tightly knit and the old Macinghi house so

170. Sassetti Chapel, S. Trinita, Florence, Ghirlandaio fresco in spandrel to right of Francesco Sassetti's tomb, 'ADLOCVTIO'.

171. Villa La Pietra, the 'sala grande dipinta' on the first floor (34).

172. Villa La Pietra, the view towards Camerata from the 'sala grande dipinta' on the first floor (34).

173. Villa La Pietra, oratory (32) on first floor.

transformed by the vigour and clarity of the new concept that it could indeed be called a 'palatium muratum et constructum per dictum Franciscum'.[103]

The rooms in the north-western corner are more elusive. For example, the ground-floor chapel listed in the document of division is shown on Vasari the Younger's plan in the corner of the house. However, this may be another example of the unreliability of his plan since the chapel is now next door (18), and the widespread tendency to retain consecrated chapels or altars in their original locations, together with the presence of the chapel in its modern position in the

Capponi inventory of 1828,[104] means that it is likely to have been in the same place since the fifteenth century. Unfortunately, the division does not clarify the arrangement of this part of the house, except that the order of rooms as they are listed in the document would support the placing of the 'camera del maestro' beside the main entrance (19) and the kitchen on the north façade (16) between the entrance to the *orto* and the factor's room (17).[105]

Upstairs the major post-fifteenth-century alterations were the creation of new corridors around the old courtyard (converting the *verone* into a corridor

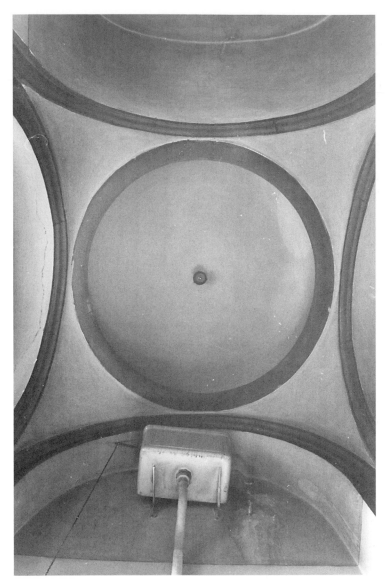

174. Villa La Pietra, dome of oratory (32).

(24), the new staircase into another (35), and building a third corridor on the east side of the *rotonda* (49)), together with the transformation of the 'sala di sopra che ghuarda verso la Pietra al Migliaio' (25) into a ballroom with a minstrel's gallery, which entailed raising the ceiling.

Many of the rooms retain the beamed, coffered wooden ceilings characteristic of first-floor rooms in fifteenth-century palaces. That of the 'sala grande dipinta che ghuarda verso Camerata' (34) is the finest example (Fig. 171). The dark patterns along the bevelled strips where the main beams meet the coffers

may be the oily traces of the original paint work. The console brackets of a simple, sturdy type may well be original too. The impressive scale, fine proportions and the views over the descending garden to Camerata and towards the distant Casentino, together with the sunny south-easterly aspect, make this perhaps the most beautiful room in the house (Fig. 172). It is safe to assume that the adjective 'dipinta' used to describe this room referred to wall paintings since panels or painted hangings would hardly be described as an integral part of the room in the context of the division that mentions no movable furnishings or decoration. Since there are windows on the long east wall and doors on the short north and south walls the most obvious space for frescoes would be the long west wall with its back to the courtyard. However no traces of such paintings were known to Arthur Acton when he restored the room in the early twentieth century and stretched green cloth across the intonaco walls. It is tempting to wonder whether there might have been a mural similar to Antonio Pollaiuolo's dancing nudes in the Villa Gallina at Arcetri, probably commissioned by the brothers Jacopo and Giovanni Lanfredini in the early 1470s.[106] More plausibly, the celebration of family events within a humanist setting painted by Botticelli c. 1486 for the villa of Giovanni Tornabuoni (a close business associate and friend of Sassetti's) might indicate the sort of subject Sassetti would have chosen for Montughi.[107] We know of no painter commissioned to work for Sassetti before Ghirlandaio's portrait of Francesco and his son and the frescoes in Santa Trinita,[108] although a painter like Alesso Baldovinetti (who worked in Santa Trinita, may have been a master of Ghirlandaio[109] and whose family was close to Francesco's brother Bartolommeo) might be a candidate for such a commission, which could have been issued when construction was over in the late 1460s or early 1470s. Unfortunately, no evidence has come to light to support such speculation.

Nevertheless, the set of rooms adjoining the 'sala grande dipinta', which were those intended for Francesco's own private use, provide one of the architectural highlights of the palace. The *camera* (33) retains its early ceiling with wooden console brackets and coffers that are less refined than those of the 'sala' and may have been modified since the fifteenth century, but opening off the *camera* (33) is the oratory (32) (Figs. 173 and 174). Although it was converted into a lavatory by Arthur Acton, its form remains unchanged. Entry is by way of a rectangular vestibule on an extremely small scale (1.86 × 1.36 metres). This space is defined by a separate groin vault resting on corner imposts (Fig. 175). A cupboard set in a niche in the external wall suggests that this area may also have functioned as a sort of sacristy for keeping the accessories pertaining to private prayer:

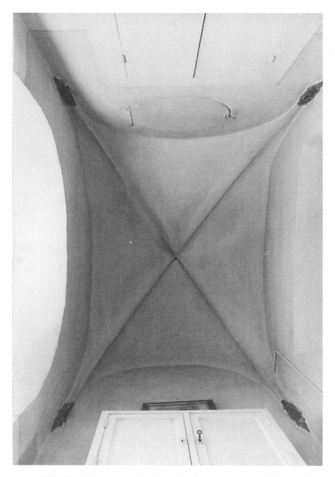

175. Villa La Pietra, vault of vestibule to oratory (32) on first floor.

lamps, candles, candlesticks, prayer books, altar cloths and so forth.

The plan of the oratory reads like a miniature Greek cross, although it is simply a square room (c. 2.28 square metres) with the corners filled in. The arches that frame each side of the central space support a dome shallow enough to be set into the ceiling and still allow room for attics on the floor above. The arches are articulated with *pietra serena* mouldings that fuse together below the squinches and form a single, wide, undulating band that bites into each corner. Recent restoration has revealed the scarred remains of what may be late-fifteenth- or sixteenth-century frescoes representing the four evangelists in the squinches (in the same position as Brunelleschi's Pazzi Chapel

Evangelists) while, much later, angels were painted in the dome.

The oratory occupies the south-eastern corner of the house. It is lit by two windows, a rectangular one facing east and a porthole facing south. Together they fill the tiny space with light. The round window that is in line with the doors to the *camera* and the 'sala grande dipinta' has been designed to maximum effect. The splayed reveals create a halo effect round the light itself that intensifies its power; they widen the beam of light as it enters the house and allow it to reach a greater area, while the diminishing perspective lends greater depth and scale to the tiny oratory.

11 · THE VILLA AT LA PIETRA IN THE CONTEXT OF CONTEMPORARY ARCHITECTURE

Comparison with other local villas and palaces makes it possible to judge whether Francesco Sassetti's country palace was typical of its day. Its relation to other buildings also throws light on the evolution of its design. Did the architect make use of contemporary or ancient models? Of local or foreign elements? Of urban or rural prototypes? In such a search the most obvious place to begin is closest to home. In the Florentine *contado* many more houses need to be surveyed and documents found to date them before detailed comparative analysis is possible; yet it is clear from accumulated evidence in tax returns, household inventories and *ricordanze*, from the depiction of villas in paintings from Lorenzetti to Gozzoli and from surviving early buildings (such as the Strozzi villas examined in Part One and Bartolommeo Sassetti's at Macia and Valcenni) that most *case da signore* were asymmetrical structures, built piecemeal over a long period and modified as the demand arose. Towers, outer porticoes and additional lean-tos were characteristic elements. The size, grandeur and symmetrical plan of Sassetti's villa obviously set it apart from this genre. Can it then be related to more prestigious, modern designs?

Two villas, lying within sight of La Pietra, had recently been built for the Medici, whose close connections with the Sassetti would also ensure that these houses were well known to Francesco. Careggi, on the western foot of Montughi, can be taken as representative of the fortified type of villa that maintained its appeal throughout the fifteenth century (eg, the

Medici villas of Trebbio and Cafaggiolo, the Pazzi villa of Trebbio, the Nerli villa at Scandicci, the Villa Salviati).[1] Careggi and La Pietra share their proximity to town, their large dimensions, internal courtyards with classicising loggias, and probably a similar taste for modern comfort and magnificence inside.[2] Michelozzo's new additions to a pre-existing structure would also have involved the same sort of compromise as that entailed at La Pietra. The slanting east wall following the curve of the road suited the fortified aspect of Careggi (Fig. 176). The courtyard behind was of necessity irregular, but its shape was not disguised so much as played off against the pair of classicising loggias which introduced the perpendicular system of the interior rooms (Fig. 177). There were modern features such as barrel vaults, rooms with special functions, and probably a series of distinct apartments. However, if the architects' briefs were similar, it only serves to emphasise what different solutions were chosen for the plan and elevations of these two villas. Comparison of Careggi's crenellated profile, the oblique line of its east façade, and the asymmetrical disposition of rooms, with La Pietra's compact regular shape, the clarity of its plan and the lack of any fortification, shows that La Pietra lies outside that tradition.

The plan of Giovanni de' Medici's villa built on the steep slope below Fiesole is more likely to have influenced La Pietra (Fig. 178).[3] In 1460 it was perhaps the only Florentine villa built *ex novo* according to a symmetrical plan without a tower or fortification. Its extraordinarily lucid ground plan was generated

176. Careggi, Villa Medici, east façade.

around the concept of external loggias opening onto gardens on the east and west, yoked by a central *sala*, with the flanking spaces occupied by a corridor, three *camere* and an *anticamera*. From the 1492 inventory[4] it appears that on the first floor there were three further *camere* and an *anticamera* for the owners' use, a kitchen and two servants' rooms and a granary in the attic.[5] Living quarters were therefore not provided on the grand scale of La Pietra, but on an altogether more modest scale, sufficient for short stays or day visits. The site, with its spectacular views and hanging gardens, was clearly the great attraction at Fiesole and the house was designed to accomodate it. At La Pietra the loggia looks in towards the central courtyard and the similarities in plan do not extend beyond its compact form, the principle of symmetry and the idea that the central *sala* at Fiesole replaced the courtyard in palaces like La Pietra. At La Pietra access was convenient, the site commodious and the apartments for living and entertaining were plentiful and extensive. While the design of Fiesole emphasised the rural ad-

vantages of the site, which could only supplement a palace in town (and other villas), La Pietra could fully substitute a palace in town by offering all the comfort and magnificence of urban life transported into a rural setting.

It is therefore not surprising that the design of Sassetti's country house should resemble a town palace. The features that typified a whole range of rural houses – crenellated walls, towers and outer porticoes – were all absent from La Pietra. On the other hand, the large regular block, the three-storeyed elevation, the interior courtyard, and the comprehensive range of apartments are suggestive of urban palace design. The sequence of spaces revealed on entering the Sassetti villa is common in fifteenth-century Florentine palaces including the Da Uzzano, Medici, Rucellai and Pazzi palaces. In each case a long vaulted *androne* leads into a porticoed courtyard placed towards the back of the house.[6]

Of those Florentine palaces completed by 1462, the plan of the Palazzo Medici bears the closest

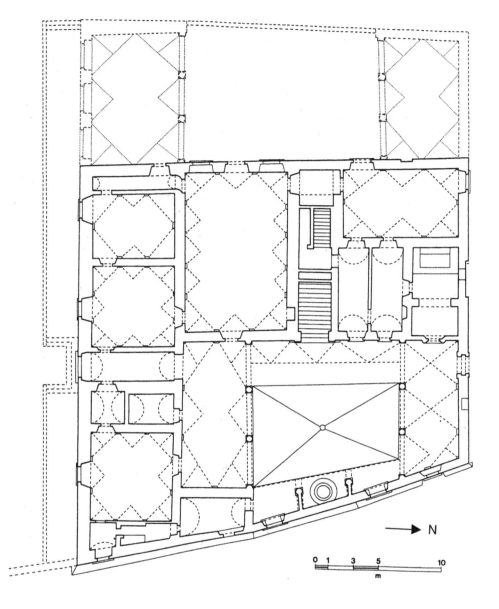

177. Careggi, Villa Medici, ground plan (adapted from Ferrara and Quinterio, *Michelozzo*, p. 248).

N

0 1 3 5 10
m

resemblance to La Pietra (Figs. 179 and 180). In both cases, their outer form appears to be a massive square block, although La Pietra is slightly more trapezoid and its dimensions are somewhat smaller.[7] While the courtyard in both houses gives the impression of centrality, it is actually placed to the left and towards the back (northeast at La Pietra, southwest at Palazzo Medici) with only a curtain wall dividing the courtyard loggia from the garden. Although the portico extends around all four sides of the Palazzo Medici courtyard and only on one side at the villa, the loggia

facing the main entrance in the Palazzo Medici, which is almost twice as deep as the other sides of the courtyard, is almost the same depth as its counterpart at La Pietra.[8] There were *veroni*[9] and *sgraffito* decoration on the upper levels of both courtyards.

Although it could not be claimed that the interior arrangement at La Pietra is perfectly symmetrical, the three *androni* and the loggia on the ground floor do divide the structure evenly into four parts, three of which form distinct apartments.[10] It is above all the three *androni* that set it apart from Palazzo Medici,

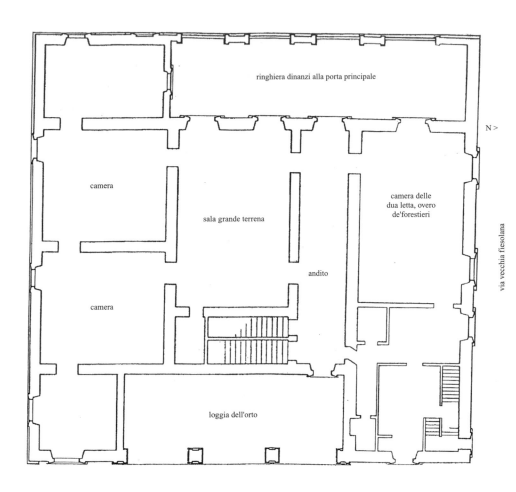

ringhiera dinanzi alla porta principale

N >

camera

sala grande terrena

camera delle
dua letta, overo
de'forestieri

via vecchia fiesolana

camera

andito

loggia dell'orto

178. Fiesole, Villa Medici,
ground plan (after Benucci,
adapted from du Prey, *The
Villas of Pliny*, p. 49).

clarifying the division into apartments and lending the whole plan greater coherence. In addition, the symmetrical organisation of the three ground-floor apartments at La Pietra (the *sala* and the 'due camere in su essa' (3, 4 and 5), the *camere* flanking the loggia with their *anticamere* (10, 9 and 8; 12, 13 and 14) and the central position of the 'sala grande dipinta' on the *piano nobile* with private chambers either side,[11] is distinctly more systematic than the disposition of rooms in Palazzo Medici.[12]

Although there is not a close similarity in the interior division of space, there is an equivalence in the provision of rooms and fulfillment of function. The space that La Pietra loses in overall dimensions is saved in its courtyard where the ground occupied by porticoes in the Medici palace is used in interior rooms at the villa. Thus, each ground floor has a *sala*, five principal *camere*, with at least three *anticamere*,

a kitchen and a servants' hall. The *scrittoio* and *stufa* downstairs in Cosimo's palace, are situated upstairs in Sassetti's house. The main chapel on the ground floor at La Pietra has its equivalent on the *piano nobile* at Palazzo Medici. Extra rooms provided for the estate manager and resident tutor at the villa were given to the chancellors' office and the street corner loggia in town.

Pius II's palace at Pienza, built by Bernardo Rossellino (1459–62), drew closely on the Palazzo Medici for its plan but regularised it further (Figs. 181 and 182). The portico running around all four sides in the square courtyard of the Palazzo Medici and Palazzo Piccolomini are closely comparable. Yet the greater regularity in the disposition of rooms in Pienza is closer to La Pietra, especially the way in which the six-door *sala* with the view towards Monte Amiata is placed over the lower loggia and flanked by square

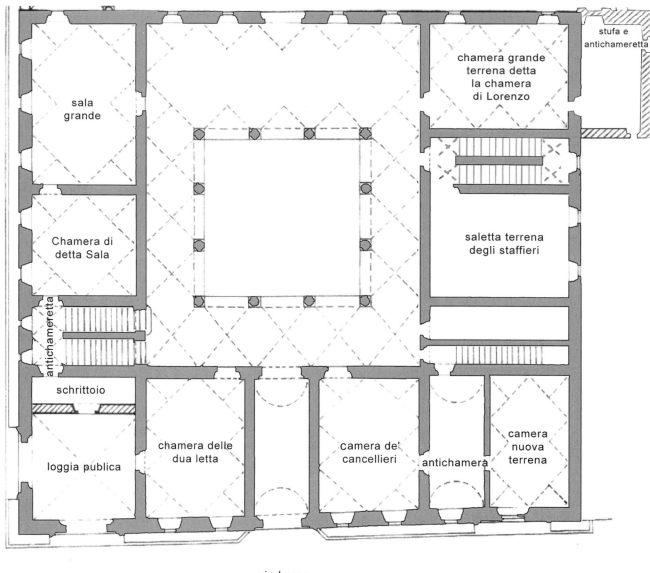

stufa e antichameretta

chamera grande terrena detta la chamera di Lorenzo

sala grande

Chamera di detta Sala

saletta terrena degli staffieri

antichameretta

schrittoio

camera nuova terrena

loggia publica

chamera delle dua letta

camera de' cancellieri

antichamera

via Larga

→ N

179. Palazzo Medici, Florence, ground-floor plan (after ASF, Guardaroba medicea, 1016, Rossi, Bartoli and Bossi in Cherubini and Fanelli, *Palazzo Medici*, pp. 125–6, 328–31, and Clarke, *Roman House*, fig. 87; showing room functions listed in the 1492 inventory, identified by Bulst, ibid., pp. 107–12).

corner *camere* is very similar to the 'sala grande dipinta che guarda verso Camerata' with its flanking *camere* at La Pietra. Pius II's private apartment included the south-east *camera*, just as Francesco's (although on the opposite side of the *sala*) was also on the south-east corner of the house. At both Pienza and La Pietra the owner's *camera* was placed between a secret stair-

case and a grand *sala* overlooking the countryside.[13] Most fundamental of all, however, is the principle by which the plan of both upper floors mirrors that of the ground floor, lending greater cohesion and symmetry to the whole palace at both Pienza and La Pietra.

When the plan of Francesco Sassetti's villa was established in the early 1460s, Cosimo de' Medici's

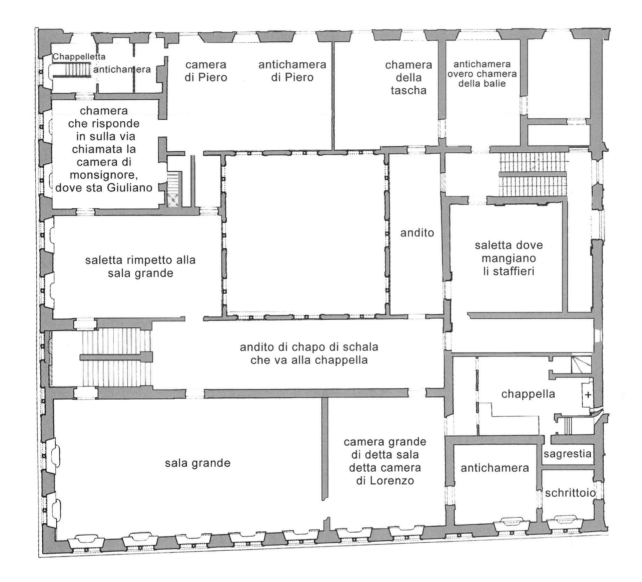

Chappelletta
antichamera

chamera
che risponde
in sulla via
chiamata la
camera di
monsignore,
dove sta Giuliano

camera
di Piero

antichamera
di Piero

chamera
della
tascha

antichamera
overo chamera
della balie

saletta rimpetto alla
sala grande

andito

saletta dove
mangiano
li staffieri

andito di chapo di schala
che va alla chappella

chappella

sala grande

camera grande
di detta sala
detta camera
di Lorenzo

antichamera

sagrestia

schrittoio

 N

180. Palazzo Medici, Florence, first-floor plan (after ASF, Guardaroba medicea, 1016; Rossi, Bartoli and Bossi in Cherubini and Fanelli, *Palazzo Medici*, pp. 126–7, 332–5, and Clarke, *Roman House*, Fig. 94; showing room functions listed in the 1492 inventory, identified by Bulst, ibid., pp. 112–18).

palace was recently completed, much admired and already widely influential.[14] Francesco's close association with the Medici family, as their trusted senior employee, political ally and friend, as well as his brother Bartolommeo's role as accountant for the construction of the Medici palace, makes the architectural connection seem almost inevitable. However close the plans, examination of the surviving architectural and decorative detail at the villa reveals only some general correspondence with the Medici palace and demonstrates that La Pietra's architectural vocabulary was drawn from a wider repertory current in Florence and its surroundings, as well as proposing some new developments on those themes.

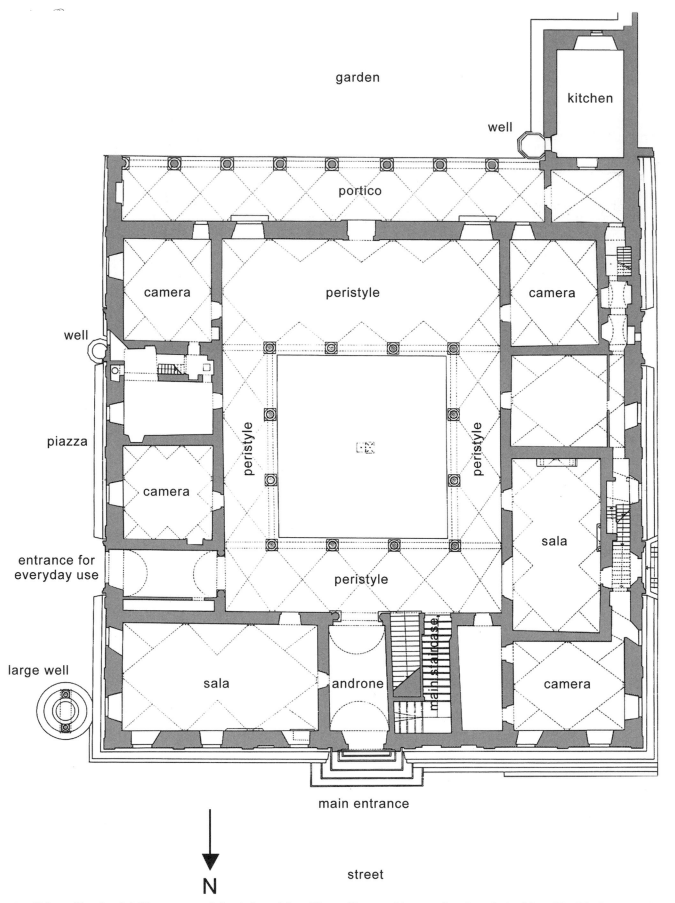

garden

kitchen

well

portico

camera

peristyle

camera

well

camera

peristyle

peristyle

sala

piazza

camera

peristyle

entrance for
everyday use

peristyle

large well

sala

androne

main staircase

camera

main entrance

N

street

181. Palazzo Piccolomini, Pienza, ground plan (adapted from Pieper, *Pienza*, with room functions derived from Pius II's *Commentari*).

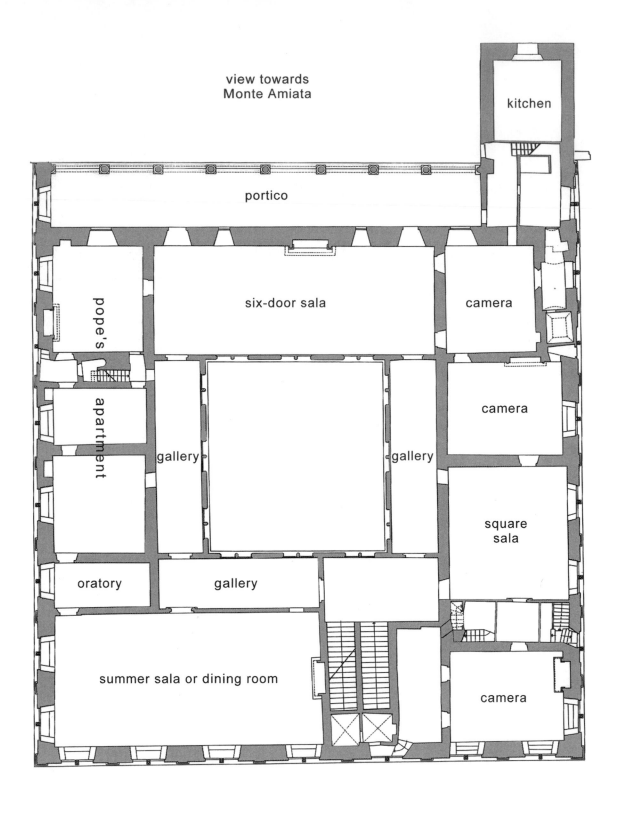

view towards
Monte Amiata

kitchen

portico

pope's

six-door sala

camera

apartment

gallery

gallery

camera

square
sala

oratory

gallery

camera

summer sala or dining room

N

182. Palazzo Piccolomini, Pienza, first-floor plan (adapted from Pieper, *Pienza*, with room functions derived from Pius II's *Commentari*).

183. Palazzo Coverelli, Florence, detail of *sgraffito* frieze with putti on façade (1470s).

Although *sgraffito* decoration is usually associated with urban buildings, it was as common in the country in the fifteenth century.[15] The grand, distinctively urban connotations of cut stone and the unwillingness to pay for revetment in the comparative isolation of the country, meant that most villas were plastered and fictive stone blocks then incised on the façades and courtyards of the smarter country houses. The *intonaco* on the outer walls at La Pietra may originally have carried a *sgraffito* design of rectangular blocks, perhaps with *all'antica* details like those in the courtyard.[16] Unfortunately, only part of the original *sgraffito* work remains in the courtyard, so that its design cannot be fully reconstructed. Still, the recent discovery of a *sgraffito* frieze in the first floor corridor reveals that a row of putti bearing festoons and ribbons ran just below the *piano nobile* windows in the original courtyard (see Figs. 147, 148 and 149 in Chapter 10).

The combination of a background of fictive ashlar with a frieze below the top storey windows depicting palmettes and acanthus between narrow courses of dentil, astragal and ovolo mouldings, and a wider frieze of dancing putti above the ground floor loggia, is closely related to the *sgraffito* schemes at the Nasi and Coverelli palaces executed according to Gunther and Christel Thiem in the 1460s and 1470s, respectively – dates that accord with the period of La Pietra's completion in the late 1460s.[17] In particular, a close comparison can be made with the upper frieze of Palazzo Coverelli, whose dancing putti carrying festoons and ribbons assume the same postures in reverse and have the same waving tufts of hair as the La Pietra putti (Fig. 183). The La Pietra putti also resemble a securely dated and more prestigious sculptural scheme, the freestanding wooden putto and garland frieze in the 'sacrestia delle messe' of Florence Cathedral, commissioned from Giuliano da Maiano and executed by a group of sculptors between 1465 and 1468 (Fig. 184).[18]

Within the house itself, there are other examples of elegant, classicising features. The barrel vaults of the *androni* (see Fig. 146 in Chapter 10) were newly popular in domestic architecture, having been adopted

184. Sacrestia delle Messe, Florence Cathedral, southeast corner, sculpted frieze with putti and garlands, Giuliano da Maiano workshop and others, 1465–68 (Photo: Antonio Quattrone).

by the Medici in the Via Larga, at Careggi and at the Badia Fiesolana.[19] The barrel vault was ideally suited to the function of hallway or entrance corridor. It was technically feasible because the span was not too wide, psychologically effective because the uninterrupted, tunnel-like curve focussed movement through space towards the final destination, and aesthetically pleasing because of the seamless sweep of the vault and straight line of the simple convex moulding that defines where the vault ends and the wall begins. At La Pietra the systematic repetition of this form is compatible with and emphasises its classical origins.

In contrast to those *androni* and to the stylish, *all'antica* imposts on the vaults of the *sala* (3), *anticamera* (13) and the *camere* beside the loggia (10 and 12), the vaults of the anticamera (9) and the two *camere* (4 and 5) adjacent to the ground-floor *sala* bear simple, trapezoid imposts with a dentilated crest that look decidedly old-fashioned (Fig. 185). It might be argued that styles outmoded in town continued to be built in the

country, but there is still not enough dated evidence for the second half of the fifteenth century on which to base that theory; in this villa the up-to-date character of so many aspects (the plan, *sgraffito*, barrel vaults, *sala* imposts and chapels) would contradict such an hypothesis. Nor is it plausible to suggest that the two contrasting types were deliberately juxtaposed in order to define the different functions of the *sala* and *camere*, since the other *camere* and even the *anticamera* carry the more modern forms, and these two *camere* were large ones in a comparatively public position, opening directly off the *sala*. Nor is there evidence to suggest that Sassetti built his palace in two separate phases or over a long extended period. On the other hand, there *is* evidence for the pre-existence of a palace owned by the Macinghi on this site. The tax returns from 1427 on suggest that the family were too poor to build, so it is far more likely that the console capitals in these *camere*, in *camera* (19) and in *anticamera* (9) survive from the time between Zanobi Macinghi's

185. Villa La Pietra, console capital in *camera* (4).

return from Naples as a rich man in the late fourteenth century and the early 1420s, than that they were carved after 1462 when reconstruction began at the villa. Datable capitals of this type are found in the Da Uzzano palace (c. 1411–21),[20] in the Zecca (after 1374 and perhaps before 1428),[21] in the Audienza of the Arte de' Vaiai and Pelliciai (Via Lambertesca before 1429),[22] in the garage behind the Chiostro delle Spese at San Marco (1437–43) (Fig. 186),[23] in the Pandolfini villa La Torre at Lastra a Signa[24] and in the courtyard of the Rucellai villa Lo Specchio at Quaracchi.[25] Although the use of these imposts cannot be anchored to an exact date, the span of its popularity lasted from c. 1370 to c. 1440, in the later years mostly confined to subordinate and service areas.

Finally, the shift in axis between this section of the house and the north-eastern part, which are not perpendicular to each other, can be explained by the pre-existence of these rooms in the earlier Macinghi house, so that an early dating of these imposts is supported by the evidence of the ground plan. If doubts remain, they are due to the masterly way in which the old structure was tailored to fit the new, and the new plan designed to accommodate the old structure.

The type of console capital found in the *sala terrena* (3), *anticamera* (13) and the *camere* flanking the loggia

(10 and 12) had come into vogue in the 1450s. Its distinguishing characteristics are the fluted *calathos* and the burgeoning *folia* that curl downwards around the volutes onto the neck and sometimes splay outwards over the adjoining wall surface. This can be found already in the discreet curl of acanthus in the Spinelli cloister (c. 1452) (Fig. 187), which have grown considerably in the capitals of the Strozzino courtyard (c. 1451–65)[26] and are still larger and more vigorous in the cloister of the Badia Fiesolana (finished mid-1460s).[27] The equivalent console capitals can be found in the *androne* of the Palazzo Rucellai (c. 1452) (Fig. 188)[28] and supporting the garden wall of the Palazzo Medici (1450s).[29] After its initial use by the Michelozzo and Rossellino workshops,[30] its popularity spread to the *contado*. It appears not far from La Pietra in the Mugnone valley in the cloister of the Conventino della Maddalena at Le Caldine (c. 1460)[31] and further afield in the *sala* of the villa attached to S. Andrea a Camoggiano in the Mugello (1470).[32] It had been exported to Pienza by Bernardo Rossellino, who used it in the capitals of the upper loggia columns and window colonettes of Pius II's palace (1459–62),[33] and to Urbino by Florentine masons working in the early phase of construction in the Palazzo Ducale.[34] The wide diffusion of this type of capital suggests

186. San Marco convent, Florence, garage, console capital.

that its appearance after c. 1460 cannot be linked to any particular architect and that its pattern had entered the repertoire of many stonemasons' yards by then.[35]

The comparison with La Pietra cannot be further advanced because two other key characteristics shared by most of the above examples – the fluted *calathos*

and the egg and dart of the upper *calathos* rim – are not always present at La Pietra. In the *sala* the fluting has been substituted by the coat of arms, and the ovolo is only sometimes included and at other times is changed to a band of leaves (see Figs. 163–166 in Chapter 10). In the *anticamera* (13), one impost carries fluting, but the other five have different variants of

187. S. Croce, Florence, Spinelli cloister, console capital.

188. Palazzo Rucellai, Florence, *androne*, console capital.

foliate motifs (see Figs. 156 and 157 in Chapter 10), while in the *camere* (10 and 12) most imposts carry diagonal striations (see Fig. 152 in Chapter 10). Nor can the treatment of console capitals at La Pietra be closely related to known examples. Within the villa itself the standard of carving varies considerably, and a number of stonemasons must have supplied the imposts, while those in the *camere* (10 and 12) are crudely cut and almost certainly restorers' copies. Those in the *anticamera* (13) and the 'sala terrena' (3) are of better quality, and their variety of motif creates a lively and decorative effect, although here, too, some imposts are cut in a dry, mechanical way with no sense of organic form nor attempt at sculptural modelling while several others, especially in the *sala*, are handled in a freer, more plastic fashion with a more loving treatment of plant forms.

The most striking feature of the *sala* console capitals is their inclusion of the family coat of arms and emblem. The Medici had already incorporated their *palle* into the console capitals of the church at Bosco ai Frati (before 1436?) (Fig. 189), and the Pazzi palace capitals (c. 1462–9) (Fig. 190) may be contemporary with those at La Pietra. Although this may be an early example of weaving a coat of arms into the architecture of a dining hall, the practice was certainly congruent

with that of the palace-owning elite who sought to display multiple versions of their family (or personal) emblems, whether on the façade, in the courtyard or inside their houses.

Only the biggest palaces could provide three *sale*. Francesco Nori's extension to the already large Palazzo di Zanobi probably included the third *sala*,[36] and the Medici palace had one on each of its three floors.[37] The wooden beamed and coffered ceilings upstairs at La Pietra are of standard quality, and even that of the 'sala grande dipinta' with its simple console brackets is no exception.[38] For the special qualities of the 'sala grande dipinta che ghuarda verso Camerata' were its dominant position in the centre of the east façade, its views over the countryside, and its mural decoration. No Florentine palace of this date could boast of a symmetrically placed *sala*,[39] and the view was clearly an advantage that could more easily be afforded in the country. Frescoes were an alternative to tapestries, painted hangings or built-in wooden panelling (*spalliere*) and were a favourite choice of wall decoration in a room that contained little furniture besides tables, benches and chairs.[40]

The 'sala grande dipinta' led directly into Francesco Sassetti's own private apartment. His *camera* was not particularly large, but it shared the same

The tiny square oratory with a pendentive dome at La Pietra can be related to larger scale Florentine chapels including the Barbadori Chapel in S. Felicita and the altar chapels of the Old Sacristy at San Lorenzo and the Pazzi Chapel at S. Croce (Fig. 191). At La Pietra, however, the arched, rectangular niches that project from the central space transform the plan into a Greek cross with an open fourth arm used as the entrance, an arrangement that is more similar to the Cardinal of Portugal's chapel at S. Miniato (1460–8) and the S. Fina Chapel in the Collegiata of S. Gimignano (1468), although neither of these contains a dome. On this small scale the elevation is streamlined and its members simplified. Thus, the arches that frame the arms of the cross form the pendentives of

189. San Francesco, Bosco ai Frati, Mugello, console capital.

wide view as the *sala* and its size was extended by the antechamber and oratory that opened off it. The relationship between the 'sala grande dipinta' and Francesco's *camera, anticamera* and oratory is similar to that between the 'sala grande' and Piero de' Medici's *camera, anticamera, scrittoio* and chapel although the Medici Chapel was also accessible from the public corridor.[41] The arrangement at La Pietra could also be compared with Giovanni di Cosimo's apartment in the southern wing of Palazzo Medici, which opened off the *saletta* and included a *camera, anticamera* and a *scrittoio* that was converted into a chapel when Giovanni di Lorenzo later lived there.[42] Another key precedent is the Palazzo Piccolomini in Pienza, where the pope's *camera* opens off a centrally placed *sala* with fine views designed for splendid entertaining and, on the other side, offers the refuge of a secret staircase leading to the outdoors.

190. Palazzo Pazzi, courtyard, capital with Pazzi heraldic dolphins.

191. Pazzi Chapel, altar chapel interior (photo: Conway Library, Courtauld Institute of Art).

the dome, and there is no horizontal entablature dividing the upper vaulted space from the lower walls. Without an entablature, there is no need for supporting members, so that the pilasters with capitals framing the entrance and in the corners of the Old Sacristy, the Pazzi, Cardinal of Portugal and S. Fina Chapels have been omitted. Instead, where the arches join at the base of the pendentives, the *pietra serena* moulding that defines each arch meets the contiguous moulding and is fused into a single undulating band like the solution adopted for the side chapels in the Badia Fiesolana (Figs. 192, 193 and 194). This unfussy so-

lution is a happy one. By emphasising the apparently simple structure with clean lines a monumental effect is achieved on a tiny scale. In fact, this structural quality is a fiction because the oratory is not a separate structure but simply a small room whose Greek cross plan is created by filling in the corners of the room and whose dome is a less than hemispherical niche nestling in the space between the first and second floors of the house.

The clear relation to Brunelleschi's prototypes and to the new chapels at S. Miniato and the Badia Fiesolana confirms the typological identity of the oratory. Even when the use of the room was grotesquely

192. Villa La Pietra, first-floor oratory (32), squinch and corner mouldings.

transformed, its original religious function was instantly recognisable in its form. Yet chapels in other contemporary palaces and villas had not adopted this formula. The Medici Chapel was not admired for its plan but for its painted walls, expensive materials and fine workmanship.[43] At Urbino an architecturally distinguished but entirely different structure with a barrel vault and an apsidal altar niche was designed for the Cappella del Perdono.[44] Although the Rucellai tabernacle is a special case, situated outside the family palace but in a parish church very close by, the same motives are evident: the desire for exclusive, private prayer combined with a taste for precious materials and monumental forms wrought in miniature. In all these cases, the scale was probably not limited through lack of space but was chosen through desire for intimacy

and in order to display rich materials and artistic skill more densely so that they seemed more profuse. At the Montughi oratory it seems likely that the reproduction of a distinguished but austere architectural formula on a small scale was more important.[45]

The practice of adapting a rectangular room for use as a chapel like those at Pienza,[46] Careggi, Cafaggiolo and the Pazzi villa of Trebbio,[47] was also followed at La Pietra but on the ground floor. Here the chapel entrance was on the main façade, perhaps located in the corner of the house as shown in Vasari's plan or in the next room where it is today. That the chapel should be available not only to the landowner's family but to the tenant farmers and any other employees on and near the estate is suggested by its accessible position at La Pietra, as was also the case in the Medici Villa of Trebbio where the chapel is a separate building some distance from the *casa da signore* in an open space that serves as a piazza for the whole estate community.[48]

The co-existence of a more public chapel and a more private oratory at La Pietra underlines this distinction in function. The same distinction must have been made in the Palazzo Medici in the 1480s when the ambitious young cleric Giovanni di Lorenzo took over Giovanni di Cosimo's old apartment and converted his *scrittoio* into a 'chappelletta'. He needed a place for private prayer apart from the chapel which already existed on the same floor of the palace.[49] Sassetti, on the other hand, did not aspire to a career in the church and, as a layman, the provision of a second chapel in his one villa might justifiably be read as a sign of special piety. Ficino certainly interpreted the chapels at La Pietra in that spirit when he wrote in his letter to Francesco:

But the ability to judge matters in such a way, and so to live happily, is something that religion alone can give us. In due course of time, it will give this to you twice as much as to others, my Francesco, if you will surpass your fellows in religion as your magnificent palace surpasses other houses. Your home, Sassetti, is twice as godly as others: for they have barely a single chapel, but yours contains two, and

193. Fiesole, Badia, side chapel.

very handsome ones at that. Live doubly more religious than others, my Francesco, fare doubly well.[50]

After all, in a domestic setting, most *camere* contained at least one religious painting or sculpture, often enclosed in a tabernacle, sometimes with a candle or lamp burning before it which served the household's informal and individual religions needs.[51] It is likely that, because of the greater distance from the parish church, chapels were more commonly attached to villas than to town palaces in the fifteenth century. Although the parish church of S. Marco Vecchio lay within half a mile of the villa, the road to it was steep and long enough to be considered inconvenient for women and to justify the existence of the ground-floor chapel to the visiting cleric in 1610.[52] Meanwhile only the desire to provide a complete range of rooms on a grand scale, together with exceptional religious devotion, or rather the wish to display such piety, could account for Francesco's own private oratory.[53]

The *stufa* or hot bath is another indication of the luxury this house provided. Francesco di Giorgio recommended that baths be situated on the ground

194. Fiesole, Badia, side chapel, corner moulding.

floor,[54] and they can be found there in the town palaces of the da Uzzano[55] and the Medici.[56] In both these cases, the *stufa* was listed as a separate entity, placed next to the principal *camera* and part of the suite of rooms belonging to the paterfamilias (Niccolò da Uzzano and Lorenzo de' Medici), which confirms the luxurious status of the object. At the villas of Careggi and La Pietra the bath seems to have been placed in (or perhaps behind a partition within) a large bedchamber,[57] and in each case the 'camera della stufa' was upstairs, part of an apartment that seems to have been second in importance after that of the owner but was not designated as belonging to anyone in particular.[58] In the case of La Pietra, the 'camera della stufa' seems to have been on the west side of the house and therefore close to the well-shaft and chim-

ney provided for the kitchen. Since the inventories for the Uzzano and the Medici do not list the bath itself among the moveable and assessable furnishings, it was almost certainly a built-in structure and not merely a wooden or tin tub of the sort depicted in some prints and paintings.[59] There is no evidence that more elaborate designs like Francesco di Giorgio's were already in use in Tuscany.[60]

Apart from the palace interior, at least one outbuilding on the estate also contributed to the convenience and magnificent status of the villa. When Francesco Sassetti built his loggia at La Pietra al Migliaio, he can have had none of the delays and difficulties that Giovanni Rucellai experienced in creating a site for his loggia in town.[61] Moreover, the site of Sassetti's loggia was entirely different from those of urban loggias, neither within close proximity to the house as in the Rucellai piazza, nor attached to the palace as the garden loggia in the Palazzo Medici was.[62] As a consequence the function must also have been quite different. The loggia at La Pietra cannot have been intended for the use of his relations or clan in the sense that the Rucellai loggia was.[63] It was not only far from the Sassetti town houses but also well away from the country district of Novoli where the other Sassetti owned estates; and it is hard to imagine that the Via Bolognese would ever have been a suitable spot for wedding banquets or funerals.[64]

The loggia beside the milestone was designed for other purposes: first of all, to serve as a link between the main road and the villa. It drew public attention to the presence of the villa (which was in sight but not within hailing distance) and to Sassetti's ownership of the surrounding lands. It may not have been intended for use by cousins or uncles, but as a device to facilitate the public appreciation of privately owned space, a loggia functioned particularly well as an advertisement for the family's wealth and power.[65] Its practical function would have been analagous to that of the gate houses which occupy that site today, or it may have been used as a stage post or setting down point for messengers and visitors.[66] Furthermore, its strategic position beside the first milestone on the main road north of Florence should not be overlooked, and if Sassetti intended his villa as a resting place for travellers on their way in or out of town, the loggia would have been the signpost to the villa. Since ceremonial entries involved stopping at specific, easily measurable distances outside the city walls to receive ambassadors and welcoming parties of dignitaries, it is very likely that Francesco intended his loggia to be used in this public way for official arrivals or departures from town.[67]

Sassetti had travelled widely and lived abroad for many years, yet there is no hint of foreign influence in the design chosen for his villa. Given that the architecture of the villa was distinctly Florentine, it might still have made use of antique models. Sassetti was certainly collecting manuscripts of ancient texts by 1456.[68] The books listed in his *Libro segreto* in 1462 included an early fifteenth-century French volume of Vitruvius, Cato and Varro, which he had probably acquired during his travels in France.[69] Although the binding together of Vitruvius's *De Architectura* with Cato's *De agri cultura* and Varro's *Rerum Rusticarum Libri Tres* should be regarded as standard practice,[70] it is tempting to look for an expression of those writings in Sassetti's own enterprise combining architecture with agriculture. The example of Careggi, the villa most often associated with the humanist movement in fifteenth-century Florence, might stand as a warning not to expect any precise or comprehensive expression of literary ideas in the actual building. Does the later design of La Pietra display a closer adherence to Vitruvian principles?

It may be unnecessary to thank the theorists for the choice of a well drained site on high ground, visible from a distance and with fine views all around. The Macinghi would have already appreciated these advantages, and this is a case in which the theory reflected common sense and the practice was widespread. The orientation of rooms within the house is sometimes in accordance with Vitruvius's recommendations, but this is barely sufficient to turn Sassetti's villa into a 'Roman house' in the Vitruvian sense. The obscure wording of the passage in Vitruvius's text describing the plan of the Roman house (Book VI, ch. 3) and the hazardous task, given the lack of plans or translations before 1486, of interpreting how the mid–fifteenth

century visualised this type of building, make it difficult to claim a Vitruvian source for the plan of Palazzo Medici and its offspring. Nevertheless, the barrel-vaulted *androni* that functioned like *vestibula*, the square courtyard with its portico and *all'antica sgraffito* decoration, the axial vistas and symmetrically arranged apartments, can all be related to ancient architectural theory and practice. As Georgia Clarke states in her study of the Roman house, the Palazzo Medici and its followers were not necessarily 'built as re-creations of ancient architecture, but they could have been read in a classical light by contemporaries versed in ancient literature'.[71]

Sassetti's villa was certainly not conceived in the predominantly agricultural terms that Vitruvius lays down in his chapter on 'villae', which begins with the recommendation that 'the size of a farm-house is to be arranged to suit the amount of land and of the crops'. Nevertheless, Vitruvius does provide an alternative for those who wished to build a grander villa, urging them to follow his design for town houses. 'If a touch of elegance is required in a farm house, it should be built in a symmetrical manner, which things are described above for town houses, yet without interfering with the needs of agriculture'. Here, then, is a Vitruvian mandate for transposing a town palace design into the countryside.[72]

Although Alberti tends to stress the differences between town and country houses and does not recommend a similar form for both, yet his description of the advantages of the *villa suburbana* applies well to La Pietra:

> There is one type of private building that combines the dignity of a city house with the delight of a villa . . . of all the buildings for practical use, I consider the *hortus* to be the foremost and healthiest: it does not detain you from business in the city, nor is it troubled by impurity of air.[73]

It is not only the site of La Pietra, close to town, near an open road, on the crest of a rise, with fine views, but the main practical advantages of Sassetti's *villa*

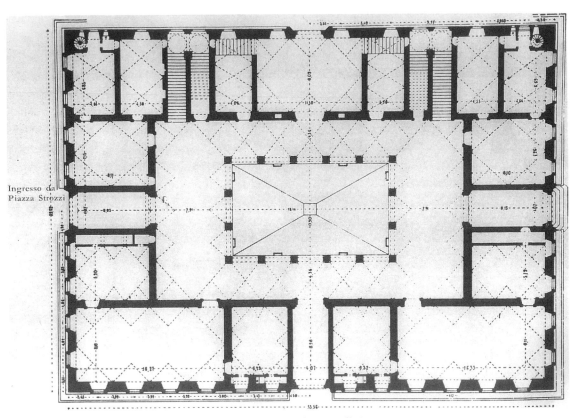

195. Palazzo Strozzi, Florence, ground plan (Stegmann and Geymüller).

suburbana, that it could be a substitute for a town house combining the dignity and convenience of an urban palace with the health and beauty of the countryside, that fits Alberti's criteria so closely.

The gradual adoption of a symmetrical system in domestic interiors can be observed if the ground plans of the Palazzo Medici (1444–c. 1453), the Palazzo Piccolomini in Pienza (1459–62), the Sassetti villa at La Pietra (1462–c. 1470) and the Palazzo Strozzi (begun 1489) are arranged in chronological sequence. At the Palazzo Medici the canon of symmetry did not yet inform the interior disposition as it did some ten or fifteen years later in the planning of Pius II's palace and soon afterwards at La Pietra. Furthermore, in Francesco Sassetti's villa the quadripartite division created by the three barrel-vaulted halls reveal it to be an important forerunner of the rigorously regular plan of Palazzo Strozzi (Fig. 195), and the range of clearly differentiated large, medium-sized and small

rooms, which systematise the apartments, set it apart from most other contemporary plans.

The bold transposition of an urban building type into the country, as well as the large scale, the innovatory plan and the up-to-date decorative features of the La Pietra villa, all point towards the contribution of a major architect. Although there is no documentary evidence, a plausible case, based on stylistic evidence, could be made for either the Rossellino workshop or Giuliano da Maiano. Since construction was under way in 1462 and Bernardo Rossellino only died in 1464 he is a possible candidate. The close resemblance between the plans of La Pietra and the Palazzo Piccolomini in Pienza would support the attribution. Although comparison with other buildings from the Rossellino workshop shows broad similarities between the oratory at La Pietra and the Cardinal of Portugal's chapel or the capitals found on the ground-floor rooms at La Pietra and the Spinelli cloister, these are not close enough to clinch the matter. On the other hand, Giuliano da Maiano, aged thirty in 1462, may have scarcely begun his architectural career. His first documented architectural work is the S. Fina Chapel in S. Gimignano (1466–70), although it is likely that Giuliano had experience in palace design by 1462 if he had indeed worked on the Palazzo Pazzi (after 1458–c. 1469) and perhaps on the Strozzino Palace (1451–65). Again the influence of Palazzo Medici (Palazzo Strozzino, Palazzo Spanocchi), the choice of a centralised chapel plan (S. Fina), and the capital types incorporating family emblems (Palazzo Pazzi) or with downward curling foliate volutes (Strozzino courtyard) are all features shared with La Pietra. In this context, the 1464 document concerning Francesco Sassetti's agreement with Giovanni di Domenico da Gaiole for the provision of wood, labour and drawings could be interpreted either way: to imply that Giuliano da Maiano, with whom Gaiole was working in the Cathedral Sacristy, had a hand in designing La Pietra, or that Gaiole himself may have worked as an architect at the villa.

A more precise morphological comparison, however, can be made between the oratory at La Pietra and the chapels of the Badia Fiesolana with their corner solution of unarticulated mouldings. Sassetti himself had a chapel in the Badia church that was only a mile from the villa and was being built at the same time. Given these factors and the Medici connection, some overlap in the workforce is likely and a *capomaestro* like Lorenzo di Antonio di Geri, who probably worked at the Badia and at Careggi, may have contributed to La Pietra. If the Rossellino were involved at the Badia, this would be another argument in their favour. There is no easy solution here, and at this point La Pietra joins the ranks of a series of midcentury Florentine palaces and villas for whom no architect is documented and attribution remains tenuous.

12 · THE ROLE OF THE VILLA AT LA PIETRA IN THE LIFE OF FRANCESCO SASSETTI

The villa at La Pietra was the concrete manifestation of Francesco Sassetti's good fortune and the proof that he had begun to realise his ambitions. It was built in his prime, it represented the peak of his financial success and was the most magnificent example of his patronage. So, too, the fate of the villa mirrored that of the family: it was sold when their wealth was exhausted and shortly before Francesco's last surviving son died.

Francesco's relations with the Medici shaped his life. The orphaned Sassetti brothers did not inherit capital that would make them independently wealthy, nor could they turn to powerful relatives for sponsorship. In return for employment and advancement from the Medici, they offered dedicated service and political loyalty.[1] After Bartolommeo had been an accountant in the Medici household for the first part of his career and improved his social and political status, he joined a separate business partnership with the Ridolfi by 1451.[2] Francesco was far more ambitious and his dependence on the Medici was greater in proportion. Thus, his early success was more spectacular, but when the bank collapsed his funds went with it.

Francesco dedicated the years between 1440 and 1459 to building his career with the Medici bank in Geneva, working his way up from junior clerk to branch manager and steadily amassing a large capital invested in share holdings and term deposits in the Medici banks of Geneva, Milan and Avignon.[3] His correpondence with the Medici in the 1450s reveals that he was already on friendly terms with the whole family. He performed special favours such as sending a falcon and sable furs to Pierfrancesco di Lorenzo[4] and linen to Piero di Cosimo's wife Lucrezia,[5] and he acted as an agent in the search for antiques and inscriptions for Piero. In 1457 he sent cameos of Camilla and a red faun to Piero for which he hoped to receive manuscripts of the orations or letters of Cicero in return.[6] In the letters accompanying these dispatches he expressed his loyalty and dependence. In 1452, he wrote to Pierfrancesco di Lorenzo de' Medici, 'don't think of saying that you cause me trouble, because it upsets me. You know that I have been and always will be, in the service of your family, and it gives me pleasure, not trouble, when I do something that gives you pleasure';[7] 'I am entirely yours and your creation and with you and yours I am bound to live and die'.[8]

The next phase of Francesco's life from 1459 to 1477 was the most fruitful in terms of his family, his political career[9] and his patronage. He married Nera di Piero Corsi in 1459 when he was thirty-eight and his bride fifteen. Over the next twenty years she bore him five sons and five daughters, of whom only one (Teodoro I) did not survive his father.[10] Even the names Francesco chose for his firstborn children reveal the same attitude that led him to build in an ostentatious manner outside his family district. Rather than expressing loyalty and adherence to the Sassetti lineage by recreating his ancestors in the names of his first progeny, he preferred to declare his affiliation with powerful figures outside the family whom he admired or whose goodwill he sought. Thus, Francesco di Giovanbattista Sassetti claims in his 'Notizie' of 1600 that Teodoro (born in 1460) was named after the Marquis of Monferrato.[11] Warburg notes that this was probably the Cardinal Legate Teodoro Paleologo (the title of Marchese actually went to his brother Giovanni) whose family had dealings with the Medici bank and whom Sassetti would have known in the north.[12] Galeazzo the second son, born in 1461, was surely named after Giangaleazzo Sforza who had visited Florence two years before and whose acquaintance Francesco may have made through the bank in Milan;[13] while Cosimo, born on 2 March 1465, was intended to recreate the virtues of Cosimo de' Medici who had died seven months before.[14] These were distinctly secular choices of children's names, revealing opportunistic motives, and a greater faith in the support of earthly patrons than in patron saints.

It was not until the late 1460s with the baptism of Lisabetta (a common name in the family), Federigo (born in 1472 to 'remake' Francesco's eldest brother who had died in 1468) and Lena (born in 1474 who was to be a reincarnation of Francesco's sister) that Francesco adopted family traditions again.[15] It may be no coincidence that these were also the years when he bought back Fiondina Sassetti's estate at Novoli (1468)[16] and returned to the Sassetti quarter in town to try to regain the ancestral patronage rights for the high altar of S. Maria Novella (1470)[17] and to buy a site for a new palace in the Via Larga dei Legniaiuoli (1472–7).[18] When seen in this light it appears that the La Pietra project, like the baptism of his first sons, was intended to create a grand first impression since the image then projected by the Sassetti establishment did not provide the magnificent associations Francesco needed to satisfy his ambitions. His choices should not be interpreted as a rejection of his kin but rather as a desire to resuscitate the lineage and reconstruct its identity. This is confirmed by the way he swiftly followed up his initially independent policy with investment and patronage that reflected traditional clannish values, but on a larger scale than his brothers or cousins were able or committed to carry out. This ambivalence is revealed in the tax returns and *Libro segreto* which show that, although in 1461 soon after his return he bought back the old family town house, he was reluctant to return to his earlier conditions and he must have retained the house purely for the sake of family tradition because it remained let throughout his life.[19] Instead, he chose to buy another house on the opposite side of town on the Canto dei Pazzi in 1465,[20] which he inhabited until he moved back to the Quarter of S. Maria Novella to live on the site of his projected palace in the mid-1470s.[21] These real estate transactions and movements between properties can be read as indicators of Francesco Sassetti's state of mind.

Another key piece of evidence from this period is Francesco Sassetti's marble portrait bust, representing him with very close cropped hair and vigorous growth of stubble, wearing a heavy robe knotted over the right shoulder in the manner of an ancient *paludamentum* (Fig. 196).[22] Since the bust is inscribed 'FRANC. SAXETTUS. FLORENT. CIVIS. ANN. XLIIII', it must have been completed between March 1464 and March 1465. Traditionally assigned to Antonio Rossellino, but reattributed to Andrea del Verrocchio by John Pope-Hennessy and Andrew Butterfield,[23] the extraordinary intensity, focus and self-assertion of this *all'antica* image fit particularly well into what we now know of this driven and productive phase of Sassetti's life. The portrait bust could even be interpreted as the sculptural equivalent of the grand new villa, each projecting an image of magnificence deriving from ancient Roman associations, and both functioning as key components in Sassetti's campaign to establish a new identity for himself in the early years after his return to the *patria*. It is tempting to assume that the bust was intended for the renovated villa, although the display of this type of portrait has been consistently located in town palaces or offices, rather than country houses. If it were intended for town, it would initially have been displayed in his house on the Canto de' Pazzi, never apparently rebuilt by Sassetti and used as a stopgap until a new palace site could be acquired.

That Sassetti was already furnishing La Pietra and the house on the Canto de' Pazzi can be inferred by

196. Portrait bust of Francesco Sassetti, aged forty-four, attributed to Andrea del Verrocchio or to Antonio Rossellino. Florence, Museo Nazionale del Bargello.

comparing the assets listed in his *Libro segreto* in 1462 and 1466.[24] This shows that while he was spending less on personal attire (his jewellery was worth 1,630 *fiorini di sugello* in 1462 and F. 1,500 *di sugello* in 1466, his clothes F. 829 *di sugello* in 1462 and F. 500 *di sugello* in 1466), his furniture (*masserizie*) rose in value from F. 2,000 *di sugello* in 1462 to F. 3,500 *di sugello* in 1466 and the silverware from F. 551 *di sugello* in 1462 to F. 1,000 *di sugello* in 1466. Unfortunately, there are no such records for the later years, although the document transferring La Pietra to Federigo's name in 1485 mentions the furnishings and contents of the villa were worth F. 1,000 *larghi* (c. F. 1,200 *di sugello*). Although there is no way of checking their accuracy, the sums listed by his great-grandson in his 'Notizie' of 1600[25] may represent the sort of increase we should expect between 1466 and 1478 when the financial crisis hit: F. 3,550 for furnishings in town and country, F. 1,600 for silver and tableware, F. 1,750 for jewellery

and goldware, F. 1,100 for his own and his family's clothes and more than F. 800 for manuscripts. Because of fluctuations in currency, the lack of dates and unspecified location of these objects, a comparative analysis of his investments and of his town and country palaces is not feasible. Nevertheless, the estate at La Pietra was the single most valuable property listed in the *Libro segreto*, and his country holdings were worth considerably more than his town houses, a state of affairs that persisted even after he had bought the site for the new urban palace in the 1470s.[26]

Although La Pietra was the first project initiated on his return, Francesco soon took on other schemes of patronage which overlapped in the late 1460s. He helped to finance the rebuilding of the chapel of Notre Dame du Pont du Rhone in Geneva for which there is a debit of 500 *scudi* (600 florins) recorded in his *Libro segreto* in 1466 and a sum of L. 228 lire 13 *soldi* and 3 *denari* under Francesco Sassetti's name in the list of debtors of the Medici bank in Lyons who were to pay the 'chonto delle fabriche della chapella fa fare a Ginevra' in April 1467.[27]

The sum of 200 florins spent on the 'capella della badia' recorded in his *Libro segreto* in 1466[28] must refer to the Badia Fiesolana, where the Sassetti arms still identify their chapel today. The date also coincides with the inscription behind the main altar commemorating the completion of the church under the supervision of Piero di Cosimo de' Medici in 1466.[29] Furthermore, the 1496 consecration of the chapels lists the patrons,[30] five of whom were employees in the Medici bank; apart from Sassetti there was Agnolo Tani, Pigello Portinari, the Martelli family and Francesco Nori.[31] The same document tells us that Sassetti was granted the privilege of (or took this opportunity to pay his respect by) dedicating his chapel to the Medicean Saints Cosmas and Damian.[32] The presence of SS. Cosmas and Damian in an enamelled terracotta altarpiece recorded in the same chapel in the eighteenth century[33] and now in the Florentine Misericordia[34] suggests that this was the altarpiece originally commissioned by Sassetti (Fig. 197). Although it is unclear whether the 200 florins recorded in the *Libro segreto* were only for patronage rights or also covered the cost of the altarpiece or furnishings, the attribution of the terracotta altarpiece to Andrea della Robbia and a dating very early in his career are compatible with the Sassetti chronology.[35]

Francesco's optimism seems to have carried through to the late 1470s. In 1468, he had invested in several big farms at Gonfienti and accumulated a group of smaller farms and pieces of land in the ancestral district of Novoli. In 1477, he bought his last big country property at Casi near Vaiano. In the same years (1472–7), he bought seven houses in the Via Larga dei Legniaouli with the intention of building a new palace there.[36]

In comparison with La Pietra, Francesco Sassetti's other rural estates now appear insignificant. Even in the fifteenth century, their houses were certainly more modest, for, unlike La Pietra, their primary function was not residential. Nevertheless, their lands were extensive, and these properties illustrate Sassetti's determination to continue developing his rural estates on

197. Madonna and Child with Saints Cosmas and Damian, God the Father with angels in the pediment, the Annunciation, Nativity and Adoration of the Magi in the predella, Sassetti altarpiece for the Badia at Fiesole, attributed to Andrea della Robbia, c. 1466, glazed terracotta. Museo dell'Arciconfraternita della Misericordia, Florence.

a large scale in a period when he was simultaneously buying the site for a new palace in town. Francesco's ambitions did not stop at La Pietra.

In 1427 Fiondina di Pellaio Sassetti, the eighty-five-year-old widow of Talano Adimari, owned a farm with a house for herself and one for the *lavoratore* in the parish of S. Maria at Novoli.[37] True to the heraldic significance of her name, Fiondina (Little Sling) made a will in 1430 leaving the Novoli farm to her relative Antonio di Piero, called Rosso,[38] and, if he should die without heirs, to Gemma di Francesco Sassetti, and, if she should leave no issue, to the Compagnia di S. Pietro Martire, and, if they should refuse to say masses for the Sassetti, to the Hospital of S. Maria Nuova. In addition there was a clause to the effect that if any member of the Sassetti family wished to buy back the farm from one of those institutions, it should

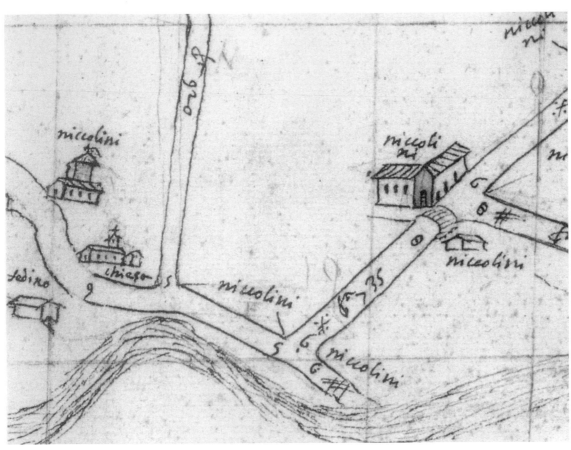

198. Parish of S. Martino a Gonfienti, with the *casa da signore* once belonging to Francesco Sassetti shown as an L-shaped house marked 'niccolini' on the right. Detail of *Piante di popoli e strade – Capitani di parte guelfa – 1580–1595*, II, c. 513.

be sold to them for twenty-five florins less than the ratable value. Rosso only kept the villa for two years before consigning the farm to the Chapter of S. Maria Novella in payment of a debt.[39]

Thirty-six years later in 1468, Francesco Sassetti requested that S. Maria Novella sell Fiondina's estate back to him in return for three pieces of land near Campi Bisenzio.[40] In the 1470s Francesco bought more land at Novoli: a piece of land on the banks of the Arno, and two farms which had belonged to his sister Caterina.[41] These were certainly not random purchases, nor were they sound financial investments. When Francesco bought back the farms that had once belonged to the Sassetti women Fiondina and Caterina, he was reclaiming family property and conserving the Sassetti presence in the district of Novoli.

Even the piece of land that was being eaten away by the river was eventually to endow the chapel in S. Trinita.[42] These properties, whose preservation was linked to the sense of family identity, were given, together with Montughi, to Federigo for safekeeping.[43] Although Francesco's other country properties were all removed from the Sassetti district, his acquisitions at Novoli reveal his desire to own land in the area associated with his ancestors and close to Macia, the villa that had long been owned by his branch of the family and was now inhabited by his brother Bartolommeo.

Gonfienti on the other hand is the sort of estate we might expect from a banker: commercially profitable, yielding large quantities of grain; easy to work on flat, alluvial ground; situated between the markets of Florence and Prato (Figs. 198 and 199). This was

199. Gonfienti, the Villa Niccolini, once Francesco Sassetti's *casa da signore*.

undoubtedly Sassetti's most valuable agricultural investment. He bought the two farms that formed the nucleus of his holdings there on 16 August 1468.[44] There was a house for the landowner as well as the tenant farmer and a huge expanse of land: 266 *staiora* planted in wheat, millet, sorghum, beans, linen, vines and osiers. In the following spring he bought three more pieces of land and altogether the estate was capitalised at 1,307 florins, 3 *soldi*, in 1480, the value of a big farm yielding 228 *staia* of grain.[45]

Sassetti continued to add to this property, buying up the surrounding land bit by bit between 1468 and 1477. It is clear that the many small purchases made during that decade were part of a plan to consolidate several big farms, a development that was completed in 1480 and 1481. Today Francesco's villa lies surrounded by large, flat fields some 500 metres from the village of Gonfienti, just beyond the banks of the Bisenzio.[46] Although the vestiges of an old tower can still be seen above the roof line, the villa seems to have been entirely rebuilt over the centuries. No description of the

fifteenth-century villa has come to light, and it is most unlikely that the *casa da signore* here was on the lavish scale of La Pietra. Yet Fonzio's inclusion of Gonfienti in his eulogies of Sassetti's patronage suggests that this estate was impressive, too.[47]

Further up the Bisenzio River, north of Prato and within the steep-sided valley, Francesco bought his last villa in the parish of S. Leonardo a Casi near Vaiano (Figs. 200 and 201).[48] Like Filippo Strozzi's villas, Francesco Sassetti's two big agricultural estates were linked by the Bisenzio River.[49] The property included flatter land on the old river terraces that provided a suitable site for the *casa da signore* and for growing wheat. From there the terrain rose steeply towards the flanks of the Montagne Pistoiesi with vines and olives growing on the lower slopes; higher up they ran herds of goats, sheep and a couple of cattle, and used the woods for timber and firewood. Like Bartolommeo Sassetti's property at Valcenni, this was bought as a hill farm outside the livestock limits imposed near town, so that its produce complemented that of the farms on

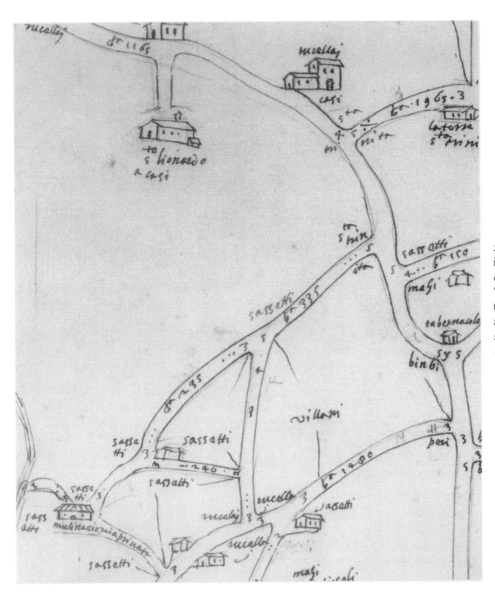

200. Parish of S. Salvatore a Vaiano with Francesco Sassetti's *casa da signore* marked 'sassetti' and 'mulinaccio' at the bottom left and the church of S. Lionardo a Casi above. Detail of *Piante di popoli e strade – Capitani di parte guelfa – 1580–1595*, II, c. 479.

flat land nearer Florence. Here Sassetti bought an estate known as 'Il Mulinaccio' from Lionardo di Stagio d'Antonio Strozzi in January 1477,[50] at the same time acquiring the patronage rights of the small but ancient *pieve* of S. Leonardo a Casi.[51]

The climate of disaster in 1478, caused by the Pazzi conspiracy, war with the papacy and the failure of the Medici banks in London, Bruges, Avignon, Venice, Milan, Naples and Rome[52] must have awoken Francesco to the need to safeguard his property from confiscation. It may also have been his sons' impending departure to work for the Medici bank abroad that

led Francesco to emancipate the two older sons and transfer much of his property to their names.[53] On 23 August 1478 a document of emancipation and donation was drawn up for Teodoro I (aged eighteen) and Cosimo (aged thirteen), making over to them all the farms at Gonfienti and nearby Mezzana and Confini together with the estate at Casi further up the Bisenzio River.[54] A year later, on 4 September 1479, a week after his eighteenth birthday, Galeazzo was given all the houses on the site of the projected town palace.[55] La Pietra and Novoli were retained in Francesco's name until Federigo reached the age of thirteen and was old

201. Casi, Il Mulinaccio, Stagio d'Antonio Strozzi's villa bought by Francesco Sassetti and rebuilt by his son Cosimo Sassetti.

enough to receive them on 5 October 1485.[56] These were cautionary measures that should be viewed in the context of looming financial disaster and even as part of Francesco's preparations for death, like the burial chapel in S. Trinita, which was planned and decorated in the same years (1478–86). If the properties were not in his name it might prevent confiscation in case of bankruptcy.

Filippo's *ultima volontà*, prompted by his departure to save the bank in Lyons in 1488, clarifies his attitude to the division of property (Fig. 202). He emphasised the importance of family unity, and the need for his sons and heirs to care for each other and to present a united front in the face of misfortune:

> Remaining united and at peace, and treating one another with love and respect, that harmony may reign among you. . . . Defend and help one another valiantly and wholeheartedly, lest you seem to be sleepers or paltry fools. Where a division must be made, let it be made discreetly, with the agreement and assistance of your brothers-in-law and your relations, if need be. Live together in love and

202. Francesco Sassetti's 'ultima volontà', copied in another hand in 1490, detail of second page dealing with 'el palagio di montughi' (Villa La Pietra). From photograph made for Aby Warburg, Warburg Institute Archive, III, 70.2 (Photo: Warburg Institute).

charity, most of all taking as much care for those younger than yourselves and for their portions as you do for yourselves.[57]

His heirs' common ownership of their property is one aspect, and a symbol for the outside world, of that unity. He goes on to say that they should each have an equal share in the whole estate and disregard the notarial contracts allocating different properties to separate members of the family:

> To Messer Federigo, to Teodoro, to Madonna Nera, and also to others of you, I have assigned the deeds and contracts concerning a number of our properties, when they were acquired, and what became of them thereafter; you will find the records in the proper place among my papers. It is still my wish that everything be shared equally between you, each receiving his portion, as if the said contracts had never been drawn up: and that, as is reasonable, no one of you shall receive more than another. Follow my wishes to the letter, like righteous and well-behaved sons and brothers, demonstrating your fraternal love and goodwill; in the knowledge, above all, that the said contracts were drawn up for a higher purpose, namely to preserve your assets, and not to give any one of you an advantage over another.[58]

Here Sassetti claims that the contracts were made solely to safeguard their estate from outside creditors and not to protect the members of the family from each other. Given his own brothers' quarrels over property, Francesco probably also intended the early donations as an extra precaution that would stand in lieu of the notarised will he chose not to make.[59]

His idealistic sentiment and earnest recommendations are, however, contradicted in the very next line when he qualifies a reminder to Galeazzo and Cosimo of money he had lent them with the phrase 'quando vi dividessi' ('when you divide the inheritance'), showing that he considered some division inevitable. Sassetti's pragmatism is most evident in his instructions for Montughi. His motive in transferring the villa to Federigo's name was that it should receive the protection of the church, and although Francesco had just stated that the properties should not remain under the name of a particular member of the family, he made a special case of La Pietra in firmly recommending that it be maintained by Federigo:

> I should like you therefore to do all you can to maintain it in the name of Messer Federigo, who holds the title deeds and to whom it has been given. . . .
>
> Leave it, I think, in Messer Federigo's name, as a clergyman, he will be best able to protect it, until time shows you the most suitable course to take.[60]

Sassetti had already devised this solution to the problem of how to protect the villa when he donated it to Federigo on 5 October 1485, for Federigo had been made apostolic protonotary seven months earlier on 28 February 1485.[61] The two elder brothers Galeazzo and Cosimo had followed in their father's footsteps and were working for the bank in France,[62] but the crises in the Medici bank may have led Francesco to lose faith in the security of financial and secular power and to pin hopes on Federigo's career in the church. An ecclesiastic was less exposed to financial disaster and his property less liable to confiscation.

Meanwhile, Lorenzo de' Medici was procuring an ecclesiastical future for his son Giovanni, and here, too, the Medici provided the model for Francesco Sassetti. Giovanni de' Medici had been made *protonotario apostolico* at the age of seven on 31 May 1483.[63] Federigo Sassetti was twelve or thirteen when he received the same benefice two years later. These events and the parallel hopes for Giovanni and Federigo's careers are certainly part of the historical context for Ghirlandaio's 'Confirmation of the Rule of S. Francis'

in the Sassetti chapel (Fig. 203),[64] and the whole foreground narrative in this fresco makes sense as a meeting between the two young clerics and their proud families. The celebration or even conferment of Federigo's benefice in 1485 fits tellingly into the 'Confirmation of the Franciscan Rule' scene[65] and employs the same type of narrative strategy as the 'Raising of the Roman Notary's Son' scene underneath in which important, recent family events are directly juxtaposed with hagiographic histories. Just as the resuscitation or rebirth of the Roman notary's/Sassetti's son legitimates the presence of the fifteenth-century family bystanders in the scene below, so the precocious boy clerics in the foreground of the lunette fresco give Sassetti and his contemporaries a reason to be there.

Sassetti's pressing anxieties and ambitions for Federigo also gave him a very specific motive to honour the Medici and display the Medici-Sassetti bond in this public way, for the surviving letters make it clear that Sassetti was dependent on Lorenzo de' Medici to sponsor Federigo in his career. The inclusion of Lorenzo and his family could therefore be read as a mark of gratitude, a sort of secular *ex voto* image, to thank Lorenzo for the support he had already given and, at the same time, to solicit his patronage for the future. Lorenzo de' Medici probably had his own particular reasons to want to be seen in these frescoes: on the one hand wishing to display his support for the S. Trinita faction in a Vallombrosan dispute[66] and, on the other hand, dependent on the continued loyalty and work of his general manager, Francesco Sassetti. For example, de Roover showed how it was one of the tasks of the Medici bank employees to find benefices for Giovanni de' Medici.[67] Lorenzo was bound into a mutually dependent relationship with Sassetti; and the 'Confirmation of the Franciscan Rule' fresco should then be interpreted as an image constructed around the reciprocal nature of patronal relations, rather than a one-sided case of the bank manager honouring the bank owner.

By 1489 Giovanni de' Medici had already been nominated as cardinal,[68] and Sassetti was asking Lorenzo to use his influence in promoting Federigo

203. Sassetti Chapel, S. Trinita, Florence, altar wall, Ghirlandaio's fresco 'The Confirmation of the Rule of St Francis' (photo: Antonio Quattrone).

from his priorship at S. Michele Berteldi to a higher office in the Cathedral of Florence.[69] After Francesco's death, his son Cosimo continued to plead for his brother, chanelling some of his own ambitions through his, only to be bitterly disappointed by Federigo's early death on 21 December 1491.[70] As Francesco had served three generations of Medici, so the next generation of Sassetti continued to depend on the favour and fortune of the Medici. Behind the conventional expression of devotion and dependence in Francesco Sassetti's letters to Lorenzo de' Medici there was also the genuine affection that derived from a shared past and sufficient parity:

> Lorenzo, this [the recovery of the Medici bank] is the greatest cause that I have or could have to face in this world, and whoever would imagine that I would not do everything in my power, would judge me mad, because I would dedicate to it my life, my sons and everything that I have in the world....[71]
>
> I take great comfort reading your helpful and loving letter and I feel as though we are discussing things together as we used to, and it reminds me of the happy, tranquil times. After so many anxieties and dangers we need to return soon to enjoy what little we have before our end is come.[72]

In the letters of Francesco's son Cosimo Sassetti, however, the tone changes to one of slavish desperation:

> Not having any recourse other than to your Excellency, I can only continue to remind you and recommend our case to you. We are left with little or no belongings and, as you

know, I have debts in Lyons. Nonetheless, we manage as well as we can to clothe ourselves. We implore you, do not abandon us, as you would not abandon any of your faithful servants, which we are and wish to be, we who were born with this bond.[73]

In his *ultima volontà* Francesco mentions the possibility that he might have no capital left to bequeath: 'if I were to leave you more debts than assets' ('quando bene vi lasciassi più debito che mobile'). The same consideration lies behind his advice for La Pietra: 'if at any time Fortune should desert you, you will have to sell the palace and let it go rather than fall into dire straits' ('quanto la fortuna vi perseguitassi, vi bisognerà restare contenti alienarlo et lasciarlo andare per non fare peggio'). This expedient attitude is the antithesis of the *fidecomesso* clause attached to many fifteenth-century wills that binds the family to its property in perpetuity.[74] Nevertheless, after Francesco's death at the end of March 1490, his heirs' tax returns show that they were slow to sell their real estate. A letter from Cosimo Sassetti to Lorenzo de' Medici, written on 28 February 1491 in reply to a request that they repay their father's debts, says that they have no cash ('mobile di danari'), but he is willing to sell small things ('mobile di cose sottili') like jewellery and silver.[75] Perhaps books fell into this category, for it was in 1491 that sixty-seven manuscripts from Francesco's library found their way into Lorenzo's possession.[76] Significantly, Cosimo does not offer to sell land, and the only properties sold soon after Francesco's death were the old house where Francesco and Bartolommeo had originally lived on the Chiasso dei Sassetti and a shop on the corner of the same block, both sold by Galeazzo.[77] Otherwise, only odd pieces of land changed hands until the 1530s.[78] Thus, Francesco's estates in the country at La Pietra, Gonfienti, Casi and Novoli, as well as his houses on the Via Larga dei Legnaiuoli, remained for the benefit of his sons, and the wisdom of converting capital into real estate was revealed. Whatever the crisis in the bank, however short of cash they may have been at Francesco's death, the immediate spectre of bankruptcy was overridden and the landed property left untouched.

The praise of Fonzio, Ficino and Verino testifies to La Pietra's fifteenth-century reputation and adds credence to Sassetti's own view:

The Palazzo di Montughi has added great lustre to my name and to our family, and it is justly famous throughout Italy and beyond; as you know, it is beautiful and costs a great deal of money.[79]

It was widely recognised that magnificent buildings lent prestige to their owners, and Sassetti's statement is another expression of this motive for building[80] but in this case applied to a villa rather than an urban palace. It is clear here that Francesco intended to create a new image for the Sassetti lineage, as it is also in his instructions for the S. Maria Novella altarpiece, in the carving of their coat of arms on the vaults in the villa and the placing of a loggia on the roadside at La Pietra. That he recommended the villa be sold rather than retained at all costs for his descendants need not be interpreted as meaning that the family and its identity meant less to him than they did to other palace owners but reflected the bad times and threatening conditions in which he was writing.

Francesco repeated how expensive the villa was to maintain ('it costs a great deal of money . . . it is an expensive luxury and produces scant revenue. It is a place for rich people . . . it carries heavy expenses',[81]) but he was also aware of the other disadvantage of owning a magnificent building. Envy accompanies magnificence.[82] Building on a grand scale is an act of arrogance ('it is a boastful luxury')[83] that requires special backing ('the clergy will be best able to protect it').[84] Pius II suggested that Cosimo de' Medici had tried to counter envy by commissioning 'noble works', but in the end, 'the people always hate superior worth'.[85] Alberti thought that only the greatest architects could obtain the approval of grand people without antagonising those who lived more modestly ('to build something praised by the magnificent, yet not rejected by the frugal').[86] Finally Francesco's method of protecting his property from a jealous society when his defences were down due to diminishing wealth was to place it under the cloak of the church.

Francesco Sassetti's attitude to his villa has been viewed through his tax returns, his *Libro segreto*, his *ultima volontà* and through the words of contemporary writers. Ultimately the building of La Pietra itself illustrates his willingness to invest in the countryside and its magnificent structure is the most concrete evidence of how highly he valued the villa. Yet one letter sent by Francesco Sassetti in Lyons to his colleague Giovanni Tornabuoni in Florence, allows us a more vivid glimpse of his sensibility towards country pleasures. Obliged to remain in Lyons until he could sort out the financial crisis in the Medici bank, Francesco dreamt of an idyllic scene at the villa of Francesco Nori:

> Remember me when you are enjoying the consoling delights of that beautiful villa, especially at Africo in that fine woody grove of Francesco Nori's, where there should be a fountain.[87]

Africo was one of Nori's farms in the hills above Antella. However, Francesco Nori, a mutual friend and co-employee of the Medici bank, had been murdered ten years before in the Pazzi Conspiracy of 1478, so that the memory of his villas and gardens is evoked here in an elegiac mood, thinking back to the good times, before the bank had sunk into decline, and before the conspiracy had introduced a climate of fear and anxiety. Writing in the subalpine cold of Lyons in late November 1488, a Florentine villa garden is the ultimate imaginary haven of health, peace and pleasure.

In examining a wider sample of villas than that provided by the narrow and exclusive Medicean canon, the notion of the villa as a pleasure house has been brought into question.[1] Much of this book has been dedicated to an alternative approach, arguing for the predominance of a functionalist and economically motivated attitude consistent with the mercantile mentality cultivated in Florence at the time. For it would seem odd if these merchants, bankers and manufacturers with their accounting habits and pecuniary concerns, were to ride into the country and leave those deeply inculcated behaviour patterns behind. The evidence for the utilitarian approach does not only come from the archives, but also from the theorists, including Alberti's writings on the villa and country life,[2] the widely disseminated ancient and medieval agricultural treatises,[3] and the 'best-selling' *Oeconomica* of the Pseudo-Aristotle.[4] But the houses themselves are, perhaps, the strongest evidence for the prevalence of this mentality. The retention of old houses and the preference for repair and renovation rather than full-scale new construction are manifestations of this value system.

If *utilità* was a fundamental part of villa ideology, this need not exclude its apparent antithesis, the pleasure principle. Although Lorenzo Strozzi perceived profit and pleasure ('rendita' and 'diletto') as distinct alternatives when he rejected Santuccio, and Alberti in his *De re aedificatoria* also divided villas into those run for profit ('per motivi d'interesse' / 'emolumenti') and those intended for pleasure ('per

semplice diletto' / 'fortassis animi gratia'),[5] the two clearly co-existed on most Florentine country estates.[6] If a productive agricultural estate could also be a delightful place to stay, and if a fine country residence could generate income from its lands, why forego the dual advantages? There are, however, signs that a more aestheticised and hedonistic attitude was gradually coming to the fore during this period. Lorenzo Strozzi's plea is the voice of someone seeking *diletto*. Francesco Sassetti's villa at La Pietra may have been a one-off case, but its disregard for modest rural decorum of the sort promoted by Alberti, and its preoccupation with urban magnificence and sophistication at the expense of pragmatic and thrifty rural values, can be seen as part of the emergence of a new villa aesthetic. Other examples begin to make more sense when seen in this context. The interior of Carlo di Marcuccio Strozzi's villa Il Palagio with its new self-sufficient apartment and its fine inlaid wooden furniture combined the useful with the comfortable and the aesthetically pleasing. It is in relation to the land, however, that the pleasure principle can most clearly be seen to be developing. The artist Zanobi Strozzi's house at Palaiuola with its garden, its *boschetto* and minimal sized vineyard, may have been acquired to serve as a workshop or living quarters near the painters Sanguigni and Fra Angelico, but he kept it long after his apprenticeship was over, and his brother's family and another cousin all moved to the same place. The attraction for an artist who painted plants, gardens and landscapes with rare delicacy and dedication, was probably Palaiuola's beautiful setting on the lower flanks of the Fiesole hill looking down the Mugnone to Florence. As Giovanni Morelli wrote, *boschetti* like Zanobi Strozzi's were key providers of *diletto*,[7] their trees planted for delight and pleasure, rather than to produce fruit, timber, firewood, stakes or withies. A grander example of this tendency is Filippo Strozzi's land above the Bay of Naples, which may have been a classic example of a farm (*masseria*) being transformed into a garden, a luxury enterprise involving a specialised gardener (*ortolano*) sent from Tuscany, and a grand new double loggia to entertain guests in the landscape.[8]

These various concepts of how to live in the country could run side by side, partly because wealthy people had more than one countryside. Each of Francesco Sassetti's rural properties was very different in character and chosen to fulfil a particular purpose. La Pietra satisfied his need for a country residence and his desire to build a grand palace as soon as possible after his return. Its farms were not especially lucrative. Gonfienti and Casi, on the other hand, supplied agricultural produce in abundance. The valley farm of Gonfienti yielded mostly grain while Casi, in more distant hill country, provided wool, meat, cheese, olive oil and wood. There were *case da signore* on both estates which would have housed the Sassetti family during summer visits, but their primary function was agricultural. The lands at Novoli were not acquired for their habitation nor their produce, but to enable Francesco to participate in the tradition of Sassetti ownership in the district of Novoli. A whole range of purposes was therefore covered by Francesco Sassetti's rural estates: the grand suburban villa suitable for dignified residence and sumptuous entertaining, the big, productive farms in hill and valley and the old family property with ancestral associations.

Despite Alberti's maxim that two villas were sufficient for one owner and three too many, the policy of acquiring complementary rural estates was widespread among the richest Florentines during the fifteenth century.[9] Palla di Nofri Strozzi's extensive properties certainly provided the full range of produce with villas serving every need from the convenient suburban estate at Novoli, to the panoramic hill site only

slightly further from town at Petraia, to the more distant villa at Poggio a Caiano near his ancestral lands in the Carmignano district and en route to his town houses and shops at Empoli and Pisa.

There are also parallels with Filippo di Matteo Strozzi's practice. Santuccio represented his desire to maintain an ancestral villa, which he renovated as his main country residence, while diversifying its crops to furnish his table. Although not close enough to be suburban and far more modest than La Pietra, Santuccio's functions were complemented by the more extensive grain-producing farms at Capalle (the equivalent of Sassetti's Gonfienti), by his new agricultural enterprise in more distant hill country at Maglio (the equivalent of Sassetti's Casi) and by his sister's elevated villa overlooking the Arno at Le Selve. The same policy could also work on a more modest scale as Bartolommeo Sassetti intended when he bought his rustic retreat in the hills at Valcenni to balance the larger, family seat in the valley near town at Macia.

In all these cases it is important to take a holistic view of rural patronage, for if complementarity was indeed a key principle underlying estate acquisition and management, then each property needs to be viewed in relation to the others. A key factor was how many estates a proprietor could afford to own. A rustic hill villa removed from main roads, villages and densely populated districts was unsuitable as the only villa for a Florentine citizen and usually functioned as an additional property for those who already possessed houses near town. Paradoxically, this apparently unsophisticated alternative was more likely to be a luxury enterprise, and was, in any case, expensive since it involved terracing hillsides, drainage, enclosure and tree planting as part of a long-term agricultural investment.

Although all these different villas fall into broad categories determined by their site and function, the categories usually overlap. Even broad architectural categories such as those identified by Heydenreich and Frommel, the villa-castle, the villa-palace, the villa-farm and the suburban villa are highly flexible ones that continually merge,[10] and do not reflect distinct or exclusive formal types. Among the Strozzi villas there are a few instances such as Loiano and the Rocca di Campi, which apparently fit the villa-castle type. Other towered villas, like Santuccio or Francesco di Benedetto's house at Brozzi, were probably not fortified for defensive purposes and could perhaps be placed in a large amorphous group labelled *case da signore*. As discussed in Chapter 4, however, in the fifteenth century the phrase *casa da signore* described the function of the villa to house the landowner and embraced the whole range of architectural forms including both castles (*fortezze*) and the bigger, grander country houses (*palagi*). Francesco Sassetti's villa at La Pietra might be classified as a villa-palace of the most modern, unfortified type. Yet no other contemporary examples of a town palace transposed into the countryside have come to light and one example does not constitute a type. On the other hand, the villa-farm could hardly be described as a distinct category in the Florentine district in this period since almost all villas were farms. Of some thirty-eight villas examined here, only one house at Palaiuola near Fiesole had no farm attached. As for the suburban villa, the label loosely describes a site, but in form the buildings might range from castellated structures like the Medici villa of Careggi to a town palace like the Sassetti villa of La Pietra to more modest farm houses of the sort shown just beyond the city walls in Buonsignori's map. The case of the Medici villa at Careggi, which belongs in all four categories since it was castellated, suburban, had farms and was described by contemporaries as a palace, argues at the very least for a highly flexible approach to typology, if it does not demonstrate the inappropriateness of the method.

As we have seen there is, therefore, no great likelihood that villas with similar functions or on similar sites should be similar in form, and in the Florentine *contado* any attempt to create a rigid architectural typology of fifteenth-century villas is likely to fail. The widespread practice of adding to villa buildings in a piecemeal fashion also makes the question of formal typology more complex. The fact that almost all villas were older surviving structures, some of which underwent major modification in the fifteenth century, means that there is enormous variety and inconsistency in ground plans and elevations that defy typological classification.

This survey was based on the selection of two families according to historical criteria in an attempt to establish a more representative view of typical country houses in the fifteenth century, rather than isolating a few architecturally outstanding buildings. It is, therefore, not surprising that historians' theories about rural building in the period have been confirmed. Christiane Klapisch-Zuber and Giuliano Pinto have suggested that in the areas surrounding the major Tuscan towns there was almost no *ex novo* construction from the period following the great plague of 1348 until the last decades of the fifteenth century.[11] Although Pinto is more concerned with the *casa poderale*, the same seems to hold true for the *casa da signore*. Both urban landlords and peasant landowners made use of old buildings constructed during the demographic boom of the thirteenth and early fourteenth centuries. To these, new wings were added, the old nuclei were refurbished and the process of conversion and renovation (*acconcimenti*) was developed into a fine art.

The art of conversion is nowhere better illustrated than in Francesco Sassetti's villa at La Pietra and Filippo Strozzi's house at Santuccio. At La Pietra the old Macinghi *palagio* was entirely subsumed within a grand new design based on the most modern and splendid palaces, the Medici palace in Florence and Pius II's palace at Pienza. The join between the old and new structures was seamless and barely recognisable. The La Pietra solution was probably unique in the Florentine *contado* and was the result of a search for a new, magnificent form of country house at a time when no distinctively rural idiom had been found to substitute traditional fortified palaces like the Medici villas of Trebbio, Cafaggiolo and Careggi. It was another fifteen to twenty years before Giuliano da Sangallo devised a classicising solution for a grand country house at Poggio a Caiano. Poggio a Caiano was also much further from Florence, and it may not have been so much the lack of a rural model as the affirmatory choice of an urban prototype that influenced the design of La Pietra. Francesco Sassetti meant La Pietra to look like a *casa da cittadino* in the *contado*.

Santuccio was an altogether more modest scheme and exemplifies a compromise solution frequently adopted in this period. The old towered wing was retained, restored and a new classicising wing with an entrance portico and upper loggia was added. The old nucleus was displayed rather than disguised or buried, the new wing being tailored to fit its scale and proportions while at the same time creating a new, *all'antica* effect. Very different in scale and form, the rebuilding projects for La Pietra and Santuccio can serve to emphasise the flexibility and range of solutions available to fifteenth-century villa owners. If a certain conformity can be said to have predominated in town, freedom and *varietà* were keynotes in the countryside.

Comparison of town and country building throws light on another key issue in this period, and it can be put forward as evidence of the urban priorities of Renaissance society. For whereas restoration and conversion campaigns were the commonest form of rural construction, a building boom in new town palaces was taking place in Florence in the mid–fifteenth century.[12] Yet the rarity of *ex novo* construction in the countryside should not be interpreted in a negative light, in contradistinction to the urban building boom. Rather, the widespread campaigns of alteration and renovation should be seen as a positive and flexible response to ensure the long-term preservation of villas, as part of a quasi-biological process in which the villa as a species – ancient, but still remarkably fit – was adapted for current use and survived.

Appendix A • Selective Genealogies of Strozzi and Sassetti Villa Owners

Key

- These tables are built around the property-owning members of the families as listed in fifteenth-century tax returns and tend therefore not to include women, those who died young or those who entered religious orders.
- The Strozzi villas are numbered according to the sequence in Appendix B and are listed in boxes below the branch of the family to whom they belonged.

- Many of the dates are approximate, since fifteenth-century and later sources provide many conflicting dates of birth.

Abbreviations

b., born
d., died
=, married
c., circa

Table 1. *Selective Genealogy of Strozzi Villa Owners*

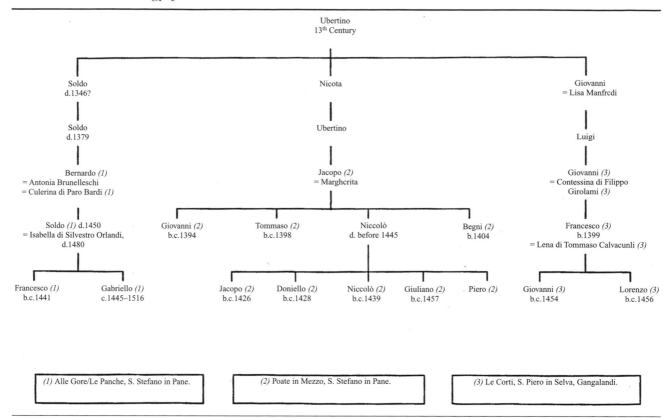

(1) Alle Gore/Le Panche, S. Stefano in Pane.

(2) Poate in Mezzo, S. Stefano in Pane.

(3) Le Corti, S. Piero in Selva, Gangalandi.

Sources: ASF Strozziane; Catasto; Litta I.

Table 2.

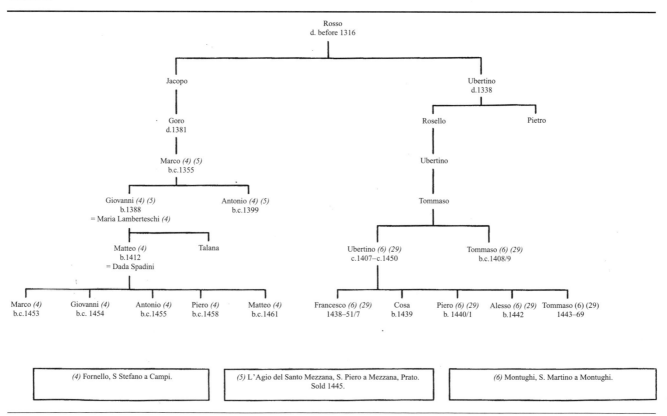

(4) Fornello, S Stefano a Campi.

(5) L'Agio del Santo Mezzana, S. Piero a Mezzana, Prato. Sold 1445.

(6) Montughi, S. Martino a Montughi.

Sources: ASF Strozziane; Catasto; Litta II.

Table 3. *Selective Genealogy of Strozzi Villa Owners*

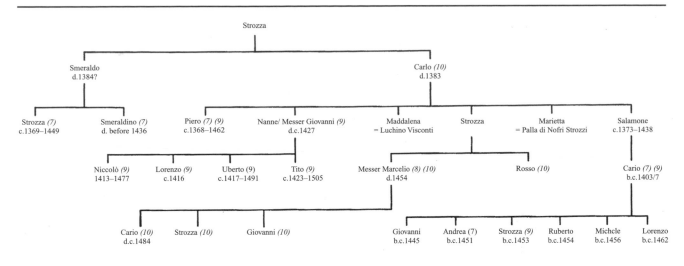

Strozza

Smeraldo
d.1384?

Carlo *(10)*
d.1383

Strozza *(7)*
c.1369–1449

Smeraldino *(7)*
d. before 1436

Piero *(7) (9)*
c.1368–1462

Nanne/ Messer Giovanni *(9)*
d.c.1427

Maddalena
= Luchino Visconti

Strozza

Marietta
= Palla di Nofri Strozzi

Salamone
c.1373–1438

Niccolò *(9)*
1413–1477

Lorenzo *(9)*
c.1416

Uberto *(9)*
c.1417–1491

Tito *(9)*
c.1423–1505

Messer Marcelio *(8) (10)*
d.1454

Rosso *(10)*

Cario *(7) (9)*
b.c.1403/7

Cario *(10)*
d.c.1484

Strozza *(10)*

Giovanni *(10)*

Giovanni
b.c.1445

Andrea *(7)*
b.c.1451

Strozza *(9)*
b.c.1453

Ruberto
b.c.1454

Michcle
b.c.1456

Lorenzo
b.c.1462

| *(7)* Loiano/Rocca di Morella, S. Stefano a Sommaia. | *(8)* Castello di Luciano, S. Michele a Luciano, Golfolina. Sold 1448. | *(9)* Querceto, S. Martino a Mensola. | *(10)* Rocca di Campi, S. Lorenozo a Campi. |

Sources: ASF Strozziane; Catasto; Litta III, IV, V, VI.

Table 4.

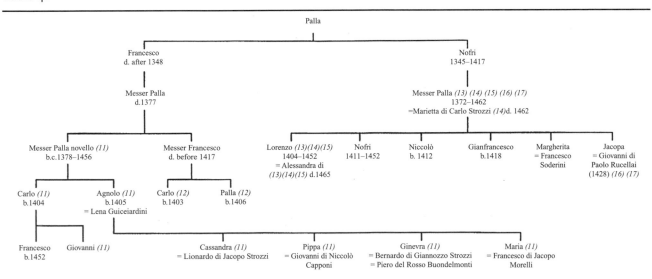

Palla

Francesco
d. after 1348

Nofri
1345–1417

Messer Palla
d.1377

Messer Palla *(13) (14) (15) (16) (17)*
1372–1462
=Marietta di Carlo Strozzi *(14)* d. 1462

Messer Palla novello *(11)*
b.c.1378–1456

Messer Francesco
d. before 1417

Lorenzo *(13)(14)(15)*
1404–1452
= Alessandra di
(13)(14)(15) d.1465

Nofri
1411–1452

Niccolò
b. 1412

Gianfrancesco
b.1418

Margherita
= Francesco
Soderini

Jacopa
= Giovanni di
Paolo Rucellai
(1428) *(16) (17)*

Carlo *(11)*
b.1404

Agnolo *(11)*
b.1405
= Lena Guiceiardini

Carlo *(12)*
b.1403

Palla *(12)*
b.1406

Francesco
b.1452

Giovanni *(11)*

Cassandra *(11)*
= Lionardo di Jacopo Strozzi

Pippa *(11)*
= Giovanni di Niccolò
Capponi

Ginevra *(11)*
= Bernardo di Giannozzo Strozzi
= Piero del Rosso Buondelmonti

Maria *(11)*
= Francesco di Jacopo
Morelli

| *(11)* Soffiano, S. Maria a Soffiano. | *(12)* Soffiano, S. Maria a Soffiano. | *(13)* Novoli, S. Maria a Novoli. Sold 1460. | *(14)* Petraia, S. Michele a Castelio. Sold 1463. | *(15)* Il Palagetto, S. Michele a Castello, Sold 1469. | *(16)* Ambra, Poggio a Calano. Confiscated 1441. | *(17)* Trefiano, S. Marco a Seano. Sold 1448 to Rucellai. |

Sources: ASF Strozziane; Catasto; Litta VIII, IX.

Table 5. *Selective Genealogy of Strozzi Villa Owners*

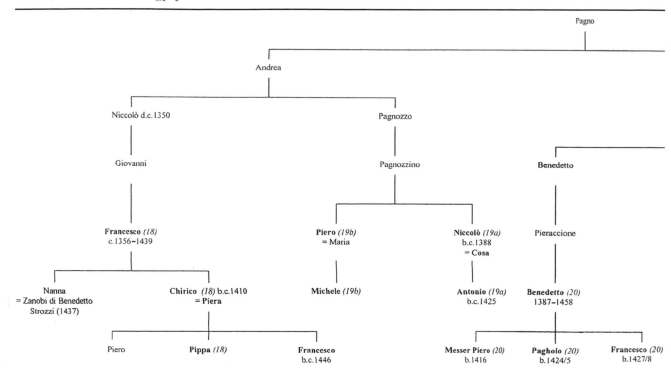

(18) Capalle, S. Quirico a Capalle.	(19) La Loggia/Macia, S. Stefano.	(20) Capalle, S. Quirico a Capalle.	(21) In Cantone, S. Martino a Brozzi.

Sources: ASF Strozziane; Catasto; Litta X, XI, XII.

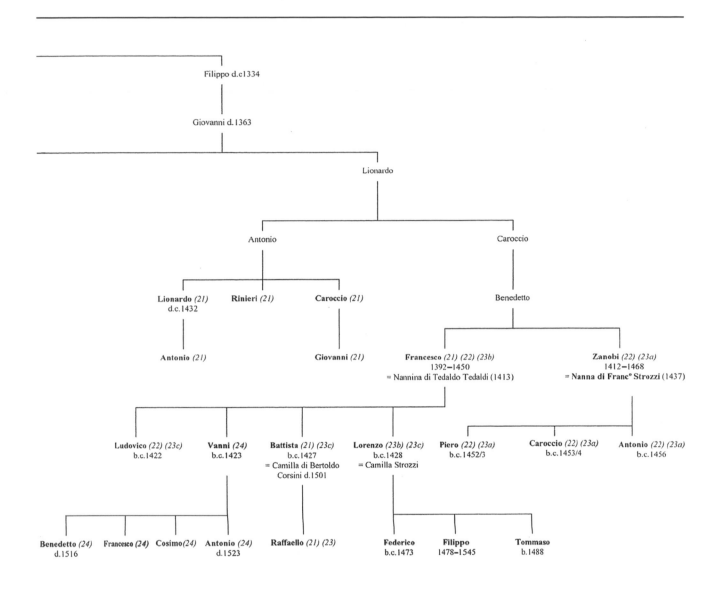

Filippo d.c1334

Giovanni d.1363

Lionardo

Antonio

Caroccio

Lionardo *(21)*
d.c.1432

Rinieri *(21)*

Caroccio *(21)*

Benedetto

Antonio *(21)*

Giovanni *(21)*

Francesco *(21) (22) (23b)*
1392–1450
= Nannina di Tedaldo Tedaldi (1413)

Zanobi *(22) (23a)*
1412–1468
= **Nanna di Francº Strozzi** (1437)

Ludovico *(22) (23c)*
b.c.1422

Vanni *(24)*
b.c.1423

Battista *(21) (23c)*
b.c.1427
= Camilla di Bertoldo
Corsini d.1501

Lorenzo *(23b) (23c)*
b.c.1428
= Camilla Strozzi

Piero *(22) (23a)*
b.c.1452/3

Caroccio *(22) (23a)*
b.c.1453/4

Antonio *(22) (23a)*
b.c.1456

Benedetto *(24)*
d.1516

Francesco *(24)*

Cosimo *(24)*

Antonio *(24)*
d.1523

Raffaello *(21) (23)*

Federico
b.c.1473

Filippo
1478–1545

Tommaso
b.1488

(22) **Brozzi, S. Martino a Brozzi.**	*(23)* **Palaiuola, Badia a Fiesole.** *(a)* **From 1430.** *(b)* **From 1469.** *(c)* **From 1464.**	*(24)* **Galluzzo, S. Maria a Travalle.** **From 1458/9.**

Table 6. *Selective Genealogy of Strozzi Villa Owners*

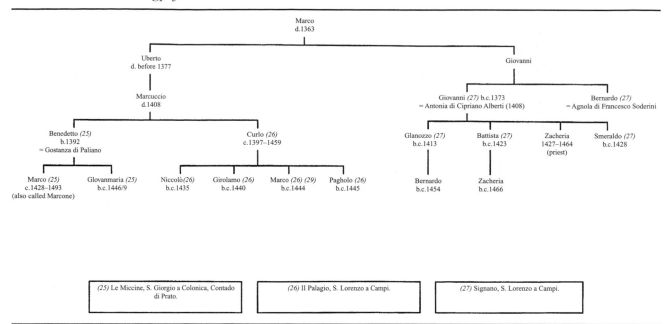

Sources: ASF Strozziane; Catasto; Litta XIII, XV, XVI.

Table 7. *Selective Genealogy of Strozzi Villa Owners*

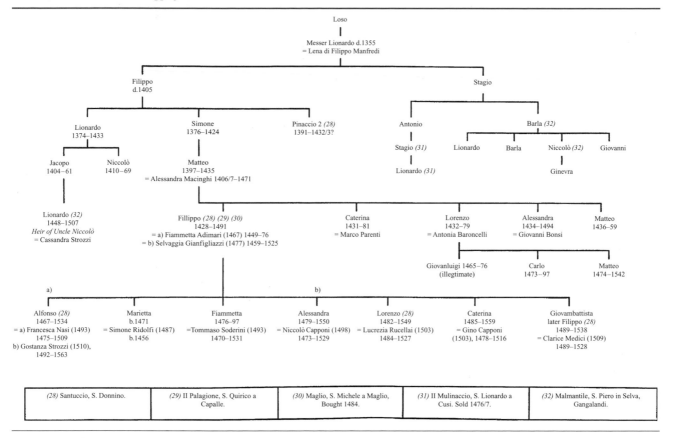

| (28) Santuccio, S. Donnino. | (29) Il Palagione, S. Quirico a Capalle. | (30) Maglio, S. Michele a Maglio, Bought 1484. | (31) Il Mulinaccio, S. Lionardo a Cusi. Sold 1476/7. | (32) Malmantile, S. Piero in Selva, Gangalandi. |

Sources: ASF Strozziane; Catasto; Litta XVII, XVIII; Fabbri; Crabb.

Table 8. *Selective Genealogy of Sassetti Family*

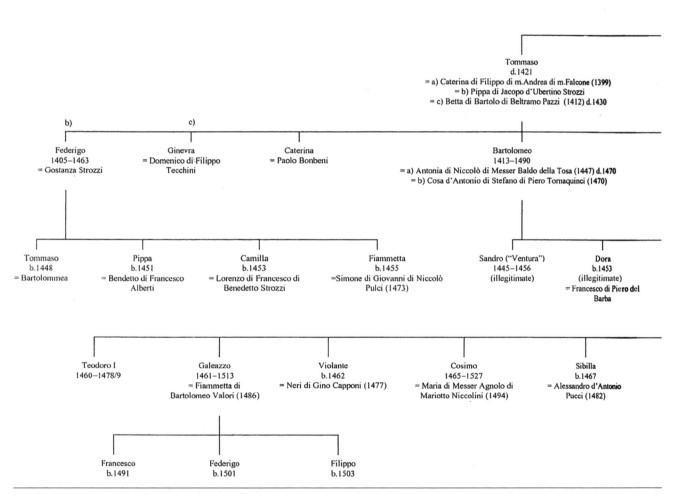

Sources: ASF Tratte (Libro dell'età), Strozziane; Catasto, Not. antecos.; Sassetti 'Notizie'; de Roover; Warburg; Borsook and Offerhaus.

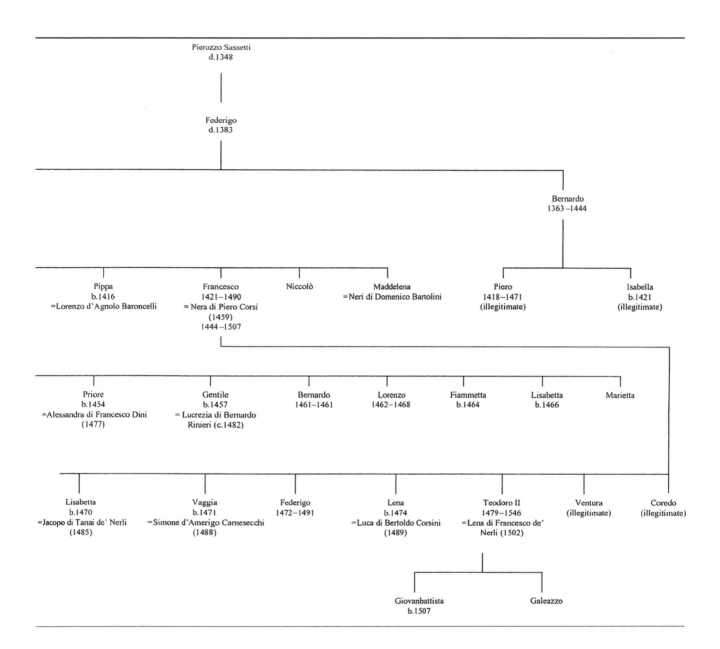

Pierozzo Sassetti
d.1348

Federigo
d.1383

Bernardo
1363–1444

Pippa
b.1416
=Lorenzo d'Agnolo Baroncelli

Francesco
1421–1490
= Nera di Piero Corsi
(1459)
1444–1507

Niccolò

Maddelena
=Neri di Domenico Bartolini

Piero
1418–1471
(illegitimate)

Isabella
b.1421
(illegitimate)

Priore
b.1454
=Alessandra di Francesco Dini
(1477)

Gentile
b.1457
= Lucrezia di Bernardo
Rinieri (c.1482)

Bernardo
1461–1461

Lorenzo
1462–1468

Fiammetta
b.1464

Lisabetta
b.1466

Marietta

Lisabetta
b.1470
=Jacopo di Tanai de' Nerli
(1485)

Vaggia
b.1471
=Simone d'Amerigo Carnesecchi
(1488)

Federigo
1472–1491

Lena
b.1474
=Luca di Bertoldo Corsini
(1489)

Teodoro II
1479–1546
=Lena di Francesco de'
Nerli (1502)

Ventura
(illegitimate)

Coredo
(illegitimate)

Giovanbattista
b.1507

Galeazzo

2. PONTE DI MEZZO/CASCIOLLE
S. Stefano in Pane

Giovanni di Jacopo d'Ubertino Strozzi
 1430 Cat. 406 fol. 210r, value F.304. 5. 9
 1433 Cat. 496 fol. 214r, value F.309. 12. 10
Giovanni, Tommaso and Begni di Jacopo d'Ubertino Strozzi
 1442 Cat. 621 fol. 222r
Tommaso di Jacopo d'Ubertino Strozzi
 1446 Cat. 673, II, fol. 690r
 1451 Cat. 709 fol. 309r
 1457 Cat. 818 fol. 121r, value F.368. 4. 6
 1469 Cat. 922 fol. 351r
Heirs of Tommaso di Jacopo Strozzi
 1480 Cat. 1014, II, fol. 220r
Heirs of Niccolò di Jacopo Strozzi
 1498 Decima Repub. 24 fol. 436r

House unidentified.

Maps: IGM *Carta d'Italia* 1:25,000, 1955, fol. 106, Firenze, c. 32TPP799516; Amministrazione Provinciale di Firenze, 1:10,000, 1979, fol. 52.

Bibl. Carocci (*I Dintorni*, I, 1906, p. 329) refers to property belonging to the Strozzi at Ponte di Mezzo between the fourteenth and sixteenth centuries, but modern roads and rebuilding have transformed the area; Zangheri, *Ville della Provincia di Firenze*, p. 256.

Litta I

3. LE CORTI
S. Piero in Selva, Gangalandi

Monna Contessina, daughter of Filippo Girolami, widow of Giovanni di Luigi Strozzi
 1427 Cat. 43 fol. 576r
 1430 Cat. 405 fol. 199r, value F.501. 19
Francesco di Giovanni di Luigi Strozzi
 1433 Cat. 495 fol. 148r, value F.503. 15
 1442 Cat. 620, I fol. 402r
 1446 Cat. 671, II fol. 695r
 1451 Cat. 707 fol. 367r
 1457 Cat. 816, II fol. 776r
 1469 Cat. 919, II fol. 289r, value F.584. 12. 11

Heirs of Francesco di Giovanni di Luigi Strozzi
 1480 Cat. 1012, II fol. 275r, value F.584. 12. 11
Monna Lena, widow of Francesco di Giovanni di Luigi Strozzi
 1498 Decima Repub. 23 fol. 370r

A house of this name in this location still exists, but no fifteenth-century features are visible in the house.

Maps: IGM *Carta d'Italia* 1:25,000, 1952, fol. 106, Montelupo Fiorentino 32TPP651449; Amministrazione Provinciale di Firenze, 1:10,000, 1979, fol. 60.

Bibl. Tampone (*Studi e ricerche sul nucleo antico di Lastra a Signa*, p. 181, Sezione F, Gavignano) notes that Le Corti has maintained its original function as a farmhouse, is much altered, but in a good state of preservation. On this family see Gregory, 'Chi erano gli Strozzi', p. 20.

Litta I

4. FORNELLO
S. Stefano a Campi

Marco di Goro Strozzi with his sons Giovanni and Antonio
 1427 Cat. 44 fol. 202r
 1430 Cat. 405 fol. 250r, value of three farms and pieces of land nearby F.2,155
 1433 Cat. 495 fol. 321v
 1442 Cat. 620, II fol. 743r
Monna Maria widow of Giovanni di Marco Strozzi
 1446 Cat. 671, II fol. 991r
Matteo di Giovanni with his brothers and mother Maria
 1451 Cat. 707 fol. 415v
 1457 Cat. 816, II fol. 810r
Heirs of Matteo di Giovanni Strozzi
 1469 Cat. 919, II fol. 342r
 1480 Cat. 1011 fol. 299r
 1498 Decima Repub. 22 fol. 318r

Villa still exists.

Maps: IGM *Carta d'Italia* 1:25,000, 1963, fol. 106, Prato 32TPP721558 'Villa Sarri'; Amministrazione

Provinciale di Firenze 1:10,000, 1979, fol. 43, 'Fornello, Villa Sarri'.

Bibl. Tempestini, *Campi Bisenzio*, p. 11; Carocci, *I Dintorni*, 1906, I, p. 353, Fornello – Villa Sarri; Righini, *Il Valdarno*, p. 133; Lensi Orlandi, *Di qua d'Arno*, p. 9, Fornello/Sarri, pl. 20; the excerpts relating to Fornello are all reprinted in Lamberini and Lazzareschi, *Campi Bisenzio*, pp. 308–11, along with Pirillo's evidence for the existence of a villa named Fornello in 1316, described then as 'podere cum domo curte puteo colombaria et domo laboratoria cum capanna aia et giardino loco dicto "al Fornello"'. Although Carocci did not mention Strozzi ownership, Tempestini noted that the Strozzi owned a villa at Fornello in the fifteenth century, and Lensi Orlandi made the connection with the present Villa Sarri. Both Tempestini and Lensi Orlandi refer to the mainly sixteenth-century structure and vestiges of a thirteenth-century tower.

Litta II

5. L'AGIO DEL SANTO/MEZZANA
S. Piero a Mezzana, Prato

Marco di Goro Strozzi with his sons Giovanni and Antonio
 1427 Cat. 44 fol. 204r
 1430 Cat. 415 fol. 249r, value of four farms
  F.2582.8.10
 1433 Cat. 495 fol. 320r, value of four farms
  F.2625.15. –
 1442 Cat. 620, II, fol. 743r

Sold 15 October 1445 for F.2,100 (*di sugello*) to the hospital of S. Maria Nuova and subsequently to Messer Dietisalvi Neroni.

Villa still exists.

Maps: IGM *Carta d'Italia* 1:25,000, 1963, fol. 106, Prato 32TPP705582, 'Mezzana'; Amministrazione Provinciale di Firenze 1:10,000, 1979, fol. 42, 'Mezzana'.

Bibl. *Prato e i Medici nel '500* (pp. 200–3, 'Villa Martini a Mezzana') notes that the villa belonged to the Martini

by 1499 and suggests that it had previously belonged to the Galli without investigating its earlier ownership. Further research is needed to establish whether the fine console capitals and windows with prominent cornices belong to renovations carried out by Dietisalvi Neroni (perhaps in the 1460s) or to subsequent owners.

Litta II

6. MONTUGHI
S. Martino a Montughi

Ubertino and Tommaso di Tommaso d'Ubertino Strozzi
 1427 Cat. 45 fol. 851r
Ubertino di Tommaso d'Ubertino Strozzi
 1430 Cat. 405 fol. 173v., value F.224. 3.
 1433 Cat. 495 fol. 491v, value F.224 2. 3
 1442 Cat. 620, II, fol. 999r
 1446 Cat. 671, II, fol. 835r
Heirs of Ubertino di Tommaso Strozzi
 1451 Cat. 707 fol. 175r
 1457 Cat. 816, I, fol. 520r, value F.202. 13. 9
 1469 Cat. 920, II, fol. 784r, value F.202. 13.
 1480 Cat. 1012, II, fol. 263r
Carlo di Niccolo di Carlo di Marco Strozzi
 1498 Decima Repub. 22, fol. 257r

House unidentified, but it may possibly be the Villa Guicciardini, Via di Montughi 49.

Maps: IGM *Carta d'Italia* 1:25,000, 1955, fol. 106, Firenze.

Bibl. Carocci (*I Dintorni*, 1906, p. 186, La Pietra – Villa Guicciardini) claims this villa had belonged to the Strozzi since the early fifteenth century and was sold by Abbot Luigi Strozzi and Senator Alessandro Strozzi in 1690. A closer study is needed to prove that this house was Ubertino di Tommaso's villa. Zangheri, *Ville della Provincia di Firenze*, p. 279. See also Strozziane IV, 639, cabreo of 1787 with drawings of Strozzi land and buildings at S. Martino a Montughi, Ginori-Lisci, *Cabrei*, p. 284.

Litta II

7. Loiano/Rocca di Morello
S. Stefano a Sommaia

Strozza and Smeraldo <Smeraldino> di Smeraldo Strozzi
    1427 Cat. 75 fol. 197r, value F.706 7. 2
Strozza di Smeraldo Strozzi
    1442 Cat. 619, II, fol. 1016r
    1446 Cat. 669, I, fol. 406r
Piero di Carlo Strozzi
    1451 Cat. 709 fol. 323v
    1457 Cat. 818 fol. 237v, value F.725. 15. 3
Carlo di Piero Strozzi
    1469 Cat. 921 fol. 192v, value F.716. 7. 9
    1480 Cat. 1013, II, fol. 216v
Andrea di Carlo di Piero Strozzi
    1498 Decima Repub. 22, fol. 89r

The villa survives.

Maps: IGM *Carta d'Italia* 1:25,000, 1952, fol. 106, Vaglia 32TPP779602, 'La Rocca'; Amministrazione Provinciale di Firenze 1:10,000, 1979, fol. 35, 'La Rocca'; Capitani di Parte Guelfa, II, c. 438, S. Stefano a Sommaia.

Bibl. P. J. Jones, 'Florentine Families', p. 188 n. 39; Lensi Orlandi, *Di Qua*, p. 31, pl. 60, 61; for a discussion of the twelfth-century nucleus and thirteenth-century fortified enclosure, together with additions such as the sixteenth-century windows on the south façade, see Lamberini, *Calenzano*, I, pp. 166–8 with full bibliography.

Litta III and IV

8. Castello di Luciano
S. Michele a Luciano, Golfolina, Val d'Arno

Messer Marcello di Strozza Strozzi
    1427 Cat. 75 fol. 131r, value F.1,167
    1442 Cat. 619, II, fol. 825r
    1446 Cat. 669, I, fol. 356r
    1451 Cat. 705 fol. 529v

Listed as sold to Bernardo and Antonio Antinori for F.1060 in 1448.

Villa unidentified.

Maps: IGM *Carta d'Italia* 1:25,000, fol. 106, 1952, Carmignano, 32TPP639475. NB. modern maps refer to this place as Luciana, although Luciano is used in the fifteenth-century documents and by Repetti.

Bibl. Carocci, *Valdarno*, p. 48; Repetti, II, pp. 913–14.

9. Querceto
S. Martino a Mensola

Niccolò, Lorenzo, Uberto and Tito di Messer Giovanni di Carlo Strozzi
    1427 Cat. 77 fol. 127v
    1430 Cat. 406 fol. 298v, value F.1,000
    1433 Cat. 496 fol. 396v, value F.1,000
Confiscated in 1436 and 1437 and sold to Piero di Carlo Strozzi by 1439
    1442 Cat. 621 fol. 596r
    1446 Cat. 673, I, fol. 307r
    1451 Cat. 709, fol. 323r
    1457 Cat. 818, fol. 235r, value of four farms F.1,020
Carlo di Piero Strozzi
    1469 Cat. 921 fol. 192r, value F.1,020
    1480 Cat. 1013, II, fol. 216r, value F.1,020
Heirs of Strozza di Carlo di Piero Strozzi
    1498 Decima Repub. 25 fol. 346r

Villa survives.

Maps: IGM *Carta d'Italia* 1:25,000, 1955, fol. 106, Firenze 32TPP861500; Amministrazione Provinciale di Firenze 1:10,000, 1979, fol. 53.

Bibl. Carocci, *I Dintorni*, 1906, I, p. 42, Palagio di Querceto – Villa dei Marchesi Strozzi-Sacrati; Lensi Orlandi, *Di Qua d'Arno*, p. 115, pl. 198–200; Zangheri, *Ville della Provincia di Firenze*, pp. 340–1, Villa 'Querceto', via Madonna delle Grazie, 18, with further bibliography. Although this is one of the few Strozzi villas to have remained in the family from the fourteenth century until the late twentieth century, and one of its original towers survives, it was transformed in the sixteenth and nineteenth centuries, and it is yet to be established how much of the late medieval structure survives.

Litta IV and V.

10. ROCCA DI CAMPI
S. Lorenzo a Campi

Messer Marcello and Rosso di Strozza Strozzi
  1427 Cat. 75 fol. 132r, value F.1,645. 14
Messer Marcello di Strozza Strozzi
  1442 Cat. 619, II, fol. 825r
  1446 Cat. 669, I, fol. 355r
  1451 Cat. 705, fol. 529r
Heirs of Messer Marcello di Strozza Strozzi
  1457 Cat. 815, I, No. 135, value F.1,002. 17. 2
Carlo and Strozza di Messer Marcello Strozzi
  1480 Cat. 1009, II, fol. 297, 446r
Giovanni di Messer Marcello Strozzi
  1498 Decima Repub. 20 fol. 610r

Villa survives.

Maps: Capitani di Parte Guelfa, II, c. 412, S. Lorenzo a Campi, the mill appears on c. 409, S. Stefano a Campi; IGM *Carta d'Italia* 1:25,000, 1963, fol. 106, Campi Bisenzio 32TPP717546; Amministrazione Provinciale di Firenze 1,10,000, 1979, fol. 43.

Bibl. Lorenzo Strozzi, *Le Vite*, p. 12; Santoni, *Campi e il Bisenzio*, pp. 27–8, 42–4; Righini, *Il Valdarno*, pp. 127–8; Tempestini, *Campi Bisenzio*, p. 23; P. J. Jones, 'Florentine Families', pp. 188–9; the exerpts relating to the Rocca at Campi are all reprinted by Lamberini and Lazzareschi, *Campi*, pp. 159, 160, 259–62, 272. P. J. Jones cites documents to support his statement that the Rocca at Campi was rebuilt by Carlo di Strozza Strozzi after 1370, p. 188 n. 39. Tempestini gives a more precise date of 1377, but it would in any case have been before Carlo's exile in 1378. Some authors have confused the *castello* or fortified village of Campi with the *fortezza* or *rocca*, a large castellated building across the bridge from the village of Campi (see Lamberini and Lazzareschi op. cit. pp. 261–2). New plans of the Rocca prepared in 1984–5 by students of the Istituto di Restauro of the Facoltà dell'Architettura at the University of Florence will greatly facilitate further study of this key surviving example of a castellated villa close to Florence.

Litta III

11. SOFFIANO
S. Maria a Soffiano

Messer Palla 'Novello' di Messer Palla di Francesco Strozzi
  1430 Cat. 405 fol. 121v, value F.121. 8. 7
  1433 Cat. 495 fol. 429r
  1442 Cat. 620, II, fol. 878r
  1446 Cat. 671, II, fol. 532v
  1451 Cat. 707, fol. 351v
Agnolo and Carlo di Messer Palla 'Novello'
  1457 Cat. 816 fol. 147v, value F.258
  1469 Cat. 919, I, fol. 39r
Carlo di Messer Palla 'Novello'
  1480 Cat. 1011 fol. 221r
Lena Guicciardini-Strozzi, widow of Agnolo di Messer Palla 'Novello' inherited this villa in repayment for her dowry in 1482 and bequeathed it to her four daughters
  1498 Decima Repub. 22 fol. 217r
  1498 Decima Repub. 22 fol. 546r

The *casa da signore* probably survives and is one of two large houses on the Via del Monasteraccio to the southwest of the church of S. Maria a Soffiano. Unfortunately, the boundaries listed in tax returns do not make it possible to determine which of these houses belonged to Palla 'Novello'.

Maps: IGM *Carta d'Italia* 1:25,000, 1955, fol. 106, Firenze, 32TPP781476; Amministrazione Provinciale di Firenze 1:10,000, 1979, fol. 52.

Bibl. Carocci, *I Dintorni*, II, 1906, pp. 404–5, Villa Pilacci-Trecci and Villa Goretti are both described as belonging to Palla Novello's branch of the Strozzi in the fifteenth century; Lensi-Orlandi, *Di là d'Arno*, p. 157, notes that one of the two towers of Villa Pilacci-Trecci was added in the nineteenth century, although some early wooden ceilings survive. Carocci's Villa Goretti is now known as the Villa S. Martino, the interior of which has been transformed for commercial purposes. Zangheri (*Ville della provincia di Firenze,* I, p. 380) presumes that the present Villa S. Martino is indeed Agnolo di Palla Novello's house and that its courtyard with Doric loggia and well and many other fifteenth-century carved stone features show that the villa was built by him.

Litta VIII

12. SOFFIANO
S. Maria a Soffiano

Palla and Carlo di Messer Francesco di Messer Palla Strozzi
    1427 Cat. 43 fol. 560r
    1430 Cat. 405 fol. 119r
    1433 Cat. 495 fol. 423r
Carlo di Messer Francesco di Messer Palla Strozzi
    1442 Cat. 620, I, fol. 273r
    1446 Cat. 671, I, fol. 117r
    1451 Cat. 707 fol. 475r
    1457 Cat. 816, II, fol. 761r
    1469 Cat. 919, I, fol. 209v, listed as sold
    1480 Cat. 1011, fol. 193r
Piero, Francesco, Palla and Lorenzo, the four sons of Carlo di Messer Francesco di Messer Palla Strozzi
    1498, Decima Repub. 23 fol. 304r

This family owned a house for their own habitation which was often described as a small one ('chasetta') in the tax returns between 1427 and 1469. This 'chasetta' was sold some time between 1457 and 1469, but in the 1498, Decima, what seems to be a new 'casa da oste' is listed with their farms at Soffiano. This may be one of the two surviving houses on the Via del Monasteraccio near Soffiano. If so, the boundaries listed in tax returns do not help to identify which house belonged to which cousin. See catalogue entry no. 11.

Maps: See no. 11.

Bibl. See no. 11.

Litta VIII

13. NOVOLI
S. Maria a Novoli

Messer Palla di Nofri Strozzi
    1427 Cat. 76 fol. 171v, value F.623. 13. 5
    1430 Cat. 405 fol. 126r, value F.612. 18. 10
    1433 Cat. 495 fol. 382v
Monna Alessandra wife of Lorenzo di Messer Palla di Nofri Strozzi
    1442 Cat. 620, I, fol. 81r
    1446 Cat. 671, II, fol. 1023r
    1451 Cat. 707 fol. 491r
    1457 Cat. 816, I, fol. 508v
    1469 Cat. 920, II, fol. 877r, listed as sold in 1460
        to Girolamo d'Adouardo Giachinotti

Villa unidentified.

Maps: IGM *Carta d'Italia* 1:25,000, 1955, fol. 106 Firenze; Amministrazione Provinciale di Firenze, 1:10,000, 1979, fol. 52.

Although this seems to have been Palla di Nofri Strozzi's most important country residence before his exile in 1434, I have found no reference to the exact whereabouts of this villa in the literature and extensive road building and industrialisation in the Novoli district make it unlikely that it would have survived.

Litta IX

14. PETRAIA
S. Michele a Castello

Messer Palla di Nofri Strozzi
    1427 Cat. 76 fol. 171v
    1430 Cat. 405 fol. 127r, value F.703. 11. 5
    1433 Cat. 495 fol. 383v
Monna Marietta wife of Messer Palla di Nofri Strozzi
    1442 Cat. 620, II, fol. 751r
    1446 Cat. 671, II, fol. 949r

In 1466 the villa was made over to the Abbott of S. Pancrazio, who let it to Alessandra wife of Lorenzo di Messer Palla di Nofri Strozzi and subsequently sold it to her in 1458.

Monna Alessandra, wife of Lorenzo di Messer Palla di Nofri Strozzi

> 1469 Cat. 920, II, fol. 877r, listed as sold in 1463 to Nerone di Nigi Dietisalvi.

Villa survives.

Maps: Capitani di Parte Guelfa, II, c. 375, S. Michele a Castello; IGM *Carta d'Italia* 1:25,000, 1955, fol. 106, Firenze 32TPP800544; Amministrazione Provinciale di Firenze 1:10,000, 1979, fol. 43, 'Villa La Petraia'.

Bibl. Chiostri (*La Petraia*) confuses the villa of Petraia with the villa called 'Il Palagetto' on the piazza below; see Chapter 1, n. 148. See also D. Wright, *The Medici Villa at Castello*, II, app. 36; Carocci, *I Dintorni*, 1906, I, pp. 281–2; Lensi-Orlandi, *Di qua d'Arno*, pp. 19–20, pl. 31–3; Studio GE 9, *Castello*, pp. 69–71; F. W. Kent, 'The Making of a Renaissance Patron', p. 23 n. 6, pp. 24, 45, 48; R. Jones, 'Palla Strozzi', pp. 44, 80–1, 99, 103; Battisti, *Brunelleschi*, pp. 47, 68, 347 n. 6; Zangheri, *Ville della provincia di Firenze*, pp. 78–95.

Litta IX

15. IL PALAGETTO, LA PIAZZA
[Villa Corsini/I Rinieri] S. Michele a Castello

Messer Palla di Nofri Strozzi

> 1427 Cat. 76 fol. 172v–173r
> 1430 Cat. 405 fol. 127v, value F.432. 2. 10
> 1433 Cat. 495 fol. 383v

Monna Alessandra, wife of Lorenzo di Messer Palla di Nofri Strozzi

> 1442 Cat. 620, I, fol. 81r
> 1446 Cat. 671, II, fol. 1023v
> 1451 Cat. 707 fol. 491r
> 1457 Cat. 826, I, fol. 508r
> 1469 Cat. 920, II, fol. 877r listed as sold in 1460 to Bernardo Rinieri.

Villa survives, known as I Rinieri or Villa Corsini.

Maps: Capitani di Parte Guelfa, II, c. 375, S. Michele a Castello; IGM *Carta d'Italia* 1:25,000, 1955, fol. 106, Firenze 32TPP796541; Amministrazione Provinciale di Firenze 1:10,000, 1979, fol. 43.

Bibl. Carocci (*I Dintorni*, 1906, I, p. 280, 'I Rinieri – Villa dei Principi Corsini') notes that this villa belonged to Palla Strozzi in the early fifteenth century and was sold by his daughter-in-law, Alessandra to Bernardo di Stoldo Rinieri, in 1460; Lensi Orlandi, *Di qua d'Arno*, p. 19, pl. 31; Studio GE 9, *Castello*, pp. 67–8; M. Dezzi Bardeschi and L. Zangheri, 'La Villa Corsini a Castello e l'intervento di Antonio Maria Ferri', *Bollettino degli Ingegneri*, 11 (1969): pp. 3–10; Zangheri, *Ville della provincia di Firenze*, pp. 120–131. Although Carocci and Zangheri clearly distinguish this villa from that of Petraia, the literature on Petraia frequently confuses the two villas, which both belonged to Palla di Nofri Strozzi; see Chapter 1, n. 148. No discernable traces of Palla's villa survive. Fifteenth-century columns imbedded in the piers of the courtyard and revealed during restoration in the 1980s probably belong to a rebuilding project by the Rinieri, whereas the baroque aspect of the present structure is due to later transformations.

Litta IX

16. AMBRA, POGGIO A CAIANO
S. Maria a Bonistallo

Messer Palla di Nofri Strozzi

> 1427 Cat. 76 fol. 185v–186r, value of farm F.682. 17
> 1430 Cat. 405 fol. 137r–v, value of farm F.761. 5.-
> 1433 Cat. 495 fol. 390r–v

The house and land were forcibly sold by the Monte officials in 1441, from whom the Venturi bought it. Giovanni Rucellai bought Ambra from Neri Venturi in 1469 and sold it again to Lorenzo de' Medici in 1474; see F. W. Kent cited in bibliography to this entry.

Palla's villa of Ambra does not appear to survive, although Lorenzo de' Medici used it while his new villa at Poggio a Caiano was being built. The boundaries listed in tax returns do not help to identify exactly where the old villa of Ambra lay in relation to the big new villa, and it is possible that the old house was subsumed within the new one.

Maps: Capitani di Parte Guelfa, II, c. 552, Bonistado; IGM *Carta d'Italia* 1:25,000, 1952, fol. 106, Carmignano 32TPP655538; for many more cartographic representations of the villa, see *Poggio a Caiano* ed. Bardazzi and Castellani cited in bibliography below.

Bibl. *Poggio a Caiano* ed. Bardazzi and Castellani; and P. Foster *A Study of Lorenzo de' Medici's Villa at Poggio a Caiano* include full bibliographies. The history of early ownership is documented and explored by F. W. Kent, in 'Lorenzo de' Medici's Acquisition of Poggio a Caiano', pp. 250–7 and 'The Making of a Renaissance Patron', pp. 46–9, 80–2; R. Jones, 'Palla Strozzi', pp. 81–2 doc.98.

Litta IX

17. TREFIANO
S. Marco a Seano

Messer Palla di Nofri Strozzi
    1427 Cat. 76 fol. 187r
    1430 Cat. 405 fol. 139r, value of home farm
        F.559. 6
    1433 Cat. 495 fol. 391v

This house was sold to a relative, Ruberto di Giovanni Altoviti, after Palla's exile in 1434 and to protect the property further it was bought by Palla's son-in-law, Giovanni Rucellai, in November 1448 on condition that Rucellai sell it back to Palla should he return to Florence; see F. W. Kent cited in bibliography to this entry. It still belonged to Giovanni Rucellai in 1469 and 1480 when it was listed in his tax returns (1469 Cat. 919 fol. 377r; 1480 Cat. 1011 fol. 341v) and was labelled as a Rucellai property on the Capitani di Parte map of 1580–95. (See Figs. 48 and 49 in Chapter 5).

    Described in Palla's 1462 will as having been built *ex novo* by his great-grandfather Jacopo and his grandfather Palla, this house was of great sentimental value to Palla di Nofri. It was in disrepair at the time of Palla's 1427 tax return, listed as 'un palagio mal abitato e mal situato', and was referred to in Palla's will

of 1462 as 'piccolissima cosa, è come un casolare'. The fourteenth-century *palagio* was transformed by Giovanni di Pandolfo Rucellai in 1570 (according to inscriptions above the windows on the east façade), and was again restored by Paolo di Orazio Rucellai between 1742 and 1745 (according to a Latin inscription above the west portal). During the eighteenth-century restoration campaign the house was enlarged, many farms were improved, an aqueduct (or new water supply) was built and *boschetti* were planted for trapping or watching birds. The house still exists; perched on a hilltop between Carmignano and Seano, it is now part of the wine-producing estate of Capezzana.

Maps: Capitani di Parte Gulefa, II. c. 553, S. Marco a Seano, labelled 'trefiano de' rucellai'; Carta del Territorio Provinciale of the Amministrazione Provinciale di Firenze, 1:10,000, 1979, fol. 42, 'Trefiano'; IGM *Carta d'Italia* 1:25,000. 1952, fol. 106, Carmignano 32TPP631542.

Bibl. F. W. Kent, 'The Making of Renaissance Patron', pp. 45, 47 n. 1, 49 n. 2; R. Jones, 'Palla Strozzi', pp. 45, 100, doc. 140 h, 104 doc. 140 k; Lillie, 'Memory of Place', pp. 209–10.

Litta IX

18. CAPALLE
S. Quirico a Capalle

Francesco di Giovanni di Messer Niccolò Strozzi
    1427 Cat. 43 fol. 674r
    1430 Cat. 405 fol. 209v, value F.392. 10
    1433 Cat. 495 fol. 170r, value F.425
Chirico di Francesco di Giovanni Strozzi
    1442 Cat. 620, I, fol. 279r
    1446 Cat. 669, I, fol. 58r
    1451 Cat. 705 fol. 520r
    1457 Cat. 814 no. 372, value F.579. 6. 5
Heirs of Chirico di Francesco Strozzi and his widow Monna Piera
    1480 Cat. 1010 fol. 429r
    1498 Decima Repub. 21 fol. 329r

The *casa da signore* probably survives. The Decima Repub. makes it clear that this estate was on the south bank of the Bisenzio ('di sotto el fiume'), and boundaries listed in tax returns, together with evidence from early maps suggest that the house may be the one that still exists to the left of the bridge over the Bisenzio, approaching from Campi into the *castello* of Capalle.

Maps: Capitani di Parte Guelfa, II, c. 410, S. Quirico a Capalle, Francesco di Giovanni's house may be the one with a small tower marked 'stroxxi', on the river bank to the left of the bridge leading into the *castello*. Another map made by the Capitani di Parte in June 1652 to illustrate their plans to redirect the course of the Bisenzio shows a house with a central courtyard and small tower in an equivalent position, illustrated in Lamberini and Lazzareschi, *Campi*, following p. 142. IGM *Carta d'Italia* 1:25,000, 1963, fol. 106, Prato 32TPP714564.

Bibl. Lamberini and Lazzareschi, *Campi*, p. 201; Tempestini, *Campi Bisenzio*, p. 44, Francesco di Giovanni's ancestor Pagno di Strozza owned lands at Capalle as early as 1315; Gregory, 'Chi erano gli Strozzi', p. 20.

Litta X

19. LA LOGGIA/MACIA
S. Stefano in Pane

a) Niccolò di Pagnozzo di Pagnozzo Strozzi
　　1427 Cat. 47 fol. 350r
　　1433 Cat. 496 fol. 399r, value F.838. 18. 8
　　1442 Cat. 621 fol. 532r
　　1446 Cat. 673, I, fol. 181r
　　1451 Cat. 709 fol. 583r
Monna Cosa, widow of Niccolò di Pagnozzo Strozzi, and their son Antonio
　　1469 Cat. 921 fol. 173r, value F.664. 11. 8
Antonio di Niccolò di Pagnozzo Strozzi
　　1480 Cat. 1013, I, fol. 44r
b) Michele di Piero di Pagnozzo di Pagnozzo Strozzi and brothers
　　1433 Cat. 496 fol. 331r
Michele di Piero di Pagnozzo di Pagnozzo Strozzi
　　1442 Cat. 620, II, fol. 731r
　　1446 Cat. 671, I, fol. 55r

Monna Maria widow of Piero di Pagnozzo Strozzi
　　1446 Cat. 671, I, fol. 56v
Michele di Piero di Pagnozzo di Pagnozzo Strozzi
　　1451 Cat. 707, fol. 291r
　　1480 Cat. 1012, I, fol. 92r
　　1498 Decima Repub. 23, fol. 166v

There were two Strozzi properties in the same district alternately called 'Macia' or 'alla Loggia' that were inherited by Niccolò and Piero, the two sons of Pagnozzo di Pagnozzo Strozzi, but were listed with no common boundaries. They may be identified with the two houses labelled by Carocci, as 'Le Sciabbie – Casa Carobbi' (1906, vol. I, p. 330) and 'La Loggia – Casa Carobbi' (1906, vol. I, p. 332). According to Carocci, 'La Loggia – Casa Carobbi' was the one that belonged to Niccolò di Pagnozzo Strozzi in 1427, whose heirs sold it to the Hospital of S. Maria Nuova, which in turn sold it to Michelangelo Buonarroti in 1512. This appears to be confirmed by the boundaries in Niccolò di Pagnozzo's tax returns, which tally with the notarial document for Michelangelo's purchase (1: the street, 2: the hospital of Messer Bonifazio Lupi, 3: Bartolommeo Sassetti). This property on what is now the Via Perfetti Ricasoli/Via Panciatichi was partly demolished and then rebuilt beyond recognition. The other Strozzi property at Macia inherited by Piero di Pagnozzo's son Michele may be the house listed by Carocci as 'Le Sciabbie – Casa Carobbi' (now the Via Accademia del Cimento 2, previously Via delle Sciabbie). It is odd, however, that this property, which is next door to Bartolommeo Sassetti's villa of Macia (see Chapter 9), was not listed with any Sassetti or Strozzi *confini* in the fifteenth century. Carocci may have confused the two Strozzi houses at Macia, and more research is needed to untangle the history of these two buildings, the difficulties being compounded by the industrialisation of this area and the transformation of the buildings in question.

Maps: IGM *Carta d'Italia* 1:25,000, 1955, fol. 106, Firenze 32TPP792521; Amministrazione Provinciale di Firenze 1:10,000, 1979, fol. 52.

Bibl. Carocci, *I Dintorni*, 1906, I, pp. 330, 332; Lensi-Orlandi, *Di quà*, p. 3; Mannini, 'Degradazione', p. 2;

Zangheri, *Ville della provincia di Firenze*, p. 255, 'Villa Carobbi, Panciatichi, Strozzi', 'Villa "La Loggia"'; Hatfield, *The Wealth of Michelangelo*, pp. 71–2, 434, 447, 462–3, 477–8, 486–7, 520–21.

Litta X

20. CAPALLE
S. Quirico a Capalle

Benedetto di Pieraccione Strozzi
    1427 Cat. 42 fol. 259r
    1430 Cat. 405 fol. 32v, total value of eight farms
        F.4,777
    1433 Cat. 495 fol. 49r
    1442 Cat. 620, I, fol. 173r
    1446 Cat. 671, I, fol. 150r
    1451 Cat. 707 fol. 396r
    1457 Cat. 816, II, fol. 777r
Messer Piero, Pagholo and Francesco di Benedetto Strozzi rejected their father's will in favour of their mother's dowry. Messer Piero inherited one large remaining farm at Capalle, while Pagholo and Francesco shared the other remaining farm and apparently the *casa da signore*, Il Cortile
Pagholo di Benedetto di Pieraccione Strozzi
    1469 Cat. 920, I, fol. 726r
    1480 Cat. 1012, I, fol. 205r
    1498 Decima Repub. 23 fol. 281r
Messer Piero di Benedetto di Pieraccione Strozzi
    1480 Cat. 1012, II, fol. 415
Francesco di Benedetto di Pieraccione Strozzi
    1469 Cat. 919, II, fol. 279r
    1480 Cat. 1011 fol. 253r, total value of two
        remaining farms F.1. 420

Villa unidentified.

The *casa da signore* belonging to this estate was situated within the walls of the *castello* of Capalle, with its garden just outside the walls.

Bibl. For the literature on Benedetto di Pieraccione Strozzi and his son Messer Piero, see Alessandra Macinghi Strozzi, *Lettere*, pp. 136, 141–2, 267; De la Mare, 'Messer Piero Strozzi', p. 56; Gregory, *A*

Florentine Family in Crisis, p. 28; Sale, *The Strozzi Chapel*, pp. 20, 62 n. 56; Lillie, 'The Patronage of Villa Oratories'.

Litta XI

21. 'BROZZI, IN CANTONE'
S. Martino a Brozzi

Lionardo d'Antonio di Lionardo Strozzi with his brothers Caroccio and Rinieri
    1427 Cat. 77 fol. 98r
    1430 Cat. 406 fol. 250v
Caroccio and Rinieri d'Antonio di Lionardo with their nephew Antonio di Lionardo
    1433 Cat. 496 fol. 99v
Rinieri d'Antonio di Lionardo with his nephew Giovanni di Caroccio
    1442 Cat. 621 fol. 462r, listed as sold in 1441 to
        Francesco di Benedetto Strozzi
Francesco di Benedetto di Caroccio Strozzi
    1442 Cat. 620, I, fol. 412r, listed as bought from
        the sons of Antonio di Lionardo Strozzi for
        F.200 on 16 June 1441
    1446 Cat. 671, I, fol. 287r
    1451 Cat. 707 fol. 431r
Sons and heirs of Francesco di Benedetto Strozzi
    1469 Cat. 920, I, fol. 565r
Battista di Francesco di Benedetto Strozzi
    1480 Cat. 1011 fol. 157r
Monna Camilla, widow of Battista di Francesco Strozzi, and their son Raphaello
    1498 Decima Repub. 22, fol. 276r

The *casa da signore* probably survives.

Maps: IGM *Carta d'Italia* 1:25,000, 1963, fol. 106, Campi Bisenzio 32TPP744514.

Bibl. Carocci (*I Dintorni*, 1906, I, pp. 359–60, La Torre – Casa Orsini Baroni) describes the towered house on the main village street at Brozzi, which once belonged to the Strozzi and is probably Lionardo d'Antonio's house with a dove-tower, which was joined to Francesco di Benedetto's house in the fifteenth century. See entry no. 22. It is clear from the boundaries listed in the tax returns and from claims for flood damage that the garden of this house went down to the river banks of the Arno.

Litta XI and XII

22. BROZZI 'IN SULLA STRADA'
S. Martino a Brozzi

Francesco and Zanobi di Benedetto di Caroccio Strozzi
    1427 Cat. 43 fol. 681r (*portata*); Cat. 76 fol. 80r (*campione*)
Francesco di Benedetto di Caroccio Strozzi
    1430 Cat. 405 fol. 48r (half the house and garden)
    1433 Cat. 495 fol. 159r (half the house and garden)
Zanobi di Benedetto di Caroccio Strozzi
    1430 Cat. 405 fol. 175r (half the house and garden)
    1433 Cat. 495 fol. 498v (half the house and garden)
Francesco di Benedetto di Caroccio Strozzi
    1442 Cat. 620, I, fol. 412r (from 1433 Francesco had sole ownership of the Brozzi house and garden)
    1446 Cat. 671, I, fol. 287r
    1451 Cat. 707 fol. 431r
Sons and heirs of Francesco di Benedetto Strozzi
    1469 Cat. 920, I, fol. 564r
Lodovico di Francesco di Benedetto Strozzi
    1480 Cat. 1012, I, fol. 11r
    1498 Decima Repub. 22, fol. 83r

    The *casa da signore* probably survives.

Maps: IGM *Carta d'Italia* 1:25,000, 1963, fol. 106, Campi Bisenzio 32TPP744514.

Bibl. Carocci, *I Dintorni*, 1906, I, pp. 359–60, La Torre – Casa Orsini Baroni, is probably the amalgamation of Lionardo d'Antonio's house on the corner with its dove-tower and Francesco di Benedetto's house next door. See entry no. 21. This property also went down to the banks of the Arno.

Litta XI and XII

23. PALAIUOLA
Badia a Fiesole

a) Zanobi di Benedetto di Caroccio Strozzi
    1430 Cat. 405 fol. 175r, no farms attached
    1433 Cat. 495 fol. 498v
    1442 Cat. 620, II, fol. 1013r
    1446 Cat. 671, I, fol. 105r
    1451 Cat. 707 fol. 483r
    1457 Cat. 816 fol. 9r
Monna Nanna, widow of Zanobi di Benedetto di Caroccio Strozzi, and their sons Piero, Caroccio and Antonio
    1469 Cat. 920, II, fol. 801v
    1480 Cat. 1012, II, fol. 225r
Monna Nanna, widow of Zanobi di Benedetto di Caroccio Strozzi
    1498 Decima Repub. 23, fol. 243r
b) Sons and heirs of Francesco di Benedetto Strozzi
    1469 Cat. 920, I, fol. 565v
Lorenzo di Francesco di Benedetto Strozzi
    1480 Cat. 1012, I, fol. 61r
Sons and heirs of Lorenzo di Francesco Strozzi
    1498 Decima Repub. 22 fol. 374r
c) Sons and heirs of Francesco di Benedetto Strozzi
    1469 Cat. 920, I, fol. 569r, acquired from Messer Otto Niccolini in May 1464.
Lorenzo di Francesco di Benedetto Strozzi
    1480 Cat. 1012, I, fol. 61r (one quarter of the house shared with his other three brothers)
Sons and heirs of Lorenzo di Francesco di Benedetto Strozzi
    1498 Decima Repub. 22, fol. 374r (one quarter of the house and land)
Batista di Francesco di Benedetto Strozzi
    1480 Cat. 1011 fol. 158r (one quarter of the house and land)
Lodovico di Francesco di Benedetto Strozzi
    1480 Cat. 1012, I, fol. 11r (one quarter of the house and land)
    1498 Decima Repub. 22 fol. 83r (one quarter of the house and land)

    The houses probably survive.

Maps: IGM *Carta d'Italia* 1:25,000, 1955, fol. 106, Firenze 32TPP837532; Amministrazione Provinciale di Firenze, 1:10,000, 1979, fol. 44.

Bibl. Carocci, *I dintorni*, 1906, I, pp. 106, 108, lists three villas at Palaiuola, Villa Pampaloni, Villa Von Buerkel and Villa Gronau, named by Lensi Orlandi, *Di qua d'Arno*, p. 76, as Villa Sacchi, Villa Costantini and Villa Gronau respectively. Further research is needed to distinguish whether these three houses are precisely those three owned by the Strozzi in the fifteenth century. See text and notes above in Chapter Three. See documentary references in Levi d'Ancona, *Miniatura*, pp. 54–59, 261–268; Levi d'Ancona, 'Zanobi Strozzi reconsidered'; Cohn, 'Il Beato Angelico e Battista di Biagio Sanguigni'.

Litta XI and XII

24. GALLUZZO
S. Maria a Travalle, Calenzano

Heirs of Francesco di Benedetto Strozzi
 1469 Cat. 920, I, fol. 567r, half the estate was bought from Forte di Simone del Bambo in June 1458 and the other half was given by Monna Antonia, daughter of Lorenzo d'Uberto Strozzi in 1459.
Vanni di Francesco di Benedetto Strozzi
 1480 Cat. 1012, II, fol. 350r
Heirs of Vanni di Francesco di Benedetto Strozzi
 1498 Decima Repub.23, fol. 387r

Villa still exists.

Maps: Capitani di Parte Guelfa, II, c. 447, S. Maria a Travalle; IGM *Carta d'Italia* 1:25,000, fol. 106, 1963, Prato, 32TPP735614.

Bibl. Lamberini, *Calenzano*, pp. 232–7, with full bibliography. This house was largely rebuilt by Vanni di Francesco Strozzi from the 1460s, as is apparent from the vaulted ground-floor *sala* (now used as a garage and storeroom) and *pietra serena* doorways. Vanni and his sons were still enlarging this estate in the 1480s and 1490s.

Litta XI and XII

25. LE MICCINE
S. Giorgio a Colonica, Contado di Prato

Benedetto di Marcuccio Strozzi
 1430 Cat. 405 fol. 16v, value of home farm F.575. 17. 11
 1433 Cat. 496 fol. 56v, value of home farm F.636.1. 6
 1442 Cat. 621 fol. 12v
 1446 Cat. 671, II, fol. 943r
 1451 Cat. 707 fol. 783r
 1457 Cat. 818 fol. 315r, value of home farm F.557
Giovanmaria di Benedetto di Marcuccio Strozzi
 1469 Cat. 921 fol. 371r

Villa unidentified.

The district known as Le Miccine covers a broad area, and it has not been possible to identify which house belonged to Benedetto di Marcuccio Strozzi.

Maps: Capitani di Parte Guelfa, II, c. 510, S. Giorgio a Colonicha; there are at least five houses marked 'stroxxi' in this parish and Strozzi lands scattered over the district in the late sixteenth century; IGM *Carta d'Italia* 1:25,000, fol. 106, 1963, Campi Bisenzio.

Bibl. Goldthwaite, 'The Building of the Strozzi Palace' pp. 120, 136–7 discusses Marco di Benedetto di Marcuccio's career as accountant to Filippo di Matteo Strozzi.

Litta XV

26. IL PALAGIO
S. Lorenzo a Campi

Carlo di Marcuccio Strozzi
 1427 Cat. 42 fol. 535r
 1430 Cat. 405 fol. 40r, value of home farm F.331.15.8
 1433 Cat. 495 fol. 103r, value of home farm F.335.10.9
 1442 Cat. 620, I, fol. 269r

1446 Cat. 671, I, fol. 230r

1451 Cat. 707 fol. 670r

1457 Cat. 819, II, fol. 647r, value of home farm F.282. 10.

Heirs of Carlo di Marcuccio Strozzi

1469 Cat. 920, II, fol. 812r, value of home farm F.313. 10

Niccolò di Carlo di Marcuccio Strozzi

1480 Cat. 1012, I, fol. 162r (one quarter of the Campi villa, shared with his brothers)

Girolamo di Carlo di Marcuccio Strozzi

1480 Cat. 1012, I, fol. 85r (half the Campi villa, shared with his brother Paolo)

Marco di Carlo di Marcuccio Strozzi

1480 Cat. 1012, I, fol. 84r (one quarter of the Campi villa)

1498 Decima Repub. 23, fol. 200r (Girolamo's quarter of the villa had gone to his widow Maddalena in repayment for her dowry, and it was then acquired by the heirs of Filippo and Lorenzo Strozzi)

The *casa da signore* still survives, Via del Paradiso, Campi Bisenzio.

Maps: Capitani di parte Guelfa, II, c.412, S. Lorenzo a Campi, a house marked 'piero stroxxi' is in the same position as the villa still known as 'Il Palagio' today; IGM *Carta d'Italia* 1:25,000, fol. 106, 1963, Campi Bisenzio 32TPP711545.

Bibl. Carocci, *I Dintorni*, 1906, I, p. 353, Il Palagio – Villa Mazzoni, notes that it used to belong to the Strozzi and then to the Bruni; Lensi Orlandi (*Di qua d'Arno*, pp. 9–10, Il Palagio Melchior) writes that the present structure dates from the eighteenth century, and I was unable to find any visible traces of the fifteenth-century house on a visit to the villa. In 1989, the property was acquired by the Arciconfraternita della Misericordia di Campi Bisenzio; see also Lamberini and Lazzareschi, *Campi*, pp. 295–6, 318–19 and plate following p. 478; Bacci, *Il Palagio, Villa Melchior*. On this branch of the family, see F. Edler de Roover, 'Per La storia dell'arte della stampa'.

Litta XV mistakenly names Marco di Carlo di Marcuccio Strozzi as Matteo.

27. SIGNANO
S. Lorenzo a Campi

Bernardo di Giovanni di Marco Strozzi

1427 Cat. 42 fol. 272r

Bernardo and Giovanni di Giovanni Strozzi

1433 Cat. 495 fol. 83r, value F.1749. 5. 9

Monna Agnola, widow of Bernardo di Giovanni Strozzi

1442 Cat. 620, I, fol. 493r

(Monna Agnola chose to enter a convent and left the villa of Signano to her nephews Giannozo, Battista, Zacheria and Smeraldo di Giovanni di Giovanni Strozzi)

Giovanni di Giovanni di Marco Strozzi

1446 Cat. 669, II, fol. 883v

(Giovanni declares that he has consigned the villa to his son Zacheria, who is a canon of S. Maria del Fiore and was emancipated in December 1446)

1451 Cat. 705 fol. 641

(The villa is in the name of Zacheria di Giovanni Strozzi)

Batista di Giovanni di Giovanni Strozzi

1457 Cat. 816, II, fol. 856r

1469 Cat. 919, I, fol. 93v

(The villa is shared between the brothers Batista and Giannozo since Zacheria's death in 1464)

Giannozo di Giovanni di Giovanni Strozzi

1469 Cat. 919, II, fol. 390r

(Giannozo has one-third of the villa, since Zacheria's share has not been reallocated after his death)

1480 Cat. 1011 fol. 425r

(Giannozo has one third of the villa, shared with his brother Batista)

Batista di Giovanni di Giovanni Strozzi

1480 Cat. 1011 fol. 121r

Giovanni and Zacheria di Battista di Giovanni Strozzi

1498 Decima Repub. 22, fol. 465r

The *casa da signore* does not survive

Bibl. Lamberini and Lazzareschi, *Campi*, pp. 305, 327–328, list this villa among those whose approximate sites are identifiable, although the buildings do not survive; Signano would have been situated just to the northeast of the Rocca di Campi near the Torre dei Buti;

see exerpts from Tempestini ibid. pp. 328 and Pirillo pp. 196, 202, 204 for fourteenth century records of the villa.

Litta XVI

28. SANTUCCIO
S. Donnino a Brozzi

Pinaccio di Filippo di Messer Lionardo Strozzi
    1427 Cat. 45 fol. 486r
    1430 Cat. 405 fol. 117v
(In 1436 the Santuccio property was received by Giannozo di Tommaso Alberti in repayment for a debt of F.496 from the merchant company of Alessandro di Francesco Ferrantini of London where Pinaccio had been working)
Giannozo di Tomaso degli Alberti
    1442 Cat. 617 fol. 450v
    1446 Cat. 664 fol. 194r
Bivigliano and Giovanni di Tommaso di Giannozo degli Alberti
    1451 Cat. 700 fol. 167v
Giovanni di Tommaso di Giannozo degli Alberti
    1469 Cat. 914 fol. 395r, value F.806. 1. 6
(Contract of sale to Filippo di Matteo Strozzi, Not. Antecos. G 618, II, fol. 188r. Messer Simone Grazzini, 14 July 1477)
Filippo di Matteo di Simone Strozzi
    1480 Cat. 1011 fol. 315r, value F.806. 1. 6
Heirs of Filippo di Matteo Strozzi
    1498 Decima Repub.23, fol. 359r

The *casa da signore* survives, Via di Ponte al Santo, between S. Donnino and S. Mauro.

Maps: Capitani di Parte Guelfa, II, c. 404 'S. Donino'; c. 421 'S. Moro'; IGM *Carta d'Italia* 1:25,000, fol. 106, 1963, Campi Bisenzio 32TPP719514; Amministrazione Provinciale di Firenze, 1979, fol. 52.

Bibl. Carocci, *I Dintorni*, 1906, I, p. 366, Il Palagio de' Vecchietti – Villa Altoviti; Lensi Orlandi, *Di qua d'Arno*, p. 4, Palagio de' Vecchietti. Carocci was unaware that the villa had once belonged to the Strozzi, while Lensi Orlandi presumed the portico was not added until the sixteenth century. Goldthwaite ('The

Building of the Strozzi Palace', pp. 108–9) identified the villa and the building accounts pertaining to its reconstruction by Filippo Strozzi in the 1480s. See also Lillie, 'Vita di palazzo, vita in villa'.

Litta XVII and XVIII

29. IL PALAGIONE, CAPALLE
Il Pelago del Gattico, S. Quirico a Capalle

Ubertino and Tommaso di Tommaso d'Ubertino Strozzi
    1427 Cat. 45 fol. 851r
Ubertino di Tommaso d'Ubertino Strozzi
    1430 Cat. 405 fol. 173v
    1433 Cat. 495 fol. 492r, value F.770. 14. 3
    1442 Cat. 620, II, fol. 999r
    1446 Cat. 671, II, fol. 835r
Heirs of Ubertino di Tommaso d'Ubertino Strozzi
    1451 Cat. 707 fol. 175r
    1457 Cat. 816, I, fol. 520r
    1469 Cat. 920, II, fol. 784r, value F.720. 9. 10
    1480 Cat. 1012, II, fol. 263v (listed as sold to Filippo di Matteo Strozzi for F.1,200 in 1474 or 1475 to pay back the dowry of Ubertino's widow Monna Nanna)
Filippo di Matteo Strozzi
    1480 Cat. 1011 fol. 314v. value F.720. 16. 7 (listed as bought on 18 May 1475 for 1,000 large florins from Marco di Carlo Strozzi)

Maps: Capitani di Parte Guelfa; II, c. 410, S. Quirico a Capalle, Ubertino's 'torrione' rebuilt by Filippo di Matteo is probably the large house with a tower shown between two gates in the *castello* walls just above the church of Capalle; IGM *Carta d'Italia* 1:25,000, fol. 106, 1963, Prato 32TPP714565; Amministrazione Provinciale di Firenze, 1:10,000, 1979, fol. 42.

Bibl. Goldthwaite, 'The Building of the Strozzi Palace', p. 107; Lamberini and Lazzareschi, *Campi*, pp. 305–7. Ubertino's 'torrione' at Capalle was probably the remains of the Florentine bishops' residence built in the early thirteenth century. (Lami, *Sanctae Ecclesiae*, II, p. 773, quoted in Lamberini and

Lazzareschi, *Campi*, p. 134) which was then acquired and rebuilt by Filippo di Matteo Strozzi in the 1470s.

Litta II and XVIII

30. MAGLIO
S. Michele a Maglio, Val di Bisenzio

Acquired after 1484, Filippo di Matteo's estate at Maglio postdates his last tax return of 1480.

Villa survives.

Maps: Capitani di Parte Guelfa, II, c. 488, S. Michele a Maglio, the towered house with an adjoining out-building is shown at a junction of four roads, labelled 'maglio delli stroxi' to the left of the parish map; IGM *Carta d'Italia* 1:25,000, fol. 106, 1960, Vaiano 32TPP713682.

Bibl. Repetti, III, p. 20, suppl. append. p. 134; Goldthwaite, 'Building of the Strozzi Palace', pp. 107; Sale, 'The Strozzi Chapel', pp. 26, 68 n. 93.

Litta XVIII

31. IL MULINACCIO/CASI
S. Lionardo a Casi, Vaiano, Prato

Stagio d'Antonio di Stagio Strozzi
  1427 Cat. 45 fol. 752r
  1430 Cat. 405 fol. 278r
  1433 Cat. 495 fol. 455v, value of four farms and
   pieces of land F.628. 2. 9
  1442 Cat. 620, II, fol. 943r
  1446 Cat. 671, I, fol. 75r
The villa was sold by Stagio's son Lionardo in January 1476/7 to Francesco Sassetti
  1480 Cat. 1013, II, fol. 320v

Galeazzo di Francesco Sassetti
  1498 Decima Repub.24, fol. 471r
Cosimo di Francesco Sassetti
  1504 Decima Repub. arroti 152, fol. 132r, Cosimo Sassetti had bought the estate at Casi from his brother Galeazzo in November 1502.

Villa survives.

Maps: Capitani di Parte Guelfa, II, c. 479, S. Salvadore a Vaiano, it is a small house labelled 'sassetti mulinaccio' on the centre left; IGM *Carta d'Italia* 1:25,000, fol. 106, 1960, Vaiano 32TPP701697.

Bibl. Repetti, I, p. 313, Petri and Paoletti, *Ville Pratesi*, pp. 33–48, Villa Vaj.

Litta XVII

32. MALMANTILE
S. Piero in Selva, Gangalandi

Barla di Stagio di Messer Lionardo Strozzi
  1427 Cat. 42 fol. 368r, he owned farms at Le
   Tesole and Poggio Chiavetti, but no *casa da*
   signore
Niccolò di Barla di Stagio Strozzi
  1442 Cat. 620, II, fol. 816r
  1446 Cat. 671, II, fol. 955r
  1469 Cat. 420, I, fol. 682r, Niccolò has now
   bought a house for his own habitation in the
   castello of Malmantile
Heirs of Niccolò di Barla di Stagio Strozzi
  1480 Cat. 1012, II, fol. 267r, value F.345. 14. 4

House unidentified.

Maps: IGM *Carta d'Italia*, 1:25,000, fol. 106, 1952, Montelupo Fiorentino: Amministrazione Provinciale di Firenze 1:10,000, 1979, fol. 60.

APPENDIX C · THE 1499 DIVISION AMONG THE SONS OF FRANCESCO SASSETTI

Copy of the 1499 division of Francesco Sassetti's villa at Montughi among his three surviving sons Galeazzo, Cosimo and Teodoro.

A.S.F. TESTAMENTI M.20, Vol.II, 1509–45, Ser Pierfrancesco Maccari.

Copia del contratto della divise di Montui infra Ghaleazzo, Cosimo et Teodoro, fratelli et figliuoli di Francesco di Tommaso Sassetti.

[fol. 449r]

In dei nomine amen. Anno Domini ab eius salutifera incarnatione MCCCC LXXXX VIIII, indictione secunda, die vero XII mensis maii. Actum in populo Sancti Marci Veteris extra muros Florentie, presentibus ibidem probis et discretis viris Domino Luca olim Bertoldi de Corsinis cive et advocato florentino, et Alexandro olim Antonii de Puccis, et Paulo Ghori de Serraglis civibus florentinis et aliis testibus ad infrascripta omnia et singhula vocatis habitis pariter et roghatis.

Cum comunio soleat plerunque parere discordias, hinc est quod nobiles viri Ghaleazius, Cosmas et Theodorus, fratres et filii olim Francisci Tomme di Sassetti, cives florentini, volentes devenire ad divisionem infrascritte domus et seu palatii positi in dicto populo Sancti Marci, Montughi nuncupato, quod disserunt inter se habere comune et pro indiviso; interventu domini Luce de Corsinis, Alexandri de Puccis, Simeonis de Carnesecchis eorum cognatorum, omni meliori modo via iure et forma quibus magis et melius de iure potuerunt et eis licuit et licet, ad infrascriptum contractum promissionem oblighationem conventionem et pactum divisionis titulo devenerunt. In primis prefati fratres de dicta domo et palatio fecerunt tres partes ut infra vulghari sermone designatas, quarum quidem partium unicuique dictorum fratrum assignetur una pars prout sorte dirimetur, factis videlicet tribus cedulis et in uno bireto positis, in quibus scripta sunt nomina dictorum fratrum, et quis primo extractus fuit possit et ei liceat eligere et capere quam partem maluit incontinenti extracta cedula et sic ordine successivo quousque omnes tres cedule extracte fuerint, et que quidem partes sunt iste videlicet.

La prima parte s'intenda essere e sia la sala di sopra, che ghuarda verso la Pietra al Migliaio con la camera della stufa, con le dua anticamere e scrittoio e con ogni altra appartenenza.

La camera dal canto in detta sala col salotto in su detta sala, la saletta da famiglia in sul verone, la cucina vecchia a capo di scala e la scala vecchia, et con tutti gli habituri che son di sopra a detti habituri insino al tetto, et più un altro habituro al tetto che è sopra la camera delle serve usata tenersi con detta cucina, et più la metà della volta maggiore a dividersi con la seconda parte per metà secondo saranno d' accordo a [fol. 449 v] spese comune, intendendosi che detta volta si habbi a dividere a requisitione di ciascuna delle parti; et più il fattoio da olio, libero con tutti e sua instrumenti et masserizie, et più la metà del sito che al presente è pollaio, el quale si habbi a dividere per metà come di sopra a spese comuni, facendo la sua entrata in su el lastrico che ghuarda verso Camerata; habbi a cchi tocca detta parte a rimurare l'uscio che va dalla cucina vecchia alla cucina terrena perchè dette scale sono della terza parte.

Que quidem prima pars sorte [sic: *sors*] et fortuna secundum premissa obvenit de necessitate Ghaleazio, qui fuit ultimus extractus ex bireto, dictis Cosimo primo et secundam dicto Teodoro secundo extractis et tertiam partes eligentibus, et quam quidem partem primam idem Ghaleazius de consensu etiam dicti Cosme et Teodori elegit et suscepit et acceptavit et de ea se bene contentum et tacitum pro parte sua vocavit.

La seconda parte la sala grande dipinta cha ghuarda verso Camerata, la camera in su quella e l'anticamera et oratorio che si chiama la camera di Francesco, la camera del salotto da verno con la camera che ha lume sul verone, che si dice anticamera delle fanciulle; la camera e anticamera che ghuarda in su l'orto che al presente abita Teodoro; la cucina in sul secondo verone, che si dice la cucina nuova, con la camera da serve che soleva servire alla cucina vecchia che si dà alla prima parte; la scala nuova, l'andito dell'orto che è fra'l pozzo e la camera del maestro in terreno. Et più con detto andito e androne il campo dalla parte che ghuarda verso Firenze per larghezza quanto la casa et lunghezza quanto va il confino con le rede di Baldo da Lutiano, cui a primo via che viene da Firenze, a secondo beni di detto Baldo, a terzo detto campo, a quarto detta casa per recta linea, con quegli sassi che si truovon dreto alla casa.

Et più la metà della volta grande, la quale si habbi a dividere a spese comune come si dice nella prima parte; et più el sito della conigl[i]era, facendo l'entrata nella parte di dreto in sul lastrico verso Camerata. Que quidem secunda pars sorte et fortuna secundum [premissa] obvenit dicto Cosmo qui primo fuit extrattus et prefatam partem modis et formis premissis [fol. 450 r] elegit incontinenti extracta dicta cedula et eam de consensu, presentia et volumptate dicti Ghaleazi et Teodori acceptavit et de ea se bene contentum et tacitum pro parte sua vocavit et asseruit.

La terza parte, la loggia terrena e corte con le dua camere, anticamere et con la entrata dell'uscio di dreto, sia libera e expedita; la camera del maestro,

l'abituro dove si tiene le legne, la sala terrena con le dua camere in su essa, el salotto da famiglia col citernino, l'entrata dell'orto con l'orto tutto et colonbaia e metà el sito del pollaio a dividersi come di sopra con la prima parte. La cucina terrena con camera da olio del fattore e forno, le dua volticine sotto l'androne dell'entrata dinanzi. Que quidem pars tertia in ordine ottigit et obvenit sorte secundum premissa dicto Teodoro, qui fuit secundus extractus ex bireto et hanc partem elegit incontinenti extracta cedula et quam quidem partem idem Teodorus de consensu, presentia et volumptate dicti Ghaleazi et Cosme acceptavit et de ea se bene contentum et tacitum pro parte sua vocavit.

Hoc tam inter dictas partes acto et per solennem stipulationem vallato quod salvis premissis inter dictas partes restet et sit comunis et pro indiviso ut primum vestibulum et seu introitus anterior dicte domus ex latere anteriori dicte domus, cum pratellis ante et retro domum et palazium, cappella puteus et seu cisterna et lodia posita super strata Lapidis Miliarii, item situs vindemmie et omnes alii situs et habitationes que secunda premissa non essent divise restent et sint pro indiviso. Que omnia ac etiam stillicidia et gronde debeant manuteneri sumptibus comunibus dictarum partium. Hoc etiam salvo et reservato et declarato quod inter ipsum Cosmum et Ghaleazzum sit liber usus veronis superioris pro aurienda aqua a dictis Ghaleazo et Cosmo, quibus obvenerunt partes superiores dicte domus. . . .

Item in Dei nomine amen. Anno Domini ab eius salutifera incarnatione MCCCCLXXXXVIIII, indictione secunda, die vero quinta junii. Actum in populo Sancti Marci Veteris extra muros Florentie, presentibus ibidem probis et discretis viris Alixandro olim Antonii de Puccis et Nanne olim Mecheri del Pecorino, testibus ad premissa omnia et singhula vocatis habitis et roghatis. Prelibati Ghaleazius, Cosmas et Teodorus fratres et filii dicti Francisci Tomme de Sassettis, volentes devenire ad divisionem predii et seu prediorem inter eos comunium, positorum circumcirca palatium de Montughi vel ut supra inter eos divisum, omni meliori modo via iure vice et forma quibus magis ac melius [et] [fol. 451 v] validius de iure potuerunt, ad infrascriptum contrattum promissionem oblighationem et pactum divisionis titulo concorditer devenerunt et quod de dictis omnibus et singhulis infrascrittis bonis rebus et iuribus comuni concordia fecerunt et constituerunt tres partes, hoc modo vulghari sermone descrittas et confinatas. Prima portio intellighatur esse et sit ista.

La casa dal lavoratore con ogni sua apartenentia verso la loggia in sulla strada, con tutte le terre dal lato di detta via insino al fossato secco della siepe, da primo via maestra, secondo via, terzo Simone Bruni, quarto l'Arte della Lana, a quinto detto rio per traverso. E con detta parte s'intenda l'anghuillare che si spiccano dal pratello e vanno insino la loggia di qua et di là, con questo inteso che della vigna del trebbiano di detto podere se ne habbi a cavare staiora cinque dal lato della via di sopra inverso la casa del poderuzzo, la qual vigna si concede alla parte di detto poderuzzo, e con questo che detto poderuzzo ha dare per ricompenso di detta parte di staiora 6 di terra del campo che confina con detta vigna et detto rio secco.

Secunda portio. El poderuzzo che lavora Nanni con casa da lavoratore e tutte sue appartenenze come habita al presente Nanni, con staiora 32 di terra in circa, cui a primo via, a secondo messer Lorenzo canonico di San Lorenzo, terzo heredi d'Agniolo Tani, a quarto via e più el resto del campo che è dalla stalla che se n'ha a dare staiora 6 per ricompenso della vigna del trebbiano e cavatone l'aia per la terza parte tanto quanto va el muro del pratello insino alla stalla, non passando uno staioro all'intorno di detta casa.

Tertia portio. Le terre che sono di verso levante verso la strada di sotto e verso et verso [sic] Firenze e più dalla parte dinanzi un campo di staiora 12 in circa, cui a primo via, a secondo rio secco, a terzo l'anghuillare del viottolo, a quarto l'arte della lana, a quinto pratello, et cum aliis confinibus dicte partis, con carico di 20 fiorini di suggello a rifare per metà a Ghaleazzo e Teodoro per ricompensa di più terre. Et

più la stalla sia di detta parte con uno staioro di terra intorno come di sopra.

E pratelli di dreto e dinanzi al palagio sieno a comune per indiviso, el simile la loggia della pietra.

[fol. 452 r]

Cum omnibus et singhulis pertinentiis dictorum bonorum sub quibuscumque dictorum bonorum confinibus vocabulis et demostrationibus quibuslibet sub quovis nomine nuncupentur et cum omnibus et singhulis que dicta bona et quodlibet ipsorum habent super se in et seu intra se [in] integrum, et cum omnibus et singulis accessibus ingressibus egressibus usibus et servitutibus suis usque in vias publicas et cum omni iure et aczione [sic] usu et seu requisitione dominio proprietate possessione vel quasi eisdem fratribus contraentibus predictis et cuilibet ipsorum in dictis de dictis aut pro dictis vel occasione dictorum bonorum vel alicuius ipsorum quomodolibet competentibus et competituris. Et quarum quidem partium sicut supra designatarum et confinatarum modis et formis premissis, prima obvenit dicto Ghaleazo, secunda vero Teodoro, tertia vero portio dicto Cosmo cum omnibus et singhulis pertinentiis et aliis predictis. Et sic dictas respective partes prefati fratres elegerunt susceperunt et acceptaverunt mutuo consensu dictarum partium hinc inde accedente, et de dictis respettive partibus cuilibet ipsarum obventis et per quemlibet ipsorum ut premittitur electis, prefati fratres vocaverunt se bene tacitos et contentos et quilibet ipsorum vocavit et asseruit, salvis infrascrittis pro omni parte et portione eisdem et cuilibet ipsorum tangente et que tangere posset quomodolibet in bonis predictis. Et cum pacto ut premittitur inter dictos fratres et contraentes expresse inito et solemni stipulatione vallato, quod pratelli ante et retro dictum palatium sint et restent in comuni et pro indiviso prout prius, et similiter lodia della Pietra al Migliaio. . . .

Notarised agreement between Francesco Sassetti and Giovanni di Domenico 'legnaiuolo' for the provision of wood, labour and drawings

A.S.F. NOTARILE ANTECOSIMIANO, 19080, Ser Silvano di Giovanni di Frosino, 1464-5.

[fol. 172r]

[^^in margin ̈Y ̈Y:] Laudum

Die XXprimo Iulii 1464

In nomine Domini amen. Anno Domini ab eius salutifera incarnatione MCCCCLXIIII, indictione xii, die xxprimo mensis Iulii. Actum Florentie in populo Sancte Marie supra Porta. Nos Iohannes olim Betti Iohannis, tintor, civis florentinus, arbiter et arbitrator, amicabilis compositor et comunis amicus electus et absumptus a Francischo Tommasi de Sassettis, civis et mercator florentinus, ex parte una, et a Iohanne Dominici, legnaiuolo populi Sancti Pieri Maioris, ex parte alia, ut de compromisso in nos facto constat manu mei Silvani, notarii infrascripti, sub die settimo presentis mensis, viso compromisso et anditis partibus et visis earum scripturis etc. et omnibus visis, Ihesu Christi nomine in vocato, inter dictas partes laudamus in hunc modum, videlicet.

Im primis visa ratione dictarum partium et reperto quod dictus Iohannes petebat dicto Francischo sibi satisfieri de quibusdam lignaminibus datis per dictum Iohannem dicto Francischo, et de quibusdam operibus quas dictus Iohannes auxiliatus fuit dictum Francischum. Et visis quibusdam designis datis et factis per dictum ser Iohannem dicto Francischo. Et computato quicquid dictus Iohannes petebat dicto Francischo occaxione quorumdam lignaminum quos dictus Iohannes emit pro dicto Francischo. Et omnibus bene consideratis, et excomputatis quicquid dictus Francischus solvit dicto Iohanni et alii pro eo, et computatis.

[^^sic ̈Y ̈Y] certa quantitate vini quem dictus Iohannes habuit a dicto Francischo, et computatis datis [et] perceptis et omnibus bene consideratis, declaramus dictum Iohannem restare et esse verum debitorem dicti Francisci librarum decem otto, soldorum decem parvorum, videlicet L.18 s.x parvorum. Et condepnamus dictum Iohannem ad dandum [fol.172 v] et solvendum dicto Francischo dictam quantitatem librarum XVIII soldorum X parvorum hinc ad per totum mensem Augusti proxime futuri sine aliqua exceptione. [*]

Item salvis predictis, absolvimus et finimus unam partem ab alia et e converso ab omnibus que insimul habuissent usque in presentem diem, imponentes dictis partibus perpetuum silentium et finem, salvis supra laudatis.

Et predicta etc. mandantes etc., sub pena, reserva etc. non intendentes etc. Lata etc. die XXprimo mensis Iulii 1464, in Arte, absentibus partibus et quelibet earum, et presentibus testibus Bartolomeo Iachopi Primerani, populi Sancti Pieri Maioris, et ser Antonio ser Christofani de Vitolino, notario et cive florentino.

[∗] [^^ in margin, this addition ŸŸ:]

Item declaramus quod dictus Franciscus te-
neatur ostendere dicto Iohanni librum suum pro
verificando denarios quos dictus Franciscus ponit
in computo dicto Iohanni solutos pro dicto Iohanne
ad aliam quamcumque personam.

NOTES

INTRODUCTION

1   Ancient examples include Varro, *On Agriculture*, I, lxix. 3; II, Introd. 1–4; III, i. 1–4; Quintilian, *Institutio Oratoria*, II, iv. 24; Juvenal, *Satires*, III; Horace, *Odes*, I, xvii; *Epodes*, II; *Epistles*, I, x; I, xiv; II, ii, 65–80; *Satires*, II, vi; see Ackerman, *The Villa*, pp. 35–43. For modern treatments of the theme, see Williams, *The Country and the City*, p. 46; Coates, *Nature*, pp. 35–6.

2   Parodies of town and country themes took very different forms, for example, in tales and verse by Franco Sacchetti, *Il Trecentonovelle*, no. 53, 195, 205, 214; *Il Libro delle rime*, 1936, p. 281; see Plaisance, 'Les Rapports ville campagne dans les nouvelles de Sacchetti, Sercambi et Sermini'; in poems by (or attributed to) Lorenzo de' Medici such as 'La Nencia di Barberino' or 'l'Uccellagione di starne'; see Gorni, 'Su Lorenzo Poeta'; in tales such as Gentile Sermini's *Novelle*, no. 3; edited as 'Scopone', by Martines, *An Italian Renaissance Sextet*, pp. 39–68.

3   Ottokar, *Il Comune di Firenze*, pp. 152–4; Plesner, *L'Emigrazione*, pp. 22–4, 105, 113; Sapori, *Studi di storia economica*, I, pp. 324–7; Fiumi, 'Sui Rapporti economici', pp. 62, 67; P. J. Jones, 'Florentine Families'; 'Medieval Agrarian Society', pp. 349–50. See also Marvin Becker, *Florence in Transition*, I, pp. 14–16, 180; II, pp. 94–9, 182–8.

4   Among many important agricultural and demographic studies of Tuscany in the late Middle Ages and fifteenth century, I have drawn most from Ildebrando Imberciadori, Elio Conti, P. J. Jones, Giovanni Cherubini, Giuliano Pinto, David Herlihy, and Christiane Klapisch-Zuber. Given this wealth of published historical evidence and analysis, it is remarkable how few detailed studies have yet been made of fifteenth-century Florentine villas. Patzak's *Palast und Villa in Toscana*, 1908–13, remains the most rigorous scholarly study of architectural development in this period. Janet Ross (*Florentine Villas* 1901), Harold Eberlein (*Villas of Florence and Tuscany* 1925), Giulio Lensi Orlandi (*Le Ville di Firenze*, first ed. 1954), and Harold Acton (*Tuscan Villas* 1973) all wrote general

surveys covering many villas from differing periods with potted histories of each building and its occupants. They were written with a general audience in mind, combining lively anecdotal history with evocative descriptions and fine illustrations. Eberlein's book goes further towards a synthetic analysis of architectural development, while Lensi Orlandi's and the recent *Ville della provincia di Firenze*, vol. I, ed. L. Zangheri, are indispensable as the most complete surveys of Florentine villas. Other recent books on villas, such as James Ackerman, *Villa*, and Margherita Azzi Visentini, *La Villa in Italia*, include one chapter on the fifteenth-century Florentine villa but only consider the Medici examples. The most important recent publication is Grazia Gobbi Sica's *La Villa fiorentina*, which considers villas in their landscape context from the late Middle Ages until the eighteenth century. Most articles on individual villas have been devoted to the Medici (eg, Gori Sassoli, Bargellini, and Ruffinière du Prey), only Poggio a Caiano has been the subject of a full monograph: P. Foster, 'A Study of Lorenzo de' Medici's Villa at Poggio a Caiano', published in Italian as *La Villa di Lorenzo de' Medici a Poggio a Caiano*.

5   See, for example, Alessandra Macinghi Strozzi, *Lettere*, pp. 49, 61, 88, 89.

6   See, for example, Rucellai, *Il Zibaldone*, I, p. 23, 'la villa di Petriuolo . . . e la villa di Brozzi'; Cherubini and Francovich, 'Forme e vicende', p. 147.

7   See, for example, Crescenzi, *Agricultura*, Lib. XI, Cap. xli; Alberti, 'I Libri della famiglia', p. 194 l.25; p. 197 l.13; p. 198 ll.6, 31; p. 199 ll.2, 11, 20, 25, 30.32, 35; p. 200 ll.2, 5; 'Villa', p. 359 l.1; p. 360 ll.4, 6; p. 362 l.22.

8   See Part 1, n. 8.

9   Najemy, *Corporatism and Consensus*, p. 323, table A 4.

10   Dale Kent, *The Rise of the Medici*, p. 357.

11   Gregory ('A Florentine Family in Crisis', pp. 160–1) discusses the Medicean sympathies of Messer Palla Novello, Messer Marcello di Strozza, and the sons of Benedetto di Caroccio Strozzi, among whom Antonio di Benedetto was the first Strozzi elected as prior under the Medici in 1450; see also

Gregory, 'The Return of the Native', pp. 7–8; Dale Kent, *The Rise of the Medici*, p. 181.

12 Brucker, *Firenze nel rinascimento*, pp. 259–60; *The Civic World of Early Renaissance Florence*, pp. 23–4.

13 P. J. Jones, 'Florentine Families', pp. 184–5.

14 Bartolommeo was elected prior in 1452 and one of the *buonomini* in 1466; Strozziane, V, 1750, cc. 186 sin., 203 des. For Francesco Sassetti's political offices, see de la Mare, 'The Library of Francesco Sassetti', p. 191, n. 11.

PART I: THE STROZZI

1 These are Trebbio, Cafaggiolo, Careggi, Fiesole and Poggio a Caiano.

2 I refer to Bentmann and Müller's 1970 study, *Die Villa als Herrschaftsarchitektur*.

3 Litta, 'Strozzi di Firenze' *Famiglie celebri italiane*; Jones, 'Florentine Families', pp. 186–90, Goldthwaite, *Private Wealth*, pp. 31–107; Gregory, 'Family in Crisis'.

4 Seventy four offices in all; Najemy, *Corporatism and Consensus*, p. 323.

5 Herlihy and Klapisch-Zuber, *Les Toscans*, p. 251; *Tuscans and Their Families*, p. 100.

6 Jones, 'Florentine Families', pp. 189–90, n. 56.

7 Conti (*L'Imposta diretta*, p. 344) noted that the total value of Strozzi real estate had dropped from 121,114 florins, declared in 1427, to 19,039 florins by 1480. For the Strozzi in exile, see Gregory, 'Chi erano gli Strozzi' and 'Family in Crisis'.

8 See Gregory, 'Chi erano gli Strozzi', pp. 15–29. The number of Strozzi households in 1427 has been variously counted as 53, 48, 45 and 39; see Gregory, 'A Family in Crisis', p. 19, n. 2: 'the total of 53 Strozzi households in 1427 counted by Herlihy and Klapisch, *Les Toscans*, p. 251, represents the number of *portate* filed, not the number of households, which was smaller'; ibid., p. 35, 'the 45 Strozzi households in 1427 can be divided into 15 different branches'. In 'Chi erano gli Strozzi', p. 16, Gregory counted 39 Strozzi households and pointed out the difficulties in defining nuclear families. Conti (*L'Imposta diretta*, p. 344) counted 48 Strozzi households in 1427.

9 Gregory, 'Chi erano gli Strozzi', pp. 26–7.

10 Molho, *Marriage Alliance*, p. 91.

11 Goldthwaite, *Private Wealth*, p. 60.

12 P. J. Jones ('Florentine Families', pp. 186–90) presents evidence for a similar 'variety of circumstance' among the Strozzi in the fourteenth century. See also F. W. Kent, *Household and Lineage*, pp. 149–63 on the 'diversity and mutability of fortunes' in the fifteenth century.

13 P. J. Jones, 'Medieval Agrarian Society', p. 350.

CHAPTER 1 THE ACQUISITION AND ALIENATION OF COUNTRY PROPERTY

1 Gregory ('Chi erano gli Strozzi', p. 19) considers the territorial identity of the Strozzi in town. See also F. W. Kent,

Household and Lineage, ch. 5; de Courcey-Bayley, 'House and Household', pp. 149, 151, 172, 173–80.

2 Herlihy, 'Family and Property', pp. 3, 15, 19, 23; F. W. Kent, *Household and Lineage*, pp. 125–49; Kuehn, 'Conflicting Conceptions of Property', pp. 310, 340, citing further bibliography; de Courcey-Bayley, 'House and Household'.

3 For further bibliography and consideration of some of the legal procedures regarding inheritance, see Kuehn, 'Law, Death, and Heirs', pp. 484–516.

4 The twenty-two villa-owning families are those who possessed a *casa da signore* for their own habitation. Where adult brothers or a father with adult sons declared shared property in 1427, I have considered them as a single family unit, although they may have inhabited separate town houses and divided their estates later in the century.

5 These estates belonged to Bernardo di Soldo at Le Gore, Jacopo d'Ubertino at Ponte di Mezzo, Giovanni di Luigi at Le Corti, Marco di Goro at Fornello, Ubertino di Tommaso at Montughi, Messer Marcello di Strozza's Rocca at Campi, Messer Palla di Messer Palla at Soffiano, Francesco di Giovanni at Capalle, Niccolò di Pagnozo at Macia, Benedetto di Pieraccione at Capalle, Francesco di Benedetto at Brozzi, Benedetto di Marcuccio at Le Miccine, Carlo di Marco's Palagio at Campi and Bernardo and Giovanni di Giovanni at Signano. The list of villas and their owners in Appendix B shows the direct lines of inheritance for these villas.

6 Strozziane, V, 10 c. 31 des., gives a list of the property Matteo di Simone inherited from his father.

7 See Chapter 8 for further discussion of this phenomenon.

8 1442 Cat. 621, fol. 462v.; Cat. 620, I, fol. 412r.; 1480 Cat. 1013, II fol. 320v.

9 Goldthwaite, *Wealth and the Demand for Art*, p. 217.

10 This tallies with F. W. Kent's analysis of the properties of the Ginori, Capponi and Rucellai families; see *Household and Lineage*, pp. 129–30, 135–6, 144, 148–9.

11 On this theme, see Lillie, 'Memory of Place'.

12 P. J. Jones ('Florentine Families', p. 118, n. 39) cites the Strozzi castles of Loiano and the Rocca di Campi for which there are no records of ownership before the fourteenth century and notes that 'this and other cases like it create the suspicion that later genealogists treated as ancient and ancestral estates first acquired with the profits of trade.'

13 Lamberini and Lazzareschi, *Campi*, pp. 92–4.

14 The first record of Strozzi purchase in the Campi area dates from 1295 (Ottokar, *Il Comune di Firenze*, p. 97), and the documents grow more numerous in the fourteenth century; Lamberini and Lazzareschi, *Campi*, pp. 181, 203, 211, 234, 255, 256, 266.

15 According to *Le Vite* of Lorenzo Strozzi, ed. Zeffi, p. 12, Carlo di Strozza Strozzi built (or rebuilt?) the Rocca di Campi. Since Litta, Tavola III, notes that Carlo fled to Ferrara in 1378, construction must have begun before that date, but after 1370 according to documents cited by P. J. Jones, 'Florentine Families', p. 188, n. 39. See also Lamberini and Lazzareschi, *Campi*, pp. 260–2, 272 (Santoni), 554 (Marcotti), who collate the sources and point out the confusion made by most authors between the fortified village

(castello) of Campi and the fortress (*rocca*) across the river Bisenzio.

16   Lamberini and Lazzareschi, *Campi*, pp. 104, 111, 116, 130–2, 134–5, 137–8, 143, 145, 149, 167, 179–80; the Florentine bishops were still extending their lands at Capalle as late as 1294.

17   Lamberini and Lazzareschi, *Campi*, p. 201; the first record of Strozzi ownership at Capalle dates from 1315.

18   The three main estates belonged to Benedetto di Pieraccione, Francesco di Giovanni and Ubertino di Tommaso, whose property was sold to Filippo di Matteo Strozzi in 1475; see Appendix B, nos. 18, 20, 29.

19   1446 Cat. 673, I, fol. 307r.

20   1442 Cat. 621, fol. 596r, 554r.

21   1442 Cat. 621, fol. 595v.

22   1451 Cat. 709, fol. 324r–v.

23   Herlihy, 'Family and Property', pp. 15, 21.

24   *Dizionario grande della lingua italiana*, ed. S. Battaglia, Turin 1971, XV, pp. 215–16, 'Primogenitura'.

25   For example, Bernardo di Soldo's widow Caterina in 1430, Giovanni di Luigi's widow Contessina in 1427, Giovanni di Marco di Goro's widow Maria in 1442 and 1451, Matteo di Giovanni di Marco's widow in 1469, Ubertino di Tommaso's widow Nanna in 1451 and 1457, Messer Marcello di Strozza's widow Margherita in 1457; see Appendix B.

26   For example, the sons of Francesco di Giovanni di Luigi at Le Corti in 1480, the sons of Jacopo d'Ubertino at Ponte di Mezzo in 1442, the sons of Matteo di Giovanni di Marco at Fornello in 1480, Strozza and Smeraldo di Smeraldo at the Rocca di Campi until Smeraldino's exile in 1434; see Appendix B.

27   1442 Cat. 620, I, fol. 412r; II, fol. 1013r–v.

28   1430 Cat. 405, fol. 48r, 175r; 1433 Cat. 495 fol. 159r, 498v.

29   1427 Cat. 75, fol. 131r, 132r, 424r.

30   See Appendix B, no. 10.

31   Kuehn, 'Law, Death, and Heirs', p. 487.

32   1430 Cat. 406, fol. 210r; 1442 Cat. 621, fol. 222r; 1446 Cat. 673, II, fol. 708r; 1451 Cat. 709, fol. 7r; 1469 Cat. 922, fol. 351r.

33   1469 Cat. 922, fol. 128r.

34   1469 Cat. 921, fol. 145r.

35   1469 Cat. 921, fol. 371r.

36   1427 Cat. 44, fol. 202r, 204r; 1430 Cat. 405, fol. 249r, 250r; 1433 Cat. 495, fol. 320r, 321v.

37   1442 Cat. 620, II, fol. 743r, 746r.

38   The practice of dividing a shared estate on paper to avoid paying tax on each property was probably a common one, for example, the Sassetti made a similar arrangement with their town houses, see Chapter 9. See de Courcey-Bayley, 'House and Household', p. 18, citing Cat. 2, fol. 31r.

39   Herlihy, 'Family and Property', p. 15; Molho, *Marriage Alliance*, p. 27.

40   Kirshner and Molho, 'The Dowry Fund', pp. 403–10; Kirshner, 'Pursuing Honor', p. 2; Molho, *Marriage Alliance*, Part I.

41   Gregory, 'A Florentine Family in Crisis', p. 100.

42   1442 Cat. 620, I, fol. 283r.

43   1427 Cat. 43, fol. 675r.

44   1442 Cat. 620, I, fol. 283v; 1446 Cat. 671, I, fol. 9r.

45   Bellomo, *La Condizione giuridica della donna*, pp. 41–2.

46   1442 Cat. 620, I, fol. 273; II, fol. 914r.

47   1446 Cat. 671, II, fol. 964r.

48   1433 Cat. 495, fol. 320v: Giovanni di Marco di Goro's daughter Spinetta had married Messer Giovanni di Bernardo da Prato.

49   1442 Cat. 620, II, fol. 743v.

50   Strozziane, V, 44, c. 173 sin. Heather Gregory ('Chi erano gli Strozzi', p. 28) cites this as an example of familial benevolence.

51   See Chapter 5, Lecceto.

52   1480 Cat. 1014, I, fol. 65r: 'La quale mezza chasa era per mio abitare. Vendela che mi ttrovavo debito e lle fanciulle senzza dota e non avevo altro modo nel aiustare i' debito nella ffare le dote se non chol vendere la metà questa chasa; però ci sto la più partte in villa.' [This half house was my own residence. I sold it since I was in debt and my daughters without dowries and I had no means of paying the debts or providing the dowries except by selling half this house; therefore I am living most of the time in the country.]

53   1427 Cat. 42, fol. 325r.

54   Kirshner and Molho, 'The Dowry Fund', p. 435.

55   Alessandra Macinghi Strozzi, *Lettere*, pp. 62–4, 128, 131–2; Alessandra's brother Zanobi had made over his villa at Antella to her in 1451 in repayment for taxes which Alessandra had paid on his behalf and for board and lodging he had received from her. When Alessandra attempted to sell the villa in 1454, her half-brother Antonio Macinghi took her to court with the support of other Macinghi relatives.

56   According to Bellomo, *La Condizione giuridica della donna*, p. 17, a woman could not transmit the inheritance from her own agnatic family to her sons, although there are examples of women bequeathing their own property to their daughters, for example, Selvaggia Gianfigliazzi Strozzi and her sister inherited lands in the Val d'Elsa from their mother.

57   1469 Cat. 920, I, fol. 567r–569v; 1480 Cat. 1012, II, fol. 398r.

58   1427 Cat. 43, fol. 676r.

59   Kuehn, *Law, Family, and Women*, pp. 198–9.

60   Bellomo, *La Condizione giuridica della donna*, pp. 43–5; Herlihy, 'Marriage at Pistoia', p. 10. The plight of poor widows and the many difficulties and delays women faced before obtaining restitution of their dowries are documented and discussed by Isabelle Chabot, 'Widowhood and Poverty', pp. 291–311, and Anne Crabb, *The Strozzi of Florence*, ch. 2.

61   See Baxendale, 'Exile in Practice', pp. 728–36, 739–45, 751, for an analysis of the behaviour of Alberti women during their husbands' exile, which closely corroborates the Strozzi evidence.

62   Gregory, 'A Florentine Family in Crisis', p. 231, a *procura generale* enabled Marietta to carry out property transactions on Palla's behalf. Kirshner, 'Wives Claims against Insolvent Husbands', pp. 275–6, 278, discusses the claims of wives whose husbands were exiled.

63   Antonio di Benedetto di Caroccio Strozzi was of great support to Alessandra until his death in 1454; Gregory, 'A Florentine Family in Crisis', pp. 116, 187, 191; 'The Return of the Native', pp. 7–8; Alessandra Macinghi Strozzi *Lettere*, pp. 9,

79–80, 91, 96–8, 112, 116–17, 122–3, as was Alessandra's son-in-law Marco Parenti from the time of his marriage in 1447; Alessandra Macinghi Strozzi, *Lettere*, pp. 3, 12.

64 See note 55, this chapter. Alessandra Macinghi Strozzi's letter describing the quarrel with Antonio Macinghi over her sale of the villa at Antella shows how she was looking forward to Filippo's presence and support, but that the initiative and arguments were hers, *Lettere*, pp. 125–6.

65 Kuehn, *Law, Family, and Women*, pp. 203–6; Kirshner, 'Pursuing Honor', p. 8, n. 23.

66 See also Kirshner, 'Wives Claims against Insolvent Husbands', p. 302, and Baxendale, 'Exile in Practice', p. 742, who notes that the Alberti women often used 'artisan passers-by' as *mundualdi* or guarantors.

67 Strozziane, V, 54, cc. 1 des., 5 des., 6 sin.

68 Strozziane, V, 60; V, 61.

69 Strozziane, V, 60, cc. 20 sin., 40 sin.

70 Strozziane, V, 60, cc. 45 sin.(1503); V, 61, cc. 126 sin.–131 sin.(1518–1521).

71 Strozziane, V, 54, cc. 74, 100, 102, 112, 113. Strozziane, V, 55, is a farm account book kept by Piero di Messer Michele Strozzi.

72 Strozziane, V, 61, cc. 30 des.(1515), 31 sin.(1517), 35 sin.(1518), 40 sin.(1519), 44 sin.(1521), 126 sin.–131 sin.

73 Strozziane, V, 61, cc. 32 des.(1518), 33 sin.(1518).

74 Gregory, 'A Florentine Family in Crisis', pp. 65–6, with assets worth more than 11,000 florins in 1427, Francesco was the second richest member of the Strozzi clan.

75 1469, Cat. 920, I, fol. 566v.

76 For the later history of Galluzzo and neighbouring Travalle, see Lamberini, *Calenzano*, I, pp. 231–2.

77 1469 Cat. 920, I, fol. 567r–v.

78 1480 Cat. 1012, II, fol. 398r.

79 The houses at Novoli, Petraia and Ambra at Poggio a Caiano were declared for Palla's personal use in 1433.

80 See Belle, 'A Renaissance Patrician', pp. 31–2, 88, 92–3.

81 R. Jones, 'Palla Strozzi', pp. 10–11.

82 Lillie, 'Lorenzo de' Medici's Rural Investments', pp. 54, 64–5.

83 A comparison of Palla's tax returns of 1427, 1430 and 1433 demonstrates this; see Belle, 'A Renaissance Patrician'.

84 Strozziane, V, 22, cc. 45 des., 99 sin.; see Lillie, 'Vita di palazzo, vita in villa', p. 169.

85 Strozziane, V, 22, cc. 46 des., 100 des.; 1480 Cat. 1011, fol. 314v.

86 Lillie, 'Vita di palazzo, vita in villa', p. 169; Strozziane, V, 22 cc. 67 des., 69 sin., 103 sin.; see also loose leaves tucked inside the back cover of this volume headed, 'Nota di più chiareze per la conpera del podere di Gio[vanni] delli Alberti'.

87 1427 Cat. 45, fol. 486r; 1430 Cat. 405, fol. 117v.

88 1442 Cat. 617, fol. 450v; 1446 Cat. 664, fol. 194r.

89 Strozziane, V, 1165, Inserta 17.

90 Alessandra Macinghi Strozzi, *Lettere*, p. 340 (A). Strozziane, V, 21 is the account book for this oratory.

91 Lillie, 'Vita di palazzo, vita in villa', p. 173; Strozziane, V, 22 cc. 86 sin., 207 sin.; V, 41, cc. 31 sin., 35 des., 58 des., 60 sin., 62 sin.–des., 94 sin., 155 des.–163 des., 176 des.

92 Strozziane, V, 22 c. 197 sin.; V, 36 c. 260 sin.

93 Strozziane, V, 22 cc. 197 sin.–des.; V, 41 cc. 27 sin., 36 des.; 95 des., 168 des., 175 des.; V 36 cc. 177 des., 297 des.

94 Strozziane, V, 41 cc. 82 sin., 167 sin.

95 Strozziane, V, 54 cc. 106 sin., 115 sin.; 1498 Decima Repub. 23, fol. 359r–v.

96 See Chapter 8, Villeggiatura.

97 Strozziane, V, 22, c. 108 des. Although apparently Lucrezia never lived at Santuccio herself, it would have been convenient for travellers on their way to the recently aquired Medici estate at Poggio a Caiano, since the Strozzi villa lay just off the Via Pistoiese half way between Florence and Poggio.

98 1446 Cat. 671, I, fol. 105r: 'il quale o affittato a 4 donne vedove cioè a Monna Angela pinzochera da Luchardo, a Monna Nanna donna fu di Guido Deti, a Monna Tancia donna fu di Angnolo Machiavegli, a Monna Lisa de' Gianfigliazi; danomene l'anno di pigione F. 5 e v'è ne di spesa anno per anno F. 1 1. 2'. Although Zanobi does not say how long the lease will last, the house is recorded 'per mio habitare' in the previous tax return of 1442 (Cat. 620, II, fol. 1013r) and in the following tax return of 1451 (Cat. 707, fol. 483r). For documentation concerning Zanobi Strozzi's career, see Levi d'Ancona, *Miniatura e miniatori*, pp. 54–8, 261–8. For the necessity of widows to retire to the countryside, see Chabot, 'Widowhood and Poverty', pp. 299–300.

99 1430 Cat. 406, fol. 298v.

100 1433 Cat. 496, fol. 396v; 1442 Cat. 621, fol. 596r–v.

101 1469 Cat. 921, fol. 145r.

102 1480 Cat. 1014, I, fol. 65r: 'Ci sto la più partte in villa e quando vengho a Ffirenze mi tornno quanddo chon uno e quando chon un'altro de' mie' parentti, e pure n'a bisogna torre una chasa a ppigione'.

103 1457 Cat. 816, II, fol. 1072r. Niccolò di Lionardo Strozzi was resident in Rome at the time, three years after the date inscribed on his marble portrait bust carved by Mino da Fiesole in Rome in 1454.

104 On urban rents see the important analysis by de Courcey-Bayley, *House and Household*, ch. 3.

105 1442 Cat. 621, fol. 597v.

106 1442 Cat. 621, fol. 462r.

107 1446 Cat. 673, I, fol. 307r.

108 See Chapter 8, The Villa as Principal Residence.

109 1442 Cat. 620, I, fol. 174v–175r.

110 1469 Cat. 920, I, fol. 565v; 1480 Cat. 1012, fol. 61r.

111 1427 Cat. 43, fol. 681; Cat. 42, fol. 534r.

112 1442 Cat. 620, I, fol. 173v, 178r; 1446 Cat. 671, I, fol. 151r–v; 1469 Cat. 919, II, fol. 279r; Cat. 920, I, fol. 726r.

113 1457 Cat. 819, II, fol. 647r. See Chapter 8, The Villa as Principal Residence.

114 1442 Cat. 621, fol. 462r.

115 1427 Cat. 45, fol. 752r–753r; 1430 Cat. 405, fol. 278r–279r.; 1433. Cat. 495, fol. 455v–456r; 1442 Cat. 620, II, fol. 943r–945r; 1446 Cat. 671, I, fol. 75r–77v; 1480 Cat. 1013, II, fol. 320v.

116 P. J. Jones, 'Florentine Families', p. 189 and n. 55.

117 1451 Cat. 707, fol. 417r; 1469 Cat. 919, II, fol. 343v.

118 1427 Cat. 44, fol. 204r; 1430 Cat. 405, fol. 249r.

119 Gregory, 'A Florentine Family in Crisis', p. 167. Palla Novello's bank failed in 1426.

120 1457 Cat. 816, fol. 151r–152r.

121 1469 Cat. 919, I, fol. 39r–41r.

122 Fabriczy, 'Giuliano da Maiano in Siena', pp. 332–4; Belli, 'Il Palazzo dello Strozzino', pp. 39–41, see also Chapter 11.

123 Litta, 'Strozzi', VIII.

124 1427 Cat. 43, fol. 560r–561r; 1446 Cat. 671, I, fol. 117r; 1446 Cat. 671, II, fol. 713r–v; 1469 Cat. 919, I, fol. 209r.

125 1442 Cat. 619, II, fol. 1016r; 1451 Cat. 709, fol. 324r.

126 F. W. Kent, 'The Making of a Renaissance Patron', p. 23, n. 6, pp. 26–7, 46–9; and 'Poggio a Caiano', pp. 250–1. For the sequestration of exiles' property, see Baxandale, 'Exile in Practice'.

127 Gregory, 'A Florentine Family in Crisis', p. 239, nn. 121 and 122.

128 F. W. Kent, 'The Making of a Renaissance Patron', p. 23, n. 6, pp. 27, 47–49, 'Poggio a Caiano', p. 250.

129 1446 Cat. 671, II, fol. 1023r. On the manoeuvres of exiled Alberti wives, see Baxandale, 'Exile in Practice', pp. 731–6.

130 1442 Cat. 620, II, fol. 751r; 1446 Cat. 671, II, fol. 949r.

131 F. W. Kent, 'The Making of a Renaissance Patron', p. 48, n. 3.

132 Palla's two *case da signore* at Petraia have been confused in the literature. The estate consisted of the main residence of Petraia, called 'Petraia alta' in Palla's will of 1462 (R. Jones, 'Palla Strozzi', p. 103, doc. 140), which was bought from Attaviano di Boccaccio Brunelleschi on 9 June 1419 (D. Wright, *The Medici Villa at Olmo a Castello*, II, n. 9, pp. 476–8), and a house at the foot of the hill at La Piazza called 'Il Palagetto', which was bought from Jacopo di Ceccherino Brunelleschi and his mother Agnola on 16 December 1423 (R. Jones, 'Palla Strozzi', p. 80, doc. 94). The sites of the two houses are clearly marked on the Capitani di Parte Guelfa map of c. 1580–95 with the towered villa of Petraia represented in elevation and Il Palagetto shown as a ground plan labelled 'Rineri' [sic: Rinieri], the family to whom Alessandra Bardi-Strozzi sold it in 1460. It is now referred to by the name of its later owners, the Corsini; Carocci, *I Dintorni*, I, p. 280; Lensi Orlandi, *Di Qua d'Arno*, p. 19, pl. 30; *Castello: campagna medicea*, pp. 67–8, 142–3; Lydecker, *The Domestic Setting*, pp. 100–1; Zangheri, 'La Villa Corsini a Castello'. After Palla's exile it was the Palagetto on the piazza that was confiscated by the commune and sold to Brunetto the butcher (R. Jones, 'Palla Strozzi, p. 94, doc. 139), not Petraia itself as F. W. Kent presumed ('The Making of a Renaissance Patron', p. 23, n. 6). When Palla's son Lorenzo had managed to retrieve the Palagetto, it was consigned to his wife, Alessandra, and claimed as security against her dowry in subsequent tax returns; 1442 Cat. 620, I, fol. 81r; 1446 Cat. 671, II, fol. 1023r; 1451 Cat. 707, fol. 491r; 1457 Cat. 816, I, fol. 508r.

133 Novoli remained in the hands of Alessandra from the time of her husband's exile in 1438 until its sale; see the preceeding note for references to Alessandra's tax returns.

134 1469 Cat. 920, II, fol. 877r.

135 Matteo left Florence in exile for Pesaro on 12 November 1434; Alessandra Macinghi Strozzi, *Lettere*, p. xxi. He died in Pesaro between July 1435 and March 1436; Gregory, 'A Florentine Family in Crisis', p. 184.

136 Alessandra Macinghi Strozzi, *Lettere*, pp. xx, xxv; 1451 Cat. 707, fol. 782r.

137 1427 Cat. 44, fol. 237r; 1430 Cat. 405, fol. 103v; 1433 Cat. 495, fol. 337v.

138 1442 Cat. 620, I, fol. 397v.

139 1457 Cat. 816, II, fol. 1011r–v.

140 No letters from Alessandra Macinghi Strozzi survive from these years, but already in February 1452 Alessandra had written to her son Lorenzo suggesting that she sell her brother's farm at Antella 'per uscire di spesa e di noia, e ancora per aiutarvi far bene . . . e facevo conto tra tu e Filippo gli avessi a trafficare, acciò voi cominciassi avanzare l'anno qualche cosa'; *Lettere*, p. 128. Alessandra sold the Antella farm in 1454 (*Lettere*, p. 63), and the sale of the Calicarza farms in January 1456 probably reflected the same policy.

141 Alessandra Macinghi Strozzi, *Lettere*, pp. xxxii–xxxiv; 146–50.

142 1469 Cat. 919, I, fol. 47v.

143 Alessandra Macinghi Strozzi, *Lettere*, pp. 581–2.

144 Goldthwaite, *Wealth and the Demand for Art*, p. 217.

145 See, for example, the statement attributed to Cosimo de' Medici that he preferred the family estate at Cafaggiolo in the Mugello to their suburban villa at Fiesole because at Cafaggiolo everything he could see belonged to them, which was not true of Fiesole; A. Wesselski, ed., *Polizianos Tagebuch [1477–9]*; Jena, 1929, p. 3.

146 This argument was first strongly sustained by P. J. Jones, 'Florentine Families', p. 203, and 'Medieval Agrarian Society', p. 352; F. W. Kent, *Household and Lineage*, p. 250, confirms this for the Capponi, Ginori and Rucellai families up until 1530.

147 Goldthwaite, *Private Wealth*, pp. 60–4.

CHAPTER 2 THE AGRICULTURAL ESTATE

1 Alberti, 'Villa', p. 359: 'Alla possessione se manca la casa, meno gli manca che se alla casa mancano e' terreni'.

2 Historians have written extensively on the decisive role played by urban landowners in the development of new farming methods in late medieval Italy, particularly in the introduction of sharecropping (*mezzadria*), consolidated farms (*appoderamento*) and diversified crops; Slicher van Bath, p. 22; Luzzato, 'Contributo', p. 81; Fiumi, 'Sui rapporti economici', pp. 41, 63–4; Cherubini, 'Qualche considerazione', pp. 81–2, 92–5; Pinto, 'Ordinamento', pp. 223–77, 'Forme', p. 287; P. J. Jones, 'Florentine Families', p. 188; P. J. Jones, 'Medeval Agrarian Society', p. 410; Pirillo, *Costruzione di un contado*.

3 See the many letters from Medici factors in MAP, e.g., Francesco Fracassini MAP VI, 217, 420, 513, 557, 571, 648, 654; VII, 187, 280, 333; X, 4, 204; Ormanno Foraboschi MAP V, 492, 543, 578; VI, 327, 479, 538, 615, 633, 764; X, 10, 304, 371, 428, 432, 438, 448, 516; Sandro Pagagnotti, MAP VI, 163; VIII, 241; IX, 68.

4   Vespasiano da Bisticci, *Le Vite*, pp. 194–5.

5   Foster, 'A Study of Lorenzo de' Medici's Villa', p. 97.

6   Crescenzi, *Agricultura*, Lib. XI, Cap. vii: 'La presentia del signore utilità è del campo e chi abandona la vigna sarà abandonato dallei. Da lavoratori la importunevole voracità niente teme se non la presentia del signori e la cautela'; see also Lib. I, cap. v.

7   Alberti, 'I Libri della famiglia', Lib. III, p. 197. See also Tanaglia, *De Agricultura*, Lib. I, 11, 331–4.

8   1427 Cat. 44, fol. 257v: 'E più tengho una chavalchatura per andare a sollecitare le mie possesioni. Non si facendo chosì non sene trarebe nulla'.

9   Also known in English as the land agent, overseer, bailiff or steward.

10   On the factor's role at Camaldoli, see P. J. Jones, 'A Tuscan Monastic Lordship', p. 179.

11   1427 Cat. 76, fol. 172v–173r, Petraia: 'Uno abituro chasefante . . adopero per miei bisongni e stavi uno fattore'; 186r, Poggio a Caiano: 'Abituro detto l'Anbra tutto rovinato e in gran parte v'è s'abita per lo mio fattore e ripovisi la richolta'; 187r, Trefiano: 'Uno Palagio male abitato e situato . . . abitaxi per llo mio fattore e tiene staiora xiiii di vingna a suo mani'.

12   Conti, *Le Fonti*, p. 53, n. 42.

13   Marco's building account books are Strozziane, V, 39 (Santuccio); IV, 358 (Maglio); V, 49 and 50 (the new palace in town).

14   Strozziane, IV, 358.

15   Strozziane, V, 51, c. 15 sin.–des.

16   Strozziane, V, 44, c. 136 des.

17   Strozziane, V, 41, c. 58 sin.

18   Strozziane, V, 44, c. 98 sin. After employing three relatives in quick succession at Maglio, Filippo found factors from outside the family in the 1490s, Strozziane, V, 55, cc. 11 sin., 40 sin.

19   Strozziane, V, 42, c. 3 sin.; Strozziane, V, 44, c. 165 sin. Lorenzo Strozzi, *Le Vite*, ed. Zeffi, p. 67.

20   Women were also employed as farm accountants at La Pietra in the early seventeenth century when the Capponi hired a succession of women from country towns and villages as *cassiere* and *fattoresse*; BNF, Capponi, 91, cc. 51, 99, 130, 148, 206 (1614–19); Capponi, 93, c. 206.

21   Strozziane, V, 55, cc. 14 sin., 40 sin.

22   1442 Cat. 620, II, fol. 744v.

23   1457 Cat. 816, II, fol. 812r.

24   1480 Cat. 1011, fol. 300r: 'Tegniamo lo fattore d'età d'anni 60, che 'a ne bisogno essere servito lui e dia' ll'i lira 30 l'anno, e non val nulla'.

25   Strozziane, V, 10, cc. 108 des.; V, 11, c. 47 sin., c. 130 sin., 147 sin., 155 sin.; V, 12, c. 10 sin.

26   Strozziane, V, 12, c. 24 des.

27   Strozziane, V, 10, cc. 129 sin., 139 des., 136 sin.; V, 11, cc. 8 des., 47 des.

28   Alessandra Macinghi Strozzi, *Lettere*, p. 48. My understanding of this passage differs from Gregory, *Selected Letters of Alessandra Strozzi*, p. 47.

29   Alessandra Macinghi Strozzi, *Lettere*, pp. 89, 102.

30   Alessandra Macinghi Strozzi, *Lettere*, p. 53. See also p. 148 for Matteo's letter of 24 August 1449, when he was staying with 'Agnolone' during an outbreak of plague.

31   For a definition of *mezzadria classica*, see Luzzato, 'Contributo', pp. 70–1; for comparisons between *mezzadria* and *fitto* contracts and conditions, see P. J. Jones, 'Medieval Agrarian Society', pp. 413–4; 'From Manor to Mezzadria', pp. 223–5; Pinto, 'Forme', pp. 291–5; Conti, *Le Campagne* p. 1, and *Monografie* p. 19.

32   Imberciadori, 'I Due poderi', pp. 837–44; Molho, 'Cosimo de' Medici: "pater patriae" or *padrino*', pp. 9–13.

33   Alessandra Macinghi Strozzi, *Lettere*, p. 438: 'Quest'anno credo non arò a comperar vino, se altra disgrazia non viene. Pure n'è molto poco per tutto; e del grano ancora è pochi gambi; ma è molto granato, e dà buon peso, migliore che l'avessi parecchi anni fa. Non so ancora come n'arò a Pazzolatico, che non v'ho lavoratore fermo, e Dio sa come gli è ridotto: ancora vive Piero e mona Cilia, tramendua infermi. Ho allogato il podere per quest'altro anno, e me lo conviene mettere in ordine; e que' due vecchi, se non muoiono, hanno andare accattare. Iddio provvegga'. See also, Crabb, *The Strozzi of Florence*, pp. 69–70.

34   Alessandra Macinghi Strozzi, *Lettere*, p. 525: 'I'ho tolto un lavoratore a Pazzolaticho, che ora al febbraio comincia a lavorare: e perche il podere è pure in disordine e'l temporale è forte, mi sono distesa a fargli aiuto d'una bestia perchè possa portare del concime; che n'ha bisogno el podere, che francherà la spesa. Se'l podere si fussi aiutato pel passato, sare' d'altra rendita, e col suo medesimo si potrebbe aiutare: ma non si può per ora. S'i' potrò fare sanza torre danari dal banco per questo, i' lo farò: s'io no ne potrò trarre d'altrove, i' gli torrò dal banco: che v'ho a fare dell' altre ispese in sul podere, che sono di nicistà, chè peggio non può stare che si stia. Piero vive ancora; e bisogna che se n'esca, e andrà accattando: pure i' non posso più ch'i' mi possa. Arà pazienza: che iddio lo chiami a sè, se'l meglio debb'essere.' Compare this with Ser Lapo Mazzei's painstaking search for a new farm for his aging, single *lavoratore*, Origo, *The Merchant of Prato*, pp. 249–50.

35   1427 Cat. 42, fol. 262r.

36   1430 Cat. 405, fol. 33v.

37   1430 Cat. 405, fol. 34v. One of the ways in which the landowner could show generosity towards his tenant farmers was in the size of the loan or *prestanza* that was written into the *mezzadria* contract.

38   Strozziane, V, 10, cc. 4 sin., 9 sin., 29 sin., 60 sin., 62 sin., 100 sin., 129 sin.; V, 11, cc. 9 sin., 39 sin., 142 sin., 143 sin., 147 sin., 154 sin., 155 sin.; V, 12, cc. 10 sin.–12 des. Matteo inherited many of these tenants and farmers from his father Simone (Strozziane, V, 2 cc. 36 des., 37 des.; V, 7, cc. 15 sin.–des., 97 des., 98 sin.), and some were still retained by his widow Alessandra (Strozziane, V, 15 cc. 2 sin., 3 sin., 4 sin.–des.).

39   1430 Cat. 405, fol. 131r, 'lavoralo a mezo e a fitto . . . rende l'anno grano di fitto, vino di 1/2.'

40   Pinto, 'Forme', p. 305.

41   Strozziane, V, 22, cc. 76 sin., 86 sin., 153 des., 176 sin.; V, 44, cc. 22 sin., 100 sin., 141 sin., 192 sin.

42 For the advantages of *fitto* versus *mezzadria*, see Luzzato, 'Contributo' p. 82; Pinto, 'Forme' pp. 308–10, 312, 315.

43 Strozziane, V, 22, c. 101 sin. Cieptto and Matteo del Paneraio were to live in the *casa da lavoratore* and received a loan of thirty florins to stock the farm. In return their rent was to be ten *moggia* of the best wheat delivered at their own expense to Florence in July, five *cogna* of wine left at the villa and 100 lire in cash to be paid in two installments in October and December. An additional two brace of cocks and hens and six dozen eggs were required at All Saints and Christmas. The contract included a final pledge to improve the farm. Unlike many *mezzadria* contracts of this period, however, the proprietor was not obliged to provide manure, nor stakes for the orchard and vineyard, nor seeds. This *fitto* contract can be compared with a *mezzadria* contract for the same farm at Capalle in 1489, Strozziane, V, 41, c. 173 des. For other contracts, see Pinto, 'Forme', pp. 291–4, 300–5; P. J. Jones, 'Medeival Agrarian Society', pp. 413–15, 'A Tuscan Monastic Lordship', p. 176.

44 Strozziane, V, 22, c. 103 sin. This confirms that by the 1470s labour was more plentiful, because even at such a high rent Filippo had no difficulty in finding tenant farmers.

45 The presence of the landlord and concentration of holdings in one area were two of the main factors that favoured *mezzadria*, whereas the absence of the landlord and dispersal of holdings over a large area favoured *affitto*; Pinto, 'Forme', pp. 286–7.

46 1427 Cat. 45, fol. 486r; 1430 Cat. 405, fol. 117v; Strozziane, V, 10, c. 129 sin.

47 1427 Cat. 44, fol. 67r–v; 1430 Cat. 405, fol. 233v–4r.

48 Pinto, 'Forme', p. 314.

49 1446 Cat. 671, II, fol. 943v: 'tutti detti poderi e ttereni [at Le Miccine] sono sanza buoi perchè quando mi parti della città per bisognio avevo, ebbi a vendere e buoi e ritorre le preste; e i poderi afitti di luglio 1441.... Tutti questi beni rendono chome si dice disopra per afito lira 200 e staia 50 di grano, e al primo chatasto essi e gli altri furono achatastati per molto più e questo perchè allora stavo di chontinouo alla villa ed era chome mia bottegha, e oggi per nicistà lo affittare e ssono male in ordine perchè sono luoghi di gran sollecetudine e sanza l'oste nulla sene chava e chi la afito credo ne faccia pocho profitto'.

50 1451 Cat. 707, fol. 783v: 'per non ci essere io stato a provederlle, che sono divenute meze pasture.'

51 1457 Cat. 818, fol. 315v–316r.

52 Here the Strozzi data tally with the analysis of yields provided by Pinto, 'Coltura', pp. 240–6.

53 Pinto, 'Ordinamento', pp. 235–40. Of twelve areas studied by Conti, nine had over 40% of their yield in wheat and cereals. In the other three areas, wine was of greater value, but unlike the Strozzi estates, half of which were in the valley, Conti's samples were all in low to high hill country, which produced more wine and slightly less wheat, *Monografie*, pp. 28, 46, 65, 84, 102, 112, 139, 151, 167, 187, 201, 222.

54 P. J. Jones, 'Florentine Families', p. 201, n. 154.

55 1427 Cat. 76, fol. 171v, 185v; 1430 Cat. 405, fol. 127r, 137r–v; 1433 Cat. 495, fol. 383v, 390r–v.

56 1427 Cat. 42, fol. 259–62v.

57 1427 Cat. 75, fol. 131r, 132r. Messer Marcello's other estate at Luciano yielded 11 *moggia* of wheat.

58 1427 Cat. 44, fol. 202r–205r.

59 Bernardo and Giovanni di Giovanni's farm at Signano yielded 16 *moggia* (384 *staia*) of wheat in 1433, Cat. 495, fol. 83r. Francesco di Benedetto's many scattered lands at Brozzi and Quaracchi produced over 14 *moggia* (345 *staia*), 1442 Cat. 620, I, fol. 412r–413v. Pinaccio Strozzi's single productive farm at Santuccio was let for a big grain rent of 11 *moggia* (264 *staia*) per annum, 1427 Cat. 45, fol. 486r.

60 Benedetto di Pieraccione, for example, was forced to sell some of his Capalle estate to pay taxes and dowries.

61 See Chapter 1, Sale.

62 1451 Cat. 707, fol. 417v; 1457 Cat. 816, II, fol. 812v–813r; 1469 Cat. 919, II, fol. 342r–343v.

63 At Santuccio, tenure was swapped between *fitto* and *mezzadria* several times during the century. When Pinaccio Strozzi was in London, he let his farm for a high grain rent of 11 *moggia* (1427 Cat. 45, fol. 486r, 1430 Cat. 405, fol. 117v). After Giannozo Alberti acquired the farm in 1436, it was sharecropped, producing only three *moggia* of wheat and four *moggia* of other cereals in 1442, and the same amount of wheat but two *moggia* of other cereals and five barrels of wine in 1446. By 1451, Giannozo's grandsons Bivigliano and Giovanni di Tommaso Alberti had reverted to *fitto* for nine *moggia* of wheat a year (Cat. 700, fol. 167v), which was eight *moggia*, 60 lira cash and 25 lb. of linen in 1469. Filippo Strozzi first let the house and its lands separately for nine florins and eight *moggia* of wheat, respectively, (1480 Cat. 1011, fol. 315r), but when he began to live in the house himself in 1486, he changed to *mezzadria* and received a greater range of produce including more wine and linen (Decima Repub. 23, fol. 359r). For a record of crops at Santuccio in 1526, see Strozziane, V, 1221, I, c.1 des.

64 Tanaglia, *De Agricultura*, Lib. I, 1012–14; Crescenzi, *Agricultura*, Lib. IX, cap. lxxxix, noted that a basket of *colombina* was worth a whole cartload of any other manure. Filippo Strozzi's factor at Capalle sold 199 *staia* of *colombina* that had accumulated over three years for four florins and seventeen *soldi*; Strozziane, V, 44 c. 134 des.

65 Crescenzi, *Agricultura*, Lib. IX, cap. xci.

66 Crescenzi, *Agricultura*, Lib. IX, cap. xc.

67 Strozziane, V, 22 c. 62 sin.

68 Strozziane, V, 11, c. 26 des.

69 Strozziane, V, 11, c. 142 des.

70 Strozziane, V, 22, cc. 63–4, 175 sin.; V, 36, c. 18.

71 Conti, *Le Fonti*, pp. 46–7, tables 10 and 11, gives the wine prices set for the 1427 *catasto*, which range from the Trebbiani valued at 40 *soldi* per barrel and Chianti at 36 *soldi*, to 14 *soldi* for the wine from the valley around Pistoia, Prato and the Valdibisenzio and 12 *soldi* for the Arno valley from Empoli westwards.

72 1427 Cat. 42, fol. 259r–262r; 1442 Cat. 620, I, fol. 173r–176v.

73 Pinto, 'Ordinamento', p. 254.

74 1442 Cat. 621, fol. 595r–596v; 1480 Cat. 1013, II, fol. 216r.

75 1430 Cat. 405, fol. 199r; 1433 Cat. 495, fol. 148v; 1469 Cat. 919, II, fol. 289r.

76 1430 Cat. 405, fol. 105r–v.

77 Alberti, 'I Libri della famiglia', p. 195: 'Così adunque farei io, provederei che la possessione in prima fusse atta a darci tutto quello bisognasse per pascere la familglia, e se non tutto, almeno insieme le più necessarie cose, pane, vino'. Translation from Watkins, *The Family in Renaissance Florence*, p. 189.

78 Strozziane, V, 11, c. 31 des.(1425): 'Calicarza, dove si ricoglie legnie e tiennisi bestie e grano . . . Pazolaticho in sul quale si ritaglie l'olio e biade e frutte e vino'. Each of the three districts in which Matteo owned land had some produce which the others had not. Thus, while all grew some wheat and wine, spelt was common to Campi and Calicarza, and beans to Calicarza and Pozzolatico, but only Campi produced flax, sorghum and Italian millet; only Calicarza produced barley, firewood, pigs and sheep; and only Pozzolatico grew fruit, olive oil, and saffron.

79 Comparisons between the capitalised values of valley and hill farms show that the valley farms were consistently larger and more profitable. The same pattern emerges in Pinto's analysis of the lands belonging to the hospital of San Gallo; 'Forme', pp. 266–70.

80 Strozziane, V, 41 cc. 56 sin., 60 sin., 78 sin., 94 sin., 97 sin., 100 sin.; V, 44, cc. 47, 113 sin., 141 sin., 173.

81 Strozziane, V, 1221, cc. 4 des.–5 sin.

82 See Chapter 1, Purchase.

83 See Chapter 9, Bartolommeo Sassetti's villa at Valcenni.

84 Pinto, 'Ordinamento', pp. 250–2, 260, 262, 269, 276.

85 1427 Cat. 76, fol. 172r; 1430 Cat. 405, fol. 127r; 1433 Cat. 495, fol. 383v.

86 1427 Cat. 75, fol. 197r; 1451 Cat. 709, fol. 323v; 1480 Cat. 1013, II, fol. 216v.

87 1442 Cat. 621, fol. 595r–596v.

88 These farms were Matteo di Simone's and Francesco di Piero's at Pozzolatico, and Niccolo di Barla's and Francesco di Giovanni's at Gangalandi. Francesco Datini only produced under three barrels from his farms.

89 The remaining oil producing farms were at Soffiano, Montughi, Travalle and Maglio.

90 Pinto, 'Ordinamento', p. 263.

91 P. J. Jones, 'Medieval Agrarian Society', p. 256.

92 Crescenzi, *Agricultura*, Lib. IX, cap. lxxv, 'villanissimi villani . . . i quali di continue fatiche si travaglino'. Neither lamb nor mutton appear among the prices for meat in the account book of the heirs of Lorenzo di Francesco Strozzi; Goldthwaite, *Building of Renaissance Florence*, p. 443.

93 Crescenzi, *Agricultura*, Lib. IX, cap. lxxv.

94 Alessandra Macinghi Strozzi, *Lettere*, pp. 109, 153, 167, 265.

95 Strozziane, V, 22, cc. 95 des.–96 sin. (1473). Together with larger presents – a painted *lettuccio*, marble busts, chess sets and a mirror – Filippo gave sheep's cheeses to King Ferdinand, Alfonso Duke of Calabria and the Duke's brothers Don Federigo and Don Giovanni. They also received other luxury foods: fennel, salame, dried figs and *bischotelli*.

96 Far larger herds were kept in high country in the Appennines and the Casentino. The monastery of Camaldoli kept at least 500 sheep, produced large quantities of cheese and practised transhumance; P. J. Jones, 'A Tuscan Monastic Lordship', pp. 180–1.

97 1427 Cat. 75, fol. 131v. Strozziane, V, 36, c. 19 des.

98 *Statuti 1322–25*, II, Lib. 3, cap. lvii, p. 221: 'De capris non tenendis'; Statuti 1415, Vol. II, rub. 43, p. 419: 'De capris non tenendis infra quatuordecim milliaria'. Crescenzi refers to the damage caused by goats in cultivated areas: 'Questo bestiame ha certa proprietade che cioè che più si dilecta di pascere in selvatichi boschi . . . e ne luoghi cultivati stiantono [*sic*: schiantono] e rompono e rodono i piccioli arbucegli, e impero da carpendo son dette chapre per la qual cosa insulla allogagione del podere si vuole fare exceptione [*sic*: patti] che illavoratore non pasca la capra in sul podere'; Crescenzi, *Agricultura*, Lib. IX, cap. lvii.

99 Filippo Strozzi kept goats at Maglio in the Val di Bisenzio, Strozziane, V, 41, c. 56 sin., 60 sin., 78 sin.; Palla di Nofri ran goats at San Michele a Ciereto in the mountains above Prato, 1427 Cat. 76, fol. 176v; Marco di Goro's widow had a dozen goats in the Mugello, 1442 Cat. 671, II, fol. 993v; and Benedetto di Marcuccio's son Bernardo inherited a farm at Gricignano in the Mugello with goats and sheep, 1469 Cat. 921, fol. 145r, while Francesco di Giovanni had a herd of 50 at Gangalandi, 1433 Cat. 495, fol. 148v.

100 1427 Cat. 76, fol. 197v. According to Crescenzi, hills and woodland were also suitable for pigs, which could rummage for acorns and chestnuts that gave the meat a better flavour; Lib. IX, cap. lxxvii. Pigs are certainly more common on hill farms among the Strozzi.

101 Crescenzi, *Agricultura*, Lib. IX, cap. lxvi. Filipp di Matteo Strozzi is one of the few to keep a cow. He regularly had one or two cows and several calves at Maglio; Strozziane, V, 41, cc. 56 sin., 97; V, 44, c. 173. The Medici herd of cows at Cafaggiolo was an unusual feature, as was Lorenzo's later initiative in importing a large herd of dairy cows for Poggio a Caiano.

102 Crescenzi, *Agricultura*, Lib. IX, cap. lxvi; Goldthwaite, *Building of Renaissance Florence*, p. 443.

103 Strozziane, V, 11, c. 37 des.(1427).

104 Strozziane, V, 51, c. 190.

105 Strozziane, V, 51, cc. 154 sin., 155 sin.

106 Goldthwaite, *Building of Renaissance Florence*, pp. 238–9. Wood was transported to the villas and stored there before being sold, used as fuel or transported to one of Filippo's building sites; Strozziane, V, 41, cc. 35, 58 des., 75 des., 98 des; Strozziane, V, 51, c. 197. River transport was used for large consignments of timber, which made Filippo Strozzi's villa at Santuccio useful as a timber yard, since it was on the banks of the Bisenzio close to its junction with the Arno, and timber could easily be ferried to and from the site.

107 Crescenzi, *Agricultura*, Lib. VIII, cap. v: 'Ne campi dilecta molto il loro bello e adorno sito. Ancho che non siano piccioli e rustichi campicielli ma gran quantita in uno sanza intervallo e che habbia dirotto [*sic*: diritto] i suoi fini overo extremitadi: e percio dee procurare ciascuno che dicio si dilecta di comperare apresso de' suoi campi piutosto che altrove e vendere in altri parti i campicielli e coi vicini premutare le

superflue e torte de campi e drizare il suo campo col suo vicino'.

108 P. J. Jones, 'Medieval Agrarian Society', pp. 394, 397, 415–17; Pinto, 'Ordinamento', pp. 232–3; Cherubini, 'Qualche considerazione', pp. 80–2, 92.

109 For the piecemeal composition of farms and the very slow process of consolidation see Conti, *Le Campagne*, p. 1; Klapisch-Zuber, 'Mezzadria e insediamenti rurali'.

110 Klapisch-Zuber, 'Mezzadria e insediamenti rurali'.

111 1433 Cat. 495, fol. 498v; 1457 Cat. 816, fol. 9r; 1480 Cat. 1012, II. fol. 252r.

112 W. Cohn, 'Il beato Angelico e Battista di Biagio Sanguigni'; Levi d'Ancona, 'Zanobi Strozzi reconsidered'; Levi d'Ancona, *Miniatura e miniatori*, pp. 55–8, 261–5. Levi d'Ancona does not distinguish between Zanobi's house at Palaiuola and the property next door in which Sanguigni lived.

113 This is in direct opposition to Ackerman, *The Villa*, pp. 9–11.

114 Strozziane, V, 10, c. 31 des., V, 11, c. 31 des., and V, 12, cc. 10 sin., 28 des.; 1427 Cat. 44, fol. 237r–238v.; 1430 Cat. 405, fol. 106v.

115 1427 Cat. 43, fol. 681r–683v.

116 Klapisch-Zuber, *Una Carta*, p. 34: the *piviere* of Brozzi, only five parishes stretching for four kilometres along the Via Pistoiese from Petriolo to San Donnino, had a population of 1,763 in 1427, not including Florentine citizens who were villa owners.

117 1427 Cat. 42, fol. 367r–368v; 1469 Cat. 420, I, fol. 682r.

118 P. J. Jones ('Medieval Agrarian Society', p. 424) considers a farm of 300 *staiora* of land to be very big.

119 1427 Cat. 75, fol. 132r.

120 P. J. Jones, 'Florentine Families', p. 188, n. 39.

121 See Appendix B, n. 10.

122 P. J. Jones, 'Florentine Families', p. 189, n. 55.

123 1457 Cat. 816, II, fol. 813r: 'Tengho per soprire alle mie terre che ssono chattive e anche per non m'avere a chontendere chon vicini che tanti mi sono in chorpo'. 1469 Cat. 919, II, fol. 343v, 'E tiensi perchè è incorporato con la maggior parte della nostra terra per non avere a contendere con altri . . . e perchè sono in mezzo d'altra nostra terra per non esser stropiciati da altri . . . E sopradetti fitti si tenghono per fugire chontesa e schandoli perchè e sono tutti a confini e quali in mezzo del nostro'. Communal statutes made a special provision to prevent such quarrels, making it legal to cross or lead oxen over neighbouring lands in order to carry out necessary work, as long as the route taken caused the least possible damage to land and crops (*Statuti 1322–25*, II, lib. 2, cap. xxxiii; *Statuta 1415*, Vol. II, Rubrica LXII, p. 429, 'Quod liceat unicuique ire per terram vicinorum ad terram suam.').

124 1442 Cat. 620, II, fol. 744v. Crescenzi recommends that communication between the various parts of the farm be convenient, *Agricultura*, Lib. VIII, cap. v. Pinto affirms that consolidation led to higher yields, 'Ordinamento', pp. 232–3.

125 1427 Cat. 42, fol. 259r–261v; 1433 Cat. 495, fol. 49v–51r.

126 1457 Cat. 816, II, fol. 777r–778v.

127 1427 Cat. 43, fol. 674v.

128 1451 Cat. 705, fol. 520v–521r.

129 Decima Repub. 21, fol. 379r–v.

130 Litta, tav. III; P. J. Jones, 'Florentine Families', p. 187.

131 1442 Cat. 621, fol. 596r–v; 1446 Cat. 673, I, fol. 307r–v.

132 1427 Cat. 42, fol. 272r–273v.

133 1451 Cat. 705, fol. 642r; 1446 Cat. 669, II, fol. 882v.

134 1427 Cat. 45, fol. 851r–852v; 1469 Cat. 920, II, fol. 784r–v. The other compact villas were Niccolo and Piero di Pagnozzo's villa La Loggia at Macia, 1427 Cat. 47, fol. 350r; Benedetto di Marco's property at Le Miccine, 1433 Cat. 496, fol. 56v; Carlo di Marco's Palagio in the parish of S. Lorenzo at Campi, 1427 Cat. 42, fol. 535r. Other examples of single-farm villas are Le Corti at Gangalandi, Ponte di Mezzo and La Gora. At Soffiano, a villa intended mainly for the owner's habitation with little commercial return from the land, Palla Novello's sons had a walled garden beside their house but only a small farm that produced a nominal quantity of wheat and a more generous amount of wine. At first there was not even a *casa da lavoratore* provided; 1433 Cat. 495, fol. 429r; 1469, Cat. 919, I, fol. 39r; 1480, Cat. 1011, fol. 221r; 1498, Decima Repub. 22, fol. 217r.

135 P. J. Jones, 'Florentine Families', p. 188 n. 39.

136 1451 Cat. 709, fol. 324v; 1457 Cat. 818, fol. 240r–v; 1469 Cat. 921, fol. 193r–v.

137 1469 Cat. 921, fol. 193r.

138 1480 Cat. 1013, II, fol. 217r.

139 1498 Decima Repub. 22, fol. 90r.

CHAPTER 3 SITES

1 Alberti, *L'Architettura*, IX, ii, p. 788: 'nella casa di città occorre regolare molti particolari tenendo conto della conformazione degli edifici vicini, mentre nella villa ci si comporta con maggiore libertà . . . la villa non è suggetta a tali limitazioni.'

2 The reasons for this are explored in Lillie, 'Memory of Place'.

3 1451 Cat. 707, fol. 417r.

4 1451 Cat. 705, fol. 529v. Repetti, II, pp. 913–14; The castle of Luciano came into the possession of the Florentine Republic who in gave it c. 1363 to their mercenary captain Melano Rastrelli d'Asti in recognition of his services. His son Giuliano sold it to Strozza di Carlo Strozzi; 1457 Cat. 815, I, No. 135. See Appendix B, No. 8.

5 See Chapter 10.

6 See F. W. Kent, 'Poggio a Caiano', pp. 251–2, 255; Chiostri, *La Petraia*, pp. 15–17.

7 Lillie, 'Memory of Place'.

8 Cato, *De Agri cultura*, I, pp. 2–5.

9 Varro, *Rerum Rusticarum Libri Tres*, I, vi, pp. 192–3; I, vii, pp. 194–5; I, ix, pp. 202–5; I, xvi, pp. 218–19, 222–3; Crescenzi, *Agricultura*, Lib. I, cap. i – v, xiii; Alberti, *L'Architettura*, V, xiv, pp. 400–3.

10 There was a clear distinction between unwalled villages (*borghi*), such as Quaracchi and Brozzi, and walled settlements (*castelli*), such as Campi and Capalle. On the 'typology

or rural settlements', see Cherubini and Francovich, 'Forme e vicende', pp. 145–52.

11 Carocci, *I Dintorni*, I, pp. 359–60, 'La Torre', Casa Orsini-Baroni.

12 Rucellai, 'Il Zibaldone', I, p. 23.

13 The *catasti* of Ubertino di Tommaso and his heirs nearly all refer to the *torrione* within the walls of Capalle: 1427 Cat. 45, fol. 851r; 1430 Cat. 405, fol. 173v; 1433 Cat. 495, fol. 492r; 1442 Cat. 620, II, fol. 999r; 1446 Cat. 671, II, fol. 835r; 1457 Cat. 816, I, fol. 5120r; 1480 Cat. 1012, II, fol. 263v.

14 Strozziane, V, 22, c. 99 sin.

15 See Chapter 1, n. 16.

16 Strozziane, V, 22, cc. 46 des., 100 des.; 1480 Cat. 1011, fol. 314v.

17 De la Roncière, *Florence*, III, ii, pp. 837–9.

18 The only other Strozzi house in a *castello* was Niccolò di Barla's at Malmantile, bought for a mere ninety florins so that he could supervise his nearby farm, which had no *casa da signore*.

19 Klapisch-Zuber, *Una Carta*.

20 Alberti, 'Villa', pp. 359–60: 'sia la villa non come una casa posta lungi dalla piazza, tale che da mercato bisogni comperare ogni cosa e portarvi, ma sia tale che indi t'avanzi, da sale in fuori, se puoi, d'ogni cosa, qual possi portare e vendere a mercato'.

21 De la Roncière, *Florence*, III, ii, pp. 894–6, 899, 901, quoted in Lamberini and Lazzareschi, *Campi*, pp. 207, 222–3.

22 Rucellai, 'Il Zibaldone', I, p. 21: 'Uno albereto presso a chasa . . . del quale se ne riceve gran consolazione, non tanto noi di chasa e del paese, quanto anchora i forastieri e' viandanti al tempo de' gram chaldi, perchè da una parte gli confina la strada pistoiese . . . che niuno foristiere non passa, che per uno quarto d'ora non si fermi a vedere el detto giardino'.

23 F. W. Kent, *Household and Lineage*, pp. 236–7, n. 29: 'rispecto alle possessioni abbiamo su questa strada tegnano molte amicitie nel contado di Pistoia'. F. W Kent, 'Poggio a Caiano', p. 253.

24 Palladio, *I Quattro libri*, Lib. II, cap. xii, p. 45.

25 *Statuta*, 1415, Vol. II, Rubrica CX, pp. 462–3: 'Quod cuilibet liceat lavare, et abeverare, et alia facere in flumine, et aquis civitate vel comitatus Florentie.' See Trexler, 'Measures against water pollution'.

26 *Statuta*, 1415, Vol. I, Rubrica CLXXXIV, p. 384: 'De poena facientis, vel tenentis cannatum in flumine arni'.

27 *Statuta*, 1415, Vol. II, Rubrica CXV, pp. 464–5: 'De poena non facientis callariam in piscaris molendinorum'.

28 *Statuta*, 1415, Vol. II, Rubrica CVII, p. 462: 'Quod cuilibet aedificandi liceat coadunare lapides in quolibet flumine'.

29 1427 Cat. 43, fol. 674r.

30 'Il fiume d'Arno vicino, nel quale tengo uno navicello e channai e truovomi rete da peschare d'ogni ragione': Rucellai, 'Il Zibaldone', I, p. 21. Rucellai says that the road or path leading from his villa straight to the Arno measured 'braccia secento diricto a corda', that is, about 400 metres, which is about 100 metres less than the distance measured on a modern map.

31 Rucellai, 'Il Zibaldone', I, p. 21: 'istando io a mensa in sala posso vedere le barghe che passano a dirinpetto per Arno'.

32 See Chapter 2, n. 106.

33 On Palazzo Gianfigliazzi see, Preyer, 'Florentine Palaces and Memories of the Past', p. 178. Caroline Elam informed me that Niccolò di Giovanni di Micho Capponi enlarged the Palazzo Coverelli between 1457 and 1469, so that the loggia facing the Arno was probably built in those years.

34 'Sarà situato non bene quel campo a cui stia di petto il fiume'; Alberti, 'Villa', p. 359. 'Fiume che lievi non gli sie confino'; Tanaglia, *De Agricultura*, Lib. I, line 291.

35 1446 Cat. 664, fol. 194r: 'El detto podere è forte manchato per il fiume di Bisenzio e'l fiume di Ghavina che ogni ano lo chuopre quando crescono e speso voltta si perde la racolta del grano'.

36 1469 Cat. 914, fol. 395v: 'Dammi al detto podere una grande noia il fiume di Bisenzio l'anno quando e' viene grosso e forte; mancha per detto fiume e più mancherebbe se non che ongni anno ne spendo 4.0.5 fiorini in fare palate e altri ripari'.

37 1427 Cat. 42, fol. 261r–v.

38 1442 Cat. 620, II, fol. 999v.

39 1446 Cat. 671, II, fol. 835r; 1469 Cat. 920, fol. 784r.

40 Lensi Orlandi, *Di Qua d'Arno*, p. 76, pl. 127.

41 The house is not listed in Zanobi and Francesco's joint tax return in 1427, Cat. 43, fol. 681r–684r, but it appears in Zanobi's first independent tax return of 1430. The descriptions of Zanobi's house are fairly consistent throughout the century: 1430 Cat. 405, fol. 175r, 'Una chasa con tre staiora di terra posta nel popolo della Badia di Fiesole Luogho detto Palaioula'; 1433 Cat. 495, fol. 498v., 'Una casetta con staiora 3 d'orto per suo abitare . . .'; 1442 Cat. 620, II, fol. 1013r, 'Una chasetta chon staiora tre d'orto o circha'; 1446 Cat. 671, I, fol. 105r: 'Una chasa chon circha staiora 3 d'orto . . . chon un pocho di boschetto'; 1451 Cat. 707, fol. 483: 'una chasa con circha di staiora tre d'orto e boschetto.' In 1457, Zanobi bought the small farmer's house next door (Cat. 816, fol. 9r): 'Una chasa chon circha a staiora 3 d'orto chon un pocho di boschetto tengho per mio habitare. . . . Una chasetta trista allato alla mia habitatione dal lavoratore chon staiora sei o circha di terra sodi chon alchuni viti e querciuoli'. His heirs declared the same property in 1469, Cat. 920, I, fol. 801r and 1480, Cat. 1012, II, fol. 225r.

42 W. Cohn, 'Il Beato Angelico e Battista di Biagio Sanguigni'; Levi d'Ancona, 'Zanobi Strozzi Reconsidered'; Levi d'Ancona, *Miniatura e miniatori*, pp. 55–8, 261–5.

43 At the time of my research Carmen Gronau kindly allowed me to explore and photograph her house. Carocci (*I Dintorni*, I, p. 107), who names the house 'Le Paglaijole ora Le Palazzine', cites the Migliori as the fifteenth-century owners followed by Lorenzo di Filippo Strozzi at the beginning of the sixteenth century. Further research is necessary to clear up the confusion surrounding these villas, but the entries in Carocci and Lensi Orlandi, which do not tally with the Strozzi tax returns, are unhelpful. Carocci records that a second house called Le Palaijole had belonged jointly to Batista Sanguigni and Chimenti Sernigi and was sold by them to Lorenzo di Francesco Strozzi in 1460; he identifies this house with that now belonging to the Costantini (previously Von Buerkel and Self), which retains a sixteenth-century Strozzi coat of

arms on the garden door but was rebuilt in the nineteenth century; Lensi Orlandi, *Di Qua d'Arno*, p. 76.

44 Lamberini (*Calenzano*, pp. 167–71) provides a lucid analysis of the site and architecture of Loiano.

45 In 1427 and 1457 the Rocca di Campi is described as 'Uno palagio adatto a fortezza', whereas in 1446 and 1451 it is described as 'una fortezza'.

46 In 1427, 1442, 1446, 1451 and 1469 Loiano is described as 'chasa da signore'; in 1457 as 'chasa da cittadino'; in 1480 and 1498 as 'Chasa da oste'.

47 1427 Cat. 45, fol. 752r, 'uno palagio disfacto et male in punto . . . è lungy da Firenze circa di miglia diciotto o venti'.

48 1433 Cat. 495, fol. 455v, 'sopra in montangnia'.

49 1446 Cat. 671, I, fol. 7r.

50 See Chapter 12, pp. 246–7.

CHAPTER 4   THE VILLA COMPLEX

1 For other uses of the word *villa*, see the Introduction and the beginning of Chapter 2.

2 Four Strozzi houses were consistently called 'casa da signore': Ponte di Mezzo, Le Miccine, Le Chorti and Le Panche. Three others oscillated between 'casa da signore', 'casa da oste' and 'casa da cittadino': Montughi, Macia and Loiano. Another two houses were only called 'chasa': Francesco di Giovanni's at Capalle and Francesco di Benedetto's at Brozzi, whereas three others varied between 'casa' and 'casa da signore': Fornello, Signano and Benedetto di Piero's house at Capalle. It is therefore unlikely that these variations in terminology signaled variations in form, type or function, and I have treated them as synonomous.

3 1427 Cat. 42, fol. 535r; 1430 Cat. 405, fol. 40r; 1433 Cat. 495, fol. 103r; 1442 Cat. 620, I, fol. 269r; 1446 Cat. 671, I, fol. 230r.

4 1427 Cat. 75, fol. 132r; 1457 Cat. 815, I, No. 135; 1446 Cat. 669, I, fol. 355r; 1451 Cat. 705, fol. 529r; 1442 Cat. 619, II, fol. 825r; 1480 Cat. 1009, II, fol. 446r.

5 1427 Cat. 76, fol. 487r.

6 1427 Cat. 45, fol. 752r.

7 1430 Cat. 406, fol. 298v; 1433 Cat. 496, fol. 396v; 1442 Cat. 621, fol. 596r; 1446 Cat. 673, I, fol. 307r; 1451 Cat. 709, fol. 323r; 1457 Cat. 818, fol. 235r; 1469 Cat. 921, fol. 192r; 1480 Cat. 1013, II, fol. 216r.

8 1469 Cat. 919, I, fol. 39r; 1480 Cat. 1011, fol. 221r.

9 1457 Cat. 816, fol. 9r.

10 The sons of Zanobi's brother, Francesco, owned two houses at Palaiuola with gardens and a small amount of land; see Chapter 3, n. 41.

11 1427 Cat. 76, fol. 178r.

12 1427 Cat. 76, fol. 182r.

13 1427 Cat. 76, fol. 195v.

14 1498 Decima Repub. 20, fol. 610r.

15 1427 Cat. 45, fol. 852r; 1457 Cat. 816, fol. 520r.

16 1427 Cat. 45, fol. 486r; 1430 Cat. 405, fol. 117v; 1442 Cat. 617, fol. 450v; 1446 Cat. 664, fol. 194r; 1451 Cat. 700, fol. 167v; Santuccio still only had accommodation for farmers in the last tax return before it was sold back to the Strozzi (1469 Cat. 914, fol. 395r) although in the sale contract of 14 July 1477, both an owner's house and a labourer's house are mentioned: 'Unum podere cum domo pro domino et pro laboratore', Not. Antecos., G. 618, vol. II (Ser Simone Grazini), fol. 188r.

17 Strozziane, V, 41, c. 74 sin. (1487), contains an account for construction at Maglio, 'E nella chasa da oste in murare unita chon quella de' lavoratore'.

18 Heers, *Le Clan familial*, pp. 3–5.

19 Bentmann and Müller, *Die Villa als Herrschaftsarchitektur*.

20 Appendix B, No. 4. The relation of the *casa da signore* to its group of outlying farmhouses is still evident on modern maps.

21 1433 Cat. 495, fol. 320r, 'Una chasa da singiore chon chorte, porticho e altre chose e con una chorticiella, torriciella dove soleva essere cholonbaia e al presente non v'è e chon una chasa perchè si fa la vendemmia'; 1442 Cat. 620, II, fol. 746r, 'Una chasa da signiore chon chorte, porticho, orto, stalla e chanali e volte'; 1446 Cat. 671, II; fol. 991r, 'Una chasa da signiore chon pozzo, chorte, cholonbaia e stalla e con staiora 12 d'orti'.

22 In 1427 Cat. 44, fol. 202v–203v, four *poderi* were listed, all with *aia, orto* and *canneto*. The 1442 description, Cat. 620, II, fol. 743r–744r, also mentions porticoes for three houses and a *stalla* beside one house, and in 1446, Cat. 671, II, fol. 991r–992r, three houses have *stalle* and one also has a *forno*.

23 The seven big Strozzi estates are listed in Chapter 2, pp. 34–37.

24 In distant hill country the frequent absence of the owner and the need to provide security for the villa community and its crops favoured a more compact unit.

25 For example, Ubertino di Tommaso's villa at Montughi, 1427 Cat. 45, fol. 851r; Carlo di Marcuccio's Palagio at Campi, 1427 Cat. 42, fol. 535r.

26 1427 Cat. 45, fol. 852r.

27 These are at Fornello, Mezzana, the three main Capalle villas, the three main Campi villas (the Rocca, Signano, Il Palagio), Le Miccine, Santuccio, Lionardo d'Antonio's villa at Brozzi and Querceto.

28 1433 Cat. 494, fol. 321v; 1446 Cat. 671, II, fol. 991r; 1451 Cat. 707, fol. 415v.

29 1430 Cat. 406, fol. 250v.

30 Strozziane, V, 41, c.74 sin.

31 1427 Cat. 75, fol. 132r: 'una torre ch'è cholonbaia alato a detta forteza'.

32 1446 Cat. 669, II, fol. 632r, 'una toraccia per abitare nela quale bisogna metere e lavoratore perchè la chasa da lavoratore è rovinata'.

33 1451 Cat. 705, fol. 528r.

34 1457 Cat. 815, I, No. 135: 'una torricella che fu già cholonbaia apresso a detta fortezza sotto la quale torre è una pigione di lire 12 l'anno tiella a pigione Berto di Marcho fabro'.

35 1480 Cat. 1009, II, fol. 297r; 1480 Cat. 1009, II, fol. 446r: 'Una torre ch'aveva sotto una bottegha da fabbro la quale tengho per mio abitare . . . e la detta bottegha 'o disfatta che mi'o fatto la cella pel vino.'

36   1498 Decima repub. 20, fol. 610r, 'una torre abitava Charllo mio fratello, e al presente abita Nanni charadore del popolo di San Lorenzo a Campi e perchè lavora mia terre'.

37   Strozziane, V, 41, c. 95 sin. (1489), 'per alzare la corte e cholonbaia della mia abitazione al Santucio'.

38   The Palagione at Capalle (Fig. 15 in Chapter 3 and Fig. 52 in Chapter 5) has undergone many transformations, but the vestiges of a large tower probably remain in the main block of the house (where a later arch has been filled in with rough blocks of *alberese*). In his 1480 *catasto* Filippo di Matteo called the Torrione/Palagione, 'La chaxa alla tore della nostra abitazione', Cat. 1011, fol. 314v.

39   The tenant farmers at Capalle delivered their wheat to the factor Paolo di Benedetto Strozzi, who stored it in the Palagione; Strozziane, V, 22, c.66 des (1478).

40   Strozziane, V, 7, c. 34 des.

41   See Chapter 9, p. 170 Bartolommeo Sassetti's granary was next to an upstairs *camera* at Macia.

42   Strozziane, V, 41, c. 74 sin.(1487) contains an account to 'rachonciare la stalla de' lavoratore e farvi disopra il granaio', and another account for making wooden windows and doors for the granary at Santuccio.

43   Crescenzi, *Agricultura*, see Lib. V, VI, VII, VIII and XI.

44   1433 Cat. 495, fol. 429r; 1442 Cat. 620, II, fol. 878r.

45   Coffin (*Gardens and Gardening*, p. 217) points this out but consistently translates *orto* as 'kitchen garden'.

46   1469 Cat. 924, I, fol. 295r: 'Uno palagio cho' loggia e orto e altri 'defici'; 1480 Cat. 1016, II, fol. 451r: 'Uno palagio chon loggia e horto e altri hedifici'; 1498 Decima Repub. 28, fol. 450r: 'Uno palagio chon loggia e orto e altri edifici'. It may, however, be significant that the Medici sculpture garden at San Marco was usually referred to as *giardino*, whereas Clarice Orsini-Medici's garden further up the Via Larga was generally known as the 'orto [di Francesco Orafo]': see Elam, 'Lorenzo de' Medici's Sculpture Garden', pp. 75–83.

47   For example, *giardino* was never used for the gardens attached to *case da lavoratore*.

48   Those without *orti* tend to be secondary villas (eg, Loiano, Luciano, Maglio), the owners of which resided more frequently at other country houses where there was a garden, or villas in the process of construction (eg, Travalle, Poggio a Caiano) or dilapidation (eg, Trefiano).

49   1427 Cat. 42, fol. 535r: 'L'orto ch'è cholla chasa ch'io abito rende l'anno staia 3 di fave, un 1/4 di peselli, uno moggio quarto di cicei [sic: ceci], dodici mazzi d'agli, l'uve si loghoron tra per mangiare e per agresto, tutte l'altra frutte si loghorono la 'state sanz'utile niuno'.

50   For Filippo Strozzi's new *pratello* at Santuccio see p. 72, for Bartolommeo's *pratello* at Valcenni see p. 177.

51   For the meadow gardens of the *Hypnerotomachia Poliphili* and their relationship to contemporary practice, see Segre, 'Untangling the Knot', pp. 82, 86–8.

52   1480 Cat. 1011, fol. 435r.

53   1427 Cat. 45, fol. 752r.

54   1427 Cat. 44, fol. 204r; 1442 Cat. 620, II, fol. 745r.

55   1427 Cat. 45, fol. 851r.

56   1446 Cat. 671, I, fol. 105r.

57   Morelli, *Ricordi*, p. 92: 'Più di presso all'abitazioni v'è gran quantità di boschetti di be' querciuoli, e molti ve n'ha acconci per diletto, netti di sotto, cioè il terreno a modo di prato, da'ndarvi iscalzo sanza temere di niente che offendesse il piè'.

58   Tanaglia, *De Agricultura*, Lib. I, line 177: 'E per boschetti di vari ucce' pieni, / Che lor dolze cantare è tanto grato'.

59   'Il Zibaldone', I, p. 21, Rucellai's description of the 'albereto . . . da potervi stare al fresco . . . al tempo de' gram chaldi', suggests that it was the equivalent of a *boschetto* rather than an orchard, since fruit trees do not provide good shade.

60   See p. 253.

61   This supports Ada Segre's view that these 'status symbols' were groves or 'tree plantations', rather than wildernesses, 'Untangling the Knot', pp. 85–6.

62   *Libro d'inventario dei beni di Lorenzo il Magnifico*, p. 179 (MAP CLXV, c. 86): 'Uno giardino drieto al detto palagio con più orticini murati e ricinti di mura e uno pezzo di terra in detto giardino con arcipressi, abeti e altro, a uso di boschetto et uno pezzo d'ortaccio a piè del detto palagio, chiuso atorno chon uno stechato, tutte le sopradette chose a uno tenere di staiora 6 incircha'.

63   See n. 78 in this Chapter.

64   For a full analysis of the Villa Medici garden, see Galletti, 'Una Committenza medicea', pp. 74–82. For the construction of the garden at Fiesole, see Lillie, 'Giovanni di Cosimo', pp. 196–9.

65   Francesco di Benedetto's *casa da signore* at Brozzi is described as 'Una casa con un pezo d'orto la quale tegnamo a uso di nostra abitazione in contado', followed by 'una casetta da lavoratore con circha staiora 3 d'ortale posta allato alla sopradetta'; 1427 Cat. 43, fol. 681r. Niccolò di Pagnozzo's declarations of his villa at Macia also distinguish between the *orto* next to the *casa da signore* and the *casa da lavoratore* with its *ortale*; 1427 Cat. 47, fol. 350r. The same distinction is made at the Rocca di Campi between the *orto* next to the Rocca and the *ortora* beside the farmhouses, the threshing yards and the sheds (1427 Cat. 75, fol. 132r), and also at Capalle, where Chirico di Francesco's house had its *orto* beside the river, with labourers' houses and their *ortora* further along the river bank; 1427 Cat. 43, fol. 674r.

66   Filippo Strozzi bought a gate and chains for the walled gardens at Santuccio in 1488, Strozziane, V, 44, c. 154 sin. The walled gardens of Bartolommeo Sassetti at Macia and Valcenni are discussed in Chapter 9.

67   See Carl, 'La Casa Vecchia dei Medici'.

68   A factor looked after the *orto* at Fornello and at Chirico di Francesco's Capalle villa, while Filippo di Matteo had a bridge built over the Marinella stream so that his factor, Paolo di Benedetto Strozzi, could move easily between the Palagione and his *orto*, Strozziane, V, 36, c. 290 sin. (1483).

69   Marco di Goro's heirs at Fornello maintained a vineyard at Capalle, a cane thicket, four hay meadows and groves of trees on the river bank all for their own use; 1427 Cat. 44, fol. 202r–203v. Giovanni di Luigi's widow at Le Corti kept an

extra vineyard (1427 Cat. 43, fol. 576r), as did Piero di Carlo at Querceto until 1446 when he handed it over to the *lavoratori* (Cat. 673, II, fol. 307v). Benedetto di Piero reserved a vineyard to produce white wine for himself (1442 Cat. 620, I, fol. 176v); other proprietors – Palla di Nofri, Niccolò di Barla and Lorenzo di Francesco di Benedetto – all owned supplementary personal vineyards. Marco di Nofri di Palla had no *casa da signore* but kept a large meadow for hay near Prato (1427 Cat. 44, fol. 254v), and Carlo di Marco also found it worthwhile to keep his own hay fields near his villa Il Palagio (1427 Cat. 42, fol. 536v).

70 Strozziane, V, 41, c. 51 des., an account dated 7 April 1486 for expenses incurred 'nella chasa e horto del Santuccio in fare truocholi, muriciuoli e uno pozo nel orto e fare il pratello e l'orto'.

71 Strozziane, V, 41, c. 51 sin.–des., 9 January 1485–6: 'matonare le corti e horticini', refers to the paving of paths and to creating beds or compartments in the *orto* or *pratello*.

72 Strozziane, V, 41, c. 95 sin., 5 December 1489: 'per ... merlare e ariciare il muro del'orto tranne eredi di Barone Spini'.

73 Strozziane, V, 41, c. 20 sin., 31 October 1486: 'per più manifature a lengnaiuolo in fare l'uscio del pratello e altre chose e in 800 charate di terra mena al pratello'.

74 Ibid. and Strozziane, V, 41, c. 35 des., 28 January 1485–6 gives a payment for wood 'per i tetti del'uscio del pratello'.

75 Strozziane, V, 41, c. 74 sin.

76 F. W. Kent, 'Poggio a Caiano' p. 251.

77 Strozziane, III, 133, c. 149, 11 March 1488–9, from Roberto Strozzi in Ferrara to Filippo Strozzi in Florence: 'priegovi gli faciati dare qualche piantolina con radice de fichi brusochi'. These figs were probably those known as 'fichi brugiotti' with a dark purple skin and red flesh.

78 Two letters from agents concern ordering plants from Naples for the garden of the Villa Medici at Fiesole, so that at least two plant-hunting trips to Naples must have been carried out for Giovanni di Cosimo de' Medici. MAP CXXXVIII, 46, 5 October 1454, from Bartolomeo Serragli in Rome to Giovanni di Cosimo de' Medici in Florence: 'E fra iiii dì parto per Napoli mandi idio di buono arò a arretir qualche buona pianta per l'ortto di Fiesole'. MAP V, 722, 11 April 1455, from Giovanni di Luca Rossi in Florence to Giovanni di Cosimo de' Medici at Bagni Petriuolo: 'Barto[lomeo] Seragli va in fra 8 dì a Napoli 'o gli fatto uno richordo di più chosse vogliamo per a Fiesole cioè melaghrani, melaranci, limonciegli, faetri [?] e alchuna altra chosa ch'io vegho si è per'l nostro bisongnio'. Other garden owners were soon requesting special plants from Giovanni di Cosimo; MAP IX, 196r, 10 March 1457, from Giovanfrancesco della Torre in Ferrara to Giovanni di Cosimo de' Medici in Florence: 'pigliarò a dire e chiedervi de quelle cosse che nui havemo carestia e vui di rata: piaquavi adunque per lo apportatore di questa che serà uno cavalaro di questo mio Ill[ustrissimo] S[ignore] mandarmi parechi piedi di rose di quelle bianche incarnatte: et similmente se havesti pianton di quelli garofalli bianchi incarnati da tante foglie e deli rossi belli che intendo ne' siti

molto ben forniti: et se non havesti deli piantoni mandateme dele semente che l'haverò ultra modo gratissimo'. For a full interpretation of these documents, see Galletti, 'Una Committenza medicea', pp. 75, 80–1.

79 Lorenzo Strozzi, *Le Vite*, ed. Zeffi, p. 16: 'Aveva vicino alla citta di Napoli un giardino chiamato Masseria il quale ... per natura e bonta eccedeva tutti gli altri. Dove spesse volte, per rifrigerio suo e dilletazione degli amici, andava, e tanto piacere prendeva della cultura di quello, che con le proprie mani vi operava molte cose, cogliendosi in esso con le piu rare e prime frutte che in Napoli venissero: donde dipoi non manco d'ornare anco la Patria di nobilissime piante, trasportandone i fichi gentili e' carciofi, che prima non erano state condotte in queste nostre parti'.

80 Strozziane, V, 22, c. 168 des.; Strozziane, V, 42, c. 3 sin.; Sale, *The Strozzi Chapel*, p. 16, n. 40.

81 Filippo returned to Florence in 1466, although he continued to visit Naples frequently, especially until his brother Lorenzo's death in 1480: Strozziane, V, 17, cc. 153 sin., 172 des.; Strozziane, V, 18, c. 130 des.; Strozziane, V, 19, cc. 120 des.–122 des.; Sale, *Strozzi Chapel*, pp. 13–14, nn. 29–30; Goldthwaite, *Private Wealth*, p. 57; Gregory, 'A Florentine Family in Crisis', p. 259.

82 Piero de' Crescenzi dedicated his treatise to Charles II of Anjou, and Michelangelo Tanaglia his to Alfonso of Aragon, Duke of Calabria in the 1480s.

83 Sale, *Strozzi Chapel*, pp. 13, 36, 73, n. 138.

84 Pontano, *I Trattati delle virtù sociali*, 'De splendore', VIII, De Hortis ac villis, pp. 136–8; quoted by Comito, *The Idea of the Garden in the Renaissance*, pp. 3–4.

85 P. J. Jones, 'Medieval Agrarian Society', p. 394 [CHECK]. See also Chapter 3.

86 Capitalised at 71 or 85 florins, 1427 Cat. 42, fol. 534v; 1430 Cat. 405, fol. 40r; 1433 Cat. 495, fol. 103r; 1442 Cat. 620, I, fol. 269r; 1446 Cat. 671, I, fol. 230r; 1451 Cat. 707, fol. 670r; 1457 Cat. 819, II, fol. 647r.

87 1442 Cat. 620, I, fol. 492r. Compare these rents with those analysed by de Courcey-Bayley, who noted that the large urban domiciles of the Florentine élite 'tended to bring over F.15 a year' when let, whereas shops in town brought proportionately more; 'House and Household', pp. 104, 117–22.

88 1469 Cat. 920, II, fol. 812r: 'detta chasa tegniamo per nostro uso per biada a ghrano e per rifugio di nostre choxe e di nostri lavoratori per tenpi di sospetto o di ghuerra'.

89 1442 Cat. 620, I, fol. 279v.

90 1430 Cat. 405, fol. 34v.

91 Strozziane, V, 22, cc. 99–100, 120 sin., 197 sin.; 1480 Cat. 1011, fol. 314v.

92 1427 Cat. 44, fol. 255v: 'Una chasetta la quale abiamo nel Chastello di Prato nella quale mettiamo tutto nostra richolta e di grano e di biade e di vino. ... E in detta chasa è più masserizie di bungnole e di botti e chose di picchola valuta'. Salamone di Carlo did likewise, keeping a house for storing crops in the village of Quaracchi (1427 Cat. 45, fol. 708r), whereas Piero di Carlo, whose villas were some distance away on Monte Morello and San Martino a Mensola, needed a

storage house at Campi to serve his farms in Le Miccine (1446 Cat. 673, I, fol. 308v).

93 1427 Cat. 76, fol. 173v, 176r, 179r–v, 190r, 196v.

94 Courcey-Bayley, 'House and Household', ch. 3.

95 Carocci assumes a very low level of comfort: 'Antichi alberghi di campagna', pp. 83–6: 'Qualche cameruccia con più d'un letto, una stalla per i cavalli, un'osteria dove i passanti si fermavano per rifocillarsi, così dovevano essere questi albergucci della campagna', but some of the evidence presented here suggests a higher standard of accomodation.

96 P. J. Jones, 'Medieval Agrarian Society', p. 387. Strozziane, V, 11, c. 130 sin.: Piero di Bartolo, Matteo's innkeeper at Quaracchi, bought wine for the hotel from Matteo's vineyards in the same district. See also Pinto, 'Ordinamento', p. 255.

97 1427 Cat. 76, fol. 185v: Pieroccio di Francescho Alberghatore paid 28 florins a year in 1427 (capitalised at 400 florins): 'Una chaxa d'albergho posta al Pogo a Chaiano nel popolo di Santa Maria Bonistallo comune di Charmignano, da p[rim]o e s[second]o via, 1/3, 1/4 Messer Palla; tiella fitto Pierocio di Francescho aberghatore e dame l'anno F. vent'otto che a 7 per c[ent]o a rendità vale F.CCCC. Una chaxa dirinpetto al sopradetto abergho si fa di nuovo per tenervi il passagiere per mantenere il sopradetto abergho'.1430 Cat. 405, fol. 137r: Marco di Pierone paid 30 florins in 1430 (capitalised at 478.11.5 florins; 1433 Cat. 495, fol. 390r), but only 25 florins in 1433 (capitalised at F.357.2.10). Palla's rent may have diminished because he had been hit by enormous taxes and was unwilling to carry out repairs; see Belle, 'A Renaissance Patrician', pp. 104–6.

98 1430 Cat. 405, fol. 143v.

99 1433 Cat. 495, fol. 395r.

100 Strozziane, V, 12, c. 10 sin.

101 Strozziane, V, 11, cc. 4 des., 45 sin.: Andrea di Moringo da Peretola and sons rented the *taverna* or *albergo* at Quaracchi in 1425 and until 1 November 1426. Strozziane, V, 11, cc. 41 sin., 44: Andreasso di Michele da Campi rented the tavern from 1 December 1426 until 11 April 1428 for 36 florins a year. Strozziane, V, 11, cc. 130 sin. 133 sin.: Domenico di Nencio da Quaracchi rented the inn from 11 May 1428 until his death there in 1429. Strozziane, V, 10, c. 111 sin.; V, 11, c. 130 sin.: Piero di Bartolo da Quaracchi detto Mazone rented the hotel for three years from 1 November 1429 until 1 November 1432 for 132 lire a year. Strozziane, V, 10, c. 136: Agnolo di Papi di Buto, Matteo's factor and Ser Domenico d'Agniolo 'Prete a S. Piero a Quaracchi' ran the hotel from 1 November 1432. Strozziane, V, 11, cc. 139 sin., 147 sin.: Pagolo di Giunta is called 'Oste a Quaracchi' from November 1432. Strozziane, V, 11, c. 156 sin.: Andrea di Bartolo da Petriolo rented the hotel for one year from 1 February c. 1433–44 for 30 florins.

102 Strozziane, V, 10, cc. 47 sin., 100 sin., 108 des.: V, 12, c. 10 sin.

103 Strozziane, V, 10, cc. 82 des., 108 sin., 138 sin.; V, 11, c. 29 des.

104 Strozziane, V, 10, c. 39 des.; V, 11, c. 39 des.

105 Strozziane, V, 10 and 11, cc. 41 sin. and 43 des.

106 Strozziane, V, 11, c. 41 sin.; V, 10, c. 111.

107 Strozziane, V, 10, c. 136 sin.

108 1457 Cat. 816, II, fol. 1010r.

109 These were Messer Marcello's at the Rocca di Campi, Andrea di Carlo's at Loiano, Vanni di Francesco's at Valigari or Sassiglioni in the Val di Marina, Messer Palla Novello's at Cintoia and San Donnino, Lionardo d'Antonio's at San Donnino and San Piero a Lechore, Filippo di Matteo's at Santuccio and Maglio and Palla di Nofri's at Prato, Signa and Poggio a Caiano.

110 Capitani di Parte, Numeri Neri, Vol. 965, 12 Sept. 1564: 'Dinanzi a voi Magistri Signori Chapitani di Parte . . . uficial di fiumi si raporte per me Piero di Francescho di Donnino al presente vostro capom[aestr]o eletto da vostre signiorie per andare a vedere e livellare la chaduta e pendio del letto di Bisenzio dall mulino d'Anfolso [sic: Alfonso] e Lor[enz]o Strozi a presso al ponte di Chanpi per insino all primo mulino di sopra a Chanpi il quale è oggi di Lorenzo del Vignia'. My thanks to Daniela Lamberini who showed me this document.

111 Strozziane, V, 61, c. 33 sin. It cost 190 florins. It is not to be confused with the double-arched structure spanning the Fosso Gavina at its confluence with the Bisenzio to the south of Santuccio, shown in the Capitani di Parte maps of S. Moro and S. Donnino, where it is labelled 'mulina del Santuccio'.

112 Strozziane, V, 61, cc. 17 des., 21 des., 29 sin.

113 Strozziane, V, 1221, I, c. 1 des.

114 Messer Palla di Nofri's mill at the Ponte a Tigliano on the Ombrone next to Poggio a Caiano was also highly productive, let for 198 *staia* of wheat in 1430, which, at 19 *soldi* per *staia*, was the cash equivalent of 188 lire, 5 *soldi* (capitalised at F.671.15), although his mill at Signa yielded half that amount (capitalised at F.346.1.7) and that at Prato only 25 *staia* (capitalised at F.81.5) in 1430; 1430 Cat. 405, fol. 130r, 132r, 137v.

115 Strozziane, V, 11, c. 2 des. (1424). When Matteo di Simone discovered that the miller Santi di Jacopo had cheated him by underweighing his grain by 20 lb., he demanded F.20.2.7 to cover the discrepancy.

116 1430 Cat. 405, fol. 121v; 1442 Cat. 620, II, fol. 878r; 1446 Cat. 671, II, fol. 533r; 1451 Cat. 707, fol. 353r.

117 1427 Cat. 76, fol. 186r.

118 This high sum may have covered the cost of rebuilding the Poggio mill since the maintenance charge was much lower in subsequent years: 1427 Cat. 76, fol. 199v, F. 496; 1430 Cat. 405, fol. 151v, F. 385.14.4; 1433 Cat. 495, fol. 400v, F. 150.

119 1480 Cat. 1012, II, fol. 300r. Muendel ('The Grain Mills of Pistoia', pp. 42–43) notes that many mills in the province of Pistioa 'were equipped with more than one set of mill-stones (*palmento*) and the most profitable had over 100 *staia* in profit', with the highest yield from one of 258 mills in the area being 214 *staia* a year in 1350.

120 These were Palla di Nofri, Filippo di Matteo, Piero di Carlo and Giovanni di Messer Marcello. See Goldthwaite, *The Building of Renaissance Florence*, pp. 177–212, for a detailed account of the manufacture of bricks and baked lime near Florence.

121 Goldthwaite, *The Building of Renaissance Florence*, pp. 191–2.

122 1427 Cat. 76, fol. 186v, 189v; R. Jones, 'Palla Strozzi', p. 87, doc. 118, (Strozziane, IV, 343, c. 140v).

123 R. Jones, 'Palla Strozzi', p. 90, doc.135 (Strozziane, IV, 343, c. 204v).

124 R. Jones, 'Palla Strozzi', p. 70, doc. 51 (Strozziane, IV, 343, c. 23), p. 81, doc. 97 (Strozziane, IV, 363, cc. 7, 11, 17, 26, 28).

125 1430 Cat. 405, fol. 127r.

126 Palla himself had a dismantled kiln at la Mirandola near Carmignano (1427 Cat. 76, fol. 186v), and Giovanni di Messer Marcello's *fornace* in the Mugello was described as 'rovinata' (1498 Decima Repub. 20, fol. 610v).

127 Strozziane, V, 41, c. 82 sin.

128 Goldthwaite, 'The Building of the Strozzi Palace', p. 113.

129 Strozziane, V, 41, c. 167 sin.: 'ii fornaci chontighue, una da lavoro e una da chalcina chon chase apichate e per 2 abitazioni e corti intorno e chon staiora 4 1/2 incircha di terra lavoratia e alborata alato a dette fornaci.' The purchase contract survives: *Strozziane*, V, 1250, Inserta 11 (1489, 27 March) c. 2 sin.–des. See also Goldthwaite, 'The Building of the Strozzi Palace', p. 158.

130 Strozziane, V, 41, cc. 167 sin., 179 sin.

131 Goldthwaite, *Building of Renaissance Florence*, pp. 181–2.

132 1433 Cat. 495, fol. 383v, 'la quale fornacie non si trouva s'affittare perche non n'ha terreno; adopirala per suoi bisongni.'

133 Goldthwaite (*Building of Renaissance Florence*, p. 181) refers to the statutes prohibiting kilns from the centre of town because of the danger of fire.

CHAPTER 5 REPAIR, CONSTRUCTION AND RURAL PATRONAGE

1 1427 Cat. 76, fol. 199v.

2 1451 Cat. 709, fol. 324r. On the other hand, Ubertino di Tommaso only needed 20 lire (c. 3 florins) at Montughi, 1427 Cat. 45, fol. 851r, whereas Francesco and Zanobi di Benedetto only claimed 3 lire 10 *soldi*, for maintenance at Brozzi, 1427 Cat. 43, fol. 684r.

3 1427 Cat. 43, fol. 674r. See Appendix B, no. 18.

4 1427 Cat. 43, fol. 675v; 1451 Cat. 705, fol. 520v.

5 Strozziane, III, 133, cc. 25–27, see n. 36 in this chapter; 1427 Cat. 45, fol. 851r, 'uno podere . . . chon torrione tutto ghuasto non s'abita, chon chasa da lavoratore e più chasolari de' quali non si vede vestigio, tutto posto nel popolo di San Chiricho a Chapalle'.

6 1442 Cat. 620, I, fol. 177v; 1446 Cat. 671, I, fol. 150r; 1451 Cat. 707, fol. 396r.

7 1446 Cat. 669, I, fol. 356v: 'Per mantenere la chasa di Firenze e luoghi da Chanpi e quelli da Luciano bisognia gran danaro, avisandovi che nonn'è ancora uno anno che lla saetta perchosse la chasa da Chanpi e fece gran danno in modo mi chosterà un buon danaro a rachonciarla, e chosì bisognia spendere assai nella chasa di Firenze che tutta rovina in più luoghi'.

8 Cherubini and Francovich, 'Forme e vicende', pp. 148–9, 172; Pinto, 'Forme', p. 262.

9 See Paolo Pirillo's important thesis for the Facoltà di Lettere and Filosofia, Università di Firenze, 1976–7, *Case rurali, castelli ed altri insediamenti nel contado fiorentino*.

10 1446 Cat. 671, I, fol. 117r–v.

11 The farm with 'Una toraccia e casolari' at Le Miccine was jointly owned by Giovanni di Francesco Strozzi (1427 Cat. 43, fol. 907v), Strozza di Rinaldo Strozzi (1427 Cat. 45, fol. 722r), Bartolommeo di Loderigo Strozzi (1427 Cat. 42, fol. 325v) and Lotto di Ridolfo da Prato.

12 P. J. Jones ('Medieval Agrarian Society', p. 394) refers to the abandonment of many medieval *castra* in favour of houses in the open countryside, which had taken place by the fifteenth century.

13 The old family palace of Trefiano was situated in the parish of S. Marco a Seano, in the district of Carmignano. See Appendix B, no. 17.

14 1427 Cat. 76, fol. 187r, 195v.

15 R. Jones, 'Palla Strozzi', pp. 44–5, 80–3, docs. 95–108.

16 See Chapter 12, pp. 246–7.

17 See Appendix B, no. 26.

18 R. Jones, 'Palla Strozzi', p. 104, doc. 140 k; Archivio di Stato, Ferrara, Archivio Bentivoglio, busta 6, no. 34, fol. 51, 'E questo fo perché da' fondamenti fu edificato dagli nostri antichi e padri messer Jacopo e Palla suo figluolo padre di Nofri mio padre e mio avolo. E voglio quanto possibile m'è provedere che decto sito luogo e podere abbia a rimanere nella casa nostra e ne' nostri discendenti, per memoria di chi lo edificò e fa principio, e per rispecto del luogo dove egli è, cioè a Carmignano sempre suti quegli uomini quel medesimo che noi e di casa nostra. Posto che decto luogo sia al presente piccolissima cosa, e come un casolare, ma già fu grande e bella e magnifica'. See also F. W. Kent, 'The Making of a Renaissance Patron', p. 45.

19 See Lillie, 'Memory of Place'.

20 'Avendomi choncieduto Iddio de' beni tenporali, liene voglio essere ricordevole. E principiando dalle chose sua, potreno venire uno dì alle nostre. Di che fo quello posso ma per anchora non risurgie niuna chonchruxione e quanto più s'inchalciasino, più richulono. Manfredi è di quelli che sta duro a mille fiorini e inanzi non voglio murare o mi dischosterei di vicinanza'. The whole text of this letter is published by Eve Borsook, 'Documenti relativi', doc. 18; Strozziane, III, 133, c. 60v. Sale (*Strozzi Chapel*, pp. 17–18) takes Filippo Strozzi's statement at face value, oversimplifying the chronology and Filippo's procedure when he says, 'Filippo began in the late 1470's a program of building, first with religious foundations, then country estates, and finally with his monumental town house'.

21 I have interpreted the phrase in the letter, 'Di che fo quello posso', as referring to the immediately preceeding clause, 'potreno venire uno dì alle nostre [cose]', meaning that Filippo is doing all he can towards furthering their own family interests. The next passage almost certainly refers to plans for

the big palace site and the reluctance of his neighbours to sell because Manfredi was not a builder, as Borsook ('Documenti relativi', p. 4) thought, but Filippo Strozzi's neighbour in town, Manfredi d'Antonio Squarcialupi, who would not sell his house for less than 1,000 florins. See Filippo's 1480 *catasto*, 1011, fol. 314r., which lists a house on the site of the new palace finally bought from the *sons* of Manfredi Squarcialupi for only 540 florins *di sugello* on 28 February 1480, confirmed in Filippo's *ricordanze*, Strozziane, V, 22 c. 156 sin. Manfredi had married the first cousin of Filippo's father, Caterina di Piero di Filippo di Messer Lionardo Strozzi, 1446 Cat. 671, II, fol. 965v; Litta, Tav. XVII.

22 'Della spesa fo al Santucio, chonoscho ho traxandato; ma poi v'avevo messo mano, non era da lasciare quella hopera inperfetta, esendo chosa nostra. Avendocy Iddio choncieduto della grazia sua, non è male che nne faciamo qualche richonoscienzia. Il mio hogietto fu che avendo Giovan Luigi el beneficio, avessi da abitarvy e che l'anno per la festa vi potesimo andare. E sendo manchato, se non fussi suta inanzi, mene ritraevo. Ma il principio era fatto; e l'ò apigionata, che in questo Ongnisanti vi torneranno. E dove prima se n'avea tra gh[r]ano e danari circha lire 110, l'ò tirato chon la pigione a 160 e fo conto che pigliamo tanto le rendite che siamo paghati e verreno avere fatto questo bene'; Borsook, 'Documenti relativi', doc. 18. Giovanluigi, whom Filippo hoped would receive the benefice of the Santuccio oratory, was the illegitimate son of his brother Lorenzo; Alessandra Macinghi Strozzi, *Lettere*, pp. 451–2, 586, 588. The increased profit from Santuccio was the result of letting the house and garden to Lucrezia Tornabuoni's agent for nine florins a year, the equivalent of the extra 50 lire to which Filippo refers.

23 Lillie, 'Vita di palazzo, vita in villa'.

24 Strozziane, V, 17, cc. 19 sin., 40 sin., 43 sin., 131 sin.–des.

25 Strozziane, V, 12, c. 27 sin.; Gregory, 'A Florentine Family in Crisis', pp. 191–2; Goldthwaite, *Private Wealth*, p. 37, n. 15; building accounts for Simone's renovation of this house (1420–1) are in Strozziane, V, 7, cc. 72–95; V, 8, cc. 22 sin.–26 des.

26 Pampaloni, *Palazzo Strozzi*, pp. 48–50, n. 54.

27 According to Gregory ('A Florentine Family in Crisis', pp. 239–40), this house had originally belonged to Messer Palla di Nofri Strozzi, who sold it provisionally to his wife's nephew, Messer Marcello Strozzi, when he went into exile. See also Goldthwaite, 'The Building of the Strozzi Palace', p. 106.

28 Elam, 'Piazza Strozzi', fig. 10; Goldthwaite, 'The Building of the Strozzi Palace', p. 106, n. 8; Pampaloni, *Palazzo Strozzi*, pp. 55, 113.

29 Strozziane, V, 36, c. 247.

30 Sale, *The Strozzi Chapel*, pp. 20–1, nn. 60–3, appendix A, doc. 2. Filippo also bought hangings and vestments for S. Maria Ughi in 1472 and 1476; Borsook, 'Documenti relativi', n. 4; Strozziane, V, 1086, Inserta 2. In 1482 Filippo paid Domenico Ghirlandaio for a fresco of the Madonna surrounded by angels, seraphim and the Strozzi coat of arms in the lunette above the main door; Sale, p. 20, n. 61, appendix A, doc. 27; Strozziane, V, 36, c. 138 sin.

31 Borsook, 'Documenti for Filippo Strozzi's Chapel in Santa Maria Novella', I and II; and Sale, *The Strozzi Chapel*, ch. IV and V.

32 Alessandra Macinghi Strozzi, *Lettere*, pp. 331, 336, 340, 343.

33 Sale, p. 20, n. 56; Strozziane, V, 21, c. 61 sin.

34 This *quaderno* survives; Strozziane, V, 21: 'È un libro di debitori e creditori e ricordi relativi all'oratorio di San Giovanni Battista a San Donnino detto il Santuccio'.

35 The rebuilding and decoration of the oratory did not take place until 1487–8, after the villa had been rebuilt, Strozziane, V, 21, cc. 14–20.

36 Strozziane, III, 133, cc. 25–27, 27 April 1474: 'Io sono per chonprare uno podere a Chanpi di pregio di circha a 1,200 Fiorini; non v'è la chasa da abitare, è solo da rendita, e perchè non escha di chasa mixi sieno volto; è di Girolamo e fratelli e lo vendono per una don[n]a cha 'anno a rendere d'Ubertino overo di T[ommas]o d'Ubertino, che da lui l'ebono. Non chredo abbi l'animo averne parte, pure parendoti lo chonpri per la chonp[agn]a. Lo farò se non lo pagherò de' mia, che tale fine l'o fatto.' Although this letter was written a whole year before Filippo's purchase of Capalle and describes the location as Campi, the larger village next door to Capalle, it certainly does refer to the same estate because a number of documents refer to the purchase from Girolamo, Marco, Niccolo and Paolo di Carlo Strozzi on behalf of Mona Nanna the widow of Ubertino Strozzi, for 1,200 *fiorini di sugello* or 1,000 large gold florins; Strozziane, V, 22, cc. 45 des., 99 sin.–des.; V, 52, c. 5 sin.; 1480 Cat. 1012, II, fol. 263v.

37 'nella muraglia fatta a Chapalle nel palagione'; Strozziane, V, 22, cc. 46 des., 54 des.

38 Strozziane, V, 22, c. 100 des.

39 Strozziane, V, 22, cc. 120 sin., 197 sin.; V, 36, c. 234.

40 Strozziane, V, 22, c. 197 des.; V, 36, cc. 297 des., 192 sin., 206 sin.–des.

41 Strozziane, V, 41, cc. 35 des., 58 sin., 62 sin.; V, 44, cc. 8 des., 30 des., 96 sin., 236 des.

42 Alessandra di Matteo Strozzi married Giovanni di Donato Bonsi in May 1451. Giovanni Bonsi rented a house in town, and since he was not well-off, in 1459 his mother-in-law Alessandra Macinghi Strozzi invited her daughter and husband to come and share her house in town. From this time Alessandra Macinghi Strozzi visited Le Selve regularly; Macinghi Strozzi, *Lettere*, pp. 119, 153, 184, 188, 190, 326.

43 Sale, *The Strozzi Chapel*, p. 21, n. 65; Strozziane, V, 22, c. 93 des.

44 Sale, *The Strozzi Chapel*, appendix A, doc. 3; Strozziane, V, 1165, inserta 23.

45 Borsook, 'Documenti relativi', p. 7, n. 80; Sale, *The Strozzi Chapel*, p. 21, nn. 64, 67; Strozziane V, 22, cc. 56 sin., 31 des. Filippo spent 28 florins on pipes for fresh water and a trough ('nel chondotto del'aqua viva e bottino') and later 21 florins on a stone fountain or water basin ('uno aquale di choncio') and in making ceilings and a stone bench in front of the door ('murare e palchetti e rifare el muriciuolo dinanzi al'uscio').

46 Borsook, 'Documenti relativi', doc. 18; Strozziane, III, 113, c. 60v, in Filippo's letter of 22 April, 1477 to his brother

Lorenzo, he wrote, 'Avixandoti che alla chiesa delle Selvi spendo ora da 100 fiorini'.

47 Borsook, 'Documenti relativi', doc. 54, 55, 56; Strozziane, V, 22, cc. 70 sin., 83 sin.

48 Borsook, 'Documenti relativi', pp. 6, 8, docs. 39–45.

49 Borsook, 'Documenti relativi', pp. 7–8; Craven, 'Aspects of Patronage', appendix, 2, pp. 166–7.

50 Strozziane, V, 41, cc. 22 sin., 29 sin; V, 44, c. 197 sin.

51 Craven, 'Aspects of Patronage', appendix 2, p. 163; Strozziane, V, 1185; Carocci, 'Chiesa e Convento dei SS. Jacopo e Filippo a Lecceto', pp. 61–7; Romagnoli, *L'Eremo di Lecceto*, pp. 10, 16.

52 Romagnoli, *L'Eremo di Lecceto*, p. 10; Craven, 'Aspects of Patronage', p. 164; the sale of a vineyard for 20 florins seems to have funded the initial construction of the church: 'Et fu fondato e cominciata del prezzo e danari d'una vigna la quale donò el magnifico huomo Piero del Pugliese e frate Domenicho Guerrucci per principare detta chiesa si vende fiorini 20 larghi.' Carocci ('Chiesa e Convento de' SS. Jacopo e Filippo a Lecceto') published a copy of Guerrucci's account of the founding of the convent on land donated by the commune of Gangalandi. With the donation of the vineyard by Pugliese, they were able to build the church up to half its height and complete the front façade ('fece . . . fundare la chiesa in sino al mezo e la facia dinanzi'); Borsook, 'Documenti relativi', p. 4, nn. 25, 26. This is confirmed by a payment of 10 florins in January 1478, published by Craven, p. 165: 'spesi a fare tirare su le mure della chiesa infino a braccia cinque o circa da ogni parte e nelle cose come sassi, calcina, rena, manovali e magisterio.' An account for the large stone oculus in the main façade was also billed to Piero del Pugliese in 1477.

53 Borsook, 'Documenti relativi', doc. 18; Strozziane, III, 133, c. 60v, 'in un'altra chiexa in lasù credo spenderne 2 volte tanti'.

54 Borsook ('Documenti relativi', doc. 26) described this as a builders' contract, but it is a stonemasons' contract, as Goldthwaite noted ('The Building of the Strozzi Palace', p. 110, n. 11). The contract was signed by Filippo Strozzi and three *scarpellini*, Bernardo di Simone di Giovanni da Fiesole, Chimenti di Nanni di Niccolo from Signa and Nichodemo di Giovanni from Fiesole. In the event, Bernardo di Simone dropped out, and the local man, Chimenti di Nanni, was placed in charge with Nichodemo and another mason, Fantasia, working under him. See n. 60, this chapter.

55 Borsook, 'Documenti relativi', p. 4, n. 41; Strozziane, III, 93 (Spogli), c. 159r. This is interesting evidence for the switch in patrons, since Pugliese had funded construction of the façade, but Strozzi was now permitted to place his own coat of arms there. For an illuminating analysis of the patronage rights at Lecceto, see Jill Burke, 'Form and Power', ch. 5, "Patronage Rights and Wrongs: Building Identity at Santa Maria a Lecceto."

56 Borsook, 'Documenti relativi', doc.19; Strozziane, V, 22, c. 108r–v.

57 The first account referring to Stefano Rosselli's work for Lecceto are payments for large pieces of timber and for builders

working for him on 23 June 1480; Strozziane, V, 36, c. 39 sin.

58 The main accounts for construction at Lecceto during this busy period are Strozziane, V, 36, cc. 11, 39, 44, 46, 48.

59 Strozziane, V, 36, c. 48 sin., 6 October 1480.

60 A detailed and precise account for stonework lists the carved stone features with their measurements; Strozziane, V, 36, c. 48 sin, (1480), partly published by Borsook, 'Documenti relativi', doc. 27. 'E adì xiiii di settenbre F. sei s.iii d.viii a oro larghi . . . paghamo per lui [Guerrucci] a Chimenti e Fantasia e compagni scharpellini, ebono contanti, portò Chimenti detto; sono per resto di L. 395 s. 8 piccioli per vi pezzi di lastronciegli lunghi braccia 1 1/2 e larghi 2/3 di braccio, e per 185 inchatoie inpionbate nel lavorio della chappella, e viii braccia di bastone sotto l'arco del chanpanile, e ii finestre inn archo di soglia di braccia x l'una, e xx pezi di schaglioncieglì a bracia 1 1/2 l'uno per la schala del chanpanile, e una balestiera pel chanpanile e 24 pietruzze ferrate per le finestre, usci a braccia l'una, e per rifare ii arche alle finestre e braccia 30 di chantoni a ii chanti della chapella e 65 braccia di chornicie a braccia 10 di recholi sotto la chornice di Matteo Bazani e 4 leghatoi per la tronba delle finestre e per la livrea in tondo nel cholmo della chappella e una finestra doppia sopra alla sachrestia di braccia 12, e per rifacimento di dua usci che l'anno a ffare chola soglia a bastone. In tutto monta chome detto d'acordo . . . F.6 s.3 d.8'.

61 A series of major payments to Maestro Stefano Rosselli for the builders and carpenters contracted by him was made on 29 December 1480 for work done between 19 June and 18 November 1480. Stefano Rosselli's final payment was made on 23 March 1481, suggesting that his role as contractor and supervisor for the project was over by then; Strozziane, V, 36, c.46 sin. Burke ('Form and Power', p. 100, n. 54) found a payment for whitewashing the church interior on 8 September 1480, showing that construction was over by then.

62 Borsook, 'Documenti relativi', p. 4, n. 40.

63 Borsook, 'Documenti relativi', pp. 5, 20, doc. 64; Strozziane, V, 36, c. 66 sin.

64 Borsook, 'Documenti relativi', pp. 3, 4, 14, doc. 15; Strozziane, V, 36, c. 66 sin., 'una pila di marmo chol piedistallo'.

65 Borsook, 'Documenti relativi', pp. 5–7, 17; docs. 32, 34–36, p. 20, docs. 67, 68.

66 Borsook, 'Documenti relativi', pp. 4, 7, 17; doc. 38, Strozziane, V, 1769, c. 42 des.; p. 18; doc. 53, Strozziane, V, 36, c. 381 sin.

67 Borsook, 'Documenti relativi', p. 5, n. 42; Goldthwaite, 'The Building of the Strozzi Palace', p. 109. Timber was sent from Santuccio in March 1487, 'per la muraglia della chasa d'abitazione a Licieto', Strozziane, V, 41, c. 35, des.; V, 44, c. 29. In 1487 Fra Alessandro da Pistoia was in charge, 'per farvi una chasa da potervi abitare i forestieri, uno forno e una stalla'; Strozziane, V, 44, c. 235 des.

68 Strozziane, V, 41, c. 29 sin.: 'Limoxine deono dare . . . s. 13 d. 11 . . . a Frate Domenicho Gueruci romito al Licieto per socerimento della festa fatta il dì di Santo Jaco[po] e di San

Filippo'. There are similar accounts in 1486, 1489 and 1491; Strozziane, V, 51, cc. 51 sin., 112 sin, 127 sin.

69   Repetti, II, p. 666: the church was reconsecrated to Saints James and Philip in 1587.

70   Strozziane, V, 36, c. 361 sin.

71   Strozziane, V, 41, c. 29 sin., December 1484. Strozziane, V, 36, c. 369 sin., March 1486.

72   Strozziane, V, 36, c. 369.

73   Burke, 'Form and Power', p. 96.

74   Fischer, *Fra Bartolommeo. Master Draughtsman*, pp. 395–8; Fischer, 'Fra Bartolommeo's Landscape Drawings', pp. 319, 322, 324.

75   Richa, *Notizie storiche*, VII, 1758, 2, p. 113.

76   Carocci, 'Chiesa e convento de' SS. Iacopo e Filippo a Lecceto', p. 62. Guerrucci was succeeded by Fra Alessandro da Pistoia from 1486 to 1488 (Strozziane, V, 36, cc. 369 sin., 390 sin.; V, 41, cc. 35 des., 75 des.); Fra Michelangelo da Cortona, *vicario* in 1489 (Strozziane, V, 51, c. 51 sin); Fra Bartolommeo *vicario* in 1490 (Strozziane, V, 51, c. 112 sin.), perhaps Fra Bartolommeo da Faenza, who was later prior at San Marco; Fra Ambrogio da Milano, also *priore* in 1490 (Strozziane, V, 36, c. 390 sin.), Fra Domencio di Maxo, *vicario* from 1491 (Strozziane, V, 51, c. 112 sin.; V, 36, c. 414 sin.), and Fra Girolamo d'Ascoli *vicario* in 1496 (Strozziane, III, 133, cc. 179–180).

77   Fra Bartolommeo was living at the convent of San Marco in 1498 and joined the order as a novice at S. Domenico in Prato in July 1500; his presence at Lecceto is documented in 1516, although Fischer considers the drawings more likely to have been executed between 1498 and 1504; Fischer, *Fra Bartolommeo. Master Draughtsman*, pp. 27, 30, 398.

78   This added height also accounts for the odd position of the Strozzi coat of arms at the end of the dormitory, since it would originally have been in the usual position at the top of the building.

79   Romagnoli (*L'Eremo di Lecceto*, pp. 17, 20) uses a description of the building written by a Dominican friar Serafino Razzi in 1596 and evidence from the nineteenth-century renovations to draw slightly different conclusions.

80   Borsook, 'Documenti relativi', p. 4, nn. 31–34, p. 16 doc. 26; Strozziane, III, 93 (Spogli), pp. 199–200.

81   See Borsook, 'Documenti relativi', for illustrations of the church at Lecceto. Borsi (*Alberti*, p. 289) suggests that the divergent pilasters framing the apse of San Martino a Gangalandi may be part of an optical experiment devised by Alberti and executed inaccurately by local builders. Spallanzani ('L'Abside dell'Alberti a San Martino a Gangalandi', pp. 247–50) published the documents for the construction of the apse, demonstrating that it was almost entirely built after Alberti's death. It seems to me unlikely that this was an error on the part of clumsy local builders, especially since it was repeated by another group of stonemasons within a decade at Lecceto and at the Badia a Settimo. See now Morolli, 'Gangalandi'.

82   See letter quoted on p. 84.

83   The correspondence between Filippo and his brother Lorenzo over the purchase of the villa at Santuccio was reported by Filippo in his *ricordi*, Strozziane, V, 22, c. 102 des. (1477). See Chapter 8, pp. 148–9.

84   Strozziane, V, 22, c. 109 des.(1478).

85   The building accounts survive: Strozziane, V, 39. The cover is inscribed: 'Debitori e Coreditori dela Muraglia del Santuccio. 1482. Segnato "A".' I dealt with the building of the villa at Santuccio at greater length in my M. A. report for the Courtauld Institute of Art, University of London, 1977, 'Santuccio: One of Filippo Strozzi's Villas near Florence'.

86   Construction at Santuccio was timed to overlap with the building of Filippo's provisional town house begun in April 1482 and structurally complete by August 1483.

87   Strozziane, V, 39, c. 29 sin.

88   Strozziane, V, 39, c. 45 sin.

89   Strozziane, V, 39, cc. 45 des., 61 sin.

90   Strozziane, V, 39, c. 65 sin.

91   Goldthwaite, 'The Building of the Strozzi Palace', pp. 106, 109.

92   1427 Cat. 45, fol. 486r; 1430 Cat. 405, fol. 117v; 1442 Cat. 617, fol. 450v; 1446 Cat. 664, fol. 194r; 1451 Cat. 700, fol. 167v; 1469 Cat. 914, fol. 395r.

93   (Simone Grazzini) Not. antecos. 10189 (1476–8), fol. 188r (14 July 1477).

94   Strozziane, V, 41, c. 51 sin, 'tanti asengnia avere spesi in murare l'agiunta alla chasa da signiore del mio podere al Santucio da dì 22 di febraio 1482 sino a dì iii di questo [January 1486] in a fare palcho e schale e volte ala chasa vechia, e logia detro chon chamere, verone, volte, pollaio, chucina, stalle e matonare le corti e horticini'.

95   Strozziane, V, 39, cc. 4, 8, 37, 66.

96   Strozziane, V, 39, c. 45 sin. (5 February 1484), 'per più conci di priete cioè davanzali, finestre, cholonne e altro, tutto posto al Santuccio . . . L.340'. I have not found reference to Girolamo d'Antonio on any of Filippo Strozzi's other buidling projects.

97   Strozziane, V, 39, c. 61 sin. (16 December 1484), 'Una bandiera chon uno palo di ferro coll'arme degli Strozi pesò libbre 20 in tutto per al Santuccio'; ibid. (12 February 1485) a payment to Marchino Ottavio, 'per doratura della palla della bandiera'.

98   Strozziane, V, 21, c. 18 des. (4 November 1487), 'F.1 . . . per 2 croci per detto oratorio cioè una per in sul chanpanella e ll'altra sulla chiesa di detto oratorio'.

99   Strozziane, V, 39, c. 45 sin. (24 December 1483), 'L.38 . . . per dipintura di regholi 330 a L. 5 al cento e braccia 230 di liste e chornice a L. 9 s. 6 al cento'; c. 61 sin. (16 October 1484), 'L. 6 s. 3 . . . per isgraffiare fregi e archali e pillastri'. Painted celings were one of Bernardo di Stefano Rosselli's specialities, but he often contracted the work out; see Thomas, *The Painter's Practice*, p. 266; Rizzo, 'Soffiti lignei', p. 97.

100 Strozziane, V, 21, c. 18 sin. (7 November 1487), 'L. 10 . . . per dipintura di detta chrocie per l'altare di detto oratorio'; Sale pp. 20, 62 n. 59, 521 doc. 26.

101 Strozziane, V, 21, c. 20 sin. (16 January 1488–9), 'F. 2 s. 2 d. 3 . . . per dipintura del'archeto sopra alla porta di detto horatorio fattovi uno San Giovanni nel diserto'; Sale, pp. 20,

62, n. 59, 521 doc. 24. Bartoli (*Biagio d'Antonio*, pp. 104–6) has misunderstood the documents and assumes that the 'oratorio di S. Giovanni' was part of the church of Lecceto, whereas it certainly refers to the oratory beside the villa of Santuccio. Although the oratory survives, its doorway was demolished, leaving no trace of a fresco.

102 Strozziane, V, 41, cc. 155 des.–156 des.; V, 22, c. 86 sin.

103 Strozziane, V, 41, cc. 156 des.–157 des., 161 des.–162 sin., 163 des., 171 des., 176 des.

104 Strozziane, V, 41, c. 36 sin. (1484); Lillie, 'The patronage of villa chapels', nn. 70–1.

105 Strozziane, V, 44, c. 113 sin, 'per tanti n'asegnia aver spesi sino a questo dì in fare raconciare la casa da oste per potervi abitare sul podere di Maglio congiunta con la casa del suo lavoratore, e una chapanna e uno' dificio da olio dirinpitto a detta chasa; e fare una chasa nuova dal lavoratore dal champo di Piso dove sta Ghabriello di Giovenale chon una stalla e chapanna; e per uno condotto d'acqua viva chondotta dove disegnia fare una chaxa il nostro maggiore . . . F. 623. 10. 2'. The much larger sum of 1,797 florins recorded by Sale (*The Strozzi Chapel*, p. 26, n. 93) included the purchase of land and farmhouses. Comparatively little was spent on construction itself, but a considerable amount on land and agricultural improvement.

106 Strozziane, V, 41, c. 161 des: 'Una presa di terra di staiora iii incircha asieme, parte lavoratia e ulivata, parte soda e parte boschata posta sul pogetto dove disengnio f[a]re la casa per abitare'.

107 Strozziane, IV, 358.

108 Filippo Strozzi's father Matteo used the local priest as paymaster at Quaracchi; see Chapter 4, p. 75. Bartolommeo Sassetti also made use of a priest to supervise construction of his villa at Valcenni; see Chapter 9, p. 178.

109 Goldthwaite, 'The Building of the Strozzi Palace', pp. 119–20, 136–42.

110 De la Mare, 'Messer Piero Strozzzi', pp. 55–67.

111 Strozziane, V, 22, c. 57 des. (1476): Filippo paid F. 21 for the papal bull granting him the patronage of the church of S. Piero a Ripoli; c. 59 sin. (1476): 'Il padronagio della chiexa di San Piero in Piano di Ripoli chonciedutoci Papa Sisto a stanza dello Maestà del Signor Re Ferdinando, cioè a Lorenzo e a me, chon condizione che in fra 4 anni da dì dela data che fu di luglio 1475 dobiamo spendere in aumentatazione delle rendite F. 1,500 d'oro. De' dare adì xxx di dicienbre F. 21 s. 1 d. 3 larga per la mia metà di F. 42 s. 2 d. 6 a oro s'è speso sino a questo dì e trane la bolla e cioè la prexentata fatta quì in Firenze al Rettore della chiesa, cioè a Messer Piero degli Strozzi'; c. 98 des. (1475), 'Ricordo come del prexente mese di luglio la Santita di Papa Sisto a chontenplatione e richiesta della Maesta del Re Ferrando' a chonciedato a me e a Lorenzo mio [fratello] che siamo da ogi inanzi padroni della chiesa di San Piero a Ripoli; chon questa chondizione che in fra 4 anni dobiamo aver speso in beni di rendita a detta chiexa F. 500 d'oro e che da ora ne dobiamo dare mallevadore. E più dobiamo hobrigharci alla chamera apostolicha che ongni volta che detta chiexa vacassi e noi avesimo eletto il piovano o rettore che infra 6 mesi arà paghato la tassa hordinata a

Roma overo a detta chamera, se non di pagharlla noi'. See also Borsook, 'Documenti relativi', n. 4 and doc. 18; De la Mare, 'Messer Piero Strozzi', nn. 16 and 19, pl. 16b, publishes a letter from Messer Piero Strozzi to Filippo Strozzi of 27 August 1474 which seems to be a reply to Filippo's request for information about the church at Ripoli, its status, its dependent clergy, its patrons and the population of its parish. King Ferrante of Naples' intervention on behalf of Filippo and Lorenzo Strozzi was probably also a way of bestowing charity on Messer Piero Strozzi, who had made fine copies of manuscripts for Ferrante, his father Alfonso I and his brother Alfonso Duke of Calabria; De la Mare, p. 58, n. 33, appendix II, no. 4, 26, 27, 28, 32, 33, 36.

112 Sale, *The Strozzi Chapel*, p. 20, n. 56; Strozziane, V, 21, c. 60 des.

113 Strozziane, V, 22, c. 96 (1473).

114 Goldthwaite, 'The Building of the Strozzi Palace', pp. 106–7, n. 8.

115 Goldthwaite, 'The Building of the Strozzi Palace', p. 109.

116 Strozziane, V, 36, cc. 11 sin., 39 sin., 44 sin., 48 sin., 66 sin.

117 Strozziane, V, 36, c. 66 sin, 'per sua faticha d'esser ito più volte al Lecieto quando visi murano a ddare disegni e per prestatura di chanapi e taglie e altre cose'.

118 Strozziane, IV, 358.

119 Strozziane, V, 44, c. 12 des, 'per suo salario d'aver tenuto conto della muraglia di Maglio e solecitato e maestri e quello è achaduto per bisogni di detta muraglia dal dì si cominciò sino finita'.

120 Goldthwaite, 'The Building of the Strozzi Palace', pp. 136–7.

121 Strozziane, V, 39, c. 61 sin.

122 1480 Cat. 1014, I, fol. 65r-v: 'Vendela [his half of a town house] che mi ttrovavo debito e lle fanciulle senza dota e non avevo altro modo nel'aiutare il debito nellaffare le dote, se non chol vendere la metà questa chasa; però ci sto la più partte in villa e quanddo vengho a Ffirenze me ttornno quanddo chon uno e quando chon un'altro de' mie' parentti, epure n'a bisognia torre una chasa a ppigione e però vi priego mi difalchiate F. 24 per detta pigione'.

123 Strozziane, V, 36, c. 362 sin.; V, 44, c. 134 sin.

CHAPTER 6   THE ARCHITECTURE OF A *CASA DA SIGNORE*: SANTUCCIO

1 The analysis of Santuccio which follows is based on close examination and photographic and measuring campaigns carried out in 1976 and 1980, before the recent conversion to apartments. I am most grateful to Giuliana Salvadore and her family, who originally gave me permission to survey the building, and to Maresa D'Arcangelo and all the present occupants of Santuccio, who so generously allowed me to visit and rephotograph the house.

2 The fortified structure of the Villa Salviati was retained through successive renovation campaigns in 1445, 1493–1526 and 1568–73; *Archivio Salviati*, pp. 48–54.

3　At Petraia the tower and castellated aspect were preserved during the renovation campaigns of the 1590s and 1620s; Zangheri, *Ville della Provincia di Firenze*, p. 79.

4　The document is quoted in full in Chapter 5, n. 94.

5　See Chapter 5, p. 96.

6　P. J. Jones ('Florentine Families', p. 188, n. 39, p. 189) states that the Rocca di Campi was not built until after 1370. If Litta (tav. III) is right in saying that Carlo di Strozza was declared a rebel in 1378, left for Ferrara and died away from Florence in 1383, it is likely that the Rocca was mostly built between 1370 and 1378. See also Lamberini and Lazzereschi, *Campi*, pp. 259–62, 272.

7　The Medici villas of Trebbio, Cafaggiolo and Careggi were all machicolated as were the Strozzi castles of Loiano and the Rocca di Campi.

8　Gori-Sassoli, 'Michelozzo'.

9　Saalman, 'The Palazzo Comunale in Montepulciano', pp. 18–28.

10　Strozziane, V, 41 c. 95 sin., 'E adì V di dicienbre [1489] . . . asengnia Piero di Messer Michele Strozzi avere speso da dì primo di giungio sino a questo dì per alzare la corte e cholonbaia della mia abitazione al Santucio'.

11　The Capitani di Parte map of c. 1585 shows what are probably farm buildings between the *casa da signore* and the river, which would support the suggestion that this area was mostly designated for agricultural purposes. The late eighteenth- or nineteenth-century mural in the villa, now destroyed, showed a walled garden on that side of the house.

12　Strozziane, V, 41, cc. 35 des., c. 96 sin., the 'portico della corte del forno' and the 'corte della chucina' were probably the same thing and may well have been where the old bread oven existed until the 1980s, at the far eastern end of the new wing, beyond the Ionic portico.

13　Foster, 'A Study of Lorenzo de' Medici's Villa', pp. 88–91; whenever Lorenzo de' Medici visited Poggio a Caiano from the time he bought the estate in 1475 until his death in 1492, he stayed in the old villa called Ambra.

14　See Chapter 10, p. 186.

15　John Shearman informed me that the covered parapet around the tower at the Medici villa of Trebbio had been used for drying flax.

16　Goldthwaite and Rearick, 'Michelozzo and the Ospedale of San Paolo', pp. 252–8.

17　Carocci, *I Dintorni*, I, pp. 174–5; Patzak, *Palast und Villa*, II, pp. 134–5, n. 331, pl. LVIII.

18　The work on the apse of San Martino a Gangalandi, completed in 1473 and 1474 with funds left by Leon Battista Alberti in his will, did not include the portico on the side of the church; Spallanzani, 'L'Abside dell'Alberti a San Martino a Gangalandi', pp. 241–50.

19　Calzolai (*La Storia della Badia a Settimo*, p. 123) records that Filippo di Ubertino Peruzzi donated funds in 1449 to build a cloister at Settimo modelled on the one at San Lorenzo. It was begun in 1461–62.

20　Onians (*Bearers of Meaning*, pp. 190–1) notes that the 'simple forms' of Ionic were associated 'with the simple villa life, perhaps by analogy with the use of the simple Ionic in

monasteries'. Onians cites the small entrance loggia of the Villa Cardinal Bessarion in Rome (1460s–70s) and Poggio a Caiano, as examples of the use of Ionic in fifteenth-century villas.

21　1469 Cat. 925, I, fol. 64r; 1480 Cat. 1019, II, fol. 6v–7r. Querci ('L'Architettura di villa', p. 43) dates the villa on stylistic grounds to c. 1455, but the tax returns document a construction date in the 1470s.

22　Querci ('L'architettura di villa', pp. 35–54) dates La Bartolina and Villa da Cignano on stylistic grounds to the mid–fifteenth century, whereas I believe they are more likely to date from the period between 1460 and 1490. For other examples of the use of the Ionic order, see Patzak, *Palast und Villa*, vol. II, pp. 135–6, 138, pl. LX: Villa Bombicci-Pontelli at S. Donato; pl. LXI: Villa Coroni at Smilea; pl. LXII: Villa Belevedere at Careggi.

23　Strozziane, V, 39 c. 45 sin., 'per più concci di priete cioè davanzali, finestre, cholonne e altro tutto posto al Ssanttuccio'.

24　Sale (*The Strozzi Chapel*, pp. 83–100) deals at length with the Strozzi coat of arms and Filippo's personal devices and their meanings.

25　Strozziane, V, 39, c. 61 sin.

26　Thiem, *Fassaden-Dekoration*, pp. 59–60, 72, pl. 21–4, 50–2; the façades of Palazzo Gerini (c.1450) and Palazzo Nasi (c. 1460–70) include *sgraffito* pilasters between the *piano nobile* windows. The Palazzo Spinelli façade decoration (1460–70) includes elaborate play with the family *imprese*; ibid. pp. 73–74, pl. 53–4. A fragment of an urn once visible in the frieze at Santuccio is very similar to the urns incised in the courtyard of the Palazzo Coverelli, (c. 1470), ibid. pp. 81–2, pl. 68–9.

27　Neilson, *Filippino Lippi*, pp. 68–9; see also Chapter 7, pp. 140–43.

28　Strozziane, V, 39 c. 45 sin.

29　Restored *lavabi* still survive in the Strozzi Palace in Florence; Pampaloni, *Palazzo Strozzi*, pl. XXXIII.

CHAPTER 7　VILLA INTERIORS

1　Klapisch-Zuber, 'Mezzadria e insediamenti rurali', p. 162, 'Casa il più delle volte rudimentale e poco confortevole, se si deve fare affidamento sugli inventari delle ricordanze. . . . Il più delle volte è ammobiliata soltanto con qualche lettiera, panche, tavole, e forzieri necessari all'accampamento estivo di una famiglia urbana. Nelle immediate vicinanze di Firenze, la *casa da signore* è più spesso equipagiata e arredata riccamente, per divenire un simbolo della vita nobile, un segno di prestigio sociale.' See also Mazzi, 'Arredi e masserizie della casa rurale'.

2　Only one of the three kitchens was equipped for daily use.

3　Strozziane, IV, 66, cc. 1v–3r. The Palagio at Campi was rebuilt in the eighteenth century, and no trace of its fifteenth-century interiors are visible.

4　For the form and functions of the *lettuccio*, see Trionfi Honorati, 'A proposito del "lettuccio"'; P. Thornton, *Italian Renaissance Interior*, pl. 90, pp. 90, 94; pl. 162, 167, pp. 149–53; Goldthwaite, *Wealth and the Demand for Art*, p. 229; Lydecker,

The Domestic Setting, p. 71; D. Thornton, *The Scholar in His Study*, pp. 59–62; Quinterio, *Giuliano da Maiano*, p. 61. The *cappellinaio* frequently referred to in inventories attached to *lettucci* was not a hat rack as has sometimes been supposed, but the high back, often topped by a cornice, visible in many prints and paintings of the period.

5 Edler de Roover, 'Per la storia dell'arte della stampa'; Gregory, 'A Florentine Family in Crisis', pp. 195, 218, n. 97.

6 Strozziane, IV, 66, c. 2v.; the *granaio* is listed between the first floor *camera* and the *androne*.

7 Strozziane, IV, 66, cc. 3r–v.

8 Strozziane, IV, 66, cc. 41r–v., 42r, 91v, 154 des., 156 sin.–des., 157 sin.–des., 158 des., 159 des., 161 des., 164 sin.–des., 167 des.

9 Strozziane, IV, 66, cc. 156 des., 'MCCCCLXVIII Anto[nio] di Nanni da Settignano de' avere adì primo d'aprile per questi conci qui a pie 'di soglia overo pichiati per s.vii il braccio, ii stipiti di braccia 3 1/8, e ii becchategli di braccia iii, una tavola di braccia 4, una cornice di braccia v, per un cammino per la sala a Campi, in tutto braccia XV 1/8 per soldi vii il braccia, montano in tutto lire cinque soldi xii . . . L. 5 s. 12 d. – / Uno navicello doppio di braccia 5 1/8, ii stipiti di braccia V 1/8, un cardinale di braccia ii 1/2, una corrente di braccia iii 1/8, in tutto braccia XVII 5/8, monta per s.vii il braccia, in tutto per l'acquaio per la sala detta, lire sei soldi iii, denari iiii piccoli . . . L. 6 s. 3 d. 4/ Uno uscio, una soglia di braccia ii 1/4, ii stipiti di braccia vii, uno cardinale di braccia ii 1/4, una cornice di braccia ii 1/2 per detto uscio per la sala detta per s.vii il braccia, monta in tutto braccia xiii, lire quatro soldi xviii piccoli . . . L. 4 s. 4 d. – / Una finestra per a Campi, uno davanzale di braccia ii 1/4, ii stipiti di braccia viii 1/2, per s. vii il braccia, monta in tutto lire dua s. xviii d. vi piccoli, posto spese di murare dare in questo in una partita a c. 184 L. 2 s. 19 d. 6. This stonemason was working in the nave of Arezzo cathedral in 1471; Quinterio, *Giuliano da Maiano*, p. 223.

10 Strozziane, IV, 66, c. 164 des., 'E adì detto [9 June 1470] lire dodici s.xi e per lui a Francesco di Salvadore legniauolo e per noi a Girolamo Strozzi sono per acconciatura dell'uscio del necessario di chamera terrena e per il descho, palchetti e panche e uscio dello scriptoio e per uno uscio a mezza scala della cucina posto Girolamo avere in questo c. 167 . . . L. 12 s. 11 d. -.'

11 See D. Thornton, *The Scholar in His Study*, for an important investigation into the significance and development of the study in this period, and especially pp. 27–9 for an analysis of their position within the house. See Goldthwaite, *Wealth and the Demand for Art*, pp. 224–43 on the development of luxury and specialisation of function in the domestic interior.

12 Lydecker, *The Domestic Setting of the Arts*, pp. 145–65. See also Goldthwaite, *Wealth and the Demand for Art*, p. 228.

13 'Mi par meglio vada a mio conto acioché ogniuno possa, togliendo donna, spendere il suo a suo modo'; Strozziane, IV, 66, c. 187 des.

14 Strozziane, IV, 66, c. 178 des., 'E adì detto [20 March 1470] lire novantacinque e per noi a Batista di Giovanni dello Squarta sono per una lettiera di braccia v con cassapanche

intorno e chappellinaio e lettuccio di che fece mercato Zanobi Bellandini posto masserizie di casa in questo c. 186 . . . L. 95 -'.

15 Strozziane, IV, 66, fol. 42 r.: 'MCCCCLXVIIII, Martedi adì xviiii di dicembre/ A masserizie di casa lire cinque s.xiiii e per loro a Giuliano legniauolo portò Paolo Strozzi e noi sono per resto ripiallatura d'una lettiera e uno paio di predelle datorno . . . L. 5 s. 14 d. -'. For Giuliano da Maiano's Strozzi commissions, see n. 33 to this chapter; Borsook, 'Documenti relativi', doc. 1; Sale, *The Strozzi Chapel*, pp. 526–7; Quinterio, *Giuliano da Maiano*, pp. 61–2, 68.

16 Strozziane, IV, 66, c. 161 des.: 'E adì viii di febraio lire trentotto s.iiii piccoli e per loro al Mancino legnaiuolo porto contanti per la monta d'un paio di cassoni coperchio piano comprati dallui essermi aportatori gli recharono a nostra in questo c. 48 . . . L. 38 s. 4 d. -'.

17 Strozziane, IV, 66, c. 172 sin.: 'Andrea di Lorenzo legniauolo de' dare adì primo di febraio lire cinque s. xiiii porta detto in F. uno largo sono per arte d'un fornimento mi debbe fare di braccia 4 1/2 coperto di noce in cassapanche e lettuccio a cassone colla predella e tutto mi debbe fare d'asse di mezzo mezzano Papino di Cerbino e tutto mi debbe avere fatto per tutto di xxii di febraio a uscita in questa a c. 42 . . . L. 5 s. 14 d. -'.

18 Strozziane, IV, 66, c. 167 des.: 'E adì xii di maggio 1471 lire venticinque fatti buoni a Francseco di Salvadore legniauolo per facitura d'un desco, una finestra, uno uscio per lo scriptoio; e per uno uscio, una finestra per il necessario; e per uno lettuccio a cassone e per braccia xviiii 1/2 di panche con regoli e cornici e braccia iiii 1/2 di cassette apicchate con dette panche, e per tre palchetti all'acquaio, e per ripiallatura d'una tavola di braccia vi, e ricommettitura di un descho biancho, e peruno uscio alla sala; e per rissettare una lettiera in camera grande a Campi a conto di spesa di casa in questo c. 192'.

19 Lydecker (*The Domestic Setting of the Arts*, pp. 89–90, 100) shows that this was also the case for Marco Parenti and Bernardo Rinieri.

20 See Chapter 9 for the new apartments created in Bartolommeo Sassetti's town house.

21 *Libro d'inventario dei beni di Lorenzo il Magnifico*, pp. 131–62; Pupilli 181, fol. 141r–144r, heirs of Giovanni di Francesco Tornabuoni.

22 Sale, *The Strozzi Chapel*, pp. 12–13, 23–5, 35–6; Borsook, 'Documenti relativi, pp. 3–4, docs. 1–11, 30.

23 Strozziane, V, 22, c. 109 des. (1478), 'Restorono di mio in chasa panche nuove alla sala di giù e'l quella di sù'.

24 Strozziane, V, 22, c. 86 des. (1478): 'per più maserizie . . . ch'erano a Sa' Moro, cioè una letiera chon 2 chassapanche e uno letucio e 4 chasoni e una choltricie e sacone'.

25 Strozziane, V, 36, c. 2 sin. (1482), 17 September: Filippo Strozzi paid F. 10 s. 15 d. 6 to Bernardo di Giovanni and Company, *linaiuoli*, of which 26 lire were for 'una lettiera chole casse compratoci a Enpoli più dì fa per mettere nella chaxa da San Moro nella camera del magiore nostro, e soldi 9 per andarlo a comprare e per mettere ferro alla nostra mula che fu di bracia 5, e lire 6 soldi 19 per braccia 28 1/2 di

schampolone e braccia 5 di lonbardo azurro per fare il sacchone di dua pezze de detto letto e lire 8 soldi 8 denari 9 per braccia 37 1/2 di verde azurro e lire 14 soldi 14 per libre 105 di lana sardescha per una materassa e lire 2 soldi 16 per braccia 11 1/2 di verde azurro e libre 35 di capicchio per uno materassino per il letuccio di detta chamera e lire 2 soldi 19 per fattura del saccone e materassa e materassino sopradetti per detto letto'. The manufacture of beds, *lettucci* and mattresses are a major item in household expense accounts. Beds were the largest, most expensive and grandest object in most houses, and the sums spent on mattresses, hangings, covers and cushions were far greater than those spent on paintings and sculptures. It is easier for us to understand the large cost of mattresses if we remember that these were the upholstery of the fifteenth century, and it was the addition of a *materassino*, cushions and a small carpet or tapestry that turned a hard wooden *lettuccio* into a comfortable daybed or sofa. See Lydecker, *The Domestic Setting of the Arts*, pp. 94–5.

26 Strozziane, V, 36, c. 260, 24 March 1483: 'spese fatte per aconciare la chasa da singniore a San Moro...sono per fare aconciare il letto e letuccio e una pancha drieto a detto letto e per paglia pel sacchone di detto letto per la chamera terena'.

27 Strozziane, V, 36, c. 295 sin., 23 August 1483: 'a Nicholo di Francesco e Co. fanno le tarsie...sono per xvii pezze di più ragione tarsie'; Strozziane, V, 39, c. 29 sin., 23 August 1483: 'a Niccholo delle Tarsie per 17 pezi di tarssie de' quale ne venne 15 al Santuccio.'

28 Strozziane, V, 44, c. 118 sin. 29 December 1487: 'Fiorino uno largho d'oro in oro per loro [Masserizie di chaxa] a Bernardo di Stefano Rossegli dipintore...per oro di foglia e suo faticha messo a dorare ii telai, uno d'una nostra donna e uno della giraffa, sono al Santuccio...F. I s. I d. III.' cf. Sale, *The Strozzi Chapel*, appendix A doc. 19, p. 520. This painted canvas of the Madonna cannot have been Filippino's Strozzi Madonna in the Metropolitan Museum, which is on panel.

29 Strozziane, V, 44, c. 154 sin.; Borsook, 'Documenti relativi', doc. 33: 'F. I d'oro largo per manifatura di dua quadri fiandreschi messi d'oro più fa al Santuccio'. The different cost and dates make it certain that these two Flemish paintings were not the canvasses of the Madonna and the giraffe framed in December 1487. The Strozzi were also involved in the export of Flemish pictures on at least one occasion. Filippo Strozzi's brother Lorenzo sent three canvasses or 'panni dipinti' to his mother from Bruges when he was working in his cousin Jacopo's bank there. One was an Adoration of the Magi, another a peacock, and the third Saint Veronica with the Holy Shroud. Alessandra intended to sell them if she could get a good price, although she thought that being small, they could only fetch three florins each in 1460; Alessandra Macinghi Strozzi, *Lettere*, pp. 224, 230–1, 246. See also Nuttall, 'The Medici and Netherlandish Painting'.

30 In 1481, Bernardo di Stefano Rosselli painted a pair of *cassoni* for Filippo Strozzi, Strozziane, V, 36, c. 138 sin. In January 1483 he was paid to decorate a pair of small chests and to paint shields or roundels, probably with coats of arms; Strozziane, V, 36, c. 240: 'per fornitura e dipintura d'un paio di forzeretti e di VI targiette e sua spese d'ogni fornimento...F. I s. – d. X'. In 1483, he also painted the *scrittoio* in Filippo's reconstructed town house (Borsook, 'Documenti relativi', p. 6, doc. 30) and restored another pair of old coffers (Strozziane, V, 36, c. 317), 'per ripingniere e rasettare uno paio di nostri forzeretti vecchi...F. I s. – d. VIII'. In 1488 he painted the Strozzi coat of arms and Filippo's device of a falcon on six small chests (Borsook, 'Documenti relativi', p. 6, doc. 33) and in 1491 he painted yet another pair of coffers with the family arms and *impresa*, as well as a roundel with the arms of the Strozzi Company (Strozziane, V, 51, c. 138, 4 May 1491): 'per dipintura di uno paio di forzeretti dipintoli a suo livrea con l'arme degli Strozzi e d'un tondo con l'arme degli Strozzi e di conpagni dipintoli più fa...F. I s. I d. VII'. Borsook published the document for the altar frontal at Lecceto, 'Documenti relativi', p. 5–6, doc. 32; and Sale (*The Strozzi Chapel*, p. 67 n. 91) and Pampaloni (*Palazzo Strozzi* p. 41, n. 48) note that Bernardo Rosselli worked on the sgrafitto decoration for Santuccio. He also painted ceilings at the villa, Strozziane, V, 39, c. 45 sin., 46 des. For Bernardo Rosselli's oeuvre, see Padoa Rizzo, 'La Cappella della compagnia di Santa Barbara', pp. 8–9, 11; Padoa Rizzo, 'Ricerche sulla pittura del '400', pp. 20–7; Thomas, *The Painter's Practice*, pp. 266, 305–8, n. 37.

31 Strozziane, V, 44, c. 26 sin.: 'una choltricie nuova piena di penna di pollo...per il letto della schiavetta per al Santuccio'; c. 118 sin. (16 December 1487), 'uno charucio da portare sassi e terra e per piane di castagno per sedili e per uno pomato grande...per al Santuccio'; c. 197 sin. (11 November 1488), 'a Giovanni di Filippo lignaiuolo...sono per 5 opere al Santucio a ffare una littiera per Arigho [Filippo Strozzi's man-servant] e uno chanciello all'orto a soldi 10 il dì...'; Strozziane, V, 51, cc. 58 des., 84 sin.: sheets, blankets, mattresses bought for Santuccio.

32 Strozziane, V, 65, c. 13 des. Another copy of Lorenzo and Filippo the Younger's share of the contents of Santuccio is recorded in Strozziane, V, 54, c. 7 des.–9 sin.

33 Giuliano and Benedetto da Maiano each made a *cassone* for Filippo Strozzi; Giuliano's cost F. 3 s. 3 d. 4 in 1466 and was described as, 'uno chassone choperto di nocie, intarsiato, auto da lui per la chamera di Filippo' (Borsook, 'Documenti relativi', doc. 1); Benedetto's cost eight florins in 1479, 'uno chassone grande intarsiato, chol falchone, arme e divisa, per tenere le mia scriture propie', Borsook, 'Documenti relativi', doc. 14. In 1482 Benedetto da Maiano carved a frame for a steel mirror for Filippo and provided him with a piece of porphyry column and a serpentine roundel; Sale, *The Strozzi Chapel*, appendix A, docs. 44 and 45, p. 526. In 1486 Guiliano da Maiano carved a tabernacle for Filippo's bedroom Madonna; Sale, *The Strozzi Chapel*, appendix A, doc. 46, pp. 526–7. Sale also quotes from the list of objects inherited by Alfonso after his father's death (Strozziane, V, 65, cc. 19 sin.– 20 des.; *The Strozzi Chapel* p. 25 and nn. 85, 86), but, like Craven, he confuses the contents of the town house with those at Santuccio. For Alfonso's share of the works of art inherited from the town house, see n. 51, this chapter.

34 Strozziane, V, 65, c. 14 sin: '1 nostra donna in piano e 3 panni dipinti in telai, cioè 1a nave, 1 chasa che arde con più fantasie e 1a nostra donna per lire 26.'

35 Strozziane, V, 65, c. 15 sin: '5 panni 5 dipinti in telai, cioè 1a oferta di magi, ii lioni, ii chani alani, 1a giraffa e 1a nostra donna, lire 52'.

36 See n. 28, this chapter.

37 Landucci, *Diario Fiorentino*, p. 52; Ildefonso di San Luigi, *Delizie*, vol. 23, pp. 246–7; Lloyd, *African Animals*, p. 49. Although the date when the giraffe painting was gilded makes it most likely that this was a portrait of Lorenzo di Medici's giraffe, Filippo Strozzi would probably have seen King Ferrante's giraffe in Naples at an earlier date, and it is possible that this was an image of the Neapolitan giraffe.

38 Lloyd, *African Animals*, pl. 32 and 33.

39 Strozziane, V, 22, c. 34 sin: '2 panni dipinti, uno di 2 chani e uno di 2 lioni e lioncini'; Sale, *The Strozzi Chapel*, p. 66, n. 86.

40 Villani, *Cronica*, X, 187; Janson, *Donatello*, p. 43, n. 3.

41 *Libro d'inventario dei beni di Lorenzo il Magnifico*, p. 26.

42 Signorini (*Opus hoc tenue*, p. 186) follows Camesasca (*Mantegna*, p. 277) in identifying the two large dogs held by servants to the left of the 'Meeting' as Molossian hounds or mastifs, the category of dog to which Great Danes, or *cani alani*, belong. Ludovico Gonzaga ordered a portrait of one of his Great Danes in 1458 when he wrote to his wife requesting that 'Jacomo iminiatore' paint his 'cani alano da naturale', Signorini, 'Two Notes', p. 319, n. 20.

43 Callmann, *Apollonio di Giovanni*, figs. 53, 54, 55, 147, 186, 205.

44 Borsook, 'Documenti relativi', p. 5, fig. 4, nn. 50, 51; D. Hannema, *Meesterwerkenn uit de Verzameling D. G. van Beuningen* n. 92, pl. 124. Jill Burke ('Form and Power', pp. 102, 106–7) has recently argued that this predella panel is an Annunciation to the Shepherds (rather than a Nativity), in which Filippo Strozzi the patron appears as one the three shepherds.

45 Signorini, *Opus hoc tenue*, pp. 200–9, figs. 89, 112, 113.

46 On the term *fantasìa* and its association with Piero di Cosimo, see Fermor, *Piero di Cosimo*, pp. 29–37. None of Piero di Cosimo's surviving paintings of fire includes a burning house; Fermor, *Piero di Cosimo*, pp. 73–4, 87. Craven (in 'Aspects of Patronage', pp. 102–4, 108–11, and 'Three Dates', pp. 575–6) gives evidence for Filippo Strozzi the Younger's participation in the Triumph of Death Masque in 1506 to which Piero di Cosimo contributed. In 1510, Filippo the Younger paid Piero di Cosimo five florins for unspecified work in his *camera*. Craven suggests this may have been a part payment for Piero di Cosimo's *Liberation of Andromeda* in the Uffizi.

47 *Libro d'inventario dei Beni di Lorenzo il Magnifico*, p. 6; Nuttall, 'The Medici and Netherlandish Painting', p. 144.

48 The Ideal City view in Berlin includes ships in the background.

49 Sale, *The Strozzi Chapel*, appendix A, docs. 14, 16, p. 518.

50 The first of these *lettucci*, ordered for himself from Giuliano da Maiano in 1466, is probably the same *lettucio* recorded in Filippo's *camera* after his death, described as six *braccia* long, with a view of Naples inlaid ('chomesso vi dentro Napoli'), Strozziane, V, 65, c. 19 sin., see the following n. 51. He ordered another, four times more expensive, for King Ferrante of Naples from Benedetto da Maiano in 1473, included in the list of gifts he sent to influential Neapolitans, with the view of Naples described as, 'ritratovi dentro di prospettiva Napoli, el chastello e loro circhustanzie'; Sale, *The Strozzi Chapel*, appendix A, doc. 4, p. 514. Although the latter has recently been interpreted as the definitive document referring to the painting known as the 'Tavola Strozzi' (del Treppo, 'Le aventure storiografiche', pp. 483–515; de Seta, 'The Urban Structure of Naples', p. 370), the terms 'chomesso' and 'prospettiva' were often used in relation to intarsia work in this period, and it is likely that these were both intarsia views of Naples expertly executed by Giuliano da Maiano, and not paintings; see Sricchia Santoro, 'Tra Napoli e Firenze', pp. 44–6. Nevertheless, the dimensions of the Naples picture (2.45 metres x 0.82 metres) make it likey that it was incorporated into a piece of furniture like Strozzi's 6 *braccia* (ie, 3.50 metres) *lettuccio*.

51 Strozziane, V, 65, cc. 19 sin.– 20 des. (1492): 'Apresso sarà nota di masserizie di Firenze'a auto Alfonso . . .

E' legniame bello della chamera di Filippo che si chiama lla chamera nuova . . .

Uno lettuccio di braccia VI in che [? hole] chomesso vi dentro Napoli . . .

Una nostra donna di rilievo . . .

Quatro panni in telaio cioe una chaccia di tori e lioni grande e pichole, e una nostra donna, e una introvi Otranto che è in telaio di legnio, e uno Napoli di legnio in charta pechora in tavola di legnio . . .

Uno tondo di marmo entrovi II teste

Uno tondo introvi una testa di Nerone cholorita di marmo

Una charta di navichare in una ghuaina verde

Una charta in su uno legnio dipintovi Napoli . . .

Uno panno grande dipintovi lioni e chavagli in uno telaio di legnio

Una testa di marmo in impronta di Nico[lo] Strozzi stava nel bancho . . .'

It is tempting to link this document listing two paintings of Naples owned by Filippo Strozzi ('uno Napoli di legnio in charta pechora in tavola di legnio' e 'una charta in su uno legnio dipintovi Napoli') with the view of Naples known as the 'Tavola Strozzi' (Sale, *The Strozzi Chapel*, pp. 24–5), but their supports – one on parchment and the other on paper – attached to wood, do not match the painting now in the Convento di San Martino in Naples. Thus, although Filippo Strozzi commissioned or owned at least four representations of Naples, none of these can be demonstrated unequivocally to be the surviving 'Tavola Strozzi'.

52 Sale, *The Strozzi Chapel*, pp. 110, 135, n. 28; Federico Zeri and Elizabeth Gardner, *Italian Paintings, A Catalogue of the Collection of the Metropolitan Museum of Art*, New York 1971, pp. 167–9, pl. 168; Scharf, *Filippino Lippi*, p. 108; Neilson, *Filippino Lippi*, p. 68.

53   Sale, *The Strozzi Chapel*, pp. 25, 66–7, n. 87, appendix A, doc. 30, p. 522.

54   The number and function of rooms can only be roughly estimated from the plan, the surviving rooms and from scattered references in the documents.

55   See n. 51, this chapter; Strozziane, V, 65, cc. 19 sin.–20 des. (1492); Sale, *The Strozzi Chapel*, p. 25 and n. 85 and 86.

56   Sale published the account for Filippo Strozzi's purchase of the marble roundel from Mino da Fiesole for four florins; *The Strozzi Chapel*, appendix A, docs. 36, 37, p. 24, n. 37.

57   Sale, *The Strozzi Chapel*, p. 15, n. 37. The bust of Niccolò, who had established the bank from which Filippo's wealth derived, was appropriately placed in the Strozzi bank in Florence.

58   The table is based on the following inventories: (Da Uzzano) Bombe, *Nachlass-Inventare*; (Francesco Nori) Pupilli 174, fol. 228r–237v; (Giovanni Tornabuoni) Pupilli 181, fol. 141r–150v; (Pierfrancesco de Medici) Shearman, 'The Collections', appendix, pp. 22–7; and (Lorenzo de' Medici) *Libro d'inventario dei beni di Lorenzo il Magnifico*.

59   Bombe, *Nachlass-Inventare*, p. 36.

60   For 'panni dipinti', see Nuttall, 'The Medici and Netherlandish Painting', pp. 139–44.

61   The predominance of religious images in fifteenth-century domestic interiors is an art-historical commonplace; see Wackernagel, *The World of the Florentine Renaissance Artist*, pp. 94, 102–3, 172, 175.

62   What makes the Palazzo Medici unusual is not simply the larger proportion of secular subjects, but the fact that only four of the paintings were plain Madonnas (although there were also nine sculptures of the Madonna) and the religious works tended to be by famous painters (Giotto, Masaccio, Fra Angelico, Pesellino, Squarcione, Jan Van Eyck and Petrus Christus) or to have narrative subjects (eg, the Agony in the Garden, the Judgment of Solomon and Moses Crossing the Red Sea), or to be a favourite theme of the family (eg, the six Adorations of the Magi, the four St. Jeromes, Judith with the Head of Holofernes).

63   *Libro d'inventario dei beni di Lorenzo il Magnifico*, p. 202: 'Otto tavolette dipintovi più figure di Nostra Donna e altri santi per uso delle chamere, chi di legno e chi di que' panni franzesi'.

64   It is important to distinguish as far as possible between different types of animal subject matter and to see whether these relate to their location. For example, in the Strozzi town house, the two large animal pictures allotted to Alfonso – a hunt with lions and bulls and a picture of lions and horses – almost certainly relate to the revival of ancient Roman games such as the fight with lions and horses put on in the Piazza Signoria to entertain Pope Pius II and Galeazzo Sforza in 1459, rather than to hunting in the normal sense; Landucci, *Diario Fiorentino*, p. 347; Cambi, XX, p. 370; Lloyd, *African Animals*, pp. 39–40; Trexler, *Public Life*, p. 263. This type of picture therefore belonged in town rather than at the villa. Filippo's predilection for animal paintings is also documented in the list of objects in his Neapolitan palace in 1487. The works of art there included two painted dogs and a picture of animals; Strozziane, V, 46, c. 109 des., 'due chane

dipinte'; c. 110 des., 'Una tavola dipinta d'animali'. Likewise, Lorenzo de' Medici hung a battle between dragons and lions by Uccello and a hunt by Pesellino as part of a series with the Battles of San Romano in his ground-floor *camera*, while another large canvas by Pesellino depicting lions in a cage was hung above a doorway in the *sala* on the *piano nobile* of Palazzo Medici; *Libro d'inventario dei beni di Lorenzo il Magnifico*, p. 26. Although the hunt by Pesellino might have been appropriate in the country, the chivalric battle between dragons and lions was congruent with the other Uccello battles, whereas Pesellino's lions in a cage may have related to the real lions owned by the Florentine Signoria. Pierfrancesco de' Medici owned no animal paintings in his villas, but in town he hung a canvas simply described as 'animali', together with a hunt of lions and bulls, that may have been another version of Filippo Strozzi's picture of the same subject; Shearman, 'The Collections', p. 25, no. 46 and 47. No animal pictures are mentioned in the other inventories examined here, although it is important to remember that they are featured in many tapestries. In Pierfrancesco de' Medici's house, the two animal paintings were hung together with a tapestry of animals and verdure; Shearman, 'The Collections' p. 25.

65   In the context of the Medici *sala*, lions were an appropriate adjunct to the Hercules cycle as heraldic civic icons as well as being part of the Hercules story; Bulst, 'Uso e trasformazione del Palazzo Mediceo, p. 113, and 'Die *sala grande* des Palazzo Medici', pp. 100, 106–9; A. Wright, 'The Myth of Hercules', pp. 325–6.

CHAPTER 8   VILLA FUNCTIONS AND ATTITUDES

1   Herlihy, 'The Problem of the "Return to the Land"', pp. 401, 405; Cherubini, 'Qualche considerazione', p. 77.

2   Conti, *Le Campagne*, p. 2; P. J. Jones, 'Medieval Agrarian Society', p. 350; Pinto 'Ordinamento', p. 228; Herlihy, 'The Problem of the "Return to the Land"', pp. 401–2.

3   Cherubini, 'Qualche considerazione', p. 95; Alberti, *I Libri della famiglia*, p. 195.

4   Fiumi, 'Sui Rapporti economici', p. 67: 'quella professione per la quale non si muore mai di fama nè si ha mai un soldo in tasca'.

5   Alberti, *I Libri della famiglia*, Lib. III, pp. 198–9: 'Quale uomo fusse, il quale non si traesse piacere della villa? Porge alla villa utile grandissimo, onestissimo e certissimo. E pruovasi qualunque altro essercizio intopparsi in mille pericoli, hanno seco mille sospetti, seguongli molti danni e molti pentimenti: in comperare cura, in condurre paura, in serbare pericolo, in vendere sollicitudine, in credere sospetto, in ritrarre fatica, nel commutare inganno. E così sempre degli altri essercizii ti premono infiniti affanni e agonie di mente. La villa sola sopra tutti si truova conoscente, graziosa, fidata, veridica. Se tu la governi con diligenza e con amore, mai a lei parerà averti satisfatto; sempre agiugne premio a' premii';

trans. Watkins, *The Family in Renaissance Florence*, pp. 191–2 [translation amended by the author].

6 Alberti, *L'Architettura*, V, xiv; *I Libri della famiglia*, p. 199.

7 Pinto, 'Coltura', pp. 277–9.

8 Klapisch-Zuber, 'Blood Parents and Milk Parents'.

9 Alessandra Macinghi Strozzi, *Lettere*, p. 61: 'ed è fatto un bello garzoncello in questo tempo è stato in villa; che avendol veduto prima, e vedendo ora, è rimutato'; trans. Gregory, *Selected Letters of Alessandra Strozzi*, pp. 51–3.

10 Alberti, *Della Famiglia*, p. 201: 'Quanto io, a vivere con manco vizio, con meno maninconie, con minore spesa, con più sanità, maggiore suavità del vivere mio, sì bene, figliuoli miei, che io lodo la villa'.

11 Alessandra Macinghi Strozzi, *Lettere*, p. 89, 22 October 1450: 'mentre è la moria...le genti dabbene son tutti fuori Firenze'. See also her letter of 22 March 1463/4, p. 274: 'Credo bene che fatto pasqua, chi arà villa che vi sia buona istanza, vi s'andrà a stare.'

12 Alessandra Macinghi Strozzi, *Lettere*, p. 91 (A).

13 Alessandra Macinghi Strozzi, *Lettere*, p. 85.

14 Alessandra Macinghi Strozzi, *Lettere*, p. 89.

15 Alessandra Macinghi Strozzi, *Lettere*, p. 92 (A).

16 Alessandra Macinghi Strozzi, *Lettere*, p. 55, 26 December 1449: 'cominciando la moria a Quaracchi, allato a noi'. The following year it spread further into the *contado*; ibid., p. 82, 5 June 1450; 'Non si potrà quest'anno fuggire pelle ville, chè quasi per tutto il contado fa gran danno, e massimo in questo nostro piano; che da Peretola insino a Prato non è villa che non ne muoia; eccetto che a Quaracchi non v'è nulla ancora; ma a Campi fa gran fracasso.'

17 Strozziane, III, 131, c. 38: 'Io mi sto in villa chome gli altri, che in Firenze è pocha gente e nulla vi si fa e in pochi dì stimo andarne in Mugello dove si chiama Pulicciano e conta e vi fuggito tutto Firenze per migliore stanza sia nel chontado. In Firenze ve muore da X in XVI per dì.'

18 Strozziane, III, 131, c. 40: 'No' siamo, in mentre che la stanza è buona qui a Quaracchi nella casa di Agnolone; e se nulla ci sarà, andremo in Mugiello in chasa di Marcho e della Chaterina, overamente andremo a Fegine [*sic*: Figline] di Prato che per ora v'è buona istanza nel'un luogo e nel'altro'; for Guasti's transcription, see Alessandra Macinghi Strozzi, *Lettere*, p. 53.

19 Rucellai, 'Il Zibaldone', I, p. 123, n. 4. See also Corradi, *Annali delle epidemie*, I, pp. 188–299 (1348–1457).

20 Strozziane, V, 10, cc. 58 sin., 75 sin., 77 des., 125.

21 1446 Cat. 671, II, fol. 534r: 'Una possessione ch'i'o comprata da Michele di Nofri Parenti in quel di Monterchio chon una chasa in detto chastello per abitazione mia. E una vigna di fuori soda e disfatta e terre da pane, per tutto F.CC; non se n' chava per ancora nulla perchè non v'è su famiglia di lavoratori ne buoi ne altro bestiame; tolsela per farla raconciare e fuggirci la moria'.

22 Strozziane, V, 22, c. 102 des: 'Risposemi per sua de dì 26 detto che non era dala partito suo perchè avrebbe amato podere per abitare e di qualche diletto insieme chomodità; ma che ne chonferissi chon Marcho [Parenti] e quando tutti e 2 ci achordasino avessi a essere il bisongnio suo per rendità lo pigliasimo per lui overo sarebbe contento torllo'.

23 Published by Borsook, 'Documenti relativi', doc. 18; quoted earlier p. 84.

24 Strozziane, V, 22, c. 102 des: 'sono suto chon Marcho e mostroli l'oste mi fai sopra il podere e che sarebbe intenzione tua. In fine li pare che dobiamo precisare a luogho più al ghusto tuo e che questo tolgha per me e quando ci sarai e n'avessi voglia ci achadra l'aver achomodar l'uno l'altro'.

25 Strozziane, V, 22, c. 102 des: 'Trovandosi poi in Firenze Lorenzo del mese di giungno 1478 e avendo visto detto podere e domandandolo io se aveva l'animo a volerllo, mi disse che nno. E che quando fussi ripatriato s'ingegnierebbe d'avere chosa che li andassi più a ghusto'.

26 Alberti, *I Libri della famiglia*, p. 200: 'Agiugni qui che tu puoi ridurti in villa e viverti in riposo...senza sentire romori, o relazioni, o alcuna altra di quelle furie quali dentro alla terra fra' cittadini mai restano, – sospetti, paure, maledicenti, ingiustizie...puoi alla villa fuggire questi strepiti, questi tumulti, questa tempesta della terra, della piazza, del palagio.'

27 Lorenzo Strozzi, *Vita di Filippo Strozzi*, ed. Bini e Bigazzi pp. 50–1; partly cited and translated by F. W. Kent, 'Palaces, Politics and Society', pp. 69–70: 'Ho caro commendi la vita mia del starmi alla Villa e godermi la quiete, unico refugio della mia indisposizione, e quello che io stimo non manco, senza offensione di niuno... Quanto alle nuove, trovandomi io al Santuccio, non ho da renderti il cambio; dove sto non solo per conto dell'aria, ma per non intendere sì spesso e sì tosto infinite cose che mi dispiacciono, e talvolta anche non vere...Dal Santuccio, il dì 6 di Giugno 1537'.

28 Lillie, 'Memory of Place', pp. 206–8.

29 For example, Gregory, *Selected Letters of Alessandra Strozzi*, 8 November 1448, p. 39; Alessandra Macinghi Strozzi, *Lettere*, 26 December 1449, pp. 54–61; 8 February 1449/50, p. 69.

30 Villani, *Cronica*, XI, 94, 'la maggior parte de' ricchi e nobili e agiati cittadini con loro famiglie stavano quattro mesi l'anno in contado, e tali più'.

31 Strozziane, V, 36, c. 18.

32 Strozziane, V, 36, cc. 111 sin., 164 sin.

33 Strozziane, V, 36, c. 202 sin.

34 Strozziane, V, 36, cc. 263, 300.

35 See, for example Boccaccio, 'Decameron', giornata V, novella ix.

36 Strozziane, V, 36, c. 237. Forty-eight *staia* of wheat was considered sufficient to feed twelve people over four months.

37 Strozziane, V, 36, c. 215: 'uno paio di parete da uciellini...di braccia 16 per uciellare'.

38 Strozziane, V, 36, c. 263: 'nella pescagione si fa fare in Bisenzio'.

39 Strozziane, V, 44, c. 34 des., 17 May 1488: 'un navicello per tenere al Santuccio'; c. 55 sin., 27 April 1487: 'braccia 40 di rizze per al Santuccio e per rife per raconciare una ragnia e raconciatura di uno giachio a porto'.

40 Strozziane, V, 36, c. 397: Fra Bernardo di Francesco Frate Ingexuato was paid for 'una paia di reti d'ottone da uciellini per al Santuccio fattali fare el nostro Filippo'.

41 Strozziane, V, 44, cc. 50 sin., 163 sin.

42 Strozziane, V, 44, cc. 163 sin., 287 des.

43 Strozziane, V, 44, c. 287 des.

44   Strozziane, V, 44, c. 291 sin.

45   Bartolommeo Sassetti preferred to baptise his sons in the Florentine Baptistery even when they were born at the villa, but he was apparently content that his daughters be baptised in the country; Strozziane, V, 1750, cc. 188 des., 193 des., 208 des.

46   Filippo Strozzi's sister Caterina went to their Mugello villa for the birth of her first son in 1449 although it was early February; Alessandra Macinghi Strozzi, *Lettere*, p. 77 (D).

47   For Sassetti weddings at the villa, see Strozziane, II, 4, c. 113 des.; Not. antecos. 391 (Ser Andrea di Angiolo da Terranova 1472–75) fol. 100 v; Not. antecos. 392 (Ser Andrea di Angiolo da Terranova, 1482–86), fol. 20v.

48   Strozziane, V, 22, cc. 90 des.; 94 des., cited by Sale, *The Strozzi Chapel*, p. 21.

49   Strozziane, V, 22, c. 90 des.

50   Strozziane, V, 53, c. 71 des.

51   Strozziane, V, 22, c. 105 des.

52   Giovanni Boccaccio, *The Decameron*, trans. Richard Aldington, Bury St Edmunds 1982, Fifth Day, Ninth Tale, p. 357 [translation here emended by the author]; Boccaccio, 'Decameron', ed. Branca, vol. IV, giornata V, novella 9, p. 510: 'e esso rimase povero, senza altra cosa che un suo poderetto piccolo essergli rimasa, delle rendite del quale strettissimamente vivea, e oltre a questo un suo falcone de' miglior del mondo. Per che, amando più che mai né parendogli più potere essere cittadino come disiderava, a Campi, là dove il suo poderetto era, se n'andò a stare. Quivi, quando poteva uccellando e senza alcuna persona richiedere, pazientemente la sua povertà comportava.'

53   F. W. Kent, *Household and Lineage*, pp. 249–50; Gregory, 'Chi erano gli Strozzi', p. 19; Chabot, Widowhood and Poverty', pp. 299–300.

54   1446 Cat. 673, I, fol. 307r: 'al presente per amore delle gravezze ch'io non posso paghare mi chonviene stare in villa'.

55   F. W. Kent, *Household and Lineage*, pp. 249–50; Gregory, 'Chi erano gli Strozzi', p. 19.

56   1427 Cat. 42, fol. 534v; 1430 Cat. 405, fol. 40r; 1433 Cat. 495, fol. 103r.

57   1442 Cat. 620, I, fol. 270r: 'Mi truovo cholle sustanze vedete e cholla schoncia e di gentile famiglia e di qui a dua mesi aspetto un'altro figliuolo che mmi truovo chon dua balia che'o faticha di vivere quando non paghassi nulla in chomune e sono dell'età vedete [45] senza inviamento niuno e senza eserciziо ed'o debito chon i spezial persona. . . . E stommi in chontado per povertà'.

58   1451 Cat. 707, fol. 670r: 'Volendo tornare a Firenze non'o di che vivere, e figliuoli miei diventano lavoratori. . . . Come vedete'o 9 figliuoli che v'è ne 5 femine elle quali per povertà non'o potuto loro fare dota in sul monte di niuna quantità. . . . E poderi non rendono a un buon pezo quello gli do ch'è molto bene'.

59   1457 Cat. 819, II, fol. 647r.

60   1469 Cat. 920, II, fol. 813r.

61   1446 Cat. 671, II, fol. 836r: 'Io no' mmi truovo chome vedete ne cchasa ne avviamento già ffa più che anni XIIII, e in questo tempo 'o ppaghato senpre le gravezze dal chapitale perche lli

62   1451 Cat. 708, No. 173: 'Troviamci non ne avere chaxa in Firenze e debito chon più persone amettendo il chomune F.400 d'oro . . . e avere venduto F.90 di maserizie per la malattia d'Ubertino nostro padre di che si morì, e di Francesco sua ereda in parte, stato malato mexi sei ed è di modo che poche ciene rimane. E stiamo tutti in villa per non ne potere paghare pigione ne tenere fante. E per nonn essere nostra madre molto sana. E abbiamo de sirocchie grande sanza dota chome per le bocche vedrete. E non ne abbiamo chi ci aiuti e chonxigli. Piacivi intendere che choxì è il vero, fate diferenza da chi dicie il vero a chi no'llo dicie; che diventiamo chontadini per forza chome intendete perche altro non ne possiamo fare'.

63   P. J. Jones, 'Florentine Families', p. 189, n. 55.

64   1427 Cat. 44, fol. 202r: 'per nicistà ci riducemo in chontado'.

65   1451 Cat. 707, fol. 418r.

66   1433 Cat. 495, fol. 320v.

67   1442 Cat. 620, II, fol. 743v.

68   1469 Cat. 919, II, fol. 343r–v.

69   1480 Cat. 1011, fol. 300r: 'Piero attende a servire la madre per levale [la] faticha del ghoverno della chasa [e] de' quelle poche tere abiamo . . . [Matteo] si sta per charestia de' parenti in villa; daci spesa assai di vestire e calzare e di mangiare e di bere e utile veruno non se n'a'.

70   1442 Cat. 621, fol. 532r: 'Io mi truovo chon sette bocche chome vedete sanza nessuna guadagno; per lla povertà no' posso istare a Firenze ed io sono in età 62 1/2 ch'esendo a Firenze non trovo chon chi starre'. Messer Niccolò was already claiming poverty in his 1427 tax return in which no town house is mentioned; Cat. 47, fol. 380r.

71   1469 Cat. 921, fol. 173r: 'istanti in villa per povertà e steti più di 30 anni passati'.

72   1442 Cat. 620, I, fol. 283r: 'sanza alchuno exercitio e sempre sono stato in villa'.

73   1480 Cat. 1010, fol. 429r; 1498 Decima Repub. 21, fol. 379r.

74   These six were (1) Bernardo di Giovanni, who apparently lived at Signano between c. 1430 when he returned from Bologna and c. 1450; (2) Benedetto di Piero, whose town house was bequeathed to only one son, leaving Pagholo to live at Capalle; (3) Niccolò di Barla, who let his town property and lived at Malmantile in the 1460s and 1470s; (4) Messer Marcello, who owned the Rocca di Campi but only rented property in town; (5) Francesco and Zanobi di Benedetto, whose villas at Brozzi and Palaiuola were maintained, while they initially rented town houses and Francesco's sons were later obliged to sell the town house bought while business was flourishing in the 1440s; and (6) Benedetto di Marco.

75   1446 Cat. 671, II, fol. 943r: 'la rivorrò [his town house] per la mia brighata però che qui non ne stanno sani e per nicistà di non tenerli qui infermi gli arò a rimandare chosì [ie, back to the town house] e aranno abitare detta chasa per loro'.

76   1480 Cat. 1014, I, fol. 65v.

77   1498 Decima Repub. 24, fol. 373r.

78   See Chapter 5, p. 103, nn. 122 and 123.

79   Battista di Francesco di Benedetto's claim is a typical example of the poorer rentier's position: 'non'o chasa in Firenze e sto

alla villa [Brozzi] cholla famiglia perche mi bixogna torre a pigione e non'o il modo. Vivo sopra le posessioni'; 1480 Cat. 1011, fol. 158r.

80 This was the final degradation from which Boccaccio's hero Alberighi was saved, first by his falcon and then by the love of his lady.

PART TWO: THE SASSETTI

1 A. Warburg, 'Francesco Sassettis letztwillige Verfügung', 1907, reprinted in *Gesammelte Schriften*, I, Leipzig and Berlin 1932; in Italian translation, 'Le Ultime volontà di Francesco Sassetti', pp. 213–46, in *La Rinascita del paganesimo antico*, ed. Gertrud Bing; and in English, 'Francesco Sassetti's Last Injunctions to his Sons', pp. 223–62, 451–66, in *The Renewal of Pagan Antiquity*, trans. David Britt. All references are made to the English edition.

2 Lillie, 'Francesco Sassetti and his villa at La Pietra'.

CHAPTER 9   THE SASSETTI FAMILY AND THEIR PROPERTY

1 My main sources are the *ricordanze* of Tommaso's son Bartolommeo, Strozziane, V, 1747, 1750 and 1751; and the tax returns of Tommaso's brother Bernardo and sons Federigo, Bartolommeo and Francesco (see the following *catasto* references). Marco Parenti described the Sassetti in just these terms in his letter to Filippo Strozzi of 11 August 1469, when he pointed out that the daughter of Federigo Sassetti would not be a suitable match because of her father's poor situation, although her uncle Francesco lent reputation to the family; Molho, *Marriage Alliance*, pp. 231–2.

2 According to Francesco di Giambatista Sassetti's 'Notizie' of 1600 (pp. xxxi, xxxiv), Tommaso worked for the bankers Ruggeri di Messer Giovanni de' Ricci and Giovanni d'Arrigo da Prato, travelling to Lombardy and Venice on their behalf until the failure of that company in 1396, after which he settled in Florence and took a wife. His first wife, Caterina di Filippo di Messer Andrea Falcone da Lucignano, died without issue; his second wife, Pippa di Jacopo d'Ubertino Strozzi, gave birth to Federigo; and the third wife, Betta di Bartolo di Beltramo de' Pazzi, whom he married in 1412, was the mother of Bartolommeo, Francesco and other children.

3 Strozziane, V, 1750 c. 180 des.

4 1427 Cat. 46, fol. 285r; Cat. 77, fol. 202 des.

5 1427 Cat. 46, fol. 582r.

6 Federigo was probably born in 1405 according to the average age declared in his tax returns and to a *ricordo* of his brother Bartolommeo, which refers to Federigo being only a few months old in January 1406; Strozziane, V, 1751 c.154 des. Federigo died on 5 September 1463; Strozziane, V, 1750, c.195 des.

7 1427 Cat. 46, fol. 582r: 'Truovomi sanza chasa; prieghovi mi riserbiate se io togliesi chasa o chonperasi masserizie d'achonciarlle'.

8 1430 Cat. 406, fol. 184r.

9 Strozziane, V, 1750, c. 182 des.

10 1427 Cat. 46, fol. 582r.

11 Strozziane, V, 1750, c. 182 des.; V, 1749 c. 161 des.

12 Strozziane, V, 1750, c. 182 des.

13 1442 Cat. 621, fol. 308r

14 Molho, *Florentine Public Finances*, pp. 104–6.

15 Strozziane, V, 1750, c. 183 sin.

16 1442 Cat. 621, fol. 308r. Federigo worked as a silk merchant in Rimini; Strozziane, V, 1749, c. 14 sin.

17 Strozziane, V, 1750, c. 183 des., V, 1749, cc. 28, 31 sin.

18 1446 Cat. 673, I, fol. 103r.

19 1451 Cat. 709, fol. 28v.

20 1457 Cat. 818, fol. 692v–693r; 1469 Cat. 921, fol. 282r.

21 Pupilli 159 (1425), fol. 317r.

22 Pupilli 165 (1429), fol. 109r; Strozziane, V, 1747, c. 1 des.

23 Neither Carocci's map based on the boundaries listed in the 1427 *catasto* nor the 1888 map of the centre before demolitions help to resolve the precise locations of these houses; nor do they help to determine which of them might be identified with the surviving Palazzo Sassetti now occupied by the Steinhauslin bank; see Lensi Orlandi, *Il Palazzo dei Sassetti*.

24 Strozziane, V, 1747, c. 2 des.

25 Strozziane, V, 1747, cc. 52 sin., 56 sin., 59 des., 104 sin.

26 Strozziane, V, 1747, c. 155 des.

27 Strozziane, V, 1747, c. 1 des.

28 Strozziane, V, 1750, c. 180 des.

29 Strozziane, V, 1747, c. 1 des.

30 Strozziane, V, 1750, c. 182 sin.: 'della quale divisa [1433] non fo particulare menzione perchè fu fittizia e facemola a cautela per potere ognuno di noi andare da per se alla distribuzione che ssi fe del catasto, maggiore perchè spigionamo la casa grande e ciascuno di noi portò una casa per suo abitare che cci fe sciemare assai di quello che aremo auto di graveza. Non istante la detta divisa siamo pure a comune così dell'entrate come di qualunque spese come per libri nostri aparisci perchè intendiamo non di meno essere a comune. Ma la divisa vera si fe tra noi l'anno 1440'.

31 Strozziane, V, 1750, c. 180 des.

32 Strozziane, V, 1750, c. 181 sin. (1455): Bartolommeo describes the division in his *ricordo*: 'Ricordo come insino adì 29 di febbraio 1439 [n.s. 1440], essendo stati insino allora insieme Francesco mio fratello e io deliberamo di dividerci e dallui venne, e però faciemo detto dì gienerale conpromesso in Neri di Domenico Bartolini nostro cognato, rogato di Ser Matteo di Martino da San Ghuentino di Val d'Elsa notaio Fiorentino durante tutti dì 31 di marzo 1440'.

33 Strozziane, V, 1750, c. 181 des.

34 This is a more precise estimate than those given by Raymond de Roover, *The Rise and Decline*, p. 362; or Bergier, 'Lettres genevoises' p. 283; whereas Florence Edler de Roover ('Francesco Sassetti', p. 65) mistakenly followed Francesco di Giambatista's 'Notizie' (p. xxxv) in stating that he went to Avignon rather than Geneva c. 1440.

35 Bergier ('Lettres genevoises', p. 283) notes that Francesco became a partner in Geneva in 1446 and branch manager in 1448; according to R. de Roover (*The Rise and Decline*, p. 362), Francesco became branch manager in 1446.

36 Bartolommeo wrote Francesco's 1442 tax return on his behalf, Cat. 621, fol. 146r.

37 1451 Cat. 709, fol. 681r.

38 Strozziane, V, 1750, c. 184 des.(1455).

39 Molho, *Florentine Public Finances*, pp. 105–6, n. 64.

40 There are five volumes of Bartolommeo's *ricordanze* in the Archivio di Stato in Florence: Strozziane, V, 1747 (1429–33) and Strozziane, V, 1748 (1435–7) are joint account books shared with his brother Francesco, whereas Bartolommeo's fuller *ricordanze* are Strozziane, V, 1749 (1440–54), V, 1750 (1455–71) and V, 1751 (1471–7). There are also some *ricordi* in Bartolommeo's *giornale*; Strozziane, V, 1752 (1476–87).

41 This is the date given by Passerini (BNF, Passerini mss: 'Sassetti') and R. de Roover, *The Rise and Decline*, p. 389. According to his age declared in tax returns, he was born between 1412 and 1415.

42 There are twenty-seven letters from Bartolommeo Sassetti to Giovanni di Cosimo de' Medici in the MAP archive: V, 309, 311, 312, 412, 426, 464, 500, 516, 560, 564, 570, 584, 592, 600, 714; VI, 20, 23, 27; VIII, 156, 158, 166, 191, 204, 385, 465; IX, 525, 549.

43 MAP V, 309, 311, 312.

44 MAP V, 312.

45 Hyman, *Florentine Studies*, pp. 126, 133, 272, 302, 311.

46 MAP V, 500, 564, 584.

47 MAP V, 312, 500; VIII, 158.

48 MAP VI, 20; IX, 549; VI, 4, 26; IX, 525.

49 D. V. and F. W. Kent, 'Two Comments', pp. 795–6, Bartolommeo's letter of 1445 refers to the Medici palace site in passing and not as though it were the main focus of his work.

50 Strozziane, V, 1749, c. 164 des., V, 1750, c. 185 des.

51 According to the 'Notizie' of 1600 (p. xxix), having belonged to the Ghibelline faction, no member of the Sassetti family was made prior or *Gonfaloniere di Giustizia* until 1450.

52 Strozziane, V, 1750, c. 186 sin; BNF Passerini mss: Sassetti. In 1466 he was one of the twelve *Buonomini*; Strozziane, V, 1750, c. 203 des.

53 Arlotto, *Motti e Facezie*; Manni, *Vita di Arlotto Mainardi*; F. W. Kent and A. Lillie, 'The Piovano Arlotto: New Documents'.

54 *Motti e Facezie*, motto 36: 'nostro onesto concittadino ed importante e leale mercante, molto amico del nostro Piovano Arlotto'.

55 Strozziane, V, 1750, c. 214 sin.

56 Strozziane, V, 1749, cc. 55 sin., 58 sin.–des., 59 des., 61 sin.–des. A *muratore*, Bonagio di Dino received the contract to carry out the alterations and supervised payment for all the workmen and suppliers except for the stone- and iron-work. Checcho di Domenicho called Caprino, a stonecutter and quarryman from Settignano provided the stone ready carved and delivered it to the site. Bartolommeo was already acquainted with Caprino at San Lorenzo and the Palazzo Medici where, as the owner of a quarry, he regularly supplied *macigno* to the Medici building projects.

57 Strozziane, V, 1749, c. 58 sin.: 'per uno cardinale e due bechatelli e una corniciе per l'uscio di camera mia L.3 s.12'.

58 Strozziane, V, 1749, c. 54 sin.

59 Strozziane, V, 1749, c. 59 des.: Chimenti also painted the walls and ceiling of the nuptial *camera* as well as the whole *sala*:

'Chimenti di Lorenzo dipintore de avere adì 13 di magio 1447 per dipintura della sala che furono braccia 278 quadre per s.1 d.8 il braccio L.23
— per braccia 65 quadre di dipintura fattami in camera nel sopalcho di sopra al letto e intorno al letto per s.2 il braccio L.6 s.10
— per dipintura fattami nel muro in camera per uno tabernacolo di donna L.2 s.10
— per stagno dorato per la corniciе del sopalco di camera s.30 L.1 s.10
— per dare colore a 4 finestre di sala s.30 L.1 s.10'.

Chimenti's workshop carried out extensive house painting and decoration; Colnaghi, *Dictionary*, p. 231.

60 Strozziane, V, 1749, c. 54 sin.

61 Strozziane, V, 1749, c. 54 sin.: 'Masserizie conprate deono dare adì 22 di febraio [n.s. 1447] lire quaranta paghai a Domenicho dipintore in due volte per costo di uno colmo di nostra donna conprai dallui F.– L.40'.

62 This price was far more than Bartolommeo paid for other paintings, such as Chimenti di Lorenzo's (see n. 61), which may have been a mural enclosed within a tabernacle, or Zanobi di Giovanni's 'tavola di nostra donna che adora il figluolo e con San Giovanni Battista' painted for his son's *camera* in 1470 and costing three florins (c. 17 lire). Another painting of a similar shape by Domenico Veneziano was listed in Lorenzo de' Medici's 1492 inventory and valued at a comparable price of c. 53 lire, described as 'uno colmetto con dua sportelli, dipintovi dentro una testa di una donna di mano di maestro Domenico da Vinegia F.8'; Wohl, *The Paintings of Domenico Veneziano*, p. 350. At this date, Domenico was certainly working on this type of domestic commission as his *cassoni* for Marco Parenti of 1448 show; Wohl, 'Domenico Veneziano Studies', pp. 635–641.

63 Callmann, *Apollonio di Giovanni*, pp. 76–77, no. 11, 19. The entries in the artist's account book are corroborated by his client's accounts; Strozziane, V, 1749, c.168 sin.: 'Ricordo delle cose recò l'Antonia mia donna le quali furono stimate . . . uno paio di forzieri dipinti costorono . . . F.32 d'oro'.

64 Strozziane, V, 1750, cc. 213 sin., 214 sin.

65 Strozziane, V, 1751, cc. 24 des., 153 sin.

66 Strozziane, V, 1751, c. 24 sin.

67 See Chapter 7.

68 Strozziane, V, 1751, c. 182 des.

69 Strozziane, V, 1751, cc. 128 sin.–des., 130 sin., 135 des.

70 Strozziane, V, 1751, c. 135 sin., 'E adì 14 detto [December 1476] fiorini tre larghi diedi contanti a Zanobi di Giovanni dipintore per costo di una tavola di nostra donna che adora il figluolo e con San Giovanni Batista per la camera di Priore F.3 . . . E adì detto soldi sei per costo di uno candelliere fornito con uno cerotto e lucerna stagnata per tenere dinanzi a nostra donna F.– s.6'.

71 Strozziane, V, 1751, c.127 des.: 'E per costo di due cassoni grandi intarsiati col coperchio a sepoltura . . . F. 15'.

72 See Lydecker, *The Domestic Setting*, for discussion of this pattern.

73 IGM Carta d'Italia, fol. 106, 1955, Firenze, 52:79; Amministrazione Provinciale di Firenze, 1979, fol. 52.

74 Carocci (*I Dintorni*, I, p. 331) notes that apart from the Sassetti, the Strozzi, Davizzi, Soldani, Della Badessa, Agli and Giachinotti families owned property at Macia. See Appendix B, no. 19, for the two Strozzi villas at Macia.

75 For site descriptions, see 1427 Cat. 77, fol. 72r, Cat. 46, fol. 582r; 1446 Cat. 673, I, fol. 522v; 1451 Cat. 709, fol. 170r; 1469 Cat. 921, fol. 130r; 1480 Cat. 1013, I, fol. 110r. It belonged to the Rosselli del Turco during the nineteenth century and was identified by Carocci, *I Dintorni*, I, p. 330.

76 Strozziane, II, 4, c.90 des. Earlier notarial records describe a farm at Macia with the same components as those that appear in fifteenth-century descriptions of the Sassetti villa, (Ser Mazzingo Gennari) Not. antecos. 8745 (1326–30), 1328, May 28, fol. 104r: 'podere cum domibus, columbaria, palmentis, et curia, vinea, puteo et orto'; my thanks to Paolo Pirillo who provided me with this reference.

77 Strozziane, II, 4, cc. 101 sin., 107 des.

78 Strozziane, V, 1751, c. 154 des.

79 In the tax returns they declared the same annual harvest from 1430 throughout most of the century until 1498: eighty-four *staia* of wheat, thirty-six *staia* each of barley and sorghum and twenty-four barrels of wine: 1430 Cat. 406, fol. 184r; 1433 Cat. 496, fol. 177r; 1442 Cat. 621, fol. 1r; 1446 Cat. 673, I, fol. 522v; 1451 Cat. 709, fol. 170r; 1469 Cat. 921, fol. 130r; 1480 Cat. 1013, I, fol. 110r; 1498 Decima Repub. 24, fol. 515r.

80 Strozziane, V, 1750, cc. 6 des., 22 des., 32 sin.

81 The house has now been divided into many apartments, making access and reconstruction difficult. The plan made by students of the Istituto di Restauro della Facoltà di Architettura of the University of Florence in 1974 is reproduced here in Fig. 121.

82 A clumsy solution is employed at this corner, where the two arches springing from different heights meet (Fig. 130).

83 Preyer, 'The "chasa overo palagio" of Alberto di Zanobi', p. 387, n. 4.

84 Rubinstein, *The Palazzo Vecchio*, pp. 25–6.

85 Chamfered cubic capitals of the Macia type are also found in the second courtyard of S. Maria Nuova (1420–30), in the second cloister at San Lorenzo, in the small cloister of S. Francesco at Fiesole, in the cloister at Lecceto (c. 1486) and in villa courtyards such as Le Pergole at Bagno a Ripoli (Patzak, *Palast und Villa*, I, p. 109, figs. 142, 143), the Villa Mini at Careggi (Lensi Orlandi, *Di Qua d'Arno*, p. 39, pl. 67) and the Strozzi Rocca of Loiano. Shields could conveniently be carved on cubic capitals as in the loggia of the Palazzo Larioni-Canigiani or the Rucellai villa Lo Specchio at Quaracchi. *Foglie d'acqua* capitals remained popular into the 1420s and 1430s, as is suggested by their appearance in the courtyard of Palazzo Da Uzzano (c. 1411–24), in the Palazzo di Parte Guelfa courtyard, in the second cloister at Impruneta

86 and flanking the well in the courtyard of the Medici villa of Careggi.

86 Strozziane, II, 4, c. 113 des.

87 Strozziane, V, 1750, c. 183 des.

88 Strozziane, V, 1751, c. 6 sin., 1471: 'Il podere da Nuovoli de' dare per costo di detto podere il quale conprai la metà dagl'uficiali delle vendite e l'altra metà degl'uficiali del monte con volontà di Federigo mio fratello come tutto apare distesamente al mio libro vecchio nero S[egnato] D, c.183

    [the first half]......................................F.155
    [the second half].................................F.156
    [200 Venetian ducats].........................F.220
    – per diritto degl'uficiali e per la gabella de contratti e carta F.40
    – per raconciare la colonbaia e fare impianellare il tetto e per correnti e per 3 abeti e maistero F. 35
    – per fare il palco alla camera disopra e per alzare il tetto e farlo impianellare e per maistero F. 25
    – per fare ismaltare la volta e farvi uno muro di mattoni intorno e rifare uno uscio F. 25
    – per abassare il palco della camera diverso tramontana e farvi una trameza per farne una camera in sul verone e una anticamera alla camera mia e amattonarle F. 20
    – per fare i truoghi de' granai e fare una trameza che divide i granai da una camera fattavi F. 15
    – per fare uno lavatoio nella via da lavare panni e per una tavola di macigno nell'orto e per orticini murati F. 15
    – per fare una scala che va in colonbaia che prima vi s'andava di sala per scala a piuoli; e per mura e usci e finestra e amattonarvi e farvi e truoghi per biada F. 18
    – per fare una trameza nella stalla e uno palco nella stalluza e per pilastri per porvi le tina e per costo di 2 alberi per sedili da tini F. 12 c.6 des [debit continued]
    E de' dare F.[crossed out] per fare la stalla da lavoratore della via e per fare la camera di verso tramontana e per alzare le mura e fare una altra camera sopra a essa e per fare il palco e amattonare la camera disotto e quella disopra e per usci e finestre fattevi per tutto F. 24
    – per fare uno cammino alla casa da lavoratore e per rifare l'usci da via e per farvi un forno e levarlo da casa nostra per tutto F. 12
    – per una condanagione mi feconli uficiali del monte per aver pagato di polize conprate parte del prezo di detto podere F.202 s.2 –'.

89 Strozziane, V, 1750, c. 41 sin: 'Una lettiera di braccia 5 con 2 casse d'atorno e col trespolo e cannaio e con lettuccio e capellinaio tutto con uno poco di tarsia'.

90 For the pergola in 1467, Piovano Arlotto sent down two tree trunks (*colonne*) from the Baldovinetti villa at Calicarza, together with ten beams, six tie bars and stakes to support young vines; Strozziane, V, 1750, c. 71 sin.

91 Strozziane, V, 1747, cc. 133 sin., 162 des.; V, 1748, cc. 57 sin., 163 sin., 165 sin.

92 Strozziane, V, 1747, c. 156 des.

93 Strozziane, V, 1750, c. 183 des. (1455), 'Dirinpetto ci parisce nel modo che io conprai il podere da Novoli che ffu di

Federigo mio fratello. Dipoi l'anno 1444 sendo Federigo tornato da Rimino per istare a Firenze e tornandosi in casa mia, mi fecie dire che volentieri rivorrebbe il detto podere e che mi renderebbe i miei denari. E io rispondendo che lla sua domanda non mi pare gusta, massime perchè ero assai cresciuto della graveza e lui sciemato e anche perchè v'aveo murato e coltivato. Finalmente lui non l'ebbe per bene e cominciomi a muovere lite diciendo che io gli avevo promesso renderglele e venimo a magiori contese che qui nonna cagione dire'.

94   Strozziane, V, 1751, c. 155 des. (1471): 'mai non si troverra vero ne verosimile che io promettessi mai a Federigo di renderglene [il podere di Novoli]. Ma bene si fforzò lui insieme con Francesco di tormelo. Idio lo perdoni loro se lo meritano'.

95   Strozziane, V, 1750, and V, 1751.

96   See Valcenni di Sopra and Valcenni di Sotto on the map of the Amministrazione Provinciale di Firenze, 1:10,000, 1979, fol. 44, as well as the IGM map, 1:25,000, 1959, fol. 106, Vaglia, 56:81. These houses are almost certainly those marked with the names of their later owners, Bonifatio and Dini on the map of S. Sivestro a Rufignano made for the Capitani di Parte Guelfa in the 1580s; see Fig. 131. In one version of the map, the name 'Valcenni' is marked under these houses; *Castello: campagna medicea*, pp. 156–7. In the sixteenth century Valcenni was known as the spot where fresh water sprang from the hill and was led by aqueduct to supply the Medici villas of Castello and Petraia below.

97   Strozziane, V, 1750, c. 52 sin.

98   Strozziane, V, 1750, c. 205 sin.

99   Strozziane, V, 1751, cc. 67 sin., 113 des.

100   Strozziane, V, 1750, cc. 54 sin., 71 sin., 73 sin.

101   Strozziane, V, 1750, c. 72 des.: 1464, 'per più conci di macigno auti da lui per lire 28. I' lavorio auto dal lui fu questo, coè:

30 scaglioni di braccia 1 3/4 l'uno a s.8 il
braccio . . . L.12
2 davanzali per l'aquaio di braccia 5 a s.9 il
braccio . . . L.2.5
1 cardinale per camino di braccia 4 a s.10 il
braccio . . . L.2
1 cardinale per camino di braccia 3 1/2 a s.10 il
braccio . . . L.1.15
2 beccatelli per camino di braccia 1 3/4 l'uno . . . L.1.8
5 finestre ferrate di braccia 30 a s.8 il braccio . . . L.12
4 pezi di sogle di braccia 8 a s.3 1/2 il braccio . . . L.1.8
3 pezi di cardinaletti in tutto braccia 5 a s.8 il
braccio . . . L.2
1 uscio intaccato di braccia 9 a s.8 il braccio . . . L.3.12
2 usci con 3 stipiti di braccia 19 a s.8 il
braccio . . . L.7.12
1 armario di braccia 5 1/2 . . . L.-.16
[total] . . . . L.46.16'.

102   Strozziane, V, 1750, c. 41 sin., 31 January 1463/4: 'a Bastiano d'Antonio Martini per costo di una lettiera vechia di braccia 4 7/8 con 2 casse e una panca e uno lettuccio comprai per mezanità di Papi di Nofri ferravechio per a Valcenni . . . l.20'.

103   Strozziane, V, 1750, c. 41 sin., 3 April 1465: 'a Domenico legnaiuolo fuori della Porta a Faenza per costo di una lettiera per a Valcenni di braccia 4 1/2 con 2 cassapanche basse L.18'.

104   Strozziane, V, 1750, c. 41 sin., 3 April 1465: 'per costo di uno capellinaio usato di braccia 3 e per una panchetta bassa di braccia 4 1/2 usata comprai tra rigattieri per luogo da Valcenni . . . L. 1 s.12 d.6'.

105   Strozziane, V, 1750, c. 41 sin., 10 April 1465: 'per costo di 3 tavole di Nostra Donna comprai coè[sic] una con più figure con li sportelli soldi 12; e un'altra molto vechia per la camera della fante per a Valcenni soldi 8; e l'altra per la camera terrena a Valcenni soldi 33 . . . L.2 s.13'.

106   For example, Maestro Antonio Lombardo, called Maestrino, lived at Valcenni from November 1464 to February 1465 while he built walls assisted by two locals; Strozziane, V, 1750, c. 73 sin.–des.

107   Strozziane, V, 1750, c.73 sin: 'venne a ritrovare dove fusse aqua per fare una fonte'.

108   Strozziane, V, 1750, cc. 92 des., 93 sin., 94 sin.

109   Strozziane, V, 1750, c. 56 sin. and des.

110   Strozziane, V, 1750, cc. 93 des.

111   Strozziane, V, 1750, c. 54 sin.: 'per costo di 16 doccioni comprai in Firenze e mandai a Valcenni per necessario della camera della torre'.

112   Strozziane, V, 1750, c. 53 sin., 20 October 1464: 'Checcho Salucci e figluoli mi fecono carta di uno pezo di terra che è di sopra alla casa loro e mia della quale terra voglio fare parte pratello e parte orto. E io debbo dare in cambio parte della mia vigna di sotto che è presso alla strada dalla Cavallina'.

113   Strozziane, V, 1750, cc. 73 sin.–des., 93 sin.–des., 99 des.

114   Strozziane, V, 1750, c. 107 sin., 3 March 1468/9: '17 arcipressi colle barbe compriamo . . . per porre in sul pratello da Valcenni L.2'.

115   Strozziane, V, 1750, c. 99 des.

116   Strozziane, V, 1750, cc. 61 sin., 62 sin. and des., 63 sin., 66 sin., 77 sin.

117   Strozziane, V, 1750, c. 87 sin., 97 des.

118   Strozziane, V, 1750, c. 90 sin. and des.

119   Strozziane, V, 1750, c. 95 sin., 105 sin.

120   Strozziane, V, 1750, c. 107 des., 'una fossa feci fare e porre allori e altri fructi et pruni per fare siepe per tendervi la ragna lungo el fossato fra noi e l'abate di San Felice Piaza che parte ne feci fare in somma per di braccia 10 larghi braccia due et adrento braccia 1 1/2 L.7 s.2 d.4'.

121   Strozziane, V, 1750, c. 94 sin.

122   Strozziane, V, 1750, cc. 196 sin., 201 des., 203 des., 205 sin., 210 sin.

123   Strozziane, V, 1750, cc. 53 sin., 56 sin., 64 sin., 93 sin., 99 sin., 105 sin.–des., 107 sin., 146 des.; V, 1751, cc. 12 des., 82 des.

124   Strozziane, V, 1750, c. 71 des.: 'Messer Antonio piovano di Cercina de avere adì 29 di luglio 1464 lire secentoventi sono per più lavorio m'a fatto fare a luogo mio da Valcenni . . . posti a spese in questo c.54'. Strozziane, V, 1750, c.54 des.: 'E insino adì 30 di luglio 1464 lire secentoventi posto messer Antonio piovano di Cercina debe avere in questo c.71, sono

per più lavorio m'a fatto fare a Valcenni per murare la casa mia e quella de' lavoratore ad ogni sua spesa dacordo con lui L.620'. The phrase 'm'a fatto fare' suggests that Messer Antonio was carrying out the day-to-day supervision of the work, as well as acting as paymaster.

125 Daniela Lamberini kindly informed me of the role of priests in supervising later building at Poggio a Caiano.

126 Strozziane, V, 1750, cc.71 sin., 141 des.; V, 1751, cc. 27 sin.–des., c. 63 sin., 105 sin.

127 Arlotto, *Facezie, motti e burle*, ed. Amerighi, pp. 33, 89, 102, 186; see Kent and Lillie, 'The Piovano Arlotto: New Documents'.

128 Strozziane, 1750, c. 188 sin.; V, 1751, cc. 77 sin.–des., 91 des., 109 des.

129 See also n. 124, in which Bartolommeo's own house ('la casa mia') is clearly distinguished from the farmers' house ('quella de' lavoratore').

CHAPTER 10 FRANCESCO SASSETTI'S VILLA AT LA PIETRA

1 R. de Roover (*The Rise and Decline*, p. 361; F. Edler de Roover, 'Francesco Sassetti', p. 66) gives 1458 as the year in which Sassetti returned to Florence and married. Passerini (BNF Passerini Mss 'Sassetti') also notes 1458 as the year in which Sassetti married. It may have been early in 1459 (ie, before 25 March 1458 according to the Florentine calendar).

2 F. Edler de Roover, 'Francesco Sassetti', pp. 68–73.

3 R. de Roover, *The Rise and Decline*, pp. 74–5.

4 R. de Roover, *The Rise and Decline*, pp. 279–91; Cassandro, 'Banca e commercio', pp. 567–611.

5 F. Edler de Roover, 'Francesco Sassetti', pp. 68–71.

6 1457 Cat. 818, fol. 694r–v.

7 The document of sale was notarised by Ser Niccolò di Francesco Galeotti (not. antecos. 8523, 1456–60) on 7 April 1460. The purchase was also recorded in Sassetti's *Libro segreto*; Strozziane, II, 20, fol. 2r, 9r.

8 C. Lewis and C. Short, *A Latin Dictionary*, Oxford 1879, p. 265, *cesalibus* derived from the military term *caesa* [Vegetius] here referring to things which had been cut down or dug up. Alternative expansions of the notary's abbreviation are as follows: *cespitibus* deriving from *cespes/caespes* meaning sods or a mound of earth, or the Italian *cespo*, in this context meaning a clump of plants; or in conjunction with rocky caves [*grottis*] and ditches [*foveis*] another possible expansion could be *cesternibus*, a Latinised version of *cisterna*, a well or cistern; I am grateful to Gino Corti for reading this document with me.

9 Not. antecos. 8523 (Ser Niccolo di Francesco Galeotti, 1456–60), 7 April 1460, pages unnumbered: 'Unum podere cum domo sive palatio pro habitatione domini et cum domibus pro lavoratore et cum factorio et orto murato in parte et pratellis cum tinis, vegetibus bigongiis canalibus strectoribus et omnibus alii[s] instrumentis actis ad recondendum fructus pertinentes ad dictum podere et cum terris laborativis vineatis olivatis et arboratis arboribus fructiferis et non fructiferis...positum in populo Sancti Marci Veteris comitatis florentie loco dicto Montughi sive Le Citine cui et quibus a primo via a secondo heredum Bartholomei Ser Santis a terzo hospitalis di Domini Bonifazi Lupi a quarto bona Capitoli Sancti Laurentii de Florentia...Una cum omnibus grottis cesalibus[?] foveis et aliis suis pertinentibus'.

10 Not. antecos. 5239, fol. 14r, 26 February 1343/4. Paolo Pirillo very kindly provided me with this reference.

11 Davidsohn VII, p. 477; by the thirteenth century, suburbs had encroached into this area and a new ring road had been built through it.

12 From the nineteenth century there are references to the Villa Capponi at La Pietra, Repetti, IV, p. 204.

13 1427 Cat. 61, fol. 570r; Cat. 81, fol. 220v.

14 Stefani, 'Cronaca fiorentina,' ed. Rodolico, vol. 30, pt. 1, p. 277, Rubrica 726; Zanobi di Neri Macinghi had been disqualified from holding public office in Florence by Rosso de' Ricci in 1372, and left for Naples where he became a favourite of Charles of Durazzo. According to Manoscritti 252, Priorista Mariani, Vol. V, 1225, he was made Gonfaloniere di Giustizia in Florence on 1 March 1393.

15 Cat. 81, fol. 220v; Cat. 61, fol. 570r; Cat. 390, fol. 419r. Carlo only declared half a house in town, a farm in the Mugello and the villa at Montughi in his tax returns of 1427, 1430 and 1433.

16 Cat. 628, fol. 978r; Cat. 720, fol. 46r; Cat. 832, fol. 220r.

17 Cat. 929, fol. 870r–871v. Of this sum the Macinghi spent 425 florins on their sister's dowry and 1,150 florins on two farms near Prato and Montemurlo. This shows that the Macinghi were not content to remain without a villa for long. Their new farm at Montemurlo included 'un pocho di chasa d'abitare per noi.'

18 Although the Capponi bought many other properties around it, the estate attached to the Sassetti palace remained discrete and was recorded in the Capponi *decimari* throughout the seventeenth and eighteenth centuries; Archivio Capponi, Patrimonio Vecchio, 53, LIIII, c. 10; Pat. Vec. 60 fol. 261v; Pat. Nuovo 64, fol. 22r.

19 Not. antecos. 393 (Ser Andrea di Angiolo da Terranuova, 1482–86), fol. 171r–174r; see below pp. 247–8,250. Rab Hatfield found this document and kindly gave me a copy of his transcription.

20 Warburg ('Francesco Sassetti's Last Injunctions', p. 254, n. 44) gives 21 December 1491 as the date of Federigo's death.

21 Not. antecos. 12482, Testamenti (Ser Pierfrancesco Maccari, 1509–45), fol. 449r–453v; transcribed in Appendix C; henceforth cited as the division. I am most grateful to Elaine Rosenthal who found this document and generously brought it to my attention.

22 According to the family tree in Francesco di Giovambatista Sassetti's 'Notizie' of 1600, p. xix, Galeazzo died in 1513 and Cosimo in 1527.

23 BNF, Passerini mss.; Sassetti, 'Notizie', p. xxxix.

24 This document is referred to in Warburg, 'Francesco Sassetti's Last Injunctions', p. 254, n. 44, as 'inserto Dei no. 17', where it is described as a deed of sale, but no buyer or price is mentioned, and it seems to be a ratification of the agreement to sell by all those who owned shares in the villa.

25 Mary Ellen Hoelscher Lawrence found the deed of sale (Not. antecos., 12480, fol. 275r–v) giving the date as 19 August 1545, although in later documents it is frequently recorded as 1546; for example, Decima Granducale 3622, fol. 503r under 'Beni alienati of M[adonn]a Fiametta vedova e donna fu di Ghaleazo di Franc[esc]o Sassetti'; and in the Capponi Decimari, ASF: Capponi, Pat. Nuovo, vol. 60, fol. 261v: 'Un Palazzo con tre poderuzzi, con case da lavoratori, posti nel Popolo di S. Marco Vecchio, Potesteria di Fiesole luogo d[ett]o Montui, overo a Sassetti...E quali Beni comperò Piero di Niccolo Capponi proprio da Teodoro di Francesco Sassetti la terza parte e li 2/3 da Federigo di Galeazzo Sassetti per Fiorini 3,500 d'oro di moneta roggi Ser Pier Franc[esc]o Macchalli sotto dì 19 di Agosto 1546'; with similar records in vol. 64, fol. 22r.

26 The loan was probably settled within the terms of the business partnership then existing between Giuliano di Piero di Gino Capponi and his nephew Piero di Niccolò di Piero Capponi; Goldthwaite, *Private Wealth*, pp. 224, 227–8. The later payments were made by the heirs of Piero di Niccolò Capponi to the heirs of Nera di Federigo di Galeazzo Sassetti; BNF: Capponi, 91 cc. 40, 75, 95.

27 Francesco Capponi inherited the villa when his father Piero died in 1568 and passed it on to his widow Cassandra de' Bardi and sons Luigi, Piero and Filippo; BNF, Capponi 91 and 93. *Dizionario Biografico degli Italiani*, vol. 19, 'Francesco Capponi'; Litta, vol. 10, tav. 15.

28 BNF: Capponi, 91, cc.123, 139; BNF: Capponi, 93, cc. 72, 88, 185.

29 Certainly by 1705, it took 50 *opere* or days' work to trim the cypresses on the avenue to La Pietra, 'per tagliature di cipressi della viottola di Montui'; BNF: Capponi, 199, 16 December 1705.

30 Gherardo Silvani was paid eight *scudi* on 4 May 1622: 'per il disegno delle dette porte e acconcimi'; BNF: Capponi, 93, c. 122. I hope to include a full analysis of the baroque refurbishment of the villa in a forthcoming study.

31 Mary Ellen Hoelscher Lawrence, 'The Villa La Pietra: New Findings, History and Myth'; on Silvani in 1650s, see BNF: Capponi Commercio, 150, fol. 70r, 140v, 150v; BNF: Capponi Commercio, 152, fol, 150v; BNF: Capponi Commercio, 157, fol. 134r, 200v; on renovations in the 1750s, see BNF: Capponi Commercio, 217, fol. 49v; BNF: Capponi Commercio, 216, fol. 88v.

32 Tabarrini, *Gino Capponi*, pp. 338–40.

33 Repetti, III, p. 604.

34 Bargellini and Guarnieri, *Le Strade*, I, pp. 136–7.

35 Repetti, IV, p. 204; Bargellini and Guarnieri, *Le Strade*, I, p. 137.

36 Division fol. 450r, 451v. There is no mention of the loggia in the early documents concerning the villa so I have presumed it was built by Francesco.

37 Division fol. 451v.

38 BNF, Capponi 93, c. 25: 'il cancello della viottola che va alla Pietra'.

39 The elevation of the driveway above the surrounding fields with retaining walls and buttresses was almost certainly a later development, although the avenue is walled in the eighteenth-century fresco of the villa which still survives at La Pietra and is reproduced in Acton, *Tuscan Villas*, pl. 33.

40 Strozziane, II, 20, c. 10.

41 Eve Borsook first suggested to me that word play on the Sassetti name and the topographical name La Pietra may have been exploited by Francesco.

42 Sassetti, 'Notizie', p. xxxvi: 'accarezzati, alloggiati in casa sua, e magnificamente trattenuti e pasteggiati'; reprinted in Warburg, 'Francesco Sassetti's Last Injunctions', pp. 224, 227.

43 For a similar deployment of a *viottola* and *anguillari* in another fifteenth-century villa garden, see Rucellai, 'Il Zibaldone', p. 22.

44 Cat. 921, fol. 282r.

45 Division fol. 451v.

46 1427 Cat. 61, fol. 570r; 1430 Cat. 390, fol. 419r; 1442 Cat. 628 fol. 978r; 1451 Cat. 720 fol. 46r; 1457 Cat. 832 fol. 220r.

47 Decima Repub. 25, fol. 441r.

48 Division, fol. 451r. The other witness was Alessandro di Antonio Pucci, Sibilla Sassetti's husband.

49 Decima Repub. 25, fol. 441r; 24, fol. 470r.

50 BNF, Capponi 91, 93, 199 contain frequent payments to factors at Montughi.

51 In 1469 Cat. 921, fol. 282r, and 1470 Cat. 1013 pt. 11, fol. 319r, one ox and a donkey were kept at Montughi and the two farms produced 48 *staia* of wheat, 50 barrels of wine, 4 barrels of olive oil, and 3 *staia* of lupin and vetch. In 1498, Decima Repub. 25, fol. 441r; 24, fol. 470r, the three brothers received a total of 42 *staia* of grain, 21 barrels of wine, 6 barrels of olive oil and 12 *staia* of spelt.

52 1469, Cat. 921, fol. 282r: 'Tutti i sopradetti poderi sono insieme e rendonmi più spesa che utile per essere picholi e chattivi terreni, oltre alla spesa ordinaria che bixongna tenere nella chasa; credo potrei darli per incarico'; 1480, Cat. 1013, II, fol. 319r., 'tragho piutosto incharicho et spesa che utilità per rispetto del sito et della chasa et potrei dargli per incharicho chome è noto a ciaschuno'; 1498 Decima Repub. 24, fol. 470r; 25, fol. 441r: 'Et notate che detta possessione m'è incharicho ciascuno anno quello che io ne tragho e più rispecto al sito della casa che è grande e bisogna per forza tenervi spesa di factori e riparare tetti et altro come accade in simili luoghi.'

53 Alberti, 'Villa', p. 359.

54 See Sassetti's 'ultima volontà' published by Warburg, 'Francesco Sassetti's Last Injunctions', pp. 236, 238, discussed in Chapter 12.

55 Many thanks to Brenda Preyer who found this document and generously brought it to my attention. Not. antecos. 4376 (Ser Antonio di Giovanni Carsidoni, 1457–69), fol. 251v; 'Item postia dictis anno indicitone secunda [et] die

tertio Maii actum Florentie in populo Sancti Simonis de Florentia presentibus testibus etcetera Francisco [et] Antonio fratribus et filiis olim Tommasii dei Businis et allis. Franciscus olim ... de Sassettis civis et me[r]chator florentinus citra revocationem etcetera omni modo fecit etcetera eius procuratorem Pierum Lap del Tovaglia presentem etcetera generaliter ad fac[i]endum omnia que ipse constituens facere posset pro muraglia quam facit in loco suo a Montug[h]i.' The items before and after this are dated 1462. Letters show that Francesco Sassetti returned to Florence at the end of July 1462 but went away again on business and was only home for a few days in September; MAP, XVII, 335 and LXVIII, 55 published by Bergier, 'Lettres genevoises', pp. 303–4. For Piero del Tovaglia's role at SS. Annunziata, see Brown, 'The Patronage and Building History,' pp. 90–2, 94, 98–108.

56 Strozziane, II, 20, c. 2 des.

57 Strozziane, II, 20, c. 70 sin.–71 des.

58 Sassetti, 'Notizie', p. xxxvii, reprinted in Warburg, 'Francesco Sassetti's Last Injunctions', pp. 226, 228.

59 Montughi was by far the most valuable piece of real estate owned by Sassetti in 1466, as is clear when its value of 5,000 *fiorini di sugello* is compared with his town house valued at 3,400 *fiorini di sugello* and his other farms totalling 2,000 *fiorini di sugello*; *Libro segreto*, Strozziane, II, 20, cc.70 sin.–71 des.

60 Not. antecos., 19080 (Ser Silvano di Giovanni di Frosino, 1464–5), fol. 172r–v. See Appendix D. I am very grateful to Brenda Preyer who found this document and generously brought it to my attention.

61 Haines, *The Sacrestia delle Messe*, pp. 136–9.

62 Haines, *The Sacrestia delle Messe*, p. 136; Borsi, Morolli and Quinterio, *Brunelleschiani*, pp. 46–50, 277–87.

63 It may be significant that early in 1472 Francesco began to acquire the site for a big palace in town. It might be inferred that with his first major building project over, he could now turn to the next. In the intervening years he had been content to buy two houses with stables on the Canto de' Pazzi and the farming estate at Gonfienti.

64 MAP XCVIII, 544.

65 BNF, mss. Magl. XXIV, 108, c. 2, published by Borsook and Offerhaus, *Francesco Sassetti and Ghirlandaio*, p. 59, appendix 1, 4.

66 See Lillie, 'Francesco Sassetti and his Villa at La Pietra', pp. 83–6.

67 De la Mare, 'The Library of Francesco Sassetti', p. 195, n. 49.

68 Ibid.

69 Fontius, *Carmina*, I, 3, pp. 2–3: 'Cui dic, Montugia me culta expectet in aula; / Nil collata valet Gallia Montugio.'

70 Fontius, *Carmina*, I, 7, p. 6: 'Non ego Montugium, non iam Ghonfientia posco, / Divite non auro, non pretio afficior.'

71 Fontius, *Carmina*, I, 5, p. 5: 'Sed gentis patriae vertis in omne decus. / Montugium testis, testis Gonfentia Tempe, / Hic bene quaesitas tu bene ponis opes. / Praeteriens Gallus miratur saxula tecta / Et stupet auratam Celtiber ipse domum.'

72 Ficino, *Opera Omnia*, I, pt. 2, Liber V, pp. 799–800, also cited by Warburg, 'Francesco Sassetti's Last Injunctions', pp. 232–3; Kristeller, *Supplementum Ficinianum*, I, p. ci.

73 Not. antecos. 391 (Ser Andrea di Angiolo da Terranova, 1472–75), fol. 100v. Rab Hatfield generously showed me this and the following marriage contract.

74 Not. antecos. 393 (Ser Andrea di Angiolo da Terranova, 1482–86), fol. 20v.

75 Gabinetto Disegni e Stampe degli Uffizi, Vasari il Giovane, 4914; reproduced in Vasari il Giovane, *La Città ideale*, pp. 249–50; *disegno* no. 200, p. 130 (according to Vasari's numeration).

76 See n. 95, this chapter.

77 This scheme contrasts with that of the Medici villa of Trebbio, for example, where there is conformity within the irregularity, i.e. the trapezoid traced by the external walls dictates the shape of the courtyard and the rest of the rooms are fitted into the remaining spaces; Gori-Sassoli, 'Michelozzo', p. 18, figs. B, C.

78 See Appendix C. The division of the palace was witnessed by Francesco Sassetti's three sons-in-law: Lena's husband, Luca Corsini; Sibilla's husband, Alessandro Pucci; and Vaggia's husband, Simone Carnesecchi. The identification of rooms 16, 17, 18 and 19 differs from those published in Lillie, 'The Humanist Villa revisited'.

79 D. Thornton, *The Scholar in His Study*, p. 28.

80 Rotondi, *Il Palazzo ducale di Urbino*, II, pl. 286.

81 *Libro d'inventario dei beni di Lorenzo il Magnifico*, p. 146 (c. 70r).

82 The approximate ages of Sassetti's daughters are calculated from the *catasti* of 1469 and 1480, which are inconsistent. The sons' births, with the exception of Federigo, are recorded in ASF, Tratte, Libro dell'Età.

83 Alberti emphasises the need to provide for all levels of inhabitant as well as visitors: *L'Architettura*; IX, viii, pp. 840–1.

84 Shearman, 'The Collections', p. 22, n. 89. At Fiesole the room with two beds is identified as a guestroom and opens off the front hallway on the ground floor: 'la chamera ch'è su l'andito, detta la camera delle dua letta, overo de' forestieri', *Libro d'inventario dei beni di Lorenzo il Magnifico*, p. 172 (c. 83r). At Palazzo Medici the 'camera delle dua letta' is immediately to the right of the front *androne* and beside the 'loggia publica im cantone'; Bulst, 'Aufteilung', p. 377, fig. 3, "Plan 1", room no. 11.

85 Alberti's recommendations take account of this factor: *L'Architettura*, I, ix, p. 67. For recent discussion of this question, see D. Thornton, *The Scholar in His Study*, pp. 27–8; and Preyer, 'Planning for Visitors'.

86 Francesco di Giorgio Martini, in his *Trattati* (I, p. 74), prescribes a similar if more elaborate sequence from *sala* to *salotto* to *anticamare*: 'e a dette anticamare due camare per ciascuna dato serà con destri, studi e camini in nelle streme parti d'esse'; and similarly elsewhere (II, p. 152), a progression up the stairs to a loggia, into the 'sala grande e principale' with a salotto at either end, 'li quali salotti dieno avere camare e postcamere et anticamare, cappella e studii'.

87 This is also Alberti's system, *L'Architettura (De Re aedificatoria)*, I, ix, p. 67: 'sed alia delectabunt, si maiora sint, alia et istorum mediocritate laudem assequentur'.

88 Francesco di Giorgio emphasises the need for privacy in the chapel and the private apartments, *Trattati*, II, p. 152. In

Palazzo Medici the two first-floor apartments of Piero and Giovanni di Cosimo are in analogous positions to those at La Pietra and also make use of the corners for the most private rooms; Bulst, 'Aufteilung', pp. 378–80, fig. 4, "Plan 2", Piero's *scrittoio* no. 7–8 and Giovanni's *scrittoio* (later Giovanni di Lorenzo's *chappelleta*) no. 13.

89 This would certainly have been the case on the first floor at La Pietra where the *verone* may have been the only corridor, while the ground floor was well provided with three *androni*, the loggia and the courtyard.

90 Preyer, 'Planning for Visitors'.

91 Pius II explained the provision of three superimposed kitchens at Pienza as a way of serving food conveniently to all floors while being near the cistern and avoiding the spread of smoke throughout the house, *Memoirs of a Renaissance Pope*, ed. Gragg and Gabel, p. 285. Francesco di Giorgio recommends the same practice, *Trattati*, I, p. 77.

92 Vitruvius, *On Architecture*, Book VI, ch. iv, p. 35. Vitruvius's main recommendations are that the baths and winter dining rooms should face the winter setting sun; that private rooms, libraries and spring and autumn dining rooms face east; while the summer dining rooms should look north. Alberti (*L'Architettura*. I, ix, p. 66) emphasises that summer rooms be larger, better ventilated and in the shade, whereas winter rooms should be smaller. Francesco di Giorgio (*Trattati*, II, p. 329) considers it better for summer rooms to have thick walls and simplifies Vitruvius's orientation by saying that winter rooms should face south and summer rooms north.

93 Madame Charles de Bunsen, *In Three Legations*, p. 200, n. 1: 'The Usedoms [Prussian Ambassador to the Italian Government in 1864] had taken the splendid villa Capponi, situated on the hills under Fiesole. It was an ideal residence, with complete summer and winter apartments, and beautiful views on all sides'.

94 This was the rural equivalent of facing the street or piazza, as Francesco di Giorgio suggests the main *sala* should (*Trattati*, II, p. 152) and as was the usual practice in Florence (eg, the Medici, Rucellai and Pazzi palaces).

95 According to the plan made for Arthur Acton's restoration, the east wall of the courtyard measures 12.85 metres, the west wall 12.88 metres, the north and south walls 12.85–90 metres. These measurements for the north and south sides include the depth of what is now an enclosed corridor (2) which was part of the original courtyard. Vasari the Younger draws a diagonally crossed rectangle on his plan as if to show that there were overhanging *veroni* on three sides of the courtyard and only the crossed central space around the well was open to the sky. As I discuss shortly, however, it seems very unlikely that there were balconies on the north and south sides, and Vasari is inaccurate in other similar cases. Compare Vasari il Giovane, *La Città ideale*, pp. 238–9, disegno 178, p. 108, 'Palazzo de' Borgherini a bellosguardo,' with the courtyard in what is now Villa Mercedes, Lensi-Orlandi *Di Là d'Arno*, pl. 207, showing there are not cantilevered balconies on the shorter sides of the courtyard, as Vasari's plan might suggest.

96 Vasari the Younger's other plans represent columns by their square bases, so there is no reason to suppose that this portico

had rectangular piers (eg, Villa Salviati, *La Città ideale*, p. 241, disegno 183, p. 113).

97 Gunther Thiem and Christel Thiem, *Fassaden-Dekoration*, Palazzo Nasi p. 72, pl. 50–2; Palazzo Spinelli pp. 73–7, pl. 53–6; Palazzo Benizzi-Guicciardini pp. 77–9, pl. 57–8; Palazzo del Comune Antico, Colle Alto di Val d'Elsa pp. 79–80, pl. 62–3; Palazzo Coverelli pp. 80–1, pl. V, 22, 66.

98 While *sgraffito* survives on the north, east and south walls of the old courtyard, it is much harder to establish what took place on the west wall. The north-west corner has been altered by the installation of a lift and the piece of wall visible in the south corner of the west wall is covered in modern plaster.

99 The Palazzo Vecchietti seems to have had two superimposed *veroni* on its upper floors supported by a groined semi-vault below, although those *veroni* run round two sides of the courtyard, unlike Montughi, and the core of the palace was transformed in the sixteenth century; G. and C. Thiem, p. 70, pl. 41.

100 See below p. 230 for further discussion of this point.

101 The vault of the western room (4) is less sharply delineated than that of room 5, but this is most likely the result of different restoration and it (4) has probably been plastered less recently, as is suggested by the remnants of an incised pattern on the south wall.

102 Warburg ('Francesco Sassetti's Last Injunctions,' p. 244 and n. 59) discussed the use of the device of a sling with pebbles which, according to the 'Notizie', had first been used by Niccolò Sassetti in 1360 and was an established part of the coat of arms by the fifteenth century. The most valuable item of jewellery listed in Filippo's *Libro segreto* was a necklace with a gold sling and seventy-two *sassetti* of pearls worth 250 florins; the next most expensive piece was a diamond brooch valued at 200 florins, in the shape of a mermaid or nereid (*serena*), the personal emblem of Nera Sassetti which was later to be featured on her sarcophagus in S. Trinita, Strozziane, II, 20 c. 2 v.

103 This was the phrase used in the document of donation when Francesco placed the villa in the name of his son Federigo on 5 October 1485. Not. antecos. 393 (Ser Andrea di Angiolo da Terranuova, 1482–86), fol. 171r–174r.

104 Archivio Capponi, Patrimonio Vecchio, 53, LIIII, unpaginated insert.

105 See Appendix C. The 'camera del maestro' is listed just before the 'sala terrena' just the other side of the main entrance, while the 'cucina terrena' is listed between the 'entrata dell'orto' and the 'camera da olio del fattore'. The logical sequence of the list of rooms suits this arrangement best, but seems to be contradicted by the earlier reference to the 'andito dell'orto ch'e fra il pozzo e la camera del maestro in terreno'.

106 A. Wright, 'Dancing Nudes'.

107 Lightbown, *Botticelli*, I, pp. 94–7; II, pp. 61–3; INAIL, *Villa Tornabuoni Lemmi di Careggi*, pp. 133, 231. According to first-hand accounts, when Botticelli's frescoes were still in place at the Villa Tornabuoni, three of the walls of the *sala* were

painted. The position of the 'sala grande dipinta' at La Pietra is analogous to the upper loggia with Botticelli's frescoes at Chiasso Macerelli, which had doors opening into adjoining rooms on both short walls and the long walls facing the courtyard on one side and the view on the other.

108 For his chapel in the Badia Fiesolana he chose an enamelled terracotta altarpiece by Andrea della Robbia; see below p. 244.

109 Kennedy, *Baldovinetti*, pp. 157–61.

CHAPTER 11 THE VILLA AT LA PIETRA IN THE CONTEXT OF CONTEMPORARY ARCHITECTURE

1 Lillie, 'The Humanist Villa', pp. 199–200.

2 For Careggi see Stegmann and Geymüller, II, p. 27 fig. 27; Patzak, *Palast und Villa*, II, pp. 74–84, nn. 78–106; Gori Sassoli, 'Michelozzo', pp. 28–32; Ferrara and Quinterio, *Michelozzo*, pp. 245–52, 311–13. Note that the attribution of Careggi to Michelozzo is undocumented.

3 Bartolommeo Sassetti was close to Giovanni de' Medici in the period when the Fiesole villa was built, see above p. 163.

4 *Libro d'Inventario dei beni di Lorenzo il Magnifico*, pp. 168–79 (cc. 81v–86v.).

5 Lillie, 'The Humanist Villa', pp. 201–7.

6 For a convenient juxtaposition of the four plans, see Ginori Lisci, *I Palazzi di Firenze*, II, pp. 810–11. See Bulst, 'Aufteilung', p. 386; and Pius II's description of the entrance to his new palace in Pienza, *Memoirs*, ed. Gragg and Gabel, p. 286.

7 The external dimensions of Palazzo Medici according to Stegmann-Geymüller's plan, II, fig. 16, are as follows: north façade c. 36.05 metres; south (via de' Gori): 38.07 metres; east (Via Larga) 40.81 metres; west (garden) c. 40.30 metres. For a recent analysis of the proportional system of Palazzo Medici, see Bartoli, 'Le Caratteristiche geometriche', and the plans by Alessandra Bossi, Maria Teresa Bartoli and Giovanna Bossi published in Cherubini and Fanelli, *Il Palazzo Medici Riccardi*, pp. 331, 335, with new measurements of the the north façade 36.5 metres; south 38.30 metres, east 40.8 metres, all very close to Stegmann-Geymüller. These are also remarkably similar to those of the Palazzo Piccolomini at Pienza recorded on Pieper's plan, *Pienza*, p. 546: north façade 36.57 metres; south 35.48 metres; east 39.40 metres; and west 39.13 metres. La Pietra's outer walls, according to the plan made for Arthur Acton's restoration, measure on the north façade 35.10 metres; south 32.05 metres; east 33.55 metres; and west 35.30 metres. In summary Palazzo Medici's and the Palazzo Piccolomini's outer measurements all fall within about 36–40 metres, whereas La Pietra's are between 32 and 35.3 metres.

8 At La Pietra the 'loggia terrena' (11) has an average width of 7 metres, whereas the equivalent loggia at Palazzo Medici measures 7.91 metres. On 'the court loggia, an important sitting area', see Preyer, 'Planning for Visitors', p. 359.

9 At Palazzo Medici, there were *veroni* only on the second storey and around all four sides of the courtyard, whereas at La Pietra, there were probably *veroni* on only one side of the court but superimposed on the first and second floors.

10 In the Palazzo Medici the ground-floor apartments are not so clearly defined by the four quarters of the square plan as they are at La Pietra.

11 At Palazzo Medici the 'sala grande' on the *piano nobile* occupied the south side of the Via Larga façade and was not centralised; Bulst, 'Aufteilung', p. 378, fig. 4.

12 The range of small, medium and large rooms came closer to being standardised at La Pietra. There, the four ground-floor *anticamere* are similar in size, whereas the Palazzo Medici contains two tiny 'antichamerette' on the ground floor and one other *anticamera*, which is almost as large as the adjoining *camera*, and the largest *camera* is close in size to the 'sala terrena'. Thus, it is not so easy to read the room functions off the plan at Palazzo Medici and it appears that the interior disposition was not so clearly worked out in the architect's mind; Bulst, 'Aufteilung', p. 387.

13 See Pieper, *Pienza*, pp. 148–51, 382–408 ; Tönnesmann, *Pienza*, p. 62, fig. 31; *Memoirs*, ed. Gragg and Gabel, p. 284.

14 The Palazzo Medici was mostly complete by April–June 1452 when the courtyard *sgraffito* was designed; Fabriczy, 'Michelozzo di Bartolomeo', Beiheft, p. 55, doc. 32; and certainly by early 1453 when the ledger for the building accounts was closed; Hyman, *Florentine Studies*, p. 302, n. 98. The Strozzino Palace may have been the first close derivation, its construction according to Brenda Preyer ('The Rucellai Palace', p. 202, n. 3), 'could have been started about 1451, or as late as 1458'. According to Gianluca Belli ('Il Palazzo dello Strozzino', pp. 39–41), demolition of part of the site was underway in 1451, at least a first stage of construction was complete by 1457, the date of 1463 is inscribed on the ground-floor façade, while a contract for the first-floor façade is dated 1465. Pius II passed through Florence in April 1459 and probably saw the Medici palace. His palace in Pienza, designed by Bernardo Rossellino, was begun in the same year and was already complete by 1462; *Memoirs*, ed Gragg and Gabel, pp. 105–13, 282. Its dependence on the plan of Palazzo Medici is noted by Bulst, 'Aufteilung', pp. 386–7, nn. 91–2; Tönnesmann, *Pienza*, pp. 60–1; Pieper, *Pienza*, p. 145.

15 Only two fifteenth-century villa schemes are illustrated in G. and C. Thiem, *Fassaden-Dekoration*, Villa Portinari-Bondi, pl. 9 and Villa Bellagio, Castello, pl. 70–3. Other examples include Bartolommeo Sassetti's villa at Macia and Filippo Strozzi's villa of Santuccio, also Jacopo di Bernardo de' Medici's villa, Il Sasso, now known as Il Palazzaccio, near Cardetole and the Pitti villa at Rusciano; Lillie, 'Memory of Place', pp. 198–9.

16 Lensi-Orlandi, *Di Qua d'Arno*, pp. 48–9: 'le facciate erano decorate a bozze graffite'. The author may have been informed of this by Arthur Acton.

17 G. and C. Thiem, *Fassaden Dekoration*, pp. 73–2, pl. 50–2; pp. 80–1, pl. V22 and 66. For a more precise dating of the Palazzo Coverelli façade see Elam, 'Viva Papa Leone' p. 178.

18 See Haines, *The Sacrestia delle Messe*, pp. 207–15, and especially p. 209 on the popularity of putto and garland friezes 'in the *sgraffito* decoration of palace exteriors ... in the years around 1460'.

19 The dating of Careggi is problematic, but the barrel vaults of its *androne* and one or two small rooms could be part of the rebuilding that included the courtyard loggias in the late 1440s or 1450s. The long superimposed halls of the dormitory wing at the Badia Fiesolana were built in 1462; Procacci, 'Cosimo de' Medici e la costruzione della Badia Fiesolana', p. 81.

20 I have accepted Brenda Preyer's statement that the Da Uzzano palace was begun by 1411, and completed by 1421: 'The 'chasa overo palagio' of Alberto di Zanobi', p. 387, n. 4. It was probably complete by the time Agnolo da Uzzano made his will in 1421 and almost certainly by the time the inventory was drawn up after Agnolo's death on 2–4 May 1424, where it is described as 'la chasa nuova dove habitavano i detti Nicholo et Agnolo'; Bombe, *Nachlass-Inventare*, pp. 2, 9–10.

21 The Zecca was probably complete before the meeting 'in domo decta Zecha in qua soliti sunt se congregari' in September 1428, perhaps during Cosimo de' Medici's first term as an official, November 1426–May 1427, and while Michelozzo was an engraver there (1410–47). Saalman preferred a date when Medicean power was consolidated during Cosimo's second term 1435–6 or last term 1450–1; 'Michelozzo Studies. The Florentine Mint', pp. 140–2, fig. 11.

22 Saalman, 'The Palazzo Comunale in Montepulciano', fig. 4. I have accepted Saalman's date here but am unaware of evidence to support it.

23 This room to the north of the Chiostro delle Spese, now used as a garage, is labelled 'Barberia' on Vasari the Younger's plan, Uffizi, A4861, reproduced by Teubner, 'S. Marco', p. 240, fig. 1. It is possible that this room belongs to the earlier Silvestrine convent since it is part of the block that includes the old cloister with octagonal piers. However this accommodating form may also belong to the phase when the dormitory was rebuilt and the cells above it constructed in 1437–8 since they all adjoined the Via Lamarmora. In any case, it would not have been built after 1442–3 when the walls surrounding the convent and its outbuildings and gardens were completed; Orlandi, *Beato Angelico*, pp. 66ff.

24 The Villa Pandolfini La Torre was originally built between c. 1380, when Filippo Pandolfini returned to Florence, and his death in 1401. The dentilated imposts and octagonal columns with *foglie d'acqua* capitals may have been part of a second building project undertaken by Filippo's son Agnolo, perhaps before 1434 when Pope Eugenius IV stayed at the villa and when Agnolo adopted it as his permanent residence until his death in 1446; Tampone, *Lastra a Signa*, pp. 95–6, figs. 17–19, 29–30.

25 This comparison does not help to date La Pietra's early wing since the construction of the Rucellai villa Lo Specchio is complex with many alterations and additions combining distinctly early forms c. 1400 with later stylistic types c. 1450, as the range of windows on the exterior of the west wall shows. The villa certainly existed but was modestly furnished in 1406. F. W. Kent has tentatively suggested a building date between the late 1440s and the 1456 marriage celebrations at the villa; 'The Making of a Renaissance Patron of the Arts', p. 40, n. 1.

26 Illustrated in Stegmann and Geymüller, I, p. 97.

27 Procacci, 'Cosimo de' Medici e la costruzione della Badia Fiesolana', p. 81; illustrated in Stegmann-Geymüller, I. p. 98.

28 Preyer, 'The Rucellai Palace', p. 166.

29 See Cherubini and Fanelli, *Il Palazzo Medici Riccardi*, pl. 42 and p. 175.

30 The type even appears in the colonettes of the bifore windows on the first floor of the Palazzo Pazzi, attributed to Giuliano da Maiano by Moscato, *Il Palazzo Pazzi*, an attribution that has been given greater credence by Haines, *The Sacrestia delle Messe*, pp. 167–8 and n. 29 and a dating of after 1458–69 supported.

31 This was originally a small hospital built c. 1460 with funds provided by Andrea di Cresci di Lorenzo Cresci: Carocci, *I Dintorni*, I, pp. 174–5; Patzak, *Palast und Villa*, II, pp. 134–5, n. 331, pl. LVIII 156–9.

32 Salmi, 'Sant'Andrea a Camoggiano', pp. 136–9, tav. LXXII. The date is inscribed on the façade.

33 In the colonettes of the first-floor garden loggia and the second-storey courtyard loggia; Carli, *Pienza*, col. pl. V, pl. 24, 46, 47; Pieper, *Pienza*, figs. 1010, 1028–34.

34 Rotondi (*Il Palazzo Ducale di Urbino*, I, pp. 199–201, II, pl. 87, 89, 90) concurs with Salmi (*Piero della Francesca e il Palazzo Ducale di Urbino*, p. 35, tav. XC, and 'Il Palazzo Ducale di Urbino e Francesco di Giorgio', p. 11) and dates these *peducci* to the years preceding Francesco Laurana's arrival in 1466.

35 Pane ('La sintassi del Brunelleschi', p. 373) remarks that the fluted *peduccio* found in the Spinelli cloister was a type 'destinato ad avere la massima diffusione anche fuori di Firenze; specialmente ad opera di Giuliano da Maiano, da Macerata fino alla vasta commitenza aragonese di Napoli.' Similarly, Goldthwaite and Rearick ('Michelozzo and the Ospedale of San Paolo', p. 293, n. 90) note that the capitals of the men's loggia at the Ospedale of San Paolo (built after 1473) derive from Alberti and Michelozzo's S. Miniato tabernacle, a type which, 'shortly after mid-century, becomes the most popular of the recent capital forms'. It appears in buildings all over the Florentine *contado*, eg. the Villa of Rusciano (Vasic Vatovec, II, p. 670, pl. 2); the Certosa of Galluzzo in the Chiostrino dei Conversi (Chiarelli and Leoncini, *La Certosa di Galluzzo*, pl. 324, 325, p. 24), built between 1484–5; at the Torre Galli at Scandicci and in Il Palazzaccio near Cardetole in the Mugello (1470s). For the most helpful recent summary of the use of this type, see the entry by Rosita Querci and Angela Rensi in Morolli, Acidini Luchinat, Marchetti, *L'Architettura di Lorenzo il Magnifico*, p. 142.

36 Preyer, 'The "chasa overo palagio" of Alberto di Zanobi', p. 399, n. 73.

37 Bulst, 'Aufteilung', p. 387, figs. 3, 4 and 5. Communal palaces such as the Bargello and Palazzo Vecchio also had a *sala* on each floor.

38 Compare them with the much more elaborately carved console brackets in the *sale principale* of the Rucellai palace;

Preyer, 'The Rucellai Palace', pp. 169–70, pl. 22 b and c, 23 a and b. La Pietra *sala grande dipinta* ceiling is more similar to that of the second-floor *sala* at the Palazzo Rucellai; ibid., pl. 22 a.

39 Frommel emphasises this feature in the evolution of palace design; Frommel, *Der römische Palastbau*, I, pp. 68–9.

40 Bulst, 'Aufteilung', pp. 387–8, n. 97; Shearman, 'The Collections', p. 17.

41 Bulst, 'Aufteilung', p. 379, fig. 4, rooms 4, 5, 6 and 7, 8. 2.

42 Bulst, 'Aufteilung', pp. 379–80, fig. 4, rooms 10, 11, 12, 13.

43 Bulst, 'Aufteilung', p. 385; Filarete, *Trattato*, II, p. 696.

44 Rotondi *Il Palazzo ducale di Urbino*, pp. 357–8, pl. 377–8, 383.

45 An inventory made for Gino Capponi in 1828 shows that both chapels were still fully furnished, the oratory upstairs containing among other things, 'un inginocchiatoio, Predella all'Altare . . . Una croce, uno quadro rappresentante la Nascita del Nostro Signore, dipinto nel muro'. This last item could have been a mural. The altarpiece in the chapel downstairs is described as 'un quadro D'Altare di terra della Robbia rappresentante la Madonna'; ASF, Capponi, (Pat. vec.) 53, LIIII.

46 Bulst, 'Aufteilung', p. 386, n. 91; Müntz, *Les Arts à la cour des papes*, I, pp. 355–6.

47 For a fuller discussion of these chapels, see Lillie, 'Cappelle e chiese delle ville medicee' and 'The Patronage of Villa Chapels and Oratories'.

48 Shearman, 'The Collections', p. 23, fol. 492r; Lillie, 'Cappelle e chiese delle ville medicee', pp. 89–90.

49 Bulst, 'Aufteilung', pp. 379–80, 390, fig. 4; Bulst, 'Uso e trasformazione del Palazzo Mediceo,' pp. 115–16. It is even possible that the idea of having a second private chapel in Palazzo Medici originated with the Sassetti; Lillie, 'The Patronage of Villa Chapels and Oratories', pp. 19–20.

50 Ficino, *Opera Omnia*, I, pt. 2, Liber V, pp. 799–800; cited and translated in Warburg, 'Francesco Sassetti's Last Injunctions,' pp. 232–3; 'Ut autem ita res existimare possumus, ideoque feliciter vivere, sola nobis potest praestare religio. Praestabit autem id tibi quandoque plus duplo, quam caeteris, mi Francisce, si tantum ipse religione alios superabis, quantum haec tuae aedes amplissimae alias superant. Duplo tibi Saxette, religiosior domus est, quam caeteris, aliae certe sacellum vix unum habent, tua vero gemina et illa quidem speciosissima continet. Vive religiosior duplo, quam caeteri, mi Francisce, vale duplo felicior.' Warburg (n. 34) did not realise that the palace to which Ficino referred still survived with its two chapels intact; see Lillie, 'Francesco Sassetti and his Villa at La Pietra' (1984), p. 86.

51 Inventories mention this arrangement: the 1497 inventory of Giovanni Tornabuoni's villa of Macerelli (Pupilli, 181, fol. 141r–144r) lists nine main *camere*, of which seven contain at least one religious painting or sculpture, as do three *anti-camere*. Of the sixteen religious works in the house, seven are mentioned as being 'in uno tabernacolo'. An inventory from 1476 of the heirs of Bartolommeo di Domenico del Frate (Pupilli, 175, fol. 133r) includes 'Una Vergine Maria di gieso

in uno tabernacholo cho una chortinuc[i]a dinanzi' followed by 'una chandeliere a bocie a deta Vergine Maria'.

52 Archivio Arcivescovile di Firenze, Oratorii 1591–1613, no. 157: 'Io P. Tommaso Barg[elli?]ni curato a S. Marcho Vecchio ho visitato la sudetta cappella, quale trovo essere remota et adorna di tutte quelle cose necessarie per dirci messa, e non essere inpregiuditi della cura ecse [= eccellenza?] ci fanno dire messa per loro divotione, et ancora quando sono in villa per più commodità, e per amore delle donne et in fide manu propria.' BNF Capponi 91 c. 84, on the 12 August 1615 a payment is recorded to 'Monsignore Antonio Segni e sono per havere cavato due licenzie dal Arcivescovo di Firenze di potere fare celebrare la messa nella cappella di Firenze e di Montui'. These documents only refer to one chapel at Montughi in the early seventeenth century, which I presume was the ground-floor chapel. This confirms that at this date the oratory was only used for private prayer. Since it did not need a license, it probably did not contain the Host and was therefore not equipped for mass, or the Capponi may have allowed its earlier status to lapse. Filarete's description of the Palazzo Medici dwells on the fact that in the chapel 'si celebra tanto sacramento, quanto è nel vero corpo e sangue di Cristo'; *Trattato*, II, Libro XXV, p. 696.

53 See Lillie, 'The Patronage of Villa Chapels', p. 32. In Bartolomeo Scala's palace (c. 1473–7), the miniature Greek cross plan and pendentive dome of the ground floor chapel is very likely derived from the Montughi oratory. Sanpaolesi, 'La Casa fiorentina di Bartolomeo Scala', pp. 275–88; Pellecchia, 'The Patron's Role', pp. 270–4. Bartolomeo Fonzio's poem written to Scala mentions the Sassetti villa of Montughi (Lillie, 'Francesco Sassetti and his Villa at La Pietra' [1984], p. 85), so Scala is likely to have known the house.

54 Francesco di Giorgio, *Trattati*, I, p. 72.

55 Bombe (*Nachlass-Inventare*, p. 13, n. 1) assumes that the bath was in a separate room of its own. Inventories do not mention any accessories connected to the bath with the exception of the Da Uzzano inventory, 'pezzi di pannolino vecchio per la stufa' (perhaps rubbing cloths or towels intended for the 'frictio' recommended by Celsus; see Burns, 'Un disegno architettonico di Alberti', p. 119, n. 10).

56 Bulst, 'Aufteilung', p. 377 and fig. 3.

57 See Chapter 10, p. 196.

58 Francesco di Giorgio (*Trattati*, I, pp. 99–101) suggests that the bath be on the west (as did Vitruvius) and near a bed, so the bather could dry himself immediately and keep warm: 'una camara o spogliatoio che quando esci del bagno in nel letto subito asciugar ti possa.' Both these factors apply at Montughi.

59 Vitruvius (*De Architectura*, trans. Cesariano, Como 1521, Liber IX, fol. cxlvi v) portrays Archimedes in a large portable wooden tub in a medium-sized vaulted room with heating apparatus built into a niche in one wall. See also Memmo di Filippuccio's frescoes in the Camera del Podesta, Palazzo del Popolo, S. Gimignano.

60 Francesco di Giorgio, *Trattati* I, tav. 42; II tav. 188.

61 Preyer, 'The Rucellai Loggia', pp. 183–98.

62 Schiaparelli, *La Casa fiorentina*, I, pp. 67–72, figs. 44, 65, 66, II figs. 49, 50, 51. I do not know of any freestanding family loggias surviving from the fifteenth century in the countryside. Bartolomeo Scala built a loggia removed from the palace on his property in the Borgo Pinti (Sanpaolesi, 'La Casa fiorentina di Bartolomeo Scala', pp. 280–1, n. 4), but this seems to have been part of his new garden and may have been more suitable for recreation than the Montughi loggia.

63 F. W. Kent, 'The Rucellai Family and its Loggia', pp. 397–401.

64 See Rucellai, 'Il Zibaldone', p. 20; F. W. Kent, 'The Rucellai Family and its Loggia', p. 397 n. 203; Bulst, 'Aufteilung', p. 382.

65 The prominent display of coats of arms on family loggias reinforces this suggestion; Schiaparelli, *La Casa fiorentina*, I, p. 69, II tav. 49a, 50, 52a, b, c.

66 Francesco Datini's villa Il Palco near Prato was set on a hill removed from the road, but a small house placed on the roadside at the foot of the hill, 'una casetta a piè del luogho in su la strada va in Bisenzio', may have functioned as a gatehouse; Imberciadori, 'Proprietà terriera di Francesco Datini', p. 257.

67 Coming from the north via Bologna this was one of the main routes into Florence in the fifteenth century with entry through the Porta San Gallo. For descriptions of official welcomes at other sites, see Pius II, *Memoirs*, ed. Gragg and Gabel, p. 105; Trexler, *Public Life*, pp. 306–8; Shearman, 'A Functional Interpretation of Villa Madama', pp. 319–21, and Coffin, *The Villa*, pp. 66–7, 149.

68 De la Mare, 'The Library of Francesco Sassetti', p. 162.

69 De la Mare, 'The Library of Francesco Sassetti', p. 163, p. 178, no. 7, Biblioteca Laurenziana, Plutei 10.

70 Krinsky ('78 Vitruvius Manuscripts', p. 37 ff.) lists three Vitruvius manuscripts certainly in Florence in the fifteenth century: Sassetti's and two belonging to the Medici (Laur, Plutei XXX, 11 and XXX, 12). Of Krinsky's seventy-eight extant manuscripts, at least twenty-seven entire texts of Vitruvius were copied and bound with other texts or excerpts to form one volume. Vegetius's *De Re militari* (7 mss.) or Faventinus's *De Agricultura* (5 mss.) were the favourite texts to combine with Vitruvius. Sassetti's manuscript is the only example in which Cato and Varro's agricultural treatises appear with the Ten Books, although Palladius's *De Agricultura* is combined with Vitruvius in three cases.

71 G. Clarke, *Roman House*, p. 176.

72 Vitruvius, *On Architecture*, trans. Granger, II, Lib. VI, cap. vi, pp. 38–41, 42–3.

73 Alberti, *On the Art of Building*, trans. Rykwert, Leach, Tavernor, Book IX, ch. 2, fol. 159v–160v, pp. 294–5.

CHAPTER 12   THE ROLE OF THE VILLA AT LA PIETRA IN THE LIFE OF FRANCESCO SASSETTI

1 Dale Kent (*The Rise of the Medici*, pp. 75–6) cites the Sassetti as one of the families who were Medicean supporters before 1434 and were then promoted in the Medici bank when Cosimo returned to power. Francesco's father-in-law Piero di Domenico Corsi had been in partnership with the Medici in a silk shop in the 1430s (R. de Roover, *The Rise and Decline*, p. 168), and another Corsi relative, Banco, was a Medici partisan (D. Kent ibid., p. 75, p. 352). See also n. 38, this chapter.

2 Cosimo de' Medici had arranged Bartolommeo's marriage to Antonia della Tosa, and it was probably through Cosimo's influence that Bartolommeo became prior in 1453; see Chapter 9. Hyman, *Florentine Studies*, p. 302, in 1451: shortly before the account books for the Medici palace closed, Bartolommeo's tax return states, 'truovomi esser conpagnio alla sservizio overo traffico della bottegha dell'oro filato che dice in Tommaso di Luigi di Messer Lorenzo Ridolfi e Comp[agn]a' (Cat 709, fol. 170v).

3 F. Edler de Roover, 'Francesco Sassetti', gives the fullest account of Sassetti's private finances although a fundamental error – that Francesco was first employed in Avignon (an error that originated in Francesco di Giovambatista's 'Notizie') – was corrected by R. de Roover, *The Rise and Decline*, p. 481, n. 20. R. de Roover's information about Sassetti's early career should be supplemented with Bergier's 'Lettres genevoises', pp. 279–310 and his *Genève et l'économie européenne*, pp. 282–8, as well as the excellent analysis of the financial situation among Italian bankers in Geneva by Cassandro, 'Banca e commercio'.

4 MAP VII, 327, 19 May 1452; Bergier ('Lettres Genevoises', pp. 290–1) thought the letter was sent to Piero di Cosimo, whereas it was clearly addressed to Pierfrancesco di Lorenzo de' Medici.

5 MAP XVII, 127, Francesco Sassetti in Geneva to Piero di Cosimo de' Medici in Florence, 24 August, 1456: 'un saggio del pannolino mi chiexe Madonna Lucretia per le camice della Bianca'.

6 De la Mare, 'The Library of Francesco Sassetti', p. 192, n. 21.

7 MAP VII, 327, 19 May 1452: 'non entrare in dire che tu mi dia faticha, che mi fai dispiacere: te sai ch'io sono stato et sarò sempre servidore della chasa vostra, et è mmi gratia et non faticha quando fo cosa che vi sia gratia'.

8 MAP XVII, 127, 24 August 1456, De la Mare, 'The Library of Francesco Sassetti', p. 192, n. 21: 'sono pure vostro et vostra creatura et con voi'o a vivere et morire'.

9 For a summary of Francesco Sassetti's political appointments and public offices, see De la Mare, 'The Library of Francesco Sassetti', p. 191, n. 11.

10 Sassetti, 'Notizie', p. xxxvi; Warburg, 'Francesco Sassetti's Last Injunctions', pp. 224–5 and n. 11, trans. p. 227.

11 Sassetti, 'Notizie', p. xxxvi; Warburg, 'Francesco Sassetti's Last Injunctions', p. 224, trans. p. 227.

12 Warburg, 'Francesco Sassetti's Last Injunctions', p. 250, n. 9; Litta Fasc. 63, Paleologo Marchesi di Monferrato, tav. I and II; for the Marquis of Monferrato's dealings with the Medici bank, see MAP XII, 221.

13 An idea of Galeazzo Sforza's popularity during his visit to Florence in 1459 can be gained from Pius II's account, *Memoirs of a Renaissance Pope*, ed. Gragg and Gabel, and from the anonymous 'Ricordi di Firenze dell'anno 1459,' ed. G. Volpi, *Rerum italicarum scriptores*, vol. 27, part I, p. 6.

14 Trexler (*Public Life*, p. 423 and n. 17) notes that this was a way to honour the Medici and refers to Giovanni Rucellai, whose grandson was named Cosimo (Rucellai, 'Il Zibaldone', p. 35).

15 Klapisch-Zuber, 'Childhood in Tuscany', pp. 99–100; 'The Name "Remade"', pp. 290–309; F. W. Kent provides similar evidence in *Household and Lineage*, pp. 254–5.

16 See below pp. 244–5.

17 Borsook and Offerhaus, *Sassetti and Ghirlandaio*, pp. 12–14; Hatfield, 'Giovanni Tornabuoni', pp. 112–13.

18 1480 Cat. 1013, II, fol. 319r.

19 *Libro segreto*, Strozziane, II, 20, 1462, fol. 2r; Cat. 921, fol. 282r; Cat. 1013, pt. II, fol. 319r. This house was the first to be sold after Francesco's death; Decima Repub. 24, fol. 471v.

20 Cat. 921, fol. 282r.

21 1480 Cat. 1013, II, fol. 319r.

22 Butterfield, *The Sculptures of Andrea del Verrocchio*, p. 16.

23 Warburg, 'Francesco Sassetti's Last Injunctions', pp. 252–3, n. 35; Pope-Hennessy, *The Study and Criticism of Italian Sculpture*, pp. 31–5; Butterfield, *The Sculptures of Andrea del Verrocchio*, pp. 15–16, 203.

24 *Libro segreto*, Strozziane, II, 20, fol. 2r, 70v–71r.

25 Sassetti, 'Notizie', p. xxxvii; Warburg, 'Francesco Sassetti's Last Injunctions', pp. 225–6, trans p. 228.

26 1480 Cat. 1013, II, fol. 319r–321r.

27 Lillie, 'Francesco Sassetti and his Villa at La Pietra', pp. 88–9; Warburg, 'Francesco Sassetti's Last Injunctions', pp. 225–6, trans. p. 228, n. 18; and Bergier, *Genève et l'économie européenne*, p. 284.

28 *Libro segreto*, Strozziane, II, 20, fol. 71; Warburg, 'Francesco Sassetti's Last Injunctions', p. 226, trans. p. 228, n. 20.

29 Viti, *La Badia Fiesolana*, p. 54.

30 Viti, *La Badia Fiesolana*, pp. 63–5.

31 R. de Roover, *The Rise and Decline*, pp. 377–9. These four chapels, whose patrons were all Medici bank managers, were in a row occupying the whole right-hand side of the nave; Viti, *La Badia Fiesolana*, pp. 63–5; Nuttall, 'The Patrons of Chapels at the Badia of Fiesole', pp. 97–112; Rohlmann, 'Flämische Tafelmalerei', p. 184.

32 Viti, *La Badia Fiesolana*, pp. 65–6.

33 Bandini, *Lettere XII*, p. 50.

34 Gentilini, *La Misericordia di Firenze*, I, cat. no. 39, pp. 228–31.

35 Marquand, *Andrea della Robbia*, II, p. 62, attributed the altarpiece to the workshop of Andrea della Robbia. Gentilini, *La Misericordia di Firenze*, I, pp. 228–31, and *Andrea della Robbia*, I, *Madonne*, p. 6, has linked the altarpiece to Sassetti's payment and argues that it was executed by Andrea della Robbia before he left Luca's workshop.

36 See Lynn Hartloff's paper on Sassetti's project for a big palace in town, supervised by Rab Hatfield. Sassetti bought the nucleus and largest part of the palace site from the sons of Francesco di Benedetto di Caroccio Strozzi, one of whom, Lorenzo, was married to Francesco Sassetti's niece Camilla di Federigo Sassetti.

37 Cat. 1427, S. Giovanni, Leon d'Oro, Fiondina Sassetti; although an inventory of Fiondina's estate in 1431 described the farm as having all the necessary appurtenances – a tower, loggia, courtyard, threshing floor and oven – it was only

capitalised at 238 florins, 18 *soldi*, 8 *denari*, in 1427 and in 1430 yielded 38 *staia* of wheat, 8 *staia* of barley, 8.5 *staia* of sorghum and 13 barrels of wine – a modest property. I am grateful to Rab Hatfield for showing me his transcription of documents concerning Fiondina's estate of which this is one.

38 Cat. 373, fol. 124r, the 1430 tax return of Antonio di Piero Sassetti 'vocato Rosso'. Rosso was a Medici partisan before 1434; see Dale Kent, *The Rise of the Medici* p. 75. Bartolommeo and Francesco may even have owed their initial employment by the Medici to Rosso's loyalty.

39 This summary is based on the archival material collected by Rab Hatfield; see Hatfield, 'Giovanni Tornabuoni', pp. 112–13.

40 Borsook and Offerhaus, *Sassetti and Ghirlandaio* pp. 65–6, documents no. 19 and 20.

41 1480 Cat. 1013, II, fol. 319v.

42 Borsook and Offerhaus, *Sassetti and Ghirlandaio* p. 61 document no. 11, the first item, as is clarified in the donation to Federigo and a further notarial document found by Hatfield.

43 On Federigo's death they passed to his mother Nera; 1498 Decima Repub. 25, fol. 203r–v. Since the previous taxation of 1480, Francesco Sassetti had bought one more piece of land at Novoli in March 1482 from the church of S. Pancrazio in Florence.

44 1469 Cat. 921, fol. 282v.

45 1480 Cat. 1013, II, fol. 319v.

46 Repetti, cf. Confienti, I, p. 791.

47 Lillie, 'Francesco Sassetti and his Villa at La Pietra', p. 85. In Fonzio's poem to Sassetti, *Carmina*, p. 5, I, 5, the complementary sites of the two villas are accentuated through juxtaposition: 'Montugium testis, testis Ghonfentia Tempe, / Hic bene quaesitas tu bene ponis opes'. The name Montughi already conveys its elevation, while 'Tempe' is a reference to the valley in Thessaly, so that with this metaphor Fonzio associates pastoral and mythological charm with Gonfienti and the Arno valley as well as commenting on its topography.

48 Repetti, I, p. 513.

49 Filippo Strozzi's estates at Capalle and Maglio were similar to Francesco Sassetti's Gonfienti and Casi in function and site and in their relation to each other.

50 1480 Cat. 1013, II, fol. 320v; 1534 Decima Granducale Campone 3624, M–Z, fol. 404r; Decima Repub. Arroti 152, fol. 132r; 153, fol. 119r. The farm owned by Stagio d'Antonio Strozzi was already known as Il Mulinaccio when he filed his tax return in 1430, Cat. 405, fol. 278r. It retains the same name today. Although there are no discernable remains of the fifteenth-century structure, the nucleus of the villa appears to date from the early sixteenth century, with a large seventeenth-century addition and many subsequent alterations. Cosimo Sassetti's purchases of land in the area at the beginning of the sixteenth century suggest that there may be truth in Francesco di Giambatista Sassetti's statement that Cosimo built a fine villa at Casi from scratch ('Notizie', p. xxxix), and the style of the portals is consistent with a construction date between c. 1505 and Cosimo's death in 1527. In 1527 the estate passed to his brother Teodoro and

subsequently from Teodoro's son Giovanbattista to his son Filippo the explorer, who sold it back to the Strozzi. Pietro d'Amerigo Strozzi sold it to Ferrante Vai and Marco Roncioni in 1661, and it remained in the Vai family until c. 1960; Petri and Paoletti, *Ville Pratesi*, pp. 33–48, 'Villa Vai'. My thanks to the Franchi family who kindly allowed me to explore their house in 1981.

51 This is stipulated in the notarial document of sale shown to me by Rab Hatfield. Although this small church appears on Capitani di Parte maps (c. 1580), and the name Casi still refers to several crumbling, uninhabited houses; none of these is recognisable as a church or chapel.

52 The London branch was in debt by 1465 (R. de Roover, *The Rise and Decline*, p. 330), and the Medici withdrew in 1472 (ibid., p. 334). The Bruges branch took unwarrented risks from 1473 (ibid., p. 346), crisis struck with the death of Charles the Bold in 1477 (ibid., p. 348) and the partnership with Tommaso Portinari was wound up in 1480 (ibid., p. 353). In Avignon, trade was decaying by 1476 and the branch had been closed by 1480 (ibid., p. 315). The bank in Milan was liquidated in 1478 (ibid., p. 274), and the Venice bank was liquidated for the second time in 1479–81 (ibid., p. 253). Anti-Medicean support for the Pazzi conspiracy meant that all Medici property was seized in Rome and Naples and the banks were closed in 1478. The Naples branch reopened the following year, but business did not pick up until 1487 (ibid., pp. 258–9). The Rome bank returned in 1481 but was in debt in the later 1480s (ibid., pp. 221–3).

53 Fonzio's poem, 'Somnium Theodori Saxetti', *Carmina*, p. 10, I, 12, makes it clear that Teodoro I died in Lyons ('Qua Rhodanum celerem lenior implet Arar: / Saxettus Theodorus amans invisere Gallos / Accessit Rhodani nobile nomen aquis'.). I presume he had begun to work for the Medici bank there, as his brothers soon did; de Roover, *The Rise and Decline*, pp. 302, 310.

54 Not. antecos. 392 (Ser Andrea di Angiolo da Terranuova, 1476–81), fols. 156v–158r. I am grateful to Rab Hatfield, who gave me his transcriptions of this and the following documents of emancipation and donation which form part of his documentary study of the Sassetti family.

55 Not. antecos. 392 (Ser Andrea di Angiolo da Terranuova 1476–81), fols. 228v–230r. *Statuta* of 1415, I, pp. 206–7: 'aetas ligitima' was reached at eighteen years.

56 Not. antecos. 393 (Ser Andrea di Angiolo da Terranuova, 1482–6), fols. 171r–174r.

57 'stando pacifichi et uniti et portando amore et riverenza l'uno all'altro immodo che tra voi sia ogni concordia...Difendetevi et aiutatevi valentemente et con buono animo, immodo non siate giunti al sonno nè giudicati imbecilli o da poco; et habbiendo a dividere, fatelo segretamente et d'accordo con l'aiuto di cognati et parenti vostri, bisogniando, vivendo in amore et carità et vivere insieme, maxime habbiendo cura de' minori di voi et della loro parte come di voi medesimi'; Warburg, 'Francesco Sassetti's Last Injunctions', p. 235, trans p. 237. Warburg gives the archival reference for the 1490 copy of the *ultima volontà* as ASF Appendice Carte Bagni, Inserto no. 25 ('Francesco Sassetti's Last

Injunctions', p. 233, n. 36). Although this document has been lost, there are photographs of the manuscript made for Aby Warburg in the Warburg Institute Archive, III, 70.2. See Fig. 202.

58 'A Messer Federigo et a Teodoro et a Madonna Nera, et anche in alcuno di voi, ho facto carta et contracti d'alcuno nostri beni, quando si sono comperati et prima et poi secondo ch'è accaduto, come troverrete pe' libri miei al luogho suo; voglio non dimancho che ogni cosa sia comune tra voi, ciascuno per la rata sua, come se e' decti contracti non fussino facti, et che nessuno vantaggio sia dall'uno all'altro, come è ragionevole. Così seguite interamente et unitamente come giusti e buoni figliuoli et frategli, immodo apparischa et si dimostri la vostra carità et benivolenza fraternale, maxime sappiendo decti contracti essersi fatto a altro fine: cioè, per salvare i vostri beni et non per fare vantaggio l'uno dall'altro'; Warburg, 'Francesco Sassetti's Last Injunctions', p. 238.

59 Sassetti makes it quite clear in the *ultima volontà* that he had annulled his earlier will; Warburg, 'Francesco Sassetti's Last Injunctions,' p. 235, trans p. 237. Rab Hatfield has found notarial documents that confirm this statement.

60 'vorrei faciessi ciò che potessi di mantenerlo sotto il nome et titolo di Messer Federigo, in cui è cartoreggiato et fattogliene donazione...lo lasciate in decto nome di Messer Federigo, perchè con la cherica lo saprà et potrà meglio difendere, in quanto il tempo vi dimostri così essere il meglio'; Warburg, 'Francesco Sassetti's Last Injunctions', p. 236, trans pp. 238–9.

61 Not. antecos. 393 (Ser Andrea di Angiolo da Terranuova, 1482–6), 27–8 February 1484/5, fols. 139r–141r.

62 R. de Roover, *The Rise and Decline*, pp. 302, 310.

63 Del Piazzo, *Protocolli*, p. 449.

64 Borsook and Offerhaus (*Sassetti and Ghirlandaio*, pp. 37–8) emphasise the support given to Giovanni de' Medici's ecclesiastical career by the Vallombrosans of S. Trinita and by Sassetti's sons Cosimo and Galeazzo. However, the authors do not point out that, having assisted Giovanni de' Medici, the Sassetti now hoped that the Medici would reciprocate on behalf of Federigo Sassetti. The letters (see nn. 69 and 70, this chapter) requesting a benefice in S. Maria del Fiore also show that they had higher ambitions for Federigo than to become abbot of S. Trinita.

65 The date of 28 February 1485 for Federigo's benefice would support Welliver's argument for late changes to the fresco cycle ('Alterations in Ghirlandaio's S. Trinita Frescoes') but still gives time for completion before the consecration date for the chapel in December 1485, inscribed on the altarpiece.

66 Borsook and Offerhaus, *Sassetti and Ghirlandaio*, pp. 17–18, n. 18; 38, n. 132; Elam and Gombrich, 'Lorenzo de' Medici and a Frustrated Villa Project', letter on p. 485.

67 R. de Roover, *The Rise and Decline*, pp. 308–9. See also Cosimo Sassetti's letters reporting on the state of the abbey of Fonte Dolce (MAP XXVI, 501 and XXXIX, 461) and recommending measures to be taken to restore its buildings and provide furnishings.

68 Roscoe, *Leo X*, pp. 24, 31. Giovanni de' Medici was nominated cardinal on 9 October 1488. Because of his youth,

he remained on probation until his investiture on 9 March 1491/2.

69 MAP LXXXVIII, 199, 24 December [1488], Francesco Sassetti in Lyons to Lorenzo de' Medici in Florence: 'Ancora vi raccomando Federigo prete. Dexidero una prebenda per lui in Santa Maria Del Fiore. Priegovi non mene manchiate quando vacasse o vi paresse tempo perchè questo è il maggiore stimolo ch'io abbia in questo mondo. / Io non dubitai mai del cappello di Messer G[iovanni], benchè molti mello [meglio?] sara locati in sule vostra badie. Tengo al continuo le mani. Aspettovi da Fonte Dolce al Bellina fra pochi giorni'.

70 Cosimo Sassetti's requests for promotion on behalf of his brother Federigo begin soon after his father's death: MAP XLII, 60, 10 May 1490 to Lorenzo de' Medici: 'Vogliate prestare favore in avere la possessione dell' archidiachanato di Santa Liperata suto resengnato a Federigho nostro fratello'. MAP XLII, 114, 16 July 1490, same correspondents: 'ancora vi priegho a porgiervi aiuto in avere la posessione del calonachato di Federigho nostro fratello el quale 'a pocho di rendita et velo racommando'. Finally after Federigo's death he wrote to Piero da Bibbiena on 15 January 1491/2, MAP CXXIV, 33: 'trouvomi alquanto in dispiaciere della perdita del mio caro fratello, la quale m'a dato et dà gran molestia, parendomi restare vedovo da delle più care cose avessi, perchè in esso avevo messo la mira d'alchuni mie disegni che speravo con tenpo m'avessino a riuscire . . . Dopo el dispiacemento mi sono assai rallegrato del buono animo dimostrò el maggiore [Lorenzo de' Medici] verso di noi et le cose nostre di fare conferire el benefizio che teneva Messer Federigo al nostro nipote [probably Federigo di Tomaso di Federigo Sassetti, Francesco Sassetti's great-nephew], che quantunque io mai faciessi dubbio della sua beningnità verso di noi mi ghode l'animo'.

71 'Lorenzo questo è il maggior caso ch'io habbi o possa havere in questo mondo et chi stimassi ch'io non ne facessi ogni cosa mi giudicherebbe pazzo: perchè c'impegnerei la vita e figluoli et ciò che ho in questo mondo' (Francesco Sassetti in Florence writing to Lorenzo de' Medici at the Bagni di Morba, 22 May 1486, MAP XXXIX, 510).

72 'Piglo gran conforto leggiendo la vostra lettera aiutativa e piena d'amore parendomi ragionare con voi come già solevamo e ricordomi de' tempi felici e tranquilli dopo tanti affanni e pericoli abbiamo a ritornare presto a godere qualche poco avanti il nostro fine' (24 December 1488, MAP LXXXVIII, 199). There is no year given but according to internal evidence 1488 is the most likely; in which case Francesco Sassetti was writing from Lyons during his final trip to try and save the bank there to Lorenzo de' Medici in Florence.

73 'Non abbiendo noi altro ricorso che alla V(ostra) M(agnificenza) non posso fare che del continuo non ricordi et racomandi a quella ongni nostro caso. Restiamo con pocho o non punto di mobile et ch'o debiti vi sapete a Lione. Non di manco ci aiutiamo quanto possiamo per vestirre. Prieghovi non ci vogliate abandonare come mai non faciesti nessuno vostro fidele servidore come siamo et volgliamo essere, noi che siamo nati con questo leghame' (Cosimo Sassetti in Tours to Lorenzo de' Medici in Florence, 16 July 1490, MAP XLII, 114).

74 See F. W. Kent, *Household and Lineage*, pp. 75–7, 142–4, and 'The Making of a Renaissance Patron', pp. 53–4; also Preyer, 'The Rucellai Palace', p. 203.

75 MAP XLII, 26, Cosimo Sassetti in Amboise to Lorenzo de' Medici in Florence: 'nostro padre non ci'a lasciato alchuno mobile di danari cho' quali possiamo chancellare detti debiti; et di questo mene potete agiustare fede, che mai trouverrete che io vi radia [?] se non con la verità, perchè desidero piu mantenere la fede et amore vostro che preservare la vita mia. Vero è che abbiamo qualche mobile di cose sottili come gioie et arienti diche a ogni modo vogliamo fare fine per sodisfare parte de' sopradetti debiti'.

76 De la Mare, 'The Library of Francesco Sassetti', pp. 170–1 and n. 102.

77 Decima Repub. 24, fol. 471v, sold on 12 October 1491 to Niccolò d'Adouardo Tosinghi.

78 See the *Decime* of 1498 submitted by Teodoro (Decima Repub. 25, fol. 441r–442r), Galeazzo (Decima Repub. 24, fol. 470r–472r) and their mother Nera (Decima Repub. 25, fol. 203r – v) with marginal annotations from 1532. For Cosimo's and his widow's tax returns, see 1504 Decima Repubblicana Arroti 152, fol. 132r; and 1534 Decima Granducale Campione 3624, fol. 14v–15r. Other useful tax returns for this later period are for Galeazzo's widow (Decima Granducale Campione 1534, 3622, A–F, fol. 502r–503r) and Teodoro, the only one of Francesco's sons still alive in 1534 (Decima Granducale Campione 1534, 3624, M–Z, fol. 403v–405r).

79 'El palagio di Montughi come sapete ha dato gran fama e reputatione al nome mio e alla famiglia nostra et è molto celebrato per Italia et altrove non inmerito, perchè come sapete è bello et costa danari assai' (Warburg, 'Francesco Sassetti's Last Injunctions', p. 236, trans p. 238).

80 This theme is explored in the writings of Goldthwaite, F. W. Kent and Preyer with reference to the Strozzi, the Rucellai, the Capponi, the di Zanobi and the Nori families, among others.

81 Warburg, 'Francesco Sassetti's Last Injunctions', p. 236: 'costa danari assai . . . di pocha rendita et luogho da richi . . . si tira drieto grande spesa'; trans. pp. 238–9.

82 Warburg, 'Francesco Sassetti's Last Injunctions', p. 236: 'si tira drieto . . grande invidia'; trans. p. 328, 'it invites envy'.

83 Warburg, 'Francesco Sassetti's Last Injunctions', p. 236: 'per essere di molta burbanza'.

84 Warburg, 'Francesco Sassetti's Last Injunctions', p. 236: 'la cherica lo saprà e potrà meglio difendere'.

85 *Memoirs*, ed. Gragg and Gabel, p. 107.

86 Alberti, *L'Architettura [De Re aedificatoria]*, II, p. 855, Lib. IX cap. x, 'verum ita aedificasse, ut lauti approbent, frugi non respuant'; trans., *On the Art of Building*, p. 315.

87 'Ricordasi di me quando siate nella consolatione di cotesta bella villa, maxime d'Africo in quel bel boschetto di Franc[esc]o Nori dove vi dovrebbe essere una fontana' (MAP, XCVI, 195; 26 November 1488). Africo was a property in the parish of S. Maria at Antella, which included a house for

Nori's own use with a garden, two farms, a farmhouse, two kilns, an olive press and many pieces of woodland scattered across the district; Pupilli 174, fol. 236r–237r. The unusual mention of a fountain in the 1478 inventory of the properties belonging to the heirs of Francesco d'Antonio di Tomaso Nori (Pupilli, 174, fol. 235v) makes it likely that Sassetti was also referring to the Nori villa of Lonchio in the parish of S. Lorenzo a Montisone near Antella: 'Una chasa cho[n] logg[i]a e prategli e orto murato cho[n] una chapella e vincio [?] e fonte e sala e chamere e cholonbaia e stala e altre sue apartenenze posta nel popolo di Sa[n] Lorenzo a Montisoni luogho detto a Lonchio da p[rim]o, 1/2, 1/3, 1/4 dette redi di Franc[esco] Nori dove abitava detto Franc[esc]o'. See Preyer, 'Florentine Palaces and Memories', p. 187, and A. De la Mare, 'Vespasiano da Bisticci', pp. 349, 384.

CONCLUSION

1   On the villa as a 'pleasure house', see, for example, Ackerman, *The Villa*, pp. 9, 10.

2   Alberti, 'I Libri della famiglia' and 'Villa'.

3   For example, Cato, Varro, Columella and Piero de' Crescenzi.

4   Aristotle, *Oeconomica*, trans. Armstrong, pp. 329, 339–43; Soudek, 'Leonardo Bruni and his Public'; Soudek, 'A Fifteenth-Century Humanist Bestseller'.

5   Alberti, *L'Architettura*, Book V, cap. xv, pp. 404–5; *On the Art of Building*, p. 141.

6   Here I would argue against Judith Brown's statement ('Prosperity or Hard Times', p. 764) that 'the attitude towards the land and its people expressed by those seeking a retreat is bound to be different from those seeking to exploit the land for economic returns', and ask what if people sought both?

See Azzi Visentini, *La Villa in Italia*, p. 13, on the ancient Roman combination of agriculture and pleasure.

7   Morelli, *Ricordi*, p. 92, 'boschetti . . . acconci per diletto'.

8   Lorenzo Strozzi, *Le Vite*, ed. Zeffi, p. 16.

9   Alberti, 'Villa', p. 360.

10   See, for example, the subdivisions made by Frommel, 'La Villa Madama', p. 47, and Heydenreich, 'La Villa: genesi e sviluppi', p. 12.

11   Klapisch-Zuber, 'Mezzadria e insediamenti rurali', pp. 152–3, 156: 'Il rinnovo del patrimonio immobiliare non avviene dunque brutalmente ma attraverso ritocchi successivi . . . la documentazione disponibile – i libri di ricordi ad esempio – indica che i proprietari si sono accontentati di riadattare edifici esistenti; e dopo l'avvento e il rotorno della peste, quando molto delle case abbandonate e minaccianti rovina offrono strutture ancora recuperabili, gli osti hanno semplicemente assicurato i restauri indispensabili ai migliori fra di esse per destinarle ai bisogni di un nuovo podere. Una vecchia torre è divenuta così colombaia o casa da signore, una vecchia casa è divenuta stala, un forno dipendente da una azienda abbandonata viene ristrutturato per servire a un altro podere. Così facendo, gli osti contribuiscono a promuovere l'inserimento dei poderi nel vecchio tessuto dell'habitat, cambiandone la destinazione e la funzione'. Pinto, 'Storia delle dimore mezzadrili', pp. 160–1: 'è significativo che nelle fonti toscane del '300 e della prima metà del 400 siano rarissimi i casi di costruzioni *ex-novo* di case poderali'. This view is confirmed by Conti, *Le Campagne*, I, p. 60; Jones, 'From Manor to Mezzadria', pp. 231–3; Herlihy, 'Santa Maria Impruneta', p. 155; de la Roncière, 'Un changeur florentin', pp. 122–30; and Pirillo, 'Case rurali, castelli ed altri insediamenti', pp. 441 ff.

12   Goldthwaite, 'The Florentine Palace as Domestic Architecture', p. 977.

BIBLIOGRAPHY

Ackerman, James S., 'Sources of the Renaissance Villa', *Studies in Western Art: Acts of the Twentieth International Congress of the History of Art*, 2 vols. (Princeton, 1963), vol. II, 6–18.

Ackerman, James S., *The Villa. Form and Ideology of Country Houses* (London, 1990).

Acton, Harold, *Memoirs of an Aesthete* (London, 1948).

Acton, Harold, *Tuscan Villas*, with photographs by A. Zielcke (London, 1973).

Alberti, Leon Battista, 'I Libri della famiglia', *Opere volgari*, ed. Cecil Grayson (Bari, 1960), vol. I, 3–341.

Alberti, Leon Battista, 'Villa', *Opere volgari*, ed. Cecil Grayson (Bari, 1960), vol. I, 359–63.

Alberti, Leon Battista, *L'Architettura* [*De re aedificatoria*], Latin text, ed. and Italian trans. Giovanni Orlandi, introduction and notes Paolo Portoghesi, 2 vols. (Milan, 1966).

Alberti, Leon Battista, *The Family in Renaissance Florence*, trans. Renée Neu Watkins [of 'I Libri della famiglia'] (Columbia, S.C., 1969).

Alberti, Leon Battista, *On the Art of Building in Ten Books*, trans. Joseph Rykwert, Neil Leach and Robert Tavernor (Cambridge, Mass. and London, 1988).

Archivio Salviati. Documenti sui beni immobiliari dei Salviati: palazzi, ville, feudi. Piante del territorio, ed. Ewa Karwacka Codini and Milletta Sbrilli (Pisa, 1987).

Aristotle, *Oeconomica* and *Magna Moralia*, trans. G. Cyril Armstrong (London and Cambridge, Mass., 1935).

Arlotto, Piovano, *Motti e Facezie del Piovano Arlotto*, ed. Gianfranco Folena (Milan and Naples, 1953).

Arlotto, Piovano, *Facezie, motti e burle del Piovano Arlotto*, ed. Chiara Amerighi (Florence, 1980).

Azzi Visentini, Margherita, *La Villa in Italia. Quattrocento e Cinquecento* (Milan, 1995).

Bacci, Giovanni, *Il Palagio, Villa Melchior* (Florence, 1988).

Bandini, Angelo Maria, *Lettere XII ad un amico nelle quali si ricerca e s'illustra l'antica e moderna situazione della città di Fiesole e suoi contorni* (Florence, 1776).

Bardazzi, Silvestro, and Castellani, Eugenio, *La Villa Medicea di Poggio a Caiano*, 2 vols. (Prato, 1981).

Bargellini, Clara, and du Prey, Pierre de la Ruffinière, 'Sources for a Reconstruction of the Villa Medici, Fiesole', *Burl. Mag.* 111 (1969), 597–605.

Bargellini, P., and Guarnieri, E., *Le Strade di Firenze* (Florence, 1977).

Bartoli, Maria Teresa, 'Le Caratteristiche geometriche e numeriche di Palazzo Medici', *Il Palazzo Medici Riccardi di Firenze*, ed. G. Cherubini and G. Fanelli (Florence, 1990).

Bartoli, Roberta, *Biagio d'Antonio* (Milan, 1999).

Battisti, Eugenio, *Brunelleschi, the Complete Work* (London, 1981).

Baxendale, Susannah Foster, 'Exile in Practice: The Alberti Family in and out of Florence 1401–1428', *Renaissance Quarterly* 44 (1991), 720–56.

Becker, Marvin, *Florence in Transition*, 2 vols. (Baltimore, 1967–8).

Belle, Lawrence William, 'A Renaissance Patrician: Palla di Nofri Strozzi 1372–1462', Ph.D. diss., University of Rochester, 1971.

Belli, Gianluca, 'Il Palazzo dello Strozzino', *Michelozzo. Scultore e Architetto (1396–1472)*, ed. Gabriele Morolli (Florence, 1998), 35–44.

Bellomo, Manlio, *La Condizione giuridica della donna in Italia* (Turin, 1970).

Bentmann, Reinhard, and Müller, Michael, *Die Villa als Herrschafts-architektur*, Frankfurt, 1970, trans. Tim Spence and David Craven as *The Villa as Hegemonic Architecture* (New Jersey and London, 1992).

Bergier, Jean-Francois, *Genève et l'économie européenne de la Renaissance* (Paris, 1963).

Bergier, Jean-Francois, 'Lettres genevoises des Medicis 1425–1475', *Studi in memoria di Federigo Melis*, 3 vols. (Naples, 1978), III, 279–310.

Biasutti, Renato, *La Casa rurale nella Toscana* (Bologna, 1938).

Bierman, Hartmut, 'Lo Sviluppo della villa toscana sotto l'influenza umanistica della corte di Lorenzo il Magnifico', *Bollettino del Centro Internazionale di studi di architettura Andrea Palladio* 11 (1969), 36–46.

Bisticci, Vespasiano da, *Le vite*, ed. Aulo Greco, 2 vols. (Florence, 1970).

Boccaccio, Giovanni, 'Decameron', *Tutte le opere*, ed. Vittore Branca, vol. IV (Milan, 1976).

Boccaccio, Giovanni, *The Decameron*, trans. Richard Aldington (Bury St Edmonds, 1982).

Bombe, Walter, *Nachlass-Inventare des Angelo da Uzzano und des Lodovico di Gino Capponi* (Leipzig and Berlin, 1928, reprinted Hildesheim, 1972).

Borsi, Franco, *Leon Battista Alberti* (Milan, 1975).

Borsi Franco, Morolli Gabriele and Quinterio Francesco, *Brunelleschiani: Francesco della Luna, Andrea di Lazzaro Cavalcanti detto il Buggiano, Antonio Manetti Ciaccheri, Giovanni di Domenico da Gaiole, Betto d'Antonio, Antonio di Betto, Giovanni di Piero del Ticcia, Cecchino di Giaggio, Salvi d'Andrea, Maso di Bartolomeo* (Rome, 1979).

Borsook, Eve, 'Documenti relativi alle cappelle di Lecceto e delle Selve di Filippo Strozzi', *Antichità Viva* 9 (1970), part 3, 3–20.

Borsook, Eve, 'Documents for Filippo Strozzi's Chapel in S. Maria Novella and Other Related Papers', part I, *Burl. Mag.* 112 (1970), 737–55; part II, 'The Documents', *Burl. Mag.* 112 (1970), 800–4.

Borsook, Eve, 'Ritratto di Filippo Strozzi il Vecchio', *Palazzo Strozzi. Metà millennio 1489–1989*, Atti del convegno di studi, Firenze, 3–6 Luglio 1989, ed. D. Lamberini (Rome, 1991), 1–14.

Borsook, Eve, and Offerhaus J., *Francesco Sassetti and Ghirlandaio at Santa Trinita, Florence* (Doornspijk, 1981).

Brown, Beverly L., 'The Patronage and Building History of the Tribuna of SS. Annunziata in Florence' *Mitt.KhIF.* 25 (1981), 59–145.

Brown, Beverly L., 'Leonardo and the Tale of Three Villas: Poggio a Caiano, the Villa Tovaglia in Florence and Poggio Reale in Mantova', *Atti del convegno "Firenze e la Toscana dei Medici nell'Europa del Cinquecento"* (Florence, 1983), vol. III, 1053–62.

Brown, Judith C., 'Prosperity or Hard Times in Renaissance Italy?', *Renaissance Quarterly* 42 (1989), 761–80.

Brucker, Gene, *The Civic World of Early Renaissance Florence* (Princeton, 1977).

Brucker, Gene, *Firenze nel rinascimento* (Florence, 1980).

Bulst, Wolfger A., 'Die ursprüngliche innere Aufteilung des Palazzo Medici in Florenz', *Mitt.KhIF.* 14 (1970), 369–92.

Bulst, Wolfger A., 'Uso e trasformazione del palazzo mediceo fino ai Riccardi', *Il Palazzo Medici Riccardi di Firenze*, ed. G. Cherubini and G. Fanelli (Florence 1990), 98–129.

Bulst, Wolfger A., 'Die *sala grande* des Palazzo Medici in Florenz. Rekonstruktion und Bedeutung', *Piero de' Medici "il Gottoso" (1416–1469)*, ed. A. Beyer and B. Boucher (Berlin 1993), 89–127.

Burke, Jill, 'Form and Power: Patronage and the Visual Arts in Florence, c. 1480–151', PhD diss., Courtauld Institute, University of London, 1999.

Burns, Howard, Fairbairn, Lynda, and Boucher, Bruce, *Andrea Palladio 1508–1580. The Portico and the Farmyard*, exhib. cat. (London, 1975).

Burns, Howard, 'Un disegno architettonico di Alberti e la questione del rapporto fra Brunelleschi ed Alberti', *Filippo Brunelleschi, la sua opera e il suo tempo*, 2 vols. (Florence, 1980), vol. I, 105–23.

Butterfield, Andrew, *The Sculptures of Andrea del Verrocchio* (New Haven and London, 1997).

Callmann, Ellen, *Apollonio di Giovanni* (Oxford, 1974).

Calzolai, Carlo Celso, *La Storia della Badia a Settimo* (Florence, 1976).

Calzolai, Carlo Celso, *Capalle, comunità prestigiosa* (Florence, 1980).

Cambi, Giovanni, *Istorie di Giovanni Cambi, Cittadino Fiorentino*, in *Delizie degli Eruditi Toscani*, ed. Ildefonso di San Luigi, 24 vols. (Florence, 1770–89).

Camesasca, Ettore, *Mantegna* (Florence, 1981).

Cantini, Lorenzo, *Saggi istorici d'antichità toscane*, 10 vols. (Florence, 1796–1800).

Carl, Doris, 'La Casa Vecchia dei Medici e il suo giardino', in *Il Palazzo Medici Riccardi di Firenze*, ed. Giovanni Cherubini and Giovanni Fanelli (Florence, 1990), 38–43.

Carli, Enzo, *Pienza, la città di Pio II* (Rome, 1967).

Carocci, Guido, 'Chiesa e convento de' SS. Filippo e Jacopo a Lecceto nel comune di Lastra a Signa', *L'Illustratore fiorentino: calendario storico per l'ano 1904* (Florence, 1903), 63–7.

Carocci, Guido, *Il Valdarno da Firenze al mare* (Bergamo, 1906).

Carocci, Guido, *I Dintorni di Firenze*, 2 vols. (Florence, 1906–7, reprinted Rome, 1968).

Carocci, Guido, 'Antichi alberghi di campagna', *L'Illustratore fiorentino: calendario storico per l'ano 1915* (Florence, 1914), 83–6.

Carunchio, Tancredi, *Origini della villa rinascimentale: la ricerca di una tipologia, Studi di storia dell'arte* (Rome, 1974), vol. 4.

Cassandro, Michele, 'Banca e commercio fiorentini alle fiere di Ginevra nel secolo XV', *Rivista storica svizzera* 26 (1976), 567–611.

Castello: campagna medicea, periferia urbana, Studio GE9 (Florence, 1984).

Cato, Marcus Porcius, *On Agriculture (De Agri cultura)*, trans. William Davis Hooper, rev. Harrison Boyd Ash (London and Cambridge, Mass., 1979).

Cavalcanti, G., *Istorie fiorentine*, ed. G. di Pino (Milan, 1944).

Chabot, Isabelle, 'Widowhood and Poverty in Late Medieval Florence', *Continuity and Change* 3 (1988), 91–311.

Chaney, Edward, and Ritchie, Neil, eds., *Oxford, China and Italy. Writings in Honour of Sir Harold Acton on his Eightieth Birthday* (London, 1984).

Chastel, André, *Art et humanisme à Florence au temps de Laurent le Magnifique. Etudes sur la Renaissance et l'humanisme platonicien* (Paris, 1959).

Cherubini, Giovanni, 'La proprietà fondiaria di un mercante toscano del Trecento (Simo d'Ubertino di Arezzo)', *Signori, contadini, borghesi* (Florence, 1974), 313–93.

Cherubini, Giovanni, 'Qualche considerazione sulle campagne dell'Italia centro-settentrionale tra l'XI e il XV secolo. Rinascita cittadina e trasformazione del mondo rurale', *Signori, contadini, borghesi* (Florence, 1974), 51–119.

Cherubini, Giovanni, *Signori, contadini, borghesi. Ricerche sulla società italiana del Basso Medioevo* (Florence, 1974).

Cherubini, Giovanni, and Fanelli, Giovanni, *Il Palazzo Medici Riccardi di Firenze* (Florence, 1990).

Cherubini, Giovanni, and Francovich, Riccardo, 'Forme e vicende degli insediamenti nella campagna toscana dei secoli XIII–XV', *Signori, contadini, borghesi* (Florence, 1974), 145–75.

Chiarelli, C., and Leoncini G., *La Certosa di Galluzzo* (Florence, 1982).

Chiostri, Ferdinando, *La Petraia, villa e giardino. Settecento anni di storia* (Florence, 1972).

Chittolini, Giorgio, *La Formazione dello stato regionale e le istituzioni del contado. Secoli XIV e XV* (Turin, 1979).

Clarke, Georgia, *Roman House – Renaissance Palaces Inventing Antiquity in Fifteenth-Century Italy* (Cambridge, 2003).

Coates, Peter, *Nature. Western Attitudes since Ancient Times* (Oxford, 1998).

Coffin, David, *The Villa in the Life of Renaissance Rome* (Princeton University Press, 1979).

Coffin, David, *Gardens and Gardening in Papal Rome* (Princeton University Press, 1991).

Cohn, Werner, 'Il Beato Angelico e Battista di Biagio Sanguigni', *Rivista d'Arte,* 30 (1956), 211–15.

Colnaghi, D. E., *A Dictionary of Florentine Painters from the Thirteenth to the Seventeenth Centuries,* ed. P. Konody and S. Brinton (London, 1938).

Comito, T., *The Idea of the Garden in the Renaissance* (Hassocks, 1979).

Conti, Elio, *La Formazione della struttura agraria moderna nel contado fiorentino,* Istituto storico italiano per il medio evo, Studi storici, fasc. 51–5, vol. I, *Le Campagne nell'età precomunale* (Rome, 1965).

Conti, Elio, *I Catasti agrari della Repubblica fiorentina e il catasto particellare toscano (secoli 14–19). La Formazione della struttura agraria moderna,* Istituto storico italiano per il medio evo, vol. III, parte 1, sez. 1, *Le Fonti* (Rome, 1966).

Conti, Elio, *La Formazione della struttura agraria moderna nel contado fiorentino,* Istituto storico italiano per il medio evo, Studi storici, fasc. 64–8, vol. III, parte 2, *Monografie e tavole statistiche* (Rome, 1965).

Conti, Elio, *L'Imposta diretta a Firenze nel Quattrocento (1427–1494)* (Rome, 1984).

Corradi, Alfonso, *Annali delle epidemie occorse in Italia dalle prime memorie fino al 1850,* vol. I (Bologna, 1863).

Corradini, E., *Prato e i suoi dintorni* (Bergamo, 1905).

Courcey-Bayley, Crispin de, 'House and Household. A Study of Families and Property in the Quarter of Santa Croce, Florence during the Fifteenth Century', PhD diss., University of York, 1998.

Crabb, Ann, *The Strozzi of Florence. Widowhood and Family Solidarity in the Renaissance* (Ann Arbor, Mich., 2000).

Craven, Stephanie J., 'Aspects of Patronage in Florence 1494–1512', PhD diss., Courtauld Institute of Art, University of London, 1973.

Craven, Stephanie J., 'Three Dates for Piero di Cosimo', *Burl. Mag.* 117 (1975), 572–6.

Crescenzi, Piero de', *Trattato della agricultura,* Italian trans., 3 vols. (Milan, 1805).

Davidsohn, Robert, *Storia di Firenze,* 8 vols. (Florence, 1965).

de Bunsen, Madame Charles, *In Three Legations: Turin, Florence, The Hague* (London, 1908).

De la Mare, Albinia, 'Messer Piero Strozzi, a Florentine Priest and Scribe', *Calligraphy and Paleography: Essay Presented to Alfred Fairbank on His Seventieth Birthday,* ed. A. S. Osley (London, 1965), 55–68.

De la Mare, Albinia, 'Vespasiano da Bisticci, Historian and Bookseller', PhD diss., Warburg Institute, University of London, 1966.

De la Mare, Albinia, 'The Library of Francesco Sassetti (1421–90)', *Cultural aspects of the Italian Renaissance: Essays in honour of Paul Oskar Kristeller,* ed. C. H. Clough (Manchester, 1976), 160–201.

de la Roncière, Charles, *Un changeur florentin du Trecento: Lippo di Fede del Sega (c. 1285–1363)* (Paris, 1973).

de la Roncière, Charles, *Florence: centre économique regional au XIVe siècle,* 5 vols. (Aix-en-Provence, 1976).

Del Piazzo, Marcello, *Protocolli del carteggio di Lorenzo il Magnifico per gli anni 1473–74, 1477–92* (Florence, 1956).

Del Treppo, Mario, 'Le Avventure storiographiche della tavola Strozzi', *Fra Storia e storiografia. Scritti in onore di Pasquale Villari,* ed. P. Macry and A. Massafra (Bologna, 1994), 483–515.

de Roover, Raymond, *The Rise and Decline of the Medici Bank, 1397–1494* (Cambridge, Mass., 1968).

De Seta, Cesare, 'The Urban Structure of Naples: Utopia and Reality', *The Renaissance from Brunelleschi to Michelangelo. The Representation of Architecture,* ed. Henry A. Millon and Vittorio Magnago Lampugnani (Milan, 1994), 349–70.

Dezzi Bardeschi, Marco, and Zangheri, Luigi, 'La Villa Corsini a Castello', *Bollettino degli Ingegneri* 11 (1969), 3–10.

du Prey, Pierre de la Ruffinière, *The Villas of Pliny from Antiquity to Posterity* (Chicago, 1994).

Eberlein, Harold Donaldson, *Villas of Florence and Tuscany* (Philadelphia, 1925).

Edler de Roover, Florence, 'Francesco Sassetti and the Downfall of the Medici Banking House', *Bulletin of the Business Historical Society* Boston [Mass.] 17 (1943), 65–80.

Edler de Roover, Florence, 'Per la storia dell'arte della stampa in Italia', *Bibliofilia* 55 (1953), 107–17.

Elam, Caroline, 'Piazza Strozzi. Two Drawings by Baccio d'Agnolo and the Problems of a Private Renaissance Square', *I Tatti Studies* 1 (1985), 103–35.

Elam, Caroline, 'Lorenzo de' Medici's Sculpture Garden', *Mitteilungen des Kunsthistorischen Institutes in Florenz* 36 (1992), 41–84.

Elam, Caroline, '*Vira Papa Leone*: Baccio d'Agnolo and the Palazzo Lanfredini in Florence', *Coming About . . . A Festschrift for John Shearman,* ed. L. R. Jones and L. C. Matthew (Cambridge Mass., 2001), 173–181.

Elam, Caroline, and Gombrich, Ernst, 'Lorenzo de' Medici and a Frustrated Villa Project at Vallombrosa', *Florence and Italy. Renaissance Studies in Honour of Nicolai Rubinstein,* ed. Peter Denley and Caroline Elam, Westfield College (University of London, 1988), 481–92.

Ettlinger, Leopold D., *Antonio and Piero Pollaiuolo* (Oxford, 1978).

Fabbri, Lorenzo, *Alleanza matrimoniale e patriziato nella Firenze del Quattrocento. Studio sulla famiglia Strozzi* (Florence, 1991).

Fabriczy, Cornelius von, 'Giuliano da Maiano in Siena', *Jahrbuch der Königlich Preussischen Kunstsammlungen* 24 (1903), 320–34.

Fabriczy, Cornelius von, 'Michelozzo di Bartolomeo', *Jahrbuch der Königlich Preussischen Kunstsammlungen* 25 (1904), Beiheft, 34–110.

Fermor, Sharon, *Piero di Cosimo: Fiction, Invention and "Fantasia"* (London, 1993).

Ferrara, Miranda, and Quinterio, Francesco, *Michelozzo di Bartolomeo* (Florence, 1984).

Ferrari, Giovan Battista, *Hesperides: sive de malorum aureorum cultura et usu* (Rome, 1646).

Ficino, Marsilio, *Opera omnia* (Basel, 1576); reprint edited by M. Sancipriano, 2 vols. (Turin, 1962).

Filarete, Antonio Averlino, *Trattato di Architettura*, ed. A. M. Finoli and L. Grassi, 2 vols. (Milan, 1972).

Fischer, Chris, 'Fra Bartolommeo's Landscape Drawings', *Mitteilungen des Kunsthistorischen Institutes in Florenz* 32 (1989), 301–42.

Fischer, Chris, *Fra Bartolommeo. Master Draughtsman of the High Renaissance. A selection from the Rotterdam Albums and Landscape Drawings from various Collections* (Rotterdam, 1990).

Fiumi, Enrico, 'Sui rapporti economici tra città e contado nell'età comunale', *Archivio storico italiano* (1956), 18–68.

Fontius, Bartholomaeus, *Carmina*, ed. I. Fogel and L. Juhasz (Leipzig, 1932).

Forster, Kurt, 'Back to the Farm. Vernacular Architecture and the Development of the Renaissance Villa', *Architectura* (1974), 1–12.

Forster, Kurt, Review of Martin Kubelik, *Die Villa im Veneto; zur typologischen Entwicklung im Quattrocento* (Munich, 1977), *Journal of the Society of Architectural Historians* 38 (1979), 189–91.

Foster, Philip, 'Lorenzo de' Medici's Cascina at Poggio a Caiano', *Mitt.KhIF.* 14 (1969), 47 ff.

Foster, Philip, *A Study of Lorenzo de' Medici's Villa at Poggio a Caiano*, 2 vols. (London and New York, 1978).

Foster, Philip, *La Villa di Lorenzo de' Medici a Poggio a Caiano* (Poggio a Caiano, 1992).

Francesco di Giorgio Martini, *Trattati di architettura, ingegneria e arte militare*, ed., C. Maltese, 2 vols. (Milan, 1967).

Francovich, Riccardo, *I Castelli del contado fiorentino nei secoli XII e XIII* (Florence, 1976).

Frey, Karl, *Michelagniolo Bunarotti. Quellen und Forschungen zu seiner Geschichte und Kunst* (Berlin, 1907).

Frommel, Christoph Luitpold, 'La Villa Madama e la tipologia della villa romana nel rinascimento', *Bollettino del Centro Internazionale di Studi di Architettura "Andrea Palladio"* 11 (1969), 47–64.

Frommel, Christoph Luitpold, *Der römische Palastbau der Hochrenaissance*, 3 vols. (Tübingen, 1973).

Galletti, Giorgio, 'Una Committenza medicea poco nota: Giovanni di Cosimo e il giardino di villa Medici a Fiesole', *Giardini Medicei. Giardini di palazzo e di villa nella Firenze del Quattrocento*, ed. Cristina Acidini Luchinat (Milan, 1996), 60–89.

Gentili, Sebastiano, Niccoli, Sandra, and Viti, Paolo, *Marsilio Ficino e il ritorno di Platone. Mostra di manoscritti, stampe e documenti*, Biblioteca Medicea Laurenziana (Florence, 1983).

Gentilini, Giancarlo, ed., *La Misericordia di Firenze. Catalogo*, vol. I, *Archivio e raccolta d'arte*, Sculpture section (Florence, 1981).

Gentilini, Giancarlo, *Andrea della Robbia*, vol. I, *Madonne*, Museo Nazionale del Bargello (Florence, 1983).

Gentilini, Giancarlo, *I Della Robbia. La Scultura invetriata nel Rinascimento*, 2 vols. (Milan, 1992).

Ginori Lisci, Leonardo, *I Palazzi di Firenze nella storia e nell'arte*, 2 vols. (Florence, 1972).

Gnoli, Raniero, *Marmora romana* (Rome, 1971).

Gobbi, Grazia, *La Villa Fiorentina. Elementi storici per una lettura* (Florence, 1980).

Gobbi Sica, Grazia, *La Villa Fiorentina. Elementi storici per una lettura* (Florence, 1998).

Goldthwaite, Richard, A., *Private Wealth in Renaissance Florence: A Study of Four Families* (Princeton, 1968).

Goldthwaite, Richard, A., 'The Florentine Palace as Domestic Architecture', *American Historical Review* 77 (1972), 977–1005.

Goldthwaite, Richard, A., 'The Building of the Strozzi Palace: The Construction Industry in Renaissance Florence', *Studies in Medieval and Renaissance History* 10 (1973), 99–174.

Goldthwaite, Richard, A., *The Building of Renaissance Florence* (Baltimore and London, 1980).

Goldthwaite, Richard, A., 'The Economy of Renaissance Italy: The Preconditions for Luxury Consumption', *I Tatti Studies* 2 (1987), 15–39.

Goldthwaite, Richard, A., *Wealth and the Demand for Art in Italy* (Baltimore and London, 1993).

Goldthwaite, Richard A., and Rearick, W. R., 'Michelozzo and the Ospedale di San Paolo in Florence', *Mitt.KhIF.* 21 (1977), 221–306.

Gori-Sassoli, Mario, 'Michelozzo e l'architettura di villa nel primo rinascimento', *Storia dell'Arte* 23 (1975), 5–51.

Gorni, Guglielmo, 'Su Lorenzo Poeta: Parodia, diletti e noie della caccia', *Lorenzo il Magnifico e il suo mondo*, ed. Gian Carlo Garfagnini (Florence, 1994), 205–23.

Gregory, Heather J., 'A Florentine Family in Crisis: The Strozzi in the Fifteenth Century', Ph.D. diss., University of London, 1981.

Gregory, Heather J., 'The Return of the Native: Filippo Strozzi and Medicean Politics', *Renaissance Quarterly* 38 (1985), 1–21.

Gregory, Heather J., 'Chi erano gli Strozzi nel Quattrocento', *Palazzo Strozzi. Metà millennio 1489–1989*, Atti del Convegno di Studi, Firenze, 3–6 Luglio 1989, ed. D. Lamberini (Rome, 1991), 15–29.

Gregory, Heather J., see Strozzi, Alessandra Macinghi.

Haines, Margaret, *The Sacrestia delle Messe of the Florentine Cathedral* (Florence, 1983).

Hannema, Dirk, *Meesterwerken uit de Verzameling D.G. van Beuningen. Catalogue of the D.G. van Beuningen Collection* (Rotterdam, 1949).

Hartloff, Lynn, 'The Unconstructed Palace of Francesco Sassetti', Symposium Paper, Syracuse University Florence, 1981.

Hartt, Frederick, Corti, Gino, and Kennedy, Clarence, *The Chapel of the Cardinal of Portugal, 1434–59, at San Miniato in Florence* (Philadelphia, 1964).

Hatfield, Rab, 'Giovanni Tornabuoni, i fratelli Ghirlandaio e la cappella maggiore di Santa Maria Novella', *Domenico Ghirlandaio 1449–1494, Atti del Convegno Internazionale Firenze, 16–18 ottobre 1994*, ed. Wolfram Prinz and Max Seidel (Florence, 1996), 112–17.

Hatfield, Rab, *The Wealth of Michelangelo* (Rome, 2002).

Heers, Jacques, *Le Clan familial au Moyen Age: étude sur les structures politiques et sociales des milieux urbains* (Paris, 1974).

Hellerforth, Brigitte, *Der Dom von Faenza. Ein Beitrag zur Problematik der Basilika-Architektur in der 2. Hälfte des Quattrocento* (Bonn, 1975).

Herlihy, David, 'Santa Maria Impruneta: A Rural Commune in the Late Middle Ages', *Florentine Studies*, ed. Nicolai Rubinstein (London, 1968), 242–76.

Herlihy, David, 'Marriage at Pistoia in the Fifteenth Century', *Bollettino storico pistoiese* 7 (1972), 3–21.

Herlihy, David, 'Family and Property in Renaissance Florence', *The Medieval City*, ed. Harry A. Miskimin, David Herlihy, A. L. Udovitch (New Haven and London, 1977), 3–24.

Herlihy, David, 'The Problem of the "Return to the Land" in Tuscan Economic History of the Fourteenth and Fifteenth Centuries', *Civiltà ed economia agricola in Toscana nei secoli XIII–XV: Problemi della vita delle campagne nel tardo medioevo* (Pistoia, 1981), 401–16.

Herlihy, David, and Klapisch-Zuber, Christiane, *Les Toscans et leur familles. Une étude du catasto florentin de 1427* (Paris, 1978).

Herlihy, David, and Klapisch-Zuber, Christiane, *Tuscans and Their Families. A Study of the Florentine Catasto of 1427* (New Haven and London, 1985).

Heydenreich, Ludwig, 'La Villa: genesi e sviluppi fino al Palladio', *Bollettino del Centro Internazionale di Studi di Architetture "Andrea Palladio"* 11 (1969), 11–22.

Horace, *Satires, Epistles, and Ars Poetica*, trans. H. Rushton Fairclough (London and Cambridge, Mass., 1961).

Horace, *The Odes and Epodes*, trans. C. E. Bennet (London and Cambridge, Mass., 1964).

Horster, Marita, *Andrea del Castagno* (Oxford, 1980).

Hyman, Isabelle, *Fifteenth-Century Florentine Studies: The Palazzo Medici and a Ledger for the Church of San Lorenzo* (New York and London, 1977).

Ildefonso di San Luigi, *Delizie degli eruditi toscani*, 24 vols. (Florence, 1776–89).

Imberciadori, Ildebrando, 'I Due poderi di Bernardo Machiavelli ovvero mezzadria poderale nel '400', *Studi in onore di Armando Sapori* (Milan, 1957), vol. II, 835–46.

Imberciadori, Ildebrando, 'Proprietà terriera di Francesco Datini e parziaria mezzadrile nel '400', *Economia e Storia* 5 (1958), 254–73.

INAIL [Istituto Nazionale per l'assicurazione contro gli infortuni sul lavoro], *Villa Tornabuoni Lemmi di Careggi* (Rome, 1988).

Jacks, Philip, and Carferro, William, *The Spinelli of Florence. Fortunes of a Renaissance Merchant Family* (University Park, Penn., 2001).

Janson, Horst W., *The Sculpture of Donatello* (Princeton, 1963).

Jones, Philip J., 'A Tuscan Monastic Lordship in the Later Middle Ages: Camaldoli', *Journal of Ecclesiastical History* 5 (1954), 168–83.

Jones, Philip J., 'Florentine Families and Florentine Diaries in the Fourteenth Century', *Papers of the British School at Rome* 24 (1956), 183–205.

Jones, Philip J., 'Medieval Agrarian Society in its Prime: Italy', *Cambridge Economic History of Europe*, vol. I, *The Agrarian Life of the Middle Ages*, ed. M. M. Postan (Cambridge, 1966), 2nd ed., 340–451.

Jones, Philip J., 'From Manor to Mezzadria: A Tuscan Case-Study in the Medieval Origins of Modern Agrarian Society', *Florentine Studies*, ed., Nicolai Rubinstein (London, 1968), 193–241.

Jones, Philip J., *Economia e società nell'Italia medievale* (Turin, 1980).

Jones, Roger, 'Palla Strozzi e la sagrestia di Santa Trinita', *Rivista d'Arte* 37 (1984), 9–106.

Juvenal, *The Satires*, trans. G. G. Ramsay (London and Cambridge, Mass., 1961).

Kennedy, Ruth Wedgwood, *Alesso Baldovinetti. A Critical and Historical Study* (New Haven and London, 1938).

Kent, Dale V., *The Rise of the Medici: Faction in Florence, 1426–1434* (Oxford, 1978).

Kent, Dale V., and Francis William, 'Two Comments of March 1445 on the Medici Palace', *Burl. Mag.* 121 (1979), 795–6.

Kent, Francis William, 'The Rucellai Family and its Loggia', *JWCI* 35 (1972), 397–401.

Kent, Francis William, *Household and Lineage in Renaissance Florence: The Family Life of the Capponi, Ginori and Rucellai* (Princeton, 1977).

Kent, Francis William, '"Più superba de quella de Lorenzo": Courtly and Family Interest in the Building of Filippo Strozzi's Palace', *Renaissance Quarterly* 30 (1977), 311–23.

Kent, Francis William, 'Lorenzo de' Medici's Acquisition of Poggio a Caiano in 1474 and an Early Reference to his Architectural Expertise', *JWCI* 43 (1979), 250–7.

Kent, Francis William, 'The Making of a Renaissance Patron of the Arts', *Giovanni Rucellai ed il suo Zibaldone*, vol. II, *A Florentine Patrician and his Palace* (London, 1981), 9–95.

Kent, Francis William, 'Palaces, Politics and Society in Fifteenth-Century Florence', *I Tatti Studies* 2 (1987), 41–70.

Kent, Francis William, and Lillie, Amanda, 'The Piovano Arlotto: New Documents', *Florence and Italy. Renaissance Studies in Honour of Nicolai Rubinstein*, ed. Peter Denley and Caroline Elam, Westfield College (University of London, 1988), 347–67.

Kirshner, Julius, 'Pursuing Honor while Avoiding Sin. The Monte delle Doti of Florence', *Quaderni di Studi Senesi* 41 (1975), 2 ff.

Kirshner, Julius, 'Wives Claims against Insolvent Husbands in Late Medieval Italy', *Women in the Medieval World. Essays in Honor of John H. Mundy*, ed. J. Kirshner and S. Wemple (Oxford, 1985), 256–304.

Kirshner, Julius, and Molho, Anthony, 'The Dowry Fund and the Marriage Market in Early Quattrocento Florence', *Journal of Modern History* 50 (1978), 403–38.

Klapisch-Zuber, Christiane, 'Mezzadria e insediamenti rurali alla fine del medioevo', *Civiltà ed economia agricola in Toscana nei secoli XIII–XV: Problemi della vita delle campagne nel tardo medioevo* (Pistoia, 1981), 149–64.

Klapisch-Zuber, Christiane, *Una Carta del popolamento toscano negli anni 1427–1430*, trans. Franco Saba (Milan, 1983).

Klapisch-Zuber, Christiane, 'Blood Parents and Milk Parents: Wet Nursing in Florence, 1300–1530', *Women, Family and Ritual in Renaissance Italy*, trans. Lydia G. Cochrane (Chicago and London, 1985), 132–64.

Klapisch-Zuber, Christiane, 'Childhood in Tuscany at the Beginning of the Fifteenth Century', *Women, Family and Ritual in Renaissance Italy*, trans. Lydia G. Cochrane (Chicago and London, 1985), 94–116.

Klapisch-Zuber, Christiane, 'The Name "Remade": The Transmission of Given Names in Florence in the Fourteenth and Fifteenth Centuries', *Women, Family and Ritual in Renaissance Italy*, trans. Lydia G. Cochrane (Chicago and London, 1985), 283–309.

Krinsky, Carol Herselle, '78 Vitruvius Manuscripts', *JWCI* 30 (1967), 36–70.

Kristeller, Paul Oskar, *Supplementum Ficinianum*, 2 vols. (Florence, 1937).

Kubelik, Martin, *Die Villa im Veneto. Zur typologischen Entwicklung im '400*, 2 vols. (Munich, 1977).

Kuehn, Thomas, '"Cum consensu mundualdi": Legal Guardianship of Women in Quattrocento Florence', *Viator* 13 (1982), 309–33.

Kuehn, Thomas, 'Conflicting Conceptions of Property in Quattrocento Florence', *Quaderni fiorentini per la storia del pensiero giuridico moderno* 14 (1985), 303 ff.

Kuehn, Thomas, *Law, Family, and Women. Toward a Legal Anthropology of Renaissance Italy* (Chicago, 1991).

Kuehn, Thomas, 'Law, Death, and Heirs in the Renaissance: Repudiation of Inheritance in Florence', *Renaissance Quarterly* 45 (1992), 484–516.

Lamberini, Daniela, *Calenzano e la Val di Marina. Storia di un territorio fiorentino* (Prato, 1987).

Lamberini, Daniela, and Lazzereschi, Luigi, *Campi Bisenzio: Documenti per la storia del territorio* (Prato, 1982).

Lami, Giovanni, *Sanctae ecclesiae florentinae monumenta*, 4 vols. (Florence, 1758).

Landucci, Luca, *Diario Fiorentino dal 1450 al 1516 continuato da un anonimo fino al 1542*, ed. Iodoco del Badia (Florence, 1883, reprinted 1985).

Lawrence, Mary Ellen Hoelscher, 'The Villa La Pietra: New Findings, History and Myth,' Symposium Paper, Syracuse University Florence, 1996.

Lazzari, Alfonso, *Ugolino e Michele Verino* (Turin, 1897).

Lensi Orlandi, Giulio, *Il Palazzo Vecchio di Firenze* (Florence, 1977).

Lensi Orlandi, Giulio, *Le Ville di Firenze, di Qua d'Arno, di Là d'Arno*, 2 vols. (Florence, 1978), 3rd ed.

Lensi Orlandi, Giulio, *Il Palazzo dei Sassetti, Banchieri Fiorentini* (Florence, 1990).

Levi d'Ancona, Mirella, 'Zanobi Strozzi reconsidered', *La Bibliofilia* 61 (1959), 1–38.

Levi d'Ancona, Mirella, *Miniatura e miniatori a Firenze dal XIV al XVI secolo. Documenti per la storia della miniatura* (Florence, 1962).

Libro d'inventario dei beni di Lorenzo il Magnifico, ed. Marco Spallanzani and Giovanna Gaeta Bertelà (Florence, 1992).

Lightbown, Ronald, *Sandro Botticelli*, 2 vols. (London, 1978).

Lillie, Amanda, 'Francesco Sassetti and his Villa at La Pietra', *Oxford, China and Italy. Writings in honour of Sir Harold Acton on his Eightieth Birthday*, ed. Edward Chaney and Neil Ritchie (London, 1984), 83–93.

Lillie, Amanda, 'Vita di palazzo, vita in villa: l'attività edilizia di Filippo il Vecchio', *Palazzo Strozzi. Metà millennio 1489–1989*, Atti del convegno di studi, Firenze, 3–6 Luglio 1989, ed. Daniela Lamberini (Rome, 1991), 167–82.

Lillie, Amanda, 'Giovanni di Cosimo and the Villa Medici at Fiesole', *Piero de' Medici "il Gottoso" (1416–1469)*, ed. Andreas Beyer and Bruce Boucher (Berlin, 1993), 189–205.

Lillie, Amanda, 'Lorenzo de' Medici's Rural Investments and Territorial Expansion', *Rinascimento* 33 (1993), 53–67.

Lillie, Amanda, 'The Humanist Villa Revisited', *Language and Images of Renaissance Italy*, ed. Alison Brown (Oxford, 1995), 193–215.

Lillie, Amanda, 'Cappelle e chiese delle ville medicee ai tempi di Michelozzo', *Michelozzo Scultore e Architetto (1396–1472)* ed. Gabriele Morolli (Florence, 1998), 89–98.

Lillie, Amanda, 'The Patronage of Villa Chapels and Oratories near Florence: a typology of private religion', *With and Without the Medici: Studies in Tuscan Art and Patronage 1435–1530*, ed. Eckart Marchand and Alison Wright (Aldershot, 1998), 19–46.

Lillie, Amanda, 'Memory of Place: *Luogo* and Lineage in the Fifteenth-Century Florentine Countryside', *Art, Memory and Family in Renaissance Florence*, ed. Giovanni Ciappelli and Patricia Lee Rubin (Cambridge, 2000), 195–214.

Litta, Pompeo, *Famiglie celebri italiane*, 11 vols. (Milan and Turin, 1819–99), ser. 2 (Turin 1902–23).

Lloyd, Joan Barclay, *African Animals in Renaissance Literature and Art* (Oxford, 1971).

Lowe, Kate J. P., *Church and Politics in Renaissance Italy. The Life and Career of Cardinal Francesco Soderini, 1453–1524* (Cambridge, 1993).

Luzzatto, Mario, 'Contributo alla storia della mezzadria nel medioevo', *Nuova Rivista Storica* 32 (1948), 69–84.

Lydecker, John Kent, 'The Domestic Setting of the Arts in Renaissance Florence', PhD diss., Johns Hopkins University, 1988.

Manni, Domenico Maria, *Vita di Arlotto Mainardi, piovano di S. Cresci a Maciuoli* (Venice, 1763).

Mannini, Marcello, 'Degradazione e rovina dei valori ambientali nella periferia fiorentina', *Bollettino tecnico degli Architetti* 37 (1972), 1–7.

Marchini, Giuseppe, *Giuliano da Sangallo* (Florence, 1942).

Marchini, Giuseppe, 'Aggiunte a Michelozzo', *Rinascita* 35 (1944), 24–51.

Marquand, Allan, *Andrea della Robbia and his Atelier*, 2 vols. (Princeton and London, 1922).

Marshall, David, 'A View of Poggioreale by Viviano Codazzi and Domenico Gargiulo', *Journal of the Society of Architectural Historians* 45 (1986), 32–46.

Martines, Lauro, *An Italian Renaissance Sextet. Six Tales in Historical Context*, trans. Murtha Baca (New York, 1994).

Masson, Georgina, 'Palladian Villas as Rural Centres', *The Architectural Review* 118 (1955), 17–20.

Masson, Georgina, *Italian Villas and Palaces* (London, 1959).

Masson, Georgina, *Italian Gardens* (London, 1966).

Mazzi, Maria Serena, 'Arredi e masserizie della casa rurale nelle campagne fiorentine del XV secolo', *Archeologia Medievale* 7 (1980), 137–52.

Mazzi, Maria Serena, and Raveggi, Sergio, *Gli Uomini e le cose nelle campagne fiorentine del Quattrocento* (Florence, 1983).

Medici, Lorenzo il Magnifico, see *Libro d'inventario dei beni di Lorenzo il Magnifico*.

Molho, Anthony, *Florentine Public Finances in the Early Renaissance 1400–1433* (Cambridge, Mass., 1971).

Molho, Anthony, 'Cosimo de' Medici: "pater patriae" or *padrino*?', *Stanford Italian Review* I (1979), 5–33.

Molho, Anthony, *Marriage Alliance in Late Medieval Florence* (Cambridge, Mass., 1994).

Morelli, Giovanni di Pagolo, *Ricordi*, ed. Vittore Branca (Florence, 1956).

Morolli, Gabriele, Acidini Luchinat, Cristina, and Marchetti, Luciano, *L'Architettura di Lorenzo il Magnifico*, exhib. cat. (Milan, 1992).

Morolli, Gabriele, *Michelozzo. Scultore e Architetto (1396–1472)*, Atti del Convegno Internazionale 'Michelozzo, Scultore e Architetto nel suo tempo (1396–1472), 2–5 October 1996 (Florence, 1998).

Morolli, Gabriele, 'Gangalandi: da un Brunelleschi apocrifo a un Alberti postumo', *S. Martino a Gangalandi*, ed. R.C. Proto Pisani and G. Romagnoli (Florence, 2001), 25–51.

Moscato, Arnoldo, *Il Palazzo Pazzi a Firenze* (Rome, 1963).

Muendel, J., 'The Grain Mills at Pistoia in 1350', *Bollettino Storico Pistoiese* 7 (1972), 39–64.

Müntz, Eugène, *Les Arts à la cour des papes pendant le 15e e le 16e siècle*, 3 vols. (Paris, 1878–82).

Müntz, Eugène, *Les Collections des Médicis au XVe siècle* (Paris and London, 1888).

Muzzoli, Giovanni, *Catalogo della mostra storica nazionale della miniatura* (Florence, 1953).

Najemy, John M., *Corporatism and Consensus in Florentine Electoral Politics, 1280–1400* (Chapel Hill, N.C., 1982).

Neilson, Katherine B., *Filippino Lippi. A Critical Study* (Cambridge, Mass., 1938).

Niccolai, Francesco, *Guida del Mugello e della Val di Sieve* (Rome, 1914, reprinted 1974).

Nuttall, Paula, 'The Patrons of Chapels at the Badia of Fiesole', *Studi di Storia dell'Arte* 3 (1992), 97–112.

Nuttall, Paula, 'The Medici and Netherlandish Painting', F. Ames-Lewis ed., *The Early Medici and their Artsists* (London, 1995), 135–52.

Onians, John, *Bearers of Meaning. The Classical Orders in Antiquity, the Middle Ages, and the Renaissance* (Cambridge, 1988).

Origo, Iris, *The Merchant of Prato, Francesco di Marco Datini* (New York, 1979).

Orlandi, Stefano, *Beato Angelico. Monografia storica della vita e delle opere con un'appendice di nuovi documenti inediti* (Florence, 1964).

Ottokar, Nicola, *Il Comune di Firenze alla fine del dugento* (Florence, 1926).

Palladio, Andrea, *I Quattro libri dell'architettura* (Venice, 1570; facsimilie ed., Milan, 1980).

Palmieri, Matteo, *Ricordi fiscali (1427–1474)*, ed. E. Conti (Rome, 1983).

Pampaloni, Guido, *Palazzo Strozzi* (Rome, 1963).

Pane, Roberto, 'La Sintassi del Brunelleschi fra il linguaggio dell'antico e l'eredità medioevale toscana', *Filippo Brunelleschi, la sua opera e il suo tempo* (Florence, 1980), II, 357–79.

Pansini, Giuseppe, see *Piante di popoli e strade*.

Patzak, Bernhard, *Palast und Villa in Toscana*, 3 vols. (Leipzig, 1908–13).

Pellecchia, Linda, 'The Patron's Role in the Production of Architecture: Bartolomeo Scala and the Scala Palace', *Renaissance Quarterly* 42 (1989), 258–91.

Petri, A., and Paoletti C., *Ville Pratesi*, vol. I, *Val di Bisenzio* (Prato, 1964).

Piante di popoli e strade. Capitani di Parte Guelfa 1580–1595, ed. Giuseppe Pansini (Florence, 1989).

Piccolomini, Eneas Silvio, *Memoirs of a Renaissance Pope. The Commentaries of Pius II*, trans. Florence Gragg, intro. Leona Gabel (London, 1960).

Pieper, Jan, *Pienza. Der Entwurf einer humanistischen Weltsicht* (Stuttgart, 1997).

Pinto, Giuliano, 'Ordinamento colturale e proprietà fondiaria cittadina nella Toscana del tardo Medioevo', *Contadini e proprietari nella Toscana moderna. Atti del convegno di studi in onore di Giorgio Giorgetti* (Florence, 1979), vol. I, 223–77.

Pinto, Giuliano, 'Forme di conduzione e rendita fondiaria nel contado fiorentino (secoli XIV e XV): Le terre dell'Ospedale di San Gallo', *Studi di storia medievale e moderna per Ernesto Sestan* (Florence, 1980), vol. I, 259–337.

Pinto, Giuliano, 'Per una storia delle dimore mezzadrili nella Toscana medievale', *Archeologia Medievale* 7 (1980), 153–71.

Pinto, Giuliano, 'Coltura e produzione dei cereali in Toscana nei secoli XIII–XV', *Civiltà ed economia agricola in Toscana nei secoli XIII-XV: Problemi della vita delle campagne nel tardo medioevo* (Pistoia, 1981), 221–85.

Pirillo, Paolo, 'Case rurali, castelli ed altri insediamenti nel contado fiorentino della prima metà del Trecento', tesi di laurea, University of Florence, 1976–7.

Pirillo, Paolo, *Costruzione di un contado. I Fiorentini e il loro territorio nel Basso Medioevo* (Florence, 2001).

Pius II, see Piccolomini

Plaisance, Michel, 'Les rapports ville campagne dans les nouvelles de Sacchetti, Sercambi et Sermini', *Culture et Société en Italie du Moyen-Age à la Renaissance. Hommage à André Rochon* (Paris, 1985), 61–73.

Plesner, Johan, *L'Emigrazione dalla campagna all città libera di Firenze nel XIII secolo* (Florence, 1979).

Pliny (Plinius Secundus, Gaius), *Natural History (Historia naturalis)*, ed. H. Rackham and W. R. S. Jones, 10 vols. (London, 1962).

Pontano, Giovanni, *I Trattati delle virtù sociali*, ed. Francesco Tateo (Rome, 1965).

Pope-Hennessy, John, *Giovanni di Paolo 1403–1483* (London, 1937).

Pope-Hennessy, John, *Fra Angelico* (London, 1974).

Pope-Hennessy, John, *The Study and Criticism of Italian Sculpture* (Princeton, 1980).

Prato e i Medici nel '500. Società e cultura artistica (Prato, 1980).

Preyer, Brenda, 'The Rucellai Loggia', *Mitt.KhIF.* 21 (1977), 183–98.

Preyer, Brenda, 'The Rucellai Palace', *Giovanni Rucellai ed il suo Zibaldone*, II, *A Florentine Renaissance Patrician and his Palace* (London, 1981), 155–225.

Preyer, Brenda, 'The "chasa overo palagio" of Alberto di Zanobi: A Florentine palace of about 1400 and its later remodelling', *Art Bulletin* 65 (1983), 387–401.

Preyer, Brenda, 'Planning for Visitors at Florentine Palaces', *Renaissance Studies* 12, no. 3 (1998), 357–74.

Preyer, Brenda, 'Florentine Palaces and Memories of the Past', *Art, Memory and Family in Renaissance Florence*, ed. Giovanni Ciappelli and Patricia Lee Rubin (Cambridge, 2000), 176–94.

Procacci, Ugo, 'Cosimo de' Medici e la construzione della Badia Fiesolana', *Commentari* 19 (1968), 80–97.

Procacci, Ugo, *Studio sul catasto fiorentino* (Florence, 1996).

Puccioni, N., *La Vallombrosa e la Val di Sieve inferiore* (Bergamo, n.d.).

Querci, Rosita, 'L'Architettura di villa del primo rinascimento nel Mugello', *Annali*, Fondazione di Studi di Storia dell'arte Roberto Longhi – Firenze, (1984), vol. I, 35–54.

Quinterio, Francesco, *Giuliano da Maiano "Grandissimo Domestico"* (Rome, 1996).

Quintilian, Marcus Fabius, *Institutio Oratoria*, trans. H. E. Butler, 4 vols. (London and Cambridge, Mass., 1989).

Relazioni degli ambasciatori veneti al senato, III, 1, 'Firenze', ed. Arnaldo Segarizzi (Bari, 1916).

Repetti, Emanuele, *Dizionario geografico fisico storico della Toscana*, 6 vols. (Florence, 1833; reprinted Rome, 1969).

Richa, Giuseppe, *Notizie storiche delle chiese fiorentine divise ne' suoi quartieri*, 10 vols. (Florence, 1754–62).

'Ricordi di Firenze dell'anno 1459 di autore anonimo', ed. Guglielmo Volpi, *Rerum italicarum scriptores*, ed. Lodovico Antonio Muratori (Città di Castello, 1903–55), vol. 27, part 1.

Righini, G., *Il Valdarno fiorentino e la Val di Bisenzio* (Florence, [1961]).

Rizzo, Anna Padoa, 'La Cappella della compagnia di Santa Barbara della "nazione tedesca" alla Santissima Annunziata di Firenze nel secolo XV. Cosimo Rosselli e la sua 'impresa' artistica', *Antichità Viva* 26 (1987), 3–18.

Rizzo, Anna Padoa, 'Ricerche sulla pittura del '400 nel territorio fiorentino: Bernardo di Stefano Rosselli', *Antichità Viva* 26, part 5–6 (1987), 20–27.

Rizzo, Anna Padoa, 'Soffitti lignei dipinti di Bernardo di Stefano Rosselli (1450–1526)', *Legno e restauro: Ricerche e restauri su architetture e manufatti lignei*, ed. Gennaro Tampone (Florence, 1989).

Rodolico, Francesco, *Le Pietre delle città d'Italia* (Florence, 1953).

Rohlmann, Michael, 'Flämische Tafelmalerei im Kreis des Piero de' Medici', *Piero de' Medici "il Gottoso" (1416–1469). Art in the Service of the Medici*, ed. Andreas Beyer and Bruce Boucher (Berlin 1993), 181–7.

Romagnoli, Gioia, *L'Eremo di Lecceto* (Lastra a Signa, 1991).

Roscoe, William, *The Life and Pontificate of Leo the Tenth*, 2 vols. (London, 1846).

Ross, Janet, *Florentine Villas* (London, 1901).

Rotondi, Pasquale, *Il Palazzo Ducale di Urbino* (Urbino, 1951).

Rowley, George, *Ambrogio Lorenzetti*, 2 vols. (Princeton, 1958).

Rubinstein, Nicolai, *The Palazzo Vecchio 1298–1532. Government, Architecture and Imagery in the Civic Palace of the Florentine Republic* (Oxford, 1995).

Rucellai, Giovanni, *Giovanni Rucellai ed il suo zibaldone*, 'Il Zibaldone quaresimale', vol. I, ed. Alessandro Perosa (London, 1960). (For vol. II, see Kent and Preyer.)

Saalman, Howard, 'The authorship of the Pazzi Palace', *Art Bulletin* 46 (1964), 388–94.

Saalman, Howard, 'The Palazzo Comunale in Montepulciano. An unknown work by Michelozzo', *Zeitschrift für Kunstgeschichte* 28 (1965), 1–46.

Saalman, Howard, 'Michelozzo Studies. The Florentine Mint', *Festschrift Ulrich Middeldorf*, ed. Antje Kosegarten and Peter Tigler (Berlin, 1968), 140–2.

Sabatini, Attilio, 'La chiesa di S. Creci a Macioli', *Rivista d'Arte* 24 (1942), 180–92.

Sacchetti, Franco, *Il Libro delle rime*, ed. Alberto Chiari (Bari, 1936).

Sacchetti, Franco, *Il Trecentonovelle*, ed. Antonio Lanza (Florence, 1984).

Sale, John Russel, *The Strozzi Chapel by Filippino Lippi in Santa Maria Novella* (Ann Arbor and London, 1979).

Salmi, Mario, *Piero della Francesca e il Palazzo Ducale di Urbino* (Florence, 1945).

Salmi, Mario, 'Il Palazzo Ducale di Urbino e Francesco di Giorgio', *Studi artistici urbinati* (Urbino, 1949).

Salmi, Mario, 'Sant'Andrea a Camoggiano e la Cappella de' Pazzi', *Festschrift Ulrich Middeldorf*, ed. Antje Kosegarten and Peter Tigler (Berlin, 1968), 136–9.

Sanpaolesi, Piero, 'La casa fiorentina di Bartolomeo Scala', *Studien zur Toskanischen Kunst. Festschrift für Ludwig H. Heydenreich* (Munich, 1964), 275–88.

Santoni, P., *Campi e il Bisenzio che Dante rammenta* (Florence, 1966).

Sapori, Armando, *Studi di storia economica, secoli XIII–XIV–XV*, 2 vols. (Florence, 1955).

Sassetti, Francesco di Giambatista, 'Notizie dell'origine e nobiltà della famiglia de' Sassetti', *Lettere edite e inedite di Filippo Sassetti*, ed. E. Marcucci (Florence, 1855).

Scharf, Alfred, *Filippino Lippi* (Vienna, 1935).

Schiaparelli, Attilio, *La Casa fiorentina e i suoi arredi nei secoli XIV e XV*, 2 vols., ed. Maria Sframeli and Laura Pagnotta (Florence, 1983).

Segre, Ada, 'Untangling the Knot: Garden Design in Francesco Colonna's "Hypnerotomachia Poliphili"', *Word and Image* 14 (1998), 82–107.

Sereni, Emilio, *Storia del paesaggio agrario italiano* (Rome and Bari, 1979).

Sermini, Gentile, *Novelle*, ed. Giuseppe Vettori, 2 vols. (Rome, 1968).

Shearman, John, 'The Collections of the Younger Branch of the Medici', *Burl. Mag.* 117 (1975), 12–27.

Shearman, John, 'A Functional Interpretation of Villa Madama', *Römisches Jahrbuch für Kunstgeschichte* 20 (1983), 313–27.

Shepherd, John C., and Jellicoe, Geoffrey A., *Italian Gardens of the Renaissance* (London, 1953).

Signorini, Rodolfo, 'Two Notes from Mantua: A Dog Named Rubino and Hozi . . . Cadette il naso a Virgilio', *JWCI* 41 (1978), 317–21.

Signorini, Rodolfo, *Opus hoc tenue. La camera dipinta di Andrea Mantegna, Lettura storica, iconografica, iconologica* (Mantua, 1985).

Slicher van Bath, Bernard Hendric, *The Agrarian History of Western Europe AD 500–1850*, trans. O. Ordish (London, 1963).

Soudek, J., 'Leonardo Bruni and his Public: A statistical and interpretative Study of his annotated Latin Version of the (Pseudo-) Aristotelian *Economics*', vol. 5. *Studies in Medieval and Renaissance History* (London, 1968), 51–136.

Soudek, J., 'A Fifteenth-Century Humanist Bestseller: The Manuscript Diffusion of Leonardo Bruni's annotated Latin Version of the (Pseudo-) Aristotelian *Economics*,' *Philosophy and Humanism: Essays in Honour of Paul Oskar Kristeller*, ed. E. P. Mahoney (London, 1976), 129–43.

Spallanzani, Marco, 'L'Abside dell'Alberti a San Martino a Gangalandi. Nota di storia economica', *Mitt.KhIF.* 29 (1975), 241–50.

Spinazzola, Vittorio, 'Di Napoli antica e della sua topografia in una tavola del XV secolo', *Bollettino d'Arte* 4 (1910), 125–45.

Sricchia Santoro, Fiorella, 'Tra Napoli e Firenze: Diomede Carafa, gli Strozzi e un celebre lettuccio', *Prospettiva* 100 (2000), 41–54.

Statuta Populi et Communis Florentine, publica auctoritate collecta castigata et praeposita anno salutis 1415, 3 vols. (Freiburg, 1778–83).

Statuti della Repubblica Fiorentina, vol. I, *Statuto del Capitano del Popolo 1322–25*, ed. Romolo Caggese (Florence, 1910).

Stefani, Marchionne di Coppo, 'Cronaca fiorentina', ed. Niccolò Rodolico, *Rerum italicarum scriptores*, series ed. L. A. Muratori (Città di Castello, 1903–55), vol. 30, part 1.

Stegmann, Carl von, and Geymüller, Heinrich von, *Die Architektur der Renaissance in Toscana*, 2 vols. (Munich, 1885–93).

Stopani, Renato, *Medievali "case da signore" nella campagna fiorentina* (Florence, 1977).

Stopani, Renato, *Medievali "case da lavoratore" nella campagna fiorentina* (Florence, 1978).

Stopani, Renato, and Carnasciali Maurizio, *La Casa rurale nel Chianti. Indagine su una zona campione: Il territorio comunale di Radda* (Florence, 1978).

Strozzi, Lorenzo, *Vita di Filippo Strozzi il vecchio scritta da Lorenzo suo figlio*, ed. Giuseppe Bini and Pietro Bigazzi (Florence, 1851).

Strozzi, Lorenzo, *Le Vite degli uomini illustri della casa Strozzi, commentario di Lorenzo di Filippo Strozzi*, ed. Francesco Zeffi (Florence, 1892).

Strozzi, Alessandra Macinghi, *Lettere di una gentildonna fiorentina del secolo XV ai figliuoli esuli*, ed. Cesare Guasti (Florence, 1877, reprinted 1972).

Strozzi, Alessandra Macinghi, *Selected Letters of Alessandra Strozzi. Bilingual edition*, trans. and ed. Heather Gregory (Berkeley, 1997).

Studio GE9, Castello: see Castello.

Tabarrini, Marco, *Gino Capponi, i suoi tempi, i suoi studi, i suoi amici* (Florence, 1879).

Tampone, Gennaro, *Studi e ricerche sul nucleo antico di Lastra a Signa* (Florence, 1980).

Tanaglia, Michelangelo, *De Agricultura*, ed. A Roncaglia (Bologna, 1953).

Tempestini, Italo, *Campi Bisenzio: documenti, note, ricordi e appunti storici* (Sesto Fiorentino, 1890).

Teubner, Hans, 'S. Marco in Florenz: Umbauten vor 1500. Ein Beitrag zum Werk des Michelozzo', *Mitt. KhIF.* 23 (1979), 239–72.

Thiem, Gunther, and Thiem, Christel, *Toskanische Fassaden-Dekoration in Sgraffito und Fresko 14. bis 17. Jahrhundert* (Munich, 1964).

Thomas, Anabel, *The Painter's Practice in Renaissance Tuscany* (Cambridge, 1995).

Thomason, David, R., ' "Rusticus": Reflections of the Pastoral on Renaissance Art and Literature', master's thesis, Warburg Institute, University of London, 1968.

Thornton, Dora, *The Scholar in his Study* (New Haven and London, 1997).

Thornton, Peter, *The Italian Renaissance Interior, 1400–1600* (London, 1991).

Toesca, Elena Berti, *Benozzo Gozzoli: gli affreschi della Cappella Medicea* (Milan, 1969).

Tönnesmann, Andreas, *Pienza: Städtebau und Humanismus* (Munich, 1990).

Trexler, Richard, 'Measures against water pollution in fifteenth-century Florence', *Viator* 5 (1974), 455–67.

Trexler, Richard, *Public Life in Renaissance Florence* (Ithaca, N.Y., 1991).

Trionfi Honorati, Maddalena, 'A proposito del "letuccio" ', *Antichita Viva* 20 (1981), 39–48.

Varro, Marcus Terentius, *On Agriculture*, (*Rerum Rusticarum Libri Tres*), trans. William Davis Hooper, rev. Harrison Boyd Ash (London and Cambridge, Mass., 1979).

Vasari, Giorgio, *Le Vite de' più eccellenti pittori, scultori ed architettori*, ed. Gaetano Milanesi, 9 vols. (Florence, 1878–85).

Vasari, Giorgio, il Giovane, *La Città ideale. Piante di Chiese [Palazzi e Ville] di Toscana e d'Italia*, ed. Virginia Stefanelli (Florence, 1970).

Vasic Vatovec, Corinna, 'La Villa di Rusciano', *Filippo Brunelleschi, la sua opera e il suo tempo* (Florence, 1980), II, 663–77.

Villani, Giovanni, *Cronica*, ed. Giovanni Aquilecchia (Turin, 1979).

Viti, Vincenzo, *La Badia Fiesolana* (Florence, 1926).

Vitruvius, Marcus V. Pollio, *De Architectura*, Italian trans. with commentary and illustrations by Cesare di Lorenzo Cesariano (Como, 1521; reissued New York and London, 1968).

Vitruvius, Marcus V. Pollio, *On Architecture (De Architectura)*, trans. Frank Granger, 2 vols. (London and Cambridge, Mass., 1970).

Wackernagel, Martin, *The World of the Florentine Renaissance Artist*, trans. A. Luchs (Princeton, 1981).

Warburg, Aby, *Bildniskunst und florentinisches Bürgertum* (Leipzig, 1902); reprinted in *Gesammelte Schriften*, vol. I (Leipzig and Berlin, 1932), 89–126.

Warburg, Aby, 'Francesco Sassettis letztwillige Verfügung', *Kunstwissenschaftliche Beiträge August Schmarsow gewidmet* (Leipzig, 1907), 129–52; reprinted in *Gesammelte Schriften*, vol. I (Leipzig and Berlin, 1932).

Warburg, Aby, 'Arte del ritratto e borghesia fiorentina: Domenico Ghirlandajo in Santa Trinita: I ritratti di Lorenzo de' Medici e dei suoi familiari', *La Rinascita del paganesimo antico*, trans. Emma Cantimori, ed. Gertrud Bing (Florence, 1966), 109–46.

Warburg, Aby, 'Le ultime volontà di Francesco Sassetti', *La Rinascita del paganesimo antico*, trans. Emma Cantimori, ed. Gertrud Bing (Florence, 1966), 213–46.

Warburg, Aby, 'Francesco Sassetti's Last Injunctions to his Sons', *The Renewal of Pagan Antiquity*, trans. David Britt (Los Angeles, 1999), 223–62, 451–66.

Warburg, Aby, 'The Art of Portraiture and the Florentine Bourgeoisie. Domenico Ghirlandaio in Santa Trinita: The Portraits of Lorenzo de' Medici and His Household', *The Renewal of Pagan Antiquity*, trans. David Britt (Los Angeles, 1999), 185–221, 435–50.

Welliver, Warman, 'Alterations in Ghirlandaio's S. Trinita Frescoes', *Art Quarterly* 32 (1969), 269–81.

Wesselski, Albert, ed., *Polizianos Tagebuch (1477–1479)* (Jena, 1929).

Williams, Raymond, *The Country and the City* (London, 1993).

Wohl, Helmut, 'Domenico Veneziano Studies: The Sant'Egidio and Parenti Documents', *Burl. Mag.* 113 (1971), 635–41.

Wohl, Helmut, *The Paintings of Domenico Veneziano c.1410–1461* (Oxford, 1980).

Wright, Alison, 'The Myth of Hercules', in *Lorenzo il Magnifico e il suo Mondo*, ed. Gian Carlo Garfagnini (Florence, 1994), 323–39.

Wright, Alison, 'Dancing Nudes in the Lanfredini Villa at Arcetri', *With and Without the Medici. Studies in Tuscan Art and Patronage 1434–1530* (Aldershot, 1998), 47–77.

Wright, David R., *The Medici Villa at Olmo a Castello: Its History and Iconography*, 2 vols. (Ann Arbor, 1976).

Zangheri, Luigi, 'La Villa Corsini a Castello e l'intervento di Antonio Maria Ferri', *Bollettino degli Ingegneri* 17 (1969), 3–10.

Zangheri, Luigi, *Ville della Provincia di Firenze. La città* (Milan, 1989).

Zeri, Federico, and Gardner, E., *Italian Paintings. A Catalogue of the Collection of the Metropolitan Museum of Art* (New York, 1971).

NA 7594
.L55
2005